1st Workshop on Representation Learning for NLP 2016

Held at ACL 2016

Berlin, Germany
11 August 2016

ISBN: 978-1-5108-2762-2

ACL 2016

The 54th Annual Meeting of the Association for Computational Linguistics

Proceedings of the 1st Workshop on Representation Learning for NLP

August 11th, 2016
Berlin, Germany

Introduction

Welcome to the 1st Workshop on Representation Learning for NLP (RepL4NLP), held on August 11, 2016 and hosted by the 54th Annual Meeting of the Association for Computational Linguistics (ACL) in Berlin, Germany. The workshop is sponsored by DeepMind, Facebook AI Research, and Microsoft Research.

Representation Learning for NLP aims to continue the spirit of previously successful workshops at ACL/NAACL/EACL, namely VSM at NAACL'15 and CVSC at ACL'13/EACL'14/ACL'15, which focussed on vector space models of meaning, compositionality, and the application of deep neural networks and spectral methods to NLP. It provides a forum for discussing recent advances on these topics, as well as future research directions in linguistically motivated vector-based models in NLP.

Organizers:

Phil Blunsom, DeepMind and Oxford University
Kyunghyun Cho, New York University
Shay Cohen, University of Edinburgh
Edward Grefenstette, DeepMind
Karl Moritz Hermann, DeepMind
Laura Rimell, University of Cambridge
Jason Weston, Facebook
Scott Yih, Microsoft

Program Committee:

Marco Baroni, University of Trento
Antoine Bordes, Facebook
Leon Bottou, Facebook
Xavier Carreras, Xerox
Stephen Clark, University of Cambridge
Hal Daumé III, University of Maryland
Kevin Duh, Johns Hopkins University
Pino Di Fabbrizio, Amazon
Manaal Faruqui, Carnegie Mellon University
Dean Foster, University of Pennsylvania
Yoav Goldberg, Bar Ilan University
Jamie Ryan Kiros, Toronto
Tomáš Kočiský, DeepMind
Omer Levy, Bar Ilan University
Wang Ling, DeepMind
Graham Neubig, NAIST
Ankur Parikh, Google
John Platt, Google
Roi Reichart, Technion
Sebastian Riedel, UCL
Tim Rocktaschel, UCL
Diarmuid O Seaghdha, University of Cambridge / VocalIQ
Richard Socher, Salesforce MetaMind
Mark Steedman, University of Edinburgh
Karl Stratos, Columbia University
Peter Turney, Allen Institute for Artificial Intelligence (AI2)
Lyle Ungar, University of Pennsylvania
Oriol Vinyals, DeepMind
Guillaume Wisniewski, LIMSI-CNRS

Table of Contents

Conference Program

Thursday, August 11, 2016

9:30–9:40   **Welcome and Opening Remarks**

9:40–10:30   **Keynote: Katrin Erk (University of Texas at Austin)**

10:30–11:00   **Coffee Break**

11:00–11:50   **Keynote: Animashree Anandkumar (University of California, Irvine)**

11:50–12:10   **Best Papers**

12:10–13:30   **Lunch Break**

13:30–14:20   **Keynote: Hal Daumé III (University of Maryland)**

14:20–15:10   **Keynote: Raia Hadsell (DeepMind)**

15.10–15.30   **Poster Session**

Decoding Neural Activity Patterns Associated with Sentences by Combining Experiential Attribute and Text-Based Semantic Models
Andrew Anderson, Jeffrey Binder, Leonardo Fernandino, Colin Humphries, Lisa Conant, Katrin Erk and Rajeev Raizada

Explaining Predictions of Non-Linear Classifiers in NLP
Leila Arras, Franziska Horn, Grégoire Montavon, Klaus-Robert Müller and Wojciech Samek

Joint Learning of Sentence Embeddings for Relevance and Entailment
Petr Baudiš, Silvestr Stanko and Jan Šedivý

Combining String Kernels and Gaussian Processes for Richer Text Representations.
Daniel Beck

Why "Blow Out"? A Structural Analysis of the Movie Dialog Dataset
Richard Searle and Megan Bingham-Walker

Learning Word Importance with the Neural Bag-of-Words Model
Imran Sheikh, Irina Illina, Dominique Fohr and Georges Linarès

A Vector Model for Type-Theoretical Semantics
Konstantin Sokolov

Towards Generalizable Sentence Embeddings
Eleni Triantafillou, Jamie Ryan Kiros, Raquel Urtasun and Richard Zemel

Domain Adaptation for Neural Networks by Parameter Augmentation
Yusuke Watanabe, Kazuma Hashimoto and Yoshimasa Tsuruoka

Neural Associative Memory for Dual-Sequence Modeling
Dirk Weissenborn

MuFuRU: The Multi-Function Recurrent Unit
Dirk Weissenborn and Tim Rocktäschel

15.30–16.00   Poster Session Continues and Coffee break

16.00–17.20   Panel Discussion

Explaining Predictions of Non-Linear Classifiers in NLP

Leila Arras[1], Franziska Horn[2], Grégoire Montavon[2],
Klaus-Robert Müller[2,3], and Wojciech Samek[1]
[1]Machine Learning Group, Fraunhofer Heinrich Hertz Institute, Berlin, Germany
[2]Machine Learning Group, Technische Universität Berlin, Berlin, Germany
[3]Department of Brain and Cognitive Engineering, Korea University, Seoul, Korea
{leila.arras, wojciech.samek}@hhi.fraunhofer.de
klaus-robert.mueller@tu-berlin.de

Abstract

Layer-wise relevance propagation (LRP) is a recently proposed technique for explaining predictions of complex non-linear classifiers in terms of input variables. In this paper, we apply LRP for the first time to natural language processing (NLP). More precisely, we use it to explain the predictions of a convolutional neural network (CNN) trained on a topic categorization task. Our analysis highlights which words are relevant for a specific prediction of the CNN. We compare our technique to standard sensitivity analysis, both qualitatively and quantitatively, using a "word deleting" perturbation experiment, a PCA analysis, and various visualizations. All experiments validate the suitability of LRP for explaining the CNN predictions, which is also in line with results reported in recent image classification studies.

1 Introduction

Following seminal work by Bengio et al. (2003) and Collobert et al. (2011), the use of deep learning models for natural language processing (NLP) applications received an increasing attention in recent years. In parallel, initiated by the computer vision domain, there is also a trend toward understanding deep learning models through visualization techniques (Erhan et al., 2010; Landecker et al., 2013; Zeiler and Fergus, 2014; Simonyan et al., 2014; Bach et al., 2015; Lapuschkin et al., 2016a) or through decision tree extraction (Krishnan et al., 1999). Most work dedicated to understanding neural network classifiers for NLP tasks (Denil et al., 2014; Li et al., 2015) use gradient-based approaches. Recently, a technique called layer-wise relevance propagation (LRP) (Bach et

al., 2015) has been shown to produce more meaningful explanations in the context of image classifications (Samek et al., 2015). In this paper, we apply the same LRP technique to a NLP task, where a neural network maps a sequence of *word2vec* vectors representing a text document to its category, and evaluate whether similar benefits in terms of explanation quality are observed.

In the present work we contribute by (1) applying the LRP method to the NLP domain, (2) proposing a technique for quantitative evaluation of explanation methods for NLP classifiers, and (3) qualitatively and quantitatively comparing two different explanation methods, namely LRP and a gradient-based approach, on a topic categorization task using the *20Newsgroups* dataset.

2 Explaining Predictions of Classifiers

We consider the problem of explaining a prediction $f(x)$ associated to an input x by assigning to each input variable x_d a score R_d determining how relevant the input variable is for explaining the prediction. The scores can be pooled into groups of input variables (e.g. all *word2vec* dimensions of a word, or all components of a RGB pixel), such that they can be visualized as heatmaps of highlighted texts, or as images.

2.1 Layer-Wise Relevance Propagation

Layer-wise relevance propagation (Bach et al., 2015) is a newly introduced technique for obtaining these explanations. It can be applied to various machine learning classifiers such as deep convolutional neural networks. The LRP technique produces a *decomposition* of the function value $f(x)$ on its input variables, that satisfies the conservation property:

$$f(x) = \sum_d R_d. \tag{1}$$

1

Proceedings of the 1st Workshop on Representation Learning for NLP, pages 1–7,
Berlin, Germany, August 11th, 2016. ©2016 Association for Computational Linguistics

The decomposition is obtained by performing a backward pass on the network, where for each neuron, the relevance associated with it is redistributed to its predecessors. Considering neurons mapping a set of n inputs $(x_i)_{i\in[1,n]}$ to the neuron activation x_j through the sequence of functions:

$$z_{ij} = x_i w_{ij} + \frac{b_j}{n}$$
$$z_j = \sum_i z_{ij}$$
$$x_j = g(z_j)$$

where for convenience, the neuron bias b_j has been distributed equally to each input neuron, and where $g(\cdot)$ is a monotonously increasing activation function. Denoting by R_i and R_j the relevance associated with x_i and x_j, the relevance is redistributed from one layer to the other by defining messages $R_{i\leftarrow j}$ indicating how much relevance must be propagated from neuron x_j to its input neuron x_i in the lower layer. These messages are defined as:

$$R_{i\leftarrow j} = \frac{z_{ij} + \frac{s(z_j)}{n}}{\sum_i z_{ij} + s(z_j)} R_j$$

where $s(z_j) = \epsilon \cdot (1_{z_j \geq 0} - 1_{z_j < 0})$ is a stabilizing term that handles near-zero denominators, with ϵ set to 0.01. The intuition behind this local relevance redistribution formula is that each input x_i should be assigned relevance proportionally to its contribution in the forward pass, in a way that the relevance is preserved ($\sum_i R_{i\leftarrow j} = R_j$).

Each neuron in the lower layer receives relevance from all upper-level neurons to which it contributes

$$R_i = \sum_j R_{i\leftarrow j}.$$

This pooling ensures layer-wise conservation: $\sum_i R_i = \sum_j R_j$. Finally, in a max-pooling layer, all relevance at the output of the layer is redistributed to the pooled neuron with maximum activation (i.e. winner-take-all). An implementation of LRP can be found in (Lapuschkin et al., 2016b) and downloaded from www.heatmapping.org[1].

2.2 Sensitivity Analysis

An alternative procedure called sensitivity analysis (SA) produces explanations by scoring input variables based on how they affect the decision output locally (Dimopoulos et al., 1995; Gevrey et al., 2003). The sensitivity of an input variable is given by its squared partial derivative:

$$R_d = \left(\frac{\partial f}{\partial x_d}\right)^2.$$

Here, we note that unlike LRP, sensitivity analysis does not preserve the function value $f(\boldsymbol{x})$, but the squared l_2-norm of the function gradient:

$$\|\nabla_{\boldsymbol{x}} f(\boldsymbol{x})\|_2^2 = \sum_d R_d. \qquad (2)$$

This quantity is however not directly related to the amount of evidence for the category to detect. Similar gradient-based analyses (Denil et al., 2014; Li et al., 2015) have been recently applied in the NLP domain, and were also used by Simonyan et al. (2014) in the context of image classification. While recent work uses different relevance definitions for a group of input variables (e.g. gradient magnitude in Denil et al. (2014) or *max*-norm of absolute value of simple derivatives in Simonyan et al. (2014)), in the present work (unless otherwise stated) we employ the squared l_2-norm of gradients allowing for decomposition of Eq. 2 as a *sum* over relevances of input variables.

3 Experiments

For the following experiments we use the *20newsbydate* version of the *20Newsgroups*[2] dataset consisting of 11314/7532 train/test documents evenly distributed among twenty fine-grained categories.

3.1 CNN Model

As a document classifier we employ a word-based CNN similar to Kim (2014) consisting of the following sequence of layers:

```
Conv → ReLU → 1-Max-Pool → FC
```

By 1-Max-Pool we denote a max-pooling layer where the pooling regions span the whole text length, as introduced in (Collobert et al., 2011). Conv, ReLU and FC denote the convolutional layer, rectified linear units activation and fully-connected linear layer. For building the CNN numerical input we concatenate horizontally 300-dimensional pre-trained *word2vec*[3] vectors (Mikolov et al., 2013), in the same order the corresponding words appear in the pre-processed

---

[1]Currently the available code is targeted on image data.

[2]http://qwone.com/%7Ejason/20Newsgroups/
[3]GoogleNews-vectors-negative300,
https://code.google.com/p/word2vec/

document, and further keep this input representation fixed during training. The convolutional operation we apply in the first neural network layer is one-dimensional and along the text sequence direction (i.e. along the horizontal direction). The receptive field of the convolutional layer neurons spans the entire word embedding space in vertical direction, and covers two consecutive words in horizontal direction. The convolutional layer filter bank contains 800 filters.

3.2 Experimental Setup

As pre-processing we remove the document headers, tokenize the text with NLTK[4], filter out punctuation and numbers[5], and finally truncate each document to the first 400 tokens. We train the CNN by stochastic mini-batch gradient descent with momentum (with l_2-norm penalty and dropout). Our trained classifier achieves a classification accuracy of 80.19%[6].

Due to our input representation, applying LRP or SA to our neural classifier yields one relevance value per word-embedding dimension. From these single input variable relevances to obtain word-level relevances, we sum up the relevances over the word embedding space in case of LRP, and (unless otherwise stated) take the squared l_2-norm of the corresponding word gradient in case of SA. More precisely, given an input document d consisting of a sequence $(w_1, w_2, ..., w_N)$ of N words, each word being represented by a D-dimensional word embedding, we compute the relevance $R(w_t)$ of the tth word in the input document, through the summation:

$$R(w_t) = \sum_{i=1}^{D} R_{i,t} \qquad (3)$$

where $R_{i,t}$ denotes the relevance of the input variable corresponding to the ith dimension of the tth word embedding, obtained by LRP or SA as specified in Sections 2.1 & 2.2.

---

[4]We employ NLTK's version 3.1 recommended tokenizers `sent_tokenize` and `word_tokenize`, module `nltk.tokenize`.

[5]We retain only tokens composed of the following characters: alphabetic-character, apostrophe, hyphen and dot, and containing at least one alphabetic-character.

[6]To the best of our knowledge, the best published *20Newsgroups* accuracy is 83.0% (Paskov et al., 2013). However we notice that for simplification we use a fixed-length document representation, and our main focus is on explaining classifier decisions, not on improving the classification state-of-the-art.

In particular, in case of SA, the above word relevance can equivalently be expressed as:

$$R_{\text{SA}}(w_t) = \|\nabla_{w_t} f(d)\|_2^2 \qquad (4)$$

where $f(d)$ represents the classifier's prediction for document d.

Note that the resulting LRP word relevance is signed, while the SA word relevance is positive.

In all experiments, we use the term *target* class to identify the function $f(x)$ to analyze in the relevance decomposition. This function maps the neural network input to the neural network output variable corresponding to the target class.

3.3 Evaluating Word-Level Relevances

In order to evaluate different relevance models, we perform a sequence of "word deletions" (hereby for deleting a word we simply set the word-vector to zero in the input document representation), and track the impact of these deletions on the classification performance. We carry out two deletion experiments, starting either with the set of test documents that are initially classified correctly, or with those that are initially classified wrongly[7]. We estimate the LRP/SA word relevances using as target class the true document class. Subsequently we delete words in decreasing resp. increasing order of the obtained word relevances.

Fig. 1 summarizes our results. We find that LRP yields the best results in both deletion experiments. Thereby we provide evidence that LRP positive relevance is targeted to words that *support* a classification decision, while LRP negative relevance is tuned upon words that *inhibit* this decision. In the first experiment the SA classification accuracy curve decreases significantly faster than the random curve representing the performance change when randomly deleting words, indicating that SA is able to identify relevant words. However, the SA curve is clearly above the LRP curve indicating that LRP provides better explanations for the CNN predictions. Similar results have been reported for image classification tasks (Samek et al., 2015). The second experiment indicates that the classification performance increases when deleting words with the lowest LRP relevance, while small SA values points to words that have less influence on the classification performance than random word selection. This result

---

[7]For the deletion experiments we consider only the test documents whose pre-processed length is greater or equal to 100 tokens, this amounts to a total of 4963 documents.

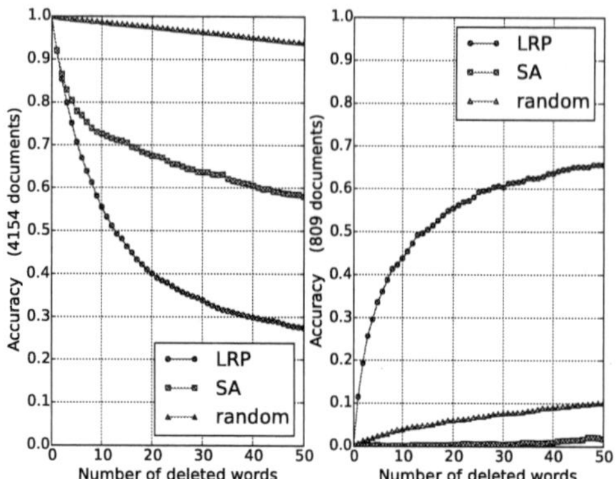

Figure 1: Word deletion on initially correct (left) and false (right) classified test documents, using either LRP or SA. The target class is the true document class, words are deleted in decreasing (left) and increasing (right) order of their relevance. Random deletion is averaged over 10 runs (std < 0.0141). A steep decline (left) and incline (right) indicate informative word relevances.

can partly be explained by the fact that in contrast to SA, LRP provides *signed* explanations. More generally the different quality of the explanations provided by SA and LRP can be attributed to their different objectives: while LRP aims at decomposing the *global* amount of evidence for a class $f(x)$, SA is build solely upon derivatives and as such describes the effect of local *variations* of the input variables on the classifier decision. For a more detailed view of SA, as well as an interpretation of the LRP propagation rules as a *deep Taylor decomposition* see Montavon et al. (2015).

3.4 Document Highlighting

Word-level relevances can be used for highlighting purposes. In Fig. 2 we provide such visualizations on one test document for different relevance target classes, using either LRP or SA relevance models. We can observe that while the word `ride` is highly negative-relevant for LRP when the target class is not `rec.motorcycles`, it is positively highlighted (even though not heavily) by SA. This suggests that SA does not clearly discriminate between words speaking *for* or *against* a specific classifier decision, while LRP is more discerning in this respect.

3.5 Document Visualization

Word2vec embeddings are known to exhibit linear regularities representing semantic relation-

ships between words (Mikolov et al., 2013). We explore if these regularities can be transferred to a document representation, when using as a document vector a linear combination of *word2vec* embeddings. As a weighting scheme we employ LRP or SA scores, with the classifier's predicted class as the target class for the relevance estimation. For comparison we perform uniform weighting, where we simply sum up the word embeddings of the document words (SUM).

For SA we use either the l_2-norm or squared l_2-norm for pooling word gradient values along the *word2vec* dimensions, i.e. in addition to the standard SA word relevance defined in Eq. 4, we use as an alternative $R_{\text{SA}(l_2)}(w_t) = \|\nabla_{w_t} f(d)\|_2$ and denote this relevance model by $\text{SA}(l_2)$.

For both LRP and SA, we employ different variations of the weighting scheme. More precisely, given an input document d composed of the sequence $(w_1, w_2, ..., w_N)$ of D-dimensional *word2vec* embeddings, we build new document representations d' and $d'_{\text{e.w.}}$[8] by either using word-level relevances $R(w_t)$ (as in Eq. 3), or through element-wise multiplication of word embeddings with single input variable relevances $(R_{i,t})_{i\in[1,D]}$ (we recall that $R_{i,t}$ is the relevance of the input variable corresponding to the ith dimension of the tth word in the input document d). More formally we use:

$$d' = \sum_{t=1}^{N} R(w_t) \cdot w_t$$

or

$$d'_{\text{e.w.}} = \sum_{t=1}^{N} \begin{bmatrix} R_{1,t} \\ R_{2,t} \\ \vdots \\ R_{D,t} \end{bmatrix} \odot w_t$$

where $\odot$ is an element-wise multiplication. Finally we normalize the document vectors d' resp. $d'_{\text{e.w.}}$ to unit l_2-norm and perform a PCA projection. In Fig. 3 we label the resulting 2D-projected test documents using five top-level document categories.

For word-based models d', we observe that while standard SA and LRP both provide similar visualization quality, the SA variant with simple l_2-norm yields partly overlapping and dense clusters, still all schemes are better than uniform[9]

---

[8] The subscript e.w. stands for *element-wise*.

[9] We also performed a TFIDF weighting of word embeddings, the resulting 2D-visualization was very similar to uniform weighting (SUM).

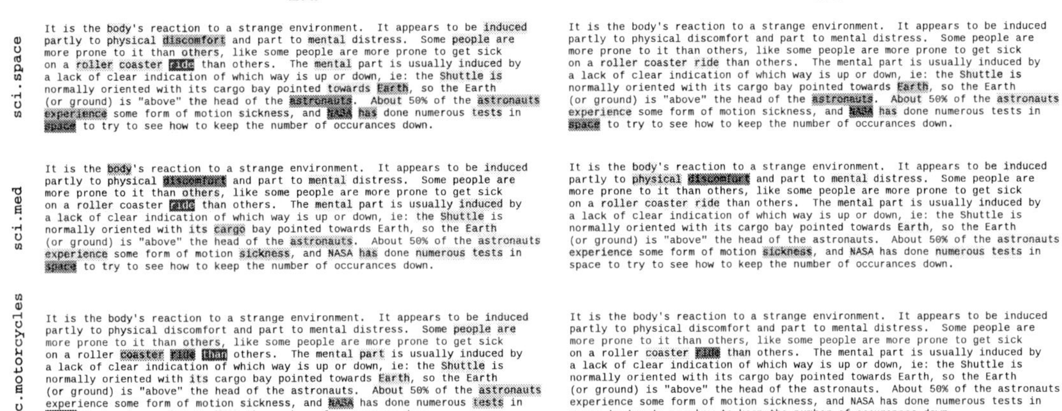

Figure 2: Heatmaps for the test document `sci.space 61393` (correctly classified), using either layer-wise relevance propagation (LRP) or sensitivity analysis (SA) for highlighting words. Positive relevance is mapped to red, negative to blue. The target class for the LRP/SA explanation is indicated on the left.

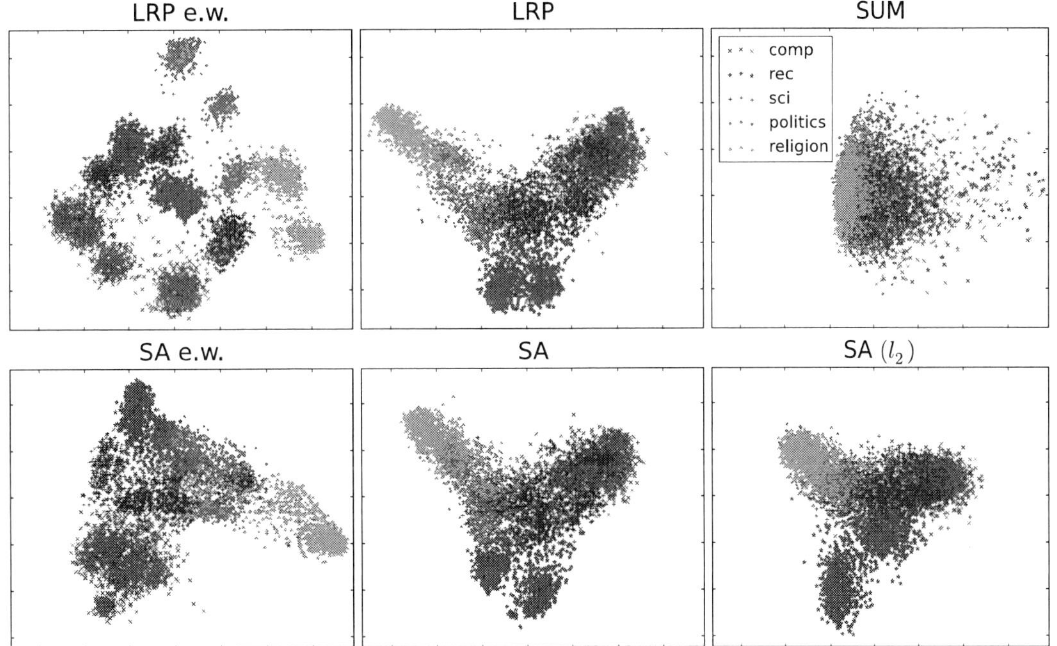

Figure 3: PCA projection of the *20Newsgroups* test documents formed by linearly combining *word2vec* embeddings. The weighting scheme is based on word-level relevances, or on single input variable relevances (e.w.), or uniform (SUM). The target class for relevance estimation is the predicted document class. SA(l_2) corresponds to a variant of SA with simple l_2-norm pooling of word gradient values. All visualizations are provided on the same equal axis scale.

weighting. In case of SA note that, even though the power to which word gradient norms are raised (l_2 or l_2^2) affects the present visualization experiment, it has no influence on the earlier described "word deletion" analysis.

For element-wise models $d'_{e.w.}$, we observe slightly better separated clusters for SA, and a clear-cut cluster structure for LRP.

4 Conclusion

Through word deleting we quantitatively evaluated and compared two classifier explanation models, and pinpointed LRP to be more effective than SA. We investigated the application of word-level relevance information for document highlighting and visualization. We derive from our empirical analysis that the superiority of LRP stems from the fact that it reliably not only links to determinant words that *support* a specific classification decision, but further distinguishes, within the preeminent words, those that are *opposed* to that decision.

Future work would include applying LRP to other neural network architectures (e.g. character-based or recurrent models) on further NLP tasks, as well as exploring how relevance information could be taken into account to improve the classifier's training procedure or prediction performance.

Acknowledgments

This work was supported by the German Ministry for Education and Research as Berlin Big Data Center BBDC (01IS14013A) and the Brain Korea 21 Plus Program through the National Research Foundation of Korea funded by the Ministry of Education.

References

S. Bach, A. Binder, G. Montavon, F. Klauschen, K.-R. Müller, and W. Samek. 2015. On Pixel-Wise Explanations for Non-Linear Classifier Decisions by Layer-Wise Relevance Propagation. *PLoS ONE*, 10(7):e0130140.

Y. Bengio, R. Ducharme, P. Vincent, and C. Jauvin. 2003. A Neural Probabilistic Language Model. *JMLR*, 3:1137–1155.

R. Collobert, J. Weston, L. Bottou, M. Karlen, K. Kavukcuoglu, and P. Kuksa. 2011. Natural Language Processing (Almost) from Scratch. *JMLR*, 12:2493–2537.

M. Denil, A. Demiraj, and N. de Freitas. 2014. Extraction of Salient Sentences from Labelled Documents. Technical report, University of Oxford.

Y. Dimopoulos, P. Bourret, and S. Lek. 1995. Use of some sensitivity criteria for choosing networks with good generalization ability. *Neural Processing Letters*, 2(6):1–4.

D. Erhan, A. Courville, and Y. Bengio. 2010. Understanding Representations Learned in Deep Architectures. Technical report, University of Montreal.

M. Gevrey, I. Dimopoulos, and S. Lek. 2003. Review and comparison of methods to study the contribution of variables in artificial neural network models. *Ecological Modelling*, 160(3):249–264.

Y. Kim. 2014. Convolutional Neural Networks for Sentence Classification. In *Proc. of EMNLP*, pages 1746–1751.

R. Krishnan, G. Sivakumar, and P. Bhattacharya. 1999. Extracting decision trees from trained neural networks. *Pattern Recognition*, 32(12):1999–2009.

W. Landecker, M. Thomure, L. Bettencourt, M. Mitchell, G. Kenyon, and S. Brumby. 2013. Interpreting Individual Classifications of Hierarchical Networks. In *IEEE Symposium on Computational Intelligence and Data Mining (CIDM)*, pages 32–38.

S. Lapuschkin, A. Binder, G. Montavon, K.-R. Müller, and W. Samek. 2016a. Analyzing Classifiers: Fisher Vectors and Deep Neural Networks. In *Proc. of the IEEE Conference on Computer Vision and Pattern Recognition (CVPR)*.

S. Lapuschkin, A. Binder, G. Montavon, K.-R. Müller, and W. Samek. 2016b. The Layer-wise Relevance Propagation Toolbox for Artificial Neural Networks. *JMLR*. in press.

J. Li, X. Chen, E. Hovy, and D. Jurafsky. 2015. Visualizing and Understanding Neural Models in NLP. *arXiv*, (1506.01066).

M. Mikolov, K. Chen, G. Corrado, and J. Dean. 2013. Efficient Estimation of Word Representations in Vector Space. In *Workshop Proc. ICLR*.

G. Montavon, S. Bach, A. Binder, W. Samek, and K.-R. Müller. 2015. Explaining NonLinear Classification Decisions with Deep Taylor Decomposition. *arXiv*, (1512.02479).

H.S. Paskov, R. West, J.C. Mitchell, and T. Hastie. 2013. Compressive Feature Learning. In *Adv. in NIPS*.

W. Samek, A. Binder, G. Montavon, S. Bach, and K.-R. Müller. 2015. Evaluating the visualization of what a Deep Neural Network has learned. *arXiv*, (1509.06321).

K. Simonyan, A. Vedaldi, and A. Zisserman. 2014. Deep Inside Convolutional Networks: Visualising Image Classification Models and Saliency Maps. In *Workshop Proc. ICLR*.

M. D. Zeiler and R. Fergus. 2014. Visualizing and Understanding Convolutional Networks. In *ECCV*, pages 818–833.

Joint Learning of Sentence Embeddings for Relevance and Entailment

Petr Baudiš, Silvestr Stanko and **Jan Šedivý**
FEE CTU Prague
Department of Cybernetics
Technická 2, Prague,
Czech Republic
`baudipet@fel.cvut.cz`

Abstract

We consider the problem of Recognizing Textual Entailment within an Information Retrieval context, where we must simultaneously determine the relevancy as well as degree of entailment for individual pieces of evidence to determine a yes/no answer to a binary natural language question.

We compare several variants of neural networks for sentence embeddings in a setting of decision-making based on evidence of varying relevance. We propose a basic model to integrate evidence for entailment, show that joint training of the sentence embeddings to model relevance and entailment is feasible even with no explicit per-evidence supervision, and show the importance of evaluating strong baselines. We also demonstrate the benefit of carrying over text comprehension model trained on an unrelated task for our small datasets.

Our research is motivated primarily by a new open dataset we introduce, consisting of binary questions and news-based evidence snippets. We also apply the proposed relevance-entailment model on a similar task of ranking multiple-choice test answers, evaluating it on a preliminary dataset of school test questions as well as the standard MCTest dataset, where we improve the neural model state-of-art.

1 Introduction

Let us consider the goal of building machine reasoning systems based on knowledge from fulltext data like encyclopedic articles, scientific papers or news articles. Such machine reasoning systems, like humans researching a problem, must be able to recover evidence from large amounts of retrieved but mostly irrelevant information and judge the evidence to decide the answer to the question at hand.

A typical approach, used implicitly in information retrieval (and its extensions, like IR-based Question Answering systems (Baudiš, 2015)), is to determine evidence relevancy by a keyword overlap feature (like tf-idf or BM-25 (Robertson et al., 1995)) and prune the evidence by the relevancy score. On the other hand, textual entailment systems that seek to confirm hypotheses based on evidence (Dagan et al., 2006) (Marelli et al., 2014) (Bowman et al., 2015) are typically provided with only a single piece of evidence or only evidence pre-determined as relevant, and are often restricted to short and simple sentences without open-domain named entity occurences. In this work, we seek to fuse information retrieval and textual entailment recognition by defining the **Hypothesis Evaluation** task as deciding the truth value of a hypothesis by integrating numerous pieces of evidence, not all of it equally relevant.

As a specific instance, we introduce the **Argus Yes/No Question Answering** task. The problem is, given a real-world event binary question like *Did Donald Trump announce he is running for president?* and numerous retrieved news article fragments as evidence, to determine the answer for the question. Our research is motivated by the Argus automatic reporting system for the Augur prediction market platform. (Baudis et al., 2016b) Therefore, we consider the question answering task within the constraints of a practical scenario that has limited available dataset and only minimum supervision. Hence, authentic news sentences are the evidence (with noise like segmentation errors, irrelevant participial phrases, etc.), and whereas we have gold standard for the correct answers, the model must do without explicit super-

Proceedings of the 1st Workshop on Representation Learning for NLP, pages 8–17,
Berlin, Germany, August 11th, 2016. ©2016 Association for Computational Linguistics

vision on which individual evidence snippets are relevant and what do they entail.

To this end, we introduce an open dataset of questions and newspaper evidence, and a neural model within the Sentence Pair Scoring framework (Baudiš et al., 2016a) that (A) learns sentence embeddings for the question and evidence, (B) the embeddings represent both relevance and entailment characteristics as linear classifier inputs, and (C) the model aggregates all available evidence to produce a binary signal as the answer, which is the only training supervision.

We also evaluate our model on a related task that concerns ranking answers of multiple-choice questions given a set of evidencing sentences. We consider the MCTest dataset and the AI2-8grade/CK12 dataset that we introduce below.

The paper is structured as follows. In Sec. 2, we formally outline the Argus question answering task, describe the question-evidence dataset, and describe the multiple-choice questions task and datasets. In Sec. 3, we briefly survey the related work on similar problems, whereas in Sec. 4 we propose our neural models for joint learning of sentence relevance and entailment. We present the results in Sec. 5 and conclude with a summary, model usage recommendations and future work directions in Sec. 6.

2 The Hypothesis Evaluation Task

Formally, the Hypothesis Evaluation task is to build a function $y_i = f_h(H_i)$, where $y_i \in [0, 1]$ is a binary label (*no* towards *yes*) and $H_i = (q_i, E_i)$ is a hypothesis instance in the form of question text q_i and a set of $E_i = \{e_{ij}\}$ evidence texts e_{ij} as extracted from an evidence-carrying corpus.

2.1 Argus Dataset

Our main aim is to propose a solution to the Argus Task, where the **Argus** system (Baudis, 2015) (Baudis et al., 2016b) is to automatically analyze and answer questions in the context of the **Augur** prediction market platform.[1] In a prediction market, users pose questions about future events whereas others bet on the *yes* or *no* answer, with the assumption that the bet price reflects the real probability of the event. At a specified moment (e.g. after the date of a to-be-predicted sports match), the correct answer is retroactively determined and the bets are paid off. At a larger vol-

ume of questions, determining the bet results may present a significant overhead for running of the market. This motivates the Argus system, which should partially automate this determination — deciding questions related to recent events based on open news sources.

To train a machine learning model for the f_h function, we have created a dataset of questions with gold labels, and produced sets of evidence texts from a variety of news paper using a pre-existing IR (information retrieval) component of the Argus system. We release this dataset openly.[2]

To pose a reproducible task for the IR component, the time domain of questions was restricted from September 1, 2014 to September 1, 2015, and topic domain was focused to politics, sports and the stock market. To build the question dataset, we have used several sources:

- We asked Amazon Mechanical Turk users to pose questions, together with a golden label and a news article reference. This seeded the dataset with initial, somewhat redundant 250 questions.

- We manually extended this dataset by derived questions with reversed polarity (to obtain an opposite answer).

- We extended the data with questions auto-generated from 26 templates, pertaining top sporting event winners and US senate or gubernatorial elections.

To build the evidence dataset, we used the **Syphon** preprocessing component (Baudis et al., 2016b) of the Argus implementation[3] to identify semantic roles of all question tokens and produce the search keywords if a role was assigned to each token. We then used the IR component to query a corpus of newspaper articles, and kept sentences that contained at least 2/3 of all the keywords. Our corpus of articles contained articles from The Guardian (all articles) and from the New York Times (Sports, Politics and Business sections). Furthermore, we scraped partial archive.org historical data out of 35 RSS feeds from CNN, Reuters, BBC International, CBS News, ABC News, c—net, Financial Times, Skynews and the Washington Post.

---

[1] https://augur.net/

[2] https://github.com/brmson/dataset-sts directory data/hypev/argus

[3] https://github.com/AugurProject/argus

	Train	Val.	Test
Original $\#q$	1829	303	295
Post-search $\#q$	1081	167	158
Average $\#m$ per q.	19.04	13.99	16.66

Figure 1: Characteristics of the Argus QA dataset.

For the final dataset, we kept only questions where at least a single evidence was found (i.e. we successfuly assigned a role to each token, found some news stories and found at least one sentence with 2/3 of question keywords within). The final size of the dataset is outlined in Fig. 1 and some examples are shown in Fig. 2.

2.2 AI2-8grade/CK12 Dataset

The **AI2 Elementary School Science Questions** (no-diagrams variant)[4] released by the Allen Institute cover 855 basic four-choice questions regarding high school science and follows up to the Allen AI Science Kaggle challenge.[5] The vocabulary includes scientific jargon and named entities, and many questions are not factoid, requiring real-world reasoning or thought experiments.

We have combined each answer with the respective question (by substituting the *wh*-word in the question by each answer) and retrieved evidence sentences for each hypothesis using Solr search in a collection of CK-12 "Concepts B" textbooks.[6] 525 questions attained any supporting evidence, examples are shown in Fig. 3.

We consider this dataset as *preliminary* since it was not reviewed by a human and many hypotheses are apparently unprovable by the evidence we have gathered (i.e. the theoretical top accuracy is much lower than 1.0). However, we released it to the public[7] and still included it in the comparison as these qualities reflect many realistic datasets of unknown qualities, so we find relative performances of models on such datasets instructive.

2.3 MCTest Dataset

The **Machine Comprehension Test** (Richardson et al., 2013) dataset has been introduced to provide a challenge for researchers to come up with models that approach human-level reading comprehen-

sion, and serve as a higher-level alternative to semantic parsing tasks that enforce a specific knowledge representation. The dataset consists of a set of 660 stories spanning multiple sentences, written in simple and clean language (but with less restricted vocabulary than e.g. the bAbI dataset (Weston et al., 2015)). Each story is accompanied by four questions and each of these lists four possible answers; the questions are tagged as based on just *one* in-story sentence, or requiring *multiple* sentence inference. We use an official extension of the dataset for RTE evaluation that again textually merges questions and answers.

The dataset is split in two parts, MC-160 and MC-500, based on provenance but similar in quality. We train all models on a joined training set.

The practical setting differs from the Argus task as the MCTest dataset contains relatively restricted vocabulary and well-formed sentences. Furthermore, the goal is to find the single key point in the story to focus on, while in the Argus setting we may have many pieces of evidence supporting an answer; another specific characteristics of MCTest is that it consists of stories where the ordering and proximity of evidence sentences matters.

3 Related Work

Our primary concern when integrating natural language query with textual evidence is to find sentence-level representations suitable both for relevance weighing and answer prediction.

Sentence-level representations in the retrieval + inference context have been popularly proposed within the Memory Network framework (Weston et al., 2014), but explored just in the form of averaged word embeddings; the task includes only very simple sentences and a small vocabulary. Much more realistic setting is introduced in the Answer Sentence Selection context (Wang et al., 2007) (Baudiš et al., 2016a), with state-of-art models using complex deep neural architectures with attention (dos Santos et al., 2016), but the selection task consists of only retrieval and no inference (answer prediction). A more indirect retrieval task regarding news summarization was investigated by (Cao et al., 2016).

In the entailment context, (Bowman et al., 2015) introduced a large dataset with single-evidence sentence pairs (Stanford Natural Language Inference, SNLI), but a larger vocabulary and slightly more complicated (but still conservatively formed)

---

[4] http://allenai.org/data.html
[5] https://www.kaggle.com/c/the-allen-ai-science-challenge
[6] We have also tried English Wikipedia, but the dataset is much harder.
[7] https://github.com/brmson/dataset-sts directory data/hypev/ai2-8grade

Will Andre Iguodala win NBA Finals MVP in 2015?
Should Andre Iguodala have won the NBA Finals MVP award over LeBron James?
12.12am ET Andre Iguodala was named NBA Finals MVP, not LeBron.
Will Donald Trump run for President in 2016?
Donald Trump released Immigration Reform that will make America Great Again last weekend —
...his first, detailed position paper since announcing his campaign for the Republican nomination
...for president.
The Fix: A brief history of Donald Trump blaming everything on President Obama
DONALD TRUMP FOR PRESIDENT OF PLUTO!

Figure 2: Example pairs in the Argus dataset.

pedigree chart model **is used to show the pattern of traits that are passed from one generation to the next in a family?**
A pedigree is a chart which shows the inheritance of a trait over several generations.
Figure 51.14 In a pedigree, squares symbolize males, and circles represent females.
energy pyramid model **is used to show the pattern of traits that are passed from one generation to the next in a family?**
Energy is passed up a food chain or web from lower to higher trophic levels.
Each step of the food chain in the energy pyramid is called a trophic level.

Figure 3: Example pairs in the AI2-8grade/CK12 dataset. Answer texts substituted to a question are shown in italics.

sentences. They also proposed baseline recurrent neural model for modeling sentence representations, while word-level attention based models are being studied more recently (Rocktäschel et al., 2015) (Cheng et al., 2016).

In the MCTest text comprehension challenge (Richardson et al., 2013), the leading models use complex engineered features ensembling multiple traditional semantic NLP approaches (Wang and McAllester, 2015). The best deep model so far (Yin et al., 2016) uses convolutional neural networks for sentence representations, and attention on multiple levels to pick evidencing sentences.

4 Neural Model

Our approach is to use a sequence of word embeddings to build sentence embeddings for each hypothesis and respective evidence, then use the sentence embeddings to estimate relevance and entailment of each evidence with regard to the respective hypothesis, and finally integrate the evidence to a single answer.

4.1 Sentence Embeddings

To produce sentence embeddings, we investigated the neural models proposed in the `dataset-sts` framework for deep learning of sentence pair scoring functions. (Baudiš et al., 2016a)

We refer the reader to (Baudiš et al., 2016a) and its references for detailed model descriptions.

We evaluate an **RNN** model which uses bidirectionally summed GRU memory cells (Cho et al., 2014) and uses the final states as embeddings; a **CNN** model which uses sentence-max-pooled convolutional filters as embeddings (Kim, 2014); an **RNN-CNN** model which puts the CNN on top of per-token GRU outputs rather than the word embeddings (Tan et al., 2015); and an **attn1511** model inspired by (Tan et al., 2015) that integrates the RNN-CNN model with per-word attention to build hypothesis-specific evidence embeddings. We also report the baseline results of **avg** mean of word embeddings in the sentence with projection matrix and **DAN** Deep Averaging Network model that employs word-level dropout and adds multiple nonlinear transformations on top of the averaged embeddings (Iyyer et al., 2015).

The original **attn1511** model (Baudiš et al., 2016a) (as tuned for the Answer Sentence Selection task) used a softmax attention mechanism that would effectively select only a few key words of the evidence to focus on — for a hypothesis-evidence token t scalar attention score $a_{h,e}(t)$, the focus $s_{h,e}(t)$ is:

$$s_{h,e}(t) = \exp(a_{h,e}(t)) / \sum_{t'} \exp(a_{h,e}(t'))$$

A different focus mechanism exhibited better performance in the Hypothesis Evaluation task, modelling per-token attention more independently:

$$s_{h,e}(t) = \sigma(a_{h,e}(t)) / \max_{t'} \sigma(a_{h,e}(t'))$$

We also use relu instead of tanh in the CNNs.

As model input, we use the standard GloVe embeddings (Pennington et al., 2014) extended with binary inputs denoting token type and overlap with token or bigram in the paired sentence, as described in (Baudiš et al., 2016a). However, we introduce two changes to the word embedding model — we use 50-dimensional embeddings instead of 300-dimensional, and rather than building an adaptable embedding matrix from the training set words preinitialized by GloVe, we use only the top 100 most frequent tokens in the adaptable embedding matrix and use fixed GloVe vectors for all other tokens (including tokens not found in the training set). In preliminary experiments, this improved generalization for highly vocabulary-rich tasks like Argus, while still allowing the high-frequency tokens (like interpunction or conjunctions) to learn semantic operator representations.

As an additional method for producing sentence embeddings, we consider the **Ubu. RNN** transfer learning method proposed by (Baudiš et al., 2016a) where an RNN model (as described above) is trained on the Ubuntu Dialogue task (Lowe et al., 2015).[8] The pretrained model weights are used to initialize an RNN model which is then fine-tuned on the Hypothesis Evaluation task. We use the same model as originally proposed (except the aforementioned vocabulary handling modification), with the dot-product scoring used for Ubuntu Dialogue training replaced by MLP point-scores described below.

4.2 Evidence Integration

Our main proposed schema for evidence integration is **Evidence Weighing**. From each pair of hypothesis and evidence embeddings,[9] we produce two $[0, 1]$ predictions using a pair of MLP point-scorers of `dataset-sts` (Baudiš et al., 2016a)[10] with sigmoid activation function. The predictions are interpreted as $C_i \in [0, 1]$ entailment (0 to 1 as *no* to *yes*) and relevance $R_i \in [0, 1]$. To integrate the predictions across multiple pieces of evidence, we propose a weighed average model:

$$y = \frac{\sum_i C_i R_i}{\sum_i R_i}$$

We do not have access to any explicit labels for the evidence, but we train the model end-to-end with just y labels and the formula for y is differentiable, carrying over the gradient to the sentence embedding model. This can be thought of as a simple passage-wide attention model.

As a baseline strategy, we also consider **Evidence Averaging**, where we simply produce a single scalar prediction per hypothesis-evidence pair (using the same strategy as above) and decide the hypothesis simply based on the mean prediction across available evidence.

Finally, following success reported in the Answer Sentence Selection task (Baudiš et al., 2016a), we consider a **BM25 Feature** combined with Evidence Averaging, where the MLP scorer that produces the pair scalar prediction as above takes an additional BM25 word overlap score input (Robertson et al., 1995) besides the element-wise embedding comparisons.

5 Results

5.1 Experimental Setup

We implement the differentiable model in the Keras framework (Chollet, 2015) and train the whole network from word embeddings to output evidence-integrated hypothesis label using the binary cross-entropy loss as an objective[11] and the Adam optimization algorithm (Kingma and Ba, 2014). We apply $\mathbb{L}_2 = 10^{-4}$ regularization and a $p = 1/3$ dropout.

Following the recommendation of (Baudiš et al., 2016a), we report expected test set question accuracy[12] as determined by average accuracy in 16 independent trainings and with 95% confidence intervals based on the Student's t-distribution.

---

[8]The Ubuntu Dialogue dataset consists of one million chat dialog contexts, learning to rank candidates for the next utterance in the dialog; the sentences are based on IRC chat logs of the Ubuntu community technical support channels and contain casually typed interactions regarding computer-related problems, resembling tweet data, but longer and with heavily technical jargon.

[9]We employ Siamese training, sharing the weights between hypothesis and evidence embedding models.

[10]From the elementwise product and sum of the embeddings, a linear classifier directly produces a prediction; contrary to the typical setup, we use no hidden layer.

[11]Unlike (Yin et al., 2016), we have found ranking-based loss functions ineffective for this task.

[12]In the MCTest and AI2-8grade/CK12 datasets, we test and rank four hypotheses per question, whereas in the Argus dataset, each hypothesis is a single question.

Model	train	val	test
avg	0.872 ±0.009	0.816 ±0.008	0.744 ±0.020
DAN	0.884 ±0.012	0.822 ±0.011	0.754 ±0.025
RNN	0.906 ±0.013	0.875 ±0.005	0.823 ±0.008
CNN	0.896 ±0.018	0.857 ±0.006	0.822 ±0.007
RNN-CNN	0.885 ±0.010	0.860 ±0.007	0.816 ±0.009
attn1511	0.935 ±0.021	0.877 ±0.008	0.816 ±0.008
Ubu. RNN	0.951 ±0.017	0.912 ±0.004	**0.852** ±0.008

Figure 4: Model accuracy on the Argus task, using the evidence weighing scheme.

Model	Mean Ev.	BM25 Feat.	Weighed
avg	0.746 ±0.051	0.770 ±0.011	0.744 ±0.020
RNN	0.822 ±0.015	0.828 ±0.015	0.823 ±0.008
attn1511	0.819 ±0.013	0.811 ±0.012	0.816 ±0.008
Ubu. RNN	0.847 ±0.009	0.831 ±0.018	0.852 ±0.008

Figure 5: Comparing the influence of the evidence integration schemes on the Argus test accuracy.

Model	train	val	test
avg	0.505 ±0.024	0.442 ±0.022	0.401 ±0.016
DAN	0.556 ±0.038	0.491 ±0.015	0.391 ±0.008
RNN	0.712 ±0.053	0.381 ±0.016	0.361 ±0.012
CNN	0.676 ±0.056	0.442 ±0.012	0.384 ±0.011
RNN-CNN	0.582 ±0.057	0.439 ±0.024	0.376 ±0.014
attn1511	0.725 ±0.069	0.384 ±0.012	0.358 ±0.015
Ubu. RNN	0.570 ±0.059	0.494 ±0.012	**0.441** ±0.011

Figure 6: Model (question-level) accuracy on the AI2-8grade/CK12 task, using the evidence weighing scheme.

Model	Mean Ev.	BM25 Feat.	Weighed
avg	0.366 ±0.010	**0.415** ±0.008	**0.401** ±0.016
CNN	0.385 ±0.020		0.384 ±0.011
Ubu. RNN	0.416 ±0.011	0.418 ±0.009	**0.441** ±0.011

Figure 7: Comparing the influence of the evidence integration schemes on the AI2-8grade/CK12 test accuracy.

5.2 Evaluation

In Fig. 4, we report the model performance on the Argus task, showing that the Ubuntu Dialogue transfer RNN outperforms other proposed models by a large margin. However, a comparison of evidence integration approaches in Fig. 5 shows that evidence integration is not the major deciding factor and there are no statically meaningful differences between the evaluated approaches. We measured high correlation between classification and relevance scores with Pearson's $r = 0.803$, showing that our model does not learn a separate evidence weighing function on this task.

In Fig. 6, we look at the model performance on the AI2-8grade/CK12 task, repeating the story of Ubuntu Dialogue transfer RNN dominating other models. However, on this task our proposed evidence weighing scheme improves over simpler approaches — but just on the best model, as shown in Fig. 7. On the other hand, the simplest averaging model benefits from at least BM25 information to select relevant evidence, apparently.

For the MCTest dataset, Fig. 8 compares our proposed models with the current state-of-art ensemble of hand-crafted syntactic and frame-semantic features (Wang and McAllester, 2015), as well as past neural models from the literature, all using attention mechanisms — the Attentive Reader of (Hermann et al., 2015), Neural Reasoner of (Peng et al., 2015) and the HABCNN model family of (Yin et al., 2016).[13] We see that averaging-based models are surprisingly effective on this task, and in particular on the MC-500 dataset it can beat even the best so far reported model of HABCNN-TE. Our proposed transfer model is statistically equivalent to the best model on both datasets (furthermore, previous work did not include confidence intervals, even though their models should also be stochastically initialized).

As expected, our models did badly on the multiple-evidence class of questions — we made no attempt to model information flow across ad-

---

[13](Yin et al., 2016) also reports the results on the former models.

Model	joint all (train)	MC-160			MC-500		
		one	multi	all	one	multi	all
hand-crafted		0.842	0.678	0.753	0.721	0.679	0.699
Attn. Reader		0.481	0.447	0.463	0.444	0.395	0.419
Neur. Reasoner		0.484	0.468	0.476	0.457	0.456	0.456
HABCNN-TE		0.633	**0.629**	**0.631**	0.542	**0.517**	0.529
avg	0.577 ±0.009	0.653 ±0.027	0.471 ±0.020	0.556 ±0.012	0.587 ±0.018	0.506 ±0.010	**0.542** ±0.011
DAN	0.590 ±0.009	0.681 ±0.017	0.486 ±0.010	0.577 ±0.010	**0.636** ±0.013	0.496 ±0.007	**0.560** ±0.007
RNN	0.608 ±0.030	0.583 ±0.033	0.490 ±0.018	0.533 ±0.020	0.539 ±0.016	0.456 ±0.013	0.494 ±0.012
CNN	0.658 ±0.021	0.655 ±0.020	0.511 ±0.012	0.578 ±0.014	0.571 ±0.013	0.483 ±0.012	0.522 ±0.009
RNN-CNN	0.597 ±0.039	0.617 ±0.041	0.493 ±0.021	0.551 ±0.020	0.554 ±0.023	0.470 ±0.016	0.508 ±0.014
attn1511	0.687 ±0.061	0.611 ±0.052	0.485 ±0.025	0.544 ±0.033	0.571 ±0.036	0.454 ±0.011	0.507 ±0.021
Ubu. RNN	0.678 ±0.035	**0.736** ±0.033	0.503 ±0.016	**0.612** ±0.023	**0.641** ±0.017	0.452 ±0.017	**0.538** ±0.015
* Ubu. RNN		0.786	0.547	0.658	0.676	0.494	0.577

Figure 8: Model (question-level) accuracy on the test split of the MCTest task, using the evidence weighing scheme. The first column shows accuracy on a train split joined across both datasets.
* The model with top MC-500 test set result (across 16 runs) that convincingly dominates HABCNN-TE in the *one* and *all* classes and illustrates that the issue of reporting evaluation spread is not just theoretical. 5/16 of the models have MC-160 *all* accuracy > 0.631.

Model	Mean Ev.	BM25 Feat.	Weighed
avg	0.423 ±0.014	0.506 ±0.012	**0.542** ±0.011
CNN	0.373 ±0.036	**0.509** ±0.027	**0.522** ±0.009
Ubu. RNN	0.507 ±0.014	0.509 ±0.012	**0.538** ±0.015

Figure 9: Comparing the influence of the evidence integration schemes on the MC-500 (all-type) test accuracy.

jacent sentences in our models as this aspect is unique to MCTest in the context of our work.

Interestingly, evidence weighing does play an important role on the MCTest task as shown in Fig. 9, significantly boosting model accuracy. This confirms that a mechanism to allocate attention to different sentences is indeed crucial for this task.

5.3 Analysis

While we can universally proclaim Ubu. RNN as the best model, we observe many aspects of the Hypothesis Evaluation problem that are shared by the AI2-8grade/CK12 and MCTest tasks, but not by the Argus task.

Our largest surprise lies in the ineffectivity of evidence weighing on the Argus task, since observations of irrelevant passages initially led us to investigate this model. We may also see that non-pretrained RNN does very well on the Argus task while CNN is a better model otherwise.

An aspect that could explain this rift is that the latter two tasks are primarily *retrieval* based, where we seek to judge each evidence as irrelevant or essentially a paraphrase of the hypothesis. On the other hand, the Argus task is highly *semantic* and compositional, with the questions often differing just by a presence of negation — recurrent model that can capture long-term dependencies and alter sentence representations based on the presence of negation may represent an essential improvement over an n-gram-like convolutional scheme. We might also attribute the lack of success of evidence weighing in the Argus task to a more conservative scheme of passage retrieval employed in the **IR** pipeline that produced the dataset. Given the large vocabulary and noise levels in the data, we may also simply require more data to train the evidence weighing properly.

We see from the training vs. test accuracies that RNN-based models (including the word-level attention model) have a strong tendency to overfit on our small datasets, while CNN is much more resilient. While word-level attention seems appealing for such a task, we speculate that we simply might not have enough training data to properly train it.[14] Investigating attention transfer is a point for future work — by our preliminary experiments on multiple datasets, attention models appear more task specific than the basic text comprehension models of memory based RNNs.

One concrete limitation of our models in case of the Argus task is a problem of reconciling particular named entity instances. The more obvious form of this issue is *Had Roger Federer beat Martin Cilic in US OPEN 2014?* versus an opposite *Had Martin Cilic beat Roger Federer in US OPEN 2014?* — another form of this problem is reconciling a hypothesis like *Will the Royals win the World Series?* with evidence *Giants Win World Series With Game 7 Victory Over Royals.* An abstract embedding of the sentence will not carry over the required information — it is important to explicitly pass and reconcile the roles of multiple named entities which cannot be meaningfully embedded in a GloVe-like semantic vector space.

6 Conclusion

We have established a general Hypothesis Evaluation task with three datasets of various properties, and shown that neural models can exhibit strong performance (with less hand-crafting effort than non-neural classifiers). We propose an evidence weighing model that is never harmful and improves performance on some tasks. We also demonstrate that simple models can outperform or closely match performance of complex architectures; all the models we consider are task-independent and were successfully used in different contexts than Hypothesis Evaluation (Baudiš et al., 2016a). Our results empirically show that a basic RNN text comprehension model well trained on a large dataset (even if the task is unrelated and vocabulary characteristics are very different) outperforms or matches more complex architectures trained only on the dataset of the task at hand.[15]

Finally, on the MCTest dataset, our best proposed model is better or statistically indistinguishable from the best neural model reported so far (Yin et al., 2016), even though it has a simpler architecture and only a naive attention mechanism.

We would like to draw several recommendations for future research from our findings: (A) encourage usage of basic neural architectures as evaluation baselines; (B) suggest that future research includes models pretrained on large data as baselines; (C) validate complex architectures on tasks with large datasets if they cannot beat baselines on small datasets; and (D) for randomized machine comprehension models (e.g. neural networks with random weight initialization, batch shuffling or probabilistic dropout), report expected test set performance based on multiple independent training runs.

As a general advice for solving complex tasks with small datasets, besides the point (B) above our analysis suggests convolutional networks as the best models regarding the tendency to overfit, unless semantic composionality plays a crucial role in the task; in this scenario, simple averaging-based models are a great start as well. Preinitializing a model also helps against overfitting.

We release our implementation of the Argus task, evidence integration models and processing of all the evaluated datasets as open source.[16]

We believe the next step towards machine comprehension NLP models (based on deep learning but capable of dealing with real-world, large-vocabulary data) will involve research into a better way to deal with entities without available embeddings. When distinguishing specific entities, simple word-level attention mechanisms will not do. A promising approach could extend the flexibility of the final sentence representation, moving from attention mechanism to a memory mechanism[17] by allowing the network to remember a set of "facts" derived from each sentence; related work has been done for example on end-to-end differentiable shift-reduce parsers with LSTM as stack cells (Dyer et al., 2015).

Acknowledgments

This work was co-funded by the Augur Project of the Forecast Foundation and financially supported by the Grant

---

[14]Just reducing the dimensionality of hidden representations did not yield an improvement.

[15]Even if these use multi-task learning, which was employed in case of the HABCNN models that were trained to also predict question classes.

[16]`https://github.com/brmson/dataset-sts` task *hypev*

[17]Not necessarily "memories" in the sense of Memory Networks.

Agency of the Czech Technical University in Prague, grant No. SGS16/ 084/OHK3/1T/13. Computational resources were provided by the CESNET LM2015042 and the CERIT Scientific Cloud LM2015085, provided under the programme "Projects of Large Research, Development, and Innovations Infrastructures."

We'd like to thank Peronet Despeignes of the Augur Project for his support. Carl Burke has provided instructions for searching CK-12 ebooks within the Kaggle challenge.

References

Petr Baudiš, Jan Pichl, Tomáš Vyskočil, and Jan Sedivý. 2016a. Sentence pair scoring: Towards unified framework for text comprehension. *CoRR*, abs/1603.06127.

Petr Baudis, Silvestr Stanko, and Peronet Despeignes. 2016b. Argus: An artificial-intelligence assistant for augur's prediction market platform reporters.

Petr Baudis. 2015. Argus: Deciding questions about events.

Petr Baudiš. 2015. YodaQA: A Modular Question Answering System Pipeline. In *POSTER 2015 - 19th International Student Conference on Electrical Engineering*.

Samuel R. Bowman, Gabor Angeli, Christopher Potts, and Christopher D. Manning. 2015. A large annotated corpus for learning natural language inference. In *Proceedings of the 2015 EMNLP Conference*. ACL.

Ziqiang Cao, Wenjie Li, Sujian Li, and Furu Wei. 2016. Attsum: Joint learning of focusing and summarization with neural attention. *arXiv preprint arXiv:1604.00125*.

Jianpeng Cheng, Li Dong, and Mirella Lapata. 2016. Long short-term memory-networks for machine reading. *CoRR*, abs/1601.06733.

KyungHyun Cho, Bart van Merrienboer, Dzmitry Bahdanau, and Yoshua Bengio. 2014. On the properties of neural machine translation: Encoder-decoder approaches. *CoRR*, abs/1409.1259.

Franois Chollet. 2015. Keras. https://github.com/fchollet/keras.

Ido Dagan, Oren Glickman, and Bernardo Magnini. 2006. The PASCAL recognising textual entailment challenge. In *Machine learning challenges. evaluating predictive uncertainty, visual object classification, and recognising tectual entailment*, pages 177–190. Springer.

Cícero Nogueira dos Santos, Ming Tan, Bing Xiang, and Bowen Zhou. 2016. Attentive pooling networks. *CoRR*, abs/1602.03609.

Chris Dyer, Miguel Ballesteros, Wang Ling, Austin Matthews, and Noah A. Smith. 2015. Transition-based dependency parsing with stack long short-term memory. *CoRR*, abs/1505.08075.

Karl Moritz Hermann, Tomas Kocisky, Edward Grefenstette, Lasse Espeholt, Will Kay, Mustafa Suleyman, and Phil Blunsom. 2015. Teaching machines to read and comprehend. In *Advances in Neural Information Processing Systems*, pages 1684–1692.

Mohit Iyyer, Varun Manjunatha, Jordan Boyd-Graber, and Hal Daumé III. 2015. Deep unordered composition rivals syntactic methods for text classification.

Yoon Kim. 2014. Convolutional neural networks for sentence classification. *arXiv preprint arXiv:1408.5882*.

Diederik Kingma and Jimmy Ba. 2014. Adam: A method for stochastic optimization. *arXiv preprint arXiv:1412.6980*.

Ryan Lowe, Nissan Pow, Iulian Serban, and Joelle Pineau. 2015. The ubuntu dialogue corpus: A large dataset for research in unstructured multi-turn dialogue systems. *CoRR*, abs/1506.08909.

Marco Marelli, Luisa Bentivogli, Marco Baroni, Raffaella Bernardi, Stefano Menini, and Roberto Zamparelli. 2014. Semeval-2014 task 1: Evaluation of compositional distributional semantic models on full sentences through semantic relatedness and textual entailment. *SemEval-2014*.

Baolin Peng, Zhengdong Lu, Hang Li, and Kam-Fai Wong. 2015. Towards neural network-based reasoning. *arXiv preprint arXiv:1508.05508*.

Jeffrey Pennington, Richard Socher, and Christopher D Manning. 2014. Glove: Global vectors for word representation. *Proceedings of the EMNLP 2014*, 12:1532–1543.

Matthew Richardson, Christopher JC Burges, and Erin Renshaw. 2013. Mctest: A challenge dataset for the open-domain machine comprehension of text.

Stephen E Robertson, Steve Walker, Susan Jones, et al. 1995. Okapi at trec-3.

Tim Rocktäschel, Edward Grefenstette, Karl Moritz Hermann, Tomás Kociský, and Phil Blunsom. 2015. Reasoning about entailment with neural attention. *CoRR*, abs/1509.06664.

Ming Tan, Bing Xiang, and Bowen Zhou. 2015. Lstm-based deep learning models for non-factoid answer selection. *CoRR*, abs/1511.04108.

Hai Wang and Mohit Bansal Kevin Gimpel David McAllester. 2015. Machine comprehension with syntax, frames, and semantics. *Proceedings of ACL, Volume 2: Short Papers*:700.

Mengqiu Wang, Noah A Smith, and Teruko Mitamura. 2007. What is the jeopardy model? a quasi-
synchronous grammar for qa. In *EMNLP-CoNLL*,
volume 7, pages 22–32.

Jason Weston, Sumit Chopra, and Antoine Bordes.
2014. Memory networks. *CoRR*, abs/1410.3916.

Jason Weston, Antoine Bordes, Sumit Chopra, and
Tomas Mikolov. 2015. Towards ai-complete ques-
tion answering: A set of prerequisite toy tasks.
CoRR, abs/1502.05698.

Wenpeng Yin, Sebastian Ebert, and Hinrich Schütze.
2016. Attention-based convolutional neural
network for machine comprehension. *CoRR*,
abs/1602.04341.

A Joint Model for Word Embedding and Word Morphology

Kris Cao and Marek Rei
Computer Lab
University of Cambridge
United Kingdom
kc391@cam.ac.uk

Abstract

This paper presents a joint model for performing unsupervised morphological analysis on words, and learning a character-level composition function from morphemes to word embeddings. Our model splits individual words into segments, and weights each segment according to its ability to predict context words. Our morphological analysis is comparable to dedicated morphological analyzers at the task of morpheme boundary recovery, and also performs better than word-based embedding models at the task of syntactic analogy answering. Finally, we show that incorporating morphology explicitly into character-level models helps them produce embeddings for unseen words which correlate better with human judgments.

1 Introduction

Word embedding models associate each word in a corpus with a vector in a semantic space. These vectors can either be learnt to optimize performance in a downstream task (Bengio et al., 2003; Collobert et al., 2011) or learnt via the distributional hypothesis: words with similar contexts have similar meanings (Harris, 1954; Mikolov et al., 2013a). Current word embedding models treat words as atomic. However, words follow a power law distribution (Zipf, 1935), and word embedding models suffer from the problem of sparsity: a word like 'unbelievableness' does not appear at all in the first 17 million words of Wikipedia, even though it is derived from common morphemes. This leads to three problems:

1. word representations decline in quality for

rarely observed words (Bullinaria and Levy, 2007).

2. word embedding models handle out-of-vocabulary words badly, typically as a single 'OOV' token.

3. the word distribution has a long tail, and many parameters are needed to capture all of the words in a corpus (for an embedding size of 300 with a vocabulary of 10k words, 3 million parameters are needed)

One approach to smooth word distributions is to operate on the smallest meaningful semantic unit, the morpheme (Lazaridou et al., 2013; Botha and Blunsom, 2014). However, previous work on the morpheme level has all used external morphological analyzers. These require a separate pre-processing step, and cannot be adapted to suit the problem at hand.

Another is to operate on the smallest orthographic unit, the character (Ling et al., 2015; Kim et al., 2016). However, the link between shape and meaning is often complicated (de Saussure, 1916), as alphabetic characters carry no inherent semantic meaning. To account for this, the model has to learn complicated dependencies between strings of characters to accurately capture word meaning. We hypothesize that explicitly introducing morphology into character-level models can help them learn morphological features, and hence word meaning.

In this paper, we introduce a word embedding model that jointly learns word morphology and word embeddings. To the best of our knowledge, this is the first word embedding model that learns morphology as part of the model. Our guiding intuition is that the words with the same stem have similar contexts. Thus, when considering word segments in terms of context-predictive power, the

Proceedings of the 1st Workshop on Representation Learning for NLP, pages 18–26,
Berlin, Germany, August 11th, 2016. ©2016 Association for Computational Linguistics

segment corresponding to the stem will have the most weight.

Our model 'reads' the word and outputs a sequence of word segments. We weight each segment, and then combine the segments to obtain the final word representation. These representations are trained to predict context words, as this has been shown to give word representations which capture word semantics well (Mikolov et al., 2013b). As the root morpheme has the most context-predictive power, we expect our model to assign high weight to this segment, thereby learning to separate root+affix structures.

One exciting feature of character-level models is their ability to represent open-vocabulary words. After training, they can predict a vector for any word, not just words that they have seen before. Our model has an advantage in that it can split unknown words into known and unknown components. Hence, it can potentially generalise better over seen morphemes and words and apply existing knowledge to new cases.

To evaluate our model, we evaluate its use as a morphological analyzer (§4.1), test how well it learns word semantics, including for unseen words (§4.2), and examine the structure of the embedding space (§4.3).

2   Related Work

While words are often treated as the fundamental unit of language, they are in fact themselves compositional. The smallest unit of semantics is the morpheme, while the smallest unit of orthography is the grapheme, or character. Both have been used as a method to go beyond word-level models.

2.1   Morphemic analysis and semantics

As word semantics is compositional, one might ask whether it is possible to learn morpheme representations, and compose them to obtain good word representations. Lazaridou et al. (2013) demonstrated precisely this: one can derive good representations of morphemes distributionally, and apply tools from compositional distributional semantics to obtain good word representations. Luong et al. (2013) also trained a morphological composition model based on recursive neural networks. Botha and Blunsom (2014) built a language model incorporating morphemes, and demonstrated improvements in language modelling and in machine translation. All of these approaches incorporated external morphological knowledge, either in the form of gold standard morphological analyses such as CELEX (Baayen et al., 1995) or an external morphological analyzer such as Morfessor (Creutz and Lagus, 2007).

Unsupervised morphology induction aims to decide whether two words are morphologically related or to generate a morphological analysis for a word (Goldwater et al., 2005; Goldsmith, 2001). While they may use semantic insights to perform the morphological analysis (Soricut and Ochs, 2015), they typically are not concerned with obtaining a semantic representation for morphemes, nor of the resulting word.

2.2   Character-level models

Another approach to go beyond words is based on on character-level neural network models. Both recurrent and convolutional architectures for deriving word representations from characters have been used, and results in downstream tasks such as language modelling and POS tagging have been promising, with reductions in word perplexity for language modelling and state-of-the-art English POS tagging accuracy (Ling et al., 2015; Kim et al., 2016). Ballesteros et al. (2015) train a character-level model for parsing. Zhang et al. (2015) do away with words completely, and train a convolutional neural network to do text classification directly from characters.

Excitingly, character-level models seem to capture morphological effects. Examining nearest neighbours of morphologically complex words in character-aware models often shows other words with the same morphology (Ling et al., 2015; Kim et al., 2016). Furthermore, morphosyntactic features such as capitalization and suffix information have long been used in tasks such as POS tagging (Xu et al., 2015; Toutanova et al., 2003). By explicitly modelling these features, one might expect good performance gains in many NLP tasks.

What is less clear is how well these models learn word semantics. Classical word embedding models seem to capture word semantics, and the nearest neighbours of a given word are typically semantically related words (Mikolov et al., 2013a; Mnih and Kavukcuoglu, 2013). In addition, the correlation between model word similarity scores and human similarity judgments is typically high (Levy et al., 2015). However, no previous work (to our knowledge) evaluates the similarity judgments

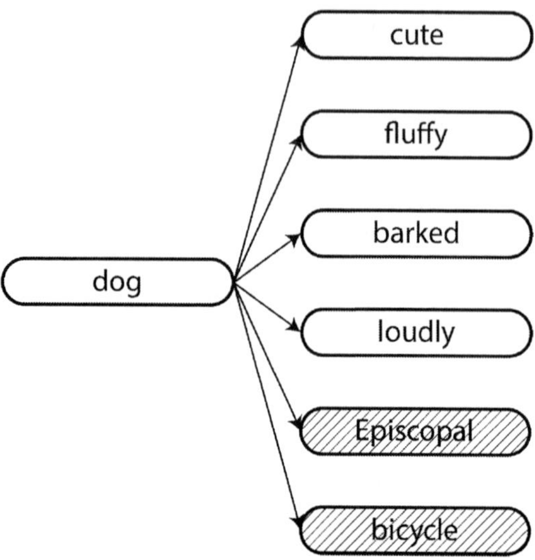

Figure 1: A graphical illustration of SGNS. The target vector for 'dog' is learned to have high inner product with the context vectors for words seen in the context of 'dog' (no shading), while having low inner product with random negatively sampled words (shaded)

of character-level models against human annotators.

3 The Char2Vec model

We hypothesize that by incorporating morphological knowledge directly into a character-level model, one can improve the ability of character-level models to learn compositional word semantics. In addition, we hypothesize that incorporating morphological knowledge helps structure the embedding space in such a way that affixation corresponds to a regular shift in the embedding space. We test both hypotheses directly in §4.2 and §4.3 respectively.

The starting point for our model is the skip-gram with negative sampling (SGNS) objective of Mikolov et al. (2013b). For a vocabulary V of size $|V|$ and embedding size N, SGNS learns two embedding tables $W, C \in \mathbb{R}^{N \times |V|}$, the target and context vectors. Every time a word w is seen in the corpus with a context word c, the tables are updated to maximize

$$\log \sigma(w \cdot c) + \sum_{i=1}^{k} \mathbb{E}_{\tilde{c}_i \sim P(w)}[\log \sigma(-w \cdot \tilde{c}_i)] \quad (1)$$

where $P(w)$ is a noise distribution from which we draw k negative samples. In the end, the target vector for a word w should have high inner product with context vectors for words with which it is typically seen, and low inner products with context vectors for words it is not typically seen with. Figure 1 illustrates this for a particular example. In Mikolov et al. (2013b), the noise distribution $P(w)$ is proportional to the unigram probability of a word raised to the 3/4th power (Mikolov et al., 2013b).

Our innovation is to replace W with a trainable function f that accepts a sequence of characters and returns a vector of length N (i.e. $f : A^{<\omega} \to \mathbb{R}^N$, where A is the alphabet we are considering and $A^{<\omega}$ denotes the finite length strings over the alphabet A). We still keep the table of context embeddings C, and our model objective is still to minimize

$$\log \sigma(f(w) \cdot c) + \sum_{i=1}^{k} \mathbb{E}_{\tilde{c}_i \sim P(w)}[\log \sigma(-f(w) \cdot \tilde{c}_i)] \quad (2)$$

where we now treat w as a sequence of characters. After training, f can be used to produce an embedding for any sequence of characters, even if it was not previously seen in training.

The process of calculating f on a word is illustrated in Figure 2. We first pad the word with beginning and end of word tokens, and then pass the characters of the word into a character lookup table. As the link between characters and morphemes is non-compositional and requires essentially memorizing a sequence of characters, we use LSTMs (Hochreiter and Schmidhuber, 1997) to encode the letters in the word, as they have been shown to capture non-local and non-linear dependencies. We run a forward and a backward LSTM over the character embeddings. The forward LSTM reads the beginning of word symbol, but not the end of word symbol, and the backward LSTM reads the end of word symbol but not the beginning of word symbol. This is necessary to align the resulting embeddings, so that the LSTM hidden states taken together correspond to a partition of the word into two without overlap.

The LSTMs output two sequences of vectors $h_0^f, \ldots, h_n^f$ and $h_n^b, \ldots, h_0^b$. We then concatenate the resulting vectors, and pass them through a shared feed-forward layer to obtain a final sequence of vectors h_i. Each vector corresponds to two half-words: one half read by the forward LSTM, and the other by the backward LSTM.

We then learn an attention model over these hid-

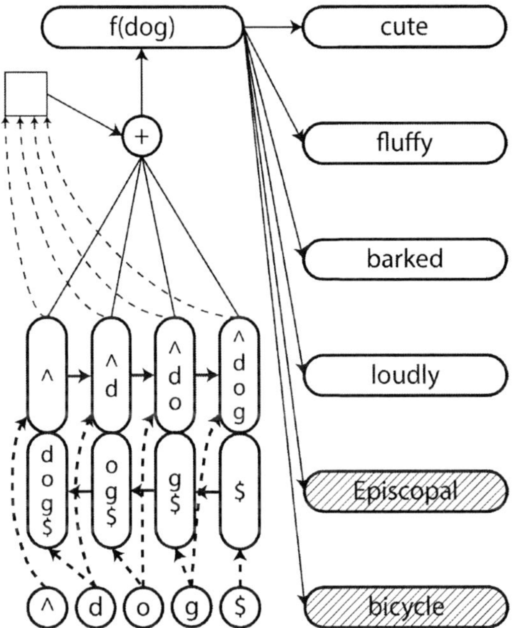

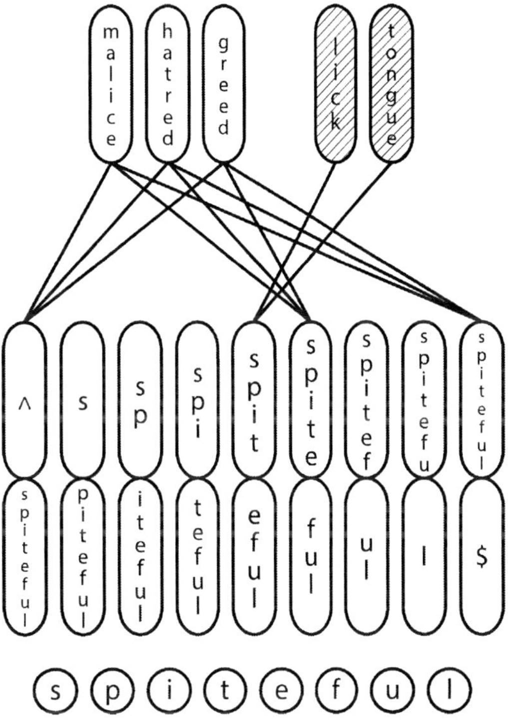

Figure 2: An illustration of Char2Vec. A bidirectional LSTM reads the word (start and end of word symbols represented by ^ and $ respectively), outputting a sequence of hidden states. These are then passed through a feed-forward layer (not shown), weighted by an attention model (the square box in the diagram) and summed to obtain the final word representation.

Figure 3: An illustration of the attention model (start and end of word symbols omitted). The root morpheme contributes the most to predicting the context, and is upweighted. In contrast, another potential split is inaccurate, and predicts the wrong context words. This is downweighted.

den states: given a hidden state h_i, we calculate a weight $\alpha_i = a(h_i)$ such that $\sum \alpha_i = 1$, and then calculate the resulting vector for the word w as $f(w) = \sum \alpha_i h_i$. Following Bahdanau et al. (2014), we calculate a as

$$a(h_i) = \frac{\exp(v^T \tanh(W h_i))}{\sum_j \exp(v^T \tanh(W h_j))} \qquad (3)$$

i.e. a softmax over the hidden states.

3.1 Capturing morphology via attention

Previous work on bidirectional LSTM character-level models used both LSTMs to read the entire word (Ling et al., 2015; Ballesteros et al., 2015). This can lead to redundancy, as both LSTMs are used to capture the full word. In contrast, our model is capable of splitting the words and optimizing the two LSTMs for modelling different halves. This means one of the LSTMs can specialize on word prefixes and roots, while the other memorizes possible suffixes. In addition, when dealing with an unknown word, it can be split into

known and unknown components. The model can then use the semantic knowledge it has learnt for a known component to predict a representation for the unknown word as a whole.

We hypothesize that the natural place to split words is on morpheme boundaries, as morphemes are the smallest unit of language which carry semantic meaning. We test the splitting capabilities of our model in §4.1.

4 Experiments

We evaluate our model on three tasks: morphological analysis (§4.1), semantic similarity (§4.2), and analogy retrieval (§4.3). We trained all of the models once, and then use the same trained model for all three tasks – we do not perform hyperparameter tuning to optimize performance on each task.

We trained our Char2Vec model on the Text8 corpus, consisting of the first 100MB of a 2006 cleaned-up dump of Wikipedia[1]. We only trained on words which appeared more than 5 times in our corpus. We used a context window size of 3 words either side of the target word, and took 11 negative samples per positive sample, using the same smoothed unigram distribution as `word2vec`. The model was trained for 3 epochs using the Adam optimizer (Kingma and Ba, 2015). All experiments were carried out using Keras (Chollet, 2015) and Theano (Bergstra et al., 2010; Bastien et al., 2012). We initialized the context lookup table using `word2vec`[2], and kept it fixed during training. [3] In all character-level models, the character embeddings have dimension $d_C = 64$, while the forward and backward LSTMs have dimension $d_{LSTM} = 256$. The concatenation of both therefore has dimensionality $d = 512$. The concatenated LSTM hidden states are then compressed down to $d_{word} = 256$ by a feed-forward layer.

As baselines, we trained a SGNS model on the same dataset with the same parameters. To test how much the attention model helps the character-level model to generalize, we also trained the Char2Vec model without the attention layer, but with the same parameters. In this model, the word embeddings are just the concatenation of the final forward and backward states, passed through a feedforward layer. We refer to this model as C2V-NO-ATT. We also constructed count-based vectors using SVD on PPMI-weighted co-occurence counts, with a window size of 3. We kept the top 256 principal components in the SVD decomposition, to obtain embeddings with the same size as our other models.

4.1 Morphological awareness

The main innovation of our Char2Vec model compared to existing recurrent character-level models is the capability to split words and model each half independently. Here we test whether our model segmentations correspond to gold-standard morphological analyses.

We obtained morphological analyses for all the words in our training vocabulary which were in the English Lexicon Project (Balota et al., 2007). We then converted these into surface-level segmenta-

tions using heuristic affix-matching, and used this as a gold-standard morphemic analysis. We ended up with 14682 words, of which 7867 have at least two morphemes and 1138 have at least three.

Evaluating morphological segmentation is a long-debated issue (Cotterell et al., 2016). Traditional hard morphological analyzers are normally evaluated on border F_1 – that is, how many morpheme borders are recovered. However, our model does not actually posit any hard morpheme borders. Instead, it just associates each character boundary with a weight. Therefore, we treat the problem of recovering intra-word morpheme boundaries as a ranking problem. We rank each inter-character boundary of a word according to our model weights, and then evaluate whether our model ranks morpheme boundaries above non-morpheme boundaries.

We use mean average precision (MAP) as our evaluation metric. We first calculate precision at N for each word, until all the gold standard morpheme boundaries have been recovered. Then, we average over N to obtain the average precision (AP) for that word. We then calculate the mean of the APs across all words to obtain the MAP for the model.

We report results of a random baseline as a point of comparison, which randomly places morpheme boundaries inside the word. We also report the results of the Porter stemmer[4], where we place a morpheme boundary at the end of the stem, then randomly thereafter.

Finally, we trained Morfessor 2.0[5] (Creutz and Lagus, 2007) on our corpus, using an initial random split value of 0.9, and stopping training when the difference in loss between successive epochs is less than 0.1% of the total loss. While Morfessor is no longer state-of-the-art in morpheme recovery (see, e.g. Narasimhan et al. (2015) for more recent work), it has previously been as a component in pipelines to build compositional word representations (Luong et al., 2013; Botha and Blunsom, 2014). We then used our trained Morfessor model to predict morpheme boundaries[6], and randomly permuted the predicted morpheme boundaries and ranked them ahead of randomly permuted non-morpheme boundaries to calculate MAP.

---

[1]available at `mattmahoney.net/dc/text8`

[2]We use the Gensim implementation: `https://radimrehurek.com/gensim/`

[3]We experimented with updating the initialized context lookup tables, and with randomly initialized context lookups, but found they were influenced too much by orthographic similarity from the character encoder.

[4]We used the NLTK implementation

[5]We used the Python implementation

[6]We found Morfessor to be quite conservative by default in its segmentations. The 2nd ranked segmentation gave better MAPs, which are the results we describe.

Model	All word MAP	Rich-morphology MAP
Random	0.233	0.261
Porter Stemmer	**0.705**	0.446
Morfessor	0.631	0.500
Char2Vec	0.593	**0.586**

Table 1: Results at retrieving intra-word morpheme boundaries.

Word	Model analysis	Gold-standard analysis
carrying	carry |ing	carry |ing
leninism	lenin |ism	lenin |ism
lesbianism	lesbia |nism	lesbian |ism
buses	buse |s	bus |es
government	gove |rnment	govern |ment
unrepentant	un |repent |ant	un |repent |ant
weaknesses	weak |nes |ses	weak |ness |es

Table 2: Morphological analyses for sample words from the corpus. We take the top N model predictions as the split points, where N is the number of gold-standard morphemes in the word.

As the test set is dominated by words with simple morphology, we also extracted all the morphologically rich words with 3 or more morphemes, and created a separate evaluation on this subsection. We report the results in Table 1.

As the results show, our model performs the best out of all the methods at analysing morphologically rich words with multiple morphemes. On these words, our model even outperforms Morfessor, which is explicitly designed as a morphological analyzer. This shows that our model learns splits which correspond well to human morphological analysis, even though we build no morphological knowledge into our model. However, when evaluating on all words, the Porter stemmer has a great advantage, as it is rule-based and able to give just the stem of words with great precision, which is effectively giving a canonical segmentation for words with just 2 morphemes.

We show some model analyses against the gold standard in Table 2.

4.2 Capturing semantic similarity

Next, we tested our model similarity scores against human similarity judgments. For these datasets, human annotators are asked to judge how similar two words are on a fixed scale. Model word vectors are evaluated based on ranking the word pairs according to their cosine similarity, and then measuring the correlation (using Spearman's

Model	WordSim353	MEN Test	RW
PPMI-SVD	0.607	**0.601**	0.293
SGNS	**0.667**	0.557	**0.388**
C2V-NO-ATT	0.361	0.298	0.317
CHAR2VEC	0.345	0.322	0.282

Table 3: Similarity correlations of in-vocabulary word pairs between the models and human annotators.

Model	WordSim353	MEN Test	RW	RW OOV
C2V-NO-ATT	**0.358**	0.292	**0.273**	0.233
CHAR2VEC	0.340	**0.318**	0.264	**0.243**

Table 4: Similarity correlations of all word pairs between the character-level models and human annotators. RW OOV indicates results specifically on pairs in the RW dataset with at least one word not seen in the training corpus.

ρ) between model judgments and human judgments (Levy et al., 2015).

We use the WordSim353 dataset (Finkelstein et al., 2002), the test split of the MEN dataset (Bruni et al., 2014), and the Rare Word (RW) dataset (Luong et al., 2013). The word pairs in the WordSim353 and MEN datasets are typically simple, commonly occurring words denoting basic concepts, whereas the RW dataset contains many morphologically derived words which have low corpus frequencies. This is reflected by how many of the test pairs in each dataset contain out of vocabulary (OOV) items: 3/353 and 6/1000 of the word pairs in WordSim353 and MEN, compared with 1083/2034 for the RW dataset.

We report results for in-corpus word pairs in Table 3, and for all word pairs for those models able to predict vectors for unseen words in Table 4.

Overall, word-based embedding models learn vectors that correlate better with human judgments, particularly for morphologically simple words. However, character-based models are competitive with word-based models on the RW dataset. While the words in this dataset appear rarely in our corpus (of the in-corpus words, over half appear fewer than 100 times), each morpheme may be common, and the character-level models can use this information. We note that on the entire RW dataset (of which over half contain an OOV word), the character-based models still perform reasonably. We also note that on word pairs in the RW test containing at least one OOV word, the

	In-vocabulary			Out-of-Vocabulary	
	germany	*football*	*bible*	*foulness*	*definately*
Char2Vec unfiltered	*germaine*	*footballer*	*bibles*	*illness*	*definitely*
	germanies	*footballing*	*testament*	*seriousness*	*indefinitely*
	germain	*footballing*	*librarianship*	*sickness*	*enthusiastically*
	germano	*foosball*	*literature*	*loudness*	*emphatically*
	germaniae	*footballers*	*librarian*	*cuteness*	*consistently*
Char2Vec filtered	*poland*	*footballer*	*testament*	*illness*	*definitely*
	german	*basketball*	*literature*	*blindness*	*consistently*
	spain	*tennis*	*hebrew*	*consciousness*	*drastically*
	germans	*rugby*	*judaism*	*hardness*	*theoretically*
	france	*baseball*	*biblical*	*weakness*	*infinitely*

Table 5: Filtered and unfiltered model nearest neighbours for some in-vocabulary and out-of-vocabulary words

full Char2Vec model outperforms the C2V model without morphology. This suggests that character-based embedding models are learning to morphologically analyse complex word forms, even on unseen words, and that giving the model the capability to learn word segments independently helps this process.

We also present some word nearest neighbours for our Char2Vec model in Table 5, both on the whole vocabulary and then filtering the nearest neighbours to only include words which appear 100 times or more in our corpus. This corresponds to keeping the top 10k words, which is common among language models (Ling et al., 2015; Kim et al., 2016). We note that nearest neighbour predictions include words that are orthographically distant but semantically similar, showing that our model has the capability to learn to compose characters into word meanings.

We also note that word nearest neighbours seem to be more semantically coherent when rarely-observed words are filtered out of the vocabulary, and more based on orthographic overlap when the entire vocabulary is included. This suggests that for rarely-observed words, the model is basing its predictions on orthographic analysis, whereas for more commonly observed words it can 'memorize' the mapping between the orthography and word semantics.

4.3 Capturing syntactic and semantic regularity

Finally, we evaluate the structure of the embedding space of our various models. In particular,

Model	All Acc	Sem. Acc	Syn. Acc
PPMI-SVD	0.365	**0.444**	0.341
SGNS	**0.436**	0.339	0.513
C2V-NO-ATT	0.316	0.016	0.472
CHAR2VEC	0.355	0.025	**0.525**

Table 6: Results on the Google analogy task

we test whether affixation corresponds to regular linear shifts in the embedding space.

To do this, we use the Google analogy dataset (Mikolov et al., 2013a). This consists of 19544 questions of the form "A is to B as C is to X". We split this collection into semantic and syntactic sections, based on whether the analogies between the words are driven by morphological changes or deeper semantic shifts. Example semantic questions are on capital-country relationships ("*Paris* is to *France* as *Berlin* is to *X*") and currency-country relationships ("*pound* is to *Great Britain* as *dollar* is to *X*"). Example syntactic questions are adjective-adverb relationships ("*amazing* is to *amazingly* as *apparent* is to *X*") and opposites formed by prefixing a negation particle ("*acceptable* is to *unacceptable* as *aware* is to *X*"). This results in 5537 semantic analogies and 10411 syntactic analogies.

We use the method of Mikolov et al. (2013a) to answer these questions. We first ℓ_2-normalize all of our word vectors. Then, to answer a question of the form "A is to B as C is to X", we find the word

w which satisfies

$$w = \underset{w \in V - \{a,b,c\}}{\mathrm{argmax}}\ \cos(w, b - a + c) \qquad (4)$$

where a, b, c are the word vectors for the words A, B and C respectively.

We report the results in Table 6. The most intriguing result is that character-level models are competitive with word-level models for syntactic analogy, with our Char2Vec model holding the best result for syntactic analogy answering. This suggests that incorporating morphological knowledge explicitly rather than latently helps the model learn morphological features. However, on the semantic analogies, the character-based models do much worse than the word-based models. This is perhaps unsurprising in light of the previous section, where we demonstrate that character-based models do worse at the semantic similarity task than word-level models.

5   Discussion

We only report results for English. However, English is a morphologically impoverished language, with little inflection and relatively few productive patterns of derivation. Our morphology test set reflects this, with over half the words consisting of a simple morpheme, and over 90% having at most 2 morphemes.

This is unfortunate for our model, as it performs better on words with richer morphology. It gives consistently more accurate morphological analyses for these words compared to standard baselines, and matches word-level models for semantic similarity on rare words with rich morphology. In addition, it seems to learn morphosyntactic features to help solve the syntactic analogy task. Most of all, it is language-agnostic, and easy to port across different languages. We thus expect our model to perform even better for languages with a richer morphology than English, such as Turkish and German.

6   Conclusion

In this paper, we present a model which learns morphology and word embeddings jointly. Given a word, it splits the word in to segments and ranks the segments based on their context-predictive power. Our model can segment words into morphemes, and also embed the word into a representation space.

We show that our model is competitive at the task of morpheme boundary recovery compared to a dedicated morphological analyzer, beating dedicated analyzers on words with a rich morphology. We also show that in the representation space word affixation corresponds to linear shifts, demonstrating that our model can learn morphological features.

Finally, we show that character-level models, while outperformed by word-level models generally at the task of semantic similarity, are competitive at representing rare morphologically rich words. In addition, the character-level models can predict good quality representations for unseen words, with the morphologically aware character-level model doing slightly better.

References

Harald R. Baayen, Richard Piepenbrock, and Leon Gulikers. 1995. *The CELEX Lexical Database. Release 2 (CD-ROM)*. Linguistic Data Consortium, University of Pennsylvania, Philadelphia, Pennsylvania.

Dzmitry Bahdanau, Kyunghyun Cho, and Yoshua Bengio. 2014. Neural machine translation by jointly learning to align and translate. *ICLR*.

Miguel Ballesteros, Chris Dyer, and Noah A Smith. 2015. Improved transition-based parsing by modeling characters instead of words with LSTMs. *EMNLP*.

David A. Balota, Melvin J. Yap, Keith A. Hutchison, Michael J. Cortese, Brett Kessler, Bjorn Loftis, James H. Neely, Douglas L. Nelson, Greg B. Simpson, and Rebecca Treiman. 2007. The english lexicon project. *Behavior Research Methods*.

Frédéric Bastien, Pascal Lamblin, Razvan Pascanu, James Bergstra, Ian J. Goodfellow, Arnaud Bergeron, Nicolas Bouchard, and Yoshua Bengio. 2012. Theano: new features and speed improvements. Deep Learning and Unsupervised Feature Learning NIPS 2012 Workshop.

Yoshua Bengio, Réjean Ducharme, Pascal Vincent, and Christian Janvin. 2003. A neural probabilistic language model. *J. Mach. Learn. Res.*, 3:1137–1155, March.

James Bergstra, Olivier Breuleux, Frédéric Bastien, Pascal Lamblin, Razvan Pascanu, Guillaume Desjardins, Joseph Turian, David Warde-Farley, and Yoshua Bengio. 2010. Theano: a CPU and GPU math expression compiler. In *Proceedings of the Python for Scientific Computing Conference (SciPy)*, June.

Jan A. Botha and Phil Blunsom. 2014. Compositional Morphology for Word Representations and Language Modelling. In *ICML*, Beijing, China, jun. *Award for best application paper*.

Elia Bruni, Nam Khanh Tran, and Marco Baroni. 2014. Multimodal distributional semantics. *J. Artif. Int. Res.*

John A. Bullinaria and Joseph P. Levy. 2007. Extracting semantic representations from word co-occurrence statistics: A computational study. *Behavior Research Methods*.

Franois Chollet. 2015. Keras. https://github.com/fchollet/keras.

Ronan Collobert, Jason Weston, Léon Bottou, Michael Karlen, Koray Kavukcuoglu, and Pavel Kuksa. 2011. Natural language processing (almost) from scratch. *JMLR*, 12:2493–2537, November.

Ryan Cotterell, Tim Vieira, and Hinrich Schütze. 2016. A joint model of orthography and word segmentation. In *NAACL*.

Mathias Creutz and Krista Lagus. 2007. Unsupervised models for morpheme segmentation and morphology learning. *ACM Trans. Speech Lang. Process.*, 4(1):3:1–3:34, February.

Ferdinand de Saussure. 1916. *Course in General Linguistics*.

Lev Finkelstein, Evgeniy Gabrilovich, Yossi Matias, Ehud Rivlin, Zach Solan, Gadi Wolfman, and Eytan Ruppin. 2002. Placing search in context: The concept revisited. *ACM Trans. Inf. Syst.*

John Goldsmith. 2001. Unsupervised learning of the morphology of a natural language. *Computational Linguistics*, 27(2):153–198, June.

Sharon Goldwater, Mark Johnson, and Thomas L. Griffiths. 2005. Interpolating between types and tokens by estimating power-law generators. In Y. Weiss, B. Schlkopf, and J. Platt, editors, *NIPS*, pages 459–466. MIT Press, Cambridge, MA.

Zelig S. Harris. 1954. Distributional structure. *Word*.

Sepp Hochreiter and Jürgen Schmidhuber. 1997. Long short-term memory. *Neural Computation*, 9(8):1735–1780, November.

Yoon Kim, Yacine Jernite, David Sontag, and Alexander M. Rush. 2016. Character-aware neural language models. *AAAI*.

Diederik P. Kingma and Jimmy Ba. 2015. Adam: A method for stochastic optimization. *ICLR*.

Angeliki Lazaridou, Marco Marelli, Roberto Zamparelli, and Marco Baroni. 2013. Compositional-ly derived representations of morphologically complex words in distributional semantics. *ACL*.

Omer Levy, Yoav Goldberg, and Ido Dagan. 2015. Improving distributional similarity with lessons learned from word embeddings. *Transactions of the Association for Computational Linguistics*, 3:211–225.

Wang Ling, Tiago Luís, Luís Marujo, Ramón Fernandez Astudillo, Silvio Amir, Chris Dyer, Alan W. Black, and Isabel Trancoso. 2015. Finding function in form: Compositional character models for open vocabulary word representation. *EMNLP*.

Minh-Thang Luong, Richard Socher, and Christopher D. Manning. 2013. Better word representations with recursive neural networks for morphology. In *CoNLL*.

Tomas Mikolov, Kai Chen, Greg Corrado, and Jeffrey Dean. 2013a. Efficient estimation of word representations in vector space. *ICLR Workshop*.

Tomas Mikolov, Ilya Sutskever, Kai Chen, Greg Corrado, and Jeffrey Dean. 2013b. Distributed representations of words and phrases and their compositionality. *NIPS*.

Andriy Mnih and Koray Kavukcuoglu. 2013. Learning word embeddings efficiently with noise-contrastive estimation. In C. J. C. Burges, L. Bottou, M. Welling, Z. Ghahramani, and K. Q. Weinberger, editors, *Advances in Neural Information Processing Systems 26*, pages 2265–2273. Curran Associates, Inc.

Karthik Narasimhan, Regina Barzilay, and Tommi S. Jaakkola. 2015. An unsupervised method for uncovering morphological chains. *TACL*.

Radu Soricut and Franz Ochs. 2015. Unsupervised morphology induction using word embeddings. *NAACL*.

Kristina Toutanova, Dan Klein, Christopher D. Manning, and Yoram Singer. 2003. Feature-rich part-of-speech tagging with a cyclic dependency network. In *In Proceedings of NAACL*.

Wenduan Xu, Michael Auli, and Stephen Clark. 2015. CCG supertagging with a recurrent neural network. *ACL*.

Xiang Zhang, Junbo Zhao, and Yann LeCun. 2015. Character-level convolutional networks for text classification. *NIPS*.

George Kingsley Zipf. 1935. *The psycho-biology of language*.

On the Compositionality and Semantic Interpretation of English Noun Compounds

Corina Dima
Collaborative Research Center 833
University of Tübingen, Germany
`corina.dima@uni-tuebingen.de`

Abstract

In this paper we present a study covering the creation of *compositional distributional representations* for English noun compounds (e.g. *computer science*) using two compositional models proposed in the literature. The compositional representations are first evaluated based on their similarity to the corresponding corpus-learned representations and then on the task of automatic classification of semantic relations for English noun compounds. Our experiments show that compositional models are able to build meaningful representations for more than half of the test set compounds. However, using pre-trained compositional models does not lead to the expected performance gains for the semantic relation classification task. Models using compositional representations have a similar performance as a basic classification model, despite the advantage of being pre-trained on a large set of compounds.

1 Introduction

Creating word representations for multiword expressions is a challenging NLP task. The challenge comes from the fact that these constructions have "idiosyncratic interpretations that cross word boundaries (or spaces)" (Sag et al., 2002). A good example of such challenging multiword expressions are noun compounds (e.g. *finger nail, health care*), where the meaning of a compound often involves combining some aspect or aspects of the meanings of its constituents.

Over the last few years distributed word representations (Collobert et al., 2011b; Mikolov et al., 2013; Pennington et al., 2014) have proven very successful at representing single-token words, and there have been several attempts at creating compositional distributional models of meaning for multi-token expressions, in particular adjective-word phrases (Baroni and Zamparelli, 2010), determiner phrases (Dinu et al., 2013b) or verb phrases (Yin and Schütze, 2014).

Studying the semantics of multiword units, and in particular the semantic interpretation of noun compounds has been an active area of research in both theoretical and computational linguistics. Here, one train of research has focused on understanding the mechanism of compounding by providing a label for the relation between the constituents (e.g. in *finger nail*, the *nail* is PART OF the *finger*) as in (Ó Séaghdha, 2008; Tratz and Hovy, 2010) or by identifying the preposition in the preferred paraphrase of the compound (e.g. *nail of the finger*) as in (Lauer, 1995).

In this paper, we explore compositional distributional models for English noun compounds, and analyze the impact of such models on the task of predicting the compound-internal semantic relation given a labeled dataset of compounds. At the same time, we analyze the results of the compositional process through the lens of the semantic relation annotation, in an attempt to uncover compounding patterns that are particularly challenging for the compositional distributional models.

2 Context and Compound Interpretation

There are two possible settings for compound interpretation: *out-of-context interpretation* and *context-dependent interpretation*.

Bauer (1983, pp. 45) describes a continuum of types of complex words, arranged with respect to their formation status and to how dependent their interpretation is on the context: (i)*"nonce formations*, coined by a speaker/writer on the spur of the moment to cover some immediate need", where there is a large ambiguity with respect to the meaning of the compound which cannot be resolved without the immediate context (e.g. Nakov's (2013) example compound *plate length*,

Proceedings of the 1st Workshop on Representation Learning for NLP, pages 27–39,
Berlin, Germany, August 11th, 2016. ©2016 Association for Computational Linguistics

for which a possible interpretation in a given context could be *what your hair is when it drags in your food*); (ii) *institutionalized lexemes*, whose potential ambiguity is canceled by the frequency of use and familiarity with the term, and whose more established meaning could be inferred based on the meanings of the constituents and prior world experience, without the need for an immediate context (e.g. *orange juice*); (iii) *lexicalized lexemes*, where the meaning has become a convention which cannot be inferred from the constituents alone and can only be successfully interpreted if the term is familiar or if the context provides enough clues (e.g. *couch potato*[1]).

The available datasets we use (described in Section 3) are very likely to contain some very low frequency items of type (i), whose actual interpretation would necessitate taking the immediate context into account, as well some highly lexicalized compounds of type (iii), where the meaning can only be deduced from context. Nevertheless, because of a lack of annotated resources that provide the semantic interpretation of a compound together with its context, we will focus on the out-of-context interpretation of compounds.

3   Datasets

3.1   English Compound Dataset for Compositionality

The English compound dataset used for the composition tests was constructed from two existing compound datasets and a selection of the nominal compounds in the WordNet database. The first existing compound dataset was described in (Tratz, 2011) and contains 19158 compounds[2]. The second existing compound dataset was proposed in (Ó Séaghdha, 2008) and contains 1443 compounds[3].

Additional compounds were collected from the WordNet 3.1 database files [4], more specifically from the noun database file `data.noun`. The WordNet compound collection process involved 3 steps: (i) collecting all candidate compounds,

i.e. words that contained an underscore or a dash (e.g. *abstract_entity*, *self-service*); (ii) filtering out candidates that included numbers or dots, or had more than 2 constituents; (iii) filtering out candidates where either one of the constituents had a part-of-speech tag that was different from `noun` or `verb`. The part-of-speech tagging of the candidate compounds was performed using the *spaCy* Python library for advanced natural language processing[5]. The reason for allowing both `noun` and `verb` as accepted part-of-speech tags was that given the extremely limited context available when PoS-tagging a compound the tagger would frequently label as `verb` multi-sense words that were actually nouns in the given context (e.g. *eye drop*, where *drop* was tagged as a verb). The final compound list extracted from WordNet 3.1 contained 18775 compounds.

The compounds collected from all three resources were combined into one list. The list was deduplicated and filtered for capitalized compounds (the Tratz (2011) dataset contained a small amount of person names and titles). A final filtering step removed all the compounds where either of the two constituents or the compound itself did not have a minimum frequency of 100 in the *support corpus* (presented later, in Section 4.1). The frequency filtering step was motivated by the assumption that the compositional process can be better modeled using "well-learned" word vectors that are based on a minimum number of contexts.

The final dataset contains 27220 compounds, formed through the combination of 5335 modifiers and 4761 heads. The set of unique modifiers and heads contains 7646 words, with 2450 words appearing both as modifiers and as heads. The dictionary for the final dataset contains therefore 34866 unique words. The dataset was partitioned into `train`, `test` and `dev` splits containing 19054, 5444 and 2722 compounds respectively.

3.2   English Compound Datasets for Semantic Interpretation

The Tratz (2011) dataset and the Ó Séaghdha (2008) dataset are both annotated with semantic relations between the compound constituents. The Tratz (2011) dataset has 37 semantic relations and 19158 compounds. The Ó Séaghdha (2008) dataset has 1443 compounds annotated with 6 coarse relation labels (ABOUT, ACTOR, BE, HAVE,

---

[1] a *couch potato* is not a potato, but a person who exercises little and spends most of the time in front of a TV.

[2] The dataset is part of the semantically-enriched parser described in (Tratz, 2011) which can be obtained from `http://www.isi.edu/publications/licensed-sw/fanseparser/`

[3] Available at `http://www.cl.cam.ac.uk/~do242/Resources/1443_Compounds.tar.gz`

[4] Available at `http://wordnetcode.princeton.edu/wn3.1.dict.tar.gz`

[5] `https://spacy.io/`

IN, INST). Appendix A lists the relations in the two datasets together with some example annotated compounds.

For both datasets a small fraction of the constituents had to be recoded to the artificial underscore-based form described in Section 4.1, in order to maximize the coverage of the word representations for the constituents (e.g. *database* was recoded to *data_base*).

4 Composition Models for English Nominal Compounds

A common view of natural language regards it as being inherently compositional. Words are combined to obtain phrases, which in turn combine to create sentences. The composition continues to the paragraph, section and document levels. It is this defining trait of human language, its *compositionality*, that allows us to produce and to understand the potentially infinite number of utterances in a human language.

Gottlob Frege (1848-1925) is credited with phrasing this intuition into the form of a principle, known as the Principle of Compositionality: "The meaning of the whole is a function of the meaning of the parts and their mode of combination" (Dowty et al., 1981, p.8).

The adoption of distributional vectors as a proxy for the meaning of individual words (in other words, having a "meaning of the parts") encouraged researchers to focus their attention on finding *composition models* which could act as the "mode of combination".

When applied to vector space models of language, the idea of looking for a "mode of combination" translates to finding a composition function f which takes as input some n-dimensional distributional representations for the two constituents constructed using a support corpus, $u^{corpus}, v^{corpus} \in \mathbb{R}^n$ and outputs another n-dimensional representation for the compound $p^{composed} \in \mathbb{R}^n$,

$$p^{composed} = f(u^{corpus}, v^{corpus})$$

Additionally, we consider $p^{corpus} \in \mathbb{R}^n$, the learned representation for the compound, to be the "gold standard" for the composed representation of the compound $p^{composed}$. Therefore the composition function f should minimize J_{MSE}, the mean squared error between the composed and the corpus-induced representations:

$$J_{MSE} = \sum_{i=1}^{nc} \frac{1}{n} \sum_{j=1}^{n} (p_{ij}^{composed} - p_{ij}^{corpus})^2$$

where nc is the number of compounds in our dataset.

Previous studies like (Guevara, 2010; Baroni and Zamparelli, 2010) evaluate their proposed composition functions on training data created using the following procedure: first, they gather a set of word pairs to model. Then, a large corpus is used to construct distributional representations both for the word pairs as well as for the individual words in each pair. In order to derive word pair representations the corpus is first pre-processed such that all the occurrences of the word pairs of interest are linked with the underscore character '_'. This tricks the tokenizer into considering each pair a singe-unit word, thus making it possible to record its co-occurrence statistics using the same distributional methods one would use for a genuine single-unit word.

The same methodology is applied here for creating a training dataset for compositional models using the list of compounds described in Section 3.1. The process is detailed in Section 4.1.

Next, we selected two composition functions (we also refer to them as composition models) from the ones presented in the literature:

- the *full additive* model, introduced in Zanzotto et al. (2010) (in their work this model is called the *estimated additive model*) and popularized as part of the DISSECT toolkit (Dinu et al., 2013a; Dinu et al., 2013b). In this model the two constituent vectors u and $v \in \mathbb{R}^n$ are composed by multiplying them via two square matrices $\mathbf{A}, \mathbf{B} \in \mathbb{R}^{n \times n}$. $\mathbf{A}$ and $\mathbf{B}$ are the same for every u and v, so during training we only have to estimate the parameters in two $n \times n$ matrices, making the model constant in the number of parameters. The mathematical formulation of the full additive model is presented in Eq. 1.

$$p = \mathbf{A}u + \mathbf{B}v \qquad (1)$$

- the *matrix* model, introduced in Socher et al. (2011). It is a non-linear composition model where the constituent vectors $u, v \in \mathbb{R}^n$ are first concatenated, resulting in a vector

$[u; v] \in \mathbb{R}^{2n}$ and then multiplied with a matrix $\mathbf{W} \in \mathbb{R}^{2n \times n}$. The result of the multiplication is an n-dimensional vector which is passed as a final step through a non-linear function g (in this case the element-wise hyperbolic tangent `tanh`). The parameter matrix $\mathbf{W}$ which has to be estimated during the training process is the same for all the possible input vectors u and v. Since this composition function is implemented via a neural network, a bias term $b \in \mathbb{R}^n$ is added after the multiplication of the matrix $\mathbf{W}$ with the concatenated vector $[u; v]$. The complete form of this composition function is given in Eq. 2.

$$p = g(\mathbf{W}[u; v] + b) \tag{2}$$

The preference for these particular composition models is justified by their constant number of parameters with respect to the vocabulary size. This allows us to use this composition model for a significantly larger number of constituents than the one in the list of compounds it was trained on. In particular, this allows us to predict a composition vector even for the compounds that were not attested in the corpus, if their constituents are frequent enough to be part of our full vocabulary.

Both models were reimplemented using the Torch7 library (Collobert et al., 2011a), whose *nn-graph* module allows for an easy creation of architectures with multiple inputs and outputs. Reimplementing the composition models is also justified by the use of trained composition models as a form of *pre-training* for the semantic interpretation models described in Section 5.

4.1 Compound-aware Word Representations

The *support corpus* for creating English word representations for compositionality experiments (referred to in Section 3.1) was obtained by concatenating the raw text from the ENCOW14AX corpus (Schäfer, 2015) and the pre-processed 2014 English Wikipedia dump described and made available in Müller and Schütze (2015). A preprocessing step similar to the one described in Müller and Schütze (2015) was applied to the concatenated corpus: the text was lowercased and the digits were replaced with 0s. An additional preprocessing step was necessary for creating compound representations. A list of compounds (described in Section 3.1) was used to recode the initial corpus such that the two-part compounds in the list

would be considered a single token. The recoding process involved replacing different spelling variants of a compound - written as two separate words, contiguously or with a dash (as in *dress code*, *dresscode* or *dress-code*), as well as their respective plural forms (*dress codes*, *dress-codes*, *dress-codes*) with an artificial underscore-based form (e.g. *dress_code*). We did not, however, modify the plural first constituents (i.e. *savings account*), nor did we normalize the spelling variation which is the result of different spelling standards as in *color scheme* (American English) and *colour scheme* (British English). The result was a 9 billion words raw-text corpus with a corresponding vocabulary containing 424,014 words (both simplex words and compounds) with minimum frequency 100 (the full vocabulary had 16M words).

The raw-text corpus was the basis for training 300 dimensional word representations using the GloVe package (Pennington et al., 2014). The GloVe model was trained for 15 iterations using a 10-word symmetric context (20 words in total) for constructing the co-occurence matrix. The vector spaces were normalized to the *L2*-norm, first across features and then across samples using *scikit-learn* (Pedregosa et al., 2011).

4.2 Evaluation and Results

The parameters of the two composition models described in Section 4 were estimated with the help of the list of compounds in the `train` set described in Section 3.1 and the word representations presented in Section 4.1. We evaluated the performance of the composition models on the `test` split of the dataset, using the rank evaluation proposed by Baroni and Zamparelli (2010). Using a trained model, we generate *composed* representations for all the compounds in the `test` set. The composed representation of each compound is ranked with respect to all the 34866 unique words in the dictionary (the set of all compounds and their respective constituents) using the cosine similarity. The best possible result is when the corpus-learned representation is the nearest neighbor of the composed representation, and corresponds to assigning the rank 1 to the composed vector. Rank 2 is assigned when the corpus-learned representation is the second nearest neighbor, and so on. The cut-off rank 1000 is assigned to all the representations with a rank

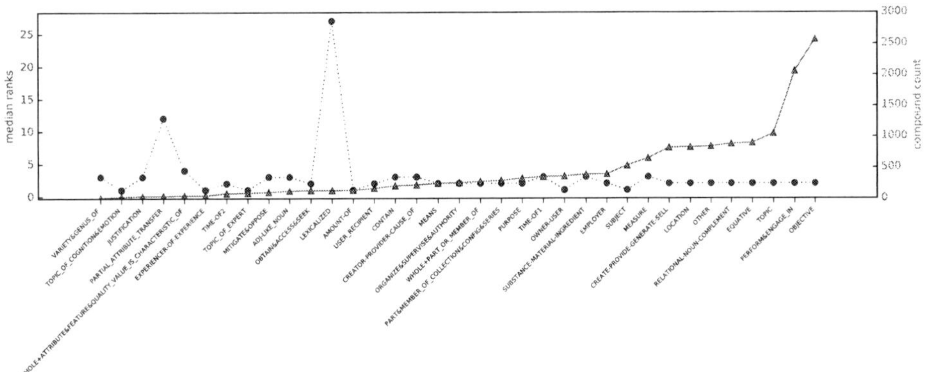

Figure 1: Semantic relations in the Tratz (2011) dataset: number of compounds labeled with a relation (green triangle) vs. the median rank assigned to their composed representations by the *full additive* model (blue circle).

≥ 1000. The first, second and third quartiles (Q1, Q2/median, Q3) are then computed for the sorted list of ranks of the composed representations of the test set compounds. The result of our evaluation are displayed in Table 1.

Model	Ranks dev				Ranks test			
	Q1	Q2	Q3	Max	Q1	Q2	Q3	Max
matrix	2	5	28	$1K$	1	5	25	$1K$
full additive	1	5	28	$1K$	1	5	25	$1K$

Table 1: Composition models results: quartiles for the ranks assigned to the `dev` and `test` composed representations (lower is better).

Both composition models obtain good results on the `test` dataset with respect to the Q1, Q2, Q3 quartiles. Ranks in the 1-5 range, which were assigned to half of the `test` set compounds correspond to a well-built compound representation which resides in the expected vectorial neighborhood. For the next quarter of the data, the rank in the 6-25 range points to a representation that might still be considered reasonable depending on the application. For the last segment of ranked compounds the constructed representations are most likely incorrect. As detailed in the next paragraph, such high ranks usually suggest a difficulty in creating a compound representation based on the constituent representations and indicate that the compound belongs to a special class (e.g. lexicalized, multi-sense etc). For both models the maximum assigned rank is the cut-off rank 1000.

To put these results into perspective, the results of compositional models were interpreted through the lens of annotated semantic relations in publicly available datasets. Figure 1 plots the median rank assigned to the compounds with a particular semantic relation against the number of compounds labeled with that semantic relation in the subset of the Tratz (2011) dataset included in the compositionality dataset described in Section 3.1. The figure confirms the intuition that recovering the meaning of lexicalized compounds like *eye candy* and *basket case* is very difficult given only the constituents: the LEXICALIZED relation, which labels 131 compounds, has the median rank 27. Another difficult semantic relation for the composition model is PARTIAL_ATTRIBUTE_TRANSFER, which labels compounds such as *hairline crack* and *bullet train*, which has a median rank of 12 for its 41 compounds. The high median rank suggests that this type of attributive relation is difficult to model using distributional representations of the individual constituents, as it is based on a common attribute which is not present in the surface form of the compound (the *width* for the *hairline* and the *crack*; the *speed* for the *bullet* and the *train*).

5 Automatic Semantic Relation Classification for English Nominal Compounds

The goal of the current section is to asses the impact of composition models on the task of *automatic semantic relation classification for English nominal compounds*. The semantic relation classification task deals with predicting the correct label for the relation between the constituents of a compound, given a fixed set of possible labels (e.g. the label of the relation linking *iron* to *fence* in *iron fence* is MATERIAL). The two datasets described in Section 3.2 are used as a testbed for the comparison of the composition models described in Section 4. The state of the art results for these datasets are 65.4% 5-fold cross-validation (CV) accuracy for the Ó Séaghdha dataset, obtained in Ó Séaghdha and Copestake (2013), 79.3% 10-fold CV accuracy for an unpublished version of the Tratz dataset, with 17509 noun pairs annotated with 43 semantic relations (Tratz and Hovy, 2010) and 77.70% 10-fold CV accuracy on a subset of the Tratz (2011) dataset obtained in (Dima and Hinrichs, 2015).

Our MLP architecture for semantic classification consists of two modules: the *composition module* which constructs the compound representation from the representations of its constituents and the *classification module* which takes as input the constructed compound representation and uses it as a basis for classifying the compound with respect to the semantic relations defined by each dataset.[6]

In the experiments described next the architecture of the composition module varies according to the method used for creating compound representations, while the classification module always follows the same architecture: a linear layer $W_{rel} \in \mathbb{R}^{n_c \times k}$ where n_c is the dimensionality of the compound representation and k is the number of semantic relations in the dataset, the nonlinearity `tanh` and a softmax layer that selects the "winning" semantic relation from the k possible relations. Another constant addition to the full architecture is a 0.1 dropout layer for regularization and a `reLU` nonlinearity between the composition and the classification modules.

All the described models are trained using a negative log-likelihood criterion, optimized with mini-batch Adagrad (Duchi et al., 2011) with a fixed initial learning rate (0.1, Tratz dataset; $5e-2$, Ó Séaghdha dataset), learning rate decay $1e - 5$, weight decay $1e - 5$ and a batch size of 100 as hyperparameters for the optimization process. The models are trained using early stopping with a patience of 100 epochs.

Our working hypothesis is that learning first how to compose, and then doing the semantic re-

lation classification task should yield better results than when the composition is learned based only on the signal provided by the classification task. We expect that pre-training the composition module would make the semantic relation classification task easier and that having a good compound representation would aid its semantic interpretation.

We define as a *basic* composition module a simple architecture that takes as input u and v, the two n-dimensional constituent representations, concatenates them, and multiplies the concatenated $2n$-dimensional vector with a matrix W. Depending on the output dimensions of the model we want to compare it to, the dimensions of W will range from $\in \mathbb{R}^{2n \times n}$ to $\in \mathbb{R}^{2n \times 4n}$.

Table 2 presents the results of the classification models, grouped according to the number of parameters in the composition module. We used the *matrix* and *full additive* composition models evaluated in Section 4.2 as pre-trained composition modules.

The first two rows in Table 2 present the results of doing semantic relation classification using the *composed* compound representations as the only input to the classifier. In these settings, which are labeled *compoM*$_{300 \times 600}$ and *compoFA*$_{300 \times 600}$, the input is the composed representation as computed by the pretrained *matrix* and *full additive* composition models. The composed representations are kept fixed during the classification process. This configuration obtained the weakest results from all the tested configurations. An explanation for this result might be that the composition models perform well for only half of our test compounds, meaning that a good portion of the compounds have a potentially suboptimal representation.

In the next two rows the pre-trained composition models are *fine-tuned* for the semantic classification task (models labeled *pretrain_matrix*$_{600 \times 300}$ and *pretrain_fullAdditive*$_{600 \times 300}$). The input in this case are the initial corpus-based vectors of the two constituents.

Contrary to our hypothesis, the classification results of the *basic*$_{600 \times 300}$ model (the last model in the first subsection) are on par or slightly better than the previous results, where the classification used the direct or fine-tuned output of a pre-trained composition module.

This effect extends to the other settings that

---

[6]The code for composing representations and for doing automatic classification of semantic relations is available at `https://github.com/corinadima/gWordcomp`

Composition module	Pre-trained?	Fine-tuned?	Tratz CV	Ó Séaghdha CV
$compoM_{300\times600}$	yes	no	74.22%	57.52%
$compoFA_{300\times600}$	yes	no	73.70%	56.62%
$pretrain\_matrix_{600\times300}$	yes	yes	78.05%	59.18%
$pretrain\_fullAdditive_{600\times300}$	yes	yes	77.89%	59.18%
$basic_{600\times300}$	no	no	78.57%	59.25%
$pretrain\_matrix\_fullAdd_{600\times600}$	yes	yes	78.92%	59.39%
$basic_{600\times600}$	no	no	78.88%	59.60%
$c1c2\_compoM_{900\times900}$	yes	no	79.06%	**61.12%**
$c1c2\_compoFA_{900\times900}$	yes	no	79.07%	59.60%
$basic_{600\times1200}$	no	no	79.03%	59.60%
$c1c2\_compoMcompoFA_{1200\times1200}$	yes	no	79.16%	59.18%
$basic_{600\times2400}$	no	no	**79.36%**	58.49%

Table 2: Semantic relation classification results on the Tratz and Ó Séaghdha datasets using accuracy as a classification measure. Results obtained through 10-fold cross-validation on the Tratz dataset and 5-fold CV on the Ó Séaghdha dataset (with the original folds).

were investigated, where:

- both pre-trained composition models are used for the composition module; the compound representation is the concatenation of the two composed representations ($pretrain\_matrix\_fullAdd_{600\times600}$); even if the combined classifier outperforms each of the classifiers based on only one composition model, its results are still on par with the ones of the basic classifier with a similar number of parameters ($basic_{600\times600}$, see results in Table 2, subsection 2).

- the initial vector representations of the constituents as well as their composed representation are used as an input ($c1c2\_compoM_{900\times900}$, $c1c2\_compoFA_{900\times900}$); the composition is in this case not fine-tuned; the results on the Tratz (2011) dataset are again similar to the comparable basic model ($basic_{600\times1200}$). The $c1c2\_compoM_{900\times900}$ obtains the best overall result, 61.12%, on the Ó Séaghdha (2008) dataset.

- the input consists of the initial vector representations and both composed representations ($c1c2\_compoMcompoFA_{1200\times1200}$); the composed vectors are fixed; the results are compared to the $basic_{600\times2400}$ model (again, with a similar number of parameters). This last section contains the best overall result for

the Tratz (2011) dataset, 79.36%, obtained by the $basic_{600\times2400}$ model.

To understand this unexpected result we analyzed the predictions made by the best performing classification models, $basic_{600\times2400}$ and $c1c2\_compoMcompoFA_{1200\times1200}$, on the Tratz (2011) dataset. The analysis targeted the distribution of errors per semantic relation for each of the two classifiers. As the distribution of compounds labeled with a particular semantic relation is rather skewed, we found it more informative to look at the percentage of errors for each class (shown in Figure 2) rather than at the absolute error values.

A first conclusion that can be drawn from this figure is that the two models have roughly the same distribution of errors: both struggle the most with the semantic relations with a low compound count (left side of the figure) and with the class of lexicalized compounds. In addition, even some of the relations with more than 500 labeled examples (starting from SUBSTANCE-MATERIAL-INGREDIENT) remain difficult to identify (in particular the heterogeneous OTHER relation, which labels compounds whose relation is not covered by the rest of the inventory, and the EQUATIVE relation, which labels compounds based on subtype or logical-and relations, i.e. *mozzarella cheese, female owner*).

An analysis of the classification errors revealed that both classifiers actually struggle to generalize above the lexical level. If a word has the majority

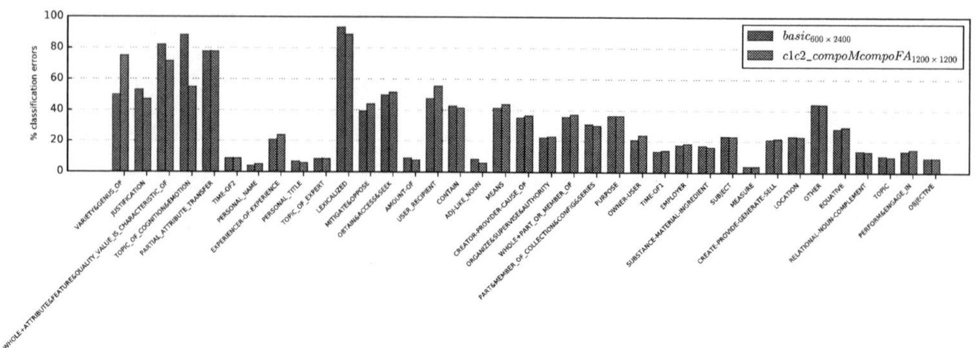

Figure 2: Error analysis for semantic relation classification on the Tratz (2011) dataset: the percentage of errors for each semantic class for the $basic_{600\times2400}$ (blue, left) and the $c1c2\_compoMcompoFA_{1200\times1200}$ (green, right) models. The semantic relations are sorted by compound count (low count to the left, high count to the right).

of compounds labeled with a relation (e.g. TOPIC for compounds with *guide*: *travel guide*, *fishing guide*), other compounds with the head *guide* will be assigned the same relation (e.g. *user guide* is labeled TOPIC although the correct relation is USER_RECIPIENT). This phenomenon where the classifier memorizes lexical associations between words in particular slots and classification labels as opposed to learning relations between the words in the two slots is referred to in Levy et al. (2015) as *lexical memorization*. To get a sense of how this phenomenon affects our classification task we plot in Figure 3 two ratios for every semantic relation in the Tratz (2011) dataset: the number of *distinct modifiers* over the total number of compounds and the number of *distinct heads* over the total number of compounds. A small ratio indicates that a large subset of the compounds labeled with a particular semantic relation share a common constituent: for example, the ADJ-LIKE_NOUN subclass has only 7 distinct modifiers for 254 compounds, resulting in a very low modifier ratio (0.03). Similarly the AMOUNT_OF subclass has 168 compounds with 15 heads (head ratio: 0.09).

Comparing Figure 3 to Figure 2, one can observe that the majority of the classes with either a low head ratio or a low modifier ratio also have the lowest percentage of errors per class. This is the case for relations like TIME_OF2, TOPIC_OF_EXPERT, AMOUNT-OF, ADJ-LIKE_NOUN and MEASURE, all of which have under 10% error rate. A notable exception is the PERSONAL_NAME semantic relation for which the classifiers manage to have a small error

rate even with very diverse modifiers and heads (both modifier and head ratio is 0.96). A more realistic estimate of the actual performance of the classifiers are the semantic relations which have both a larger number of compounds and a more diverse set of constituents, like in the case of USER_RECIPIENT, CREATOR_PROVIDER_CAUSE-OF, WHOLE+PART_OR_MEMBER_OF or PURPOSE, which have a 40-60% error rate.

As a concluding point, the best results in our study are comparable to the respective state-of-the-art counterparts (79.3%/77.70% accuracy vs. 79.36% accuracy on the Tratz data; 65.4% vs. 61.12% on the Ó Séaghdha data). However, it must be taken into account that in this study the only available information for the classifiers comes from the word embeddings themselves, and from the correlations learned in the composition process. By contrast the classifiers used in (Tratz and Hovy, 2010; Tratz, 2011) relied on an extensive feature set which included information from the WordNet (hypernyms, synonyms, gloss, part-of-speech indicators; "lexicalized" indicator if the compound had an WN entry as a single term), Roget's thesaurus, surface-level features and n-gram features extracted from the Web 1T corpus. The state-of-the-art of the Ó Séaghdha (2008) dataset is based on both lexical features (for the individual constituents, constructed on the basis of dependency relations) and relational features (for the typical interactions of constituents, constructed on the basis of contexts where the constituents appear together as separate words). The distributional representations we use as input are likely to cap-

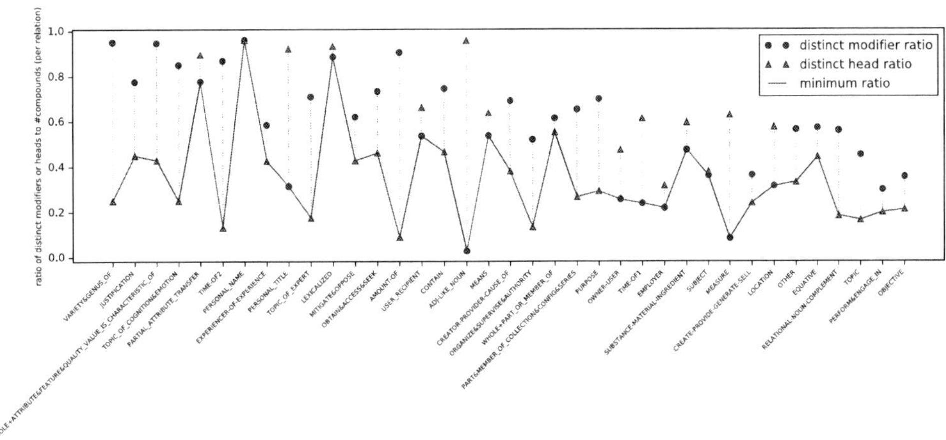

Figure 3: Diversity of modifiers and heads per relation: a low ratio for either the modifier (blue circle) or the head (green triangle) correlates with a small error rate for the classification task.

ture both lexical and relational aspects, but do not explicitly model pairwise constituent interactions.

6   Conclusions

In this paper we have presented a study covering the creation of compositional distributional representations for English noun compounds. The representations created by the compositional models were further evaluated on the task of automatic semantic relation classification for English noun compounds, using two preexisting annotated datasets. The experiments are, to the best of our knowledge, the first compositional investigations focusing on English noun compounds. The composition models have a good performance and manage to build meaningful composed vectors for half of the test set compounds.

The investigation of semantically annotated compound datasets revealed that composition models cannot represent compounds with lexicalized meaning. This suggests that the representations of compounds where the meaning of the whole is substantially different from the one of the parts should be learned directly from corpus co-occurence data. Another vocabulary-related observation concerns the extensive pre-processing necessary to create distributional representations for compounds. Spelling variation (e.g. *health care*, *health-care*, *healthcare*) artificially creates separate forms with the same meaning. Such forms should be identified and collapsed back to a single meaning representation when creating vector space models of language.

The semantic relation classification experiments showed that state-of-the-art composition models must be further refined before they can be of use for downstream semantic tasks. In our experiments compositional models were unable to improve upon a basic model for semantic relation identification, despite being pretrained on a large set of compounds. Their mediocre performance on the semantic relation classification task is likely caused by the use of individual word representations as the exclusive source of input, combined with the expectation that mathematical composition functions can directly extract and model patterns of interaction between pairs of words. We hypothesize that composition models can be improved by first modeling the semantic relations between words and then using the semantic relation representations together with the word representations as inputs to the composition process.

Acknowledgments

The author is indebted to Melanie Bell for the fruitful discussions and her comprehensive comments on the initial draft of the paper. The author would also like to thank Emanuel Dima and Erhard Hinrichs, as well as the anonymous reviewers for their insightful comments and suggestions. Financial support for the research reported in this paper was provided by the German Research Foundation (DFG) as part of the Collaborative Research Center "The Construction of Meaning" (SFB 833), project A3.

References

Marco Baroni and Roberto Zamparelli. 2010. Nouns are vectors, adjectives are matrices: Representing adjective-noun constructions in semantic space. In *Proceedings of the Conference on Empirical Methods in Natural Language Processing (EMNLP 2010)*, pages 1183–1193, Massachussetts, USA.

Laurie Bauer. 1983. *English word-formation*. Cambridge University Press.

Ronan Collobert, Koray Kavukcuoglu, and Clément Farabet. 2011a. Torch7: A Matlab-like environment for machine learning. In *BigLearn, NIPS Workshop*.

Ronan Collobert, Jason Weston, Léon Bottou, Michael Karlen, Koray Kavukcuoglu, and Pavel Kuksa. 2011b. Natural language processing (almost) from scratch. *The Journal of Machine Learning Research*, 12:2493–2537.

Corina Dima and Erhard Hinrichs. 2015. Automatic noun compound interpretation using deep neural networks and word embeddings. In *Proceedings of the 11th International Conference on Computational Semantics (IWCS 2015)*, pages 173–183, London, UK.

Georgiana Dinu, The Pham Nghia, and Marco Baroni. 2013a. DISSECT - DIStributional SEmantics Composition Toolkit. In *Proceedings of the 51st Annual Meeting of the Association for Computational Linguistics (ACL 2013)*, pages 31–36, Sofia, Bulgaria.

Georgiana Dinu, The Pham Nghia, and Marco Baroni. 2013b. General estimation and evaluation of compositional distributional semantic models. In *ACL Workshop on Continuous Vector Space Models and their Compositionality*, Sofia, Bulgaria.

David R. Dowty, Robert Wall, and Stanley Peters. 1981. *Introduction to Montague semantics*, volume 11 of *Synthese Language Library*. Springer Science & Business Media.

John Duchi, Elad Hazan, and Yoram Singer. 2011. Adaptive subgradient methods for online learning and stochastic optimization. *The Journal of Machine Learning Research*, 12:2121–2159.

Emiliano Guevara. 2010. A regression model of adjective-noun compositionality in distributional semantics. In *Proceedings of the 2010 Workshop on GEometrical Models of Natural Language Semantics*, pages 33–37. Association for Computational Linguistics.

Mark Lauer. 1995. *Designing statistical language learners: Experiments on compound nouns*. Ph.D. thesis, Macquarie University.

Omer Levy, Steffen Remus, Chris Biemann, Ido Dagan, and Israel Ramat-Gan. 2015. Do Supervised Distributional Methods Really Learn Lexical Inference Relations? In *Proceedings of the 2015 Conference of the North American Chapter of the Association for Computational Linguistics - Human Language Technologies (NAACL HLT 2015)*, Denver, CO, USA.

Tomas Mikolov, Kai Chen, Greg Corrado, and Jeffrey Dean. 2013. Efficient estimation of word representations in vector space. *arXiv preprint arXiv:1301.3781*.

Thomas Müller and Hinrich Schütze. 2015. Robust morphological tagging with word representations. In *Proceedings of the 2015 Conference of the North American Chapter of the Association for Computational Linguistics - Human Language Technologies (NAACL HLT 2015)*, Denver, CO, USA.

Preslav Nakov. 2013. On the interpretation of noun compounds: Syntax, semantics, and entailment. *Natural Language Engineering*, 19(03):291–330.

Diarmuid Ó Séaghdha and Ann Copestake. 2013. Interpreting compound nouns with kernel methods. *Natural Language Engineering*, 19(03):331–356.

Diarmuid Ó Séaghdha. 2008. *Learning compound noun semantics*. Ph.D. thesis, Computer Laboratory, University of Cambridge. Published as University of Cambridge Computer Laboratory Technical Report 735.

F. Pedregosa, G. Varoquaux, A. Gramfort, V. Michel, B. Thirion, O. Grisel, M. Blondel, P. Prettenhofer, R. Weiss, V. Dubourg, J. Vanderplas, A. Passos, D. Cournapeau, M. Brucher, M. Perrot, and E. Duchesnay. 2011. Scikit-learn: Machine learning in Python. *Journal of Machine Learning Research*, 12:2825–2830.

Jeffrey Pennington, Richard Socher, and Christopher D. Manning. 2014. GloVe: Global vectors for word representation. In *Proceedings of the Empirical Methods in Natural Language Processing (EMNLP 2014)*, volume 12.

Ivan A. Sag, Timothy Baldwin, Francis Bond, Ann Copestake, and Dan Flickinger. 2002. Multiword expressions: A pain in the neck for NLP. In *Computational Linguistics and Intelligent Text Processing*, pages 1–15. Springer.

Roland Schäfer. 2015. Processing and querying large web corpora with the COW14 architecture. In *Challenges in the Management of Large Corpora (CMLC-3)*.

Richard Socher, Jeffrey Pennington, Eric H. Huang, Andrew Y. Ng, and Christopher D. Manning. 2011. Semi-supervised recursive autoencoders for predicting sentiment distributions. In *Proceedings of the Conference on Empirical Methods in Natural Language Processing (EMNLP 2011)*, pages 151–161. Association for Computational Linguistics.

Stephen Tratz and Eduard Hovy. 2010. A taxonomy, dataset, and classifier for automatic noun compound interpretation. In *Proceedings of the 48th Annual Meeting of the Association for Computational Linguistics (ACL-10)*, Uppsala, Sweden.

Stephen Tratz. 2011. *Semantically-enriched parsing for natural language understanding*. Ph.D. thesis, University of Southern California.

Wenpeng Yin and Hinrich Schütze. 2014. An exploration of embeddings for generalized phrases. In *ACL 2014 Student Research Workshop*, pages 41–47, Baltimore, USA.

Fabio Massimo Zanzotto, Ioannis Korkontzelos, Francesca Fallucchi, and Suresh Manandhar. 2010. Estimating Linear Models for Compositional Distributional Semantics. In *Proceedings of the 23rd International Conference on Computational Linguistics*, pages 1263–1271.

A Overview of the Semantic Relations in the Tratz (2011) and Ó Séaghdha (2008) Datasets

Category name	Dataset percentage	Example
Objective		
OBJECTIVE	17.1%	leaf blower
Doer-Cause-Means		
SUBJECT	3.5%	police abuse
CREATOR-PROVIDER-CAUSE_OF	1.5%	ad revenue
JUSTIFICATION	0.3%	murder arrest
MEANS	1.5%	faith healer
Purpose/Activity Group		
PERFORM&ENGAGE_IN	11.5%	cooking pot
CREATE-PROVIDE-GENERATE-SELL	4.8%	nicotine patch
OBTAIN&ACCESS&SEEK	0.9%	shrimp boat
MITIGATE&OPPOSE	0.8%	flak jacket
ORGANIZE&SUPERVISE&AUTHORITY	1.6%	ethics authority
PURPOSE	1.9%	chicken spit
Ownership, Experience, Employment, Use		
OWNER-USER	2.1%	family estate
EXPERIENCER-OF-EXPERIENCE	0.5%	family greed
EMPLOYER	2.3%	team doctor
USER_RECIPIENT	1.0%	voter pamphlet
Temporal Group		
TIME-OF1	2.2%	night work
TIME-OF2	0.5%	birth date
Location and Whole+Part/Member of		
LOCATION	5.2%	hillside home
WHOLE+PART_OR_MEMBER_OF	1.7%	robot arm
Composition and Containment Group		
CONTAIN	1.2%	shoe box
SUBSTANCE-MATERIAL-INGREDIENT	2.6%	plastic bag
PART&MEMBER_OF_COLLECTION&CONFIG&SERIES	1.8%	truck convoy
VARIETY&GENUS_OF	0.1%	plant species
AMOUNT-OF	0.9%	traffic volume
Topic Group		
TOPIC	7.0%	travel story
TOPIC_OF_COGNITION&EMOTION	0.3%	auto fanatic
TOPIC_OF_EXPERT	0.7%	policy expert
Other Complements Group		
RELATIONAL-NOUN-COMPLEMENT	5.6%	eye shape
WHOLE+ATTRIBUTE&FEATURE&QUALITY_VALUE_IS_CHARACTERISTIC_OF	0.3%	earth tone
Attributive and Equative		
EQUATIVE	5.4%	fighter plane
ADJ-LIKE_NOUN	1.3%	core activity
PARTIAL_ATTRIBUTE_TRANSFER	0.3%	skeleton crew
MEASURE	4.2%	hour meeting
Other		
LEXICALIZED	0.8%	pig iron
OTHER	5.4%	contact lense
Personal*		
PERSONAL_NAME	0.5%	Ronald Reagan
PERSONAL_TITLE	0.5%	Gen. Eisenhower

Table 3: Semantic relations in the Tratz inventory - abbreviated version of Table 4.5 from Tratz (2011).

Relation	Frequency	Proportion	Examples
BE	191	13.2%	guide dog, rubber wheel, cat burglar
HAVE	199	13.8%	family firm, coma victim, sentence structure, computer clock, star cluster
IN	308	21.3%	pig pen, air disaster, evening edition, dawn attack
ACTOR	266	18.4%	army coup, project organiser
INST	236	16.4%	cereal cultivation, foot imprint
ABOUT	243	16.8%	history book, waterways museum, embryo research, house price

Table 4: Semantic relations in the Ó Séaghdha inventory - Table 6.2 from Ó Séaghdha (2008), augmented with examples from Table 3.1.

Functional Distributional Semantics

Guy Emerson and Ann Copestake
Computer Laboratory
University of Cambridge
{gete2,aac10}@cam.ac.uk

Abstract

Vector space models have become popular in distributional semantics, despite the challenges they face in capturing various semantic phenomena. We propose a novel probabilistic framework which draws on both formal semantics and recent advances in machine learning. In particular, we separate predicates from the entities they refer to, allowing us to perform Bayesian inference based on logical forms. We describe an implementation of this framework using a combination of Restricted Boltzmann Machines and feedforward neural networks. Finally, we demonstrate the feasibility of this approach by training it on a parsed corpus and evaluating it on established similarity datasets.

1 Introduction

Current approaches to distributional semantics generally involve representing words as points in a high-dimensional vector space. However, vectors do not provide 'natural' composition operations that have clear analogues with operations in formal semantics, which makes it challenging to perform inference, or capture various aspects of meaning studied by semanticists. This is true whether the vectors are constructed using a *count* approach (e.g. Turney and Pantel, 2010) or an *embedding* approach (e.g. Mikolov et al., 2013), and indeed Levy and Goldberg (2014b) showed that there are close links between them. Even the tensorial approach described by Coecke et al. (2010) and Baroni et al. (2014), which naturally captures argument structure, does not allow an obvious account of context dependence, or logical inference.

In this paper, we build on insights drawn from formal semantics, and seek to learn representations which have a more natural logical structure, and which can be more easily integrated with other sources of information.

Our contributions in this paper are to introduce a novel framework for distributional semantics, and to describe an implementation and training regime in this framework. We present some initial results to demonstrate that training this model is feasible.

2 Formal Framework of Functional Distributional Semantics

In this section, we describe our framework, explaining the connections to formal semantics, and defining our probabilistic model. We first motivate representing predicates with functions, and then explain how these functions can be incorporated into a representation for a full utterance.

2.1 Semantic Functions

We begin by assuming an extensional model structure, as standard in formal semantics (Kamp and Reyle, 1993; Cann, 1993; Allan, 2001). In the simplest case, a model contains a set of entities, which predicates can be true or false of. Models can be endowed with additional structure, such as for plurals (Link, 2002), although we will not discuss such details here. For now, the important point is that we should separate the representation of a predicate from the representations of the entities it is true of.

We generalise this formalisation of predicates by treating truth values as random variables,[1]

---

[1] The move to replace absolute truth values with probabilities has parallels in much computational work based on formal logic. For example, Garrette et al. (2011) incorporate distributional information in a Markov Logic Network (Richardson and Domingos, 2006). However, while their approach allows probabilistic inference, they rely on existing distributional vectors, and convert similarity scores to weighted logical formulae. Instead, we aim to learn representations which are directly interpretable within in a probabilistic logic.

Proceedings of the 1st Workshop on Representation Learning for NLP, pages 40–52,
Berlin, Germany, August 11th, 2016. ©2016 Association for Computational Linguistics

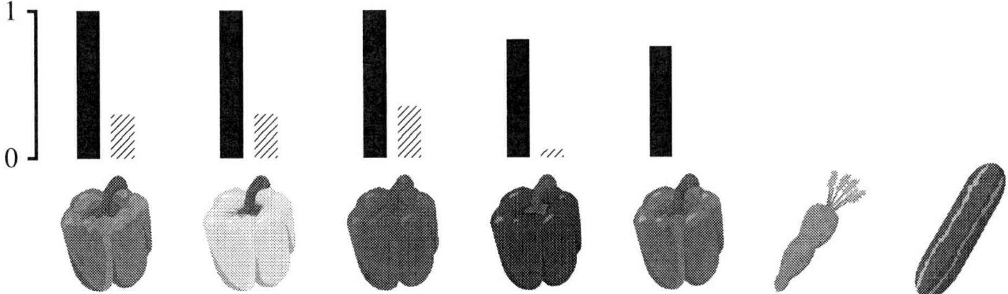

Figure 1: Comparison between a *semantic function* and a *distribution* over a space of entities. The vegetables depicted above (five differently coloured bell peppers, a carrot, and a cucumber) form a discrete semantic space $\mathcal{X}$. We are interested in the truth t of the predicate for *bell pepper* for an entity $x \in \mathcal{X}$. Solid bars: the semantic function $P(t|x)$ represents how much each entity is considered to be a pepper, and is bounded between 0 and 1; it is high for all the peppers, but slightly lower for atypical colours. Shaded bars: the distribution $P(x|t)$ represents our belief about an entity if all we know is that the predicate for *bell pepper* applies to it; the probability mass must sum to 1, so it is split between the peppers, skewed towards typical colours, and excluding colours believed to be impossible.

which enables us to apply Bayesian inference. For any entity, we can ask which predicates are true of it (or 'applicable' to it). More formally, if we take entities to lie in some semantic space $\mathcal{X}$ (whose dimensions may denote different features), then we can take the meaning of a predicate to be a function from $\mathcal{X}$ to values in the interval $[0, 1]$, denoting how likely a speaker is to judge the predicate applicable to the entity. This judgement is variable between speakers (Labov, 1973), and for borderline cases, it is even variable for one speaker at different times (McCloskey and Glucksberg, 1978).

Representing predicates as functions allows us to naturally capture vagueness (a predicate can be equally applicable to multiple points), and using values between 0 and 1 allows us to naturally capture gradedness (a predicate can be more applicable to some points than to others). To use Labov's example, the predicate for *cup* is equally applicable to vessels of different shapes and materials, but becomes steadily less applicable to wider vessels.

We can also view such a function as a classifier – for example, the semantic function for the predicate for *cat* would be a classifier separating cats from non-cats. This ties in with a view of concepts as abilities, as proposed in both philosophy (Dummett, 1978; Kenny, 2010), and cognitive science (Murphy, 2002; Bennett and Hacker, 2008). A similar approach is taken by Larsson (2013), who argues in favour of representing perceptual concepts as classifiers of perceptual input.

Note that these functions do not directly define probability distributions over entities. Rather, they define binary-valued *conditional* distribu-

tions, *given an entity*. We can write this as $P(t|x)$, where x is an entity, and t is a stochastic truth value. It is only possible to get a corresponding distribution over entities given a truth value, $P(x|t)$, if we have some background distribution $P(x)$. If we do, we can apply Bayes' Rule to get $P(x|t) \propto P(t|x)P(x)$. In other words, the truth of an expression depends crucially on our knowledge of the situation. This fits neatly within a verificationist view of truth, as proposed by Dummett (1976), who argues that to understand a sentence is to know how we could verify or falsify it.

By using both $P(t|x)$ and $P(x|t)$, we can distinguish between underspecification and uncertainty as two kinds of 'vagueness'. In the first case, we want to state partial information about an entity, but leave other features unspecified; $P(t|x)$ represents which kinds of entity could be described by the predicate, regardless of how likely we think the entities are. In the second case, we have uncertain knowledge about the entity; $P(x|t)$ represents which kinds of entity we think are likely for this predicate, given all our world knowledge.

For example, bell peppers come in many colours, most typically green, yellow, orange or red. As all these colours are typical, the semantic function for the predicate for *bell pepper* would take a high value for each. In contrast, to define a probability distribution over entities, we must split probability mass between different colours,[2]

---

[2]In fact, colour would be most properly treated as a continuous feature. In this case, $P(x)$ must be a probability density function, not a probability mass function, whose value would further depend on the parametrisation of the space.

and for a large number of colours, we would only have a small probability for each. As purple and blue are atypical colours for a pepper, a speaker might be less willing to label such a vegetable a pepper, but not completely unwilling to do so – this linguistic knowledge belongs to the semantic function for the predicate. In contrast, after observing a large number of peppers, we might conclude that blue peppers do not exist, purple peppers are rare, green peppers common, and red peppers more common still – this world knowledge belongs to the probability distribution over entities. The contrast between these two quantities is depicted in figure 1, for a simple discrete space.

2.2 Incorporation with Dependency Minimal Recursion Semantics

Semantic dependency graphs have become popular in NLP. We use Dependency Minimal Recursion Semantics (DMRS) (Copestake et al., 2005; Copestake, 2009), which represents meaning as a directed acyclic graph: nodes represent predicates/entities (relying on a one-to-one correspondence between them) and links (edges) represent argument structure and scopal constraints. Note that we assume a neo-Davidsonian approach (Davidson, 1967; Parsons, 1990), where events are also treated as entities, which allows a better account of adverbials, among other phenomena.

For example (simplifying a little), to represent *"the dog barked"*, we have three nodes, for the predicates *the*, *dog*, and *bark*, and two links: an ARG1 link from *bark* to *dog*, and a RSTR link from *the* to *dog*. Unlike syntactic dependencies, DMRS abstracts over semantically equivalent expressions, such as *"dogs chase cats"* and *"cats are chased by dogs"*. Furthermore, unlike other types of semantic dependencies, including Abstract Meaning Representations (Banarescu et al., 2012), and Prague Dependencies (Böhmová et al., 2003), DMRS is interconvertible with MRS, which can be given a direct logical interpretation.

We deal here with the extensional fragment of language, and while we can account for different quantifiers in our framework, we do not have space to discuss this here – for the rest of this paper, we neglect quantifiers, and the reader may assume that all variables are existentially quantified.

We can use the structure of a DMRS graph to define a probabilistic graphical model. This gives us a distribution over lexicalisations of the graph

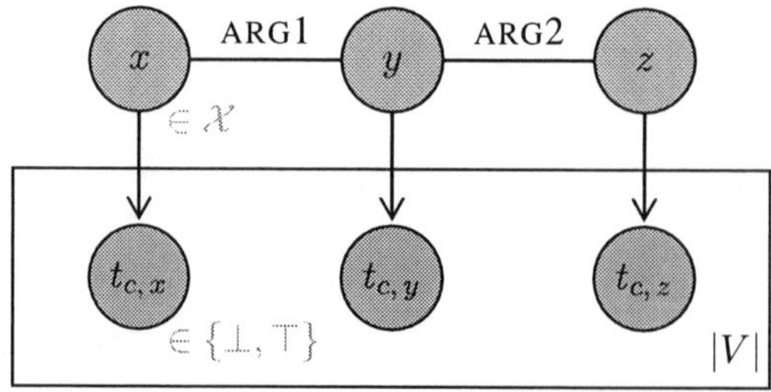

Figure 2: A situation composed of three entities. Top row: the entities x, y, and z lie in a semantic space $\mathcal{X}$, jointly distributed according to DMRS links. Bottom row: each predicate c in the vocabulary V has a stochastic truth value for each entity.

given an abstract graph structure, where links are labelled but nodes are not, we have a process to generate a predicate for each node. Although this process is different for each graph structure, we can share parameters between them (e.g. according to the labels on links). Furthermore, if we have a distribution over graph structures, we can incorporate that in our generative process, to produce a distribution over lexicalised graphs.

The entity nodes can be viewed as together representing a situation, in the sense of Barwise and Perry (1983). We want to be able to represent the entities without reference to the predicates – intuitively, the world is the same however we choose to describe it. To avoid postulating causal structure amongst the entities (which would be difficult for a large graph), we can model the entity nodes as an undirected graphical model, with edges according to the DMRS links. The edges are undirected in the sense that they don't impose conditional dependencies. However, this is still compatible with having 'directed' semantic dependencies – the probability distributions are not symmetric, which maintains the asymmetry of DMRS links.

Each node takes values in the semantic space $\mathcal{X}$, and the network defines a joint distribution over entities, which represents our knowledge about which situations are likely or unlikely. An example is shown in the top row of figure 2, of an entity y along with its two arguments x and z – these might represent an event, along with the agent and patient involved in the event. The structure of the graph means that we can factorise the joint distribution $P(x, y, z)$ over the entities as being proportional to the product $P(x, y)\,P(y, z)$.

For any entity, we can ask which predicates are true of it. We can therefore introduce a

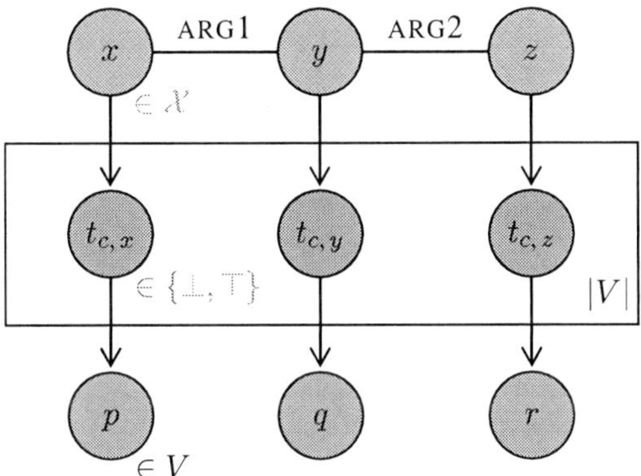

Figure 3: The probabilistic model in figure 2, extended to generate utterances. Each predicate in the bottom row is chosen out of all predicates which are true for the corresponding entity.

node for every predicate in the vocabulary, where the value of the node is either true ($\top$) or false ($\bot$). Each of these predicate nodes has a single directed link from the entity node, with the probability of the node being true being determined by the predicate's semantic function, i.e. $P\left(t_{c,x} = \top | x\right) = t_c(x)$. This is shown in the second row of figure 2, where the plate denotes that these nodes are repeated for each predicate c in the vocabulary V. For example, if the situation represented a dog chasing a cat, then nodes like $t_{dog,x}$, $t_{animal,x}$, and $t_{pursue,y}$ would be true (with high probability), while $t_{democracy,x}$ or $t_{dog,z}$ would be false (with high probability).

The probabilistic model described above closely matches traditional model-theoretic semantics. However, while we could stop our semantic description there, we do not generally observe truth-value judgements for all predicates at once;[3] rather, we observe utterances, which have specific predicates. We can therefore define a final node for each entity, which takes values over predicates in the vocabulary, and which is conditionally dependent on the truth values of all predicates. This is shown in the bottom row of figure 3. Including these final nodes means that we can train such a model on observed utterances. The process of choosing a predicate from the true ones may be complex, potentially depending on speaker intention and other pragmatic factors – but in section 3, we will simply choose a true predicate at random (weighted by frequency).

The separation of entities and predicates allows us to naturally capture context-dependent meanings. Following the terminology of Quine (1960), we can distinguish context-independent *standing* meaning from context-dependent *occasion* meaning. Each predicate type has a corresponding semantic function – this represents its standing meaning. Meanwhile, each predicate token has a corresponding entity, for which there is a posterior distribution over the semantic space, conditioning on the rest of the graph and any pragmatic factors – this represents its occasion meaning.

Unlike previous approaches to context dependence, such as Dinu et al. (2012), Erk and Padó (2008), and Thater et al. (2011), we represent meanings in and out of context by different kinds of object, reflecting a type/token distinction. Even Herbelot (2015), who explicitly contrasts individuals and kinds, embeds both in the same space.

As an example of how this separation of predicates and entities can be helpful, suppose we would like *"dogs chase cats"* and *"cats chase mice"* to be true in a model, but *"dogs chase mice"* and *"cats chase cats"* to be false. In other words, there is a dependence between the verb's arguments. If we represent each predicate by a single vector, it is not clear how to capture this. However, by separating predicates from entities, we can have two different entities which *chase* is true of, where one co-occurs with a dog-entity ARG1 and cat-entity ARG2, while the other co-occurs with a cat-entity ARG1 and a mouse-entity ARG2.

3 Implementation

In the previous section, we described a general framework for probabilistic semantics. Here we give details of one way that such a framework can be implemented for distributional semantics, keeping the architecture as simple as possible.

3.1 Network Architecture

We take the semantic space $\mathcal{X}$ to be a set of binary-valued vectors,[4] $\{0,1\}^N$. A situation s is then composed of entity vectors $x^{(1)}, \cdots, x^{(K)} \in \mathcal{X}$ (where the number of entities K may vary), along with links between the entities. We denote a link from $x^{(n)}$ to $x^{(m)}$ with label l as: $x^{(n)} \xrightarrow{l} x^{(m)}$. We define the background distribution over situations using a Restricted Boltzmann Machine

---

[3]This corresponds to what Copestake and Herbelot (2012) call an *ideal distribution*. If we have access to such information, we only need the two rows given in figure 2.

[4]We use the term *vector* in the computer science sense of a linear array, rather than in the mathematical sense of a point in a vector space.

(RBM) (Smolensky, 1986; Hinton et al., 2006), but rather than having connections between hidden and visible units, we have connections between components of entities, according to the links.

The probability of the network being in the particular configuration s depends on the *energy* of the configuration, $E^b(s)$, as shown in equations (1)-(2). A high energy denotes an unlikely configuration. The energy depends on the edges of the graphical model, plus bias terms, as shown in (3). Note that we follow the Einstein summation convention, where repeated indices indicate summation; although this notation is not typical in NLP, we find it much clearer than matrix-vector notation, particularly for higher-order tensors. Each link label l has a corresponding weight matrix $W^{(l)}$, which determines the strength of association between components of the linked entities. The first term in (3) sums these contributions over all links $x^{(n)} \xrightarrow{l} x^{(m)}$ between entities. We also introduce bias terms, to control how likely an entity vector is, independent of links. The second term in (3) sums the biases over all entities $x^{(n)}$.

$$P(s) = \frac{1}{Z} \exp\left(-E^b(s)\right) \qquad (1)$$

$$Z = \sum_{s'} \exp\left(-E^b(s')\right) \qquad (2)$$

$$-E^b(s) = \sum_{x^{(n)} \xrightarrow{l} x^{(m)}} W_{ij}^{(l)} x_i^{(n)} x_j^{(m)} - \sum_{x^{(n)}} b_i x_i^{(n)} \qquad (3)$$

Furthermore, since sparse representations have been shown to be beneficial in NLP, both for applications and for interpretability of features (Murphy et al., 2012; Faruqui et al., 2015), we can enforce sparsity in these entity vectors by fixing a specific number of units to be active at any time. Swersky et al. (2012) introduce this RBM variant as the Cardinality RBM, and also give an efficient exact sampling procedure using belief propagation. Since we are using sparse representations, we also assume that all link weights are non-negative.

Now that we've defined the background distribution over situations, we turn to the semantic functions t_c, which map entities x to probabilities. We implement these as feedforward networks, as shown in (4)-(5). For simplicity, we do not introduce any hidden layers. Each predicate c has a vector of weights $W'^{(c)}$, which determines the strength of association with each dimension of the semantic space, as well as a bias term $b'^{(c)}$. These together define the energy $E^p(x, c)$ of an entity x with the predicate, which is passed through a sigmoid function to give a value in the range $[0, 1]$.

$$t_c(x) = \sigma(-E^p(x, c)) = \frac{1}{1 + \exp\left(E^p\right)} \qquad (4)$$

$$-E^p(x, c) = W_i'^{(c)} x_i - b'^{(c)} \qquad (5)$$

Given the semantic functions, choosing a predicate for a entity can be hard-coded, for simplicity. The probability of choosing a predicate c for an entity x is weighted by the predicate's frequency f_c and the value of its semantic function $t_c(x)$ (how true the predicate is of the entity), as shown in (6)-(7). This is a mean field approximation to the stochastic truth values shown in figure 3.

$$P(c|x) = \frac{1}{Z_x} f_c t_c(x) \qquad (6)$$

$$Z_x = \sum_{c'} f_{c'} t_{c'}(x) \qquad (7)$$

3.2 Learning Algorithm

To train this model, we aim to maximise the likelihood of observing the training data – in Bayesian terminology, this is *maximum a posteriori* estimation. As described in section 2.2, each data point is a lexicalised DMRS graph, while our model defines distributions over lexicalisations of graphs. In other words, we take as given the observed distribution over abstract graph structures (where links are given, but nodes are unlabelled), and try to optimise how the model generates predicates (via the parameters $W_{ij}^{(l)}, b_i, W_i'^{(c)}, b'^{(c)}$).

For the family of optimisation algorithms based on gradient descent, we need to know the gradient of the likelihood with respect to the model parameters, which is given in (8), where $x \in \mathcal{X}$ is a latent entity, and $c \in V$ is an observed predicate (corresponding to the top and bottom rows of figure 3). Note that we extend the definition of energy from situations to entities in the obvious way: half the energy of an entity's links, plus its bias energy. A full derivation of (8) is given in the appendix.

$$\begin{aligned}
\frac{\partial}{\partial \theta} \log P(c) &= \mathbb{E}_{x|c} \left[\frac{\partial}{\partial \theta} \left(-E^b(x)\right) \right] \\
&\quad - \mathbb{E}_x \left[\frac{\partial}{\partial \theta} \left(-E^b(x)\right) \right] \\
&\quad + \mathbb{E}_{x|c} \left[(1 - t_c(x)) \frac{\partial}{\partial \theta} \left(-E^p(x, c)\right) \right] \\
&\quad - \mathbb{E}_{x|c} \left[\mathbb{E}_{c'|x} \left[(1 - t_{c'}(x)) \frac{\partial}{\partial \theta} \left(-E^p(x, c')\right) \right] \right]
\end{aligned} \qquad (8)$$

There are four terms in this gradient: the first two are for the background distribution, and the last two are for the semantic functions. In both cases, one term is positive, and conditioned on the data, while the other term is negative, and represents the predictions of the model.

Calculating the expectations exactly is infeasible, as this requires summing over all possible configurations. Instead, we can use a Markov Chain Monte Carlo method, as typically done for Latent Dirichlet Allocation (Blei et al., 2003; Griffiths and Steyvers, 2004). Our aim is to sample values of x and c, and use these samples to approximate the expectations: rather than summing over all values, we just consider the samples. For each token in the training data, we introduce a latent entity vector, which we use to approximate the first, third, and fourth terms in (8). Additionally, we introduce a latent predicate for each latent entity, which we use to approximate the fourth term – this latent predicate is analogous to the negative samples used by Mikolov et al. (2013).

When resampling a latent entity conditioned on the data, the conditional distribution $P(x|c)$ is unknown, and calculating it directly requires summing over the whole semantic space. For this reason, we cannot apply Gibbs sampling (as used in LDA), which relies on knowing the conditional distribution. However, if we compare two entities x and x', the normalisation constant cancels out in the ratio $P(x'|c)/P(x|c)$, so we can use the Metropolis-Hastings algorithm (Metropolis et al., 1953; Hastings, 1970). Given the current sample x, we can uniformly choose one unit to switch on, and one to switch off, to get a proposal x'. If the ratio of probabilities shown in (9) is above 1, we switch the sample to x'; if it's below 1, it is the probability of switching to x'.

$$\frac{P(x'|c)}{P(x|c)} = \frac{\exp\left(-E^b(x')\right)\frac{1}{Z_{x'}}t_c(x')}{\exp\left(-E^b(x)\right)\frac{1}{Z_x}t_c(x)} \tag{9}$$

Although Metropolis-Hastings avoids the need to calculate the normalisation constant Z of the background distribution, we still have the normalisation constant Z_x of choosing a predicate given an entity. This constant represents the number of predicates true of the entity (weighted by frequency). The intuitive explanation is that we should sample an entity which few predicates are true of, rather than an entity which many predicates are true of. We approximate this constant

by assuming that we have an independent contribution from each dimension of x. We first average over all predicates (weighted by frequency), to get the average predicate W^{avg}. We then take the exponential of W^{avg} for the dimensions that we are proposing switching off and on – intuitively, if many predicates have a large weight for a given dimension, then many predicates will be true of an entity where that dimension is active. This is shown in (10), where x and x' differ in dimensions i and i' only, and where k is a constant.

$$\frac{Z_x}{Z_{x'}} \approx \exp\left(k\left(W_i^{avg} - W_{i'}^{avg}\right)\right) \tag{10}$$

We must also resample latent predicates given a latent entity, for the fourth term in (8). This can similarly be done using the Metropolis-Hastings algorithm, according to the ratio shown in (11).

$$\frac{P(c'|x)}{P(c|x)} = \frac{f_{c'}t_{c'}(x)}{f_c t_c(x)} \tag{11}$$

Finally, we need to resample entities from the background distribution, for the second term in (8). Rather than recalculating the samples from scratch after each weight update, we used fantasy particles (persistent Markov chains), which Tieleman (2008) found effective for training RBMs. Resampling a particle can be done more straightforwardly than resampling the latent entities – we can sample each entity conditioned on the other entities in the situation, which can be done exactly using belief propagation (see Yedidia et al. (2003) and references therein), as Swersky et al. (2012) applied to the Cardinality RBM.

To make weight updates from the gradients, we used AdaGrad (Duchi et al., 2011), with exponential decay of the sum of squared gradients. We also used L1 and L2 regularisation, which determines our prior over model parameters.

We found that using a random initialisation is possible, but seems to lead to a long training time, due to slow convergence. We suspect that this could be because the co-occurrence of predicates is mediated via at least two latent vectors, which leads to mixing of semantic classes in each dimension, particularly in the early stages of training. Such behaviour can happen with complicated topic models – for example, Ó Séaghdha (2010) found this for their "Dual Topic" model. One method to reduce convergence time is to initialise predicate parameters using pre-trained vectors. The link parameters can then be initialised as follows: we consider a situation with just one entity, and for each predicate, we find the mean-field entity vector given the pre-trained predicate parameters; we then fix all entity vectors in our training corpus to be these mean-field vectors, and find the positive pointwise mutual information of each each pair of entity dimensions, for each link label. In particular, we initialised predicate parameters using our sparse SVO Word2Vec vectors, which we describe in section 4.2.

4 Training and Initial Experiments

In this section, we report the first experiments carried out within our framework.

4.1 Training Data

Training our model requires a corpus of DMRS graphs. In particular, we used WikiWoods, an automatically parsed version of the July 2008 dump of the full English Wikipedia, distributed by DELPH-IN[5]. This resource was produced by Flickinger et al. (2010), using the English Resource Grammar (ERG; Flickinger, 2000), trained on the manually treebanked subcorpus WeScience (Ytrestøl et al., 2009), and implemented with the PET parser (Callmeier, 2001; Toutanova et al., 2005). To preprocess the corpus, we used the python packages pydelphin[6] (developed by Michael Goodman), and pydmrs[7] (Copestake et al., 2016).

For simplicity, we restricted attention to subject-verb-object (SVO) triples, although we should stress that this is not an inherent limitation of our model, which could be applied to arbitrary graphs. We searched for all verbs in the WikiWoods treebank, excluding modals, that had either an ARG1 or an ARG2, or both. We kept all instances whose arguments were nominal, excluding pronouns and proper nouns. The ERG does not automatically convert out-of-vocabulary items from their surface form to lemmatised predicates, so we applied WordNet's morphological processor Morphy (Fellbaum, 1998), as available in NLTK (Bird et al., 2009). Finally, we filtered out situations including rare predicates, so that every predicate appears at least five times in the dataset.

As a result of this process, all data was of the form (*verb*, ARG1, ARG2), where one (but not

both) of the arguments may be missing. A summary is given in table 1. In total, the dataset contains 72m tokens, with 88,526 distinct predicates.

Situation type	No. instances
Both arguments	10,091,234
ARG1 only	6,301,280
ARG2 only	14,868,213
Total	31,260,727

Table 1: Size of the training data.

4.2 Evaluation

As our first attempt at evaluation, we chose to look at two lexical similarity datasets. The aim of this evaluation was simply to verify that the model was learning something reasonable. We did not expect this task to illustrate our model's strengths, since we need richer tasks to exploit its full expressiveness. Both of our chosen datasets aim to evaluate similarity, rather than thematic relatedness: the first is Hill et al. (2015)'s SimLex-999 dataset, and the second is Finkelstein et al. (2001)'s WordSim-353 dataset, which was split by Agirre et al. (2009) into similarity and relatedness subsets. So far, we have not tuned hyperparameters.

Results are given in table 2. We also trained Mikolov et al. (2013)'s Word2Vec model on the SVO data described in section 4.1, in order to give a direct comparison of models on the same training data. In particular, we used the continuous bag-of-words model with negative sampling, as implemented in Řehůřek and Sojka (2010)'s *gensim* package, with off-the-shelf hyperparameter settings. We also converted these to sparse vectors using Faruqui et al. (2015)'s algorithm, again using off-the-shelf hyperparameter settings. To measure similarity of our semantic functions, we treated each function's parameters as a vector and used cosine similarity, for simplicity.

For comparison, we also include the performance of Word2Vec when trained on raw text. For SimLex-999, we give the results reported by Hill et al. (2015), where the 2-word window model was the best performing model that they tested. For WordSim-353, we trained a model on the full WikiWoods text, after stripping all punctuation and converting to lowercase. We used the *gensim* implementation with off-the-shelf settings, except for window size (2 or 10) and dimension (200, as recommended by Hill et al.). In fact, our re-trained model performed better on SimLex-999 than Hill

[5]http://moin.delph-in.net/WikiWoods
[6]https://github.com/delph-in/pydelphin
[7]https://github.com/delph-in/pydmrs

Model	SimLex Nouns	SimLex Verbs	WordSim Sim.	WordSim Rel.
Word2Vec (10-word window)	.28	.11	**.69**	.46
Word2Vec (2-word window)	.30	.16	.65	.34
SVO Word2Vec	.44	.18	.61	.24
Sparse SVO Word2Vec	**.45**	**.27**	.63	.30
Semantic Functions	.26	.14	.34	**.01**

Table 2: Spearman rank correlation of different models with average annotator judgements. Note that we would like to have a *low* score on the final column (which measures relatedness, rather than similarity).

flood / water (related verb and noun)	.06
flood / water (related nouns)	.43
law / lawyer (related nouns)	.44
sadness / joy (near-antonyms)	.77
happiness / joy (near-synonyms)	.78
aunt / uncle (differ in a single feature)	.90
cat / dog (differ in many features)	.92

Table 3: Similarity scores for thematically related words, and various types of co-hyponym.

et al. reported (even when we used less preprocessing or a different edition of Wikipedia), although still worse than our sparse SVO Word2Vec model.

It is interesting to note that training Word2Vec on verbs and their arguments gives noticeably better results on SimLex-999 than training on full sentences, even though far less data is being used: $\sim$72m tokens, rather than $\sim$1000m. The better performance suggests that semantic dependencies may provide more informative contexts than simple word windows. This is in line with previous results, such as Levy and Goldberg (2014a)'s work on using syntactic dependencies. Nonetheless, this result deserves further investigation.

Of all the models we tested, only our semantic function model failed on the relatedness subset of WordSim-353. We take this as a positive result, since it means the model clearly distinguishes relatedness and similarity.

Examples of thematically related predicates and various kinds of co-hyponym are given in table 3, along with our model's similarity scores. However, it is not clear that it is possible, or even desirable, to represent these varied relationships on a single scale of similarity. For example, it could be sensible to treat *aunt* and *uncle* either as synonyms (they refer to relatives of the same degree of relatedness) or as antonyms (they are "opposite" in some sense). Which view is more appropriate will depend on the application, or on the context.

Nouns and verbs are very strongly distinguished, which we would expect given the structure of our model. This can be seen in the similarity scores between *flood* and *water*, when *flood* is considered either as a verb or as a noun.[8] SimLex-999 generally assigns low scores to near-antonyms, and to pairs differing in a single feature, which might explain why the performance of our model is not higher on this task. However, the separation of thematically related predicates from co-hyponyms is a promising result.

5 Related Work

As mentioned above, Coecke et al. (2010) and Baroni et al. (2014) introduce a tensor-based framework that incorporates argument structure through tensor contraction. However, for logical inference, we need to know how one vector can entail another. Grefenstette (2013) explores one method to do this; however, they do not show that this approach is learnable from distributional information, and furthermore, they prove that quantifiers cannot be expressed with tensors.

Balkır (2014), working in the tensorial framework, uses the quantum mechanical notion of a "mixed state" to model uncertainty. However, this doubles the number of tensor indices, so squares the number of dimensions (e.g. vectors become matrices). In the original framework, expressions with several arguments already have a high dimensionality (e.g. *whose* is represented by a fifth-order tensor), and this problem becomes worse.

Vilnis and McCallum (2015) embed predicates as Gaussian distributions over vectors. By assuming covariances are diagonal, this only doubles the number of dimensions (N dimensions for the mean, and N for the covariances). However, similarly to Mikolov et al. (2013), they simply assume

---

[8] We considered the ERG predicates `_flood_v_cause` and `_flood_n_of`, which were the most frequent predicates in WikiWoods for *flood*, for each part of speech.

that nearby words have similar meanings, so the model does not naturally capture compositionality or argument structure.

In both Balkır's and Vilnis and McCallum's models, they use the probability of a vector given a word – in the notation from section 2.1, $P(x|t)$. However, the opposite conditional probability, $P(t|x)$, more easily allows composition. For instance, if we know two predicates are true (t_1 and t_2), we cannot easily combine $P(x|t_1)$ and $P(x|t_2)$ to get $P(x|t_1, t_2)$ – intuitively, we're generating x twice. In contrast, for semantic functions, we can write $P(t_1, t_2|x) = P(t_1|x)P(t_2|x)$.

Gärdenfors (2004) argues concepts should be modelled as convex subsets of a semantic space. Erk (2009) builds on this idea, but their model requires pre-trained count vectors, while we learn our representations directly. McMahan and Stone (2015) also learn representations directly, considering colour terms, which are grounded in a well-understood perceptual space. Instead of considering a single subset, they use a probability distribution over subsets: $P(A|t)$ for $A \subset \mathcal{X}$. This is more general than a semantic function $P(t|x)$, since we can write $P(t|x) = \sum_{A \ni v} P(A|t)$. However, this framework may be *too* general, since it means we cannot determine the truth of a predicate until we know the entire set A. To avoid this issue, they factorise the distribution, by assuming different boundaries of the set are independent. However, this is equivalent to considering $P(t|x)$ directly, along with some constraints on this function. Indeed, for the experiments they describe, it is sufficient to know a semantic function $P(t|x)$. Furthermore, McMahan and Stone find expressions like *greenish* which are nonconvex in perceptual space, which suggests that representing concepts with convex sets may not be the right way to go.

Our semantic functions are similar to Cooper et al. (2015)'s probabilistic type judgements, which they introduce within the framework of Type Theory with Records (Cooper, 2005), a rich semantic theory. However, one difference between our models is that they represent situations in terms of situation types, while we are careful to define our semantic space without reference to any predicates. More practically, although they outline how their model might be learned, they assume we have access to type judgements for observed situations. In contrast, we describe how a model can be learned from observed utterances, which was necessary for us to train a model on a corpus.

Goodman and Lassiter (2014) propose another linguistically motivated probabilistic model, using the stochastic λ-calculus (more concretely, probabilistic programs written in Church). However, they rely on relatively complex generative processes, specific to individual semantic domains, where each word's meaning may be represented by a complex expression. For a wide-scale system, such structures would need to be extended to cover all concepts. In contrast, our model assumes a direct mapping between predicates and semantic functions, with a relatively simple generative structure determined by semantic dependencies.

Finally, our approach should be distinguished from work which takes pre-trained distributional vectors, and uses them within a richer semantic model. For example, Herbelot and Vecchi (2015) construct a mapping from a distributional vector to judgements of which quantifier is most appropriate for a range of properties. Erk (2016) uses distributional similarity to probabilistically infer properties of one concept, given properties of another. Beltagy et al. (2016) use distributional similarity to produce weighted inference rules, which they incorporate in a Markov Logic Network. Unlike these authors, we aim to directly learn interpretable representations, rather than interpret given representations.

6   Conclusion

We have introduced a novel framework for distributional semantics, where each predicate is represented as a function, expressing how applicable the predicate is to different entities. We have shown how this approach can capture semantic phenomena which are challenging for standard vector space models. We have explained how our framework can be implemented, and trained on a corpus of DMRS graphs. Finally, our initial evaluation on similarity datasets demonstrates the feasibility of this approach, and shows that thematically related words are not given similar representations. In future work, we plan to use richer tasks which exploit the model's expressiveness.

Acknowledgments

This work was funded by a Schiff Foundation Studentship. We would also like to thank Yarin Gal, who gave useful feedback on the specification of our generative model.

References

Eneko Agirre, Enrique Alfonseca, Keith Hall, Jana Kravalova, Marius Paşca, and Aitor Soroa. 2009. A study on similarity and relatedness using distributional and WordNet-based approaches. In *Proceedings of the 2009 Conference of the North American Chapter of the Association for Computational Linguistics*, pages 19–27.

Keith Allan. 2001. *Natural Language Semantics*. Blackwell Publishers.

Esma Balkır. 2014. Using density matrices in a compositional distributional model of meaning. Master's thesis, University of Oxford.

Laura Banarescu, Claire Bonial, Shu Cai, Madalina Georgescu, Kira Griffitt, Ulf Hermjakob, Kevin Knight, Philipp Koehn, Martha Palmer, and Nathan Schneider. 2012. Abstract meaning representation (amr) 1.0 specification. In *Proceedings of the 11th Conference on Empirical Methods in Natural Language Processing*, pages 1533–1544.

Marco Baroni, Raffaela Bernardi, and Roberto Zamparelli. 2014. Frege in space: A program of compositional distributional semantics. *Linguistic Issues in Language Technology*, 9.

Jon Barwise and John Perry. 1983. *Situations and Attitudes*. MIT Press.

Islam Beltagy, Stephen Roller, Pengxiang Cheng, Katrin Erk, and Raymond J. Mooney. 2016. Representing meaning with a combination of logical and distributional models.

Maxwell R Bennett and Peter Michael Stephan Hacker. 2008. *History of cognitive neuroscience*. John Wiley & Sons.

Steven Bird, Ewan Klein, and Edward Loper. 2009. *Natural language processing with Python*. O'Reilly Media, Inc.

David M Blei, Andrew Y Ng, and Michael I Jordan. 2003. Latent Dirichlet Allocation. *the Journal of Machine Learning Research*, 3:993–1022.

Alena Böhmová, Jan Hajič, Eva Hajičová, and Barbora Hladká. 2003. The Prague dependency treebank. In *Treebanks*, pages 103–127. Springer.

Ulrich Callmeier. 2001. Efficient parsing with large-scale unification grammars. Master's thesis, Universität des Saarlandes, Saarbrücken, Germany.

Ronnie Cann. 1993. *Formal semantics: An introduction*. Cambridge Textbooks in Linguistics. Cambridge University Press.

Bob Coecke, Mehrnoosh Sadrzadeh, and Stephen Clark. 2010. Mathematical foundations for a compositional distributional model of meaning. *Linguistic Analysis*, 36:345–384.

Robin Cooper, Simon Dobnik, Staffan Larsson, and Shalom Lappin. 2015. Probabilistic type theory and natural language semantics. *LiLT (Linguistic Issues in Language Technology)*, 10.

Robin Cooper. 2005. Austinian truth, attitudes and type theory. *Research on Language and Computation*, 3(2-3):333–362.

Ann Copestake and Aurelie Herbelot. 2012. Lexicalised compositionality. Unpublished draft.

Ann Copestake, Dan Flickinger, Carl Pollard, and Ivan A Sag. 2005. Minimal Recursion Semantics: An introduction. *Research on Language and Computation*.

Ann Copestake, Guy Emerson, Michael Wayne Goodman, Matic Horvat, Alexander Kuhnle, and Ewa Muszyńska. 2016. Resources for building applications with Dependency Minimal Recursion Semantics. In *Proceedings of the 10th International Conference on Language Resources and Evaluation (LREC 2016)*. European Language Resources Association (ELRA).

Ann Copestake. 2009. Slacker semantics: Why superficiality, dependency and avoidance of commitment can be the right way to go. In *Proceedings of 12th Conference of the European Chapter of the Association for Computational Linguistics*.

Donald Davidson. 1967. The logical form of action sentences. In Nicholas Rescher, editor, *The Logic of Decision and Action*, chapter 3, pages 81–95. University of Pittsburgh Press.

Georgiana Dinu, Stefan Thater, and Sören Laue. 2012. A comparison of models of word meaning in context. In *Proceedings of the 13th Conference of the North American Chapter of the Association for Computational Linguistics*, pages 611–615.

John Duchi, Elad Hazan, and Yoram Singer. 2011. Adaptive subgradient methods for online learning and stochastic optimization. *The Journal of Machine Learning Research*, 12:2121–2159.

Michael Dummett. 1976. What is a theory of meaning? (II). In Gareth Evans and John McDowell, editors, *Truth and Meaning*, pages 67–137. Clarendon Press (Oxford).

Michael Dummett. 1978. *What Do I Know When I Know a Language?* Stockholm University. Reprinted in Dummett (1993) *Seas of Language*, pages 94–105.

Katrin Erk and Sebastian Padó. 2008. A structured vector space model for word meaning in context. In *Proceedings of the 13th Conference on Empirical Methods in Natural Language Processing*, pages 897–906. Association for Computational Linguistics.

Katrin Erk. 2009. Representing words as regions in vector space. In *Proceedings of the 13th Conference on Computational Natural Language Learning*, pages 57–65. Association for Computational Linguistics.

Katrin Erk. 2016. What do you know about an alligator when you know the company it keeps? *Semantics and Pragmatics*, 9(17):1–63.

Manaal Faruqui, Yulia Tsvetkov, Dani Yogatama, Chris Dyer, and Noah Smith. 2015. Sparse overcomplete word vector representations. In *Proceedings of the 53rd Annual Conference of the Association for Computational Linguistics*.

Christiane Fellbaum. 1998. *WordNet*. Blackwell Publishers.

Lev Finkelstein, Evgeniy Gabrilovich, Yossi Matias, Ehud Rivlin, Zach Solan, Gadi Wolfman, and Eytan Ruppin. 2001. Placing search in context: The concept revisited. In *Proceedings of the 10th International Conference on the World Wide Web*, pages 406–414. Association for Computing Machinery.

Dan Flickinger, Stephan Oepen, and Gisle Ytrestøl. 2010. WikiWoods: Syntacto-semantic annotation for English Wikipedia. In *Proceedings of the 7th International Conference on Language Resources and Evaluation*.

Dan Flickinger. 2000. On building a more efficient grammar by exploiting types. *Natural Language Engineering*.

Peter Gärdenfors. 2004. *Conceptual spaces: The geometry of thought*. MIT Press, second edition.

Dan Garrette, Katrin Erk, and Raymond Mooney. 2011. Integrating logical representations with probabilistic information using Markov logic. In *Proceedings of the 9th International Conference on Computational Semantics (IWCS)*, pages 105–114. Association for Computational Linguistics.

Noah D Goodman and Daniel Lassiter. 2014. Probabilistic semantics and pragmatics: Uncertainty in language and thought. *Handbook of Contemporary Semantic Theory*.

Edward Grefenstette. 2013. Towards a formal distributional semantics: Simulating logical calculi with tensors. In *Proceedings of the 2nd Joint Conference on Lexical and Computational Semantics*.

Thomas L Griffiths and Mark Steyvers. 2004. Finding scientific topics. *Proceedings of the National Academy of Sciences*, 101(suppl 1):5228–5235.

W. Keith Hastings. 1970. Monte Carlo sampling methods using Markov chains and their applications. *Biometrika*, 57(1):97–109.

Aurélie Herbelot and Eva Maria Vecchi. 2015. Building a shared world: Mapping distributional to model-theoretic semantic spaces. In *Proceedings of the 2015 Conference on Empirical Methods in Natural Language Processing*, pages 22–32. Association for Computational Linguistics.

Aurélie Herbelot. 2015. Mr Darcy and Mr Toad, gentlemen: distributional names and their kinds. In *Proceedings of the 11th International Conference on Computational Semantics*, pages 151–161.

Felix Hill, Roi Reichart, and Anna Korhonen. 2015. Simlex-999: Evaluating semantic models with (genuine) similarity estimation. *Computational Linguistics*.

Geoffrey E Hinton, Simon Osindero, and Yee-Whye Teh. 2006. A fast learning algorithm for deep belief nets. *Neural computation*, 18(7):1527–1554.

Hans Kamp and Uwe Reyle. 1993. From discourse to logic; introduction to modeltheoretic semantics of natural language, formal logic and discourse representation theory.

Anthony Kenny. 2010. Concepts, brains, and behaviour. *Grazer Philosophische Studien*, 81(1):105–113.

William Labov. 1973. The boundaries of words and their meanings. In Charles-James N. Bailey and Roger W. Shuy, editors, *New ways of analyzing variation in English*, pages 340–73. Georgetown University Press.

Staffan Larsson. 2013. Formal semantics for perceptual classification. *Journal of Logic and Computation*.

Omer Levy and Yoav Goldberg. 2014a. Dependency-based word embeddings. In *Proceedings of the 52nd Annual Meeting of the Association for Computational Linguistics*, pages 302–308.

Omer Levy and Yoav Goldberg. 2014b. Neural word embedding as implicit matrix factorization. In Z. Ghahramani, M. Welling, C. Cortes, N. D. Lawrence, and K. Q. Weinberger, editors, *Advances in Neural Information Processing Systems 27*, pages 2177–2185. Curran Associates, Inc.

Godehard Link. 2002. The logical analysis of plurals and mass terms: A lattice-theoretical approach. In Paul Portner and Barbara H. Partee, editors, *Formal semantics: The essential readings*, chapter 4, pages 127–146. Blackwell Publishers.

Michael E McCloskey and Sam Glucksberg. 1978. Natural categories: Well defined or fuzzy sets? *Memory & Cognition*, 6(4):462–472.

Brian McMahan and Matthew Stone. 2015. A Bayesian model of grounded color semantics. *Transactions of the Association for Computational Linguistics*, 3:103–115.

Nicholas Metropolis, Arianna W Rosenbluth, Marshall N Rosenbluth, Augusta H Teller, and Edward Teller. 1953. Equation of state calculations by fast computing machines. *The Journal of Chemical Physics*, 21(6):1087–1092.

Tomas Mikolov, Kai Chen, Greg Corrado, and Jeffrey Dean. 2013. Efficient estimation of word representations in vector space. In *Proceedings of the 1st International Conference on Learning Representations*.

Brian Murphy, Partha Pratim Talukdar, and Tom M Mitchell. 2012. Learning effective and interpretable semantic models using non-negative sparse embedding. In *Proceedings of the 24th International Conference on Computational Linguistics (COLING 2012)*, pages 1933–1950. Association for Computational Linguistics.

Gregory Leo Murphy. 2002. *The Big Book of Concepts*. MIT Press.

Diarmuid Ó Séaghdha. 2010. Latent variable models of selectional preference. In *Proceedings of the 48th Annual Meeting of the Association for Computational Linguistics*, pages 435–444. Association for Computational Linguistics.

Terence Parsons. 1990. *Events in the Semantics of English: A Study in Subatomic Semantics*. Current Studies in Linguistics. MIT Press.

Willard Van Orman Quine. 1960. *Word and Object*. MIT Press.

Radim Řehůřek and Petr Sojka. 2010. Software framework for topic modelling with large corpora. In *Proceedings of the LREC 2010 Workshop on New Challenges for NLP Frameworks*, pages 45–50. ELRA.

Matthew Richardson and Pedro Domingos. 2006. Markov logic networks. *Machine learning*, 62(1-2):107–136.

Paul Smolensky. 1986. Information processing in dynamical systems: Foundations of harmony theory. In *Parallel Distributed Processing: Explorations in the Microstructure of Cognition*, volume 1, pages 194–281. MIT Press.

Kevin Swersky, Ilya Sutskever, Daniel Tarlow, Richard S Zemel, Ruslan R Salakhutdinov, and Ryan P Adams. 2012. Cardinality Restricted Boltzmann Machines. In *Advances in Neural Information Processing Systems*, pages 3293–3301.

Stefan Thater, Hagen Fürstenau, and Manfred Pinkal. 2011. Word meaning in context: A simple and effective vector model. In *Proceedings of the 5th International Joint Conference on Natural Language Processing*, pages 1134–1143.

Tijmen Tieleman. 2008. Training restricted Boltzmann machines using approximations to the likelihood gradient. In *Proceedings of the 25th International Conference on Machine Learning*, pages 1064–1071. Association for Computing Machinery.

Kristina Toutanova, Christoper D. Manning, Dan Flickinger, and Stephan Oepen. 2005. Stochastic HPSG parse selection using the Redwoods corpus. *Journal of Research on Language and Computation*.

Peter D. Turney and Patrick Pantel. 2010. From frequency to meaning: Vector space models of semantics. *Journal of Artificial Intelligence Research*.

Luke Vilnis and Andrew McCallum. 2015. Word representations via Gaussian embedding. In *Proceedings of the 3rd International Conference on Learning Representations*.

Jonathan S. Yedidia, William T. Freeman, and Yair Weiss. 2003. Understanding Belief Propagation and its generalizations. In *Exploring Artificial Intelligence in the New Millennium*, chapter 8, pages 239–269.

Gisle Ytrestøl, Stephan Oepen, and Daniel Flickinger. 2009. Extracting and annotating Wikipedia subdomains. In *Proceedings of the 7th International Workshop on Treebanks and Linguistic Theories*.

Appendix: Derivation of Gradients

In this section, we derive equation (8). As our model generates predicates from entities, to find the probability of observing the predicates, we need to sum over all possible entities. After then applying the chain rule to log, and expanding $P(x, c)$, we obtain the expression below.

$$\frac{\partial}{\partial\theta} \log P(c) = \frac{\partial}{\partial\theta} \log \sum_x P(x, c)$$

$$= \frac{\frac{\partial}{\partial\theta} \sum_x P(x, c)}{\sum_{x'} P(x', c)}$$

$$= \frac{\frac{\partial}{\partial\theta} \sum_x \frac{1}{Z_x} f_c t_c(x) \frac{1}{Z} \exp\left(-E^b(x)\right)}{\sum_{x'} P(x', c)}$$

When we now apply the product rule, we will get four terms, but we can make use of the fact that the derivatives of all four terms are multiples of the original term:

$$\frac{\partial}{\partial\theta} e^{-E^b(x)} = e^{-E^b(x)} \frac{\partial}{\partial\theta}\left(-E^b(x)\right)$$

$$\frac{\partial}{\partial\theta} t_c(x) = t_c(x)\left(1 - t_c(x)\right) \frac{\partial}{\partial\theta}\left(-E^p(x, c)\right)$$

$$\frac{\partial}{\partial\theta} \frac{1}{Z_x} = \frac{-1}{Z_x^2} \frac{\partial}{\partial\theta} Z_x$$

$$\frac{\partial}{\partial\theta} \frac{1}{Z} = \frac{-1}{Z^2} \frac{\partial}{\partial\theta} Z$$

This allows us to derive:

$$= \sum_x \frac{P(x,c)}{\sum_{x'} P(x',c)} \left[\frac{\partial}{\partial \theta} \left(-E^b(x) \right) \right.$$

$$+ \left(1 - t_c(x)\right) \frac{\partial}{\partial \theta} \left(-E^p(x,c) \right)$$

$$\left. - \frac{1}{Z_x} \frac{\partial}{\partial \theta} Z_x \right]$$

$$- \frac{\sum_x P(x,c)}{\sum_{x'} P(x',c)} \frac{1}{Z} \frac{\partial}{\partial \theta} Z$$

Finally, we write expectations instead of sums of probabilities:

$$= \mathbb{E}_{x|c} \left[\frac{\partial}{\partial \theta} \left(-E^b(x) \right) \right.$$

$$+ \left(1 - t_c(x)\right) \frac{\partial}{\partial \theta} \left(-E^p(x,c) \right)$$

$$\left. - \mathbb{E}_{c'|x} \left[\left(1 - t_{c'}(x)\right) \frac{\partial}{\partial \theta} \left(-E^p(x,c') \right) \right] \right]$$

$$- \mathbb{E}_x \left[\frac{\partial}{\partial \theta} \left(-E^b(x) \right) \right]$$

We can now simplify using conditional probabilities, and expand the derivatives of the normalisation constants:

$$= \sum_x P(x|c) \left[\frac{\partial}{\partial \theta} \left(-E^b(x) \right) \right.$$

$$+ \left(1 - t_c(x)\right) \frac{\partial}{\partial \theta} \left(-E^p(x,c) \right)$$

$$\left. - \frac{1}{Z_x} \frac{\partial}{\partial \theta} \sum_{c'} f_{c'} t_{c'}(x) \right]$$

$$- \frac{1}{Z} \frac{\partial}{\partial \theta} \sum_x \exp\left(-E^b(x) \right)$$

$$= \sum_x P(x|c) \left[\frac{\partial}{\partial \theta} \left(-E^b(x) \right) \right.$$

$$+ \left(1 - t_c(x)\right) \frac{\partial}{\partial \theta} \left(-E^p(x,c) \right)$$

$$\left. - \sum_{c'} \frac{f_{c'} t_{c'}(x)}{Z_x} \left(1 - t_{c'}(x)\right) \frac{\partial}{\partial \theta} \left(-E^p(x,c') \right) \right]$$

$$- \sum_x \frac{\exp\left(-E^b(x) \right)}{Z} \frac{\partial}{\partial \theta} \left(-E^b(x) \right)$$

$$= \sum_x P(x|c) \left[\frac{\partial}{\partial \theta} \left(-E^b(x) \right) \right.$$

$$+ \left(1 - t_c(x)\right) \frac{\partial}{\partial \theta} \left(-E^p(x,c) \right)$$

$$\left. - \sum_{c'} P(c'|x) \left(1 - t_{c'}(x)\right) \frac{\partial}{\partial \theta} \left(-E^p(x,c') \right) \right]$$

$$- \sum_x P(x) \frac{\partial}{\partial \theta} \left(-E^b(x) \right)$$

Assisting Discussion Forum Users using Deep Recurrent Neural Networks

Jacob Hagstedt P Suorra, Olof Mogren

Chalmers University of Technology, Sweden

`jacob.hagstedt@gmail.com`
`mogren@chalmers.se`

Abstract

We present a discussion forum assistant based on deep recurrent neural networks (RNNs). The assistant is trained to perform three different tasks when faced with a question from a user. Firstly, to recommend related posts. Secondly, to recommend other users that might be able to help. Thirdly, it recommends other channels in the forum where people may discuss related topics. Our recurrent forum assistant is evaluated experimentally by prediction accuracy for the end–to–end trainable parts, as well as by performing an end-user study. We conclude that the model generalizes well, and is helpful for the users.

1 Introduction

Discussion forums pose an interesting setting for human interaction. Chat systems, social media, and customer support systems are closely related, and in this paper, we will use the term "discussion forum" for all of them. These platforms play an increasingly important role for people, both in their professional and personal lives. For example, many software developers are familiar with web services such as Stack Overflow where you ask questions and other users can respond. Similar approaches are also used in customer support systems, allowing for quick turnaround time and a growing database of queries that can be made available to customers along with their responses.

In this paper, we will discuss how an automated system can help people make better use of existing platforms, and we propose a system that solves some of the associated problems. More specifically, our system helps people find their way around a discussion forum and gives intelli-

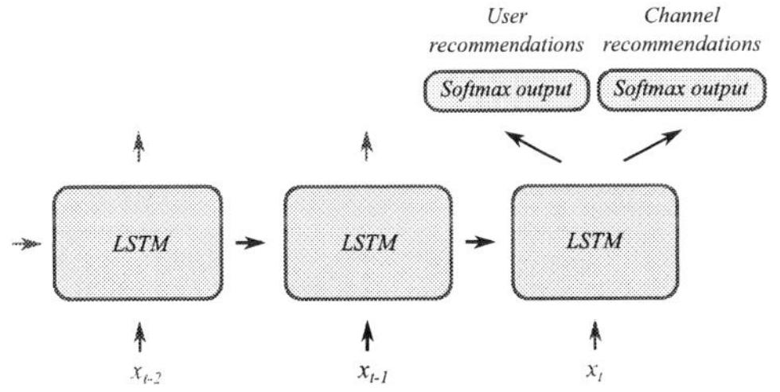

Figure 1: The layout of our recommendation model. The recommendations of users and channels are modelled as two different softmax output layers, attached to the end of a deep recurrent LSTM network modelling the input.

gent suggestions on where to get the information that they need.

The proposed system is based on deep recurrent neural networks (RNNs) and solves three different problems for discussion forum users. Firstly, faced with a question from a forum user, our system can suggest related posts from other channels in the system, based on a similarity measure computed on representations learned by a Long Short Term Memory (LSTM) RNN (Schmidhuber and Hochreiter, 1997). Secondly, we train a similar network end–to–end to recommend other forum users that might be knowledgeable about the current question. Finally, the model is also trained to suggest other channels where similar discussions have been held previously.

The assistant is evaluated on data from a corporate discussion forum on the chat-platform Slack. We show experimental results by evaluating the generalization of our model, as well as performing and analysing a study based on collecting data from users who interact with the discussion forum assistant.

Proceedings of the 1st Workshop on Representation Learning for NLP, pages 53–61,
Berlin, Germany, August 11th, 2016. ©2016 Association for Computational Linguistics

2 Background

A recurrent neural network (RNN) is an artificial neural network that can model a sequence of arbitrary length. The basic layout is simply a feedforward neural network with weight sharing at each position in the sequence, making it a recursive function on the hidden state h_t. The network has an input layer at each position t in the sequence, and the input x_t is combined with the the previous internal state h_{t-1}. In a language setting, it is common to model sequences of words, in which case each input x_t is the vector representation of a word. In the basic variant ("vanilla" RNN), the transition function is a linear transformation of the hidden state and the input, followed by a pointwise nonlinearity.

$$h_t = \tanh(W x_t + U h_{t-1} + b),$$

where W and U are weight matrices, and b is a bias term.

Basic "vanilla" RNNs have some shortcomings. One of them is that these models are unable to capture longer dependencies in the input. Another one is the vanishing gradient problem that affects many neural models when many layers get stacked after each other, making these models difficult to train (Hochreiter, 1998; Bengio et al., 1994).

The Long Short Term Memory (LSTM) (Schmidhuber and Hochreiter, 1997) was presented as a solution to these shortcomings. An LSTM is an RNN where the layer at each timestep is a cell that contains three gates controlling what parts of the internal memory will be kept (the forget gate f_t), what parts of the input that will be stored in the internal memory (the input gate i_t), as well as what will be included in the output (the output gate o_t). In essence, this means that the following expressions are evaluated at each step in the sequence, to compute the new internal memory c_t and the cell output h_t. Here "$\odot$" represents element-wise multiplication.

$$
\begin{aligned}
i_t &= \sigma(W^{(i)} x_t + U^{(i)} h_{t-1} + b^{(i)}), \\
f_t &= \sigma(W^{(f)} x_t + U^{(f)} h_{t-1} + b^{(f)}), \\
o_t &= \sigma(W^{(o)} x_t + U^{(o)} h_{t-1} + b^{(o)}), \\
u_t &= \tanh(W^{(u)} x_t + U^{(u)} h_{t-1} + b^{(u)}), \\
c_t &= i_t \odot u_t + f_t \odot c_{t-1}, \\
h_t &= o_t \odot \tanh(c_t).
\end{aligned}
\tag{1}
$$

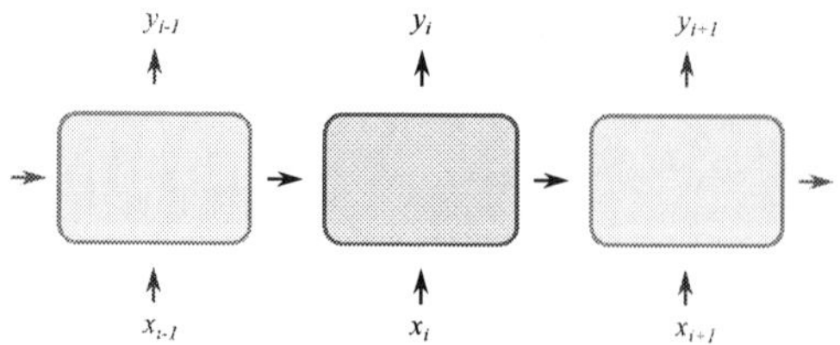

Figure 2: A recurrent neural language model. At each input x_i, the model is trained to output a prediction y_i of the next token in the sequence, x_{i+1}. In this paper, each block is a deep LSTM cell, and the network is trained using backpropagation through time (BPTT).

LSTM networks have been used successfully for language modelling (predicting the distribution of the word following after a given sequence) (see Figure 2), sentiment analysis (Tang et al., 2015), textual entailment (Rocktäschel et al., 2016), and machine translation (Sutskever et al., 2014). In the following section, we will see that the learned features are also suitable for relating forum posts to each other, and as a building block for the recommendation system in our virtual forum assistant.

3 The Recurrent Forum Assistant

In this section, we present a virtual forum assistant built using LSTM networks.

The assistant solves three different tasks in a discussion forum at an IT consultant organization. The forum is used internally and contains discussions regarding both technical topics and more everyday issues. When a user enters a question (defined simply by containing a question mark), the assistant produces one output corresponding to each task, and posts this back to the channel where the question was asked. The first task is recommending forum posts, the goal of which is to suggest related posts that might be of help to the user. The second task is to recommend other forum users that are suited to answer the question, and the third task is to suggest other forum channels where you could look for an answer to the question. See Figure 3 for an illustration of the assistant in action.

All three tasks are solved using the same underlying model, a deep recurrent LSTM network initially pretrained as a language model (see Figure 2). The pretraining is first performed using a general corpus (Wikipedia), and then using the posts from the discussion forum. Finally the model is trained in a supervised fashion to perform the recommendation tasks (see Figure 1).

The following sections will go through how the agent solves the three different tasks.

3.1 Recommending Related Posts

The subsystem for recommending related forum posts works by first feeding each post p through the recurrent network to compute the final internal representation, $r_p = c_T$ (see Equation 1). The forum post representations are then compared using cosine similarity to get a similarity score between different forum posts:

$$sim(r_1, r_2) = \frac{r_1 \cdot r_2}{\|r_1\|\|r_2\|}.\qquad(2)$$

When posed with a question q from a user, the assistant finds the post p that maximizes $sim(q, p)$.

Representing the posts using the internal representations learned by a recurrent neural network has a number of benefits. Firstly, we can represent a sequence of arbitrary length. Secondly, the structure of the LSTM cells gives us a model that takes into account the order of the words.

3.2 End–to–End Learning of Recommendations

The second part of our virtual forum assistant is trained in an end–to–end fashion with the aim of recommending relevant **(a)** forum *users*, and **(b)** forum *channels* that might be of help to the user.

The recommendation model is built on the post recommendation model, and hence first pretrained as a language model. In order to recommend users and forum channels, we attach two multiclass classification output layers to our recurrent neural network (see Figure 1 on page 1). These are softmax layers with the number of outputs corresponding to the number of users and the number of channels in the forum, respectively. During training, the author of each post is assigned as the target value for the user recommendation layer. Similarly, the channel in which the post was made, is assigned as the target value for the channel recommendation layer. This means that we can get recommendations for forum posts, forum users, and forum channels at the same time, from the same source forum post, using the same underlying model.

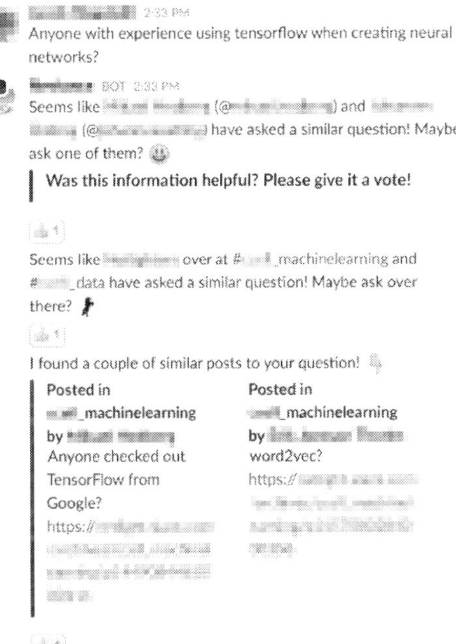

Figure 3: Screenshot of the Slack user interface when asking a question to which the recurrent assistant provides responses. Names and usernames have been anonymized.

4 Experimental Setup

This section explains the setup of the empirical study of our model. How it is designed, trained, and evaluated.

4.1 Model Layout

The same recurrent neural network is used both in the forum post recommendation step and for the recommendations for users and channels. We use a deep recurrent neural network with LSTM cells. The depth of the network is 2, and we use 650 hidden units in the LSTM cells.

For the pretraining phase, the output layer of the model is a softmax layer with 45985 outputs (the number of words in the vocabulary). For the user and channel recommendations, two softmax layers are attached to the last output of the recurrent network, one for *user* recommendations and one for *channel* recommendations (see Figure 1 on page 1). As pretraining, only the language model is trained. Then, both the recommendation output layers are trained simultaneously.

4.2 Baselines

For the related forum post recommendations, a baseline was implemented and evaluated using precomputed word embeddings from Word2Vec[1] (Mikolov et al., 2013). The precomputed model contains 300 dimensional vectors for 3 million words that were trained on the Google News corpus. For each post, a representation was computed by simply summing the vectors for each word. The forum post representations were then compared using cosine similarity (see Equation 2).

For forum user and channel recommendations, the baseline reported is a naïve solution, consistently recommending the same top-2 items; the items that maximizes the score, i.e. the 2 most common targets.

4.3 Datasets

Two datasets were used during the training; the English Wikipedia and data exported from a forum on the Slack platform.

The Wikipedia data was used to prime the model with generic English language. For this, the complete dump from 20150315 was used[2]. The dump was cleaned using Wiki-Extractor[3], and then tokenized using the Punkt tokenizer in Python NLTK.

In the discussion data from Slack, we collected all public posts made by an IT consultant organization. The discussions contain questions and answers about programming practices; different libraries and languages and what they are best suited for. The nature of the discussions are similar to that of the well known online system Stack Overflow[4], where software developers ask questions and anyone can respond. In both environments, the responses can then receive feedback and reactions.

At the time of exporting data from Slack, this forum contained 1.7 million messages written by 799 users in 664 channels. Many of these are private messages that were not used in this work. Non-public messages, inactive users (having au-

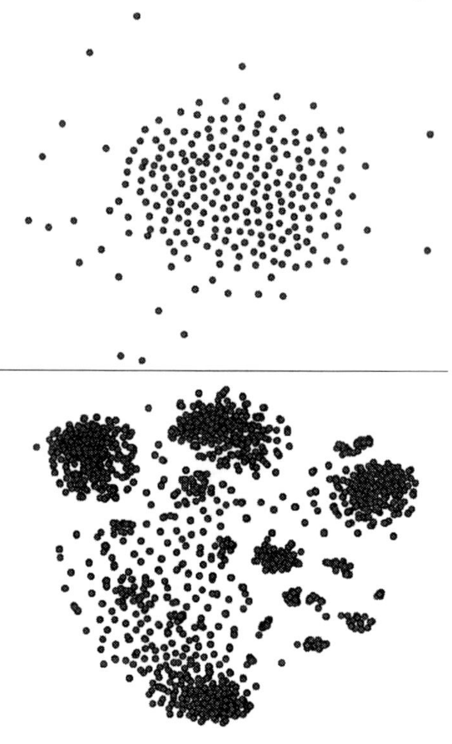

Figure 4: T-SNE projections of forum post representations.
Top: posts are represented as a sum of embeddings from Word2Vec over the words in each post.
Bottom: the internal state of an LSTM network is used as the representation.
The posts were taken from a discussion channel about mobile app development. You can see that while the word-embedding sum baseline are all clustered together, the representations created using LSTMs result in easily separable clusters.

thored less than 10 posts) and channels with fewer than 50 messages were removed, leaving 184.637 public messages, 660 users, and 321 channels that were used for training. The messages were in average 17 words long (minimum 0 and maximum 1008). A random split was made, reserving 369 posts for the validation set, and a separate export of data from the following month, resulted in 14.000 posts for the (separate) test set.

---

[1]https://code.google.com/p/word2vec/
[2]https://dumps.wikimedia.org/
[3]https://github.com/bwbaugh/
wikipedia-extractor
[4]https://stackoverflow.com/

Cosine	(a) Word Embedding Baseline
0.854	Having a edge on differen javascript frameworks would be very cool. We could have multiple [...]
0.848	So I have a lot of javascript that will be used across about 40 sites. [...]
0.842	Hey guys! Me myself and <user> are having a discussion regarding using Typescript with Angular.js [...]

Cosine	(b) Recurrent Forum Assistant
0.927	can someone recommend testing frameworks for Python?
0.921	Does anyone have experience in using Zend Server (for debugging) with Eclipse?
0.918	are you using any framework? such as phpspec?

Table 1: Top 3 responses from (a) the baseline method (see Section 4.2), (b) the recurrent forum assistant, when asking the question: "Do we have any experience with using angular and javascript two way databinding?". The first 15 words of each post was included.

4.4 Training

Preliminary results showed that training the model on the discussion forum data alone was not enough to give good suggestions of related posts. Given the limited nature of this data, we decided to pretrain the model (as a language model) using one pass through the whole Wikipedia dump. The model was then trained for 39 epochs as a language model on the discussion data from Slack, whereafter finally the two recommendation output layers (for forum user recommendations and forum channel recommendations) were trained simultaneously for 19 epochs. Using the Wikipedia pretraining substantially improved the performance of the system. Training time was decided using early stopping (Wang et al., 1994).

Training was done with backpropagation through time (BPTT) and minibatch stochastic gradient descent.

Training the user recommendation classification was done by having the author of each forum post as the classification target. Similarly, the training target for the forum channel classification was the channel in which the corresponding post was made.

4.5 Evaluation

To evaluate the performance of the proposed virtual assistant system, two different approaches were used. Firstly, a separate test set (see Section 4.3) was constructed to evaluate the generalization of the model in the user and channel recommendations. Secondly, a user study was performed, evaluating actual performance of the agent in a live setting in the live system with users interacting with it.

When evaluating the recommendations produced by the assistant on the held–out test set, several recommendations could be reasonable choices to any one question. Therefore, we employed a top-2 testing approach, where the system was allowed to produce two recommendations for each query. If the correct target was one of the two recommendations, it was counted as "correct". The top-2 evaluation also reflects the live implementation of our system, where two recommendations are always produced.

In the user study, the agent collected a number of data-points for the evaluation after each recommendation produced. These included an identifier of the questioner, the agent's response, a timestamp, what kind of recommendation that the agent provided (posts, users, or channels), and a list of reactions that was provided by the users towards the agent's action. Positive and negative reactions were then counted and reported, as well as recommendations from the assistant that did not receive any user reactions. Along with each recommendation, the assistant encourages users to provide reactions to them (see Figure 3).

For the post recommendations in the user study, each question was served either by the LSTM state representation, or by the word embedding representation baseline, randomly picked with equal probability.

5 Results

This section presents the results of the experimental evaluation of the recurrent forum assistant.

Table 1 shows example forum post recommendation outputs from the assistant using **(a)** the word-embedding sum representations, and **(b)** the LSTM representations when posed with the example question:

"Do we have any experience with using angular and javascript two way databinding?".

We present the top-3 outputs from the word-embedding baseline method and from the recurrent forum assistant, along with the cosine similarity to the representation for the question.

For recommending forum users and channels, we report accuracy scores for the test set (see Table 3). The accuracy score is the percentage of recommendations performed on the previously unseen test-set, compared to the naïve baseline of consistently recommending the top-2 users or channels respectively; the fixed recommendation that maximizes the score.

We also report results from the user study (see Table 2). For each recommendation that the assistant post in the forum, positive and negative reactions are counted. If more than 60 minutes go without a reaction, we count this as one "No reaction". Hence, you can get more than one positive reaction and more than one negative reaction for each recommendation, but only one "No reaction".

In total, 123 reactions were collected in the user study.

6 Related Work

Machines that can communicate with humans in natural language have fascinated people a long time. Alan Turing defined and gave name to a test that he meant aimed to measure a machine's ability to exhibit intelligent behavior (Turing, 1950). Taking place in a chat setting, the task is for the machine to appear like a human to a panel of judges. The test has been debated by some for not measuring intelligent behavior at all. However, the topic is at the heart of artificial intelligence, and a machine that can communicate in natural language is not only fascinating, but can also be very useful.

	Positive	Negative	No reaction
Users	70.4%	6.1%	23.5%
Channels	80.9%	4.8%	14.3%
Posts LSTM	42.1%	47.4%	10.5%
Posts W2V	35.7%	57.1%	7.1%

Table 2: The results from the live user study. Percentage is based on the total number of reactions to the agent's actions (and an action from the agent that resulted in no reaction from users is counted as "no reaction"). For users and channels recommendations most reactions are positive, suggesting that our assistant is useful to the forum users.

	User	Channel
Recurrent assistant	14.39%	22.01%
Naïve baseline	2.46%	5.54%

Table 3: Accuracy of the recommendations from the agent regarding forum users and channels, respectively, on the separate test set. The proposed assistant beats the naïve baseline by a large margin.

There has been a number of different approaches to neural representations of sentences and documents. A common way of representing sequences of words is to use some form of word embeddings, and for each word in the sequence, do an element-wise addition (Mitchell and Lapata, 2010). This approach works well for many applications, such as phrase similarity and multi-document summarization (Mogren et al., 2015), even though it disregards the order of the words. Paragraph vectors (Le and Mikolov, 2014) trains a model to predict the word following a sequence. The paragraph vectors are trained, using gradient descent, at the same time as the word vectors in the model. Our approach for embedding forum posts (as described in Section 3) is more similar to (Cho et al., 2014), where the authors use a recurrent LSTM network for machine translation, by encoding an input sequence into a fixed representation which is then decoded into a sequence in another language. Other approaches have been using convolutional neural networks (Blunsom et al., 2014), and sequential denoising autoencoders (Hill et al., 2016).

Dialog systems, also known as conversational agents, typically focus on learning to produce a well-formed response, and put less emphasis on the message that they convey in their responses. Partially observed Markov descision processes (POMDPs) have been applied to this task (Young et al., 2013), but they typically require hand-crafted features. (Sordoni et al., 2015) used a recurrent encoder–decoder model to perform response generation from questions as input, and training the model using two posts as input and the following response as target. (Serban et al., 2016) presented a dialog system built as a hierarchical recurrent LSTM encoder–decoder, where the dialogue is seen as a sequence of utterances, and each utterance is modelled as a sequence of words.

QA systems attempt to give the answer to a question given a knowledgebase as input. (Hermann et al., 2015) used LSTM networks with an attention mechanism to answer questions about an input text. (Bordes et al., 2015) used memory networks to answer questions with data from Freebase.

7 Discussion

The results in the empirical evaluation of the system proposed in this paper show some interesting points.

The accuracy of the model on the test set (see Table 3) shows that the model beats the naïve baseline by a large margin for forum user and channel recommendations. Since we employed a top-2 testing approach (see Section 4.5), the baseline system were allowed to recommend the two most frequent targets, resulting in a score of 2.46% and 5.54%, for user and channel recommendations, respectively. However, with the corresponding accuracy scores of 14.39% and 22.01% for the recurrent forum assistant, we have a solid improvement.

The user study (see Table 2) shows that forum users give positive reactions to most recommendations made by the recurrent assistant when recommending forum users and channels (70.4% and 80.9%, respectively). Some recommendations did not receive any reactions, and although people were encouraged to give reactions, it is hard to say what the reason is for the missing ones. However, even if you interpret each missing reaction as one negative reaction, the positive reactions are still many more.

For the related post recommendations, the number of positive user reactions are much lower (42.1% and 35.7%, respectively). We note that the two evaluated methods for representing forum posts give recommendations of comparable quality. You can see in the examples in Table 1 that using the LSTM state to represent forum posts results in a system that is able to generalize very well, which might be desirable or not depending on application. The system finds responses that are less specific compared to the ones found by using the word embedding representations. This seems like a reasonable result from a network that was trained as a language model. E.g: a language model will compute a similar distribution over the next word after observing the word "Python", as compared to observing the word "Java". In a forum post recommendation system, however, the difference between the two are crucial. Even if the network was in the end trained to recommend users and channels (something that we presumed would help learn features that were well suited also for the forum post recommendations), perhaps some other strategy for training the network, using more direct feedback from the learning objective, would work better for this task.

Figure 4 shows clustering of forum posts created with T-SNE, using (top) word-embedding representations, and (bottom) LSTM representations. The bottom plot shows how forum posts are clearly separated into clusters based on the LSTM representations, but this technique seems unable to separate the posts into clusters using word-embeddings. We believe that the reason might be connected to the observation in previous paragraph, as the LSTM representations are trained using a different objective.

In this paper, we stated the problem (and the three subproblems) as the task of finding relevant information (posts, users, and channels) whithin the current forum. The same approach can be used to find things from other sources. In the same setting, recommending posts in other forums, or pages on Wikipedia would be reasonable choices. In a customer support setting, a database of predefined statements or solution suggestions would be more suitable. With subtle changes to the implementation, the system can learn to choose from a number of output templates, and then fill in the related information from the context.

8   Conclusions

In this paper, we have proposed a virtual assistant for discussion forum users, built using deep recurrent neural networks with LSTM cells. Our solution relies heavily on learning useful representations for the data in discussion forums.

We found that using the representations from a deep recurrent neural network can be useful for the retrieval of relevant posts. However, in this particular task we found that using a representation based on summing word-embeddings works comparably well. We also found that pretraining the RNN as a language model with a general corpus such as Wikipedia gave substantially better suggestions of related posts.

Given an input question, the proposed model is able to give good recommendations for forum users and forum channels. This is evaluated both as a prediction task on an unseen test-set, and in a user study where we measure user reactions when interacting with our assistant.

Our joint model learns to produce recommendations for both users and channels, and generalize well to unseen data.

Our results from the user study clearly shows that the users find the suggestions from the assistant to be positive and useful. More experiments and A/B testing is left for future work to determine how the assistant can create the most useful suggestions.

In this work, we have taken an approach that we have not seen in previous work. Our aim was to create a useful virtual assistant for professional users of a discussion forum in an IT organization, and to help point users in the right directions for further reading. Vast amounts of knowledge can potentially reside inside a discussion platform, but the tools for navigating it are often primitive at best. We have seen that some of the tasks otherwise performed by helpful forum members can also be performed by a virtual recurrent forum assistant.

8.1   Future Work

Even though we have presented ways to learn good representations to perform recommendations of forum users and channels, more research is needed to find out how to best learn the representations for the post recommendation task.

We are currently working on a complete conversational agent that generates responses using a sequence–to–sequence learning approach with an attention mechanism. We believe that this, in combination with using external sources of information such as Wikipedia pages or databases containing information for customer support, can result in a promising virtual assistant.

Another exciting direction for this research will be to use the collected data from user reactions and create a model using deep reinforcement learning that can improve as it collects more data.

Acknowledgments

This work has been done within the project "Data-driven secure business intelligence", grant IIS11-0089 from the Swedish Foundation for Strategic Research (SSF).

References

Yoshua Bengio, Patrice Simard, and Paolo Frasconi. 1994. Learning long-term dependencies with gradient descent is difficult. *Neural Networks, IEEE Transactions on*, 5(2):157–166.

Phil Blunsom, Edward Grefenstette, and Nal Kalchbrenner. 2014. A convolutional neural network for modelling sentences. In *Proceedings of the 52nd Annual Meeting of the Association for Computational Linguistics*. Proceedings of the 52nd Annual Meeting of the Association for Computational Linguistics.

Antoine Bordes, Nicolas Usunier, Sumit Chopra, and Jason Weston. 2015. Large-scale simple question answering with memory networks. *CoRR*, abs/1506.02075.

Kyunghyun Cho, Bart van Merrienboer, aglar Glehre, Dzmitry Bahdanau, Fethi Bougares, Holger Schwenk, and Yoshua Bengio. 2014. Learning phrase representations using rnn encoder-decoder for statistical machine translation. In Alessandro Moschitti, Bo Pang, and Walter Daelemans, editors, *EMNLP*, pages 1724–1734. ACL.

Karl Moritz Hermann, Tomas Kocisky, Edward Grefenstette, Lasse Espeholt, Will Kay, Mustafa Suleyman, and Phil Blunsom. 2015. Teaching machines to read and comprehend. In C. Cortes, N. D. Lawrence, D. D. Lee, M. Sugiyama, and R. Garnett, editors, *Advances in Neural Information Processing Systems 28*, pages 1693–1701. Curran Associates, Inc.

F. Hill, K. Cho, and A. Korhonen. 2016. Learning Distributed Representations of Sentences from Unlabelled Data. *ArXiv e-prints*, February.

Sepp Hochreiter. 1998. The vanishing gradient problem during learning recurrent neural nets and problem solutions. *International Journal of Uncertainty, Fuzziness and Knowledge-Based Systems*, 6(02):107–116.

Quoc Le and Tomas Mikolov. 2014. Distributed representations of sentences and documents. In Tony Jebara and Eric P. Xing, editors, *Proceedings of the 31st International Conference on Machine Learning (ICML-14)*, pages 1188–1196. JMLR Workshop and Conference Proceedings.

Tomas Mikolov, Kai Chen, Greg Corrado, and Jeffrey Dean. 2013. Efficient estimation of word representations in vector space. In *ICLR*.

Jeff Mitchell and Mirella Lapata. 2010. Composition in distributional models of semantics. *Cognitive science*, 34(8):1388–1429.

Olof Mogren, Mikael Kågebäck, and Devdatt Dubhashi. 2015. Extractive summarization by aggregating multiple similarities. In *Recent Advances in Natural Language Processing*, page 451.

Tim Rocktäschel, Edward Grefenstette, Karl Moritz Hermann, Tomáš Kočiskỳ, and Phil Blunsom. 2016. Reasoning about entailment with neural attention. In *International Conference on Learning Representations*.

Jürgen Schmidhuber and Sepp Hochreiter. 1997. Long short-term memory. *Neural computation*, 7(8):1735–1780.

Iulian Vlad Serban, Alessandro Sordoni, Yoshua Bengio, Aaron C. Courville, and Joelle Pineau. 2016. Building end-to-end dialogue systems using generative hierarchical neural network models. In Dale Schuurmans and Michael P. Wellman, editors, *AAAI*, pages 3776–3784. AAAI Press.

Alessandro Sordoni, Michel Galley, Michael Auli, Chris Brockett, Yangfeng Ji, Margaret Mitchell, Jian-Yun Nie, Jianfeng Gao, and Bill Dolan. 2015. A neural network approach to context-sensitive generation of conversational responses. In Rada Mihalcea, Joyce Yue Chai, and Anoop Sarkar, editors, *HLT-NAACL*, pages 196–205. The Association for Computational Linguistics.

Ilya Sutskever, Oriol Vinyals, and Quoc V Le. 2014. Sequence to sequence learning with neural networks. In *Advances in neural information processing systems*, pages 3104–3112.

Duyu Tang, Bing Qin, and Ting Liu. 2015. Document modeling with gated recurrent neural network for sentiment classification. In *Proceedings of the 2015 Conference on Empirical Methods in Natural Language Processing*, pages 1422–1432.

Alan M Turing. 1950. Computing machinery and intelligence. *Mind*, 59(236):433–460.

C. Wang, S. S. Venkatesh, and J. S. Judd. 1994. Optimal stopping and effective machine complexity in learning. In *Advances in Neural Information Processing Systems 6*. Morgan Kaufmann.

Stephanie Young, Milica Gasic, Blaise Thomson, and John D Williams. 2013. Pomdp-based statistical spoken dialog systems: A review. *Proceedings of the IEEE*, 101(5):1160–1179.

Adjusting Word Embeddings with Semantic Intensity Orders

Joo-Kyung Kim[†]**, Marie-Catherine de Marneffe**[‡]**, Eric Fosler-Lussier**[†]
[†]Department of Computer Science and Engineering,
[‡]Department of Linguistics,
The Ohio State University,
Columbus, Ohio 43210, USA
`kimjook@cse.ohio-state.edu, mcdm@ling.ohio-state.edu,`
`fosler@cse.ohio-state.edu`

Abstract

Semantic lexicons such as WordNet and PPDB have been used to improve the vector-based semantic representations of words by adjusting the word vectors. However, such lexicons lack semantic intensity information, inhibiting adjustment of vector spaces to better represent semantic intensity scales. In this work, we adjust word vectors using the semantic intensity information in addition to synonyms and antonyms from WordNet and PPDB, and show improved performance on judging semantic intensity orders of adjective pairs on three different human annotated datasets.

1 Introduction

Word embedding models that represent words as real-valued vectors have been directly used in word-level NLP tasks such as word similarity (Mikolov et al., 2013b), antonym detection (Ono et al., 2015; Pham et al., 2015; Chen et al., 2015), knowledge relations (Toutanova et al., 2015; Socher et al., 2013; Bordes et al., 2013), and semantic scale inference (Kim and de Marneffe, 2013). Word embedding models such as Word2Vec (continuous bag-of-words (CBOW) and skip-gram) (Mikolov et al., 2013a) and GloVe (Pennington et al., 2014), widely used to generate word vectors, are trained following the distributional hypothesis (Harris, 1954) which assumes that the meaning of words can be represented by their context.

However, word embedding models based solely on the distributional hypothesis often place words improperly in vector spaces. For example, in a vector space, a word and its antonym should be sufficiently far apart, but they can be quite close because they can have similar contexts in many cases.

For better semantic representations, different approaches using semantic lexicons as well as lexical knowledge to adjust word vectors have recently been introduced. Faruqui et al. (2015) adjusted each word vector to be in the middle between the initial position and its synonymous words. Mrkšić et al. (2016) used max-margin approaches to adjust each word vector with synonyms and antonyms while keeping the relative similarities to the neighbors. While these two approaches are post-processing models that adjust preexisting word vectors, Ono et al. (2015), Pham et al. (2015), and Liu et al. (2015) jointly train models that augment the skip-gram (Mikolov et al., 2013a) objective function to include knowledge from semantic lexicons. The common goal in these approaches is to make semantically close words closer and semantically distant words farther apart while keeping each word vector not to be too far from the original position. Although the joint training models can even indirectly adjust words that are not listed in the semantic lexicons (Pham et al., 2015), the post-processing models are much more efficient and can be applied to word vectors from any kinds of models, which can eventually perform better than the joint training models (Mrkšić et al., 2016).

Although Faruqui et al. (2015), Mrkšić et al. (2016), Ono et al. (2015), Pham et al. (2015), and Liu et al. (2015)'s adjustment approaches have been shown to represent word semantics better in vector spaces, their coarse modeling of words as synonyms or antonyms may be insufficient for modeling words lying along a semantic intensity scale. For example, assume that "great" is erroneously between "bad" and "good" in a vector space ("bad" should be closer to "good" than "great"). Since semantic lexicons such as Word-

Proceedings of the 1st Workshop on Representation Learning for NLP, pages 62–69,
Berlin, Germany, August 11th, 2016. ©2016 Association for Computational Linguistics

Net (Fellbaum, 1998) and the Paraphrase Database (PPDB) (Pavlick et al., 2015) only inform us that "good" and "great" are semantically similar and "good" is semantically opposite to "bad", adjusting word vectors with those semantic lexicons does not permit to retrieve the appropriate semantic intensity ordering: bad < good < great.

Accurate representation of such semantic intensity scales can help correct processing in downstream tasks that require robust textual understanding. For instance, given an assertion such as *the movie is outstanding*, statements that contain a semantically weaker expression (e.g., *the movie is good*, *the movie is okay*) are entailed, whereas *the movie is okay* does not entail that *the movie is outstanding*. Similarly, correct information about semantic scales can also provide accurate inferences: when answers to a yes/no question that contains a gradable adjective does not explicitly contain a *yes* or a *no*, we can derive the intended answer by figuring out whether the answer entails or implicates the question (Horn, 1972; Hirschberg, 1985; de Marneffe et al., 2010). For example, for the question *Was the talk good?*, if the answer is *It was excellent*, the answer entails "yes", but if the answer is *It was okay*, "no" will be implied.

To deal with the representation of semantic intensity scales, we infer semantic intensity orders with de Melo and Bansal (2013)'s approach and then use the intensity orders to adjust the word vectors. Evaluating on three different human annotated datasets, we show that the adjustment with intensity orders in addition to adjustments with synonyms and antonyms performs best in representing semantic intensities.

2 Adjusting word embeddings with semantic lexicons

In this study, we start from one of three different off-the-shelf word vector types as a baseline for our studies: GloVe, CBOW, and Paragram-SL999 (Wieting et al., 2015); we adjust each of these sets of vectors with a variety of contrastive methods. Our first contrastive system is a baseline using synonyms and antonyms ("syn&ant") following Mrkšić et al. (2016)'s approach, which adjusts word vectors so that the sum of the following three max-margin objective functions are minimized.

Adjusting with antonyms We adjust word vectors so that the cosine similarity between each word and its antonyms is zero or lower:

$$AF(V) = \sum_{(u,w) \in A} \tau\left(\cos\left(v_u, v_w\right)\right), \quad (1)$$

where $\tau(x) = \max(0, x)$, V is the vocabulary matrix, A is the set of antonym pairs, and v_i is the i-th row of V (i-th word vector). The antonym pairs consist of the antonyms from WordNet and *Exclusion* relations from PPDB word pairs.

Adjusting with synonyms We let the cosine similarities between each word and its synonyms be increased:

$$SC(V) = \sum_{(u,w) \in S} \tau\left(1 - \cos\left(v_u, v_w\right)\right), \quad (2)$$

where S is the set of synonym pairs. The synonym pairs consist of the *Equivalence* relations from PPDB word pairs.

Keeping the similarity to the initial neighboring words We encourage the cosine similarity between the initial vectors of each word and a neighbor word to be equal to or higher than the current cosine similarity between them:

$$KN\left(V, V^0\right) =$$
$$\sum_{i=1}^{N} \sum_{j \in N(i)} \tau\left(\cos\left(v_i, v_j\right) - \cos\left(v_i^0, v_j^0\right)\right), \quad (3)$$

where V^0 is the initial vocabulary matrix, N is the vocabulary size, and $N(i)$ is the set of the initial neighbors of the i-th word. Word pairs with cosine similarities equal to or higher than 0.8 are regarded as neighbors.

The objective function for the word vector adjustment is represented as the sum of the three terms:

$$C\left(V, V^0\right) = AF(V) + SC(V) + KN\left(V, V^0\right) \quad (4)$$

This function is minimized with stochastic gradient descent with learning rate 0.1 for 20 iterations.

3 Adjusting word embeddings with semantic intensity orders

In order to better model semantic intensity ordering, we augment the synonym and antonym adjusted model with semantic intensity information to adjust word vectors. We first cluster semantically related words, infer semantic intensity orders of words in each cluster, and then adjust word vectors based on the intensity orders.

3.1 Clustering words for intensity ordering

de Melo and Bansal (2013) used WordNet dumbbells (Gross and Miller, 1990), each of which consists of an adjective antonym pair and each adjective's synonyms, to define a set of words along a semantic intensity scale. Words in each half of a dumbbell form a cluster. This clustering is effective since synonyms are semantically highly related but their intensities may be different. However, this approach can only cluster words listed in WordNet.

Shivade et al. (2015) clustered word vectors from the CBOW model with k-means++ clustering (Arthur and Vassilvitskii, 2007). This approach depends on the current word vector placement and does not require semantic lexicons. However, a word can only belong to one cluster since k-means++ is a hard clustering, thus causing issues with polysemous words. For example, "hot" is both on the temperature scale (e.g., *It's hot today*) and on the interestingness scale (e.g., *It's a hot topic*). If "hot" is adjusted for the former scale, "hot" may not properly be placed on the latter scale. Another issue of using clustering algorithms is that unrelated or antonymous words can belong to a cluster, which may hinder correct intensity ordering.

We evaluated both clustering approaches and their combination to cluster words for intensity orders. In Table 2, by default, WordNet dumbbells and *Equivalence* relations of PPDB word pairs are used as the intensity clusters. "kmeans only" denotes that only clusters from k-means++ are used, and "+kmeans" means that WordNet, PPDB, and clusters from k-means++ are used altogether. Following Shivade et al. (2015), when clustering with k-means++, we set k to be 5,798, which is the number of all observed adjectives (17,394) divided by 3 so that the average number of adjectives in a cluster is 3.

3.2 Inferring intensity ordering

We follow de Melo and Bansal (2013)'s approach to order the adjectives in each cluster. For every possible pair of adjectives in the cluster, we search for regular expressions like "⟨∗⟩ but not ⟨∗⟩" in Google N-gram (Brants and Franz, 2006). These patterns give us the direction of the ordering between the adjectives. For example, if "good but not great" appears frequently in Google N-gram, we infer that "great" is semantically stronger than "good".[1] Once we have the intensity differences of adjective pairs in a cluster, mixed integer linear programming (MILP) is used for optimal ordering of all the adjectives in the cluster given the pairwise intensity information of the adjective pairs, following de Melo and Bansal (2013).

3.3 Adjusting word vectors based on intensity orders

Now that we have word clusters whose constituent words are ordered according to their semantic intensities, we adjust the word vectors in two ways, as follows.

3.3.1 Adjusting words with the same intensity order to be closer

When intensity orders are assigned to words in a cluster, different words can have the same rank. For example, given a word cluster {"interesting", "provocative", "exciting", "sexy", "exhilarating", "thrilling"}, both "exhilarating" and "thrilling" are assigned the highest order, and "exciting" and "sexy" are assigned the second highest order. Since words in a same cluster are considered to be very close in both the meaning and the intensity, it is desirable to let them to be similar in the vector space. Therefore, we formulate a max-margin function:

$$SO\left(V\right) = \sum_{(u,w) \in E} \tau \left(1 - \cos\left(v_u, v_w\right)\right), \quad (5)$$

where E is the word pairs of the same intensities from the intensity clusters.

3.3.2 Adjusting weaker/stronger word pairs based on antonyms

For two similar words with different intensities (e.g., "good" and "great"), the similarity between the weaker word vector and its antonym vector should be higher than the similarity between the stronger word vector and the antonym vector. Figure 1 shows an example of word vectors which are wrongly ordered.

To reduce wrong orderings, we formulate a

---

[1] Shivade et al. (2015) used Tregex (Levy and Andrew, 2006) to extract patterns including more words but it is not necessary when we extract patterns from phrases consisting of less or equal to five words.

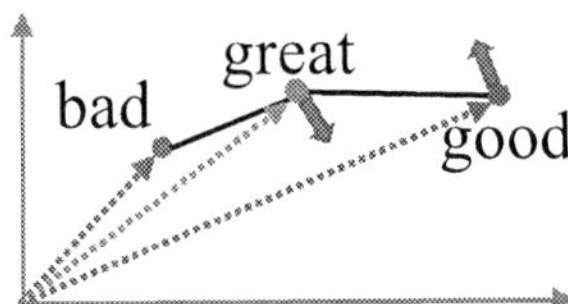

Figure 1: An example of incoherent word vector positions, where "bad" should be closer to "good" than "great" but the similarity between "bad" and "good" is lower than the similarity between "bad" and "great".

max-margin function:

$$AO\left(V\right) =$$
$$\sum_{(w,a)\in A}\sum_{s\in Str(w)} \tau\left\{\cos\left(v_s, v_a\right) - \cos\left(v_w, v_a\right)\right\},$$

$$(6)$$

where A is the set of antonym pairs and $Str\left(w\right)$ is a set of words semantically stronger than w. By minimizing this function, out-of-order vectors are adjusted so that the stronger word vector gets farther from the antonym vector and the weaker word vector gets closer to the antonym vector.

Both equations 5 and 6 can be either solely used or summed to others like equation 4 to serve as a term of the objective function.

4 Evaluation

We evaluate the representation of semantic intensities on the three following human-annotated datasets.

4.1 WordNet synset pairs

We obtained a dataset of 670 synonymous adjective pairs coming from synsets in WordNet from Christopher Potts. Each adjective pair was annotated for intensity order on Mechanical Turk. For each adjective pair <A, B> (e.g., "good" and "great"), ten different Turkers were asked to judge whether A is semantically stronger than B, B is semantically stronger than A, or A is equal to B. For consistency of annotation with the other datasets, we mapped "A is semantically stronger than B" to "no", "B is semantically stronger than A" to "yes", and "A is equal to B" to "uncertain".

For 77.3% of adjective pairs, at least 6 out of the 10 Turkers agreed with each other on the same annotation. Table 1 gives a breakdown of how often Turkers agree with each other. The inter-

Max # Turkers agreeing	Coverage (%)
10	17.5
9	17.2
8	13.3
7	14.6
6	14.9
5	16.7
4	6

Table 1: Percentage of adjective pairs and the maximum number of Turkers who agree with each other on the annotation.

annotator agreement (Fleiss' kappa) of this dataset is 0.359. Note that Fleiss' kappa is a very conservative measure given the partial order in the annotation, which is not taken into account in Fleiss' kappa.

4.2 Indirect question-answer pairs (IQAP)

IQAP (de Marneffe et al., 2010) is a corpus consisting of 127 indirect question-answer pairs in which both the question and the answer contain a gradable adjective (*Is Obama qualified? I think he's young.*). For each pair, 30 Turkers decided whether the answer implies a "yes", "no" or "uncertain" response to the question. A majority "yes" response implies that the adjective in the question entails the adjective in the answer.

The ordering between the adjectives in the question and in the answer can be used to infer a "yes" or "no" answer: if the adjective in the answer is semantically equivalent or stronger to the adjective in the question, we infer a "yes" answer (*Was the movie good? It was excellent.*); if not, we infer a "no" answer.

4.3 Word intensity orders in clusters

We also use the test set from de Melo and Bansal (2013) consisting of 507 pairs of adjectives in 88 clusters annotated by two native English speakers for intensity ordering. From this set, we generated all the possible adjective pairs from the ordered list in a cluster. For example, for "known" < "famous" < "legendary" in the test set, we generated "known" < "famous", "known" < "legendary", and "famous" < "legendary".

4.4 Evaluation results

In our evaluation of the semantic orderings of adjective pairs, we decide which adjective in a pair <A, B> is semantically stronger following Kim and de Marneffe (2013)'s approach. First, we look

Adjustment methods	WordNet synset pairs			IQAP			de Melo & Bansal (2013)		
	GloVe	CBOW	Pgrm	GloVe	CBOW	Pgrm	GloVe	CBOW	Pgrm
baseline	0.5614	0.5092	0.5224	0.7044	0.7016	0.7591	0.9468	0.9347	0.9803
syn&ant	0.5106	0.5516	0.5572	**0.8143**	**0.8045**	0.8307	0.9632	0.9444	0.9791
same_ord (kmeans only)	**0.5762**	0.5163	0.5196	0.7044	0.7016	0.7473	0.9480	0.9359	0.9791
same_ord, diff_ord	0.5505	0.5331	0.5167	0.7119	0.6889	0.7718	0.9456	0.9371	0.9701
syn&ant,same_ord	0.5364	0.5639	0.5782	0.7922	0.7818	0.8284	0.9632	0.9492	0.9803
syn&ant,diff_ord	0.5300	0.5551	0.5765	**0.8143**	0.7922	0.8307	0.9735	0.9539	**0.9825**
syn&ant,same_ord,diff_ord	0.5467	0.5730	**0.5960**	**0.8143**	0.8033	**0.8395**	**0.9758**	0.9539	**0.9825**
syn&ant,same_ord,diff_ord (kmeans only)	0.5186	0.5516	0.5729	0.8033	**0.8045**	0.8194	0.9609	0.9468	0.9803
syn&ant,same_ord,diff_ord (+kmeans)	0.5512	**0.5828**	**0.5960**	0.8033	0.8033	**0.8395**	0.9735	**0.9609**	0.9814

Table 2: F1 scores for determining semantic intensity ordering on three datasets, across three baseline models (GloVe, CBOW, Paragram), using different compositions of adjustment techniques, including **syn**onyms, **ant**onyms, **same** intensity **ord**ers, and **diff**erent intensity **ord**ers.

Datasets	# pairs	# syn	# ant
WordNet synset pairs	670	79	0
IQAP	127	7	9
de Melo & Bansal	507	54	1

Table 3: The numbers of total adjective pairs, synonymous pairs, and antonymous pairs for each dataset.

for an antonym of A.[2] Then, we check whether the word vector for B is more similar to the vector for A than to the vector for A's antonym, or whether the vector for B is more similar to the vector for A's antonym. We infer a "yes" answer in the former case, and a "no" in the other case. If A has more than one antonym, we select the antonym that is most collinear with the vectors for A and B assuming that the most collinear antonym is most semantically related to A and B.

Table 2 shows the F1 scores of different combinations of the adjustments on the three datasets,[3] whereas Table 3 shows the number of total adjective pairs in each dataset, as well as the number of pairs in which both adjectives are synonyms (*Equivalence* relations from PPDB) and the number of pairs in which both adjectives are antonyms (*Exclusion* relations from PPDB and antonyms from WordNet).

Expanding on the results in Table 2, as the baselines, we used three different 300 dimensional off-the-shelf word vectors: GloVe,[4] CBOW,[5] and Paragram-SL999.[6] Following Mrkšić et al. (2016), for each of the word vector sets, we extracted word vectors corresponding to the 76,427 most frequent words from Open-Subtitles.[7]

Table 4 indicates whether the differences in performance of the adjustment methods in Table 2 are statistically significant (McNemar's χ^2 test with p-value < 0.05). In the table, "merged" columns are the results of the concatenation of all the datasets. For each comparison, '+' denotes that the performance of the latter is significantly higher than that of the former, and '-' denotes the opposite, whereas no value indicates that the difference in performance is not statistically significant. For Paragram vectors, only one case ("baseline" vs "syn&ant,same_ord") is significantly different.

In Table 2, "baseline" shows the performance of the baseline word vectors without any adjustments. Since Paragram-SL999 are optimized to perform best on evaluating SimLex-999 dataset, the baseline performance of Paragram-SL999 on SimLex-999 as well as two of the other datasets are noticeably better than word vectors from GloVe and CBOW.

In "syn&ant", corresponding to the optimization with equation 4, 15,509 words are adjusted with the synonyms and 6,162 words are adjusted with the antonyms. This adjustment significantly

---

[2]If there are no antonyms of A in WordNet, we obtain antonyms from Roget's thesaurus (Kipfer, 2009).

[3]For simplicity of the evaluation in vector spaces, we calculate F1 scores without "uncertain" cases.

[4]Available from `http://nlp.stanford.edu/projects/glove/`

[5]Available from `https://code.google.com/p/word2vec/`

[6]Available from `https://drive.google.com/file/d/0B9w48e1rj-MOck1fRGxaZW1LU2M/`

[7]Available from `invokeit.wordpress.com/frequency-word-lists`

Compared adjustment methods	GloVe				CBOW			
	WN	IQAP	dM&B	merged	WN	IQAP	dM&B	merged
baseline v. syn&ant	-	+	+			+		
baseline v. syn&ant,same_ord,diff_ord	-	+	+			+	+	+
syn&ant v. syn&ant,same_ord,diff_ord			+	+				
baseline v. syn&ant,same_ord,diff_ord (+kmeans)		+	+	+		+	+	
syn&ant v. syn&ant,same_ord,diff_ord (+kmeans)	+			+			+	+

Table 4: McNemar's χ^2 test results (p-value < 0.05) for different methods of GloVe/CBOW adjustments across WordNet synset (WN), IQAP, and de Melo & Bansal (dM&B) datasets, as well as concatenating the three datasets (merged). For x v. y, '+' denotes that y's score is significantly higher than that of x, ''-' denotes the opposite, and no value denotes that the difference is not statistically significant.

improves the performance of CBOW vectors and Paragram vectors on the IQAP and de Melo and Bansal (2013)'s datasets. Specifically, for the IQAP dataset, where many of the pairs are either synonyms or antonyms, "syn&ant" showed better performance than including adjustments with semantic intensity orders. However, this adjustment makes GloVe vectors yield significantly worse performance on the WordNet synset pair dataset. This shows that the adjustment with just synonyms and antonyms can worsen the representation of subtle semantics considering intensities. In this case, using just the adjustment with semantic intensity orders can be helpful. "same_ord (kmeans only)", corresponding to equation 5, adjusts word vectors by just making vectors of words with the same intensity order to be more similar without using synonyms and antonyms. For GloVe vectors, "same_ord (kmeans only)" showed the highest score for the WordNet synset pair dataset. For adjustments with semantic intensity orders, 616 words are adjusted when WordNet dumbbells and *Equivalence* relations from PPDB word pairs are used as the clusters. When clusters from k-means++ are used, several hundreds of words are adjusted, where the adjusted words vary depending on the vector space for each iteration.

For the WordNet synset pair dataset and de Melo and Bansal (2013)'s dataset, where the subtle semantic intensity differences are more critical, using synonyms, antonyms, and semantic intensity orders altogether ("syn&ant,same_ord,diff_ord") showed significantly higher scores than "syn&ant" in many settings. Here, "diff_ord" corresponds to equation 6.

Table 5 shows the adjective pairs whose intensity judgements were changed by including adjustments with semantic intensity orders. The pairs are from the WordNet synset pairs and

baseline v. same_ord (kmeans only)	syn&ant v. syn&ant, same_ord,diff_ord(+kmeans)
satisfactory < superb	mediocre < severe
unfavorable < poor	troublesome < rocky
crazy < ardent	upfront < blunt
outspoken < expansive	solid < redeeming
sad < tragic	warm < uneasy
deserving < sacred	valuable < sacred

Table 5: Adjective pairs whose incorrect decisions with the former models are corrected by the latter models. For those model comparisons, there were no pairs that were correctly judged with the former models but not with the latter models.

GloVe vectors were used as the baseline. "baseline" is compared to "same_ord (kmeans only)" in the first column and "syn&ant" is compared to "syn&ant,same_ord,diff_ord(+kmeans)". In both cases, we observe that some of the incorrectly judged pairs are corrected when adding the adjustment with semantic intensity orders. In these cases, there were no pairs that were correctly judged by the adjustments without semantic intensity orders but incorrectly judged with semantic intensity orders.

Since the numbers of adjectives pairs in the datasets and the numbers of words that are adjusted with semantic intensity orders are small, not all the cases comparing the adjustments using just synonyms and antonyms to the adjustments including semantic intensity orders were significant for p-value < 0.05, as shown in Table 4. However, since many of them are slightly insignificant (like p-value=0.07) and the scores noticeably increased in many cases, using semantic intensity orders for the adjustments seem promising.

In addition, to show that the adjustments are not harmful for the representation of the general semantics of the words, we also evaluated on SimLex-999 (Hill et al., 2015), where 999 word

	GloVe	CBOW	Pgrm
baseline	0.4453	0.4567	0.6920
syn&ant	0.5969	0.5768	0.7268
same_ord (kmeans only)	0.4420	0.4585	0.6926
same_ord, diff_ord	0.4522	0.4613	0.6872
syn&ant,same_ord	0.5969	0.5768	0.7261
syn&ant,diff_ord	0.5958	0.5767	**0.7274**
syn&ant,same_ord,diff_ord	0.5962	**0.5773**	0.7271
syn&ant,same_ord,diff_ord (kmeans only)	**0.5980**	0.5769	0.7269
syn&ant,same_ord,diff_ord (+kmeans)	0.5956	0.5771	0.7273

Table 6: Spearman's ρ on SimLex-999.

pairs were annotated on Mechanical Turk to score the degree of semantic similarities. This dataset has been widely used to evaluate the quality of semantic representations of words.

Table 6 shows Spearman's ρ scores on the SimLex-999 dataset for the different adjustment methods. Since SimLex-999 dataset is not directly related to semantic intensities compared to the other evaluation datasets, there were no significant gains for the adjustments with semantic intensity orders. However, no significant drops indicate that the adjustments with semantic intensity orders are not harmful for the representation of general word semantics.

5 Discussion and Conclusion

In this work, we adjusted word vectors with inferred semantic intensity orders as well as information from WordNet and PPDB, and showed that adjusting word vectors with semantic intensity orders, synonyms, and antonyms altogether showed the best performance for all the three datasets we evaluated on. Using the semantic intensity orders for adjusting word vectors can help represent semantic intensities of words in vector spaces. In addition, we showed the adjustments including semantic intensity orders are not harmful for the representation of semantics in general by evaluating on SimLex-999.

In future work, we plan to investigate clustering techniques beyond WordNet dumbbells and k-means++ as preprocessing in the semantic ordering. The clusters using WordNet dumbbells depend on a preexisting semantic lexicon that may not cover all the semantically related words. With k-means++, clusters may contain semantically opposite words and a word can belong to only one cluster. As both techniques have limitations, by

using another clustering method, the performance could be further improved. In addition, we plan to use larger corpora than Google N-gram so that we can find more intensity orderings within clusters. We can also further improve the performance by using semantic intensity information from other linguistic resources. For example, given a list of base, comparative, and superlative forms of adjectives and adverbs, we can let those adjectives aligned more correctly in vector spaces. We can also use word definitions from dictionaries. For example, from *American Heritage Dictionary*, one of the definitions of "furious" is "extremely angry" and one of that of "excellent" is "exceptionally good". Therefore, by analyzing word definitions, we can obtain word intensity orders.

Acknowledgments

We are very grateful to Christopher Potts for sharing with us the judgements on the WordNet synset pairs that he gathered on Mechanical Turk. We also thank our anonymous reviewers for their comments.

References

David Arthur and Sergei Vassilvitskii. 2007. K-means++: The advantages of careful seeding. In *Proceedings of the 18th Annual ACM-SIAM Symposium on Discrete Algorithms (SODA)*, pages 1027–1035.

Antoine Bordes, Nicolas Usunier, Alberto Garcia-Duran, Jason Weston, and Oksana Yakhnenko. 2013. Translating embeddings for modeling multi-relational data. In *Advances in Neural Information Processing Systems 26*, pages 2787–2795.

Thorsten Brants and Alex Franz. 2006. The Google Web 1T 5-gram Version 1.1.

Zhigang Chen, Wei Lin, Qian Chen, Xiaoping Chen, Si Wei, Hui Jiang, and Xiaodan Zhu. 2015. Revisiting word embedding for contrasting meaning. In *Proceedings of ACL*, pages 106–115.

Marie-Catherine de Marneffe, Christopher D. Manning, and Christopher Potts. 2010. Was it good? It was provocative. Learning the meaning of scalar adjectives. In *Proceedings of the 48th Meeting of the Association for Computational Linguistics (ACL)*, pages 167–176.

Gerald de Melo and Mohit Bansal. 2013. Good, Great, Excellent: Global Inference of Semantic Intensities. *Transactions of the Association for Computational Linguistics (TACL)*, 1:279–290.

Manaal Faruqui, Jesse Dodge, Sujay K. Jauhar, Chris Dyer, Eduard Hovy, and Noah A. Smith. 2015. Retrofitting word vectors to semantic lexicons. In *Proceedings of NAACL*, pages 1606–1615.

Christiane Fellbaum. 1998. *WordNet: An electronic lexical database*. MIT Press.

Derek Gross and Katherine J. Miller. 1990. Adjectives in WordNet. *International Journal of Lexicography*, 3(4):265–277.

Zellig Harris. 1954. Distributional structure. *Word*, 10:146–162.

Felix Hill, Roi Reichart, and Anna Korhonen. 2015. SimLex-999: Evaluating Semantic Models with (Genuine) Similarity Estimation. *Computational Linguistics*, 41(4):665–695.

Julia B. Hirschberg. 1985. *A Theory of Scalar Implicature*. Ph.D. thesis, University of Pennsylvania.

Lawrence Horn. 1972. *On the Semantic Properties of Logical Operators in English*. Bloomington, Indiana: Indianan University Linguistics Club.

Joo-Kyung Kim and Marie-Catherine de Marneffe. 2013. Deriving Adjectival Scales from Continuous Space Word Representations. In *Proceedings of the Empirical Methods in Natural Language Processing (EMNLP)*, pages 1625–1630.

Barbara Ann Kipfer. 2009. *Rogets 21st Century Thesaurus*. Dell.

Roger Levy and Galen Andrew. 2006. Tregex and Tsurgeon: tools for querying and manipulating tree data structures. In *Proceedings of the Fifth International Conference on Language Resources and Evaluation (LREC)*, pages 2231–2234.

Quan Liu, Hui Jiang, Si Wei, Zhen-Hua Ling, and Yu Hu. 2015. Learning semantic word embeddings based on ordinal knowledge constraints. In *Proceedings of ACL*, pages 1501–1511.

Tomas Mikolov, Greg Corrado, Kai Chen, and Jeffrey Dean. 2013a. Efficient Estimation of Word Representations in Vector Space. In *International Conference on Learning Representations (ICLR) workshop*.

Tomas Mikolov, Wen-tau Yih, and Geoffrey Zweig. 2013b. Linguistic regularities in continuous space word representations. In *Proceedings of the 2013 Conference of the North American Chapter of the Association for Computational Linguistics: Human Language Technologies (NAACL-HLT)*, pages 746–751.

Nikola Mrkšić, Diarmuid Ó Séaghdha, Blaise Thomson, Milica Gašić, Lina Rojas-Barahona, Pei-Hao Su, David Vandyke, Tsung-Hsien Wen, and Steve Young. 2016. Counter-fitting word vectors to linguistic constraints. In *NAACL*, pages 142–148.

Masataka Ono, Makoto Miwa, and Yutaka Sasaki. 2015. Word embedding-based antonym detection using thesauri and distributional information. In *Proceedings of NAACL*, pages 984–989.

Ellie Pavlick, Pushpendre Rastogi, Juri Ganitkevich, Benjamin Van Durme, and Chris Callison-Burch. 2015. PPDB 2.0: Better paraphrase ranking, fine-grained entailment relations, word embeddings, and style classification. In *Proceedings of the Association for Computational Linguistics (ACL 2015)*, pages 425–430.

Jeffrey Pennington, Richard Socher, and Christopher D. Manning. 2014. Glove: Global vectors for word representation. In *Proceedings of the 2014 Conference on Empirical Methods in Natural Language Processing (EMNLP)*, pages 1532–1543.

Nghia The Pham, Angeliki Lazaridou, and Marco Baroni. 2015. A multitask objective to inject lexical contrast into distributional semantics. In *Proceedings of ACL*, pages 21–26.

Chaitanya Shivade, Marie-Catherine de Marneffe, Eric Fosler-Lussier, and Albert M. Lai. 2015. Corpus-based discovery of semantic intensity scales. In *Proceedings of NAACL*, pages 483–493.

Richard Socher, Danqi Chen, Christopher D. Manning, and Andrew Y. Ng. 2013. Reasoning With Neural Tensor Networks For Knowledge Base Completion. In *Advances in Neural Information Processing Systems 26*, pages 926–934.

Kristina Toutanova, Danqi Chen, Patrick Pantel, Hoifung Poon, Pallavi Choudhury, and Michael Gamon. 2015. Representing text for joint embedding of text and knowledge bases. In *Empirical Methods in Natural Language Processing (EMNLP)*, pages 1499–1509.

John Wieting, Mohit Bansal, Kevin Gimpel, Karen Livescu, and Dan Roth. 2015. From paraphrase database to compositional paraphrase model and back. *Transactions of the ACL (TACL)*, 3:345–358.

Towards Abstraction from Extraction: Multiple Timescale Gated Recurrent Unit for Summarization

Minsoo Kim
School of Electronics Engineering
Kyungpook National University
Daegu, South Korea
minsoo9574@gmail.com

Moirangthem Dennis Singh
School of Electronics Engineering
Kyungpook National University
Daegu, South Korea
mdennissingh@gmail.com

Minho Lee
School of Electronics Engineering
Kyungpook National University
Daegu, South Korea
mholee@gmail.com

Abstract

In this work, we introduce temporal hierarchies to the sequence to sequence (seq2seq) model to tackle the problem of abstractive summarization of scientific articles. The proposed Multiple Timescale model of the Gated Recurrent Unit (MT-GRU) is implemented in the encoder-decoder setting to better deal with the presence of multiple compositionalities in larger texts. The proposed model is compared to the conventional RNN encoder-decoder, and the results demonstrate that our model trains faster and shows significant performance gains. The results also show that the temporal hierarchies help improve the ability of seq2seq models to capture compositionalities better without the presence of highly complex architectural hierarchies.

1 Introduction and Related Works

Summarization has been extensively researched over the past several decades. Jones (2007) and Nenkova et al. (2011) offer excellent overviews of the field. Broadly, summarization methods can be categorized into extractive approaches and abstractive approaches (Hahn and Mani, 2000), based on the type of computational task. Extractive summarization is a selection problem, while abstractive summarization requires a deeper semantic and discourse understanding of the text, as well as a novel text generation process. Extractive summarization has been the focus in the past, but abstractive summarization remains a challenge.

Recently, sequence-to-sequence (seq2seq) recurrent neural networks (RNNs) have seen wide application in a number of tasks. Such RNN encoder-decoders (Cho et al., 2014; Bahdanau et al., 2014) combine a representation learning encoder and a language modeling decoder to perform mappings between two sequences. Similarly, recent works have proposed to cast summarization as a mapping problem between an input sequence and a summary sequence. Recent successes such as Rush et al. (2015);Nallapati et al. (2016) have shown that the RNN encoder-decoder performs remarkably well in summarizing short text. Such seq2seq approaches offer a fully data-driven solution to both semantic and discourse understanding and text generation.

While seq2seq presents a promising way forward for abstractive summarization, extrapolating the methodology to other tasks, such as the summarization of a scientific article, is not trivial. A number of practical and theoretical concerns arise: 1) We cannot simply train RNN encoder-decoders on entire articles: For the memory capacity of current GPUs, scientific articles are too long to be processed whole via RNNs. 2) Moving from one or two sentences, to several sentences or several paragraphs, introduces additional levels of compositionality and richer discourse structure. How can we improve the conventional RNN encoder-decoder to better capture these? 3) Deep learning approaches depend heavily on good quality, large-scale datasets. Collecting source-summary data pairs is difficult, and datasets are scarce outside of the newswire domain.

In this paper, we present a first, intermediate step towards end-to-end abstractive summarization of scientific articles. Our aim is to extend seq2seq based summarization to larger text with a more complex summarization task. To ad-

Proceedings of the 1st Workshop on Representation Learning for NLP, pages 70–77,
Berlin, Germany, August 11th, 2016. ©2016 Association for Computational Linguistics

dress each of the issues above, 1) We propose a paragraph-wise summarization system, which is trained via paragraph-salient sentence pairs. We use Term Frequency-Inverse Document Frequency (TF-IDF) (Luhn, 1958; Jones, 1972) scores to extract a salient sentence from each paragraph. 2) We introduce a novel model, Multiple Timescale Gated Recurrent Unit (MTGRU), which adds a temporal hierarchy component that serves to handle multiple levels of compositionality. This is inspired by an analogous concept of temporal hierarchical organization found in the human brain, and is implemented by modulating different layers of the multilayer RNN with different timescales (Yamashita and Tani, 2008). We demonstrate that our model is capable of understanding the semantics of a multi-sentence source text and knowing what is important about it, which is the first necessary step towards abstractive summarization. 3) We build a new dataset of Computer Science (CS) articles from ArXiv.org, extracting their Introductions from the LaTeX source files. The Introductions are decomposed into paragraphs, each paragraph acting as a natural unit of discourse.

Finally, we concatenate the generated summary of each paragraph to create a non-expert summary of the article's Introduction, and evaluate our results against the actual Abstract. We show that our model is capable of summarizing multiple sentences to its most salient part on unseen data, further supporting the larger view of summarization as a seq2seq mapping task. We demonstrate that our MTGRU model satisfies some of the major requirements of an abstractive summarization system. We also report that MTGRU has the capability of reducing training time significantly compared to the conventional RNN encoder-decoder.

The paper is structured as follows: Section 2 describes the proposed model in detail. In Section 3, we report the results of our experiments and show the generated summary samples. In Section 4 we analyze the results of our model and comment on future work.

2 Proposed Model

In this section we discuss the background related to our model, and describe in detail the newly developed architecture and its application to summarization.

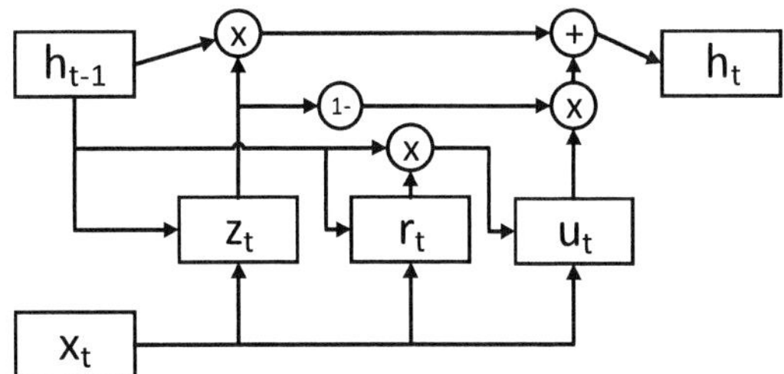

Figure 1: A gated recurrent unit.

2.1 Background

The principle of compositionality defines the meaning conveyed by a linguistic expression as a function of the syntactic combination of its constituent units. In other words, the meaning of a sentence is determined by the way its words are combined with each other. In multi-sentence text, sentence-level compositionality (the way sentences are combined with one another) is an additional function which will add meaning to the overall text. When dealing with such larger texts, compositionality at the sentence and even paragraph levels should be considered, in order to capture the text meaning completely. An approach explored in recent literature is to create dedicated architectures in a hierarchical fashion to capture subsequent levels of compositionality: Li et al. (2015) and Nallapati et al. (2016) build dedicated word and sentence level RNN architectures to capture compositionality at different levels of text-units, leading to improvements in performance.

However, architectural modifications to the RNN encoder-decoder such as these suffer from the drawback of a major increase in both training time and memory usage. Therefore, we propose an alternative enhancement to the architecture that will improve performance with no such overhead. We draw our inspiration from neuroscience, where it has been shown that functional differentiation occurs naturally in the human brain, giving rise to temporal hierarchies (Meunier et al., 2010; Botvinick, 2007). It has been well documented that neurons can hierarchically organize themselves into layers with different adaptation rates to stimuli. The quintessential example of this phenomenon is the auditory system, in which syllable level information in a short time window is integrated into word level information over a longer time window, and so on. Previous works have applied this concept to RNNs in movement tracking (Paine and Tani, 2004) and speech recog-

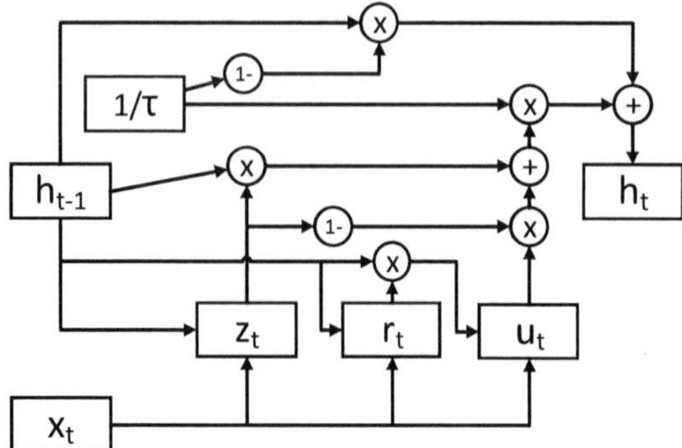

Figure 2: Proposed multiple timescale gated recurrent unit.

nition (Heinrich et al., 2012).

2.2 Multiple Timescale Gated Recurrent Unit

Our proposed Multiple Timescale Gated Recurrent Unit (MTGRU) model applies the temporal hierarchy concept to the problem of seq2seq text summarization, in the framework of the RNN encoder-decoder. Previous works such as (Yamashita and Tani, 2008)'s Multiple Timescale Recurrent Neural Network (MTRNN) have employed temporal hierarchy in motion prediction. However, MTRNN is prone to the same problems present in the RNN, such as difficulty in capturing long-term dependencies and vanishing gradient problem (Hochreiter et al., 2001). Long Short Term Memory network (Hochreiter et al., 2001) utilizes a complex gating architecture to aid the learning of long-term dependencies and has been shown to perform much better than the RNN in tasks with long-term temporal dependencies such as machine translation (Sutskever et al., 2014). Gated Recurrent Unit (GRU) (Cho et al., 2014), which has been proven to be comparable to LSTM (Chung et al., 2014), has a similar complex gating architecture, but requires less memory. The standard GRU architecture is shown in Fig. 1.

Because seq2seq summarization involves potentially many long-range temporal dependencies, our model applies temporal hierarchy to the GRU. We apply a timescale constant at the end of a GRU, essentially adding another constant gating unit that modulates the mixture of past and current hidden states. The reset gate r_t, update gate z_t, and the candidate activation u_t are computed similarly to that of the original GRU as shown in Eq.(1).

$$r_t = \sigma(W_{xr}x_t + W_{hr}h_{t-1})$$
$$z_t = \sigma(W_{xz}x_t + W_{hz}h_{t-1}) \quad (1)$$
$$u_t = \tanh(W_{xu}x_t + W_{hu}(r_t \odot h_{t-1}))$$
$$h_t = ((1 - z_t)h_{t-1} + z_t u_t)\frac{1}{\tau} + (1 - \frac{1}{\tau})h_{t-1} \quad (2)$$

The time constant τ added to the activation h_t of the MTGRU is shown in Eq.(2). τ is used to control the timescale of each GRU cell. Larger τ meaning slower cell outputs but it makes the cell focus on the slow features of a dynamic sequence input. The proposed MTGRU model is illustrated in Fig. 2. The conventional GRU will be a special case of MTGRU where $\tau = 1$, where no attempt is made to organize layers into different timescales.

$$\frac{\delta E}{\delta h_{t-1}} = \frac{1}{\tau}[\frac{\delta E}{\delta h_t} \odot (u_t - h_{t-1}) \odot \sigma'(z_t)W_{zh}]$$
$$+ \frac{1}{\tau}[((\frac{\delta E}{\delta h_t} \odot z_t \odot \tanh'(u_t))W_{uh}) \odot r_t]$$
$$+ \frac{1}{\tau}[(((\frac{\delta E}{\delta h_t} \odot z_t \odot \tanh'(u_t))W_{uh})$$
$$\odot \sigma'(r_t) \odot h_{t-1})W_{rh}]$$
$$+ \frac{1}{\tau}[\frac{\delta E}{\delta h_t} \odot (1 - z_t)] + (1 - \frac{1}{\tau})\frac{\delta E}{\delta h_t} \quad (3)$$

Eq. (3) shows the learning algorithm derived for the MTGRU according to the defined forward process and the back propagation through time rules. $\frac{\delta E}{\delta h_{t-1}}$ is the error of the cell outputs at time $t-1$ and $\frac{\delta E}{\delta h_t}$ is the current gradient of the cell outputs. Different timescale constants are set for each layer where larger τ means slower context units and $\tau = 1$ defines the default or the input timescale. Based on our hypothesis that later layers should learn features that operate over slower timescales, we set larger τ as we go up the layers.

In this application, the question is whether the word sequences being analyzed by the RNN possess information that operates over different temporal hierarchies, as they do in the case of the continuous audio signals received by the human auditory system. We hypothesize that they do, and that word level, clause level, and sentence level compositionalities are strong candidates. In this light, the multiple timescale modification functions as a way to explicitly guide each layer of the neural network to facilitate the learning of features operating over increasingly slower timescales, corre-

RNN Type	Layers	Hidden Units
GRU	4	1792
MTGRU	4	1792

Table 1: Network Parameters for each model.

sponding to subsequent levels in the compositional hierarchy.

2.3 Summarization

To apply our newly proposed multiple timescale model to summarization, we build a new dataset of academic articles. We collect LaTeX source files of articles in the CS.{CL,CV,LG,NE} domains from the arXiv preprint server, extracting their Introductions and Abstracts. We decompose the Introduction into paragraphs, and pair each paragraph with its most salient sentence as the target summary. These target summaries are generated using the widely adopted TF-IDF scoring. Fig. 3 shows the structure of our summarization model.

Our dataset contains rich compositionality and longer text sequences, increasing the complexity of the summarization problem. The temporal hierarchy function has the biggest impact when complex compositional hierarchies exist in the input data. Hence, the multiple timescale concept will play a bigger role in our context compared to previous summarization tasks such as Rush et al. (2015).

The model using MTGRU is trained using these paragraphs and their targets. The generated summaries of each Introduction is evaluated using the Abstracts of the collected articles. We chose the Abstracts as gold summaries, because they usually contain important discourse structures such as goal, related works, methods, and results, making them good baseline summaries. To test the effectiveness of the proposed method, we compare it with the conventional RNN encoder-decoder in terms of training speed and performance.

3 Experiments and Results

We trained two seq2seq models, the first model using the conventional GRU in the RNN encoder decoder, and the second model using the newly proposed MTGRU. Both models are trained using the same hyperparamenter settings with the optimal configuration which fits our existing hardware capability.

Following Sutskever et al. (2014), the inputs are divided into multiple buckets. Both GRU and MT-

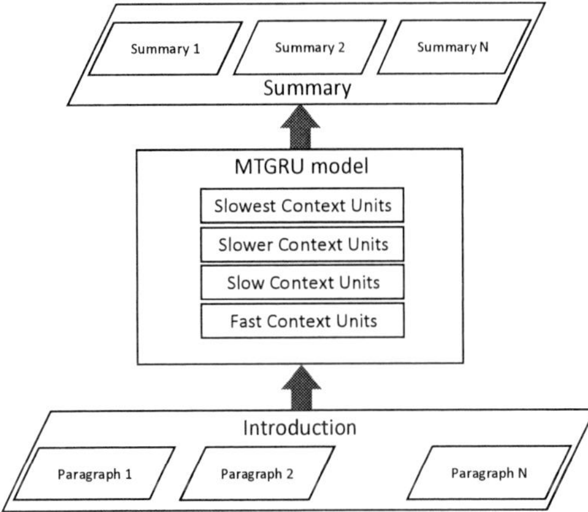

Figure 3: Paragraph level approach to summarization.

Steps	RNN	Train Perplexity	Test Perplexity
74750	GRU	6.8	29.72
74750	MTGRU	5.87	18.53

Table 2: Training results of the Models.

GRU models consist of 4 layers and 1792 hidden units. As our models take longer input and target sequence sizes, the hidden units size and number of layers are limited. An embedding size of 512 was used for both networks. The timescale constant τ for each layer is set to $1, 1.25, 1.5, 1.7$, respectively. The models are trained on 110k text-summary pairs. The source text are the paragraphs extracted from the introduction of academic articles and the targets are the most salient sentence extracted from the paragraphs using TF-IDF scores. For comparison of the training speed of the models, Fig. 4 shows the plot of the training curve until the train perplexity reaches 9.5. Both of the models are trained using 2 Nvidia Ge-Force GTX Titan X GPUs which takes roughly 4 days and 3 days respectively. During test, greedy decoding was used to generate the most likely output given a source Introduction.

For evaluation, we adopt the Recall-Oriented Understudy for Gisting Evaluation (ROUGE) metrics (Lin, 2004) proposed by Lin and Hovy (2003). ROUGE is a recall-oriented measure to score system summaries which is proven to have a strong correlation with human evaluations. It measures

Evaluation Metric	Recall	Precision	F–Score
ROUGE-1	0.48135	0.59030	0.50835
ROUGE-2	0.32399	0.39505	0.34089
ROUGE-L	0.46588	0.57218	0.49234

Table 3: ROUGE scores of GRU Model

Evaluation Metric	Recall	Precision	F–Score
ROUGE-1	0.50901	0.61571	0.53870
ROUGE-2	0.34148	0.40824	0.35925
ROUGE-L	0.49406	0.59830	0.52318

Table 4: ROUGE scores of MTGRU Model

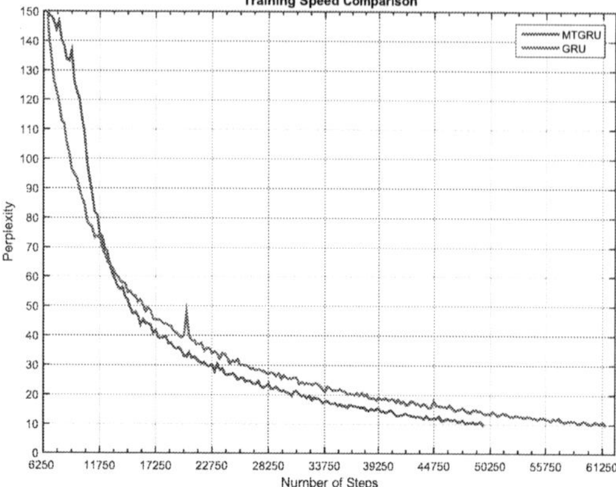

Figure 4: Comparison of Training Speed between GRU and MTGRU.

the n-gram recall between the candidate summary and gold summaries. In this work, we only have one gold summary which is the Abstract of an article, thus the ROUGE score is calculated as given in Li et al. (2015). ROUGE-1, ROUGE-2 and ROUGE-L are used to report the performance of the models. For the performance evaluation, both the models are trained up to 74750 steps where the training perplexity of GRU and MTGRU are shown in Table 2. This step was chosen as the early stopping point as at this step we get the lowest test perplexity of the GRU model. The ROUGE scores calculated using these trained networks are shown in Table 3 and Table 4 for the GRU and MT-GRU models, respectively. A sample summary generated by the MTGRU model is shown in Fig. 5.

Input Text:
The input is the Introduction of this paper.

Generated Summary:
1. Summarization has been the topic explored as a challenge of text semantic understanding
2. Recently , _UNK neural networks have emerged as a success in wide range of practical problems
3. In particular , we need to use a new way to evaluate three important questions into the algorithms
4. We use a concept to define the temporal hierarchy of each sentence in the context of paragraph
5. We demonstrate that our model outperforms a conventional _UNK system and significantly lead to optimize
6. In section # , we evaluate the experimental results on our model and evaluate our results in Section #

Figure 5: An example of the generated summary with MTGRU.

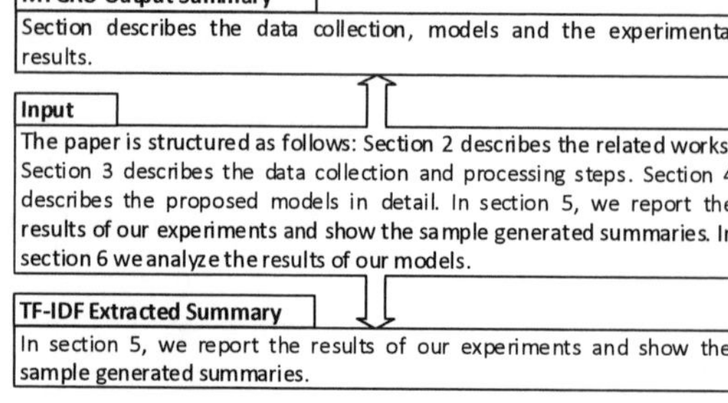

Figure 6: An example of the output summary vs the extracted targets

4 Discussion and Future Work

The ROUGE scores obtained for the summarization model using GRU and MTGRU show that the multiple timescale concept improves the performance of the conventional seq2seq model without the presence of highly complex architectural hierarchies. Another major advantage is the increase in training speed by as much as 1 epoch. Moreover, the sample summary shown in Fig. 5 demonstrates that the model has successfully generalized on the difficult task of summarizing a large paragraph into a one line salient summary.

In setting the τ timescale parameters, we follow (Yamashita and Tani, 2008) . We gradually increase τ as we go up the layers such that higher layers have slower context units. Moreover, we experiment with multiple settings of τ and compare the training performance, as shown in Fig. 7. The τ of MTRGU-2 and MTRGU-3 are set as {1, 1.42, 2, 2.5} and {1, 1, 1.25, 1.25}, respectively. MTGRU-1 is the final model adopted in our experiment described in the previous section. MTGRU-2 has comparatively slower context layers and MTGRU-3 has two fast and two slow context layers. As shown in the comparison, the training performance of MTRGU-1 is superior to the remaining two, which justifies our selection of the timescale settings.

The results of our experiment provide evidence that an organizational process akin to functional differentiation occurs in the RNN in language tasks. The MTGRU is able to train faster than the conventional GRU by as much as 1 epoch. We believe that the MTRGU expedites a type of functional differentiation process that is already ocurring in the RNN, by explicitly guiding the layers into multiple timescales, where otherwise this temporal hierarchical organization occurs more gradually.

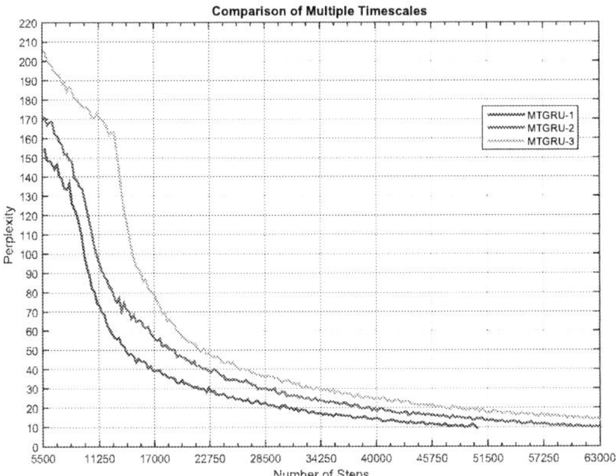

Figure 7: Comparison of Training performance between multiple time constants.

In Fig. 6, we show the comparison of a generated summary of the input paragraph to an extracted summary. As seen in the example, our model has successfully extracted the key information from multiple sentences and reproduces it into a single line summary. While the system was trained only on the extractive summary, the abstraction of the entire paragraph is possible because of the generalization capability of our model. The seq2seq objective maximizes the joint probability of the target sequence conditioned on the source sequence. When a summarization model is trained on source-extracted salient sentence target pairs, the objective can be viewed as consisting of two subgoals: One is to correctly perform saliency finding (importance extraction) in order to identify the most salient content, and the other is to generate the precise order of the sentence target. In fact, during training, we observe that the optimization of the first subgoal is achieved before the second subgoal. The second subgoal is fully achieved only when overfitting occurs on the training set. The generalization capability of the model is attributable to the fact that the model is expected to learn multiple points of saliency per given paragraph input (not only a single salient section corresponding to a single sentence) as many training examples are seen. This explains how the results such as those in Fig. 6 can be obtained from this model.

We believe our work has some meaningful implications for seq2seq abstractive summarization going forward. First, our results confirm that it is possible to train an encoder-decoder model to perform saliency identification, without the need to refer to an external corpus at test time. This

has already been shown, implicitly, in previous works such as Rush et al. (2015; Nallapati et al. (2016), but is made explicit in our work due to our choice of data consisting of paragraph-salient sentence pairs. Secondly, our results indicate that probabilistic language models can solve the task of novel word generation in the summarization setting, meeting a key criteria of abstractive summarization. Bengio et al. (2003) originally demonstrated that probabilistic language models can achieve much better generalization over similar words. This is due to the fact that the probability function is a smooth function of the word embedding vectors. Since similar words are trained to have similar embedding vectors, a small change in the features induces a small change in the predicted probability. This makes a strong case for RNN language models as the best available solution for abstractive summarization, where it is necessary to generate novel sentences. For example, in Fig. 5, the first summary shows that our model generates the word "explored" which is not present in the paper. Furthermore, our results suggest that if given abstractive targets, the same model could train a fully abstractive summarization system.

In the future, we hope to explore the organizational effect of the MTGRU in different tasks where temporal hierarchies can arise, as well as investigating ways to effectively optimize the timescale constant. Finally, we will work to move towards a fully abstractive end-to-end summarization system of multi-paragraph text by utilizing a more abstractive target which can potentially be generated with the help of the Abstract from the articles.

5 Conclusion

In this paper, we have demonstrated the capability of the MTGRU in the multi-paragraph text summarization task. Our model fulfills a fundamental requirement of abstractive summarization, deep semantic understanding of text and importance identification. The method draws from a well-researched phenomenon in the human brain and can be implemented without any hierarchical architectural complexity or additional memory requirements during training. Although we show its application to the task of capturing compositional hierarchies in text summarization only, MTGRU also shows the ability to enhance the learning speed thereby reducing training time significantly. In the future, we hope to extend our work to a fully abstractive end-to-end summarization system of multi-paragraph text.

Acknowledgment

This research was supported by Basic Science Research Program through the National Research Foundation of Korea(NRF) funded by the Ministry of Science, ICT and future Planning(2013R1A2A2A01068687) (50%), and by the Industrial Strategic Technology Development Program (10044009) funded by the Ministry of Trade, Industry and Energy (MOTIE, Korea) (50%).

References

Dzmitry Bahdanau, Kyunghyun Cho, and Yoshua Bengio. 2014. Neural machine translation by jointly learning to align and translate. *CoRR*, abs/1409.0473.

Yoshua Bengio, Réjean Ducharme, Pascal Vincent, and Christian Jauvin. 2003. A neural probabilistic language model. *journal of machine learning research*, 3(Feb):1137–1155.

Matthew M Botvinick. 2007. Multilevel structure in behaviour and in the brain: a model of fuster's hierarchy. *Philosophical Transactions of the Royal Society B: Biological Sciences*, 362(1485):1615–26, September.

Kyunghyun Cho, Bart van Merrienboer, Çaglar Gülçehre, Fethi Bougares, Holger Schwenk, and Yoshua Bengio. 2014. Learning phrase representations using RNN encoder-decoder for statistical machine translation. *CoRR*, abs/1406.1078.

Junyoung Chung, Çaglar Gülçehre, KyungHyun Cho, and Yoshua Bengio. 2014. Empirical evaluation of gated recurrent neural networks on sequence modeling. *CoRR*, abs/1412.3555.

Udo Hahn and Inderjeet Mani. 2000. The challenges of automatic summarization. *Computer*, 33(11):29–36, November.

Stefan Heinrich, Cornelius Weber, and Stefan Wermter, 2012. *Artificial Neural Networks and Machine Learning – ICANN 2012: 22nd International Conference on Artificial Neural Networks, Lausanne, Switzerland, September 11-14, 2012, Proceedings, Part I*, chapter Adaptive Learning of Linguistic Hierarchy in a Multiple Timescale Recurrent Neural Network, pages 555–562. Springer Berlin Heidelberg, Berlin, Heidelberg.

Sepp Hochreiter, Yoshua Bengio, and Paolo Frasconi. 2001. Gradient flow in recurrent nets: the difficulty of learning long-term dependencies. In J. Kolen and S. Kremer, editors, *Field Guide to Dynamical Recurrent Networks*. IEEE Press.

Karen Sparck Jones. 1972. A statistical interpretation of term specificity and its application in retrieval. *Journal of Documentation*, 28(1):11–21.

Karen Sparck Jones. 2007. Automatic summarising: the state of the art. *Information Processing and Management: an International Journal*, 43(6):1449–1481.

Jiwei Li, Minh-Thang Luong, and Dan Jurafsky. 2015. A hierarchical neural autoencoder for paragraphs and documents. *CoRR*, abs/1506.01057.

Chin-Yew Lin and Eduard Hovy. 2003. Automatic evaluation of summaries using n-gram co-occurrence statistics. In *Proceedings of the 2003 Conference of the North American Chapter of the Association for Computational Linguistics on Human Language Technology-Volume 1*, pages 71–78. Association for Computational Linguistics.

Chin-Yew Lin. 2004. Rouge: A package for automatic evaluation of summaries. In *Text summarization branches out: Proceedings of the ACL-04 workshop*, volume 8.

H. P. Luhn. 1958. The automatic creation of literature abstracts. *IBM J. Res. Dev.*, 2(2):159–165, April.

D. Meunier, R. Lambiotte, A. Fornito, K. D. Ersche, and E. T. Bullmore. 2010. Hierarchical modularity in human brain functional networks. *ArXiv e-prints*, April.

Ramesh Nallapati, Bing Xiang, and Bowen Zhou. 2016. Sequence-to-sequence rnns for text summarization. 4th International Conference on Learning Representations - Workshop Track (ICLR 2016).

Ani Nenkova, Sameer Maskey, and Yang Liu. 2011. Automatic summarization. In *Proceedings of the 49th Annual Meeting of the Association for Computational Linguistics: Tutorial Abstracts of ACL 2011*, HLT '11, pages 3:1–3:86, Stroudsburg, PA, USA. Association for Computational Linguistics.

Rainer W. Paine and Jun Tani. 2004. Motor primitive and sequence self-organization in a hierarchical recurrent neural network. *Neural Networks*, 17(89):1291 – 1309. New Developments in Self-Organizing Systems.

Alexander M. Rush, Sumit Chopra, and Jason Weston. 2015. A neural attention model for sentence summarization. In *Proceedings of the 2015 Conference on Empirical Methods in Natural Language Processing*, pages 379–389. Association for Computational Linguistics, Lisbon, Portugal.

Ilya Sutskever, Oriol Vinyals, and Quoc V Le. 2014. Sequence to sequence learning with neural networks. In Z. Ghahramani, M. Welling, C. Cortes,

N. D. Lawrence, and K. Q. Weinberger, editors, *Advances in Neural Information Processing Systems 27*, pages 3104–3112. Curran Associates, Inc.

Yuichi Yamashita and Jun Tani. 2008. Emergence of functional hierarchy in a multiple timescale neural network model: A humanoid robot experiment. *PLoS Comput Biol*, 4(11):1–18, 11.

An Empirical Evaluation of `doc2vec` with Practical Insights into Document Embedding Generation

Jey Han Lau[1,2] and **Timothy Baldwin**[2]
[1] IBM Research
[2] Dept of Computing and Information Systems,
The University of Melbourne

`jeyhan.lau@gmail.com`, `tb@ldwin.net`

Abstract

Recently, Le and Mikolov (2014) proposed `doc2vec` as an extension to `word2vec` (Mikolov et al., 2013a) to learn document-level embeddings. Despite promising results in the original paper, others have struggled to reproduce those results. This paper presents a rigorous empirical evaluation of `doc2vec` over two tasks. We compare `doc2vec` to two baselines and two state-of-the-art document embedding methodologies. We found that `doc2vec` performs robustly when using models trained on large external corpora, and can be further improved by using pre-trained word embeddings. We also provide recommendations on hyper-parameter settings for general-purpose applications, and release source code to induce document embeddings using our trained `doc2vec` models.

1 Introduction

Neural embeddings were first proposed by Bengio et al. (2003), in the form of a feed-forward neural network language model. Modern methods use a simpler and more efficient neural architecture to learn word vectors (`word2vec`: Mikolov et al. (2013b); `GloVe`: Pennington et al. (2014)), based on objective functions that are designed specifically to produce high-quality vectors.

Neural embeddings learnt by these methods have been applied in a myriad of NLP applications, including initialising neural network models for objective visual recognition (Frome et al., 2013) or machine translation (Zhang et al., 2014; Li et al., 2014), as well as directly modelling word-to-word relationships (Mikolov et al.,

2013a; Zhao et al., 2015; Salehi et al., 2015; Vylomova et al., to appear),

Paragraph vectors, or `doc2vec`, were proposed by Le and Mikolov (2014) as a simple extension to `word2vec` to extend the learning of embeddings from words to word sequences.[1] `doc2vec` is agnostic to the granularity of the word sequence — it can equally be a word n-gram, sentence, paragraph or document. In this paper, we use the term "document embedding" to refer to the embedding of a word sequence, irrespective of its granularity.

`doc2vec` was proposed in two forms: `dbow` and `dmpv`. `dbow` is a simpler model and ignores word order, while `dmpv` is a more complex model with more parameters (see Section 2 for details). Although Le and Mikolov (2014) found that as a standalone method `dmpv` is a better model, others have reported contradictory results.[2] `doc2vec` has also been reported to produce sub-par performance compared to vector averaging methods based on informal experiments.[3] Additionally, while Le and Mikolov (2014) report state-of-the-art results over a sentiment analysis task using `doc2vec`, others (including the second author of the original paper in follow-up work) have struggled to replicate this result.[4]

Given this background of uncertainty regarding the true effectiveness of `doc2vec` and confusion about performance differences between `dbow` and `dmpv`, we aim to shed light on a number of em-

---

[1] The term `doc2vec` was popularised by Gensim (Řehůřek and Sojka, 2010), a widely-used implementation of paragraph vectors: `https://radimrehurek.com/gensim/`

[2] The authors of Gensim found `dbow` outperforms `dmpv`: `https://github.com/piskvorky/gensim/blob/develop/docs/notebooks/doc2vec-IMDB.ipynb`

[3] `https://groups.google.com/forum/#!topic/gensim/bEskaT45fXQ`

[4] For a detailed discussion on replicating the results of Le and Mikolov (2014), see: `https://groups.google.com/forum/#!topic/word2vec-toolkit/Q49FIrNOQRo`

Proceedings of the 1st Workshop on Representation Learning for NLP, pages 78–86,
Berlin, Germany, August 11th, 2016. ©2016 Association for Computational Linguistics

pirical questions: (1) how effective is `doc2vec` in different task settings?; (2) which is better out of `dmpv` and `dbow`?; (3) is it possible to improve `doc2vec` through careful hyper-parameter optimisation or with pre-trained word embeddings?; and (4) can `doc2vec` be used as an off-the-shelf model like `word2vec`? To this end, we present a formal and rigorous evaluation of `doc2vec` over two extrinsic tasks. Our findings reveal that `dbow`, despite being the simpler model, is superior to `dmpv`. When trained over large external corpora, with pre-trained word embeddings and hyper-parameter tuning, we find that `doc2vec` performs very strongly compared to both a simple word embedding averaging and n-gram baseline, as well as two state-of-the-art document embedding approaches, and that `doc2vec` performs particularly strongly over longer documents. We additionally release source code for replicating our experiments, and for inducing document embeddings using our trained models.

2 Related Work

`word2vec` was proposed as an efficient neural approach to learning high-quality embeddings for words (Mikolov et al., 2013a). Negative sampling was subsequently introduced as an alternative to the more complex hierarchical softmax step at the output layer, with the authors finding that not only is it more efficient, but actually produces better word vectors on average (Mikolov et al., 2013b).

The objective function of `word2vec` is to maximise the log probability of context word (w_O) given its input word (w_I), i.e. $\log P(w_O|w_I)$. With negative sampling, the objective is to maximise the dot product of the w_I and w_O while minimising the dot product of w_I and randomly sampled "negative" words. Formally, $\log P(w_O|w_I)$ is given as follows:

$$\log \sigma(v'_{w_O}{}^\mathsf{T} v_{w_I}) +$$
$$\sum_{i=1}^{k} w_i \sim P_n(w) \left[\log \sigma(-v'_{w_i}{}^\mathsf{T} v_{w_I}) \right] \quad (1)$$

where σ is the sigmoid function, k is the number of negative samples, $P_n(w)$ is the noise distribution, v_w is the vector of word w, and v'_w is the negative sample vector of word w.

There are two approaches within `word2vec`: `skip-gram` ("`sg`") and `cbow`. In `skip-gram`, the input is a word (i.e. v_{w_I} is a vector of *one* word)

and the output is a context word. For each input word, the number of left or right context words to predict is defined by the window size hyper-parameter. `cbow` is different to `skip-gram` in one aspect: the input consists of multiple words that are combined via vector addition to predict the context word (i.e. v_{w_I} is a summed vector of *several* words).

`doc2vec` is an extension to `word2vec` for learning document embeddings (Le and Mikolov, 2014). There are two approaches within `doc2vec`: `dbow` and `dmpv`.

`dbow` works in the same way as `skip-gram`, except that the input is replaced by a special token representing the document (i.e. v_{w_I} is a vector representing the document). In this architecture, the order of words in the document is ignored; hence the name *distributed bag of words*.

`dmpv` works in a similar way to `cbow`. For the input, `dmpv` introduces an additional document token in addition to multiple target words. Unlike `cbow`, however, these vectors are not summed but concatenated (i.e. v_{w_I} is a concatenated vector containing the document token and several target words). The objective is again to predict a context word given the concatenated document and word vectors..

More recently, Kiros et al. (2015) proposed `skip-thought` as a means of learning document embeddings. `skip-thought` vectors are inspired by abstracting the distributional hypothesis from the word level to the sentence level. Using an encoder-decoder neural network architecture, the encoder learns a dense vector presentation of a sentence, and the decoder takes this encoding and decodes it by predicting words of its next (or previous) sentence. Both the encoder and decoder use a gated recurrent neural network language model. Evaluating over a range of tasks, the authors found that `skip-thought` vectors perform very well against state-of-the-art task-optimised methods.

Wieting et al. (2016) proposed a more direct way of learning document embeddings, based on a large-scale training set of paraphrase pairs from the Paraphrase Database (PPDB: Ganitkevitch et al. (2013)). Given a paraphrase pair, word embeddings and a method to compose the word embeddings for a sentence embedding, the objective function of the neural network model is to optimise the word embeddings such that the cosine similarity of the sentence embeddings for the pair is maximised. The authors explore several methods of combining word embeddings, and found that simple averaging produces the best performance.

3 Evaluation Tasks

We evaluate `doc2vec` in two task settings, specifically chosen to highlight the impact of document length on model performance.

For all tasks, we split the dataset into 2 partitions: development and test. The development set is used to optimise the hyper-parameters of `doc2vec`, and results are reported on the test set. We use all documents in the development and test set (and potentially more background documents, where explicitly mentioned) to train `doc2vec`. Our rationale for this is that the `doc2vec` training is completely unsupervised, i.e. the model takes only raw text and uses no supervised or annotated information, and thus there is no need to hold out the test data, as it is unlabelled. We ultimately relax this assumption in the next section (Section 4), when we train `doc2vec` using large external corpora.

After training `doc2vec`, document embeddings are generated by the model. For the `word2vec` baseline, we compute a document embedding by taking the component-wise mean of its component word embeddings. We experiment with both variants of `doc2vec` (`dbow` and `dmpv`) and `word2vec` (`skip-gram` and `cbow`) for all tasks.

In addition to `word2vec`, we experiment with another baseline model that converts a document into a distribution over words via maximum likelihood estimation, and compute pairwise document similarity using the Jensen Shannon divergence.[5] For word types we explore n-grams of order $n = \{1, 2, 3, 4\}$ and find that a combination of unigrams, bigrams and trigrams achieves the best results.[6] Henceforth, this second baseline will be referred to as `ngram`.

3.1 Forum Question Duplication

We first evaluate `doc2vec` over the task of duplicate question detection in a web forum setting, using the dataset of Hoogeveen et al. (2015). The dataset has 12 subforums extracted from StackExchange, and provides training and test splits in two experimental settings: retrieval and classification. We use the classification setting, where the goal is to classify whether a given question pair is a duplicate.

The dataset is separated into the 12 subforums, with a pre-compiled training–test split per subforum; the total number of instances (question pairs) ranges from 50M to 1B pairs for the training partitions, and 30M to 300M pairs for the test partitions, depending on the subforum. The proportion of true duplicate pairs is very small in each subforum, but the setup is intended to respect the distribution of true duplicate pairs in a real-world setting.

We sub-sample the test partition to create a smaller test partition that has 10M document pairs.[7] On average across all twelve subforums, there are 22 true positive pairs per 10M question pairs. We also create a smaller development partition from the training partition by randomly selecting 300 positive and 3000 negative pairs. We optimise the hyper-parameters of `doc2vec` and `word2vec` using the development partition on the *tex* subforum, and apply the same hyper-parameter settings for all subforums when evaluating over the test pairs. We use both the question title and body as document content: on average the test document length is approximately 130 words. We use the default tokenised and lower-cased words given by the dataset. All test, development and un-sampled documents are pooled together during model training, and each subforum is trained separately.

We compute cosine similarity between documents using the vectors produced by `doc2vec` and `word2vec` to score a document pair. We then sort the document pairs in descending order of similarity score, and evaluate using the area under the curve (AUC) of the receiver operating characteristic (ROC) curve . The ROC curve tracks the true positive rate against the false positive rate at each point of the ranking, and as such works well for heavily-skewed datasets. An AUC score of 1.0 implies that all true positive pairs are ranked before true negative pairs, while an AUC score of .5 indicates a random ranking. We present the full results for each subforum in Table 1.

---

[5] We multiply the divergence value by -1.0 to invert the value, so that a higher value indicates greater similarity.

[6] That is, the probability distribution is computed over the union of unigrams, bigrams and trigrams in the paired documents.

[7] Uniform random sampling is used so as to respect the original distribution.

Subforum	doc2vec		word2vec		ngram
	dbow	dmpv	sg	cbow	
android	**.97**	.96	.86	.93	.80
english	.84	**.90**	.76	.73	.84
gaming	**1.00**	.98	.97	.97	.94
gis	.93	.95	.94	**.97**	.92
mathematica	**.96**	.90	.81	.81	.70
physics	.96	**.99**	.93	.90	.88
programmers	**.93**	.83	.84	.84	.68
stats	**1.00**	.95	.91	.88	.77
tex	**.94**	.91	.79	.86	.78
unix	**.98**	.95	.91	.91	.75
webmasters	**.92**	.91	**.92**	.90	.79
wordpress	**.97**	**.97**	.79	.84	.87

Table 1: ROC AUC scores for each subforum. Boldface indicates the best score in each row.

Domain	DLS	doc2vec		word2vec		ngram
		dbow	dmpv	sg	cbow	
headlines	.83	.77	**.78**	.74	.69	.61
ans-forums	.74	**.66**	.65	.62	.52	.50
ans-students	.77	.65	.60	**.69**	.64	.65
belief	.74	**.76**	.75	.72	.59	.67
images	.86	**.78**	.75	.73	.69	.62

Table 2: Pearson's r of the STS task across 5 domains. DLS is the overall best system in the competition. Boldface indicates the best results between doc2vec and word2vec in each row.

Comparing doc2vec and word2vec to ngram, both embedding methods perform substantially better in most domains, with two exceptions (*english* and *gis*), where nqram has comparable performance.

doc2vec outperforms word2vec embeddings in all subforums except for *gis*. Despite the skewed distribution, simple cosine similarity based on doc2vec embeddings is able to detect these duplicate document pairs with a high degree of accuracy. dbow performs better than or as well as dmpv in 9 out of the 12 subforums, showing that the simpler dbow is superior to dmpv.

One interesting exception is the *english* subforum, where dmpv is substantially better, and ngram — which uses only surface word forms — also performs very well. We hypothesise that the order and the surface form of words possibly has a stronger role in this subforum, as questions are often about grammar problems and as such the position and semantics of words is less predictable (e.g. *Where does "for the same" come from?*)

Hyper-Parameter	Description
Vector Size	Dimension of word vectors
Window Size	Left/right context window size
Min Count	Minimum frequency threshold for word types
Sub-sampling	Threshold to downsample high frequency words
Negative Sample	No. of negative word samples
Epoch	Number of training epochs

Table 3: A description of doc2vec hyperparamters.

3.2 Semantic Textual Similarity

The Semantic Textual Similarity (STS) task is a shared task held as part of *SEM and SemEval over a number of iterations (Agirre et al., 2013; Agirre et al., 2014; Agirre et al., 2015). In STS, the goal is to automatically predict the similarity of a pair of sentences in the range $[0, 5]$, where 0 indicates no similarity whatsoever and 5 indicates semantic equivalence.

The top systems utilise word alignment, and further optimise their scores using supervised learning (Agirre et al., 2015). Word embeddings are employed, although sentence embeddings are often taken as the average of word embeddings (e.g. Sultan et al. (2015)).

We evaluate doc2vec and word2vec embeddings over the English STS sub-task of SemEval-2015 (Agirre et al., 2015). The dataset has 5 domains, and each domain has 375–750 annotated pairs. Sentences are much shorter than our previous task, at an average of only 13 words in each test sentence.

As the dataset is also much smaller, we combine sentences from all 5 domains and also sentences from previous years (2012–2014) to form the training data. We use the *headlines* domain from 2014 as development, and test on all 2015 domains. For pre-processing, we tokenise and lowercase the words using Stanford CoreNLP (Manning et al., 2014).

As a benchmark, we include results from the overall top-performing system in the competition, referred to as "DLS" (Sultan et al., 2015). Note, however, that this system is supervised and highly customised to the task, whereas our methods are completely unsupervised. Results are presented in Table 2.

Unsurprisingly, we do not exceed the overall performance of the supervised benchmark system DLS, although doc2vec outperforms DLS over

Method	Task	Training Size	Vector Size	Window Size	Min Count	Sub-Sampling	Negative Sample	Epoch
dbow	Q-Dup	4.3M	300	15	5	10^{-5}	5	20
	STS	.5M	300	15	1	10^{-5}	5	400
dmpv	Q-Dup	4.3M	300	5	5	10^{-6}	5	600
	STS	.5M	300	5	1	10^{-6}	5	1000

Table 4: Optimal `doc2vec` hyper-parameter values used for each tasks. "Training size" is the total word count in the training data. For Q-Dup training size is an average word count across all subforums.

the domain of *belief*. `ngram` performs substantially worse than all methods (with an exception in *ans-students* where it outperforms `dmpv` and `cbow`).

Comparing `doc2vec` and `word2vec`, `doc2vec` performs better. However, the performance gap is lower compared to the previous two tasks, suggesting that the benefit of using `doc2vec` is diminished for shorter documents. Comparing `dbow` and `dmpv`, the difference is marginal, although `dbow` as a whole is slightly stronger, consistent with the observation of previous task.

3.3 Optimal Hyper-parameter Settings

Across the two tasks, we found that the optimal hyper-parameter settings (as described in Table 3) are fairly consistent for `dbow` and `dmpv`, as detailed in Table 4 (task abbreviations: Q-Dup = Forum Question Duplication (Section 3.1); and STS = Semantic Textual Similarity (Section 3.2)). Note that we did not tune the initial and minimum learning rates (α and α_{min}, respectively), and use the the following values for all experiments: $\alpha = .025$ and $\alpha_{min} = .0001$. The learning rate decreases linearly per epoch from the initial rate to the minimum rate.

In general, `dbow` favours longer windows for context words than `dmpv`. Possibly the most important hyper-parameter is the sub-sampling threshold for high frequency words: in our experiments we find that task performance dips considerably when a sub-optimal value is used. `dmpv` also requires more training epochs than `dbow`. As a rule of thumb, for `dmpv` to reach convergence, the number of epochs is one order of magnitude larger than `dbow`. Given that `dmpv` has more parameters in the model, this is perhaps not a surprising finding.

4 Training with Large External Corpora

In Section 3, all tasks were trained using small in-domain document collections. `doc2vec` is designed to scale to large data, and we explore the effectiveness of `doc2vec` by training it on large external corpora in this section.

We experiment with two external corpora: (1) WIKI, the full collection of English Wikipedia;[8] and (2) AP-NEWS, a collection of Associated Press English news articles from 2009 to 2015. We tokenise and lowercase the documents using Stanford CoreNLP (Manning et al., 2014), and treat each natural paragraph of an article as a document for `doc2vec`. After pre-processing, we have approximately 35M documents and 2B tokens for WIKI, and 25M and .9B tokens for AP-NEWS. Seeing that `dbow` trains faster and is a better model than `dmpv` from Section 3, we experiment with only `dbow` here.[9]

To test if `doc2vec` can be used as an off-the-shelf model, we take a pre-trained model and infer an embedding for a new document without updating the hidden layer word weights.[10] We have three hyper-parameters for test inference: initial learning rate (α), minimum learning rate (α_{min}), and number of inference epochs. We optimise these parameters using the development partitions in each task; in general a small initial α (= .01) with low α_{min} (= .0001) and large epoch number (= 500–1000) works well.

For `word2vec`, we train `skip-gram` on the

---

[8] Using the dump dated 2015-12-01, cleaned using WikiExtractor: https://github.com/attardi/wikiextractor

[9] We use these hyper-parameter values for WIKI (AP-NEWS): vector size = 300 (300), window size = 15 (15), min count = 20 (10), sub-sampling threshold = 10^{-5} (10^{-5}), negative sample = 5, epoch = 20 (30). After removing low frequency words, the vocabulary size is approximately 670K for WIKI and 300K for AP-NEWS.

[10] That is, test data is held out and not including as part of `doc2vec` training.

Task	Metric	Domain	pp	skip-thought	dbow		skip-gram			ngram
			PPDB	BOOK-CORPUS	WIKI	AP-NEWS	WIKI	AP-NEWS	GL-NEWS	
Q-Dup	AUC	android	.92	.57	**.96**	.94	.77	.76	.72	.80
		english	.82	.56	.80	.81	.62	.63	.61	**.84**
		gaming	**.96**	.70	.95	.93	.88	.85	.83	.94
		gis	.89	.58	.85	.86	.79	.83	.79	**.92**
		mathematica	.80	.57	**.84**	.80	.65	.58	.59	.70
		physics	**.97**	.61	.92	.94	.81	.77	.74	.88
		programmers	.88	.69	**.93**	.88	.75	.72	.64	.68
		stats	.87	.60	.92	**.98**	.70	.72	.66	.77
		tex	.88	.65	**.89**	.82	.75	.64	.73	.78
		unix	.86	.74	**.95**	.94	.78	.72	.66	.75
		webmasters	.89	.53	.89	**.91**	.77	.73	.71	.79
		wordpress	.83	.66	**.99**	.98	.61	.58	.58	.87
STS	r	headlines	**.77**	.44	.73	.75	.73	.74	.66	.61
		ans-forums	**.67**	.35	.59	.60	.46	.44	.42	.50
		ans-students	**.78**	.33	.65	.69	.67	.69	.65	.65
		belief	**.78**	.24	.58	.62	.51	.51	.52	.67
		images	**.83**	.18	.80	.78	.72	.73	.69	.62

Table 5: Results over all two tasks using models trained with external corpora.

same corpora.[11] We also include the word vectors trained on the larger Google News by Mikolov et al. (2013b), which has 100B words.[12] The Google News `skip-gram` vectors will henceforth be referred to as GL-NEWS.

`dbow`, `skip-gram` and `ngram` results for all two tasks are presented in Table 5. Between the baselines `ngram` and `skip-gram`, `ngram` appears to do better over Q-Dup, while `skip-gram` works better over STS.

As before, `doc2vec` outperforms `word2vec` and `ngram` across almost all tasks. For tasks with longer documents (Q-Dup), the performance gap between `doc2vec` and `word2vec` is more pronounced, while for STS, which has shorter documents, the gap is smaller. In some STS domains (e.g. *ans-students*) `word2vec` performs just as well as `doc2vec`. Interestingly, we see that GL-NEWS `word2vec` embeddings perform worse than our WIKI and AP-NEWS `word2vec` embeddings, even though the Google News corpus is orders of magnitude larger.

Comparing `doc2vec` results with in-domain results (1 and 2), the performance is in general lower. As a whole, the performance difference between the `dbow` models trained using WIKI and AP-NEWS is not very large, indicating the robustness of these large external corpora for general-purpose applications. To facilitate applications us-

ing off-the-shelf `doc2vec` models, we have publicly released code and trained models to induce document embeddings using the WIKI and AP-NEWS `dbow` models.[13]

4.1 Comparison with Other Document Embedding Methodologies

We next calibrate the results for `doc2vec` against `skip-thought` (Kiros et al., 2015) and paragram-phrase (pp: Wieting et al. (2016)), two recently-proposed competitor document embedding methods. For `skip-thought`, we use the pre-trained model made available by the authors, based on the BOOK-CORPUS dataset (Zhu et al., 2015); for pp, once again we use the pre-trained model from the authors, based on PPDB (Ganitkevitch et al., 2013). We compare these two models against `dbow` trained on each of WIKI and AP-NEWS. The results are presented in Table 5, along with results for the baseline method of `skip-gram` and `ngram`.

`skip-thought` performs poorly: its performance is worse than the simpler method of `word2vec` vector averaging and `ngram`. `dbow` outperforms pp over most Q-Dup subforums, although the situation is reversed for STS. Given that pp is based on word vector averaging, these observations support the conclusion that vector averaging methods works best for shorter documents, while `dbow` handles longer documents better.

It is worth noting that `doc2vec` has the upper-

---

[11] Hyper-parameter values for WIKI (AP-NEWS): vector size = 300 (300), window size = 5 (5), min count = 20 (10), sub-sampling threshold = 10^{-5} (10^{-5}), negative sample = 5, epoch = 100 (150)
[12] https://code.google.com/archive/p/word2vec/
[13] https://github.com/jhlau/doc2vec

hand compared to pp in that it can be trained on in-domain documents. If we compare in-domain `doc2vec` results (1 and 2) to pp (Table 5), the performance gain on Q-Dup is even more pronounced.

5 Improving `doc2vec` with Pre-trained Word Embeddings

Although not explicitly mentioned in the original paper (Le and Mikolov, 2014), `dbow` does not learn embeddings for words in the default configuration. In its implementation (e.g. Gensim), `dbow` has an option to turn on word embedding learning, by running a step of `skip-gram` to update word embeddings before running `dbow`. With the option turned off, word embeddings are randomly initialised and kept at these randomised values.

Even though `dbow` can in theory work with randomised word embeddings, we found that performance degrades severely under this setting. An intuitive explanation can be traced back to its objective function, which is to maximise the dot product between the document embedding and its constituent word embeddings: if word embeddings are randomly distributed, it becomes more difficult to optimise the document embedding to be close to its more critical content words.

To illustrate this, consider the two-dimensional t-SNE plot (Van der Maaten and Hinton, 2008) of `doc2vec` document and word embeddings in Figure 1(a). In this case, the word learning option is turned on, and related words form clusters, allowing the document embedding to selectively position itself closer to a particular word cluster (e.g. content words) and distance itself from other clusters (e.g. function words). If word embeddings are randomly distributed on the plane, it would be harder to optimise the document embedding.

Seeing that word vectors are essentially learnt via `skip-gram` in `dbow`, we explore the possibility of using externally trained `skip-gram` word embeddings to initialise the word embeddings in `dbow`. We repeat the experiments described in Section 3, training the `dbow` model using the smaller in-domain document collections in each task, but this time initialise the word vectors using pre-trained `word2vec` embeddings from WIKI and AP-NEWS. The motivation is that with better initialisation, the model could converge faster and improve the quality of embeddings.

Results using pre-trained WIKI and AP-NEWS

Task	Domain	dbow	dbow + WIKI	dbow + AP-NEWS
Q-Dup	android	.97	**.99**	.98
	english	.84	**.90**	.89
	gaming	**1.00**	**1.00**	**1.00**
	gis	.93	.92	**.94**
	mathematica	**.96**	**.96**	**.96**
	physics	.96	**.98**	.97
	programmers	**.93**	.92	.91
	stats	**1.00**	**1.00**	.99
	tex	.94	**.95**	.92
	unix	**.98**	**.98**	.97
	webmasters	.92	**.93**	**.93**
	wordpress	.97	.96	**.98**
STS	headlines	.77	**.78**	**.78**
	ans-forums	.66	**.68**	**.68**
	ans-students	**.65**	.63	**.65**
	belief	.76	.77	**.78**
	images	.78	**.80**	.79

Table 6: Comparison of `dbow` performance using pre-trained WIKI and AP-NEWS `skip-gram` embeddings.

`skip-gram` embeddings are presented in Table 6. Encouragingly, we see that using pre-trained word embeddings helps the training of `dbow` on the smaller in-domain document collection. Across all tasks, we see an increase in performance. More importantly, using pre-trained word embeddings *never* harms the performance. Although not detailed in the table, we also find that the number of epochs to achieve optimal performance (based on development data) is fewer than before.

We also experimented with using pre-trained `cbow` word embeddings for `dbow`, and found similar observations. This suggests that the initialisation of word embeddings of `dbow` is not sensitive to a particular word embedding implementation.

6 Discussion

To date, we have focused on quantitative evaluation of `doc2vec` and `word2vec`. The qualitative difference between `doc2vec` and `word2vec` document embeddings, however, remains unclear. To shed light on what is being learned, we select a random document from STS — *tech capital bangalore costliest indian city to live in: survey* — and plot the document and word embeddings induced by `dbow` and `skip-gram` using t-SNE in Figure 1.[14]

---

[14]We plotted a larger set of sentences as part of this analysis, and found that the general trend was the same across all sentences.

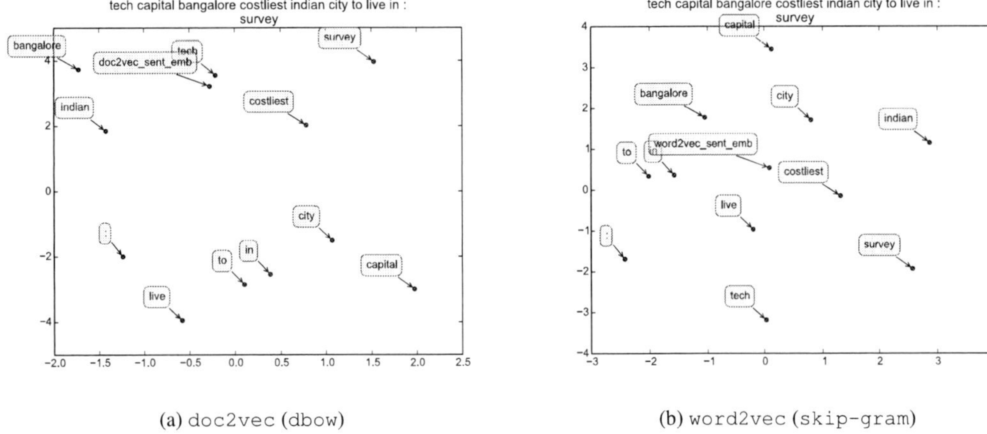

(a) <code>doc2vec (dbow)</code>   (b) <code>word2vec (skip-gram)</code>

Figure 1: Two-dimentional t-SNE projection of `doc2vec` and `word2vec` embeddings.

For `word2vec`, the document embedding is a centroid of the word embeddings, given the simple word averaging method. With `doc2vec`, on the other hand, the document embedding is clearly biased towards the content words such as *tech*, *costliest* and *bangalore*, and away from the function words. `doc2vec` learns this from its objective function with negative sampling: high frequency function words are likely to be selected as negative samples, and so the document embedding will tend to align itself with lower frequency content words.

7 Conclusion

We used two tasks to empirically evaluate the quality of document embeddings learnt by `doc2vec`, as compared to two baseline methods — `word2vec` word vector averaging and an n-gram model — and two competitor document embedding methodologies. Overall, we found that `doc2vec` performs well, and that `dbow` is a better model than `dmpv`. We empirically arrived at recommendations on optimal `doc2vec` hyper-parameter settings for general-purpose applications, and found that `doc2vec` performs robustly even when trained using large external corpora, and benefits from pre-trained word embeddings. To facilitate the use of `doc2vec` and enable replication of these results, we release our code and pre-trained models.

References

Eneko Agirre, Daniel Cer, Mona Diab, Aitor Gonzalez-Agirre, and Weiwei Guo. 2013. *sem 2013 shared task: Semantic textual similarity. In *Proceedings of the Second Joint Conference on Lexical and Computational Semantics (*SEM 2013)*, pages 32–43, Atlanta, USA.

Eneko Agirre, Carmen Banea, Claire Cardie, Daniel Cer, Mona Diab, Aitor Gonzalez-Agirre, Weiwei Guo, Rada Mihalcea, German Rigau, and Janyce Wiebe. 2014. Semeval-2014 task 10: Multilingual semantic textual similarity. In *Proceedings of the 8th International Workshop on Semantic Evaluation (SemEval 2014)*, pages 81–91, Dublin, Ireland.

Eneko Agirre, Carmen Banea, Claire Cardie, Daniel Cer, Mona Diab, Aitor Gonzalez-Agirre, Weiwei Guo, Inigo Lopez-Gazpio, Montse Maritxalar, Rada Mihalcea, German Rigau, Larraitz Uria, and Janyce Wiebe. 2015. SemEval-2015 task 2: Semantic textual similarity, English, Spanish and pilot on interpretability. In *Proceedings of the 9th International Workshop on Semantic Evaluation (SemEval 2015)*, pages 252–263, Denver, USA.

Yoshua Bengio, Réjean Ducharme, Pascal Vincent, and Christian Janvin. 2003. A neural probabilistic language model. *The Journal of Machine Learning Research*, 3:1137–1155.

Andrea Frome, Greg S Corrado, Jon Shlens, Samy Bengio, Jeff Dean, Marc Aurelio Ranzato, and Tomas Mikolov. 2013. DeViSE: A deep visual-semantic embedding model. In *Advances in Neural Information Processing Systems 26 (NIPS-13)*, pages 2121–2129.

Juri Ganitkevitch, Benjamin Van Durme, and Chris Callison-Burch. 2013. PPDB: The paraphrase database. In *Proceedings of the 2013 Conference of the North American Chapter of the Association for Computational Linguistics: Human Language Technologies (NAACL HLT 2013)*, pages 758–764, Atlanta, USA.

Doris Hoogeveen, Karin Verspoor, and Timothy Baldwin. 2015. CQADupStack: A benchmark data set for community question-answering research. In *Proceedings of the Twentieth Australasian Document Computing Symposium (ADCS 2015)*, pages 3:1–3:8, Sydney, Australia.

Ryan Kiros, Yukun Zhu, Ruslan Salakhutdinov, Richard S. Zemel, Antonio Torralba, Raquel Urtasun, and Sanja Fidler. 2015. Skip-thought vectors. In *Advances in Neural Information Processing Systems 28 (NIPS-15)*, pages 3294–3302, Montreal, Canada.

Q. Le and T. Mikolov. 2014. Distributed representations of sentences and documents. In *Proceedings of the 31st International Conference on Machine Learning (ICML 2014)*, pages 1188–1196, Beijing, China.

Peng Li, Yang Liu, Maosong Sun, Tatsuya Izuha, and Dakun Zhang. 2014. A neural reordering model for phrase-based translation. In *Proceedings of the 25th International Conference on Computational Linguistics (COLING 2014)*, pages 1897–1907, Dublin, Ireland.

Christopher D. Manning, Mihai Surdeanu, John Bauer, Jenny Finkel, Steven J. Bethard, and David McClosky. 2014. The Stanford CoreNLP natural language processing toolkit. In *Association for Computational Linguistics (ACL) System Demonstrations*, pages 55–60, Baltimore, USA.

Tomas Mikolov, Kai Chen, Greg Corrado, and Jeffrey Dean. 2013a. Efficient estimation of word representations in vector space. In *Proceedings of Workshop at the International Conference on Learning Representations, 2013*, Scottsdale, USA.

Tomas Mikolov, Ilya Sutskever, Kai Chen, Greg S Corrado, and Jeff Dean. 2013b. Distributed representations of words and phrases and their compositionality. In *Advances in Neural Information Processing Systems*, pages 3111–3119.

Jeffrey Pennington, Richard Socher, and Christopher Manning. 2014. Glove: Global vectors for word representation. In *Proceedings of the 2014 Conference on Empirical Methods in Natural Language Processing (EMNLP 2014)*, pages 1532–1543, Doha, Qatar.

Radim Řehůřek and Petr Sojka. 2010. Software Framework for Topic Modelling with Large Corpora. In *Proceedings of the LREC 2010 Workshop on New Challenges for NLP Frameworks*, pages 45–50, Valletta, Malta.

Bahar Salehi, Paul Cook, and Timothy Baldwin. 2015. A word embedding approach to predicting the compositionality of multiword expressions. In *Proceedings of the 2015 Conference of the North American Chapter of the Association for Computational Linguistics — Human Language Technologies (NAACL HLT 2015)*, pages 977–983, Denver, USA.

Md Arafat Sultan, Steven Bethard, and Tamara Sumner. 2015. DLS@CU: Sentence similarity from word alignment and semantic vector composition. In *Proceedings of the 9th International Workshop on Semantic Evaluation (SemEval 2015)*, pages 148–153, Denver, Colorado.

Laurens Van der Maaten and Geoffrey Hinton. 2008. Visualizing data using t-SNE. *Journal of Machine Learning Research*, 9(2579–2605):85.

Ekaterina Vylomova, Laura Rimell, Trevor Cohn, and Timothy Baldwin. to appear. Take and took, gaggle and goose, book and read: Evaluating the utility of vector differences for lexical relation learning. Berlin, Germany.

John Wieting, Mohit Bansal, Kevin Gimpel, and Karen Livescu. 2016. Towards universal paraphrastic sentence embeddings. In *Proceedings of the International Conference on Learning Representations 2016*, San Juan, Puerto Rico.

Jiajun Zhang, Shujie Liu, Mu Li, Ming Zhou, and Chengqing Zong. 2014. Bilingually-constrained phrase embeddings for machine translation. In *Proceedings of the 52nd Annual Meeting of the Association for Computational Linguistics (ACL 2014)*, pages 111–121, Baltimore, USA.

Jiang Zhao, Man Lan, Zheng-Yu Niu, and Yue Lu. 2015. Integrating word embeddings and traditional nlp features to measure textual entailment and semantic relatedness of sentence pairs. In *Proceedings of the International Joint Conference on Neural Networks (IJCNN2015)*, pages 1–7, Killarney, Ireland.

Yukun Zhu, Ryan Kiros, Richard Zemel, Ruslan Salakhutdinov, Raquel Urtasun, Antonio Torralba, and Sanja Fidler. 2015. Aligning books and movies: Towards story-like visual explanations by watching movies and reading books. *Arxiv*, abs/1506.06724.

Quantifying the vanishing gradient and long distance dependency problem in recursive neural networks and recursive LSTMs

Phong Le and **Willem Zuidema**
Institute for Logic, Language and Computation
University of Amsterdam, the Netherlands
{p.le,zuidema}@uva.nl

Abstract

Recursive neural networks (RNN) and their recently proposed extension recursive long short term memory networks (RLSTM) are models that compute representations for sentences, by recursively combining word embeddings according to an externally provided parse tree. Both models thus, unlike recurrent networks, explicitly make use of the hierarchical structure of a sentence. In this paper, we demonstrate that RNNs nevertheless suffer from the vanishing gradient and long distance dependency problem, and that RLSTMs greatly improve over RNN's on these problems. We present an artificial learning task that allows us to quantify the severity of these problems for both models. We further show that a ratio of gradients (at the root node and a focal leaf node) is highly indicative of the success of backpropagation at optimizing the relevant weights low in the tree. This paper thus provides an explanation for existing, superior results of RLSTMs on tasks such as sentiment analysis, and suggests that the benefits of including hierarchical structure and of including LSTM-style gating are complementary.

1 Introduction

The recursive neural network (RNN) model became popular since the work of Socher et al. (2010). It has been employed to tackle several NLP tasks, such as syntactic parsing (Socher et al., 2013a), machine translation (Liu et al., 2014), and word embedding learning (Luong et al., 2013). However, like traditional *recurrent* neural networks, the RNN seems to suffer from the vanish-

ing gradient problem, in which error signals propagating from the root in a parse tree to the child nodes shrink very quickly. Moreover, it encounters difficulties in capturing long range dependencies: information propagating from child nodes deep in a parse tree can be obscured before reaching the root node.

In the recurrent neural network world, the long short term memory (LSTM) architecture (Hochreiter and Schmidhuber, 1997) is often used as a solution to these two problems. A natural extension of the LSTM can be defined for tree structures, which we call Recursive LSTM (RLSTM), as proposed independently by Tai et al. (2015), Zhu et al. (2015), and Le and Zuidema (2015). However, while there is intensive research showing how the LSTM architecture can overcome those two problems compared to traditional recurrent models (e.g., Gers and Schmidhuber (2001)), such research is, to our knowledge, still absent for the comparison between RNNs and RLSTMs. Therefore, in the current paper we investigate the following two questions:

1. Is the RLSTM more capable of capturing long range dependencies than the RNN?

2. Does the RLSTM overcome the vanishing gradient problem more effectively than the RNN?

Supervised learning requires annotated data, which is often expensive to collect. As a result, examining a model on natural data on many different aspects can be difficult because the portion of data that fits a specific aspect could not be sufficient. Moreover, studying individual aspects separately is hard since many aspects are often correlated with each other. This, unfortunately, is true in our case: answering those two questions requires us to evaluate the examined models on datasets of dif-

Proceedings of the 1st Workshop on Representation Learning for NLP, pages 87–93,
Berlin, Germany, August 11th, 2016. ©2016 Association for Computational Linguistics

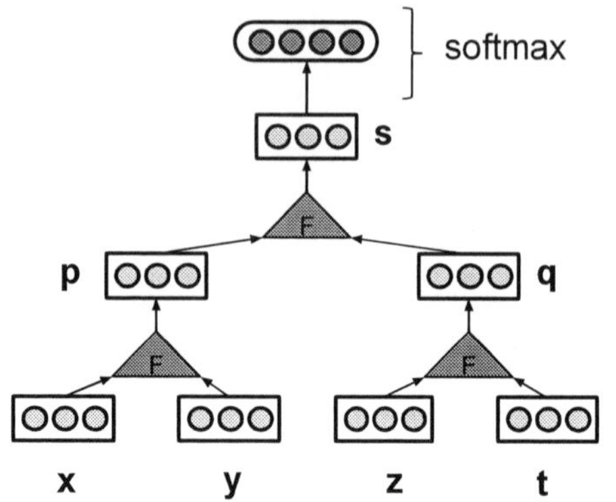

Figure 1: A recursive model (such as RNN and RLSTM) employ a composition function F in a bottom-up manner to compute a vector representation for each internal node in a tree. If the model is used for classification on the sentence level, a softmax layer is put on the top of the root node to compute a distribution over all possible classes.

ferent tree depths, in which the key nodes which contain decisive information in a parse tree must be identified. Using available annotated corpora such as the Stanford Sentiment Treebank (Socher et al., 2013b) and the Penn Treebank is thus inappropriate, as they are too small for this purpose (10k, 40k trees, respectively, compared to 240k trees in our experiments), and key nodes are not marked. Our solution is an artificial task where sentences and parse trees can be randomly generated under any arbitrary constraints on tree depth and key node's position.

2 Background

Both the RNN and the RLSTM model are instances of a general framework which takes a sentence, syntactic tree, and vector representations for the words in the sentence as input, and applies a composition function to recursively compute vector representations for all the phrases in the tree and the complete sentence. Technically speaking, given a production $p \rightarrow x\ y$, and $\mathbf{x}, \mathbf{y} \in \mathbb{R}^n$ representing x, y, we compute $\mathbf{p} \in \mathbb{R}^n$ for p by

$$\mathbf{p} = F(\mathbf{x}, \mathbf{y})$$

where F is a composition function (Figure 1).

In the RNN, F is a one-layer feed-forward neural network:

$$\mathbf{p} = f(\mathbf{W}_1\mathbf{x} + \mathbf{W}_2\mathbf{y} + \mathbf{b})$$

where $\mathbf{W}_1, \mathbf{W}_2 \in \mathbb{R}^{n \times n}$ are weight matrices and $\mathbf{b} \in \mathbb{R}^n$ is a bias vector. f is an activation function.

In the RLSTM, a node p is represented by the vector $[\mathbf{p}; \mathbf{c}_p]$ resulting from concatenating a vector representing the phrase that the node covers and a memory vector. F could be any LSTM that can compute two such concatenation vectors, such as Structure-LSTM (Zhu et al., 2015), Tree-LSTM (Tai et al., 2015), and LSTM-RNN (Le and Zuidema, 2015). In the current paper, we use the implementation[1] of Le and Zuidema (2015) where an LSTM (for binary trees) has two input gates i_1, i_2, two forget gates f_1, f_2, an output gate o, and a memory cell c. The vector representation and memory vector for node p are computed as follows:

$$\mathbf{i}_1 = \sigma\big(\mathbf{W}_{i1}\mathbf{x} + \mathbf{W}_{i2}\mathbf{y} + \mathbf{W}_{ci1}\mathbf{c}_x + \mathbf{W}_{ci2}\mathbf{c}_y + \mathbf{b}_i\big)$$
$$\mathbf{i}_2 = \sigma\big(\mathbf{W}_{i1}\mathbf{y} + \mathbf{W}_{i2}\mathbf{x} + \mathbf{W}_{ci1}\mathbf{c}_y + \mathbf{W}_{ci2}\mathbf{c}_x + \mathbf{b}_i\big)$$
$$\mathbf{f}_1 = \sigma\big(\mathbf{W}_{f1}\mathbf{x} + \mathbf{W}_{f2}\mathbf{y} + \mathbf{W}_{cf1}\mathbf{c}_x + \mathbf{W}_{cf2}\mathbf{c}_y + \mathbf{b}_f\big)$$
$$\mathbf{f}_2 = \sigma\big(\mathbf{W}_{f1}\mathbf{y} + \mathbf{W}_{f2}\mathbf{x} + \mathbf{W}_{cf1}\mathbf{c}_y + \mathbf{W}_{cf2}\mathbf{c}_x + \mathbf{b}_f\big)$$
$$\mathbf{c}_p = \mathbf{f}_1 \odot \mathbf{c}_x + \mathbf{f}_2 \odot \mathbf{c}_y +$$
$$\qquad g\big(\mathbf{W}_{c1}\mathbf{x} \odot \mathbf{i}_1 + \mathbf{W}_{c2}\mathbf{y} \odot \mathbf{i}_2 + \mathbf{b}_c\big)$$
$$\mathbf{o} = \sigma\big(\mathbf{W}_{o1}\mathbf{x} + \mathbf{W}_{o2}\mathbf{y} + \mathbf{W}_{co}\mathbf{c} + \mathbf{b}_o\big)$$
$$\mathbf{p} = \mathbf{o} \odot g(\mathbf{c}_p)$$

where $\mathbf{u}$ and $\mathbf{c}_u$ are the output and the state of the memory cell at node u; $\mathbf{i}_1, \mathbf{i}_2, \mathbf{f}_1, \mathbf{f}_2, \mathbf{o}$ are the activations of the corresponding gates; $\mathbf{W}$'s and $\mathbf{b}$'s are weight matrices and bias vectors; and g is an activation function.

3 Experiments

We now examine how the two problems, the vanishing gradient problem and the problem of how to capture long range dependencies, affect the RLSTM model and the RNN model. To do so, we propose the following artificial task, which requires a model to distinguish useful signals from noise. We define:

- a sentence is a sequence of tokens which are integer numbers in the range $[0, 10000]$;

- a sentence contains one and only one *keyword* token which is an integer number smaller than 1000;

- a sentence is labeled with the integer resulting from dividing the keyword by 100. For

---

[1] https://github.com/lephong/lstm-rnn

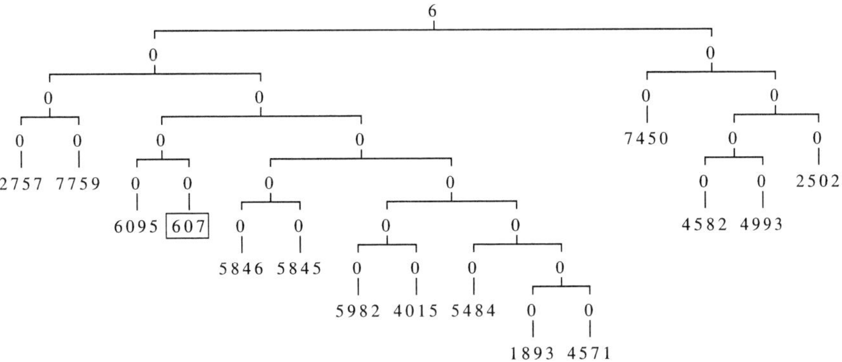

Figure 2: Example binary tree for the artificial task. The number enclosed in the box is the *keyword* of the sentence.

instance, if the keyword is 607, the label is 6. In this way, there are 10 classes, ranging from 0 to 9.

The task is to predict the class of a sentence, given its binary parse tree (Figure 2). Because the label of a sentence is determined solely by the keyword, the two models need to identify the keyword in the parse tree and allow only the information from the leaf node of the keyword to affect the root node. It is worth noting that this task resembles sentiment analysis with simple cases in which the sentiment of a whole sentence is determined by one keyword (e.g. "I like the movie"). Simulating complex cases involving negation, composition, etc. is straightforward and for future work. But here we believe that the current task is adequate to answer our two questions raised in Section 1.

The two models, RLSTM and RNN, were implemented with the dimension of vector representations and vector memories 50. Following Socher et al. (2013b), we used $tanh$ as the activation function, and initialized word vectors by randomly sampling each value from a uniform distribution $U(-0.0001, 0.0001)$. We trained the two models using the AdaGrad method (Duchi et al., 2011) with a learning rate of 0.05 and a mini-batch size of 20 for the RNN and of 5 for the RLSTM. Development sets were employed for early stopping (training is halted when the accuracy on the development set is not improved after 5 consecutive epochs). It is worth noting that we also tried other values for the hyper-parameters but did not gain significantly better results on development sets.

3.1 Experiment 1

We randomly generated 10 datasets. To generate a sentence of length l, we shuffle a list of randomly chosen $l-1$ non-keywords and one keyword. The i-th dataset contains 12k sentences of lengths from $10i-9$ tokens to $10i$ tokens, and is split into train, dev, test sets with sizes of 10k, 1k, 1k sentences. We parsed each sentence by randomly generating a binary tree whose number of leaf nodes equals to the sentence length.

The test accuracies of the two models on the 10 datasets are shown in Figure 3; For each dataset we run each model 5 times and reported the highest accuracy for the RNN model, and the distribution of accuracies (via boxplot) for the RLSTM model. We can see that the RNN model performs reasonably well on very short sentences (less than 11 tokens). However, when the sentence length exceeds 10, the RNN's performance drops so quickly that the difference between it and the random guess' performance (10%) is negligible. Trying different learning rates, mini-batch sizes, and values for n (the dimension of vectors) did not give significant differences. On the other hand, the RLSTM model achieves more than 90% accuracy on sentences shorter than 31 tokens. Its performance drops when the sentence length increases, but is still substantially better than the random guess when the sentence length does not exceed 70. When the sentence length exceeds 70, both the RLSTM and RNN perform similarly.

3.2 Experiment 2

In Experiment 1, it is not clear whether the tree size or the keyword depth is the main factor of the rapid drop of the RNN's performance. In this ex-

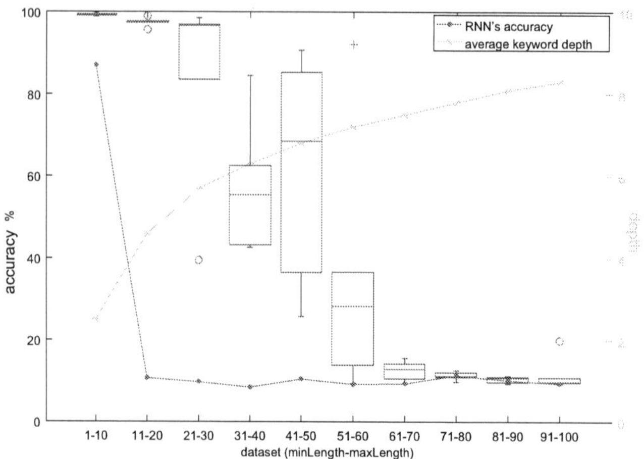

Figure 3: Test accuracies of the RNN (red solid curve, the best among 5 runs) and the RLSTM (boxplots) on datasets of different sentence lengths.

periment, we kept the tree size fixed and vary the keyword depth. We generated a pool of sentences of lengths from 21 to 30 tokens and parsed them by randomly generating binary trees. We then created 10 datasets each of which has 12k trees (10k for training, 1k for development, and 1k for testing). The i-th dataset consists of only trees in which distances from keywords to roots are i or $i + 1$ (to stop the networks from exploiting keyword depths directly).

Figure 4 shows test accuracies of the two models on those 10 datasets. Similarly in Experiment 1, for each dataset we run each model 5 times and reported the highest accuracy for the RNN model, and the distribution of accuracies for the RLSTM model. As we can see, the RNN model achieves very high accuracies when the keyword depth does not exceed 3. Its performance then drops rapidly and gets close to the performance of the random guess. This is evidence that the RNN model has difficulty capturing long range dependencies. By contrast, the RLSTM model performs at above 90% accuracy until the depth of the keyword reaches 8. It has difficulty dealing with larger depths, but the performance is always better than the random guess.

3.3 Experiment 3

We now examine whether the two models can encounter the vanishing gradient problem. To do so, we looked at the the back-propagation phase of each model in Experiment 1 on the third dataset (the one containing sentences of lengths from 21 to 30 tokens). For each tree, we calculated the ra-

tio

$$\frac{\left\| \frac{\partial J}{\partial \mathbf{x}_{keyword}} \right\|}{\left\| \frac{\partial J}{\partial \mathbf{x}_{root}} \right\|}$$

where the numerator is the norm of the error vector at the keyword node and the denominator is the norm of the error vector at the root node. This ratio gives us an intuition how the error signals develop when propagating backward to leaf nodes: if the ratio $\ll 1$, the vanishing gradient problem occurs; else if the ratio $\gg 1$, we observe the exploding gradient problem.

Figure 5 reports the ratios w.r.t. the keyword node depth in each epoch of training the RNN model. The ratios in the first epoch are always very small. In each following epoch, the RNN model successfully lifts up the ratios steadily (see Figure 7a for a clear picture at the keyword depth 10), but a clear decrease when the depth becomes larger is observable. For the RLSTM model (see Figure 6 and 7b), the story is somewhat different. The ratios go up after two epochs so rapidly that there are even some exploding error signals sent back to leaf nodes. They subsequently go down and remain stable with substantially less exploding error signals. This is, interestingly, concurrent with the performance of the RLSTM model on the development set (see Figure 7b). It seems that the RLSTM model, after one epoch, quickly locates the keyword node in a tree and relates it to the root by building a strong bond between them via error signals. After the correlation between the keyword and the label at the root is found, it tries to stabilize the training by reducing the error signals sent back

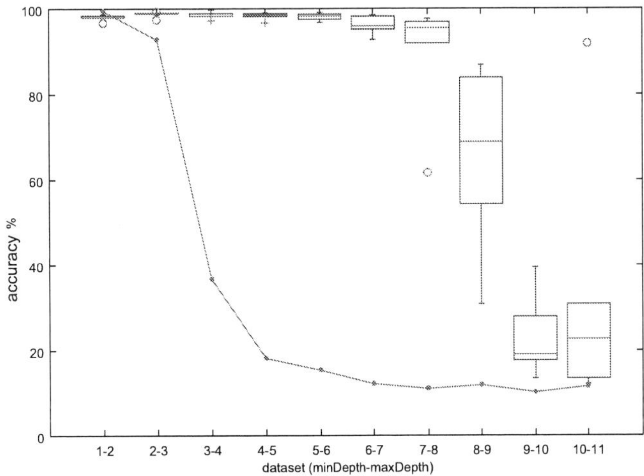

Figure 4: Test accuracies of the RNN (red solid curve, the best among 5 runs) and the RLSTM (boxplots) on datasets of different keyword depths.

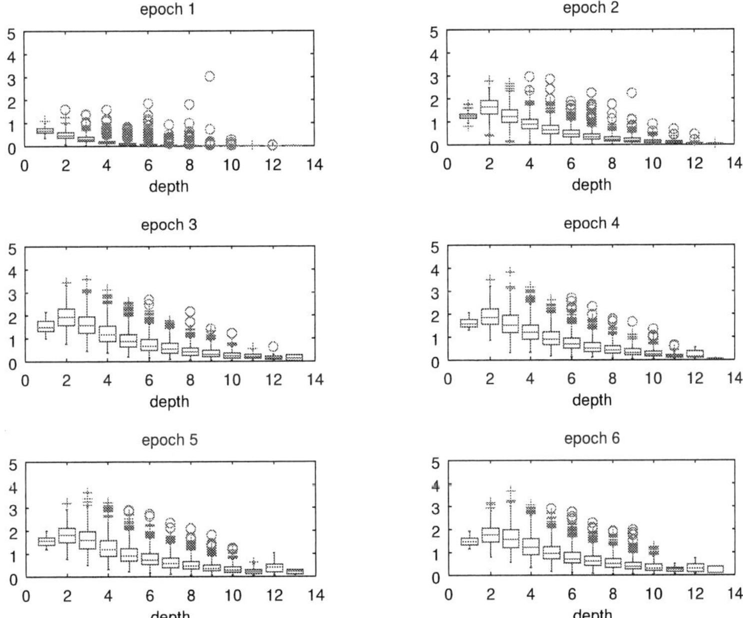

Figure 5: Ratios of norms of error vectors at keyword nodes to norms of error vectors at root nodes w.r.t. the keyword node depth in each epoch of training the RNN. Gradients gradually vanish with greater depth.

to the keyword node. Comparing the two models by aligning Figure 5 with Figure 6, and Figure 7a with Figure 7b, we can see that the RLSTM model is more capable of transmitting error signals to leaf nodes.

It is worth noting that we do see the vanishing gradient problem happening when training the RNN model in Figure 5; but Figure 7a suggests that the problem can become less serious after a long enough training time. This might be because depth 10 is still manageable for the RNN model. (Notice that in the Stanford Sentiment Treebank, more than three quarters of leaf nodes are at depths less than 10.) The fact the the RNN model still doesnot perform better than random guessing can be explained using the arguments given by Bengio et al. (1994), who show that there is a trade-off between avoiding the vanishing gradient problem

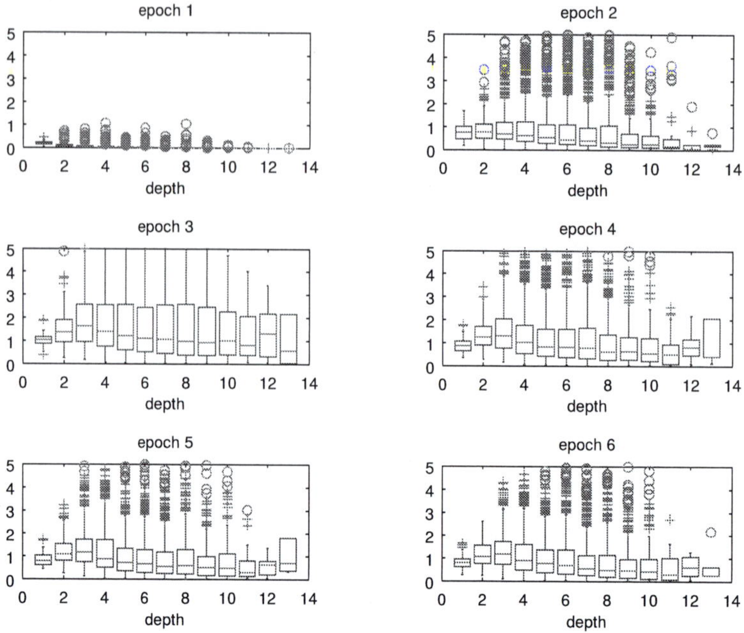

Figure 6: Ratios of norms of error vectors at keyword nodes (at different depths) to norms of error vectors at root nodes, in the RLSTM. Many gradients explode in epoch 2, but stabilize later. Gradients do not vanish, even at depth 12 and 13.

and capturing long term dependencies when training traditional recurrent networks.

4   Conclusion

Because long range dependencies and vanishing gradients are serious challenges in deep learning, evaluating how well a model overcome these challenges is necessary. In this current paper, we focus on two recursive models, RNN and RLSTM. Due to lack of natural data, we proposed a novel artificial task where the label of a sentence is solely determined by a key word it contains. The experimental results show that the RLSTM is superior to the RNN. This is in parallel with general conclusions about the power of the LSTM architecture compared to traditional Recurrent neural networks.

Although our proposed task is simple, it is sufficient for testing recursive models since solving the task requires models to be capable of capturing long range dependencies and propagating errors to leaf nodes far from the root. It is, moreover, straightforward to extend the task such that more complex cases can be taken into account. For instance, for compositionality, a sentence can contain more than one keywords and the sentence label is determined by some kind of interaction between those keywords (such as addition).

References

Yoshua Bengio, Patrice Simard, and Paolo Frasconi. 1994. Learning long-term dependencies with gradient descent is difficult. *Neural Networks, IEEE Transactions on*, 5(2):157–166.

John Duchi, Elad Hazan, and Yoram Singer. 2011. Adaptive subgradient methods for online learning and stochastic optimization. *The Journal of Machine Learning Research*, pages 2121–2159.

Felix A Gers and Jürgen Schmidhuber. 2001. Lstm recurrent networks learn simple context-free and context-sensitive languages. *Neural Networks, IEEE Transactions on*, 12(6):1333–1340.

Sepp Hochreiter and Jürgen Schmidhuber. 1997. Long short-term memory. *Neural computation*, 9(8):1735–1780.

Phong Le and Willem Zuidema. 2015. Compositional distributional semantics with long short term memory. In *Proceedings of the Joint Conference on Lexical and Computational Semantics (*SEM)*. Association for Computational Linguistics.

Shujie Liu, Nan Yang, Mu Li, and Ming Zhou. 2014. A recursive recurrent neural network for statistical machine translation. In *Proceedings of the 52nd Annual Meeting of the Association for Computational*

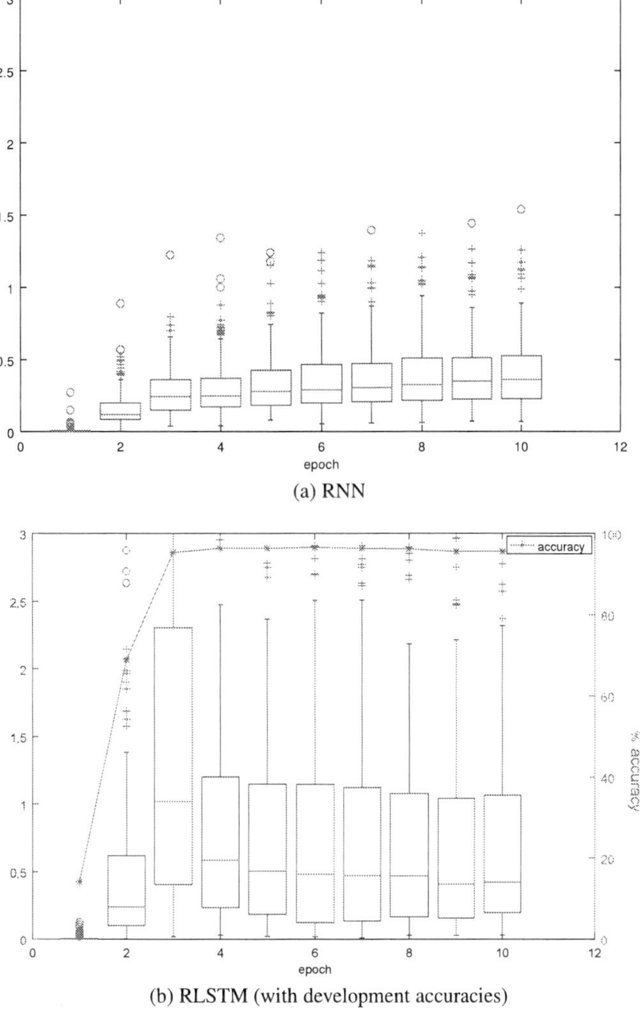

(a) RNN

(b) RLSTM (with development accuracies)

Figure 7: Ratios at depth 10 in each epoch of training the RNN (a) and the RLSTM (b).

Linguistics (Volume 1: Long Papers), pages 1491–1500, Baltimore, Maryland, June. Association for Computational Linguistics.

Minh-Thang Luong, Richard Socher, and Christopher D Manning. 2013. Better word representations with recursive neural networks for morphology. *CoNLL-2013*, 104.

Richard Socher, Christopher D. Manning, and Andrew Y. Ng. 2010. Learning continuous phrase representations and syntactic parsing with recursive neural networks. In *Proceedings of the NIPS-2010 Deep Learning and Unsupervised Feature Learning Workshop*.

Richard Socher, John Bauer, Christopher D Manning, and Andrew Y Ng. 2013a. Parsing with compositional vector grammars. In *Proceedings of the 51st Annual Meeting of the Association for Computational Linguistics*, pages 455–465.

Richard Socher, Alex Perelygin, Jean Y Wu, Jason Chuang, Christopher D Manning, Andrew Y Ng, and Christopher Potts. 2013b. Recursive deep models for semantic compositionality over a sentiment treebank. In *Proceedings EMNLP*.

Kai Sheng Tai, Richard Socher, and Christopher D. Manning. 2015. Improved semantic representations from tree-structured long short-term memory networks. In *Proceedings of the 53rd Annual Meeting of the Association for Computational Linguistics and the 7th International Joint Conference on Natural Language Processing (Volume 1: Long Papers)*, pages 1556–1566, Beijing, China, July. Association for Computational Linguistics.

Xiaodan Zhu, Parinaz Sobhani, and Hongyu Guo. 2015. Long short-term memory over recursive structures. In *Proceedings of International Conference on Machine Learning*, July.

LSTM-based Mixture-of-Experts for Knowledge-Aware Dialogues

Phong Le*
University of Amsterdam
p.le@uva.nl

Marc Dymetman, Jean-Michel Renders
Xerox Research Centre Europe
{firstname.lastname}@xrce.xerox.com

Abstract

We introduce an LSTM-based method for dynamically integrating several word-prediction experts to obtain a conditional language model which can be good simultaneously at several subtasks. We illustrate this general approach with an application to dialogue where we integrate a neural chat model, good at conversational aspects, with a neural question-answering model, good at retrieving precise information from a knowledge-base, and show how the integration combines the strengths of the independent components. We hope that this focused contribution will attract attention on the benefits of using such mixtures of experts in NLP and dialogue systems specifically.

1 Introduction

The mainstream architecture for virtual agents in dialogue systems (McTear, 2004; Jokinen and McTear, 2009; Rieser and Lemon, 2011; Young et al., 2013) involves a combination of several components, which require a lot of expertise in the different technologies, considerable development and implementation effort to adapt each component to a new domain, and are only partially trainable (if at all). Recently, Vinyals and Le (2015), Serban et al. (2015), Shang et al. (2015) proposed to replace this complex architecture by a single network (such as a Long Short Term Memory (LSTM) (Hochreiter and Schmidhuber, 1997)) that predicts the agent's response from the dialogue history up to the point where it should be produced: this network can be seen as a form of conditional neural language model (LM), where

---

*Work performed during Phong Le's internship at XRCE in 2015.

the dialogue history provides the context for the production of the next agent's utterance.

Despite several advantages over the traditional architecture (learnability, adaptability, better approximations to human utterances), this approach is inferior in one dimension: it assumes that all the knowledge required for the next agent's utterance has to be implicitly present in the dialogues over which the network is trained, and to then be precisely memorized by the network, while the traditional approach allows this knowledge to be dynamically accessed from external knowledge-base (KB) sources, with guaranteed accuracy.

To address this issue, we propose the following approach. As in Vinyals and Le (2015), we first do train a conditional neural LM based on existing dialogues, which we call our *chat model*; this model can be seen as an "expert" about the conversational patterns in the dialogue, but not about its knowledge-intensive aspects. Besides, we train another model, which this time is an expert about these knowledge aspects, which we call our *QA model*, due to its connections to Question Answering (QA). We then combine these two expert models through an LSTM-based *integration model*, which at each time step, encodes the whole history into a vector and then uses a softmax layer to compute a probability mixture over the two models, from which the next token is then sampled.

While here we combine in this way only two models, this core contribution of our paper is immediately generalizable to several expert models, each competent on a specific task, where the (soft) choice between the models is done through the same kind of contextually-aware "attention" mechanism. Additional smaller contributions consist in the neural regime we adopt for training the QA model, the way in which we reduce the memorization requirements on this model.

It is worth noting that concurrently with our

94

Proceedings of the 1st Workshop on Representation Learning for NLP, pages 94–99,
Berlin, Germany, August 11th, 2016. ©2016 Association for Computational Linguistics

work, Yin et al. (2015) have proposed a similar idea focusing only on QA in a traditional set-up. Our case is more difficult because of the chat interaction; and the integration framework we propose is generally applicable to situations where a pool of word-prediction "experts" compete for attention during the generation of text. Outside of dialogue applications, also independently and even more recently, Ling et al. (2016) have proposed a "Latent Predictor Network for Code Generation", which has some close similarities to our LSTM-based mixture of experts.

2 LSTM-based Mixture of Experts

The method is illustrated in Figure 1. Let $w_1^t = w_1...w_t$ be a history over words. We suppose that we have K models each of which can compute a distribution over its own vocabulary V_k : $p_k(w \in V_k | w_1^t)$, for $k \in [1, K]$. We use an LSTM to encode the history word-by-word into a vector $\mathbf{h}_t$ which is the hidden state of the LSTM at time step t. We then use a softmax layer to compute the probabilities

$$p(k|w_1^t) = \frac{e^{u(k,\mathbf{h}_t)}}{\sum_{k'=1}^{K} e^{u(k',\mathbf{h}_t)}}$$

where $[u(1, \mathbf{h}_t), ..., u(K, \mathbf{h}_t)]^T = \mathbf{W}\mathbf{h}_t + \mathbf{b}$, $\mathbf{W} \in \mathbb{R}^{K \times dim(\mathbf{h}_t)}$, $\mathbf{b} \in \mathbb{R}^K$. The final probability of the next word is then:

$$p(w|w_1^t) = \sum_{k=1}^{K} p(k|w_1^t)\, p_k(w|w_1^t). \quad (1)$$

Our proposal can be seen as bringing together two previous lines of research within an LSTM framework. Similar to the *mixture-of-experts* technique of Jacobs et al. (1991), we predict a label by using a "gating" neural network to mix the predictions of different experts based on the current situation. Similar to the approach of Florian and Yarowsky (1999), we dynamically combine distributions on words to produce an integrated LM. However Florian and Yarowsky (1999) focus on the combination of topic-dependent LMs, while in our case, the components can be arbitrary distributions over words — we later use a component that produces answers to questions appearing in the text. In our case, the labels are words, the gating neural network is an LSTM that stores a representation of a long textual prefix, and the combination mechanism is trained by optimizing the

parameters of this LSTM.

3 Data

Our corpus consists of 165k dialogues from a "tech company" in the domain of mobile telephony support. We split them into train, development, and test sets whose sizes are 145k, 10k, and 10k dialogues. We then tokenize and lowercase each dialogue, and remove unused information such as head, tail, chat time (Figure 2). For each response utterance found in a dialogue, we create a context-response pair whose context consists of all sentences appearing before the response. This process gives us 973k/74k/75k pairs for training/development/testing.

Knowledge-base   The KB we use in this work consists of 1,745k device-attribute-value triples, e.g., (Apple iPhone 5; camera megapixels; 8.0). There are 4729 devices and 608 attributes. Because we consider only numeric values, only triples that have numeric attributes are chosen, resulting in a set of 65k triples of 34 attributes.

Device-specification context-response pairs Our target context-response pairs are those in which the client asks about numeric value attributes. We employ a simple heuristic to select target context-response pairs: a context-response pair is chosen if its response contains a number and one of the following keywords: cpu, processor, ghz, mhz, memory, mb(s), gb(s), byte, pixel, height, width, weigh, size, camera, mp, hour(s), mah.   Using this heuristic, we collect 17.6k/1.3k/1.4k pairs for training/dev/testing. These sets are significantly smaller than those extracted above.

4 KB-aware Chat Model

4.1 Neural Chat Model

Ouur corpus is comparable to the one described in Vinyals and Le (2015)'s first experiment, and we use here a similar neural chat model.

Without going into the details of this model for lack of space, it uses a LSTM to encode into a vector the sequence of words observed in a dialogue up to a certain point, and then this vector is used by another LSTM for generating the next utterance also word-by-word. The approach is reminiscent of seq2seq models for machine translation such as (Sutskever et al., 2014), where the role of "source

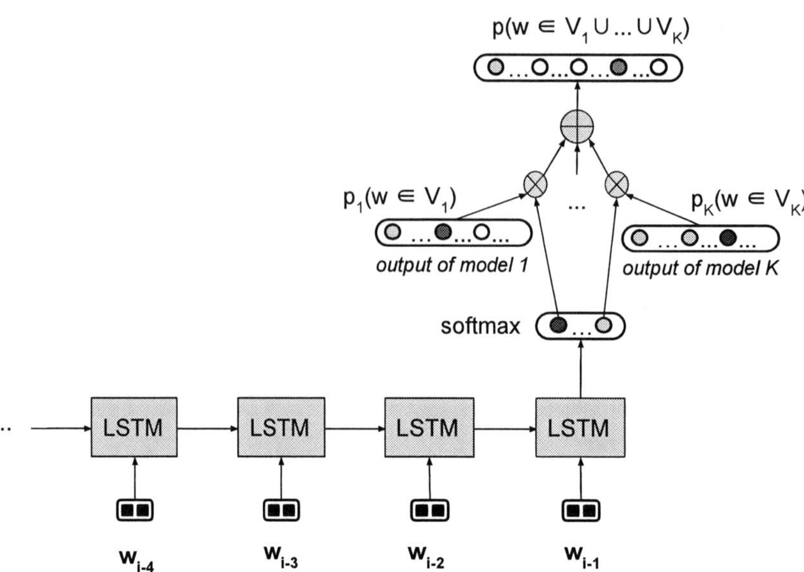

Figure 1: LSTM-based mixture-of-experts for Language modelling. $\otimes$ denotes multiplication, $\oplus$ denotes sum.

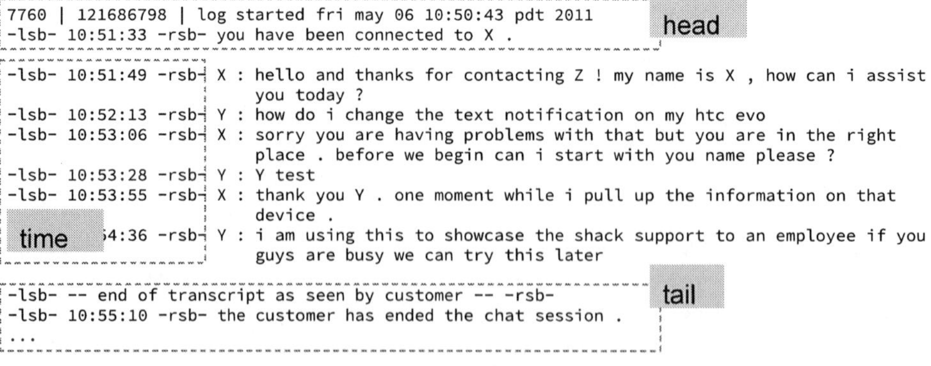

Figure 2: An example dialogue.

sentence" is played by the dialogue prefix, and that of "target sentence" by the response utterance.

4.2 Neural Question Answering Model

In a standard setting, a question to query a KB must be formal (e.g., SQL). However, because a human-like QA system should take natural questions as input, we build a neural model to translate natural questions to formal queries. This model employs an LSTM to encode a natural question into a vector. It then uses two softmax layers to predict the device name and the attribute. This model is adequate here, since we focus on the QA situation where the client asks about device specifications. For more complex cases, more advanced QA models should be considered (e.g., Bordes et al. (2014), Yih et al. (2015)).

Given question w_1^l, the two softmax layers give us a distribution over devices $p_d(\bullet|w_1^l)$ and a distribution over attributes $p_a(\bullet|w_1^l)$. We can then compute a distribution over the set V_{qa} of all values found in the KB, by marginalizing over d, a:

$$p_{qa}(v|w_1^l) = \sum_{\langle d,a,v\rangle \in T} p_d(d|w_1^l)p_a(a|w_1^l), \quad (2)$$

where T is the set of all triples in the KB.

Initial experiments showed that predicting values in this indirect way significantly improves the accuracy compared to employing a single softmax layer to predict values directly, because it does not require the hidden states to directly memorize the value for each device-attribute pair.

Data Generation One serious difficulty is that we do not have a corpus of natural questions on which to train the QA model, so we have to resort to a method for generating virtual question/answer pairs, on which to train our QA model. However, existing corpora and methods for generating such data (e.g., Fader et al. (2013)) hardly meet our needs here. This is because our case is very different from (and somewhat more difficult than) traditional QA set-ups in which questions are independent. In our case several scenarios are possible, resulting from the chat interaction (e.g., in a chat, questions can be related as in Figure 3). We therefore propose a simple heuristic method for generating artificial QA data that can cover several scenarios.

For each pair <device name, attribute>, we paraphrase the device name by randomly dropping some words (e.g., "apple iphone 4"

becomes "iphone 4"), and paraphrase the attribute using a small handcrafted dictionary and also randomly dropping some words ("battery talk time" becomes "battery life" which can become "battery"). We then draw a sequence of l words from a vocabulary w.r.t word frequency, where $l \sim Gamma(k, n)$ (e.g., "i what have"), and shuffle these words. The output of the final step is used as a training datapoint like: `have iphone 4 what battery i` $\rightarrow$ `apple_iphone_4 battery_talk_time`. To make it more realistic, we also generate complex questions by concatenating two simple ones. Such questions are used to cover the dialogue scenario where the client continues asking about another device and attribute. In this case, the system should focus on the latest device and attribute. Using this method, we generate a training set of 7.6m datapoints and a development set of 10k.

4.3 Integration

We now show how we integrate the chat model with the QA model using the LSTM-based mixture-of-experts method. The intuition is the following: the chat model is in charge of generating smooth responses into which the QA model "inserts" values retrieved from the KB. Ideally, we should employ an independent LSTM for the purpose of computing mixture weights, as in Section 2. However, due to the lack of training data, our integration model makes use of the chat model's hidden state to compute these weights. Because this hidden state captures the uncertainty of generating the next word, it is also able to detect whether or not the next word should be generated by the chat model.

The chat model is the backbone because it generates most tokens. The QA model, on the other hand, is crucial since we want the system to generate correct values. (E.g., the chat model alone cannot provide the precise information shown in Figure 3.) More importantly, in the future when new devices are released, we do not need to collect new chat data, which are often expensive, to retrain the chat model.

Let C and w_1^t be a context and words generated up to this point. $p_c(\bullet|w_1^t, C)$ and $p_{qa}(\bullet|w_1^t, C)$ are given by the chat model and the QA model. We then compute the distribution $p(\bullet|w_1^t, C)$ over $V_c \cup$

V_{qa} as a mixture of p_c and p_{qa}:

$$p(w|w_1^t, C) = \alpha.p_c(w|w_1^t, C)$$
$$+ (1 - \alpha).p_{qa}(w|w_1^t, C)$$

where $\alpha = \sigma(\mathbf{w}^T \mathbf{h}_t^c + b)$, $\mathbf{h}_t^c$ is the hidden state of the chat model, σ is the sigmoid function; $\mathbf{w} \in \mathbb{R}^{dim(\mathbf{h}_t^c)}$ and $b \in \mathbb{R}$. Note that the sigmoid is equivalent to the softmax for two output units.

Training To train this integration model, we keep the chat model and the QA model frozen, and minimize the objective:

$$J(\theta) = - \sum_{(C,w_1^l) \in D} \sum_{t=0}^{l-1} \beta(w_{t+1}) \log p(w_{t+1}|w_1^t, C; \theta)$$
$$+ \frac{\lambda}{2}||\theta||^2$$

w.r.t. $\theta = (\mathbf{w}, b)$, where $\beta(w) = 100$ if $w \in V_{qa} \setminus V_c$, $\beta(w) = 1$ otherwise. λ is the regularization parameter and D is the training set. We set $\beta(w \in V_{qa} \setminus V_c)$ high because we want the training phase to focus on those tokens representing values in the KB but not supported by the chat model.

Decoding To find the most probable responses, our decoder employs the uniform-cost-search algorithm (Russell and Norvig, 2003), which is guaranteed to find optimal solutions and is feasible with our search space. We stipulate a constraint that a response is to answer not more than one question.

5 Experiments

We implement our models in C++ using CUDA. Since automatically evaluating a conversation system is still challenging, we, following Vinyals and Le (2015), use word perplexity only. In our experiments, every LSTM has 1024 hidden units and 1024 memory cells. The vocabulary of the chat model has 19.3k words, that of the QA model 12.7k words.

We firstly train the chat model on all chat data with the learning rate 0.01, and continue training it on the device-specification data with the learning rate 0.001. Using this smaller learning rate we expect that the model will not forget what it has learnt on all the chat corpus. Next, we train the QA model on the data generated in Section 4.2 with the learning rate 0.01. Finally, we train the integration model on the device-specification training data also with the learning rate 0.01.

Our initial results are as follows. The integration slightly increases the perplexity on all tokens (15.4, compared to 14.7 of the chat model), but it does help to significantly decrease perplexity 38% on the *numeric* tokens (46.8, compared to 75.8 of the chat model). This decrease is due to the improved ability of the integration model to detect places where a numeric value associated with a device-attribute information request should be inserted and to predict this value. Not all numeric values are associated with information requests of this type, but the reported perplexities are over all numeric values. The decrease in perplexity over the numeric values is not enough to decrease overall perplexity because the numeric tokens represent only 6.7% of the tokens, and the integration model wrongly puts some small probability mass on the QA expert also in the case of the many non-numeric tokens. However, the fact that the perplexity decreases over the numeric tokens shows that the integration model is useful for predicting correct values, which are informationally much more critical to the user than general words (admittedly, perplexity is here a weak proxy for what a human evaluation of usefulness would provide.)

Figure 3 shows a chat example with our integration model.

6 Conclusions

We introduce a general LSTM-based mixture-of-experts method for language modelling and illustrate the approach by integrating a neural chat model with a neural QA model. The experimental results, while limited to measures of perplexity, do show that the integration model is capable of handling chats inside of which the user may ask about device specifications; a more thorough and convincing evaluation would require human assessments of the quality of the produced responses.

We believe that the proposed integration method has potential for a wide range of applications. It allows to pool a number of different language models, each expert in a specific domain or class of problems (possibly trained independently based on the most appropriate data) and to generate the next word based on a competition between these models, under the supervision of an LSTM-based attention mechanism.

Client: i want to know about how fast is the processor of apple ipad 2
Machine: that 's an excellent question , i can definitely help you with that !
1 ghz
was there anything else i could help you out with today ?
Client: and its ram ?
Machine: 0.5 gigabytes
Client: thanks
Machine: was there anything else i could help you out with today ?

Figure 3: A dialogue with the integration model. The first value is produced by the pair <apple_ipad_2, cpu_maximum_frequency>, the second value by <apple_ipad_2, internal_ram>.

References

Antoine Bordes, Sumit Chopra, and Jason Weston. 2014. Question answering with subgraph embeddings. In *Proceedings of the 2014 Conference on Empirical Methods in Natural Language Processing (EMNLP)*, pages 615–620, Doha, Qatar, October. Association for Computational Linguistics.

Anthony Fader, Luke S Zettlemoyer, and Oren Etzioni. 2013. Paraphrase-driven learning for open question answering. In *ACL (1)*, pages 1608–1618. Citeseer.

Radu Florian and David Yarowsky. 1999. Dynamic nonlocal language modeling via hierarchical topic-based adaptation. In *Proceedings of the 37th annual meeting of the Association for Computational Linguistics on Computational Linguistics*, pages 167–174. Association for Computational Linguistics.

Sepp Hochreiter and Jürgen Schmidhuber. 1997. Long short-term memory. *Neural computation*, 9(8):1735–1780.

Robert A Jacobs, Michael I Jordan, and Andrew G Barto. 1991. Task decomposition through competition in a modular connectionist architecture: The what and where vision tasks. *Cognitive Science*, 15(2):219–250.

Kristiina Jokinen and Michael F. McTear. 2009. *Spoken Dialogue Systems*. Synthesis Lectures on Human Language Technologies. Morgan & Claypool Publishers.

Wang Ling, Edward Grefenstette, Karl Moritz Hermann, Tomás Kociský, Andrew Senior, Fumin Wang, and Phil Blunsom. 2016. Latent predictor networks for code generation. *CoRR*, abs/1603.06744.

Michael F. McTear. 2004. *Spoken Dialogue Technology: Towards the Conversational User Interface*. Springer.

Verena Rieser and Oliver Lemon. 2011. *Reinforcement learning for adaptive dialogue systems : a data-driven methodology for dialogue management and natural language generation*. Theory and applications of natural language processing monographs. Springer, Heidelberg, New York.

Stuart J. Russell and Peter Norvig. 2003. *Artificial Intelligence: A Modern Approach*. Pearson Education, 2 edition.

Iulian V Serban, Alessandro Sordoni, Yoshua Bengio, Aaron Courville, and Joelle Pineau. 2015. Hierarchical neural network generative models for movie dialogues. *arXiv preprint arXiv:1507.04808*.

Lifeng Shang, Zhengdong Lu, and Hang Li. 2015. Neural responding machine for short-text conversation. In *Proceedings of the 53rd Annual Meeting of the Association for Computational Linguistics and the 7th International Joint Conference on Natural Language Processing of the Asian Federation of Natural Language Processing, ACL 2015, July 26-31, 2015, Beijing, China, Volume 1: Long Papers*, pages 1577–1586.

Ilya Sutskever, Oriol Vinyals, and Quoc VV Le. 2014. Sequence to sequence learning with neural networks. In *Advances in neural information processing systems*, pages 3104–3112.

Oriol Vinyals and Quoc Le. 2015. A neural conversational model. *arXiv preprint arXiv:1506.05869*.

Wen-tau Yih, Ming-Wei Chang, Xiaodong He, and Jianfeng Gao. 2015. Semantic parsing via staged query graph generation: Question answering with knowledge base. In *Proceedings of the 53rd Annual Meeting of the Association for Computational Linguistics and the 7th International Joint Conference on Natural Language Processing (Volume 1: Long Papers)*, pages 1321–1331, Beijing, China, July. Association for Computational Linguistics.

Jun Yin, Xin Jiang, Zhengdong Lu, Lifeng Shang, Hang Li, and Xiaoming Li. 2015. Neural generative question answering. *CoRR*, abs/1512.01337.

Steve Young, Milica Gasic, Blaise Thomson, and Jason D. Williams. 2013. Pomdp-based statistical spoken dialog systems: A review. *Proceedings of the IEEE*, 101(5):1160–1179.

Mapping Unseen Words to Task-Trained Embedding Spaces

Pranava Swaroop Madhyastha*   **Mohit Bansal**[†]   **Kevin Gimpel**[†]   **Karen Livescu**[†]
*Universitat Politècnica de Catalunya
`pranava@cs.upc.edu`
[†]Toyota Technological Institute at Chicago
`{mbansal,kgimpel,klivescu}@ttic.edu`

Abstract

We consider the supervised training setting in which we learn task-specific word embeddings. We assume that we start with initial embeddings learned from unlabelled data and update them to learn task-specific embeddings for words in the supervised training data. However, for new words in the test set, we must use either their initial embeddings or a single unknown embedding, which often leads to errors. We address this by learning a neural network to map from initial embeddings to the task-specific embedding space, via a multi-loss objective function. The technique is general, but here we demonstrate its use for improved dependency parsing (especially for sentences with out-of-vocabulary words), as well as for downstream improvements on sentiment analysis.

1 Introduction

Performance on NLP tasks drops significantly when moving from training sets to held-out data (Petrov et al., 2010). One cause of this drop is words that do not appear in the training data but appear in test data, whether in the same domain or in a new domain. We refer to such out-of-training-vocabulary (OOTV) words as *unseen* words. NLP systems often make errors on unseen words and, in structured tasks like dependency parsing, this can trigger a cascade of errors in the sentence.

Word embeddings can counter the effects of limited training data (Necsulescu et al., 2015; Turian et al., 2010; Collobert et al., 2011). While the effectiveness of pretrained embeddings can be heavily task-dependent (Bansal et al., 2014), there

is a great deal of work on updating embeddings during supervised training to make them more task-specific (Kalchbrenner et al., 2014; Qu et al., 2015; Chen and Manning, 2014). These task-trained embeddings have shown encouraging results but raise some concerns: (1) the updated embeddings of infrequent words are prone to overfitting, and (2) many words in the test data are not contained in the training data at all. In the latter case, at test time, systems either use a single, generic embedding for all unseen words or use their initial embeddings (typically derived from unlabelled data) (Søgaard and Johannsen, 2012; Collobert et al., 2011). Neither choice is ideal: A single unknown embedding conflates many words, while the initial embeddings may be in a space that is not comparable to the trained embedding space.

In this paper, we address both concerns by learning to map from the initial embedding space to the task-trained space. We train a neural network mapping function that takes initial word embeddings and maps them to task-specific embeddings that are trained for the given task, via a multi-loss objective function. We tune the mapper's hyperparameters to optimize performance on each domain of interest, thereby achieving some of the benefits of domain adaptation. We demonstrate significant improvements in dependency parsing across several domains and for the downstream task of dependency-based sentiment analysis using the model of Tai et al. (2015).

2 Mapping Unseen Representations

Let $\mathcal{V} = \{w_1, \ldots, w_V\}$ be the vocabulary of word types in a large, unannotated corpus. Let e_i^o denote the initial (original) embedding of word w_i computed from this corpus. The initial embeddings are typically learned in an unsupervised

Proceedings of the 1st Workshop on Representation Learning for NLP, pages 100–110,
Berlin, Germany, August 11th, 2016. ©2016 Association for Computational Linguistics

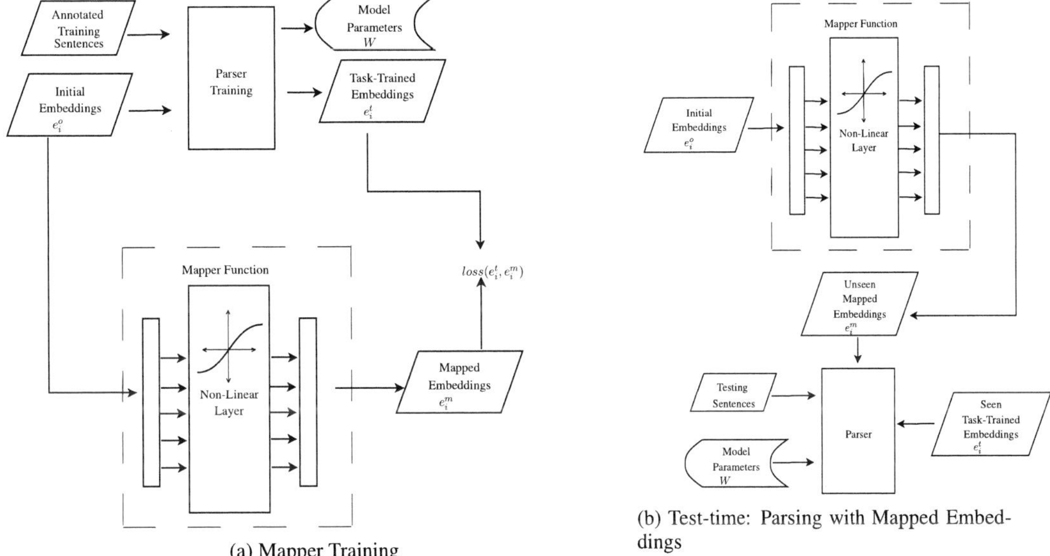

(a) Mapper Training

(b) Test-time: Parsing with Mapped Embeddings

Figure 1: System Pipeline

way, but for our purposes they can be any initial embeddings. Let $\mathcal{T} \subseteq \mathcal{V}$ be the subset of words that appear in the annotated training data for some supervised task-specific training. We define **unseen** words as those in the set $\mathcal{V} \setminus \mathcal{T}$. While our approach is general, for concreteness, we consider the task of dependency parsing, so the annotated data consists of sentences paired with dependency trees. We assume a dependency parser that learns task-specific word embeddings e_i^t for word $w_i \in \mathcal{T}$, starting from the original embedding e_i^o. In this work, we use the Stanford neural dependency parser (Chen and Manning, 2014).

The goal of the mapper is as follows. We are given a training set of N pairs of initial and task-trained embeddings $\mathcal{D} = \left\{ \left(e_1^o, e_1^t\right), \ldots, \left(e_N^o, e_N^t\right) \right\}$, and we want to learn a function G that maps each initial embedding e_i^o to be as close as possible to its corresponding output embedding e_i^t. We denote the mapped embedding e_i^m, i.e., $e_i^m = G\left(e_i^o\right)$.

Figure 1a describes the training procedure of the mapper. We use a supervised parser which is trained on an annotated dataset and initialized with pre-trained word embeddings e_i^o. The parser uses back-propagation to update these embeddings during training, producing task-trained embeddings e_i^t for all $w_i \in \mathcal{T}$. After we train the parser, the mapping function G is trained to map an initial word embedding e_i^o to its parser-trained embedding e_i^t. At test (or development) time, we use the trained

mapper G to transform the original embeddings of unseen test words to the parser-trained space (see Figure 1b). When parsing held-out data, we use the same parser model parameters (W) as shown in Figure 1b. The only difference is that now some of the word embeddings (i.e., for unseen words) have changed to mapped ones.

2.1 Mapper Architecture

Our proposed mapper is a multi-layer feedforward neural network that takes an initial word embedding as input and outputs a mapped representation of the same dimensionality. In particular, we use a single hidden layer with a hardtanh non-linearity, so the function G is defined as:

$$G(e_i^o) = W_2(\mathrm{hard\,tanh}(W_1 e_i^o + b_1)) + b_2 \quad (1)$$

where W_1 and W_2 are parameter matrices and b_1 and b_2 are bias vectors.

The 'hardtanh' non-linearity is the standard 'hard' version of hyperbolic tangent:

$$\mathrm{hard\,tanh}(z) = \begin{cases} -1 & \text{if } z < -1 \\ z & \text{if } -1 \leq z \leq 1 \\ 1 & \text{if } z > 1 \end{cases}$$

In preliminary experiments we compared with other non-linear functions (sigmoid, tanh, and ReLU), as well as with zero and more than one non-linear layers. We found that fewer or more non-linear layers did not improve performance.

2.2 Loss Function

We use a weighted, multi-loss regression approach, optimizing a weighted sum of mean squared error and mean absolute error:

$$loss(y, \hat{y}) =$$

$$\alpha \sum_{j=1}^{n} |y_j - \hat{y_j}| + (1 - \alpha) \sum_{j=1}^{n} |y_j - \hat{y_j}|^2 \quad (2)$$

where $y = e_i^t$ (the ground truth) and $\hat{y} = e_i^m$ (the prediction) are n-dimensional vectors. This multi-loss approach seeks to make both the conditional *mean* of the predicted representation close to the task-trained representation (via the squared loss) and the conditional *median* of the predicted representation close to the task-trained one (via the mean absolute loss). A weighted multi-criterion objective allows us to avoid making strong assumptions about the optimal transformation to be learned. We tune the hyperparameter α on domain-specific held-out data. We try to minimize the assumptions in our formulation of the loss, and let the tuning determine the particular mapper configuration that works best for each domain. Strict squared loss or an absolute loss are just special forms of this loss function.

For optimization, we use batch limited memory BFGS (L-BFGS) (Liu and Nocedal, 1989). In preliminary experiments comparing with stochastic optimization, we found L-BFGS to be more stable to train and easier to check for convergence (as has recently been found in other settings as well (Ngiam et al., 2011)).

2.3 Regularization

We use elastic net regularization (Liu and Nocedal, 1989), which linearly combines ℓ_1 and ℓ_2 penalties on the parameters to control the capacity of the mapper function. This equates to minimizing:

$$F(\theta) = L(\theta) + \lambda_1 \|\theta\|_1 + \frac{\lambda_2}{2} \|\theta\|_2^2$$

where θ is the full set of mapper parameters and $L(\theta)$ is the loss function (Eq. 2 summed over mapper training examples). We tune the hyperparameters of the regularizer and the loss function separately for each task, using a task-specific development set. This gives us additional flexibility to map the embeddings for the domain of interest, especially when the parser training data comes from a particular domain (e.g., newswire) and we want to use the parser on a new domain (e.g., email). We also tried dropout-based regularization (Srivastava et al., 2014) for the non-linear layer but did not see any significant improvement.

2.4 Mapper-Parser Thresholds

Certain words in the parser training data $\mathcal{T}$ are very infrequent, which may lead to inferior task-specific embeddings e_i^t learned by the parser. We want our mapper function to be learned on high-quality task-trained embeddings. After learning a strong mapping function, we can use it to remap the inferior task-trained embeddings.

We thus consider several frequency thresholds that control which word embeddings to use to train the mapper and which to map at test time. Below are the specific thresholds that we consider:

Mapper-training Threshold (τ_t) The mapper is trained only on embedding pairs for words seen at least τ_t times in the training data $\mathcal{T}$.

Mapping Threshold (τ_m) For test-time inference, the mapper will map any word whose count in $\mathcal{T}$ is less than τ_m. That is, we discard parser-trained embeddings e_i^t of these infrequent words and use our mapper to map the initial embeddings e_i^o instead.

Parser Threshold (τ_p) While training the parser, for words that appear fewer than τ_p times in $\mathcal{T}$, the parser replaces them with the 'unknown' embedding. Thus, no parser-trained embeddings will be learned for these words.

In our experiments, we explore a small set of values from this large space of possible threshold combinations (detailed below). We consider only relatively small values for the mapper-training (τ_t) and parser thresholds (τ_p) because as we increase them, the number of training examples for the mapper decreases, making it harder to learn an accurate mapping function[1].

3 Related Work

There are several categories of related approaches, including those that learn a single

---

[1] Note that the training of the mapper tends to be very quick because training examples are word types rather than word tokens. When we increase τ_t, the number of training examples reduces further. Hence, since we do not have many examples, we want the mapping procedure to have as much flexibility as possible, so we use multiple losses and regularization strategies, and then tune their relative strengths.

embedding for unseen words (Søgaard and Johannsen, 2012; Chen and Manning, 2014; Collobert et al., 2011), those that use character-level information (Luong et al., 2013; Botha and Blunsom, 2014; Ling et al., 2015; Ballesteros et al., 2015), those using morphological and n-gram information (Candito and Crabbé, 2009; Habash, 2009; Marton et al., 2010; Seddah et al., 2010; Attia et al., 2010; Bansal and Klein, 2011; Keller and Lapata, 2003), and hybrid approaches (Dyer et al., 2015; Jean et al., 2015; Luong et al., 2015; Chitnis and DeNero, 2015). The representation for the unknown token is either learned specifically or computed from a selection of rare words, for example by averaging their embedding vectors.

Other work has also found improvements by combining pre-trained, fixed embeddings with task-trained embeddings (Kim, 2014; Paulus et al., 2014). Also relevant are approaches developed specifically to handle large target vocabularies (including many rare words) in neural machine translation systems (Jean et al., 2015; Luong et al., 2015; Chitnis and DeNero, 2015).

Closely related to our approach is that of Tafforeau et al. (2015). They induce embeddings for unseen words by combining the embeddings of the k nearest neighbors. In Sec. 4, we show that our approach outperforms theirs. Also related is the approach taken by Kiros et al. (2015). They learn a linear mapping of the initial embedding space via unregularized linear regression. Our approach differs by considering nonlinear mapping functions, comparing different losses and mapping thresholds, and learning separately tuned mappers for each domain of interest. Moreover, we focus on empirically evaluating the effect of the mapping of unseen words, showing statistically significant improvements on both parsing and a downstream task (sentiment analysis).

4 Experimental Setup

4.1 Dependency Parser

We use the feed-forward neural network dependency parser of Chen and Manning (2014). In all our experiments (unless stated otherwise), we use the default arc-standard parsing configuration and hyperparameter settings. For evaluation, we compute the percentage of words that get the correct head, reporting both unlabelled attachment score (UAS) and labelled attachment score (LAS). LAS additionally requires the predicted dependency label to be correct. To measure statistical signifi-

cance, we use a bootstrap test (Efron and Tibshirani, 1986) with 100K samples.

4.2 Pre-Trained Word Embeddings

We use the 100-dimensional GloVe word embeddings from Pennington et al. (2014). These were trained on Wikipedia 2014 and the Gigaword v5 corpus and have a vocabulary size of approximately 400,000.[2]

4.3 Datasets

We consider a number of datasets with varying rates of OOTV words. We define the OOTV rate (or, equivalently, the unseen rate) of a dataset as the percentage of the vocabulary (types) of words occurring in the set that were not seen in training.

Wall Street Journal (WSJ) and OntoNotes-WSJ We conduct experiments on the Wall Street Journal portion of the English Penn Treebank dataset (Marcus et al., 1993). We follow the standard splits: sections 2-21 for training, section 22 for validation, and section 23 for testing. We convert the original phrase structure trees into dependency trees using Stanford Basic Dependencies (De Marneffe and Manning, 2008) in the Stanford Dependency Parser. The POS tags are obtained using the Stanford POS tagger (Toutanova et al., 2003) in a 10-fold jackknifing setup on the training data (achieving an accuracy of 96.96%). The OOTV rate in the development and test sets is approximately 2-3%.

We also conduct experiments on the OntoNotes 4.0 dataset (which we denote OntoNotes-WSJ). This dataset contains the same sentences as the WSJ corpus (and we use the same data splits), but has significantly different annotations. The OntoNotes-WSJ training data is used for the Web Treebank test experiments. We perform the same pre-processing steps as for the WSJ dataset.

Web Treebank We expect our mapper to be most effective when parsing held-out data with many unseen words. This often happens when the held-out data is drawn from a different distribution than the training data. For example, when training a parser on newswire and testing on web data,

---

[2] http://www-nlp.stanford.edu/data/glove.6B.100d.txt.gz; We have also experimented with the downloadable 50-dimensional SENNA embeddings from Collobert et al. (2011) and with word2vec (Mikolov et al., 2013) embeddings that we trained ourselves; in preliminary experiments the GloVe embeddings performed best, so we use them for all experiments below.

many errors occur due to differing patterns of syntactic usage and unseen words (Foster et al., 2011; Petrov and McDonald, 2012; Kong et al., 2014; Wang et al., 2014).

We explore this setting by training our parser on OntoNotes-WSJ and testing on the Web Treebank (Petrov and McDonald, 2012), which includes five domains: answers, email, newsgroups, reviews, and weblogs. Each domain contains aproximately 2000-4000 manually annotated syntactic parse trees in the OntoNotes 4.0 style. In this case, we are adapting the parser which is trained on OntoNotes corpora using the small development set for each of the sub-domains (the size of the Web Treebank dev corpora is only around 1000-2000 trees so we use it for validation instead of including it in training). As before, we convert the phrase structure trees to dependency trees using Stanford Basic Dependencies. The parser and the mapper hyperparameters were tuned separately on the development set for each domain. The unseen rate is typically 6-10% in the domains of the Web Treebank. We used the Stanford tagger (Toutanova et al., 2003), which was trained on the OntoNotes training corpus, for part-of-speech tagging the Web Treebank corpora. The tagger used bidirectional architecture and it included word shape and distributional similarity features. We train a separate mapper for each domain, tuning mapper hyperparameters separately for each domain using the development sets. In this way, we obtain some of the benefits of domain adaptation for each target domain.

Downstream Task: Sentiment Analysis with Dependency Tree LSTMs We also perform experiments to analyze the effects of embedding mapping on a downstream task, in this case sentiment analysis using the Stanford Sentiment Treebank (Socher et al., 2013). We use the dependency tree long short-term memory network (Tree-LSTM) proposed by Tai et al. (2015), simply replacing their default dependency parser with our version that maps unseen words. The dependency parser is trained on the WSJ corpus and mapped using the WSJ development set. We use the same mapper that was optimized for the WSJ development set, without further hyperparameter tuning for the mapper. For the Tree-LSTM model, we use the same hyperparameter tuning as described in Tai et al. (2015). We use the standard train/development/test splits of

6820/872/1821 sentences for the binary classification task and 8544/1101/2210 for the fine-grained task.

4.4 Mapper Settings and Hyperparameters

The initial embeddings given to the mapper are the same as the initial embeddings given to the parser. These are the 100-dimensional GloVe embeddings mentioned above. The output dimensionality of the mapper is also fixed to 100. All model parameters of the mappers are initialized to zero. We set the dimensionality of the non-linear layer to 400 across all experiments. The model parameters are optimized by maximizing the weighted multiple-loss objective using L-BFGS with elastic-net regularization (Section 2). The hyperparameters include the relative weight of the two objective terms (α) and the regularization constants (λ_1, λ_2). For α, we search over values in $\{0, 0.1, 0.2, \ldots, 1\}$. For each of λ_1 and λ_2, we consider values in $\{10^{-1}, 10^{-2}, \ldots, 10^{-9}, 0\}$. The hyperparameters are tuned via grid search to maximize the UAS on the development set.

5 Results and Analysis

5.1 Results on WSJ, OntoNotes, and Switchboard

The upper half of Table 1 shows our main test results on WSJ, OntoNotes, and Switchboard, the low-OOTV rate datasets. Due to the small initial OOTV rates ($<3\%$), we only see modest gains of 0.3-0.4% in UAS, with statistical significance at $p < 0.05$ for WSJ and OntoNotes and $p < 0.07$ for Switchboard. The initial OOTV rates are cut in half by our mapper, with the remaining unknown words largely being numerical strings and misspellings.[3] When only considering test sentences containing OOTV words (the row labeled "OOTV subset"), the gains are significantly larger (0.5-0.8% UAS at $p < 0.05$).

5.2 Results on Web Treebank

The lower half of Table 1 shows our main test results on the Web Treebank's five domains, the high-OOTV rate datasets. As expected, the mapper has a much larger impact when parsing these out-of-domain datasets with high OOTV word

---

[3]We could potentially train the initial embeddings on a larger corpus or use heuristics to convert unknown numbers and misspellings to forms contained in our initial embeddings.

	Lower OOTV word rate			Higher OOTV word rate					
	WSJ	OntoNotes	Avg.	Answers	Emails	Newsgroups	Reviews	Weblogs	Avg.
UAS	91.85→92.21	90.17→90.49	90.38→90.70	82.67→83.21	81.76→82.42	84.68→85.13	84.25→84.99	87.73→88.43	84.22→84.84
LAS	89.49→89.73	87.68→87.92	87.92→88.14	78.98→79.59	77.93→78.56	81.88→82.71	81.26→81.92	85.68→86.29	81.01→81.81
OOTV %	2.72→1.45	2.72→1.4	–	8.53→1.22	10.56→3.01	10.34→1.04	6.84→0.73	8.45→0.38	–
OOTV UAS	89.88→90.51	89.27→89.81	89.12→89.78	80.88→81.75	79.29→81.02	82.54→83.71	81.17→82.22	86.43→87.31	82.06→83.20
#Sents	337	329	–	671	644	579	632	541	–

Table 1: Results of dependency parsing on various treebanks. Entries of the form A→B give results for parsing without mapped embeddings (A) and with mapped embeddings (B). "OOTV %" entries A→B indicate that A% of the test set vocabulary was unseen in the parser training, and B% remain unknown after mapping the embeddings. "OOTV UAS" refers to UAS measured on the subset of the test set sentences that contain at least one OOTV word, and "#Sents" gives the number of sentences in this subset.

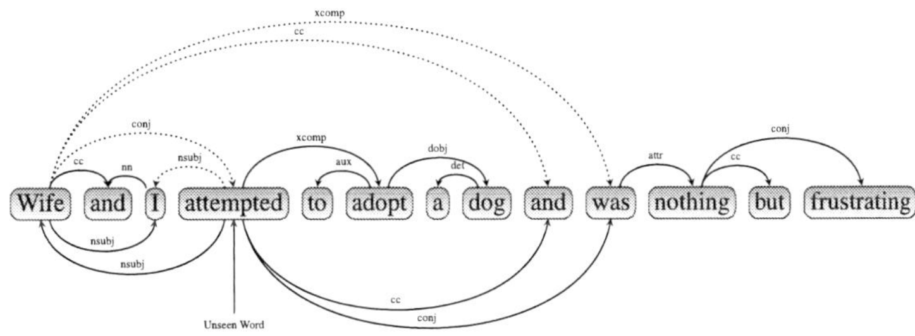

(a) We obtain correct attachments and correct tree after the mapper maps the unseen word 'attempted'.

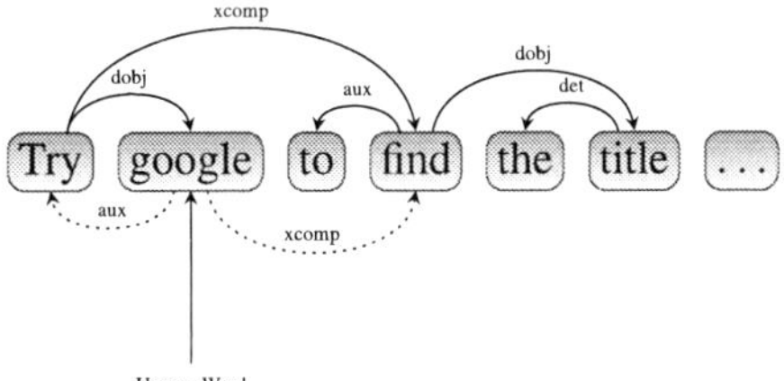

(b) The mapper incorrectly maps 'google', resulting in wrong attachments and wrong tree.

Figure 2: Examples where the mapper helps and hurts: In the above examples the top arcs are before mapping and bottom ones are after mapping; dotted lines refer to incorrect attachment.

rates.[4]

The OOTV rate reduction is much larger than for the WSJ-style datasets, and the parsing improvements (UAS and LAS) are statistically significant at $p < 0.05$. On subsets containing at least one OOTV word (that also has an initial embedding), we see an average gain of 1.14% UAS (see row labeled "OOTV subset"). In this case, all improvements are statistically significant at $p < 0.02$. We observe that the relative reduction in OOTV% for the Web Treebanks is larger than for the WSJ, OntoNotes, or Switchboard datasets. In particular, we are able to reduce the OOTV% by 71-95% relative. We also see the intuitive trend that larger relative reductions in OOTV rate correlate with larger accuracy improvements.

5.3 Downstream Results

We now report results using the Dependency Tree-LSTM of Tai et al. (2015) for sentiment analysis on the Stanford Sentiment Treebank. We consider both the binary (positive/negative) and fine-grained classification tasks ({very negative, negative, neutral, positive, and very positive}). We use the implementation provided by Tai et al. (2015), changing only the dependency parses that are fed to their model. The sentiment dataset contains approximately 25% OOTV words in the training set vocabulary, 5% in the development set vocabulary, and 9% in the test set vocabulary. We map unseen words using the mapper tuned on the WSJ development set. We use the same Dependency Tree-LSTM experimental settings as Tai et al. Re-

---

[4]As stated above, we train the parser on the OntoNotes dataset, but tune mapper hyperparameters to maximize parsing performance on each development section of the Web Treebank's five domains. We then map the OOTV word vectors on each test set domain using the learned mapper for that domain.

Fine-Grained	Binary
48.4→49.5	85.7→ 86.1

Table 2: Improvements on Stanford Sentiment Treebank test set using our parser with the Dependency Tree-LSTM.

Baseline	t_1	t_3	t_5	t_∞
84.11	84.89	84.97	84.81	84.14

Table 3: Average Web Treebank development UAS at different threshold settings.

sults are shown in Table 2. We improve upon the original accuracies in both binary and fine-grained classification. [5] We also reduce the OOTV rate from 25% in the training set vocabulary to about 6%, and from 9% in the test set vocabulary down to 4%.

5.4 Effect of Thresholds

We also experimented with different values for the thresholds described in Section 2. For the mapping threshold τ_m, mapper-training threshold τ_t, and parser threshold τ_p, we consider the following four settings:

$$t_1 : \tau_m = \tau_t = \tau_p = 1$$
$$t_3 : \tau_m = \tau_t = \tau_p = 3$$
$$t_5 : \tau_m = \tau_t = \tau_p = 5$$
$$t_\infty : \tau_m = \infty, \tau_p = \tau_t = 5$$

Using $\tau_m = \infty$ corresponds to mapping all words at test time, even words that we have seen many times in the training data and learned task-specific embeddings for.

We report the average development set UAS over all Web Treebank domains in Table 3. We see that t_3 performs best, though settings t_1 and t_5 also improve over the baseline. At threshold t_3 we have approximately 20,000 examples for training the mapper, while at threshold t_5 we have only about 10,000 examples. We see a performance drop at t_∞, so it appears better to directly use the task-specific embeddings for words that appear frequently in the training data. In other results reported in this paper, we used t_3 for the Web Treebank test sets and t_1 for the rest.

5.5 Effect of Weighted Multi-Loss Objective

We analyzed the results when varying α, which balances between the two components of the map-

per's multi-loss objective function. We found that, for all domains except Answers, the best results are obtained with some α between 0 and 1. The optimal values outperformed the cases with $\alpha = 0$ and $\alpha = 1$ by 0.1-0.3% UAS absolute. However, on the Answers domain, the best performance was achieved with $\alpha = 0$; i.e., the mapper preferred mean squared error. For other domains, the optimal α tended to be within the range $[0.3, 0.7]$.

5.6 Comparison with Related Work

We compare to the approach presented by Tafforeau et al. (2015). They propose to refine embeddings for unseen words based on the relative shifts of their k nearest neighbors in the original embeddings space. Specifically, they define "artificial refinement" as:

$$\phi_r(t) = \phi_o(t) + \sum_{k=1}^{K} \alpha_k(\phi_r(n_k) - \phi_o(n_k)) \quad (3)$$

where $\phi_r(.)$ is the vector in the refined embedding space and $\phi_o(.)$ is the vector in the original embedding space. They define α_k to be proportional to the cosine similarity between the target unseen word (t) and neighbor (n_k):

$$\alpha_k = s(t, n_k) = \frac{\phi_o(t).\phi_o(n_k)}{|\phi(t)||\phi_o(n_k)|}$$

	Avg. UAS	Avg. LAS
Baseline	84.11	81.02
k-NN	84.54	81.38
Our Mapped	84.97	81.79

Table 4: Comparison to k-nearest neighbor matching of Tafforeau et al. (2015).

Table 4 shows the average performance of the models over the development sets of the Web Treebank. On average, our mapper outperforms the k-NN approach ($k = 3$).

5.7 Dependency Parsing Examples

In Figure 2, we show two sentences: an instance where the mapper helps and another where the mapper hurts the parsing performance.[6] In the first sentence (Figure 2a), the parsing model has not seen the word 'attempted' during training. Note that the sentence contains 3 verbs: 'attempted', 'adopt', and 'was'. Even with the POS tags, the

---

[5]Note that we report accuracies and improvements on the dependency parse based system of Tai et al. (2015) because the neural parser that we use is dependency-based.

[6]Sentences in Figure 2 are taken from the development portion of the Answers domain from the Web Treebank.

parser was unable to get the correct dependency attachment. After mapping, the parser correctly makes 'attempted' the root and gets the correct arcs and the correct tree. The 3 nearest neighbors of 'attempted' in the mapped embedding space are 'attempting', 'tried', and 'attempt'. We also see here that a single unseen word can lead to multiple errors in the parse.

In the second example (Figure 2b), the default model assigns the correct arcs using the POS information even though it has not seen the word 'google'. However, using the mapped representation for 'google', the parser makes errors. The 3-nearest neighbors for 'google' in the mapped space are 'damned', 'look', and 'hash'. We hypothesize that the mapper has mapped this noun instance of 'google' to be closer to verbs instead of nouns, which would explain the incorrect attachment.

5.8 Analyzing Mapped Representations

To understand the mapped embedding space, we use t-SNE (Van der Maaten and Hinton, 2008) to visualize a small subset of embeddings. In Figure 3, we plot the initial embeddings, the parser-trained embeddings, and finally the mapped embeddings. We include four unseen words (shown in caps): 'horrible', 'poor', 'marvelous', and 'magnificent'. In Figure 3a and Figure 3b, the embeddings for the unseen words are identical (even though t-SNE places them in different places when producing its projection). In Figure 3c, we observe that the mapper has placed the unseen words within appropriate areas of the space with respect to similarity with the seen words. We contrast this with Figure 3b, in which the unseen words appear to be within a different region of the space from all seen words.

6 Conclusion

We have described a simple method to resolve unseen words when training supervised models that learn task-specific word embeddings: a feed-forward neural network that maps initial embeddings to the task-specific embedding space. We demonstrated significant improvements in dependency parsing accuracy across several domains, as well as improvements on a downstream task. Our approach is simple, effective, and applicable to many other settings, both inside and outside NLP.

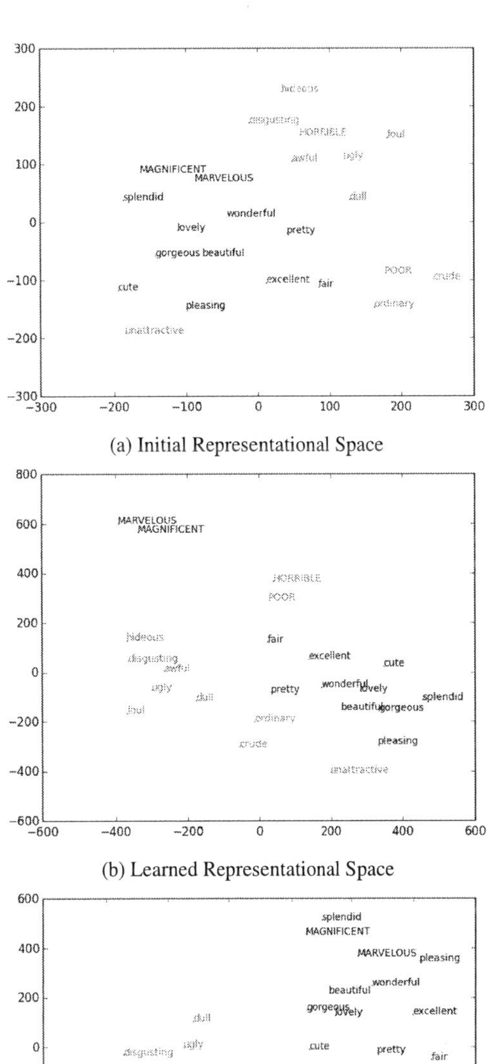

(a) Initial Representational Space

(b) Learned Representational Space

(c) Mapped Representational Space

Figure 3: t-SNE plots on initial, parser trained, and mapped representations.

Acknowledgments

We would like to thank the anonymous reviewers for their useful comments. This research was supported by a Google Faculty Research Award to Mohit Bansal, Karen Livescu and Kevin Gimpel.

References

Mohammed Attia, Jennifer Foster, Deirdre Hogan, Joseph Le Roux, Lamia Tounsi, and Josef Van Genabith. 2010. Handling unknown words in statistical latent-variable parsing models for arabic, english and french. In *Proceedings of the NAACL HLT 2010 First Workshop on Statistical Parsing of Morphologically-Rich Languages*, pages 67–75. Association for Computational Linguistics.

Miguel Ballesteros, Chris Dyer, and Noah A. Smith. 2015. Improved transition-based parsing by modeling characters instead of words with lstms. In *Proceedings of the 2015 Conference on Empirical Methods in Natural Language Processing*, pages 349–359, Lisbon, Portugal, September. Association for Computational Linguistics.

Mohit Bansal and Dan Klein. 2011. Web-scale features for full-scale parsing. In *Proceedings of ACL*.

Mohit Bansal, Kevin Gimpel, and Karen Livescu. 2014. Tailoring continuous word representations for dependency parsing. In *Proceedings of ACL*.

Jan A. Botha and Phil Blunsom. 2014. Compositional morphology for word representations and language modelling. In *International Conference on Machine Learning (ICML)*.

Marie Candito and Benoît Crabbé. 2009. Improving generative statistical parsing with semi-supervised word clustering. In *Proceedings of the 11th International Conference on Parsing Technologies*, pages 138–141. Association for Computational Linguistics.

Danqi Chen and Christopher D Manning. 2014. A fast and accurate dependency parser using neural networks. In *Empirical Methods in Natural Language Processing (EMNLP)*.

Rohan Chitnis and John DeNero. 2015. Variable-length word encodings for neural translation models. In *Proceedings of the 2015 Conference on Empirical Methods in Natural Language Processing*, pages 2088–2093, Lisbon, Portugal, September. Association for Computational Linguistics.

R. Collobert, J. Weston, L. Bottou, M. Karlen, K. Kavukcuoglu, and P. Kuksa. 2011. Natural language processing (almost) from scratch. *Journal of Machine Learning Research*, 12:24932537.

Marie-Catherine De Marneffe and Christopher D Manning. 2008. Stanford typed dependencies manual. Technical report, Stanford University.

Chris Dyer, Miguel Ballesteros, Wang Ling, Austin Matthews, and Noah A. Smith. 2015. Transition-based dependency parsing with stack long short-term memory. In *Proceedings of the 53rd Annual Meeting of the Association for Computational Linguistics and the 7th International Joint Conference on Natural Language Processing (Volume 1: Long Papers)*, pages 334–343, Beijing, China, July. Association for Computational Linguistics.

B. Efron and R. Tibshirani. 1986. Bootstrap methods for standard errors, confidence intervals, and other measures of statistical accuracy. *Statist. Sci.*, 1(1):54–75, 02.

Jennifer Foster, Özlem Çetinoglu, Joachim Wagner, Joseph Le Roux, Stephen Hogan, Joakim Nivre, Deirdre Hogan, and Josef Van Genabith. 2011. # hardtoparse: Pos tagging and parsing the twitterverse. In *AAAI 2011 Workshop on Analyzing Microtext*, pages 20–25.

Nizar Habash. 2009. Remoov: A tool for online handling of out-of-vocabulary words in machine translation. In *Proceedings of the 2nd International Conference on Arabic Language Resources and Tools (MEDAR), Cairo, Egypt*.

Sébastien Jean, Kyunghyun Cho, Roland Memisevic, and Yoshua Bengio. 2015. On using very large target vocabulary for neural machine translation. In *Proceedings of the 53rd Annual Meeting of the Association for Computational Linguistics and the 7th International Joint Conference on Natural Language Processing (Volume 1: Long Papers)*, pages 1–10, Beijing, China, July. Association for Computational Linguistics.

Nal Kalchbrenner, Edward Grefenstette, and Phil Blunsom. 2014. A convolutional neural network for modelling sentences. In *Proceedings of the 52nd Annual Meeting of the Association for Computational Linguistics (Volume 1: Long Papers)*, pages 655–665, Baltimore, Maryland, June. Association for Computational Linguistics.

Frank Keller and Mirella Lapata. 2003. Using the web to obtain frequencies for unseen bigrams. *Computational linguistics*, 29(3):459–484.

Yoon Kim. 2014. Convolutional neural networks for sentence classification. In *Proceedings of the 2014 Conference on Empirical Methods in Natural Language Processing (EMNLP)*, pages 1746–1751, Doha, Qatar, October. Association for Computational Linguistics.

Ryan Kiros, Yukun Zhu, Ruslan Salakhutdinov, Richard S Zemel, Antonio Torralba, Raquel Urtasun, and Sanja Fidler. 2015. Skip-thought vectors. *arXiv preprint arXiv:1506.06726*.

Lingpeng Kong, Nathan Schneider, Swabha Swayamdipta, Archna Bhatia, Chris Dyer, and Noah A. Smith. 2014. A dependency parser for tweets. In *Proceedings of the 2014 Conference on Empirical Methods in Natural Language Processing (EMNLP)*, pages 1001–1012, Doha, Qatar, October. Association for Computational Linguistics.

Wang Ling, Tiago Luís, Luís Marujo, Rámon Fernandez Astudillo, Silvio Amir, Chris Dyer, Alan W Black, and Isabel Trancoso. 2015. Finding function in form: Compositional character models for open vocabulary word representation. In *Proc. of EMNLP*.

D. C. Liu and J. Nocedal. 1989. On the limited memory BFGS method for large scale optimization. *Math. Programming*, 45(3, (Ser. B)):503–528.

Thang Luong, Richard Socher, and Christopher Manning. 2013. Better word representations with recursive neural networks for morphology. In *Proceedings of the Seventeenth Conference on Computational Natural Language Learning*, pages 104–113, Sofia, Bulgaria, August. Association for Computational Linguistics.

Thang Luong, Ilya Sutskever, Quoc Le, Oriol Vinyals, and Wojciech Zaremba. 2015. Addressing the rare word problem in neural machine translation. In *Proceedings of the 53rd Annual Meeting of the Association for Computational Linguistics and the 7th International Joint Conference on Natural Language Processing (Volume 1: Long Papers)*, pages 11–19, Beijing, China, July. Association for Computational Linguistics.

Mitchell P Marcus, Mary Ann Marcinkiewicz, and Beatrice Santorini. 1993. Building a large annotated corpus of english: The penn treebank. *Computational linguistics*, 19(2):313–330.

Yuval Marton, Nizar Habash, and Owen Rambow. 2010. Improving arabic dependency parsing with lexical and inflectional morphological features. In *Proceedings of the NAACL HLT 2010 First Workshop on Statistical Parsing of Morphologically-Rich Languages*, pages 13–21, Los Angeles, CA, USA, June. Association for Computational Linguistics.

Tomas Mikolov, Kai Chen, Greg Corrado, and Jeffrey Dean. 2013. Efficient estimation of word representations in vector space. *arXiv preprint arXiv:1301.3781*.

Silvia Necsulescu, Sara Mendes, David Jurgens, Núria Bel, and Roberto Navigli. 2015. Reading between the lines: Overcoming data sparsity for accurate classification of lexical relationships. In *Proceedings of the Fourth Joint Conference on Lexical and Computational Semantics*, pages 182–192, Denver, Colorado, June. Association for Computational Linguistics.

Jiquan Ngiam, Adam Coates, Ahbik Lahiri, Bobby Prochnow, Quoc V. Le, and Andrew Y. Ng. 2011. On optimization methods for deep learning. In *Proceedings of the 28th International Conference on Machine Learning (ICML-11)*, pages 265–272.

Romain Paulus, Richard Socher, and Christopher D Manning. 2014. Global belief recursive neural networks. In *Advances in Neural Information Processing Systems*, pages 2888–2896.

Jeffrey Pennington, Richard Socher, and Christopher Manning. 2014. Glove: Global vectors for word representation. In *Proceedings of the 2014 Conference on Empirical Methods in Natural Language Processing (EMNLP)*, pages 1532–1543, Doha, Qatar, October. Association for Computational Linguistics.

Slav Petrov and Ryan McDonald. 2012. Overview of the 2012 shared task on parsing the web. Notes of the First Workshop on Syntactic Analysis of Non-Canonical Language (SANCL).

Slav Petrov, Pi-Chuan Chang, Michael Ringgaard, and Hiyan Alshawi. 2010. Uptraining for accurate deterministic question parsing. In *Proceedings of the 2010 Conference on Empirical Methods in Natural Language Processing*, pages 705–713. Association for Computational Linguistics.

Lizhen Qu, Gabriela Ferraro, Liyuan Zhou, Weiwei Hou, Nathan Schneider, and Timothy Baldwin. 2015. Big data small data, in domain out-of domain, known word unknown word: The impact of word representation on sequence labelling tasks. *arXiv preprint arXiv:1504.05319*.

Djamé Seddah, Grzegorz Chrupała, Ozlem Cetinoglu, Josef van Genabith, and Marie Candito. 2010. Lemmatization and lexicalized statistical parsing of morphologically-rich languages: the case of french. In *Proceedings of the NAACL HLT 2010 First Workshop on Statistical Parsing of Morphologically-Rich Languages*, pages 85–93, Los Angeles, CA, USA, June. Association for Computational Linguistics.

Richard Socher, Alex Perelygin, Jean Wu, Jason Chuang, Christopher D. Manning, Andrew Ng, and Christopher Potts. 2013. Recursive deep models for semantic compositionality over a sentiment treebank. In *Proceedings of the 2013 Conference on Empirical Methods in Natural Language Processing*, pages 1631–1642, Seattle, Washington, USA, October. Association for Computational Linguistics.

Anders Søgaard and Anders Johannsen. 2012. Robust learning in random subspaces: Equipping NLP for OOV effects. In *Proceedings of COLING 2012: Posters*, Mumbai, India, December.

Nitish Srivastava, Geoffrey Hinton, Alex Krizhevsky, Ilya Sutskever, and Ruslan Salakhutdinov. 2014. Dropout: A simple way to prevent neural networks from overfitting. *Journal of Machine Learning Research*, 15:1929–1958.

Jeremie Tafforeau, Thierry Artieres, Benoit Favre, and Frederic Bechet. 2015. Adapting lexical representation and oov handling from written to spoken language with word embedding. In *Interspeech*.

Kai Sheng Tai, Richard Socher, and Christopher D. Manning. 2015. Improved semantic representations from tree-structured long short-term memory networks. In *Proceedings of the 53rd Annual Meeting of the Association for Computational Linguistics and the 7th International Joint Conference on Natural Language Processing (Volume 1: Long Papers)*, pages 1556–1566, Beijing, China, July. Association for Computational Linguistics.

Kristina Toutanova, Dan Klein, Christopher D Manning, and Yoram Singer. 2003. Feature-rich part-of-speech tagging with a cyclic dependency network. In *Proceedings of the 2003 Conference of the North American Chapter of the Association for Computational Linguistics on Human Language Technology-Volume 1*, pages 173–180. Association for Computational Linguistics.

Joseph Turian, Lev Ratinov, and Yoshua Bengio. 2010. Word representations: a simple and general method for semisupervised learning. In *Proceedings of the 48th annual meeting of the association for computational linguistics*, page 384394. Association for Computational Linguistics.

Laurens Van der Maaten and Geoffrey Hinton. 2008. Visualizing data using t-sne. *Journal of Machine Learning Research*, 9(2579-2605):85.

William Yang Wang, Lingpeng Kong, Kathryn Mazaitis, and William W Cohen. 2014. Dependency parsing for weibo: An efficient probabilistic logic programming approach. In *Proceedings of the 2014 Conference on Empirical Methods in Natural Language Processing (EMNLP)*, pages 1152–1158, Doha, Qatar, October. Association for Computational Linguistics.

Multilingual Modal Sense Classification using a Convolutional Neural Network

Ana Marasović and **Anette Frank**
Research Training Group AIPHES
Department of Computational Linguistics
Heidelberg University
69120 Heidelberg, Germany
`{marasovic,frank}@cl.uni-heidelberg.de`

Abstract

Modal sense classification (MSC) is a special WSD task that depends on the meaning of the proposition in the modal's scope. We explore a CNN architecture for classifying modal sense in English and German. We show that CNNs are superior to manually designed feature-based classifiers and a standard NN classifier. We analyze the feature maps learned by the CNN and identify known and previously unattested linguistic features. We benchmark the CNN on a standard WSD task, where it compares favorably to models using sense-disambiguated target vectors.

1 Introduction

Factuality recognition (de Marneffe et al., 2012; Lee et al., 2015) is a subtask in information extraction that differentiates facts from hypotheses and speculation, expressed through signals of modality, most prominently, modal verbs and adverbs. Modal verbs are, however, ambiguous between an *epistemic* sense (possibility) as opposed to non-epistemic *deontic* (permission/obligation) or *dynamic* (capability) senses, as in: *He could be at home* (epistemic), *You can enter now* (deontic) and *Only John can solve this problem* (capability).

Modal sense classification (MSC) is a special case of sense disambiguation that is also relevant in areas of dialogue act and plan recognition in AI, as well as novel tasks such as argumentation mining. Prior work (Ruppenhofer and Rehbein, 2012; Zhou et al., 2015) addressed the task with feature-based classification. However, even with carefully designed semantic features the models have difficulties beating the majority sense baseline in cases of difficult sense distinctions and when applying the models to heterogenous text genres.

We cast modal sense classification as a novel semantic sentence classification task using a convolutional neural network (CNN) architecture. Our contributions are: (i) our experiments on MSC confirm the adequacy of CNNs for modeling propositions in *semantic* sentence classification tasks (cf. Kim (2014)); (ii) we show that automatically learned features in a CNN outperform manually designed features for difficult modal verbs and novel genres; (iii) we demonstrate that the CNN approach can be generalized across languages, by adapting the model to German. (iv) We offer insights into the linguistic properties captured by the learned feature maps. Finally, (v) we benchmark the CNN on a standard WSD task, comparing it to a WSD model using rich sense-disambiguated embeddings and obtain comparable results.

2 Prior and related work

Modal sense classification (MSC). We focus on disambiguation of modal verbs, adopting the sense inventory established in formal semantics: *epistemic, deontic/bouletic* and *circumstantial/dynamic*.[1] We compare to prior work in Ruppenhofer and Rehbein (2012) and follow-up work in Zhou et al. (2015) (henceforth, R&R and Z+). R&R induced modal sense classifiers from manual annotations on the MPQA corpus (Wiebe et al., 2005) using word-based and syntactic features. Z+ propose an extended semantically informed model that significantly outperforms R&R's results. Z+ also create heuristically sense-annotated training data from parallel corpora, to overcome sparsity and bias in the MPQA corpus. However, their models do not beat the majority sense baseline for the difficult modal verbs, *may, can* and *could*.

---

[1] These senses correspond to (Baker et al., 2010)'s modal categories (with *deontic* split into *requirement* and *permissive*), and R&Rs inventory, with regrouping of *concessive, conditional* and *circumstantial*, cf. Zhou et al. (2015).

111

Proceedings of the 1st Workshop on Representation Learning for NLP, pages 111–120,
Berlin, Germany, August 11th, 2016. ©2016 Association for Computational Linguistics

Modal sense classification interacts with genre and domain differences. Prabhakaran et al. (2012) observe strong cross-genre effects and missing generalization capacities when applying their modality classifier to out-of-domain genres.

Word Embeddings and Sense Disambiguation. Taghipour and Ng (2015) investigate the impact of word embeddings on classical WSD, using pre-trained embeddings and tuning them to the task using a NN. Both variants, integrated into the state-of-the-art system IMS (Zhong and Ng, 2012), improve WSD performance on benchmark tasks.

Ordinary word embeddings do not differentiate word senses. Rothe and Schütze (2015) explore supervised WSD using sense-specific embeddings, which they induce by exploiting *sense encodings* and *constraints* given by a lexical resource.[2] Integrating the sense-specific vectors into IMS yields significant improvements and small gains relative to Taghipour and Ng (2015). Hence, word embeddings – tuned to the task or sense-specific – prove beneficial for supervised WSD.

The CNN approach we investigate in our work does not employ a fixed feature space or a pre-defined window around the target word. It flexibly learns feature maps for variable window sizes over the embedding matrix for the full sentence. In contrast to Rothe and Schütze (2015), embeddings used by our CNNs models are knowledge-lean and do not encode senses of the target words.

Sentence classification using CNNs. Recent work investigates NN architectures and their ability to capture the semantics of sentences for various classification tasks. Kalchbrenner et al. (2014) construct a dynamic CNN that builds on unparsed input and achieves performance beyond strong baselines for sentiment and question type classification. By contrast, recursive neural networks (Socher et al., 2013) take parsed input, recursively generate representations for intermediate phrases, and perform classification on the basis of the full sentence representation.

Kim (2014) evaluates a one-layer CNN on various benchmark tasks for sentence classification. CNNs trained on pre-trained (static) embeddings perform well and can be further improved by tuning them to the task (non-static). Using two chan-

nels did not significantly improve results. Overall, the CNNs show consistently strong performance, improving on state-of-the-art results in 4 out of 7 tasks, i.a., sentiment and opinion classification.

3   A CNN for modal sense classification

We aim at a NN approach to MSC that (i) improves over existing feature-based classifiers, (ii) alleviates manual crafting of features, (iii) generalizes over various text genres, and (iv) is easily portable to novel languages. Besides this, MSC is a special kind of WSD, in that modal verbs have a restricted sense inventory shared across languages, and act as operators that take a full proposition as argument. We thus cast MSC as a semantic sentence classification task in a CNN architecture, adopting the one-layer CNN model of Kim (2014), a variant of Collobert et al. (2011). Unlike Kim (2014) we will use only one channel, but experiment with various types of word vectors.

A CNN represents a sentence with a fixed size vector, passed to classifier to classify the sentence into task-specific target categories. In our case, it will classify sentences into three modal sense categories. The input layer is a matrix $\mathbf{x} \in \mathbb{R}^{s \times d}$, with each row corresponding to a d-dimensional word embedding $x_i \in \mathbb{R}^d$ of a word in the sentence of length s. Word embeddings can be randomly initialized or pre-trained vectors, e.g. word2vec (Mikolov et al., 2013) or dependency-based (Levy and Goldberg, 2014) embeddings. Based on the input layer, a CNN builds up one or more convolutional layers. A convolution is an operation between sub-matrices of the input matrix $\mathbf{x} \in \mathbb{R}^{s \times d}$ and a *filter* parametrised by a weight matrix $\mathbf{w} \in \mathbb{R}^{n \times d}$, that returns a vector usually referred to as a *feature map*. Formally, let $\mathbf{x}_{i-n+1:i}$ be the sub-matrix of the input matrix $\mathbf{x}$ from the $(i-n+1)$-th row to the i-th row and let $\langle .,. \rangle_{\mathcal{F}}$ denote the sum of elements of the component-wise inner product of two matrices, known as Frobenius inner product. The i-th component of the feature map $\mathbf{c}$ is obtained by taking the Frobenius inner product of the sub-matrix $\mathbf{x}_{i-n+1:i}$ with the filter matrix $\mathbf{w}$

$$c_i = \langle \mathbf{x}_{i-n+1:i}, \mathbf{w} \rangle_{\mathcal{F}}, \qquad (1)$$

for $i \in \{n, \dots, s\}$[3]. Afterwards, we add a bias term, $b \in \mathbb{R}$ to every component of the feature map and apply an activation function f,

$$\tilde{c}_i = f(c_i + b). \qquad (2)$$

<hr>

[3]We apply the narrow type of convolution.

Finally, *max-over-time pooling* (Collobert et al., 2011) is applied over a single feature map that extracts the maximum value $\hat{c} = max\{\tilde{\mathbf{c}}\}$, which represents the chosen feature for this feature map. Like Kim (2014) we don't use just one filter as described, but multiple filters with different region sizes n, resulting in multiple feature maps. Features obtained through max-pooling from each feature map are concatenated to a vector representation of the input sentence that is passed to the softmax layer. Parameters to learn are elements of the filter matrices and the input matrix when word vectors are tuned.

Filters are trained to be especially active when they encounter a sequence of words relevant for the given classification task. Kalchbrenner et al. (2014) present n-grams of different feature detectors that capture positive or negative sentiment phrases, and also more abstract semantic categories, such as negation or degree particles ('too') that are relevant in compositional sentiment detection. In the modal sense classification task, we expect the feature maps to capture semantic categories found to be relevant in prior work, such as tense, aspectual classes, negation and semantic properties of verbs and phrases. Moreover, prior work has shown that MSC profits from features that model the wider syntactic context, esp. subject and embedded verb and their semantics (abstractness, semantic class, aspect, tense). Explicit modeling of these features as in Z+ improves performance, but requires feature design for each new language. Also, modeling semantic features through lexical resources is subject to sparsity, and relying on parsed input leads to lack of robustness.

Given that MSC profits from semantic features in the wider syntactic context, we expect that a CNN that applies filters of variable sizes to various regions of the sentence to learn feature maps can capture diverse linguistic features, and offers greater flexibility compared to a conventional WSD model with a fixed window size centered around the target word. To investigate these special properties of the CNN model, we test it on English and German data. While in English, subject, modal and embedded verb are in a close syntactic context, in German, they can be distributed over wider distances, and the feature maps are expected to capture properties over wider distances.

We perform experiments for MSC for English and German, using various data sets. Section 4 presents the data, experimental settings and the model variations we investigate. We perform detailed quantitative and qualitative evaluation of our experimental results. In Section 5, we evaluate the CNN approach in a lexical sample WSD task, to benchmark its performance on a well-studied data set, and to investigate the potential advantage of learning feature maps based on flexible window sizes. To our knowledge, this constitutes the first attempt to apply a CNN model in a WSD task.

4 Modal sense classification

4.1 Data

Our experiments are based on three data sets. Their basic composition is given in Table 1.[4]

1) MPQA + EPOS$_E$ The English benchmark data set MPQA from R&R was further enriched through balanced heuristically tagged training data, EPOS$_E$, by Z+. The EPOS$_E$ data set was obtained using a cross-lingual sense projection approach. Z+ identified paraphrases for modal senses (e.g. *brauchen-need; erlauben-permit* for deontic, *schaffen-able to* for dynamic sense), extracted sentences from a parallel corpus with a modal verb aligned to a sense-identifying paraphrase, and tagged them with the identified modal sense. Z+ measured 0.92 accuracy on 420 instances of the heuristically tagged corpora. To alleviate distributional bias stemming from the MPQA dataset, Z+ balanced the blend of MPQA with EPOS$_E$ using under- and oversampling. We experiment with both versions ($\pm$ balanced).[5]

2) MASC A subset of the multi-genre corpus MASC (Ide et al., 2008), consisting of 19 genres was manually annotated (Anonymous) with modal senses for the same modal verbs. The annotated data consists of $\approx$100 instances for each genre.[6]

3) EPOS$_G$ Following the method of Z+, we constructed a German data set EPOS$_G$ from the Europarl and OpenSubtitles corpora of OPUS (Tiedemann, 2012) by projecting modal sense categories from English to German, using selected modal sense identifying English paraphrases. The resulting corpus with sense-tagged German modal verbs

---

[4]More detailed information will be provided through accompanying material with the final version. The annotated MASC and EPOS$_G$ data sets will be made publicly available.

[5]Their data is publicly available through their website. We omit *shall* from MPQA, due to low number of occurrences.

[6]Exceptions with less than 100 instances are journal, newspaper, technical, travel guides, and telephone.

		can	could	may	must	should
MPQA	ep	2	156	130	11	26
	de	115	17	9	83	248
	dy	271	67	–	–	–
$EPOS_E$	ep	150	40	950	800	150
	de	150	40	950	800	150
	dy	150	40	–	–	–
MASC	ep	88	144	217	29	27
	de	72	16	43	115	224
	dy	710	251	3	–	–

		dürfen	können	müssen	sollen
$EPOS_G$ (train)	ep	1000	1000	1000	1000
	de	1000	1000	1000	1000
	dy	–	1000	–	–
$EPOS_G$ (test)	ep	98	100	32	100
	de	98	47	100	100
	dy	–	100	–	–

Table 1: Composition of MPQA, $EPOS_E$, MASC and $EPOS_G$

können (can), müssen (must), sollen (should), dürfen (may) consists of a manually validated test section consisting of up to 100 instances for each sense. Annotation was done by two independent judges and one adjudicator. Balanced training data of 1000 instances per sense for each modal verb was constructed from heuristically tagged sentences that were judged high-quality by validating 20 instances for each paraphrase. For modal verbs with rare extractions, we added training data from modal verbs of shared senses, changing their verb forms to the verb form of the target verb.[7]

4.2 Experimental settings

MSC on MPQA using CNN-E$_B$ and CNN-E$_U$, CV For MSC we benchmark the CNN approach against the latest state-of-the-art results in Z+. We reimplemented their maximum entropy classifier (henceforth, *MaxEnt*) and trained it on their balanced and unbalanced blend of MPQA and EPOS.[8] As in Z+ we train independent classifiers for each modal verb on their respective training data.[9] For evaluation, we perform 5-fold cross validation as in Z+. Each fold for training holds a stratified 80% section of the MPQA data together with the full $EPOS_E$ data set, and we use the remaining 20% of MPQA data for testing. We refer to the CNN models trained on the ±balanced versions of this data as CNN-E$_B$ and CNN-E$_U$.

MSC on MASC using CNN-E$_B$ and CNN-E$_U$ Besides MPQA, we evaluate the CNN on the multi-genre MASC (sub)corpus. For comparability with Z+, for training we use one training fold from the previous setting,[10] and evaluate on MASC as test. We analyze the performance of the CNN model overall and on different genre subcorpora (not reported here).

Both English data sets are characterized by modest training set sizes and involve a considerable distributional biases, with high most frequent sense majority baselines (cf. Tables 3 and 4).

MSC on EPOS$_G$ using CNN-G In constrast to the English data sets, the German EPOS$_G$ data set provides larger training set sizes of 1000 instances for all modal verbs and senses. This eliminates distributional bias from the data, so that the discriminating power of the classifier model is not masqued by distributional information.

4.3 Model variations

Hyperparameters Model-specific hyperparameters of the CNN are the number of filters, filter region size, and the depth of the network. We restrict our model to a one-dimensional CNN architecture.

Following the advices in Zhang and Wallace (2015), we used following setting: ReLU (rectified linear unit) as activation function, filter region sizes of 3, 4, and 5 with 100 feature maps each, dropout keep probability of 0.5, l_2 regularisation coefficient of 10^{-3}, number of iterations of 1001[11] and mini-batch size of 50. Training is done with the Adam optimisation algorithm (Kingma and Ba, 2014) with learning rate of 10^{-4}. Filter weights are initialized using Glorot-Bengio strategy (Glorot and Bengio, 2010). We experimented with some parameter variations (using nested CV), but found no consistently better results. In all following MSC experiments we thus used this hyperparameter setting for CNN training.

Word embeddings In the first and third experimental setting we investigate the impact of static and tuned versions of different word vectors: word2vec (Mikolov et al., 2013), dependency-based (Levy and Goldberg, 2014) and randomly initialized embeddings.

We used publicly available `word2vec` vectors that were trained on Google News for En-

---

[7] Replacing e.g. *könnte* with *dürfte* in *Es könnte Dir gefallen* extracted from *You might get a taste for it.*

[8] We omit *shall* with a small number of instances.

[9] This holds for all our experiments.

[10] Hence, one 80% fold of MPQA plus $EPOS_E$. Despite this small difference, we refer to the CNN models as above, as CNN-E$_B$ and CNN-E$_U$.

[11] We did not perform early stopping.

glish[12] and various datasets for German (Reimers et al., 2014)[13], as well as English dependency-based vectors trained on Wikipedia[14]. The German dependency-based embeddings were trained on the SdeWaC corpus (Faaß and Eckart, 2013), parsed with Malt parser. We used 300 dimensions for English embeddings and 100 for German.

For words without a pre-trained vector and in the random initialization setting, each dimension of the random vector was sampled from $\mathcal{U} \sim [-a, a]$ with parameter a picked such that the variance of the uniform distribution equals the variance of the available pre-trained vectors.

Baselines For MPQA and MASC, the classifiers are compared against strong *majority sense baselines, BL_{maj},* due to skewed sense distributions in the training data. Further, we compare the CNN results to the reconstructed *MaxEnt* classifier from Z+, trained on the blend of MPQA and EPOS with R&R's shallow lexical and syntactic path features and the newly designed semantic features of Z+.

To our knowledge, there is no work on modal sense classification using a neural network. We thus compare our CNN models with a simple, one-layer neural network NN to investigate the impact offered by the more complex CNN architecture.

Input to the NN is the sum of all vectors of the words in the sentence. As for the CNN, we experimented with different types of word vectors.

The *hyperparameter setting* for the NN is: ReLU as activation function, l_2 regularisation coefficient of 10^{-3}, hidden layer size of 1024, number of iterations of 3001, dropout keep probability of 0.5, and mini-batch size of 50. Training is again done with the Adam optimisation algorithm (Kingma and Ba, 2014) with learning rate of 10^{-4}. Weights are initialized using Glorot-Bengio strategy (Glorot and Bengio, 2010).[15]

4.4 Results

English

In Table 2 we report results for CNN-E$_B$ and CNN-E$_U$ with diverse input representations. For balanced training, dependency based vectors yield the best (*can, could*) or equally good results (*may,*

CNN-E$_B$	can	could	may	must	should
w2v-static	65.02	51.67	**93.57**	**93.82**	**90.77**
w2v-tuned	63.73	54.17	**93.57**	**93.82**	**90.77**
dep-static	**65.78**	56.67	**93.57**	**93.82**	**90.77**
dep-tuned	59.89	**67.50**	**93.57**	93.29	90.42
rand-static	63.99	46.67	**93.57**	92.79	**90.77**
rand-tuned	64.50	48.33	**93.57**	92.79	**90.77**

CNN-E$_U$	can	could	may	must	should
w2v-static	70.10	65.27	**93.49**	**94.97**	**90.59**
w2v-tuned	70.62	66.10	**93.49**	**94.97**	**90.59**
dep-static	69.85	65.27	**93.49**	94.46	**90.59**
dep-tuned	69.59	**66.55**	**93.49**	93.95	**90.59**
rand-static	70.36	64.45	**93.49**	93.45	**90.59**
rand-tuned	**70.87**	64.86	**93.49**	93.45	**90.59**

CNN-G	dürfen	können	müssen	sollen
w2v-static	91.92	68.82	77.61	71.64
w2v-tuned	**99.49**	74.09	83.58	72.14
dep-static	91.92	63.56	75.37	73.13
dep-tuned	97.47	73.28	82.83	**74.63**
rand-static	96.46	77.33	81.34	74.13
rand-tuned	98.48	**78.95**	**85.07**	73.63

Table 2: CV accuracy for CNN-E$_B$, CNN-E$_U$, test accuracy for CNN-G, with different input representations.

must, should). *Could* is the only case with large performance differences depending on the choice of embeddings. For *can* and *could* choosing either static or tuned versions of vectors is beneficial. With unbalanced training, dependency-based vectors are outperformed by `word2vec` for *must* and by randomly initialized vectors for *can*. Large differences in the results for *could* w.r.t. the choice of embeddings, are no longer present.

In Table 3 we report overall results for CNN-E$_B$ and CNN-E$_U$ on MPQA compared to the baselines. As representations for the NN and CNN we selected, for each modal verb, the embedding type that yielded the best results (Table 2)[16].

For each training data set, scores of the CNN which are significantly better[17] than the next lower score among the baselines are underlined. If CNN does not yield the best results, significance between the baseline with the best score and CNN is reported. Overlining is used if CNN with unbalanced training performs significantly better than CNN with balanced training, and vice versa.

With balanced training, CNN outperforms all baselines for every modal verb and in terms of micro average. However, differences between CNN

---

[12]https://code.google.com/archive/p/word2vec

[13]https://www.ukp.tu-darmstadt.de/research/ukp-in-challenges/germeval-2014

[14]https://levyomer.wordpress.com/2014/04/25/dependency-based-word-embeddings

[15]This is clearly not shown to be the best hyperparameter setting, as we chose it heuristically without tuning.

[16]For NN the impact of word vectors was investigated as well.

[17]By conducting the mid-p-value McNemar test (Fagerland et al., 2013) with p <0.05.

	can	could	may	must	should	micro
BL_{rand}	33.33	33.33	50.00	50.00	50.00	41.49
MaxEnt	59.64	61.25	92.14	87.60	90.11	74.88
NN	56.01	55.42	90.00	75.24	88.68	69.74
CNN-E_B	**65.78**	**67.50**	93.57	93.82	90.77	**79.29**

	can	could	may	must	should	micro
BL_{maj}	69.92	65.00	93.57	94.32	90.81	80.18
MaxEnt	64.76	63.33	92.14	92.78	**91.48**	78.01
NN	67.29	66.08	**94.23**	86.37	90.96	77.93
CNN-E_U	**70.87**	**66.55**	93.49	**94.97**	90.59	**80.74**

Table 3: Comparison of CV accuracies on MPQA of CNN-E_B (upper table) and CNN-E_U (lower table) with baselines.

	can	could	may	must	should	micro
BL_{rand}	33.52	33.82	48.67	46.87	46.01	38.63
MaxEnt	66.74	62.86	**87.83**	83.33	84.06	72.25
CNN-E_B	**80.46**	**64.48**	86.69	**84.72**	88.84	**79.33**

	can	could	may	must	should	micro
BL_{maj}	**81.61**	35.04	82.51	79. 86	89.24	72.86
MaxEnt	73.17	**55.34**	**87.45**	86.11	**89.64**	74.41
CNN-E_U	81.03	49.15	86.31	**86.80**	89.24	**76.49**

Table 4: Accuracies on MASC dataset of classifiers trained on MPQA+EPOS$_E$.

	dürfen	können	müssen	sollen	micro
BL_{rand}	50.00	33.33	50.00	50.00	39.10
NN	77.73	43.32	73.88	50.25	57.69
CNN-G	**99.49**	**78.95**	**85.07**	**74.63**	**84.10**

Table 5: Average accuracy on EPOS$_G$.

and *MaxEnt* are significant only for *can*, *could* and micro average. Moving to unbalanced training, CNN has difficulties beating the baselines (cf. *may*, *should*), but yields the best micro average. Unbalanced training for CNN outperforms balanced training in terms of micro averages, however the difference is not significant.

Table 4 summarizes the evaluation of CNN-E_B and CNN-E_U on the MASC corpus. Note that CNN with unbalanced training, CNN-E_U, does not have enough generalization capability when applied to different genres. This behavior coincides with changes of the predominant sense between training and test. CNN-E_U, as well as *MaxEnt*, is highly sensitive to such distributional changes. Even though balanced training for CNN leads to a slightly worse micro average when evaluated on MPQA, on MASC CNN–E_B yields a +3pp gain in micro average compared to unbalanced training.[18]

In sum, our evaluation shows that the CNN model is able to outperform strong baselines in most configurations. Balanced training shows more consistent results beyond the baselines and is competitive with unbalanced training, without significant difference except for *can*. In view of genre differences in MASC, the CNN–E_B model is more robust against sense changes, and yields overall better results. The strong behaviour on balanced training data shows that the CNN model is able to learn meaningful structure from the data.

German

In Table 2 we report results for CNN-G with diverse input representations. Reasons for the slightly weaker performance of dependency-based vectors compared to word2vec (1-2 pp.) can be seen in the smaller size of the training corpus, and possibly greater noise due to parsing errors.

In Table 5 we report overall results for CNN-G compared to the NN baseline.[19] The CNN outperforms both baselines by large margins, per modal verb and in terms of micro average. Given we employed perfectly balanced training data, the classifier performances reflect their ability to learn characteristic information for the classes. Indeed, the NN has great difficulties distinguishing the senses for *können* (3 senses) and *sollen*, and is outperformed by CNN-G by +35.6 and +24.4 pp. gains. The confusion matrices for CNN-G show a clear separation of these classes, in contrast to the NN.

While German is a more difficult language than English due to its syntactic properties (word order, degree of inflection), CNN-G reaches overall higher performance levels compared to English, especially for difficult cases.[20] One reason can be the morphological distinction between indicative and subjunctive (Konjunktiv), which – in interaction with tense and other factors – can ease the distinction of epistemic vs. deontic/dynamic sense. For *sollen* this morphological division is masqued, and this can explain the weaker results compared to other binary classes. Generally, CNN-G profits from larger and perfectly balanced training data.

---

[18]In contrast to *MaxEnt*, which does not profit from balanced training.

[19]We did not construct a MaxEnt classifier for German. For NN and CNN-G we chose the best performing embedding types per modal verb.

[20]Clearly, we cannot draw any strict comparison here.

4.5 Semantic feature detectors

Z+ provided a thorough analysis of the impact of semantic features by ablating individual feature groups. Their ablation analysis confirmed that feature groups relating to tense and aspect of the embedded verb, negation, abstractness of the subject and semantic features of the embedded verb yield significant effects on classification performance.

For *must*, Z+ found clear patterns for the occurrence of specific features and the ability to properly classify a specific sense. However, they did not identify precise features that differentiate epistemic and dynamic readings with *can*. We spefically investigated whether the learned filters for *must* can be related to the semantic categories Z+ found to be important for distinguishing its senses. In addition, we investigated whether the CNN is able to capture unattested features that differentiate epistemic and dynamic readings with *can*.

For every modal verb and every filter, we sort sentences in the training data by the maximum value obtained by applying *1-max pooling* to the feature map acquired by applying the respective filter to a sentence. For each filter and each of the top-ranked 15 sentences, we extract the ngram that corresponds to the maximum value w.r.t. the filter, i.e. the argmax of the feature map. The ngram vector is the sum of all vectors of words in the ngram. The obtained ngram vectors were plotted using the t-SNE algorithm (Van der Maaten and Hinton, 2008) and textually displayed with their surrounding context.

For *must* we found many feature detectors that relate to observations in Z+. Many filters detect past (*you must have been* out last night; ep) vs. non-past (*we must make* further efforts; de) and a dynamic event (*we must develop* a policy; de) vs. stative (*you must think* me a perfect fool; ep) reading of the embedded verb. Among others the feature detectors capture passive constructions (*actual steps must be taken*; de) and negation (*we must not fear*; de). Some filters were trained to capture domain vocabulary which intuitively goes along with deontic sense (*European parliament; present regulation; fisheries policy*). One filter captures telic clauses (*to address these problems; to prevent both forum; to exert maximum influence*), identifying deontic sense. Novel features not considered in Z+ are discourse markers (*but; and (then)*) that correlate with deontic sense. All in all, the CNN learns meaningful features that are

known to be important for differentiating senses for *must*, and in contrast to manual feature design, it detects relevant unattested features by itself.

For *can* many filters recognise accomplishments which go along with dynamic sense, e.g. *You can do it/make it to NY*. Others detect words indicating *possibility* (ep), negation (de), discourse markers, animate subject (de and dy), passive construction (de and dy). However, without a systematic classification of these features it remains unclear how important they are for differentiating the senses of *can*. Also, similar to Z+ we did not find clear-cut features that recognize epistemic sense.

We performed a corresponding analysis of feature maps for German, following the same extraction procedure. We found the typical state (ep) vs. event (de) contrast for the embedded verb, negation and tense, and again previously unattested factors such as discourse relation markers[21] (*but; without; thereby; in order to* (dy)). For German we identified various indicators for epistemic sense (for *müssen* and *können*): attitude predicates (*believe, not know; tell me; have an idea, be afraid*), adverbials (*possibly*), conditionals (*if*); counterfactual and negative polarity contexts (*not be the case; how; ever*). Further detectors for epistemic sense are abstract subjects: placeholders for propositions (*it*), abstract concepts (*idea; music; grades; application*); indefinite subjects (*one*). We find a tendency for 1st or 2nd person subjects to co-occur with de/dy and 3rd person pronouns with ep. For *können* (dy) we find achievements (*present report; move mountains; find compromise*). For deontic readings, next to negation with 1st and 2nd person we find typical verb-object combinations for actions that can be granted: *use telephone; communicate with third parties*.

We extracted statistics about the distance of the extracted ngrams from the modal verb (distance overall; to the left/right and ngrams starting with the modal). There are no greater overall distances for German compared to English. However, for German we find significantly more ngrams that include the modal verb, especially for epistemic readings of *können, müssen, dürfen* that clearly mark subjunctive mood, whereas for *sollen*, with ambiguous forms for subjunctive and past tense, no such tendency is observed. Thus, the feature maps identify subjunctive marking (in conjunction with other factors) as relevant for classifying epis-

---

[21]For reasons of space we provide translations to English.

temic sense, whereas for *sollen* the lack of this indicator goes along with lower performance. Finally, we observe, for English and German, strikingly larger distances to the left of the modal verb for epistemic readings compared to non-epistemic readings. This can be traced back to indicators in the wider left-embedding context: embedding predicates, subjects, if clauses, etc.

5 Word sense disambiguation

Next to modal sense classification, we evaluate our CNN model in a classical WSD task. As benchmark corpus we chose the *SensEval-3 lexical sample* data set (Mihalcea et al., 2004), which was recently applied in Rothe and Schütze (2015) (henceforth R&S) and Taghipour and Ng (2015), using sense-specific embeddings and a NN architecture, respectively (cf. Section 2).

The training data size for the 57 target word types ranges from 14 to 263 instances. Sense labels of test instances of a given target word are predicted using the CNN model trained on the training instances for the respective word type.[22] We set the CNN hyperparameters to be the same as for MSC, except for mini-batch size and region sizes. Since the training data for some words is below 50 instances, mini-batch size was set to 10. For tuning of the region sizes, we split the training data for each word (80:20 for training and validation) and used static `word2vec` for the input representation. Among $\{(1,2,3),(2,3,4),(3,4,5),(4,5,6),(5,6,7)\}$ the best results were obtained for $(5,6,7)$.[23]

The final hyperparameter setting was used to investigate the impact of representations. Among `word2vec`, dependency-based and randomly initialised, `word2vec` performed the best, the tuned version being slightly better than static vectors. We report results for tuned `word2vec` vectors.

We compare our results to the results R&S obtained when using only sense-specific embeddings. These are not the state-of-the-art WSD results they obtain with additional features, namely POS tags of words in a small window around the target word, their discrete representation and local collocations. For sentence representation, R&S used every word in the target word sentence. For

S_{naive}-prod	62.20	S-prod	64.30
S-cosine	60.50	S-raw	63.10
		CNN	**66.50**

Table 6: WSD accuracy on *SensEval-3* dataset.

sense prediction, they used the following feature vectors that are fed into a linear SVM classifier:

$$\text{S-cosine} = \langle \cos(c, s^{(1)}), \dots, \cos(c, s^{(k)}) \rangle \,,$$

$$\text{S-product} = \langle c_1 s_1^{(1)}, \dots, c_n s_n^{(1)}, \dots, c_1 s_1^{(k)}, \dots, c_n s_n^{(k)} \rangle \,,$$

$$\text{S-raw} = \langle c_1, \dots, c_n, \dots, s_1^{(k)}, \dots, s_n^{(k)} \rangle \,,$$

where w is a target word with k senses, c is the centroid defined as the sum of all `word2vec` vectors of words in the sentence and $s^{(j)}$ is the embedding of the j-th synset of w.[24] They propose a variant of the *S-prod* feature vector, S_{naive}-*prod*, for which the synset embeddings are the sum of the `word2vec` vectors of all words in that sysnet.

The results are summarised in Table 6. The CNN model compares favorably to the competitor models of R&S using *AutoExtend* embeddings for WSD. It achieves slightly higher results without explicitly marking the target word, whereas the *AutoExtend* embeddings encode much richer information: what is the target word, how many possible sense it has, and knowledge-intense sense embeddings for each of its synsets. The CNN is able to compete with the rich *AutoExtend* model, and future work needs to investigate whether – similar to the S-product setting in R&S – the CNN model can achieve competitive state-of-the-art results by incorporating features corresponding to those of the IMS system of Zhong and Ng (2010).

6 Conclusion and future work

We presented an account for multilingual modal sense classification using a CNN architecture. We apply the same architecture in a standard WSD task and achieve competitive results compared to a system using richer embedding information.

Our one-layer CNN architecture outperforms strong baselines and prior art for MSC in English, including a NN and MaxEnt model, and proves particularly robust in cross-genre classification.

We applied the CNN model to German, on a data set of modest size, obtained using cross-lingual projection techniques. The CNN-G classifier outperforms a NN model by large margins.

---

[22]Training instances in the *SensEval-3* dataset can have more than one sense label. For training we randomly picked one of possible labels. Instances which contain more than one marked target word were omitted.

[23]However, the differences in the results were minor.

[24]Obtained using the *AutoExtend* method of R&S.

Our approach can be easily generalized to novel languages without tedious and resource-intensive feature engineering. Through analysis of learned feature maps we gave evidence that the CNN learns both known and novel features for MSC.

The attractiveness of the CNN framework lies in its ability to learn (semantic) features from flexible window regions without syntactic processing, and the ensuing robustness on difficult text genres and its ease in generalizing to novel languages.

Acknowledgments

We thank Mengfei Zhou for her support with the German corpus construction. This work has been supported by the German Research Foundation as part of the Research Training Group "Adaptive Preparation of Information from Heterogeneous Sources" (AIPHES) under grant No. GRK 1994/1.

References

Kathryn Baker, Michael Bloodgood, Bonnie J Dorr, Nathaniel W Filardo, Lori Levin, and Christine Piatko. 2010. A Modality Lexicon and its use in Automatic Tagging. In *Proceedings of LREC*, pages 1402–1407.

Aljoscha Burchardt, Marco Pennacchiotti, Stefan Thater, and Manfred Pinkal. 2009. Assessing the impact of frame semantics on textual entailment. *Natural Langugae Engineering*, 15(4):527–550.

Ronan Collobert, Jason Weston, Léon Bottou, Michael Karlen, Koray Kavukcuoglu, and Pavel Kuksa. 2011. Natural language processing (almost) from scratch. *The Journal of Machine Learning Research*, 12:2493–2537.

Marie-Catherine de Marneffe, Christopher D. Manning, and Christopher Potts. 2012. Did It Happen? The Pragmatic Complexity of Veridicality Assessment. *Computational Linguistics*, 38(2):301–333. Special Issue: Modality and Negation.

Gertrud Faaß and Kerstin Eckart. 2013. *Language Processing and Knowledge in the Web: 25th International Conference, GSCL 2013, Darmstadt, Germany, September 25-27, 2013. Proceedings.* Springer Berlin Heidelberg, Berlin, Heidelberg.

Morten W Fagerland, Stian Lydersen, and Petter Laake. 2013. The mcnemar test for binary matched-pairs data: mid-p and asymptotic are better than exact conditional. *BMC medical research methodology*, 13(1):1.

Xavier Glorot and Yoshua Bengio. 2010. Understanding the difficulty of training deep feedforward neural networks. In *International conference on artificial intelligence and statistics*, pages 249–256.

Nancy Ide, Collin Baker, Christiane Fellbaum, and Charles Fillmore. 2008. MASC: The manually annotated sub-corpus of American English. In *Proceedings of the Sixth International Conference on Language Resources and Evaluation (LREC-2008)*.

Nal Kalchbrenner, Edward Grefenstette, and Phil Blunsom. 2014. A convolutional neural network for modelling sentences. In *Proceedings of the 52nd Annual Meeting of the Association for Computational Linguistics*, pages 655–665, Baltimore, Maryland.

Yoon Kim. 2014. Convolutional neural networks for sentence classification. In *Proceedings of the 2014 Conference on Empirical Methods in Natural Language Processing (EMNLP)*, page 17461751, Doha, Qatar.

Diederik Kingma and Jimmy Ba. 2014. Adam: A method for stochastic optimization. *arXiv preprint arXiv:1412.6980*.

Kenton Lee, Yoav Artzi, Yejin Choi, and Luke Zettlemoyer. 2015. Event detection and factuality assessment with non-expert supervision. In *Proceedings of the 2015 Conference on Empirical Methods in Natural Language Processing*, pages 1643–1648, Lisbon, Portugal, September.

Omer Levy and Yoav Goldberg. 2014. Dependency-based word embeddings. In *ACL (2)*, pages 302–308.

R. Mihalcea, T. Chklovski, and A. Kilgarriff. 2004. The Senseval-3 English lexical sample task. In *Proceedings of SENSEVAL-3: Third International Workshop on the Evaluation of Systems for the Semantic Analysis of Text [CD-ROM]*, pages 25–28.

Tomas Mikolov, Ilya Sutskever, Kai Chen, Greg S Corrado, and Jeff Dean. 2013. Distributed representations of words and phrases and their compositionality. In *Advances in neural information processing systems*, pages 3111–3119.

Vinodkumar Prabhakaran, Michael Bloodgood, Mona Diab, Bonnie Dorr, Lori Levin, Christine D. Piatko, Owen Rambow, and Benjamin Van Durme. 2012. Statistical modality tagging from rule-based annotations and crowdsourcing. In *Proceedings of the Workshop on Extra-Propositional Aspects of Meaning in Computational Linguistics*, pages 57–64, Jeju, Republic of Korea, July.

Nils Reimers, Judith Eckle-Kohler, Carsten Schnober, Jungi Kim, and Iryna Gurevych. 2014. Germeval-2014: Nested named entity recognition with neural networks. In Gertrud Faaß and Josef Ruppenhofer, editors, *Workshop Proceedings of the 12th Edition of the KONVENS Conference*, pages 117–120, Hildesheim, October. Universitätsverlag Hildesheim.

Sascha Rothe and Hinrich Schütze. 2015. Autoextend: Extending word embeddings to embeddings for synsets and lexemes. In *Proceedings of the 53rd Annual Meeting of the Association for Computational Linguistics and the 7th International Joint Conference on Natural Language Processing (Volume 1: Long Papers)*, pages 1793–1803, Beijing, China.

Josef Ruppenhofer and Ines Rehbein. 2012. Yes we can !? Annotating the senses of English modal verbs. In *Proceedings of the LREC 2012 Conference*, pages 1538–1545.

Richard Socher, Alex Perelygin, Jean Wu, Jason Chuang, Christopher D. Manning, Andrew Ng, and Christopher Potts. 2013. Recursive deep models for semantic compositionality over a sentiment treebank. In *Proceedings of the 2013 Conference on Empirical Methods in Natural Language Processing*, pages 1631–1642, Seattle, Washington, USA.

Kaveh Taghipour and Hwee Tou Ng. 2015. Semi-supervised word sense disambiguation using word embeddings in general and specific domains. In *The 2015 Annual Conference of the North American Chapter of the Association for Computational Linguistics*, pages 314–323.

Jörg Tiedemann. 2012. Parallel Data, Tools and Interfaces in OPUS. In Nicoletta Calzolari, Khalid Choukri, Thierry Declerck, Mehmet Uğur Doğan, Bente Maegaard, Joseph Mariani, Jan Odijk, and Stelios Piperidis, editors, *Proceedings of LREC-2012*, pages 2214–2218, Istanbul, Turkey, May.

Laurens Van der Maaten and Geoffrey Hinton. 2008. Visualizing data using t-sne. *Journal of Machine Learning Research*, 9(2579-2605):85.

Janyce Wiebe, Theresa Wilson, and Claire Cardie. 2005. Annotating expressions of opinions and emotions in language. *Language resources and evaluation*, 39(2-3):165 – 210.

Ye Zhang and Byron C. Wallace. 2015. A sensitivity analysis of (and practitioners' guide to) convolutional neural networks for sentence classification. Technical report, University of Texas at Austin. arXiv:1510.03820v2.

Zhi Zhong and Hwee Tou Ng. 2010. It makes sense: A wide-coverage word sense disambiguation system for free text. In *Proceedings of the ACL 2010 System Demonstrations*, pages 78–83. Association for Computational Linguistics.

Zhi Zhong and Hwee Tou Ng. 2012. Word sense disambiguation improves information retrieval. In *Proceedings of the 50th Annual Meeting of the Association for Computational Linguistics (Volume 1: Long Papers)*, pages 273–282, Jeju Island, Korea.

Mengfei Zhou, Anette Frank, Annemarie Friedrich, and Alexis Palmer. 2015. Semantically Enriched Models for Modal Sense Classification. In *Proceedings of the EMNLP 2015 Workshop LSDSem: Linking Models of Lexical, Sentential and Discourse-level Semantics*, Lisbon, Portugal.

Towards cross-lingual distributed representations without parallel text trained with adversarial autoencoders

Antonio Valerio Miceli Barone
The University of Edinburgh
Informatics Forum, 10 Crichton Street
Edinburgh
amiceli@inf.ed.ac.uk

Abstract

Current approaches to learning vector representations of text that are compatible between different languages usually require some amount of parallel text, aligned at word, sentence or at least document level. We hypothesize however, that different natural languages share enough semantic structure that it should be possible, in principle, to learn compatible vector representations just by analyzing the monolingual distribution of words.

In order to evaluate this hypothesis, we propose a scheme to map word vectors trained on a source language to vectors semantically compatible with word vectors trained on a target language using an adversarial autoencoder.

We present preliminary qualitative results and discuss possible future developments of this technique, such as applications to cross-lingual sentence representations.

1 Introduction

Distributed representations that map words, sentences, paragraphs or documents to vectors real numbers have proven extremely useful for a variety of natural language processing tasks (Bengio et al., 2006; Collobert and Weston, 2008; Turian et al., 2010; Maas et al., 2011; Mikolov et al., 2013b; Socher et al., 2013; Pennington et al., 2014; Levy and Goldberg, 2014; Le and Mikolov, 2014; Baroni et al., 2014; Levy et al., 2015), as they provide an effective way to inject into machine learning models general prior knowledge about language automatically obtained from inexpensive unannotated corpora. Based on the assumption that different languages share a similar semantic struc-

ture, various approaches succeeded to obtain distributed representations that are compatible across multiple languages, either by learning mappings between different embedding spaces (Mikolov et al., 2013a; Faruqui and Dyer, 2014) or by jointly training cross-lingual representations (Klementiev et al., 2012; Hermann and Blunsom, 2013; Chandar et al., 2014; Gouws et al., 2014). These approaches all require some amount of parallel text, aligned at word level, sentence level or at least document level, or some other kind of parallel resources such as dictionaries (Ammar et al., 2016).

In this work we explore whether the assumption of a shared semantic structure between languages is strong enough that it allows to induce compatible distributed representations without using any parallel resource. We only require monolingual corpora that are thematically similar between languages in a general sense.

We hypothesize there exist a suitable vectorial space such that each language can be viewed as a random process that produces vectors at some level of granularity (words, sentences, paragraphs, documents) which are then encoded as discrete surface forms, and we hypothesize that, if languages are used to convey thematically similar information in similar contexts, these random processes should be approximately isomorphic between languages, and that this isomorphism can be learned from the statistics of the realizations of these processes, the monolingual corpora, in principle without any form of explicit alignment.

We motivate this hypothesis by observing that humans, especially young children, who acquire multiple languages, can often do so with relatively little exposure to explicitly aligned parallel linguistic information, at best they may have access to distant and noisy alignment information in the form of multisensorial environmental clues. Nevertheless, multilingual speakers are always au-

Proceedings of the 1st Workshop on Representation Learning for NLP, pages 121–126,
Berlin, Germany, August 11th, 2016. ©2016 Association for Computational Linguistics

tomatically able to translate between all the languages that they can speak, which suggests that their brain either uses a shared conceptual representations for the different surface features of each language, or uses distinct but near-isomorphic representations that can be easily transformed into each other.

2 Learning word embedding cross-lingual mappings with adversarial autoencoders

The problem of learning transformations between probability distributions of real vectors has been studied in the context of generative neural network models, with approaches such as Generative Moment Matching Networks (GMMNs) (Li et al., 2015) and Generative Adversarial Networks (GANs) (Goodfellow et al., 2014). In this work we consider GANs, since their effectiveness has been demonstrated in the literature more thoroughly than GMMNs.

In a typical GAN, we wish to train a *generator* model, usually a neural network, to transform samples from a known, easy to sample, uninformative distribution (e.g. Gaussian or uniform) into samples distributed according to a target distribution defined implicitly by a training set. In order to do so, we iteratively alternate between training a differentiable *discriminator* model, also a neural network, to distinguish between training samples and artificial samples produced by the generator, and training the generator to fool the discriminator into misclassifying the artificial examples as training examples. This can be done with conventional gradient-based optimization because the discriminator is differentiable thus it can backpropagate gradients into the generator.

It can be proven that, with sufficient model capacity and optimization power, sufficient entropy (information dimension) of the generator input distribution, and in the limit of infinite training set size, the generator learns to produce samples from the correct distribution. Intuitively, if there is any computable test that allows to distinguish the artificial samples from the training samples with better than random guessing probability, then a sufficiently powerful discriminator will eventually learn to exploit it and then a sufficiently powerful generator will eventually learn to counter it, until the generator output distribution becomes undistinguishable from the true training

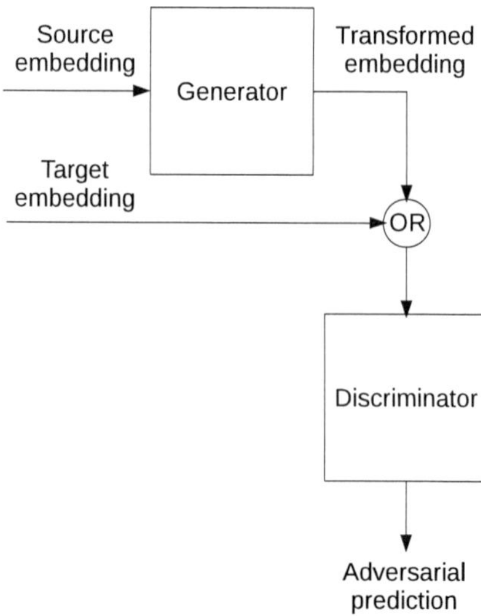

Figure 1: Generative adversarial network for cross-lingual embedding mapping

distribution. In practice, actual models have finite capacity and gradient-based optimization algorithms can become unstable or stuck when applied to this multi-objective optimization problem, though hey have been successfully used to generate fairly realistic-looking images (Denton et al., 2015; Radford et al., 2015).

In our preliminary experiments we attempted to adapt GANs to our problem, by training the generator to learn a transformation between word embeddings trained on different languages (fig. 1). Let d be the embedding dimensionality, $G_{\theta_G} : \mathcal{R}^d \to \mathcal{R}^d$ be the generator parametrized by θ_G, $D_{\theta_D} : \mathcal{R}^d \to [0, 1]$ be the discriminator parametrized by θ_D.

At each training step:

1. draw a sample $\{f\}_n$ of n source embeddings, according to their (adjusted) word frequencies

2. transform them into target-like embeddings $\{\hat{e}\}_n = G_{\theta_G}(\{f\}_n)$

3. evaluate them with the discriminator, estimating their probability of having been sampled from the true target distribution $\{p\}_n = D_{\theta_D}(\{\hat{e}\})$

4. update the generator parameters θ_G to reduce the average adversarial loss $L_a = -\log(\{p\}_n)$

5. draw a sample $\{e\}_n$ of n true target embeddings

6. update the discriminator parameters θ_D to reduce its binary cross-entropy loss on the classification between $\{e\}_n$ (positive class) and $\{\hat{e}\}$ (negative class)

repeat these steps until convergence.

Unfortunately we found that in this setup, even with different network architectures and hyperparameters, the model quickly converges to a pathological solution where the generator always emits constant or near-constant samples that somehow can fool the discriminator. This appears to be an extreme case of the know mode-seeking issue of GANs (Radford et al., 2015; Theis et al., 2015; Salimans et al., 2016), which is probably exacerbated in our settings because of the point-mass nature of our probability distributions where each word embedding is a mode on its own.

In order to avoid these pathological solutions, we needed a way to penalize the generator for destroying too much information about its input. Therefore we turned our attention to Adversarial Autoencoders (AAE) (Makhzani et al., 2015). In an AAE, the generator, now called *encoder*, is paired with another model, the *decoder* R_{θ_R} : $\mathcal{R}^d \rightarrow \mathcal{R}^d$ parametrized by θ_R which attempts to transform the artificial samples emitted by the encoder back into the input samples. The encoder and the decoder are jointly trained to minimize a combination of the average reconstruction loss $L_r(\{f\}_n, R_{\theta_R}(G_{\theta_G}(\{f\}_n)))$ and the adversarial loss defined as above. The discriminator is trained as above. In the original formulation of the AAE, the discriminator is used to enforce a known prior (e.g. Gaussian or Gaussian mixture) on the intermediate, *latent* representation, in our setting instead we use it to match the latent representation to the target embedding distribution so that the encoder can be used to transform source embeddings into target ones (fig. 2).

In our experiments, we use the cosine dissimilarity as reconstruction loss, and as a further penalty we also include the pairwise cosine dissimilarity between the generated latent samples $\{\hat{e}\}$ and the true target samples $\{e\}_n$. Therefore, the total loss incurred by the encoder-decoder at each step is

$$L_{GR} = \lambda_r L_r(\{f\}_n, R_{\theta_R}(G_{\theta_G}(\{f\}_n))) - \lambda_a \log(\{p\}_n) + \lambda_c L_r(\{e\}_n, G_{\theta_G}(\{f\}_n))$$

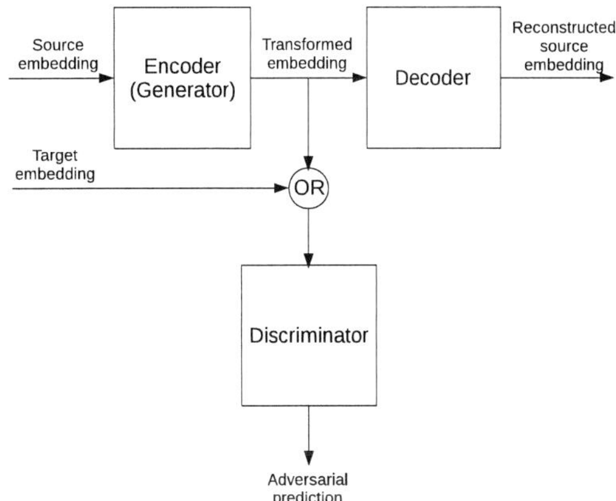

Figure 2: Adversarial autoencoder for cross-lingual embedding mapping (loss function blocks not shown).

where λ_r, λ_a and λ_c are hyperparameters (all set equal to 1 in our experiments).

3 Experiments

We performed some preliminary exploratory experiments on our model. In this section we report salient results.

The first experiment is qualitative, to assess whether our model is able to learn any semantically sensible transformation at all. We consider English to Italian embedding mapping.

We train English and Italian word embeddings on randomly subsampled Wikipedia corpora consisting of about 1.5 million sentences per language. We use word2vec (Mikolov et al., 2013b) in skipgram mode to generate embeddings with dimension $d = 100$. Our encoder and decoder are linear models with tied matrices (one the transpose of the other), initialized as random orthogonal matrices (we also explored deep non-linear autoencoders but we found that they make the optimization more difficult without providing apparent benefits).

Our discriminator is a Residual Network (He et al., 2015) without convolutions, one leaky ReLU non-linearity (Maas et al., 2013) per block, no non-linearities on the passthrough path, batch normalization (Ioffe and Szegedy, 2015) and dropout (Nitish et al., 2014). The block (layer) equation is:

$$h_{t+1} = \phi(W_t \times h_{t-1}) + h_{t-1} \qquad (1)$$

where W_t is a weight matrix and ϕ is batch normalization (with its internal parameters) followed by leaky ReLU and h_t is a k-dimensional block state (in our experiments $k = 40$). The network has $T = 10$ blocks followed by a 1-dimensional output layer with logistic sigmoid activation. We found that using a Residual Network as discriminator rather than a standard multi-layer perceptron yields larger gradients being backpropagated to the generator, facilitating training. We actually train two discriminators per experiment, with identical structure but different random initializations, and use one to train the generator and the other for monitoring in order to help us determine whether overfitting or underfitting occurs.

At each step, word embeddings are sampled according to their frequency in the original corpora, adjusted to subsample frequent words, as in word2vec. Updates are performed using the Adam optimizer (Kingma and Ba, 2014) with learning rate 0.001 for the encoder-decoder and 0.01 for the discriminator.

The code[1] is implemented in Python, Theano (Theano Development Team, 2016) and Lasagne.

We qualitatively analyzed the quality of the embeddings by considering the closest Italian embeddings to a sample of transformed English embeddings. We notice that in some cases the closest or nearly closest embedding is the true translation, for instance 'computer' (en) ->'computer' (it). In other cases, the closest terms are not translations but subjectively appear to be semantically related, for instance 'rain' (en) ->'gelo', 'gela', 'intensissimo', 'galleggiava', 'rigidissimo', 'arida', 'semi-desertico', 'fortunale', 'gelata', 'piovosa' (it 10-best), or 'comics' (en) ->'Kadath', 'Microciccio','Cugel','Promethea','flashback','episodio', 'Morimura', 'Chatwin', 'romanzato','Deedlit' (it 10-best), or 'anime' (en) ->'Zatanna', 'Alita', 'Yuriko', 'Wildfire', 'Carmilla', 'Batwoman', 'Leery', 'Aquarion', 'Vampirella', 'Minaccia' (it 10-best). Other terms, such as names of places however, tend to be transformed incorrectly, for instance 'France' (en) ->'Radiomobile', 'Cartubi', 'Freniatria', 'UNUCI', 'Cornhole', 'Internazione', 'CSCE', 'Folklorica', 'UECI', 'Rientro' (it 10-best).

We further evaluate our model on German to English and English to German embedding transformations, using the same evaluation setup as (Klementiev et al., 2012) with embeddings trained

on the concatenation of the Reuters corpora and the News Commentary 2015 corpora, with embedding dimension $d = 40$ and discriminator depth $T = 4$. On a qualitative analysis notice similar partial semantic similarity patterns. However the cross-lingual document classification task we were able to improve over the baseline only for the smallest training set size.

4   Discussion and future work

From the qualitative analysis of the word embedding mappings it appears that the model does learn to transfer some semantic information, although it's not competitive with other cross-lingual representation approaches. This may be possibly an issue of hyperparameter choice and architectural details, since, to our knowledge, this is the first work to apply adversarial training techniques to point-mass distribution arising from NLP tasks.

Further experimentation is needed to determine whether the model can be improved or whether we already hit a fundamental limit on how much semantic transfer can be performed by monolingual distribution matching alone. This additional experimentation may help to test how strongly our initial hypothesis of semantic isomorphism between languages holds, in particular across languages of different linguistic families.

Even if this hypothesis does not hold in a strong sense and semantic transfer by monolingual text alone turns out to be infeasible, our technique might help in conjunction with training on parallel data. For instance, in neural machine translation "sequence2sequence" transducers without attention (Cho et al., 2014), it could be useful to train as usual on parallel sentences and train in autoencoder mode on monolingual sentences, using an adversarial loss computed by a discriminator on the intermediate latent representations to push them to be isomorphic between languages. A modification of this technique that allows for the latent representation to be variable-sized could be also applied to the attentive "sequence2sequence" transducers (Bahdanau et al., 2014), as an alternative or in addition to monolingual dataset augmentation by backtranslation (Sennrich et al., 2015).

Furthermore, it may be worth to evaluate additional distribution learning approaches such as the aforementioned GMMs, as well as the more recent BiGAN/ALI framework (Donahue et al., 2016; Dumoulin ct al., 2016) which uscs an advcr-

---

[1]Code with full hyperparameters available at: https://github.com/Avmb/clwcadv

sarial discriminator loss both to match latent distributions and to enforce reconstruction, and also to consider more recent GAN training techniques (Salimans et al., 2016).

In conclusion we believe that this work initiates a potentially promising line of research in natural language processing consisting of applying distribution matching techniques such as adversarial training to learn isomorphisms between languages.

Acknowledgements

This project has received funding from the European Union's Horizon 2020 research and innovation programme under grant agreement 645452 (QT21).

References

Waleed Ammar, George Mulcaire, Yulia Tsvetkov, Guillaume Lample, Chris Dyer, and Noah A Smith. 2016. Massively multilingual word embeddings. *arXiv preprint arXiv:1602.01925*.

Dzmitry Bahdanau, Kyunghyun Cho, and Yoshua Bengio. 2014. Neural machine translation by jointly learning to align and translate. *arXiv preprint arXiv:1409.0473*.

Marco Baroni, Georgiana Dinu, and Germán Kruszewski. 2014. Don't count, predict! a systematic comparison of context-counting vs. context-predicting semantic vectors. In *ACL (1)*, pages 238–247.

Yoshua Bengio, Holger Schwenk, Jean-Sébastien Senécal, Fréderic Morin, and Jean-Luc Gauvain. 2006. Neural probabilistic language models. In *Innovations in Machine Learning*, pages 137–186. Springer.

Sarath Chandar, Stanislas Lauly, Hugo Larochelle, Mitesh Khapra, Balaraman Ravindran, Vikas C Raykar, and Amrita Saha. 2014. An autoencoder approach to learning bilingual word representations. In *Advances in Neural Information Processing Systems*, pages 1853–1861.

Kyunghyun Cho, Bart van Merriënboer, Dzmitry Bahdanau, and Yoshua Bengio. 2014. On the properties of neural machine translation: Encoder-decoder approaches. *arXiv preprint arXiv:1409.1259*.

Ronan Collobert and Jason Weston. 2008. A unified architecture for natural language processing: Deep neural networks with multitask learning. In *Proceedings of the 25th international conference on Machine learning*, pages 160–167. ACM.

Emily L Denton, Soumith Chintala, Rob Fergus, et al. 2015. Deep generative image models using a laplacian pyramid of adversarial networks. In *Advances in Neural Information Processing Systems*, pages 1486–1494.

J. Donahue, P. Krähenbühl, and T. Darrell. 2016. Adversarial Feature Learning. *ArXiv e-prints*, May.

V. Dumoulin, I. Belghazi, B. Poole, A. Lamb, M. Arjovsky, O. Mastropietro, and A. Courville. 2016. Adversarially Learned Inference. *ArXiv e-prints*, June.

Manaal Faruqui and Chris Dyer. 2014. Improving vector space word representations using multilingual correlation. Association for Computational Linguistics.

Ian Goodfellow, Jean Pouget-Abadie, Mehdi Mirza, Bing Xu, David Warde-Farley, Sherjil Ozair, Aaron Courville, and Yoshua Bengio. 2014. Generative adversarial nets. In *Advances in Neural Information Processing Systems*, pages 2672–2680.

Stephan Gouws, Yoshua Bengio, and Greg Corrado. 2014. Bilbowa: Fast bilingual distributed representations without word alignments. *arXiv preprint arXiv:1410.2455*.

Kaiming He, Xiangyu Zhang, Shaoqing Ren, and Jian Sun. 2015. Deep residual learning for image recognition. *arXiv preprint arXiv:1512.03385*.

Karl Moritz Hermann and Phil Blunsom. 2013. Multilingual distributed representations without word alignment. *arXiv preprint arXiv:1312.6173*.

Sergey Ioffe and Christian Szegedy. 2015. Batch normalization: Accelerating deep network training by reducing internal covariate shift. *arXiv preprint arXiv:1502.03167*.

Diederik Kingma and Jimmy Ba. 2014. Adam: A method for stochastic optimization. *arXiv preprint arXiv:1412.6980*.

Alexandre Klementiev, Ivan Titov, and Binod Bhattarai. 2012. Inducing crosslingual distributed representations of words. In *Proceedings of the International Conference on Computational Linguistics (COLING)*, Bombay, India, December.

Quoc V Le and Tomas Mikolov. 2014. Distributed representations of sentences and documents. *arXiv preprint arXiv:1405.4053*.

Omer Levy and Yoav Goldberg. 2014. Neural word embedding as implicit matrix factorization. In *Advances in Neural Information Processing Systems*, pages 2177–2185.

Omer Levy, Yoav Goldberg, and Ido Dagan. 2015. Improving distributional similarity with lessons learned from word embeddings. *Transactions of the Association for Computational Linguistics*, 3:211–225.

Yujia Li, Kevin Swersky, and Richard Zemel. 2015. Generative moment matching networks. *arXiv preprint arXiv:1502.02761*.

Andrew L Maas, Raymond E Daly, Peter T Pham, Dan Huang, Andrew Y Ng, and Christopher Potts. 2011. Learning word vectors for sentiment analysis. In *Proceedings of the 49th Annual Meeting of the Association for Computational Linguistics: Human Language Technologies-Volume 1*, pages 142–150. Association for Computational Linguistics.

Andrew L Maas, Awni Y Hannun, and Andrew Y Ng. 2013. Rectifier nonlinearities improve neural network acoustic models. In *Proc. ICML*, volume 30, page 1.

Alireza Makhzani, Jonathon Shlens, Navdeep Jaitly, and Ian Goodfellow. 2015. Adversarial autoencoders. *arXiv preprint arXiv:1511.05644*.

Tomas Mikolov, Quoc V Le, and Ilya Sutskever. 2013a. Exploiting similarities among languages for machine translation. *arXiv preprint arXiv:1309.4168*.

Tomas Mikolov, Ilya Sutskever, Kai Chen, Greg S Corrado, and Jeff Dean. 2013b. Distributed representations of words and phrases and their compositionality. In *Advances in neural information processing systems*, pages 3111–3119.

Srivastava Nitish, Geoffrey Hinton, Alex Krizhevsky, Ilya Sutskever, and Ruslan Salakhutdinov. 2014. Dropout: A simple way to prevent neural networks from overfitting. *The Journal of Machine Learning Research*, 15(1):1929–1958.

Jeffrey Pennington, Richard Socher, and Christopher D Manning. 2014. Glove: Global vectors for word representation. In *EMNLP*, volume 14, pages 1532–1543.

Alec Radford, Luke Metz, and Soumith Chintala. 2015. Unsupervised representation learning with deep convolutional generative adversarial networks. *arXiv preprint arXiv:1511.06434*.

T. Salimans, I. Goodfellow, W. Zaremba, V. Cheung, A. Radford, and X. Chen. 2016. Improved Techniques for Training GANs. *ArXiv e-prints*, June.

Rico Sennrich, Barry Haddow, and Alexandra Birch. 2015. Improving neural machine translation models with monolingual data. *arXiv preprint arXiv:1511.06709*.

Richard Socher, John Bauer, Christopher D Manning, and Andrew Y Ng. 2013. Parsing with compositional vector grammars. In *ACL (1)*, pages 455–465.

Theano Development Team. 2016. Theano: A Python framework for fast computation of mathematical expressions. *arXiv e-prints*, abs/1605.02688, May.

Lucas Theis, Aäron van den Oord, and Matthias Bethge. 2015. A note on the evaluation of generative models. *arXiv preprint arXiv:1511.01844*.

Joseph Turian, Lev Ratinov, and Yoshua Bengio. 2010. Word representations: a simple and general method for semi-supervised learning. In *Proceedings of the 48th annual meeting of the association for computational linguistics*, pages 384–394. Association for Computational Linguistics.

Decomposing Bilexical Dependencies into Semantic and Syntactic Vectors

Jeff Mitchell

mitchelljeff@hotmail.com

Abstract

Bilexical dependencies have been commonly used to help identify the most likely parses of a sentence. The probability of a word occurring as the dependent of a given head within a particular structure provides a measure of semantic plausibility that complements the purely syntactic part of the parsing model.

Here, we attempt to use the distributional information within these bilexical dependencies to construct representations that decompose into semantic and syntactic components. In particular, we compare two different approaches to composing vectors to explore how syntactic and semantic representations should interact within such a model.

Our results suggest a tensor product approach has advantages, which we believe could be exploited in making more effective use of the information captured in these bilexical dependencies.

1 Introduction

Using points within the geometry of a vector space to represent the way words are distributed across contexts has proven to be a fruitful tactic for many language processing tasks. For example, Landauer and Dumais (1997) projected raw tf-idf scores of occurrence across a set of documents down into lower dimensional vectors using a technique called singular value decomposition. The resulting semantic representations were then applied to semantic dismbiguation and to predict synonyms in a TOEFL test. Working instead with the linear structure of raw text, Collobert et al. (2011) trained a neural language model to induce word vectors in

the hidden layer of their network. These versatile representations were then applied to a wide range of tasks including part-of-speech tagging, chunking, named entity recognition, and semantic role labeling.

Two key elements within any such approach to constructing representations are the contexts across which the distribution of a word is tracked and how vectors are constructed from these occurrences. Here, we investigate the construction of distributional representations from bilexical dependencies found in a parser and explore how such vectors can be decomposed into semantic and syntactic components.

Although, distributional approaches have commonly become most strongly associated with semantic representations and tasks, they have also seen applications to syntax. In fact, distributional analysis was first applied by linguists to syntactic categories rather than the representation of meaning and Ross (1972) presented a continuous, or at least graded, conception of syntax long before the recent surge of interest in vectorial approaches to semantics.

Practical applications of these distributional techniques to syntactic problems have included work on the induction (Brown et al., 1992) or learning (Mintz, 2003) of categories and the computational problems of tagging (Tsuboi, 2014) and parsing (Socher et al., 2013). The latter problem of parsing brings to the foreground the question of how syntactic and semantic representations relate to and interact with each other, as the optimal parse must maximise both syntactic and semantic plausibility, in an integrated structure.

An unmodified PCFG, modelling just the dependencies between syntactic categories, is generally inadequate to derive robust parses, and lexicalisation is commonly used to enhance such models. In particular, bilexical dependencies introduce

Proceedings of the 1st Workshop on Representation Learning for NLP, pages 127–136,
Berlin, Germany, August 11th, 2016. ©2016 Association for Computational Linguistics

a measure of the plausibility of combining specific heads and dependents within the possible syntactic structures.

These dependencies contain much the same information used by Lin (1998) and Padó and Lapata (2007) to construct semantic representations, and we can easily see that the plausibility of *cake* as an object of *bake*, *eat* and *regret* tells us something about the semantic properties of *cake*. Nonetheless, these dependencies contain substantial quantities of syntactic information, too. The dependencies observed for *cake* and *eat*, for example, are substantially different because the former is a noun while the latter is a verb.

However, the sparsity of the resulting counts can mean these dependencies may contribute little to parser performance, particulaly on out of domain data. One solution, proposed by Rei and Briscoe (2013), is to smooth the bilexical dependencies using a similarity measure. For example, if counts for *publication* as an object of *read* are lacking we might instead leverage the similarity of *publication* to *book* to use the counts for *book* as an object of *read* to make a reasonable inference about the unseen dependency. Alternatively, we might try to use some form of dimensionality reduction to smooth out the sparsity.

Levy and Goldberg (2014) use a modified version of word2vec (Mikolov et al., 2013) to induce 300 dimensional representations from word distributions across 900,000 dependency contexts. They find that these word vectors capture a form of functional similarity, with the closest words in the space typically being cohyponyms within the same syntactic class. This syntactic specificity is not particularly surprising, as we would expect the strongest effects within these dependencies to relate to the syntactic class of a word - e.g. only a noun can be the subject of a verb - with semantic factors having a weaker influence merely on word choice within the correct syntactic class.

In this paper, we will consider a couple of approaches that attempt to separate out semantic and syntactic components of the dependencies, boosting performance on both types of task. One popular method of boosting semantic performance has been to ignore or average over syntactic structure. By treating the context a target occurs in as a bag-of-words (Landauer and Dumais, 1997; Blei et al., 2003; Mikolov et al., 2013), syntactic information is washed out and semantic information

is retained. Conversely, distributional approaches to syntactic tasks typically make use of the sequential structure contained in bigrams (Brown et al., 1992; Clark, 2003) or longer n-grams (Mintz, 2003; Redington et al., 1998).

Recent work, (Mitchell, 2013; Mitchell and Steedman, 2015), has attempted to use both types of information in a single model that decomposes representations into syntactic and semantic components. An open question, however, is the most effective way of forming these combined representations. Mitchell and Steedman (2015) explicitly employ a direct sum - i.e. concatenation - of semantic and syntactic vectors. On the other hand, the multiplicative combination used by Mitchell (2013) is much closer to a tensor product formulation.

Griffiths et al. (2005) also pursue the representation of semantics and syntax in a single distributional model. They integrate a topic model and HMM to produce a model of the sequential structure of raw text in which each word is either semantic - chosen by the topic model to fit the long range semantic context - or syntactic - chosen to fit the short range dependencies of the HMM. This either/or assumption is rejected by Boyd-graber and Blei (2009) who moreover work with parsed sentences, rather than raw text. In this model, each word is chosen based on a product of a document topic distribution and a set of syntactic transition probabilities, determined top-down within the parse tree. Socher et al. (2010) are also concerned with inducing distributional representations within the stucture of parse trees. Their neural network model composes vectors recursively from the bottom up to represent possible phrases and from those representations computes how likely each is to be a valid constituent.

Although, parsing may seem, initially, to be the ideal task in which to explore the relationship between semantic and syntactic representations, the complexity of a working system - which Bikel (2004a) describes as *an intractable behemoth* - makes it difficult to isolate and investigate just this question on its own. Parser performance depends on a multitiude of interacting components, and could only obliquely produce insights into the merit of the approaches to representation we want to consider here.

Instead, we follow the advice of Bikel (2004b) to *treat the model as data*, and make direct evaluations of distributional representations induced from the parameters of a wide coverage model. We focus in on just the bilexical dependencies within the BLLIP parser (Charniak and Johnson, 2005; McClosky et al., 2006) and explore models of these parameters in which the representation for each word decomposes into a semantic and a syntactic vector. We evaluate both a direct sum and a tensor product approach to this decomposition of the representation space and find that the latter has advantages.

In the next section, we describe the BLLIP parser and the data we extract from the wide coverage model of McClosky et al. (2006). Then in Sections 3 and 4 we describe the models applied to this data and their evaluation. Finally, we present our results and conclusions in Sections 5 and 6.

2 BLLIP Parser

The BLLIP parser (Charniak and Johnson, 2005) uses a two stage approach, based on discriminative reranking applied to candidate parses produced by a generative lexicalised PCFG. That first stage of the model takes inspiration from loglinear models to express the overall parse probability in terms of a product of multiplicative factors.

Here we are specifically interested in the bilexical dependencies, which are stored in the model as a probability, $p(d|h, t)$, of a dependent, d, given a head, h within some tree structure, t, along with a count for the occurence of that head-tree combination. The tree structure, t, is only specified in terms of the tags on the head and dependent leaves, the node from which they branch, and the category of the dependent branch below that point. Thus, many distinct trees are collapsed into a single class. For example, the model fails to distinguish between subjects and objects of a verb.

McClosky et al. (2006) expanded the domain of the standard Penn Treebank (Marcus et al., 1993) trained BLLIP model, applying self-training to 2.5M sentences from the NANC corpus (Graff, 1995). The resulting model has a large vocabulary, with reliable estimates of probabilities for many words, which provides a useful basis for our investigations.

We extract the bilexical dependencies and head-tree counts from the model file, replacing words that occur less than 5 times with an $\langle UNK \rangle$ tag, and also excluding any word that does not occur in both the head and dependent positions. The head-

tree contexts are similarly filtered, with items that occur less then 5 times replaced with a dummy catch-all context.

3 Models

The models we discuss here derive a probability of a dependent word, d, within the context of a tree, t, with a head, h, in terms of latent variables, e.g. i, j, k. So, the simplest model we will consider has the form:

$$p(d|h, t) = \sum_i p(d|i)p(i|h, t) \qquad (1)$$

It will be useful, notationally and conceptually, to think of these models in terms of vectors. The equation above already has a superficial similarity to a dot product, being a sum over a series of products.

We can rewrite this:

$$p(d|h, t) = p(d) \sum_i p(i) \frac{p(i|d)}{p(i)} \frac{p(i|h, t)}{p(i)} \qquad (2)$$

We will think of $\frac{p(i|x)}{p(i)}$ as being the components, v_i^x, of a vector, $\mathbf{v}^x$, representing x and define an inner product in terms of a weighted [1] sum of component products as follows:

$$\mathbf{u} \cdot \mathbf{v} = \sum_i \lambda_i u_i v_i \qquad (3)$$

Taking $\lambda_i = p(i)$, we can rewrite Eq. 2 as follows:

$$p(d|h, t) = p(d)\mathbf{v}^d \cdot \mathbf{v}^{ht} \qquad (4)$$

More generally, this model form will need to include normalisation:

$$p(d|h, t) = \frac{p(d)\mathbf{v}^d \cdot \mathbf{v}^{ht}}{N(h, t)} \qquad (5)$$

One of the benefits of this model form is that the normalising constant for each head-tree can be calculated fairly efficiently in terms of a single inner product.

$$N(h, t) = \mathbf{n} \cdot \mathbf{v}^{ht} \qquad (6)$$

Here, $\mathbf{n}$ is a sum over all dependent probabilities and vectors.

---

[1] The use of such a weighting implies we are working with unnormalised basis vectors.

$$\mathbf{n} = \sum_d p(d)\mathbf{v}^d \qquad (7)$$

Given this model form, we must then specify how the vectors $\mathbf{v}$ are constructed. In particular, if our representations are based on semantic vectors, $\mathbf{a}$, and syntactic vectors, $\mathbf{b}$, then we must decide how these are to be combined. One obvious choice is between a direct sum (Eq. 8) and a tensor product (Eq. 9).

$$\bar{\mathbf{v}} = \bar{\mathbf{a}} \oplus \bar{\mathbf{b}} \qquad (8)$$

$$\tilde{\mathbf{v}} = \tilde{\mathbf{a}} \otimes \tilde{\mathbf{b}} \qquad (9)$$

Although both these constructions consist of a combination of vectors, $\mathbf{a}$ and $\mathbf{b}$, the actual vectors induced during EM training will inevitably turn out to be substantially different for each approach. In fact, our purpose is precisely to investigate how this choice of combination affects the representations induced in our trained models. We therefore notationally distinguish the two approaches: using a bar, $\bar{\mathbf{v}}$, to indicate direct sum vectors and a tilde, $\tilde{\mathbf{v}}$, for tensor product vectors. However, we will also employ bare symbols without bar or tilde when discussing general properties across both types of structure.

So, if $\mathbf{a}$ and $\mathbf{b}$ are m and n dimensional vectors respectively, then Eq. 8 corresponds to forming the $n + m$ dimensional concatenation of those vectors, while Eq. 9 results in the $n \times m$ dimensional vector of all products of their components. From a probabilistic perspective, a reasonable interpretation would be that our models using the direct sum representations in Eq. 8 assume that the dependencies between head and dependent are either syntactic or semantic, whereas tensor product models, Eq. 9, assume that each word has both semantic and syntactic characteristics.

Given some method for combining vectors $\mathbf{a}$ and $\mathbf{b}$, we also need to specify the form of their components. In particular, we are interested here in separating semantic and syntactic dependencies.

Mitchell (2013) and Mitchell and Steedman (2015) both exploit word order to decompose representations into semantic and syntactic components, with semantic dependencies being modelled in terms of a similarity measure that is independent of word order, while the syntactic part of the model captures sequential information. However,

the bilexical dependencies we are working with here do not explicitly relate to surface word order. Nonetheless, the relationship is still directed, distinguishing a head and a dependent, and we can exploit this directedness to define a symmetric semantic component and an asymmetric syntactic component.

In each of the models below, any word has a single semantic vector, $\mathbf{a}$, whether it occurs in head or dependent position, with components a_j given by:

$$a_j = \frac{p(j|w)}{p(j)} \qquad (10)$$

Ignoring the syntactic component of the model for a moment, we can define a semantics only model (leaving out the normalising constant for brevity):

$$p(d|h,t) \propto p(d) \sum_j p(j)\frac{p(j|w^d)}{p(j)}\frac{p(j|w^h)}{p(j)}$$
$$= p(d)\mathbf{a}^d \cdot \mathbf{a}^h \quad (11)$$

This employs an inner product defined by $\mathbf{a}^d \cdot \mathbf{a}^h = \sum_j \lambda_j a_j^d a_j^h$ with $\lambda_j = p(j)$. However, this semantic only model ignores the tree t the words occur in and gives words the same representations whether they occur in head or dependent position. It is therefore symmetric in relation to these roles, and we can think of this model as capturing what head and dependent have in common.

In contrast, there are two forms of syntactic vectors, $\mathbf{b}^d$ and $\mathbf{b}^{ht}$, distinguishing between dependents and the head-tree contexts they occur in, with components given by:

$$b_k^{ht} = \frac{p(k|h,t)}{p(k)} \qquad (12)$$

$$b_k^d = \frac{p(k|d)}{p(k)} \qquad (13)$$

Again we can ignore the other part of the model and consider this part on its own:

$$p(d|h,t) \propto p(d) \sum_k p(k)\frac{p(k|d)}{p(k)}\frac{p(k|h,t)}{p(k)}$$
$$= p(d)\mathbf{b}^d \cdot \mathbf{b}^{ht} \quad (14)$$

This is exactly equivalent to the simple model Eq. 4 above.

Taking the direct sum approach first (Eq. 8), we concatenate the semantic vectors, $\bar{\mathbf{a}}$, and syntactic vectors, $\bar{\mathbf{b}}$, to form a combined vector, $\bar{\mathbf{v}}$, with indices ranging over both j and k.

$$\bar{v}_i = \begin{cases} \bar{a}_j & \text{if } i = j; \\ \bar{b}_k & \text{if } i = k. \end{cases} \tag{15}$$

Inner products of such vectors will consist of a sum over the j component products followed by a sum over the k component products, with some appropriate weighting. The simplest model having this structure is an interpolation of the two models above (Eq. 11 and Eq. 14) with proportions q_a and q_b.

$$p(d|ht) \propto q_a p(d)\bar{\mathbf{a}}^d \cdot \bar{\mathbf{a}}^h + q_b p(d)\bar{\mathbf{b}}^d \cdot \bar{\mathbf{d}}^{ht} \tag{16}$$

In terms of the model form of Eq. 5, this is equivalent to defining an inner product on the direct sum vectors, $\bar{\mathbf{v}}^d \cdot \bar{\mathbf{v}}^{ht}$, with weightings λ of $q_a p(j)$ and $q_b p(k)$ for the two sets of components respectively.

$$\bar{\mathbf{v}}^d \cdot \bar{\mathbf{v}}^{ht} = \begin{array}{c} q_a \sum_j p(j)\dfrac{p(j|w^d)}{p(j)}\dfrac{p(j|w^h)}{p(j)} \\ + \\ q_b \sum_k p(k)\dfrac{p(k|d)}{p(k)}\dfrac{p(k|h,t)}{p(k)} \end{array} \tag{17}$$

For the tensor product model (Eq. 9), the indices of the combined vector, $\tilde{\mathbf{v}}$, range over all combinations of j and k.

$$\tilde{v}_{jk} = \tilde{a}_j \tilde{b}_k \tag{18}$$

The components of $\tilde{\mathbf{v}}^{ht}$ are then given by products of terms, which suggests conditional independence of j and k on ht.

$$\tilde{v}_{jk} = \frac{p(k|h,t)}{p(k)}\frac{p(j|h)}{p(j)} = \frac{p(j,k|h,t)}{p(j)p(k)} \tag{19}$$

Making a similar assumption of conditional independence in relation to $\tilde{\mathbf{v}}^d$ is enough to derive a model for $p(d|h,t)$.

$$p(d|h,t) = \sum_{jk} p(d|j,k)p(j,k|h,t)$$

$$\propto p(d)\sum_{jk}\frac{p(j|d)p(k|d)}{p(j,k)}p(j|h)p(k|h,t) \tag{20}$$

This can be put into the form of Eq. 5 by defining the inner product $\tilde{\mathbf{v}}^d \cdot \tilde{\mathbf{v}}^{ht}$ as follows:

$$\tilde{\mathbf{v}}^d \cdot \tilde{\mathbf{v}}^{ht} = \sum_{j,k} \lambda_{jk}\tilde{a}_j^d\tilde{b}_k^d \times \tilde{a}_j^h\tilde{b}_k^{ht} =$$

$$\sum_{j,k} \frac{p(j)^2 p(k)^2}{p(j,k)} \left(\begin{array}{c} \dfrac{p(j|w^d)}{p(j)}\dfrac{p(k|d)}{p(k)} \\ \times \\ \dfrac{p(j|w^h)}{p(j)}\dfrac{p(k|h,t)}{p(k)} \end{array} \right) \tag{21}$$

Here, the weighting $\lambda_{jk} = \frac{p(j)^2 p(k)^2}{p(j,k)}$ is based on the assumption that j and k are both conditionally independent of d and ht.

As described above, the tensor product of a pair of vectors (Eq. 9) of dimension m and n produces a vector of dimension $n \times m$. However, these vectors only form a subset of the full $n \times m$ dimensional space. Moreover, the form of the model in both the direct sum and tensor product cases assumes that the semantic relation of head and dependent is independent of the syntactic relation. That is, we employ the same semantic vectors to represent head and dependent irrespective of the tree they occur in. We could begin to address both these issues by considering representations that lie in the full $n \times m$ dimensional tensor product space. This would essentially allow us to represent the dependence of semantic content on syntactic context. However, for now we restrict ourselves to the models described above.

We calculate the cross-entropy between the model and the BLLIP bilexical dependencies for each head-tree context and our objective function is then an average of these values, weighted by the occurence of that context. Training maximises this measure over 200 iterations of the EM algorithm.

4 Evaluation

We evaluate our models in a number of ways. We assess the quality of the word representations in terms of two similarity tasks on the semantic vectors, $\mathbf{a}$, and a POS induction task on the syntactic vectors, $\mathbf{b}$. In addition, both these tasks are applied to the raw data and to the vectors induced by the undecomposed models, Eq. 2 and Eq. 11. We also investigate the ability of our models to differentiate semantically and syntactically implausible adjective-noun constructions. Finally, we list a sample of nearest neighbours to allow a qualitative insight into the best performing model.

Our semantic similarity tasks are based on the ratings in two datasets, on both of which we evaluate our models using Spearman correlation. The first is the WordSim353 dataset (Finkelstein et al., 2002) containing ratings from 16 participants between pairs of nouns. The second dataset contains similarity ratings for noun-verb pairs (Mitchell, 2013). The former measures the ability of the model to capture semantic similarity within a POS class, while the latter tells about its representation of similarity across classes. This cross-class measure is useful in determining how effective the model has been in separating semantic from syntactic information. A model that bundles both into a single representation may identify the similarity in *disappear-vanish* but will typically fail to make the same judgement about *disappearance-vanish*. Making that judgement requires ignoring the syntactic difference between nouns and verbs, which we achieve in our models by representing that information separately.

Our syntactic task is POS induction. We cluster the vocabulary into 45 classes using k-means, and evaluate in terms of the many-to-one measure using the PTB POS classes as a gold standard. Although POS class information is already present in the bilexical dependency data, we use this task as a means of determining the quality of syntactic information contained in the vectors, rather than as an example of a practical application.

We then examine how our models differentiate semantic and syntactic plausibility. Our semantic plausibility dataset is constructed by combining a set of food nouns (e.g. *milk*, *meat*, *bread*, etc.) with either food appropriate adjectives (e.g. *hot*, *bitter*, *sweet*, etc.) or implausible political adjectives (e.g. *bipartisan*, *legislative*, *constitutional*, etc.). To create an equivalent syntactic plausibility dataset we combine common singular and plural nouns (e.g. *year - years*, *player - players*, etc.) with the modifier *several*. In each case, we calculate a semantic plausibility ($\mathbf{a}^d \cdot \mathbf{a}^h = \sum p(j)a_j^d a_j^h$) and a syntactic plausibility ($\mathbf{b}^d \cdot \mathbf{b}^{ht} = \sum p(k)b_k^d b_k^{ht}$) for the resulting adjective-noun phrase. Comparing the distribution of these measures in the high and low plausibility cases allows us to investigate further the extent to which the model separates semantic and syntactic dependencies.

Finally, we evaluate the best performing model - based on a tensor product of vectors - qualitatively by examining the closest neighbours of set of nouns, adjectives and verbs.

5 Results

Table 1 gives the correlations and many-to-one measures for the raw data, the simple undecomposed model (Eq. 2), the symmetric undecomposed model (Eq. 11), the direct sum model (Eq. 8) and the tensor product model (Eq. 9). Looking at the first two rows of the table, to compare the raw data to the simple model, we can see that the latter outpeforms the fomer on the POS clustering task, but is worse on the semantic similarity tasks. The improvement in performance on the clustering task can probably be put down to the excessive dimensionality (= number of head-tree contexts) of the input space in the case of the raw data. Reduction of this space using a latent variable model appears to make the clustering more effective. On the other hand, achieving this dimensionality reduction requires preserving the strongest, typically syntactic, dependencies and discarding weaker, frequently semantic, dependencies with the result that performance on semantic similarity tasks degrades. The predicted noun-verb similarities for both approaches is only weakly correlated with the human ratings, which we ascribe to the fact that neither model has a mechanism for finding the commonalities between words found in distinct sets of syntactic contexts.

The undecomposed symmetric model, $\mathbf{a}$, produces a better performance on the semantic tasks, but is worse on the syntactic task. This is not surprising, as the form of this model ignores the difference between heads and dependents, essentially treating the dependencies as a bag-of-words.

Both the direct sum and tensor product models also contain a similarity based component. However, only the tensor product model achieves an improvement in performance over the undecomposed models. In fact, this model outperforms the other models on all three measures, including achieving a reasonable level of correlation on the noun-verb dataset. This difference between the two decomposed models can be related to the fact that the form of the tensor product assumes that a dependent should be semantically *and* syntactically appropriate to its head-tree context, while the direct sum model uses an *or* condition between the two parts of the model.

Figures 1 and 2 present the results of exper-

Model	NV	WS353	MTO
raw	0.15	0.37	0.39
$\mathbf{v}$	-0.06	0.22	0.73
$\mathbf{a}$	0.24	0.42	0.42
$\bar{\mathbf{a}} \oplus \bar{\mathbf{b}}$	0.03	0.17	0.61
$\tilde{\mathbf{a}} \otimes \tilde{\mathbf{b}}$	0.38	0.49	0.74

Table 1: Correlations of model cosines with human similarity ratings on the noun-verb (NV) and WordSim353 (WS353) datasets, alongside many-to-one (MTO) measures of cluster quality on the POS clustering task, for the raw data (raw), the simple undecomposed model ($\mathbf{v}$), the symmetric undecomposed model ($\mathbf{a}$), the direct sum model ($\bar{\mathbf{a}} \oplus \bar{\mathbf{b}}$) and the tensor product model ($\tilde{\mathbf{a}} \otimes \tilde{\mathbf{b}}$).

iments on how these representations predict the plausibility of various adjective-noun phrases. In particular, these boxplots give an insight into the ability of these models to differentiate semantically from syntactically implausible constructions. Each plot contrasts the distribution of a logarithm of a dot product for high and low plausibility items. This dot product is either taken of semantic vectors, $\mathbf{a}$, or syntactic vectors, $\mathbf{b}$, providing a measure of, respectively, semantic and syntactic plausibility as predicted by the model. The results for each model are organised into a 2×2 array of plots, with the left hand column relating to the syntactic task and the right hand column to the semantic task.

Examining the results for the tensor product model in Figure 1 first, we find that of the syntactic plots, 1a and 1c, the contrast between high and low plausibility items is greatest for the $\ln(\tilde{\mathbf{b}} \cdot \tilde{\mathbf{b}})$ measure. This indicates that these vectors have captured more of the syntactic information necessary to identify phrases such as *several year* as implausible. In contrast, the semantic plots, 1b and 1d, show the reverse pattern. There, it is the $\ln(\tilde{\mathbf{a}} \cdot \tilde{\mathbf{a}})$ measure which shows the largest contrast between high and low plausibility items. Thus, the difference in plausibility between *hot bread* and *bipartisan bread* is more effectively captured in the $\tilde{\mathbf{a}}$ vectors.

Turning to the results for the direct sum model in Figure 2, this differentiation between semantic and syntactic plausibility is no longer as clear, and the largest contrast between high and low plausibility items is always found in the $\ln(\bar{\mathbf{b}} \cdot \bar{\mathbf{b}})$ measure. Specifically, in the plots for the semantic

Word	$\tilde{\mathbf{a}} \otimes \tilde{\mathbf{b}}$	$\tilde{\mathbf{a}}$	$\tilde{\mathbf{b}}$
black	khaki	hispanic	female
	baggy	latino	decrepit
	cashmere	midterm	handmade
	plaid	D.C.	antique
	lace	Merle	year-old
political	tribal	cultural	biomedical
	tax-and-spend	favoritism	mechanical
	populist	sect	sole
	cultural	dissidents	mystical
	staunch	enlightenment	forensic
found	discovered	evidence	unveiled
	examined	takers	snared
	pleaded	fossils	rejected
	revealed	researchers	knocked
	flagged	conclusive	backfired
help	blame	strain	permit
	reprimand	psychological	resolve
	inflict	blisters	nudge
	relieve	suffering	laugh
	prevent	suffers	jump-start
company	firm	manufacturer	think-tank
	insurer	maker	nobody
	unit	pharmacuetical	everybody
	corporation	conglomerate	everyone
	consortium	subsidiary	foreman
game	opener	missed	speech
	finale	preseason	rotation
	rout	opener	shootout
	rematch	games	balloting
	tournament	NFC	opener

Table 2: Nearest neighbours within the full tensor product space ($\tilde{\mathbf{a}} \otimes \tilde{\mathbf{b}}$) and its semantic ($\tilde{\mathbf{a}}$) and syntactic ($\tilde{\mathbf{b}}$) components for a sample of adjectives, verbs and nouns.

task, 2b and 2d, the $\ln(\bar{\mathbf{a}} \cdot \bar{\mathbf{a}})$ measure does not produce a convincingly smaller prediction for the low plausibility items. In other words, the $\bar{\mathbf{a}}$ vectors do not contain the semantic information needed to identify the implausibility of phrases such as *bipartisan bread* or *constitutional milk*.

Thus, the tensor product space appears to be most effective in separating semantic and syntactic information and its structure can be understood more concretely in terms of the sample of nearest neighbours shown in Table 2. Taking the adjective *black* as an example, the first column, $\tilde{\mathbf{a}} \otimes \tilde{\mathbf{b}}$, lists its nearest neighbours within the full tensor prod-

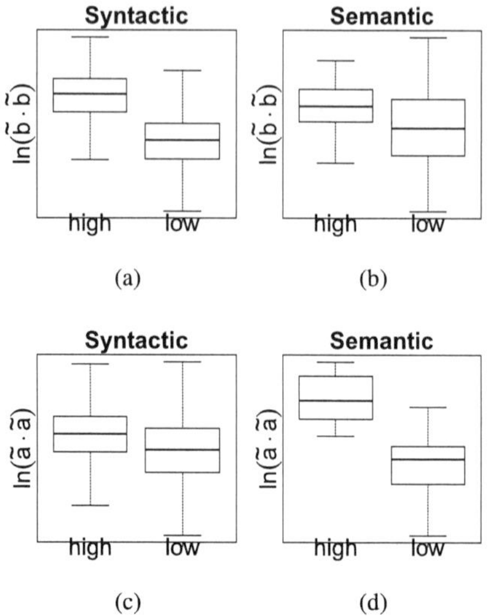

Figure 1: Boxplots of plausibility factors for tensor product representations on syntactic and semantic tasks.

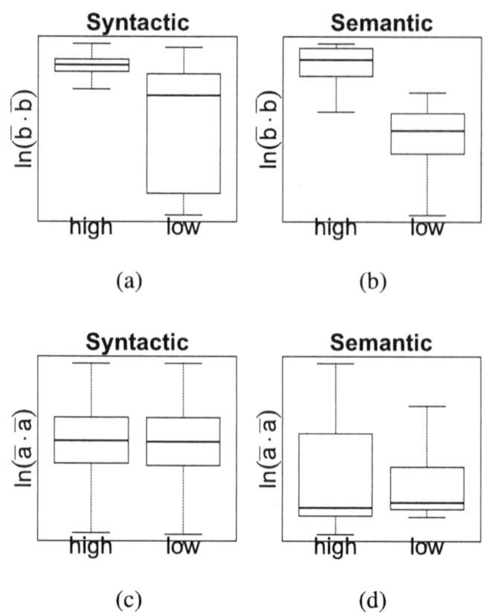

Figure 2: Boxplots of plausibility factors for direct sum representations on syntactic and semantic tasks.

uct space, which appear to be other descriptors of material appearance or structure. In contrast, the neighbours within the semantic space, $\tilde{a}$, listed in the second column, seem to be words with cultural or political associations to *black*, while the syntactic neighbours in the third column, $\tilde{b}$, are other adjectives drawn from a much wider domain.

6   Conclusions

We have shown that the bilexical dependencies within a parser capture useful semantic information, and also that it is possible to, at least partially, begin to separate out this semantic information from the syntactic information. Our experiments with vectors based on ratios of probabilities suggest that a tensor product approach to decomposing the space of representations has advantages over a direct sum approach. While the latter is conceptually simpler, being just a concatenation of the two vectors, the resulting model corresponds to an assumption that semantic and syntactic dependencies are disjoint, i.e. that the relationship between head and dependent is *either* semantic *or* syntactic. In contrast, the tensor product approach leads to a model in which a dependent must be syntactically *and* semantically appropriate to the context of tree and head word, and this seems to be more effective in practice.

These conclusions apply only to the ratio of probabilities type vectors that were investigated here. Log-linear vectors, as produced by neural network models, are likely to show substantially different behaviours. In fact, Mitchell and Steedman (2015) have shown that a direct sum approach can be effective for this type of model. Future work should investigate tensor product models in this setting.

Furthermore, there are theoretical reasons to pursue the tensor product approach further. While the models considered here are based on combining separate, independent semantic and syntactic vectors, the tensor product approach also allows us to consider the interaction of the two components. The direct sum approach, on the other hand, is less expressive.

In addition, implementation of parsers based on these representations may also be a fertile direction for future work. Our results suggest the techniques we investigated are effective in constructing semantic representations. We would also like to know whether capturing that semantic information effectively has benefits in modelling the overall probability of the whole dependency. However, our initial investigations suggest the syntactic part of the dependency needs a more sophisticated approach.

References

Daniel Bikel. 2004a. A distributional analysis of a lexicalized statistical parsing mode. In *Proceedings of the 2004 Conference on Empirical Methods in Natural Language Processing*, pages 182–189.

Daniel M. Bikel. 2004b. *On the parameter space of generative lexicalized statistical parsing models.* Ph.D. thesis, University of Pennsylvania, Philadelphia, PA, USA.

David M. Blei, Andrew Y. Ng, and Michael I. Jordan. 2003. Latent dirichlet allocation. *Journal of Machine Learning Research*, 3:993–1022, March.

Jordan L. Boyd-graber and David M. Blei. 2009. Syntactic topic models. In D. Koller, D. Schuurmans, Y. Bengio, and L. Bottou, editors, *Advances in Neural Information Processing Systems 21*, pages 185–192. Curran Associates, Inc.

Peter F. Brown, Peter V. deSouza, Robert L. Mercer, Vincent J. Della Pietra, and Jenifer C. Lai. 1992. Class-based n-gram models of natural language. *Comput. Linguist.*, 18(4):467–479, December.

Eugene Charniak and Mark Johnson. 2005. Coarse-to-fine n-best parsing and maxent discriminative reranking. In *Proceedings of the 43rd Annual Meeting on Association for Computational Linguistics*, ACL '05, pages 173–180, Ann Arbor, Michigan. Association for Computational Linguistics.

Alexander Clark. 2003. Combining distributional and morphological information for part of speech induction. In *Proceedings of the tenth Annual Meeting of the European Association for Computational Linguistics (EACL)*, pages 59–66.

Ronan Collobert, Jason Weston, Léon Bottou, Michael Karlen, Koray Kavukcuoglu, and Pavel Kuksa. 2011. Natural language processing (almost) from scratch. *J. Mach. Learn. Res.*, 12:2493–2537, November.

Lev Finkelstein, Evgeniy Gabrilovich, Yossi Matias, Ehud Rivlin, Zach Solan, Gadi Wolfman, and Eytan Ruppin. 2002. Placing search in context: The concept revisited. *ACM Trans. Inf. Syst.*, 20(1):116–131, January.

David Graff. 1995. North american news text corpus. LDC95T21.

Thomas L. Griffiths, Mark Steyvers, David M. Blei, and Joshua B. Tenenbaum. 2005. Integrating topics and syntax. In *In Advances in Neural Information Processing Systems 17*, pages 537–544. MIT Press.

Thomas K Landauer and Susan T. Dumais. 1997. A solution to platos problem: The latent semantic analysis theory of acquisition, induction, and representation of knowledge. *Psychological Review*, 104(2):211–240.

Omer Levy and Yoav Goldberg. 2014. Dependency-based word embeddings. In *Proceedings of the 52nd Annual Meeting of the Association for Computational Linguistics, ACL, Volume 2: Short Papers*, pages 302–308, Baltimore, MD, USA.

Dekang Lin. 1998. An information-theoretic definition of similarity. In *Proceedings of the Fifteenth International Conference on Machine Learning*, ICML '98, pages 296–304, San Francisco, CA, USA. Morgan Kaufmann Publishers Inc.

Mitchell P. Marcus, Mary Ann Marcinkiewicz, and Beatrice Santorini. 1993. Building a large annotated corpus of english: The penn treebank. *Comput. Linguist.*, 19(2):313–330, June.

David McClosky, Eugene Charniak, and Mark Johnson. 2006. Effective self-training for parsing. In *Proceedings of the Main Conference on Human Language Technology Conference of the North American Chapter of the Association of Computational Linguistics*, HLT-NAACL '06, pages 152–159, New York, New York. Association for Computational Linguistics.

Tomas Mikolov, Wen-tau Yih, and Geoffrey Zweig. 2013. Linguistic regularities in continuous space word representations. In *Proceedings of the 2013 Conference of the North American Chapter of the Association for Computational Linguistics: Human Language Technologies*, pages 746–751, Atlanta, Georgia, June. Association for Computational Linguistics.

Toben H. Mintz. 2003. Frequent frames as a cue for grammatical categories in child directed speech. *Cognition.*, 90(1):91–117.

Jeff Mitchell and Mark Steedman. 2015. Orthogonality of syntax and semantics within distributional spaces. In *Proceedings of the 53rd Annual Meeting of the Association for Computational Linguistics and the 7th International Joint Conference on Natural Language Processing (Volume 1: Long Papers)*, pages 1301–1310, Beijing, China, July. Association for Computational Linguistics.

Jeff Mitchell. 2013. Learning semantic representations in a bigram language model. In *Proceedings of the 10th International Conference on Computational Semantics (IWCS 2013) – Short Papers*, pages 362–368, Potsdam, Germany, March. Association for Computational Linguistics.

Sebastian Padó and Mirella Lapata. 2007. Dependency-based construction of semantic space models. *Comput. Linguist.*, 33(2):161–199, June.

Martin Redington, Nick Chater, and Steven Finch. 1998. Distributional information: A powerful cue for acquiring syntactic categories. *Cognitive Science*, 22(4):425–469.

Marek Rei and Ted Briscoe. 2013. Parser lexicalisation through self-learning. In *Proceedings of the 2013 Conference of the North American Chapter of the Association for Computational Linguistics: Human Language Technologies*, pages 391–400, Atlanta, Georgia, June. Association for Computational Linguistics.

John R. Ross. 1972. The category squish: Endstation Hauptwort. In *Papers from the Eighth Regional Meeting*, pages 316–328, Chicago. Chicago Linguistic Society.

Richard Socher, Christopher D. Manning, and Andrew Y. Ng. 2010. Learning Continuous Phrase Representations and Syntactic Parsing with Recursive Neural Networks. In *Proceedings of the Deep Learning and Unsupervised Feature Learning Workshop of NIPS 2010*, pages 1–9.

Richard Socher, John Bauer, Christopher D. Manning, and Ng Andrew Y. 2013. Parsing with compositional vector grammars. In *Proceedings of the 51st Annual Meeting of the Association for Computational Linguistics (Volume 1: Long Papers)*, pages 455–465, Sofia, Bulgaria, August. Association for Computational Linguistics.

Yuta Tsuboi. 2014. Neural networks leverage corpus-wide information for part-of-speech tagging. In *Proceedings of the 2014 Conference on Empirical Methods in Natural Language Processing (EMNLP)*, pages 938–950, Doha, Qatar, October. Association for Computational Linguistics.

Learning Semantic Relatedness in Community Question Answering Using Neural Models

Henry Nassif, Mitra Mohtarami, James Glass
MIT Computer Science and Artificial Intelligence Laboratory
Cambridge, MA 02139, USA
{hnassif, mitram, glass}@mit.edu

Abstract

Community Question Answering forums, such as Quora and Stackoverflow contain millions of questions and answers. Automatically finding the relevant questions from the existing questions and finding the relevant answers to a new question are Natural Language Processing tasks. In this paper, we aim to address these tasks, which we refer to as *similar-Question Retrieval* and *Answer Selection*. We present a neural-based model with stacked bidirectional LSTMs and MLP to address these tasks. The model generates the vector representations of the question-question or question-answer pairs and computes their semantic similarity scores, which are then employed to rank and predict relevancies. Extensive experiments demonstrate our results outperform the baselines.

1 Introduction

Community Question Answering (cQA) websites such as Quora[1] and Stackoverflow[2] are rapidly expanding. Managing such platforms has become increasingly difficult because of the exponential growth in content, triggered by wider access to the internet. Traditionally, websites used to keep track of a list of frequently asked questions (FAQ) that they expect visitors to consult before asking a question. Now, with a wider range of questions being asked, a need has emerged for a better and more scalable system to automatically identify similarities between any two questions on the platform. In addition, with many users contributing to a single question, it has become harder to identify

which answers are more relevant than others. We summarize these two problems as follows:

- *Question Retrieval:* given a new question and a list of questions, we automatically rank the questions in the list according to their relevancy to the new question.

- *Answer Selection:* given a cQA thread containing a question and a list of answers, we automatically rank the answers according to their relevance to the question.

The increase in the number of community-based Q&A platforms has lead to a rapid build up of large archives of user-generated questions and answers. When a new question is asked on the platform, the system searches for questions that are semantically similar in the archives. If a similar question is found, the corresponding correct answer is retrieved and returned immediately to the user as the final answer. The quality of the answer depends on the effectiveness of the question-similarity calculation. However, measuring semantic relatedness between questions and answers is not trivial. Sometimes, similar questions or relevant answers use very different wording. For instance, the two questions "Is downloading movies illegal?" and "Can I share a copy of a DVD online" have an almost identical meaning but are lexically very different. Traditional text-based similarity metrics for measuring sentence distance such as the Jaccard coefficient and the overlap coefficient (Manning and Schütze, 1999), perform poorly. In this paper, we present a neural-based model including stacked Bidirectional Long Short-Term Memory (BLSTM) networks and Multi-Layer Perceptron (MLP) to address the question retrieval and answer selection problems. The model computes the representations of the Q&As and then their semantic simi-

---

[1] https://www.quora.com/
[2] http://stackexchange.com/

137

Proceedings of the 1st Workshop on Representation Learning for NLP, pages 137–147,
Berlin, Germany, August 11th, 2016. ©2016 Association for Computational Linguistics

larity scores. These scores are subsequently employed to rank the list of existing questions and answers with respect to the given question. We evaluate our model on a public benchmark cQA data (Nakov et al., 2016), and show that the results of our model outperform the baselines.

2 Related Work

2.1 Question Retrieval

As explained in Section 1, two questions that are worded very differently can be similar in meaning. Three types of approaches have been developed in the literature to solve this word mismatch problem among similar questions. The first type of approach uses knowledge databases such as dictionaries. For example, Frequently Asked Question (FAQ) Finder (Burke et al., 1997) heuristically combined statistical similarities computed using conventional vector space models with semantic similarities between questions estimated using WordNet (Fellbaum, 1998) to rank FAQs. Song et al. (2007) presented an approach which is a linear combination of statistic similarity, calculated based on word co-occurrence, and semantic similarity, calculated using WordNet and a bipartite mapping. Auto-FAQ (Whitehead, 1995) applied shallow language understanding into automatic FAQ answering, where the matching of a question to FAQs is based on keyword comparison enhanced by limited language processing techniques. However, the quality and structure of current knowledge databases are, based on the results of previous experiments, not good enough for reliable performance.

The second type of approach employed manual rules or templates. These methods are expensive and hard to scale for large size collections. Sneiders (2002) proposed template based FAQ retrieval systems, while Kim and Seo (2006) proposed using user click logs to find similar queries. Lai et al. (2002) proposed an approach to automatically mine FAQs from the web; However, they did not study the use of these FAQs after they were collected. Berger et al. (2000) proposed a statistical lexicon correlation method. These previous approaches were tested with relatively small sized collections and are hard to scale because they are based on specific knowledge databases or handcrafted rules.

The third type of approach uses statistical techniques developed in information retrieval and natural language processing (Berger et al., 2000). Jeon et al. (2005) presented question retrieval methods that are based on using the similarity between answers in the archive to estimate probabilities for a translation-based retrieval model. They run the IBM model 1 (Brown et al., 1993) to learn word translation probabilities on a collection of question pairs. Given a new question, a translation based information retrieval model exploits the word relationships to retrieve similar questions from Q&A archives. They show that with this model it is possible to find semantically similar questions with relatively little word overlap.

2.2 Answer Selection

Passage reordering or reranking has always been an essential step of automatic answer selection (Radlinski and Joachims, 2005; Jeon et al., 2005; Shen and Lapata, 2007; Moschitti et al., 2007; Severyn and Moschitti, 2015a; Moschitti, 2008; Tymoshenko and Moschitti, 2015; Surdeanu et al., 2008). Many methods have been proposed, such as exploring web redundancy information for answer validation (Magnini et al., 2002) and using non-textual features (Jeon et al., 2006).

Recently, many advanced models have been developed for automating answer selection based on syntactic structures (Severyn and Moschitti, 2012; Severyn and Moschitti, 2013; Grundström and Nugues, 2014) and textual entailment. These models include quasi-synchronous grammar to learn syntactic transformations from the question to the candidate answers (Wang et al., 2007); Continuous word and phrase vectors to encode semantic similarity (Belinkov et al., 2015); Tree Edit Distance (TED) to learn tree transformations in pairs (Heilman and Smith, 2010); probabilistic model to learn tree-edit operations on dependency parse trees (Wang and Manning, 2010); and linear chain CRFs with features derived from TED to automatically learn associations between questions and candidate answers (Yao et al., 2013).

In addition to the usual local features that only look at the question-answer pair, automatic answer selection algorithms can rely on global thread-level features, such as the position of the answer in the thread (Hou et al., 2015), or the context of an answer in a thread (Nicosia et al., 2015), or dependencies between thread answers using structured prediction models (Barrón-Cedeno et al., 2015).

Joty et al. (2015) modeled the relations between

pairs of answers at any distance in the thread, which they combine in a graph-cut and in an Integer Linear Programming (ILP) frameworks. They then proposed a fully connected pairwise CRFs (FCCRF) with global normalization and an Ising-like edge potential.

2.3 Neural Networks

Neural based approaches have wide applications including speech recognition (Graves and Jaitly, 2014), language modeling (Mikolov et al., 2010; Mikolov et al., 2011; Sutskever et al., 2011), translation (Liu et al., 2014; Sutskever et al., 2014; Auli et al., 2013), and image captioning (Karpathy and Fei-Fei, 2015). In addition, recent work shows the effectiveness of neural models in answer selection (Severyn and Moschitti, 2015b; Tan et al., 2015; Feng et al., 2015) and question similarity (dos Santos et al., 2015) in community question answering.

Dos Santos et al. (2015) developed CNN and bag-of-words (BOW) representation models for the question similarity task. Cosine similarity between the representations of the input questions were used to compute the CNN and BOW similarity scores for the question-question pairs. The convolutional representations in conjunction with other vectors are then passed to a MLP to compute the similarity score of the question pair. Furthermore, recent research has shown the effectiveness of CNNs for answer ranking of *short* textual contents (Severyn and Moschitti, 2015b).

In this paper, we present a neural model based on stacked bidirectional LSTMs and MLP to capture the long dependencies in longer-length questions and answers.

3 Method

In this paper, we present a neural based model using stacked bidirectional LSTMs and MLP to address the question retrieval and answer selection problems. We first briefly explain recurrent neural networks (RNNs), Long Short-Term Memory (LSTM) networks and their bidirectional networks. Then, we present the stacked bidirectional LSTMs for capturing the semantic similarity of questions and answers in cQA.

Recurrent Neural Networks: A recurrent neural network (RNN) has the form of a chain of repeating modules of neural network. This architecture is pertinent to learning sequences of information because it allows information to persist across states. The output of each loop is utilized as input to the following loop through hidden states that capture information about the preceding sequence.

RNNs are trained using backpropagation through time (BPTT) where the gradient at each output depends on the current and previous time steps. The BPTT approach is not effective at learning long term dependencies because of the exploding gradients problem (Pascanu et al., 2012; Bengio et al., 1994). A certain type of RNN, Long Short Term Memory (LSTM) (Hochreiter and Schmidhuber, 1997) has been designed to improve the learning of long-term dependencies.

Long Short-Term Memory Recurrent Neural Networks: Similar to Recurrent Neural Networks, Long Short-Term Memory Networks (LSTM) (Hochreiter and Schmidhuber, 1997) have a chain like architecture, with a different module structure. Instead of having a single neural network layer, each module has four layers filling different purposes. Each LSTM unit contains a memory cell with self-connections, as well as three multiplicative gates - forget, input, output - to control information flow. Each gate is composed of a sigmoid neural net layer and a pointwise multiplication operation.

Given input vector x_t, previous hidden outputs h_{t-1}, and previous cell state c_{t-1}, the LSTM unit performs the following operations:

$$f_t = \sigma\left(W_f.[h_{t-1}, x_t] + b_f\right)$$
$$i_t = \sigma(W_i.[h_{t-1}, x_t] + b_i)$$
$$c_t = f_t \odot c_{t-1} + i_t \odot \tanh(W_c.[h_{t-1}, x_t] + b_c)$$
$$o_t = \sigma(W_o.[h_{t-1}, x_t] + b_o)$$
$$h_t = o_t \odot \tanh(c_t)$$

where f_t, i_t, o_t and h_t respectively represent the forget gate, input gate, output gate and the hidden layer.

Many variants of LSTMs were later introduced, such as depth gated RNNs (Yao et al., 2015), clockwork RNNS (Koutnik et al., 2014), and Gated Recurrent Unit RNNs (Cho et al., 2014).

Bidirectional Recurrent Neural Networks: Bidirectional RNNs (Schuster and Paliwal, 1997) or BRNN use past and future context sequences to predict or label each element. This is done by combining the outputs of two RNN, one

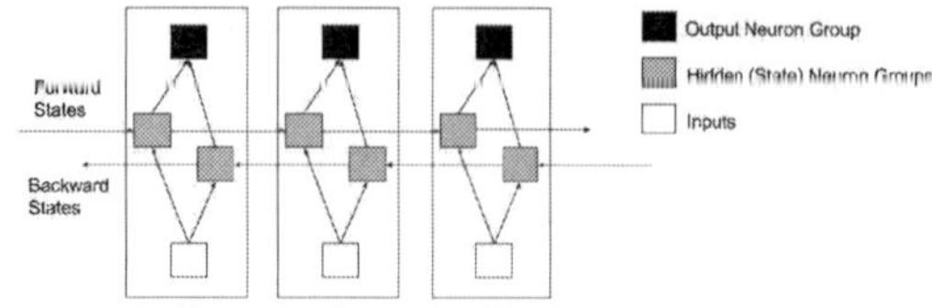

Figure 1: Bidirectional Long Short-Term Recurrent Neural Network. Bidirectional LSTMs are equivalent to two LSTMs independently updating their parameters by processing the input either in forward or backward direction.

processing the sequence forward (or left to right), the other one processing the sequence backwards (from right to left) as shown in Figure 1. This technique proved to be especially useful when combined with LSTM (Graves and Schmidhuber, 2005).

3.1 Stacked Bidirectional LSTMs for cQA

Given a question, we aim to rank a list of questions for question retrieval and a list of answers for answer selection. To address these ranking problems, we propose a neural model to compute the semantic similarities for the question-question (q, q') or question-answer (q, a) pairs. These scores are then employed to rank the list of questions and answers with respect to the given question q. Figure 2 shows the general architecture of our model. We explain our model by referring to the pair (q, a), but the same applies to the pair (q, q'). The question q and answer a contain the lists of words:

$$q = \{w_1^q, w_2^q, w_3^q, ..., w_k^q\}$$
$$a = \{w_1^a, w_2^a, w_3^a, ..., w_m^a\}$$

where w_i^q and w_i^a are the ith word of the q and a respectively.

First, the q and a are truncated to have similar length[3], and two lists of vectors corresponding to the words for the question q and a are generated and randomly initialized:

$$V_q = \{X_1, X_2, X_3, ..., X_{n/2}\}$$
$$V_a = \{X_{n/2+1}, X_{n/2+2}, X_{n/2+3}, ..., X_n\}$$

where X_i with $i \in [1, n/2]$ is the vector of w_i^q for the q, X_i with $i \in [n/2 + 1, n]$ is the vector of $w_{i-n/2}^a$ for the a[4].

***

[3]We truncate the length of questions and answers to a maximum of 100 words. The questions and answers with less than 100 words are padded with zeros.

[4]n equals to 200

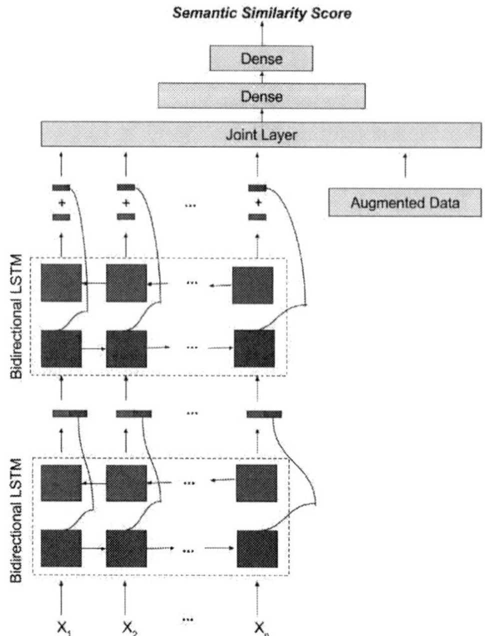

Figure 2: The general architecture of our model including the stacked Bidirectional LSTMs and MLP. The model is built on two bidirectional LSTMs whose output can be augmented with extra features and fed into the multi-layer perceptron.

The word vectors for the q (i.e., V_q) are passed to the model as shown in Figure 2. The model computes the representation of the question q after passing its last word vector to the model. Then the q representation along with the word vectors of the answer a (i.e., V_a) are passed to the model. The model generates the representation of the given pair (q, a) after processing the last word vector of the answer a affected by the representation of q. This information processing is performed at the forward layer of the first bidirectional LSTM shown in the figure (left to right). Similar processing in the reverse direction (right to left) is further applied on the given pair at the first bidirectional LSTM. The output vectors of the hidden layers for these two directions of the first bidirectional LSTM are then concatenated and inputted into the second bidirectional LSTM as shown in the Figure 2.

While the second bidirectional LSTM processes the input vectors similarly to the first one, its output vectors from two directions are summed[5] instead of concatenated. Finally, the resulting vec-

***

[5]Using summation instead of concatenation is selected based on the experimental results on the development set.

Embedding	initialized, updated
Weights for Two LSTMs	not shared
Optimizer	Adam
Learning rate	0.001
Dropout rate	0.5
Batch Size	16

Table 1: The hyper-parameters of the stacked bidirectional LSTM model.

Category	Train	Dev	Test
New Coming Questions	267	50	70
Related Questions	2,669	500	700
– Perfect-Match	235	59	81
– Relevant	848	155	152
– Irrelevant	1,586	286	467
Related Answers	17,900	2,440	7,000
– Good	6651	818	2,767
– Bad	8,139	1,209	3,090
– Potentially-Useful	3,110	413	1,143

Table 2: The statistics for the cQA data (Nakov et al., 2016) that we employ to evaluate our neural model.

Text-based features
– Longest Common Substring
– Longest Common Subsequence
– Greedy String Tiling
– Monge Elkan Second String
– Jaro Second String
– Jaccard coefficient
– Containment similarity

Vector-based features
– Normalized Averaged Word Vectors using `word2vec` (Mikolov et al., 2013)
– Most similar sentence pair for a given (q, a) using sentence vector representation
– Most similar chunk pair for a given (q, a) using chunk vector representation

Metadata-based features
– User information, like user id

Table 3: Some of the most important text- and vector- based features employed in the Bag-of-Vectors (BOV) baseline (Belinkov et al., 2015).

tors can be augmented with the additional features and passed to the MLP with two hidden layers in order to compute the semantic similarity score of the q and a.

4 Results and Discussion

Hyper-parameters: Table 1 shows the hyper-parameters used in our model. The values for the hyper-parameters are optimized with respect to the results on the development set. The word vectors are randomly initialized and updated during the training step as explained in Section 3, and the weights for the two bidirectional LSTMs of the model arc not shared. We employ *Adam* (Kingma and Ba, 2014) as the optimization method and *mean squared error* as loss function for our model. We further use the values 0.001, 0.5 and 16 for learning rate, dropout rate and batch size respectively.

Dataset: We evaluate our model on the cQA data (Nakov et al., 2016) in which the questions and answers have been manually labeled by a community of annotators in a crowdsourcing platform. Table 2 shows the statistics for the train, development and test data. The related questions are labeled as *Perfect-Match*, *Relevant* and *Irrelevant* with respect to an original question in the question retrieval task. The *Irrelevant* questions should be ranked lower than the other questions by the model. In addition, the answers are labeled as *Good*, *Bad* and *Potentially-Useful* with respect to a question in the answer selection task. The expected result is that both *Good* and *Potentially-Useful* answers have useful information, while the *Good* answers should be ranked higher than both *Potentially-Useful* and *Bad* answers.

Baselines: We compare our neural model with the BOV, BM25, IR and TF-IDF baselines that are briefly explained below:

- *Bag-of-Vectors (BOV):* This baseline employed various text- and vector- based features for the cQA problems (Belinkov et al., 2015). We highlight some of those features in Table 3.

- *BM25:* We use the BM25 similarity measure trained on the cQA raw data provided by (Màrquez et al., 2015).

- *IR:* This is the order of the related questions provided by the search engine for question retrieval task and is the chronological ranking, in which answers are ordered by their time of posting, for the answer selection task.

- *TF-IDF:* This is computed using the cQA raw data provided by (Màrquez et al., 2015), and the ranking is defined by the cosine similarity of the TF-IDF vectors for the questions and answers.

We evaluate our models using F1-score for a global assessment of the models in addition to the following ranking metrics: Mean Average Precision (MAP), Average Recall (AveRec) and Mean Reciprocal Rank (MRR). For the MAP, we use the average of MAP@1 to MAP@10.

Method	Dev					
	MAP	AveRcc	MRR	**F1**	R	P
BOV	63.18	82.56	69.36	56.84	52.08	62.56
BM25	55.16	73.18	63.33	-	-	-
IR	53.84	72.78	63.13	-	-	-
TF-IDF	52.52	72.34	60.20	-	-	-
Single LSTM - F_{aug}	61.25	81.76	68.57	-	-	-
Single BLSTM - F_{aug}	62.51	82.35	69.61	51.69	42.91	**65.00**
Single BLSTM	65.46	85.22	72.78	**62.47**	**63.69**	61.29
Double BLSTMs	**66.27**	**85.52**	**73.33**	60.36	59.66	61.08

(a) Results on development data for answer selection.

Method	Test					
	MAP	AveRec	MRR	**F1**	R	P
BOV	75.06	85.76	82.14	59.21	50.56	**71.41**
BM25	59.57	72.57	67.06	-	-	-
IR	59.53	72.60	67.83	-	-	-
TF-IDF	59.65	72.06	66.62	-	-	-
Single LSTM - F_{aug}	71.55	83.54	79.00	-	-	-
Single BLSTM - F_{aug}	73.29	84.58	80.82	53.00	42.89	69.34
Single BLSTM	74.03	85.49	82.53	62.91	59.67	66.53
Double BLSTMs	74.98	**85.98**	**83.05**	**63.53**	**59.89**	67.63

(b) Results on test data for answer selection.

Table 4: Results on (a) development and (b) test data for answer selection task in cQA.

Performance for Answer selection: The results of the answer selection task on development and test data are respectively shown in Tables 4a and 4b. In the tables, the first four rows show the baseline results, and the following rows show the neural models results. The "*Single LSTM - F_{aug}*" row shows the results of the model presented by Mohtarami et al. (2016) when only one LSTM is used instead of two bidirectional LSTMs, and no augmented features F_{aug} are used. The "*Single BLSTM - F_{aug}*" row indicates the results when one bidirectional LSTM is used in our model, and no augmented features F_{aug} are used. Using a BLSTM improves the performance compared to the single LSTM, as can be seen in Tables 4a and 4b. The "*Single BLSTM*" row shows the results for one bidirectional LSTM using F_{aug}. F_{aug} is a 10-length binary vector that encodes the order of the answers in their threads corresponding to their time of posting. F_{aug} helps improve the performance, as can be seen by comparing the results with the ones obtained using a single BLSTM without F_{aug}. The "*Double BLSTM*" row shows the results generated by the complete model illustrated in Figure 2. For the development set represented in Table 4a, the highest results over all the evaluation metrics are obtained using the neural models. The "*Double BLSTM*" achieves the highest performance over the ranking metrics. In addition, the results on the test set shown in Table 4b indicate that while the MAPs of the "*Double BLSTM*" and BOV baseline are comparable, the "*Double BLSTM*" achieves the highest performance over the other metrics, especially F1.

Performance for Question Retrieval: The results of question retrieval task on development and test data are respectively shown in Tables 5a and 5b. In the tables, the first four rows show the baseline results, and the following rows show the neural models results. The neural models are the ones described in the previous section. In this task, we employ the order of the related questions, provided by the search engine, as augmented features F_{aug} explained under *IR baseline* in Section 4. As shown in the tables, the neural models using F_{aug} outperform the models without F_{aug} for both development and test data. For the development set shown in Table 5a, the "*Double BLSTM*" model achieves the highest performance over the evaluation metrics. For the test set shown in Table 5b, the result of the "*Single BLSTM*" model is comparable with the IR and TF-IDF over the ranking metrics, while the highest F1 is obtained using BOV baseline. There are several points to highlight regarding the performance of the neural models compared to the baselines, : First, the size of the data for this task is small, which makes it harder to train our neural models. Second, the baselines have access to external resources; for example IR had ac-

Method	Dev					
	MAP	AveRec	MRR	**F1**	R	P
BOV	64.60	80.83	71.42	59.55	49.53	**74.65**
BM25	61.31	79.42	69.27	-	-	-
IR	71.35	86.11	76.67	-	-	-
TF-IDF	63.40	81.74	70.43	-	-	-
Single LSTM - F_{aug}	54.49	73.39	62.00	-	-	-
Single BLSTM - F_{aug}	57.00	74.54	62.85	51.64	51.40	51.89
Single BLSTM	67.40	83.14	75.87	44.94	37.38	56.34
Double BLSTMs	**70.75**	**86.2**	**76.83**	**62.83**	**66.36**	59.66

(a) Results on development data for question retrieval.

Method	Test					
	MAP	AveRec	MRR	**F1**	R	P
BOV	66.27	82.40	77.96	**56.81**	51.93	**62.69**
BM25	67.27	83.41	79.12	-	-	-
IR	<u>74.75</u>	<u>88.30</u>	<u>83.79</u>	-	-	-
TF-IDF	<u>73.95</u>	<u>87.50</u>	<u>84.55</u>	-	-	-
Single LSTM - F_{aug}	45.24	67.12	52.07	-	-	-
Single BLSTM - F_{aug}	48.00	70.39	54.18	40.88	48.07	35.56
Single BLSTM	<u>73.20</u>	<u>86.99</u>	<u>83.38</u>	48.15	44.64	52.26
Double BLSTMs	71.98	85.86	81.16	51.27	**64.81**	42.42

(b) Results on test data for question retrieval.

Table 5: Results on (a) development and (b) test data for question retrieval task in cQA.

cess to the click log of the users and TF-IDF is trained on a large cQA raw dataset (Màrquez et al., 2015). Finally, the number of out-of-vocabulary (OOV) words in the test data is higher than the development data, and the OOV word vectors are randomly initialized and do not get updated during the training phase. This results in a smaller improvement on the test data.

4.1 Visualization

In order to gain better intuition on our neural model, we consider our complete model with two bidirectional LSTMs as illustrated in Figure 2, and represent the outputs of the hidden layers for each bidirectional LSTM. The represented outputs correspond to the cosine similarities between word vector representations of words in question-question pairs or question-answer pairs. Figure 3 shows the heatmaps for the first bidirectional LSTM (top) and the second bidirectional LSTM (bottom) for the question retrieval task with the following two questions:

- q_1: Which is the best Pakistani school for children in Qatar ? Which is the best Pakistani school for children in Qatar ?

- q_2: Which Indian school is better for the kids ? I wish to admit my kid to one of the Indian schools in Qatar Which is better DPS or Santhinekethan ? please post your comments

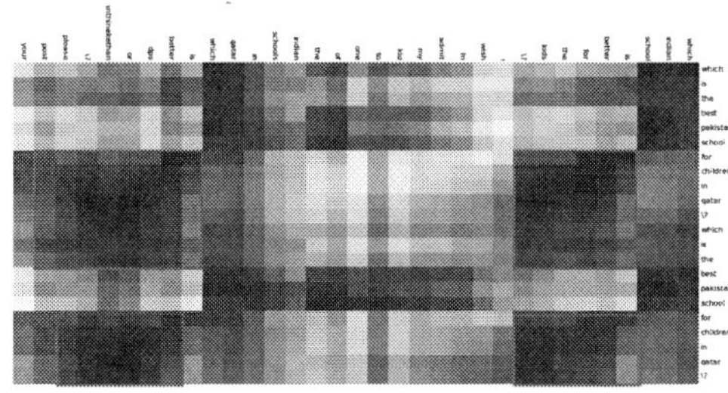

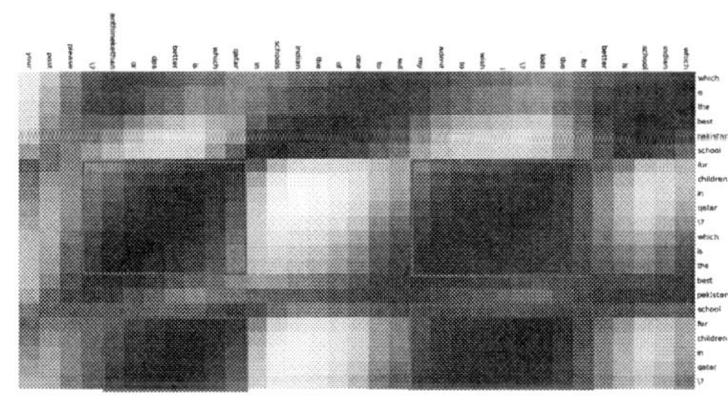

Figure 3: Example of a pair of questions that is correctly predicted as similar by the first (top) and second (bottom) bidirectional LSTMs. The dark blue squares represent areas of high similarity.

The areas of high similarity are highlighted in the red squares in figure 3. While both bidirectional LSTMs correctly predict that the questions are similar, the heatmaps show that the second bidirectional LSTM performs better than the first one, and that the areas of similarities (delimited by the red rectangles) are much better defined by the second bidirectional LSTM. For ex-

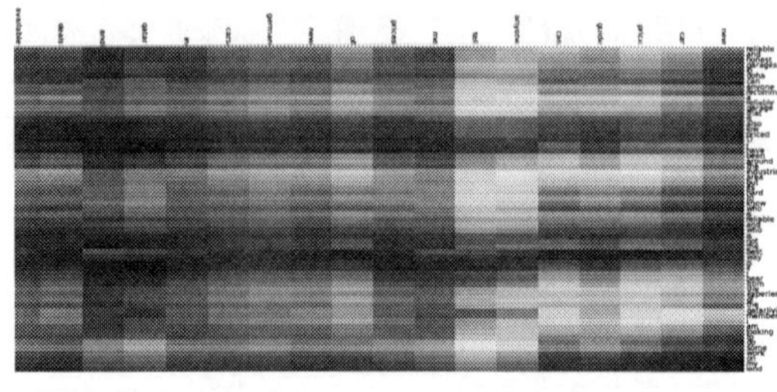

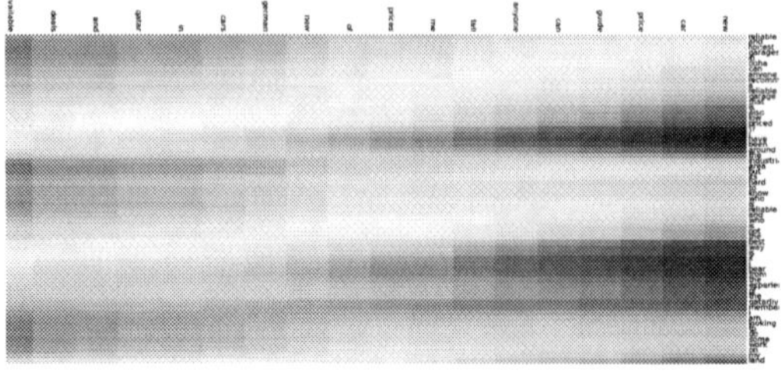

Figure 4: Example of a pair of questions that is incorrectly predicted as similar by the first bidirectional LSTM (top) and correctly predicted by the the second bidirectional LSTM (bottom). The dark blue squares represent areas of high similarity.

ample, the first bidirectional LSTM identifies similarities between the part *"for children in qatar ? Which is the"* from the question q_1 with the parts *"is better for the kids ?"* and *"is better DPS or Santhinekethan ? please post"* from the question q_2. The second bidirectional LSTM accurately updates those parts from the question q_2 to *"for the kids ? I wish to **admit** my"* and *"Qatar which is better DPS or Santhinekethan"* respectively. This shows that the second bidirectional LSTM assigns smaller values to the non-important words (e.g., *"please post"*) while highlighting important words (e.g., *"admit"*).

Figure 4 shows the heatmaps for the first bidirectional LSTM (top) and the second bidirectional LSTM (bottom) for another example of the question retrieval task with the following two questions:

- q_3: New car price guide. Can anyone tell me prices of new German cars in Qatar and deals available

- q_4: Reliable and honest garages in Doha. Can anyone recommend a reliable garage that is also low priced ? I have been around the industrial area but it is hard to know who is reliable and who is not. The best way is if I hear from the experience of the qatarliving mem-

bers . I am looking to do some work on my land cruiser

As shown in the figure, the areas highlighted in dark blue in the first bidirectional LSTM are much larger than the second bidirectional LSTM. These results show that the first bidirectional LSTM incorrectly predicts that the questions q_3 and q_4 are similar, while the second bidirectional LSTM correctly predicts that the questions are dissimilar.

5 Conclusion

In this paper, we present a neural-based model with stacked bidirectional LSTMs to generate the vector representations of questions and answers, and predict their semantic similarities. These similarity scores are then employed to rank elements in a list of questions in the question retrieval task, and a list of answers in the answer selection task for a given question. The experimental results show that our model can perform better than the baselines, even though the baselines use various text- and vector-based features and have access to external resources. We also demonstrate the impact of the OOV words, and the size of the train data on the performance of the neural model.

Acknowledgments

This work is supported by the Qatar Computing Research Institute (QCRI). We thank members of the MIT Spoken Language Systems (SLS) group and the reviewers for their helpful comments.

References

Michael Auli, Michel Galley, Chris Quirk, and Geoffrey Zweig. 2013. Joint language and translation modeling with recurrent neural networks. In *EMNLP*, volume 3.

Alberto Barrón-Cedeno, Simone Filice, Giovanni Da San Martino, Shafiq Joty, Lluıs Marquez, Preslav Nakov, and Alessandro Moschitti. 2015. Threadlevel information for comment classification in community question answering. In *Proceedings of the 53rd Annual Meeting of the Association for Computational Linguistics and the 7th International Joint Conference on Natural Language Processing, ACLIJCNLP*, volume 15, pages 687–693.

Yonatan Belinkov, Mitra Mohtarami, Scott Cyphers, and James Glass. 2015. Vectorslu: A continuous word vector approach to answer selection in community question answering systems. *SemEval-2015*, page 282.

Yoshua Bengio, Patrice Simard, and Paolo Frasconi. 1994. Learning long-term dependencies with gradient descent is difficult. *Neural Networks, IEEE Transactions on*, 5(2):157–166.

Adam Berger, Rich Caruana, David Cohn, Dayne Freitag, and Vibhu Mittal. 2000. Bridging the lexical chasm: statistical approaches to answer-finding. In *Proceedings of the 23rd annual international ACM SIGIR conference on Research and development in information retrieval*, pages 192–199. ACM.

Peter F Brown, Vincent J Della Pietra, Stephen A Della Pietra, and Robert L Mercer. 1993. The mathematics of statistical machine translation: Parameter estimation. *Computational linguistics*, 19(2):263–311.

Robin D Burke, Kristian J Hammond, Vladimir Kulyukin, Steven L Lytinen, Noriko Tomuro, and Scott Schoenberg. 1997. Question answering from frequently asked question files: Experiences with the faq finder system. *AI magazine*, 18(2):57.

Kyunghyun Cho, Bart Van Merriënboer, Caglar Gulcehre, Dzmitry Bahdanau, Fethi Bougares, Holger Schwenk, and Yoshua Bengio. 2014. Learning phrase representations using rnn encoder-decoder for statistical machine translation. *arXiv preprint arXiv:1406.1078*.

Cicero dos Santos, Luciano Barbosa, Dasha Bogdanova, and Bianca Zadrozny. 2015. Learning hybrid representations to retrieve semantically equivalent questions. In *Proceedings of the 53rd Annual Meeting of the Association for Computational Linguistics and the 7th International Joint Conference on Natural Language Processing (Volume 2: Short Papers)*, pages 694–699, Beijing, China, July. Association for Computational Linguistics.

Christiane Fellbaum. 1998. A semantic network of english verbs. *WordNet: An electronic lexical database*, 3:153–178.

Minwei Feng, Bing Xiang, Michael R. Glass, Lidan Wang, and Bowen Zhou. 2015. Applying deep learning to answer selection: A study and an open task. *CoRR*, abs/1508.01585.

Alex Graves and Navdeep Jaitly. 2014. Towards end-to-end speech recognition with recurrent neural networks. In *Proceedings of the 31st International Conference on Machine Learning (ICML-14)*, pages 1764–1772.

Alex Graves and Jürgen Schmidhuber. 2005. Framewise phoneme classification with bidirectional lstm and other neural network architectures. *Neural Networks*, 18(5):602–610.

Jakob Grundström and Pierre Nugues. 2014. Using syntactic features in answer reranking. In *AAAI 2014 Workshop on Cognitive Computing for Augmented Human Intelligence*, pages 13–19.

Michael Heilman and Noah A Smith. 2010. Tree edit models for recognizing textual entailments, paraphrases, and answers to questions. In *Human Language Technologies: The 2010 Annual Conference of the North American Chapter of the Association for Computational Linguistics*, pages 1011–1019. Association for Computational Linguistics.

Sepp Hochreiter and Jürgen Schmidhuber. 1997. Long short-term memory. *Neural computation*, 9(8):1735–1780.

Yongshuai Hou, Cong Tan, Xiaolong Wang, Yaoyun Zhang, Jun Xu, and Qingcai Chen. 2015. Hitszicrc: Exploiting classification approach for answer selection in community question answering. In *Proceedings of the 9th International Workshop on Semantic Evaluation, SemEval*, volume 15, pages 196–202.

Jiwoon Jeon, W Bruce Croft, and Joon Ho Lee. 2005. Finding similar questions in large question and answer archives. In *Proceedings of the 14th ACM international conference on Information and knowledge management*, pages 84–90. ACM.

Jiwoon Jeon, W Bruce Croft, Joon Ho Lee, and Soyeon Park. 2006. A framework to predict the quality of answers with non-textual features. In *Proceedings of the 29th annual international ACM SIGIR conference on Research and development in information retrieval*, pages 228–235. ACM.

Shafiq Joty, Alberto Barrón-Cedeno, Giovanni Da San Martino, Simone Filice, Lluis Marquez, Alessandro Moschitti, and Preslav Nakov. 2015. Global thread-level inference for comment classification in community question answering. In *Proceedings of the Conference on Empirical Methods in Natural Language Processing, EMNLP*, volume 15.

Andrej Karpathy and Li Fei-Fei. 2015. Deep visual-semantic alignments for generating image descriptions. In *Proceedings of the IEEE Conference on Computer Vision and Pattern Recognition*, pages 3128–3137.

Harksoo Kim and Jungyun Seo. 2006. High-performance faq retrieval using an automatic clustering method of query logs. *Information processing & management*, 42(3):650–661.

Diederik P. Kingma and Jimmy Ba. 2014. Adam: A method for stochastic optimization. *CoRR*, abs/1412.6980.

Jan Koutnik, Klaus Greff, Faustino Gomez, and Juergen Schmidhuber. 2014. A clockwork rnn. *arXiv preprint arXiv:1402.3511*.

Yu-Sheng Lai, Kuao-Ann Fung, and Chung-Hsien Wu. 2002. Faq mining via list detection. In *proceedings of the 2002 conference on multilingual summarization and question answering-Volume 19*, pages 1–7. Association for Computational Linguistics.

Shujie Liu, Nan Yang, Mu Li, and Ming Zhou. 2014. A recursive recurrent neural network for statistical machine translation. In *ACL (1)*, pages 1491–1500.

Bernardo Magnini, Matteo Negri, Roberto Prevete, and Hristo Tanev. 2002. Is it the right answer?: exploiting web redundancy for answer validation. In *Proceedings of the 40th Annual Meeting on Association for Computational Linguistics*, pages 425–432. Association for Computational Linguistics.

Christopher D Manning and Hinrich Schütze. 1999. *Foundations of statistical natural language processing*, volume 999. MIT Press.

Lluís Màrquez, James Glass, Walid Magdy, Alessandro Moschitti, Preslav Nakov, and Bilal Randeree. 2015. SemEval-2015 Task 3: Answer Selection in Community Question Answering. In *Proceedings of the 9th International Workshop on Semantic Evaluation (SemEval 2015)*.

Tomas Mikolov, Martin Karafiát, Lukas Burget, Jan Cernockỳ, and Sanjeev Khudanpur. 2010. Recurrent neural network based language model. In *INTERSPEECH*, volume 2, page 3.

Tomáš Mikolov, Stefan Kombrink, Lukáš Burget, Jan Honza Černockỳ, and Sanjeev Khudanpur. 2011. Extensions of recurrent neural network language model. In *Acoustics, Speech and Signal Processing (ICASSP), 2011 IEEE International Conference on*, pages 5528–5531. IEEE.

Tomas Mikolov, Ilya Sutskever, Kai Chen, Greg S Corrado, and Jeff Dean. 2013. Distributed representations of words and phrases and their compositionality. In *Advances in neural information processing systems*, pages 3111–3119.

Mitra Mohtarami, Yonatan Belinkov, Wei-Ning Hsu, Yu Zhang, Tao Lei, Kfir Bar, Scott Cyphers, and James Glass. 2016. Sls at semeval-2016 task 3: Neural-based approaches for ranking in community question answering. In *Proceedings of NAACL-HLT Workshop on Semantic Evaluation*, pages 753–760, San Diego, California, June. Association for Computational Linguistics.

Alessandro Moschitti, Silvia Quarteroni, Roberto Basili, and Suresh Manandhar. 2007. Exploiting syntactic and shallow semantic kernels for question answer classification. In *Annual meeting-association for computational linguistics*, volume 45, page 776.

Alessandro Moschitti. 2008. Kernel methods, syntax and semantics for relational text categorization. In *Proceedings of the 17th ACM conference on Information and knowledge management*, pages 253–262. ACM.

Preslav Nakov, Lluís Màrquez, Walid Magdy, Alessandro Moschitti, Jim Glass, and Bilal Randeree. 2016.

SemEval-2016 task 3: Community question answering. In *Proceedings of the 10th International Workshop on Semantic Evaluation*, SemEval '16, San Diego, California, June. Association for Computational Linguistics.

Massimo Nicosia, Simone Filice, Alberto Barrón-Cedeno, Iman Saleh, Hamdy Mubarak, Wei Gao, Preslav Nakov, Giovanni Da San Martino, Alessandro Moschitti, Kareem Darwish, et al. 2015. Qcri: Answer selection for community question answeringexperiments for arabic and english. In *Proceedings of the 9th International Workshop on Semantic Evaluation, SemEval*, volume 15, pages 203–209.

Razvan Pascanu, Tomas Mikolov, and Yoshua Bengio. 2012. On the difficulty of training recurrent neural networks. *arXiv preprint arXiv:1211.5063*.

Filip Radlinski and Thorsten Joachims. 2005. Query chains: learning to rank from implicit feedback. In *Proceedings of the eleventh ACM SIGKDD international conference on Knowledge discovery in data mining*, pages 239–248. ACM.

Mike Schuster and Kuldip K Paliwal. 1997. Bidirectional recurrent neural networks. *Signal Processing, IEEE Transactions on*, 45(11):2673–2681.

Aliaksei Severyn and Alessandro Moschitti. 2012. Structural relationships for large-scale learning of answer re-ranking. In *Proceedings of the 35th international ACM SIGIR conference on Research and development in information retrieval*, pages 741–750. ACM.

Aliaksei Severyn and Alessandro Moschitti. 2013. Automatic feature engineering for answer selection and extraction. In *EMNLP*, pages 458–467.

Aliaksei Severyn and Alessandro Moschitti. 2015a. Learning to rank short text pairs with convolutional deep neural networks. In *Proceedings of the 38th International ACM SIGIR Conference on Research and Development in Information Retrieval*, pages 373–382. ACM.

Aliaksei Severyn and Alessandro Moschitti. 2015b. Learning to rank short text pairs with convolutional deep neural networks. In *Proceedings of the 38th International ACM SIGIR Conference on Research and Development in Information Retrieval*, SIGIR '15, pages 373–382, New York, NY, USA. ACM.

Dan Shen and Mirella Lapata. 2007. Using semantic roles to improve question answering. In *EMNLP-CoNLL*, pages 12–21.

Eriks Sneiders. 2002. Automated question answering using question templates that cover the conceptual model of the database. In *Natural Language Processing and Information Systems*, pages 235–239. Springer.

Wanpeng Song, Min Feng, Naijie Gu, and Liu Wenyin. 2007. Question similarity calculation for faq answering. In *Semantics, Knowledge and Grid, Third International Conference on*, pages 298–301. IEEE.

Mihai Surdeanu, Massimiliano Ciaramita, and Hugo Zaragoza. 2008. Learning to rank answers on large online qa collections. In *ACL*, volume 8, pages 719–727.

Ilya Sutskever, James Martens, and Geoffrey E Hinton. 2011. Generating text with recurrent neural networks. In *Proceedings of the 28th International Conference on Machine Learning (ICML-11)*, pages 1017–1024.

Ilya Sutskever, Oriol Vinyals, and Quoc V Le. 2014. Sequence to sequence learning with neural networks. In *Advances in neural information processing systems*, pages 3104–3112.

Ming Tan, Bing Xiang, and Bowen Zhou. 2015. Lstm-based deep learning models for non-factoid answer selection. *CoRR*, abs/1511.04108.

Kateryna Tymoshenko and Alessandro Moschitti. 2015. Assessing the impact of syntactic and semantic structures for answer passages reranking. In *Proceedings of the 24th ACM International on Conference on Information and Knowledge Management*, pages 1451–1460. ACM.

Mengqiu Wang and Christopher D Manning. 2010. Probabilistic tree-edit models with structured latent variables for textual entailment and question answering. In *Proceedings of the 23rd International Conference on Computational Linguistics*, pages 1164–1172. Association for Computational Linguistics.

Mengqiu Wang, Noah A Smith, and Teruko Mitamura. 2007. What is the jeopardy model? a quasi-synchronous grammar for qa. In *EMNLP-CoNLL*, volume 7, pages 22–32.

Steven D Whitehead. 1995. Auto-faq: An experiment in cyberspace leveraging. *Computer Networks and ISDN Systems*, 28(1):137–146.

Xuchen Yao, Benjamin Van Durme, Chris Callison-Burch, and Peter Clark. 2013. Answer extraction as sequence tagging with tree edit distance. In *HLT-NAACL*, pages 858–867. Citeseer.

Kaisheng Yao, Trevor Cohn, Katerina Vylomova, Kevin Duh, and Chris Dyer. 2015. Depth-gated recurrent neural networks. *arXiv preprint arXiv:1508.03790*.

Learning Text Similarity with Siamese Recurrent Networks

Paul Neculoiu, Maarten Versteegh and **Mihai Rotaru**
Textkernel B.V. Amsterdam
{neculoiu, versteegh, rotaru}@textkernel.nl

Abstract

This paper presents a deep architecture for learning a similarity metric on variable-length character sequences. The model combines a stack of character-level bidirectional LSTM's with a Siamese architecture. It learns to project variable-length strings into a fixed-dimensional embedding space by using only information about the similarity between pairs of strings. This model is applied to the task of job title normalization based on a manually annotated taxonomy. A small data set is incrementally expanded and augmented with new sources of variance. The model learns a representation that is selective to differences in the input that reflect semantic differences (e.g., "Java developer" vs. "HR manager") but also invariant to non-semantic string differences (e.g., "Java developer" vs. "Java programmer").

1 Introduction

Text representation plays an important role in natural language processing (NLP). Tasks in this field rely on representations that can express the semantic similarity and dissimilarity between textual elements, be they viewed as sequences of words or characters. Such representations and their associated similarity metrics have many applications. For example, word similarity models based on dense embeddings (Mikolov et al., 2013) have recently been applied in diverse settings, such as sentiment analysis (dos Santos and Gatti, 2014) and recommender systems (Barkan and Koenigstein, 2016). Semantic textual similarity measures have been applied to tasks such as automatic summarization (Ponzanelli et al., 2015), debate analysis (Boltuzic and Šnajder, 2015) and paraphrase detection (Socher et al., 2011).

Measuring the semantic similarity between texts is also fundamental problem in Information Extraction (IE) (Martin and Jurafsky, 2000). An important step in many applications is normalization, which puts pieces of information in a standard format, so that they can be compared to other pieces of information. Normalization relies crucially on semantic similarity. An example of normalization is formatting dates and times in a standard way, so that "12pm", "noon" and "12.00h" all map to the same representation. Normalization is also important for string values. Person names, for example, may be written in different orderings or character encodings depending on their country of origin. A sophisticated search system may need to understand that the strings "李小龙", "Lee, Junfan" and "Bruce Lee" all refer to the same person and so need to be represented in a way that indicates their semantic similarity. Normalization is essential for retrieving actionable information from free, unstructured text.

In this paper, we present a system for job title normalization, a common task in information extraction for recruitment and social network analysis (Javed et al., 2014; Malherbe et al., 2014). The task is to receive an input string and map it to one of a finite set of job codes, which are predefined externally. For example, the string "software architectural technician Java/J2EE" might need to be mapped to "Java developer". This task can be approached as a highly multi-class classification problem, but in this study, the approach we take focuses on learning a representation of the strings such that synonymous job titles are close together. This approach has the advantage that it is flexible, i.e., the representation can function as the input space to a subsequent classifier, but can also be used to find closely related job titles or explore job title clusters. In addition, the architecture of the learning model allows us to learn useful representations with limited supervision.

Proceedings of the 1st Workshop on Representation Learning for NLP, pages 148–157,
Berlin, Germany, August 11th, 2016. ©2016 Association for Computational Linguistics

2 Related Work

The use of (deep) neural networks for NLP has recently received much attention, starting from the seminal papers employing convolutional networks on traditional NLP tasks (Collobert et al., 2011) and the availability of high quality semantic word representations (Mikolov et al., 2013). In the last few years, neural network models have been applied to tasks ranging from machine translation (Zou et al., 2013; Cho et al., 2014) to question answering (Weston et al., 2015). Central to these models, which are usually trained on large amounts of labeled data, is feature representation. Word embedding techniques such as word2vec (Mikolov et al., 2013) and Glove (Pennington et al., 2014) have seen much use in such models, but some go beyond the word level and represent text as a sequence of characters (Kim et al., 2015; Ling et al., 2015). In this paper we take the latter approach for the flexibility it affords us in dealing with out-of-vocabulary words.

Representation learning through neural networks has received interest since autoencoders (Hinton and Salakhutdinov, 2006) have been shown to produce features that satisfy the two desiderata of representations; that they are *invariant* to differences in the input that do not matter for that task and *selective* to differences that do (Anselmi et al., 2015).

The Siamese network (Bromley et al., 1993) is an architecture for non-linear metric learning with similarity information. The Siamese network naturally learns representations that embody the invariance and selectivity desiderata through explicit information about similarity between pairs of objects. In contrast, an autoencoder learns invariance through added noise and dimensionality reduction in the bottleneck layer and selectivity solely through the condition that the input should be reproduced by the decoding part of the network. In contrast, a Siamese network learns an invariant and selective representation directly through the use of similarity and dissimilarity information.

Originally applied to signature verification (Bromley et al., 1993), the Siamese architecture has since been widely used in vision applications. Siamese convolutional networks were used to learn complex similarity metrics for face verification (Chopra et al., 2005) and dimensionality reduction on image features (Hadsell et al., 2006). A variant of the Siamese network, the triplet network (Hoffer and Ailon, 2015), was used to learn an image similarity measure based on ranking data (Wang et al., 2014).

In other areas, Siamese networks have been applied to such diverse tasks as unsupervised acoustic modelling (Synnaeve et al., 2014; Thiolliere et al., 2015; Kamper et al., 2016; Zeghidour et al., 2015), learning food preferences (Yang et al., 2015) and scene detection (Baraldi et al., 2015). In NLP applications, Siamese networks with convolutional layers have been applied to matching sentences (Hu et al., 2014). More recently, (Mueller and Thyagarajan, 2016) applied Siamese recurrent networks to learning semantic entailment.

The task of job title normalization is often framed as a classification task (Javed et al., 2014; Malherbe et al., 2014). Given the large number of classes (often in the thousands), multi-stage classifiers have shown good results, especially if information outside the string can be used (Javed et al., 2015). There are several disadvantage to this approach. The first is the expense of data acquisition for training. With many thousands of groups of job titles, often not too dissimilar from one another, manually classifying large amounts of job title data becomes prohibitively expensive. A second disadvantage of this approach is its lack of corrigibility. Once a classification error has been discovered or a new example has been added to a class, the only option to improve the system is to retrain the entire classifier with the new sample added to the correct class in the training set. The last disadvantage is that using a traditional classifier does not allow for transfer learning, i.e., reusing the learned model's representations for a different task.

A different approach is the use of string similarity measures to classify input strings by proximity to an element of a class (Spitters et al., 2010). The advantage of this approach is that there is no need to train the system, so that improvements can be made by adding job title strings to the data. The disadvantages are that data acquisition still needs to be performed by manually classifying strings and that the bulk of the problem is now shifted to constructing a good similarity metric.

By modeling similarity directly based on pairs of inputs, Siamese networks lend themselves well to the semantic invariance phenomena present in job title normalization: typos (e.g. "Java developeur"), near-synonymy (e.g., "developer" and "programmer") and extra words (e.g., "experienced Java developer"). This is the approach we take in this study.

3 Siamese Recurrent Neural Network

Recurrent Neural Networks (RNN) are neural networks adapted for sequence data $(x_1, \ldots, x_T)$. At each time step $t \in \{1, \ldots, T\}$, the hidden-state vector h_t is updated by the equation $h_t = \sigma(W x_t + U h_{t-1})$, in which x_t is the input at time t, W is the weight matrix from inputs to the hidden-state vector and U is the weight matrix on the hidden-state vector from the previous time step h_{t-1}. In this equation and below the logistic function is denoted by $\sigma(x) = (1 + e^{-x})^{-1}$.

The Long Short-Term Memory (Hochreiter and Schmidhuber, 1997) variant of RNNs in particular has had success in tasks related to natural language processing, such as text classification (Graves, 2012) and language translation (Sutskever et al., 2014). Standard RNNs suffer from the vanishing gradient problem in which the backpropagated gradients become vanishingly small over long sequences (Pascanu et al., 2013). The LSTM model was proposed as a solution to this problem. Like the standard RNN, the LSTM sequentially updates a hidden-state representation, but it introduces a memory state c_t and three gates that control the flow of information through the time steps. An output gate o_t determines how much of c_t should be exposed to the next node. An input gate i_t controls how much the input x_t matters at this time step. A forget gate f_t determines whether the previous time step's memory should be forgotten. An LSTM is parametrized by weight matrices from the input and the previous state for each of the gates, in addition to the memory cell. We use the standard formulation of LSTMs with the logistic function (σ) on the gates and the hyperbolic tangent (`tanh`) on the activations. In the equations (1) below, $\circ$ denotes the Hadamard (elementwise) product.

$$i_t = \sigma(W_i x_t + U_i h_{t-1}) \tag{1}$$

$$f_t = \sigma(W_f x_t + U_f h_{t-1}) \tag{2}$$

$$o_t = \sigma(W_o x_t + U_o h_{t-1}) \tag{3}$$

$$\tilde{c}_t = \tanh(W_c x_t + U_c h_{t-1}) \tag{4}$$

$$c_t = i_t \circ \tilde{c}_t + f_t \circ c_{t-1} \tag{5}$$

$$h_t = o_t \circ \tanh(c_t) \tag{6}$$

Bidirectional RNNs (Schuster and Paliwal, 1997) incorporate both future and past context by running the reverse of the input through a separate RNN. The output of the combined model at each time step is simply the concatenation of the outputs from the forward and backward networks. Bidirectional LSTM models in particular have recently shown good results on standard NLP tasks like Named Entity Recognition (Huang et al., 2015; Wang et al., 2015) and so we adopt this technique for this study.

Siamese networks (Chopra et al., 2005) are dual-branch networks with tied weights, i.e., they consist of the same network copied and merged with an energy function. Figure 1 shows an overview of the network architecture in this study. The training set for a Siamese network consists of triplets (x_1, x_2, y), where x_1 and x_2 are character sequences and $y \in \{0, 1\}$ indicates whether x_1 and x_2 are similar ($y = 1$) or dissimilar ($y = 0$). The aim of training is to minimize the distance in an embedding space between similar pairs and maximize the distance between dissimilar pairs.

3.1 Contrastive loss function

The proposed network contains four layers of Bidirectional LSTM nodes. The activations at each timestep of the final BLSTM layer are averaged to produce a fixed-dimensional output. This output is projected through a single densely connected feedforward layer.

Let $f_W(x_1)$ and $f_W(x_2)$ be the projections of x_1 and x_2 in the embedding space computed by the network function f_W. We define the energy of the model E_W to be the cosine similarity between the embeddings of x_1 and x_2:

$$E_W(x_1, x_2) = \frac{\langle f_W(x_1), f_W(x_2) \rangle}{\|f_W(x_1)\| \|f_W(x_2)\|} \tag{7}$$

For brevity of notation, we will denote $E_W(x_1, x_2)$ by E_W. The total loss function over a data set $X = \left\{ \langle x_1^{(i)}, x_2^{(i)}, y^{(i)} \rangle \right\}$ is given by:

$$\mathcal{L}_W(X) = \sum_{i=1}^{N} L_W^{(i)}(x_1^{(i)}, x_2^{(i)}, y^{(i)}) \tag{8}$$

The instance loss function $L_W^{(i)}$ is a contrastive loss function, composed of terms for the similar ($y =$

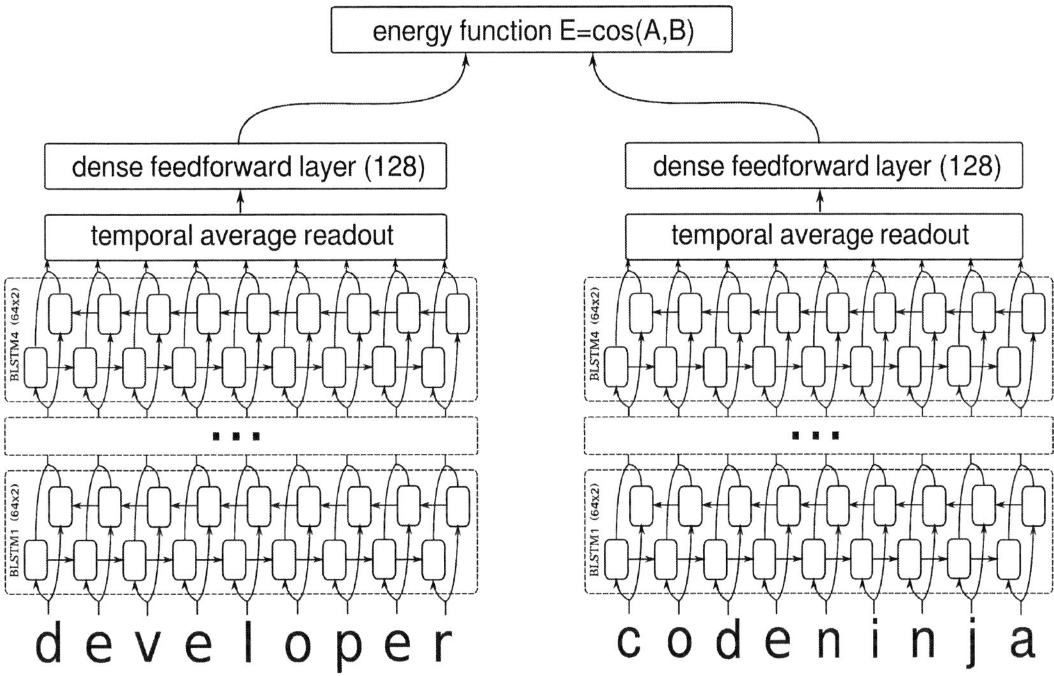

Figure 1: Overview of the Siamese Recurrent Network architecture used in this paper. The weights of all the layers are shared between the right and the left branch of the network.

1) case (L_+), and the dissimilar $(y = 0)$ case (L_-):

$$L_\mathrm{W}^{(i)} = y^{(i)} L_+(x_1^{(i)}, x_2^{(i)}) + \quad (9)$$

$$(1 - y^{(i)}) L_-(x_1^{(i)}, x_2^{(i)}) \quad (10)$$

$$(11)$$

The loss functions for the similar and dissimilar cases are given by:

$$L_+(x_1, x_2) = \frac{1}{4}(1 - E_\mathrm{W})^2 \quad (12)$$

$$L_-(x_1, x_2) = \begin{cases} E_\mathrm{W}^2 & \text{if } E_\mathrm{W} < m \\ 0 & \text{otherwise} \end{cases} \quad (13)$$

Figure 2 gives a geometric perspective on the loss function, showing the positive and negative components separately. Note that the positive loss is scaled down to compensate for the sampling ratios of positive and negative pairs (see below).

The network used in this study contains four BLSTM layers with 64-dimensional hidden vectors h_t and memory c_t. There are connections at each time step between the layers. The outputs of the last layer are averaged over time and this 128-dimensional vector is used as input to a dense feedforward layer. The input strings are padded to

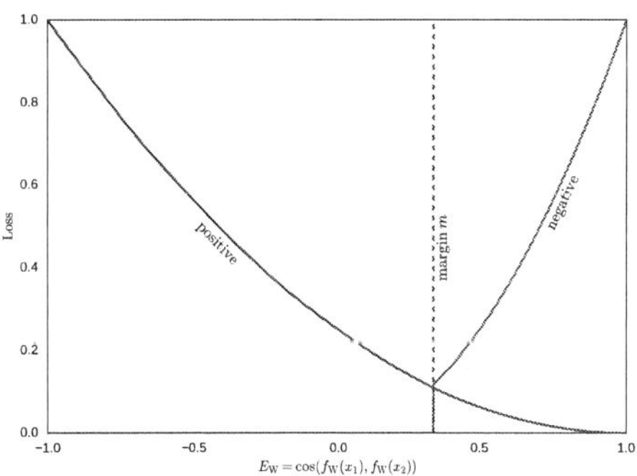

Figure 2: Positive and negative components of the loss function.

produce a sequence of 100 characters, with the input string randomly placed in this sequence. The parameters of the model are optimized using the Adam method (Kingma and Ba, 2014) and each model is trained until convergence. We use the dropout technique (Srivastava et al., 2014) on the recurrent units (with probability 0.2) and between layers (with probability 0.4) to prevent overfitting.

4 Experiments

We conduct a set of experiments to test the model's capabilities. We start from a small data set based on a hand made taxonomy of job titles. In each subsequent experiment the data set is augmented by adding new sources of variance. We test the model's behavior in a set of unit tests, reflecting desired capabilities of the model, taking our cue from (Weston et al., 2015). This section discusses the data augmentation strategies, the composition of the unit tests, and the results of the experiments.

4.1 Baseline

Below we compare the performance of our model against a baseline n-gram matcher (Daelemans et al., 2004). Given an input string, this matcher looks up the closest neighbor from the base taxonomy by maximizing a similarity scoring function. The matcher subsequently labels the input string with that neighbor's group label. The similarity scoring function is defined as follows. Let $Q = \langle q_1, \ldots, q_M \rangle$ be the query as a sequence of characters and $C = \langle c_1, \ldots, c_N \rangle$ be the candidate match from the taxonomy. The similarity function is defined as:

$$\mathrm{sim}(Q, C) = M - \mathrm{match(Q, C)}$$
$$\mathrm{match}(Q, C) = |T_Q \ominus T_C| - |T_Q \cap T_C|$$
$$\text{where}$$
$$A \ominus B = (A \setminus B) \cup (B \setminus A)$$
$$T_Q = \bigcup_{i=1}^{M-2} \{\langle q_i, q_{i+1}, q_{i+2} \rangle\}$$
$$T_C = \bigcup_{i=1}^{N-2} \{\langle c_i, c_{i+1}, c_{i+2} \rangle\}$$

This (non-calibrated) similarity function has the properties that it is easy to compute, doesn't require any learning and is particularly insensitive to appending extra words in the input string, one of the desiderata listed below.

In the experiments listed below, the test sets consist of pairs of strings, the first of which is the input string and the second a target group label from the base taxonomy. The network model projects the input string into the embedding space and searches for its nearest neighbor under cosine distance from the base taxonomy. The test records a hit if and only if the neighbor's group label matches the target.

4.2 Data and Data Augmentation

The starting point for our data is a hand made proprietary job title taxonomy. This taxonomy partitions a set of 19,927 job titles into 4,431 groups. Table 1 gives some examples of the groups in the taxonomy. The job titles were manually and semi-automatically collected from résumés and vacancy postings. Each was manually assigned a group, such that the job titles in a group are close together in meaning. In some cases this closeness is an expression of a (near-)synonymy relation between the job titles, as in "developer" and "developer/programmer" in the "Software Engineer" category. In other cases a job title in a group is a specialization of another, for example "general operator" and "buzz saw operator" in the "Machine Operator" category. In yet other cases two job titles differ only in their expression of seniority, as in "developer" and "senior developer" in the "Software Engineer" category. In all cases, the relation between the job titles is one of *semantic* similarity and not necessarily surface form similarity. So while, "Java developer" and "J2EE programmer" are in the same group, "Java developer" and "real estate developer" should not be.

Note that some groups are close together in meaning, like the "Production Employee" and "Machine Operator" groups. Some groups could conceivably be split into two groups, depending on the level of granularity that is desired. We make no claim to completeness or consistency of these groupings, but instead regard the wide variety of different semantic relations between and within groups as an asset that should be exploited by our model.

The groups are not equal in size; the sizes follow a broken power-law distribution. The largest group contains 130 job titles, the groups at the other end of the distribution have only one. This affects the amount of information we can give to the system with regards to the semantic similarity between job titles in a group. The long tail of the distribution may impact the model's ability to accurately learn to represent the smallest groups. Figure 3 shows the distribution of the group sizes of the original taxonomy.

We proceed from the base taxonomy of job titles in four stages. At each stage we introduce (1) an

Customer Service Agent	Production Employee	Software Engineer	Machine Operator	Software Tester
support specialist	assembler	developer	operator punch press	tester sip
service desk agent	manufacturing assistant	application programmer	machinist	test consultant
support staff	production engineer	software architect	buzz saw operator	stress tester
customer care agent III	factory employee	cloud engineer	operator turret punch press	kit tester
customer service agent	casting machine operator	lead software engineer	blueprint machine operator	agile java tester
customer interaction	helper production	senior developer	general operator	test engineer
customer care officer	production laborer	developer/programmer	operator nibbler	QTP tester

Table 1: Example job title groups from the taxonomy. The total taxonomy consists of 19,927 job titles in 4,431 groups.

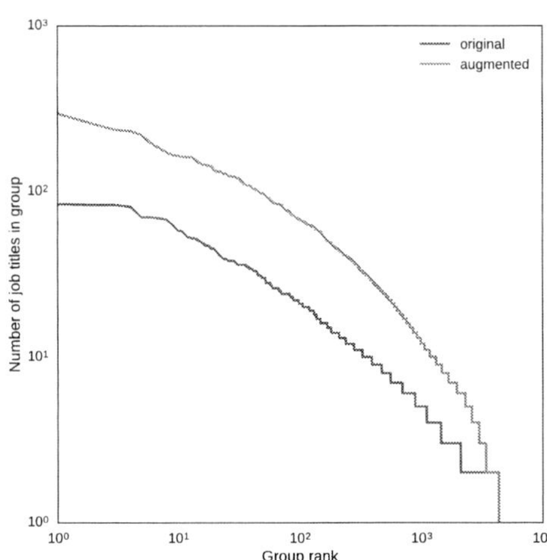

Figure 3: The distributions of group sizes in the original taxonomy (blue) and the taxonomy augmented with synonym substitutions (green) follow broken power-law distributions. Note that both axes are on a logarithmic scale. The figure shows the long tail of the distribution, in which groups contain one or only a few job titles.

augmentation of the data which focuses on a particular property and (2) a test that probes the model for behavior related to that property. Each stage builds on the next, so the augmentations from the previous stage are always included. Initially, the data set consists of pairs of strings sampled from the taxonomy in a 4:1 ratio of between-class (negative) pairs to within-class (positive) pairs. This ratio was empirically determined but other studies have found a similar optimal ratio of negative to positive pairs in Siamese networks (Synnaeve and Dupoux, 2016). In the subsequent augmentations, we keep this ratio constant.

1. Typo and spelling invariance. Users of the system may supply job titles that differ in spelling from what is present in the taxonomy (e.g., "laborer" vs "labourer") or they may make a typo and insert, delete or substitute a character. To induce invariance to these we augment the base taxonomy by extending it with positive sample pairs consisting of job title strings and the same string but with 20% of characters randomly substituted and 5% randomly deleted. Of the resulting training set, 10% consists of these typo pairs. The corresponding test set (**Typos**) consists of all the 19,928 job title strings in the taxonomy with 5% of their characters randomly substituted or deleted. This corresponds to an approximate upper bound on the proportion of spelling errors (Salthouse, 1986).

2. Synonyms. Furthermore, the model must be invariant to synonym substitution. To continue on the example given above, the similarity between "Java developer" and "Java programmer" show that in the context of computer science "developer" and "programmer" are synonyms. This entails that, given the same context, "developer" can be substituted for "programmer" in any string in which it occurs without altering the meaning of that string. So "C++ developer" can be changed into "C++ programmer" and still refer to the same job. Together with the selectivity constraint, the invariance to synonym substitution constitutes a form of compositionality on the component parts of job titles. A model with this compositionality property will be able to generalize over the meanings of parts of job titles to form useful representations of unobserved inputs. We augment the data set by substituting words in job titles by synonyms from two sources. The first source is a manually constructed job title synonym set, consisting of around 1100 job titles, each with between one and ten synonyms for a total of 7000 synonyms. The second source of synonyms is by induction. As in the example above, we look through the taxonomy for groups in which two job titles share one or two words, e.g., "C++". The complements of the matching strings form a synonym candidate, e.g., "developer" and "programmer". If the candidate meets certain requirements (neither part occurs in isolation, the parts do not contain special characters like '&', the parts consist of at most two words), then the candidate is accepted as a synonym and is substituted throughout the group. The effect of this augmentation on the group sizes is shown in figure 3. The corresponding test set (**Composition**) consists of a held out set of 7909 pairs constructed in the same way.

3. Extra words. To be useful in real-world applications, the model must also be invariant to the presence of superfluous words. Due to parsing errors or user mistakes the input to the normalization system may contain strings like "looking for C++ developers (urgent!)", or references to technologies, certifications or locations that are not present in the taxonomy. Table 2 shows some examples of real input. We augment the data set by extracting examples of superfluous words from real world data. We construct a set by selecting those input strings for which there is a job title in the base taxonomy which is the complete and strict substring of the input and which the baseline n-gram matcher selects as the normalization. As an example, in table 2, the input string "public relations consultant business business b2c" contains the taxonomy job title "public relations consultant". Part of this set ($N = 1949$) is held out from training and forms the corresponding test set (**Extra Words**).

Input string
supervisor dedicated services share plans
part II architectural assistant or architect at
geography teacher 0.4 contract now
customer relationship management developer super user â
forgot password
public relations consultant business business b2c
teaching assistant degree holders only contract

Table 2: Example input strings to the system.

4. Feedback. Lastly, and importantly for industrial applications, we would like our model to be *corrigible*, i.e., when the model displays undesired behavior or our knowledge about the domain increases, we want the model to facilitate manual intervention. As an example, if the trained model assigns a high similarity score to the string "Java developer" and "Coffee expert (Java, Yemen)" based on the corresponding substrings, we would like to be able to signal to the model that these particular instances do not belong together. To test this behavior, we manually scored a set of 11929 predic-

tions. This set was subsequently used for training. The corresponding test set (**Annotations**) consists of a different set of 1000 manually annotated held-out input strings.

4.3 Results

Table 3 shows the results of the experiments. It compares the baseline n-gram system and proposed neural network models on the four tests outlined above. Each of the neural network models (1)-(4) was trained on augmentations of the data set that the previous model was trained on.

The first thing to note is that both the n-gram matching system and the proposed models have near-complete invariance to simple typos. This is of course expected behavior, but this test functions as a good sanity check on the surface form mapping to the representations that the models learn.

In the performance of all tests except for the Annotations test, we see a strong effect of the associated augmentation. Model (1) shows 0.04 improvement over model (0) on the typo test. This indicates that the proposed architecture is suitable for learning invariance to typos, but that the addition of typos and spelling variants to the training input only produces marginal improvements over the already high accuracy on this test.

Model (2) shows 0.29 improvement over model (1) on the Composition test. This indicates that model (2) has successfully learned to combine the meanings of individual words in the job titles into new meanings. This is an important property for a system that aims to learn semantic similarity between text data. Compositionality is arguably the most important property of human language and it is a defining characteristic of the way we construct compound terms such as job titles. Note also that the model learned this behavior based largely on observations of *combinations* of words, while having little evidence on the individual meanings.

Model (3) shows 0.45 improvement over model (2) on the Extra Words test, jumping from 0.29 accuracy to 0.76. This indicates firstly that the proposed model can successfully learn to ignore large portions of the input sequence and secondly that the evidence of extra words around the job title is crucial for the system to do so. Being able to ignore subsequences of an input sequence is an important ability for information extraction systems.

The improvements on the Annotations test is also greatest when the extra words are added to the

	Typos ($N = 19928$)	Composition ($N = 7909$)	Extra Words ($N = 1949$)	Annotations ($N = 1000$)
n-gram	0.99	0.61	1.00*	0.83
(0) RNN base taxonomy	0.95	0.55	0.40	0.69
(1) + typos	0.99	0.54	0.36	0.77
(2) + synonyms	**1.00**	0.83	0.29	0.76
(3) + extra words	**1.00**	**0.84**	0.76	**0.87**
(4) + feedback	**1.00**	0.79	**0.82**	0.84

Table 3: Accuracy of the baseline and models on each of the four test cases. The best performing neural network in each column is indicated in **bold**. Note that the performance of the n-gram match system (*) on the Extra Words test is 1.00 by construction.

training set. Model (4) actually shows a decrease in performance with respect to model (3) on this test. The cause for this is likely the fact that the Extra Words test and the held out Annotations tests show a lot of similarity in the structure of their inputs. Real production inputs often consist of additional characters, words and phrases before or after the actual job title. It is unclear why model (4) shows an improvement on the Extra Words test while simultaneously showing a decrease in performance on the Composition and Annotations tests. This matter is left to future investigation.

5 Discussion

In this paper, we presented a model architecture for learning text similarity based on Siamese recurrent neural networks. With this architecture, we learned a series of embedding spaces, each based on a specific augmentation of the data set used to train the model. The experiments demonstrated that these embedding spaces captured important invariances of the input; the models showed themselves invariant to spelling variation, synonym replacements and superfluous words. The proposed architecture made no assumptions on the input distribution and naturally scales to a large number of classes.

The ability of the system to learn these invariances stems from the contrastive loss function combined with the stack of recurrent layers. Using separate loss functions for similar and dissimilar samples helps the model maintain selectivity while learning invariance over different sources of variability. The experiment shows that the explicit use of prior knowledge to add these sources of invariance to the system was crucial in learning. Without this knowledge extra words and synonyms will

negatively affect the performance of the system.

We would like to explore several directions in future work. The possibility space around the proposed network architecture could be explored more fully, for example by incorporating convolutional layers in addition to the recurrent layers, or by investigating a triplet loss function instead of the contrastive loss used in this study.

The application used here is a good use case for the proposed system, but in future work we would also like to explore the behavior of the Siamese recurrent network on standard textual similarity and semantic entailment data sets. In addition, the baseline used in this paper is relatively weak. A comparison to a stronger baseline would serve the further development of the proposed models.

Currently negative samples are selected randomly from the data set. Given the similarity between some groups and the large differences in group sizes, a more advanced selection strategy is likely to yield good results. For example, negative samples could be chosen such that they always emphasize minimal distances between groups. In addition, new sources of variation as well as the sampling ratios between them can be explored.

Systems like the job title taxonomy used in the current study often exhibit a hierarchical structure that we did not exploit or attempt to model in the current study. Future research could attempt to learn a single embedding which would preserve the separations between groups at different levels in the hierarchy. This would enable sophisticated transfer learning based on a rich embedding space that can represent multiple levels of similarities and contrasts simultaneously.

References

Fabio Anselmi, Lorenzo Rosasco, and Tomaso Poggio. 2015. On invariance and selectivity in representation learning. *arXiv preprint arXiv:1503.05938*.

Lorenzo Baraldi, Costantino Grana, and Rita Cucchiara. 2015. A deep siamese network for scene detection in broadcast videos. In *Proceedings of the 23rd Annual ACM Conference on Multimedia Conference*, pages 1199–1202. ACM.

Oren Barkan and Noam Koenigstein. 2016. Item2vec: Neural item embedding for collaborative filtering. *arXiv preprint arXiv:1603.04259*.

Filip Boltuzic and Jan Šnajder. 2015. Identifying prominent arguments in online debates using semantic textual similarity. In *Proceedings of the 2nd Workshop on Argumentation Mining*, pages 110–115.

Jane Bromley, James W Bentz, Léon Bottou, Isabelle Guyon, Yann LeCun, Cliff Moore, Eduard Säckinger, and Roopak Shah. 1993. Signature verification using a "siamese" time delay neural network. *International Journal of Pattern Recognition and Artificial Intelligence*, 7(04):669–688.

Kyunghyun Cho, Bart Van Merriënboer, Caglar Gulcehre, Dzmitry Bahdanau, Fethi Bougares, Holger Schwenk, and Yoshua Bengio. 2014. Learning phrase representations using rnn encoder-decoder for statistical machine translation. *arXiv preprint arXiv:1406.1078*.

Sumit Chopra, Raia Hadsell, and Yann LeCun. 2005. Learning a similarity metric discriminatively, with application to face verification. In *Computer Vision and Pattern Recognition, 2005. CVPR 2005. IEEE Computer Society Conference on*, volume 1, pages 539–546. IEEE.

Ronan Collobert, Jason Weston, Léon Bottou, Michael Karlen, Koray Kavukcuoglu, and Pavel Kuksa. 2011. Natural language processing (almost) from scratch. *The Journal of Machine Learning Research*, 12:2493–2537.

Walter Daelemans, Jakub Zavrel, Ko van der Sloot, and Antal van den Bosch. 2004. Timbl: Tilburg memory-based learner. *Tilburg University*.

Cícero Nogueira dos Santos and Maira Gatti. 2014. Deep convolutional neural networks for sentiment analysis of short texts. In *COLING*, pages 69–78.

Alex Graves. 2012. *Supervised sequence labelling*. Springer.

Raia Hadsell, Sumit Chopra, and Yann LeCun. 2006. Dimensionality reduction by learning an invariant mapping. In *Computer vision and pattern recognition, 2006 IEEE computer society conference on*, volume 2, pages 1735–1742. IEEE.

Geoffrey E Hinton and Ruslan R Salakhutdinov. 2006. Reducing the dimensionality of data with neural networks. *Science*, 313(5786):504–507.

Sepp Hochreiter and Jürgen Schmidhuber. 1997. Long short-term memory. *Neural computation*, 9(8):1735–1780.

Elad Hoffer and Nir Ailon. 2015. Deep metric learning using triplet network. In *Similarity-Based Pattern Recognition*, pages 84–92. Springer.

Baotian Hu, Zhengdong Lu, Hang Li, and Qingcai Chen. 2014. Convolutional neural network architectures for matching natural language sentences. In *Advances in Neural Information Processing Systems*, pages 2042–2050.

Zhiheng Huang, Wei Xu, and Kai Yu. 2015. Bidirectional lstm-crf models for sequence tagging. *arXiv preprint arXiv:1508.01991*.

Faizan Javed, Matt McNair, Ferosh Jacob, and Meng Zhao. 2014. Towards a job title classification system. In *WSCBD 2014: Webscale Classification: Classifying Big Data from the Web, WSDM Workshop*.

Faizan Javed, Qinlong Luo, Matt McNair, Ferosh Jacob, Meng Zhao, and Tae Seung Kang. 2015. Carotene: A job title classification system for the online recruitment domain. In *Big Data Computing Service and Applications (BigDataService), 2015 IEEE First International Conference on*, pages 286–293. IEEE.

H. Kamper, W. Wang, and K. Livescu. 2016. Deep convolutional acoustic word embeddings using word-pair side information. In *Proceedings ICASSP*.

Yoon Kim, Yacine Jernite, David Sontag, and Alexander M. Rush. 2015. Character-aware neural language models. *arXiv preprint arXiv:1508.06615*.

Diederik Kingma and Jimmy Ba. 2014. Adam: A method for stochastic optimization. *arXiv preprint arXiv:1412.6980*.

Wang Ling, Tiago Luís, Luís Marujo, Ramón Fernandez Astudillo, Silvio Amir, Chris Dyer, Alan W Black, and Isabel Trancoso. 2015. Finding function in form: Compositional character models for open vocabulary word representation. *arXiv preprint arXiv:1508.02096*.

Emmanuel Malherbe, Mamadou Diaby, Mario Cataldi, Emmanuel Viennet, and Marie-Aude Aufaure. 2014. Field selection for job categorization and recommendation to social network users. In *Advances in Social Networks Analysis and Mining (ASONAM), 2014 IEEE/ACM International Conference on*, pages 588–595. IEEE.

James H. Martin and Daniel Jurafsky. 2000. Speech and language processing. *International Edition*.

Tomas Mikolov, Ilya Sutskever, Kai Chen, Greg S Corrado, and Jeff Dean. 2013. Distributed representations of words and phrases and their compositionality. In *Advances in neural information processing systems*, pages 3111–3119.

Jonas Mueller and Aditya Thyagarajan. 2016. Siamese recurrent architectures for learning sentence similarity. In *Thirtieth AAAI Conference on Artificial Intelligence*.

R. Pascanu, T. Mikolov, and Y. Bengio. 2013. On the difficulty of training recurrent neural networks. *Journal of Machine Learning Research*.

Jeffrey Pennington, Richard Socher, and Christopher D. Manning. 2014. Glove: Global vectors for word representation. In *EMNLP*, volume 14, pages 1532–1543.

Luca Ponzanelli, Andrea Mocci, and Michele Lanza. 2015. Summarizing complex development artifacts by mining heterogeneous data. In *Proceedings of the 12th Working Conference on Mining Software Repositories*, pages 401–405. IEEE Press.

Timothy A. Salthouse. 1986. Perceptual, cognitive, and motoric aspects of transcription typing. *Psychological bulletin*, 99(3):303.

Mike Schuster and Kuldip K Paliwal. 1997. Bidirectional recurrent neural networks. *Signal Processing, IEEE Transactions on*, 45(11):2673–2681.

Richard Socher, Eric H. Huang, Jeffrey Pennin, Christopher D Manning, and Andrew Y. Ng. 2011. Dynamic pooling and unfolding recursive autoencoders for paraphrase detection. In *Advances in Neural Information Processing Systems*, pages 801–809.

Martijn Spitters, Remko Bonnema, Mihai Rotaru, and Jakub Zavrel. 2010. Bootstrapping information extraction mappings by similarity-based reuse of taxonomies. In *CEUR Workshop Proceedings*, volume 673. Citeseer.

Nitish Srivastava, Geoffrey Hinton, Alex Krizhevsky, Ilya Sutskever, and Ruslan Salakhutdinov. 2014. Dropout: A simple way to prevent neural networks from overfitting. *The Journal of Machine Learning Research*, 15(1):1929–1958.

Ilya Sutskever, Oriol Vinyals, and Quoc V. Le. 2014. Sequence to sequence learning with neural networks. In *Advances in neural information processing systems*, pages 3104–3112.

Gabriel Synnaeve and Emmanuel Dupoux. 2016. A temporal coherence loss function for learning unsupervised acoustic embeddings. *Procedia Computer Science*, 81:95–100.

Gabriel Synnaeve, Thomas Schatz, and Emmanuel Dupoux. 2014. Phonetics embedding learning with side information. In *Spoken Language Technology Workshop (SLT), 2014 IEEE*, pages 106–111. IEEE.

Roland Thiolliere, Ewan Dunbar, Gabriel Synnaeve, Maarten Versteegh, and Emmanuel Dupoux. 2015. A hybrid dynamic time warping-deep neural network architecture for unsupervised acoustic modeling. In *Proc. Interspeech*.

Jiang Wang, Yang Song, Thomas Leung, Chuck Rosenberg, Jingbin Wang, James Philbin, Bo Chen, and Ying Wu. 2014. Learning fine-grained image similarity with deep ranking. In *Proceedings of the IEEE Conference on Computer Vision and Pattern Recognition*, pages 1386–1393.

Peilu Wang, Yao Qian, Frank K Soong, Lei He, and Hai Zhao. 2015. A unified tagging solution: Bidirectional lstm recurrent neural network with word embedding. *arXiv preprint arXiv:1511.00215*.

Jason Weston, Antoninipe Bordes, Sumit Chopra, and Tomas Mikolov. 2015. Towards AI-complete question answering: A set of prerequisite toy tasks. *arXiv preprint arXiv:1502.05698*.

Longqi Yang, Yin Cui, Fan Zhang, John P Pollak, Serge Belongie, and Deborah Estrin. 2015. Plateclick: Bootstrapping food preferences through an adaptive visual interface. In *Proceedings of the 24th ACM International on Conference on Information and Knowledge Management*, pages 183–192. ACM.

Neil Zeghidour, Gabriel Synnaeve, Maarten Versteegh, and Emmanuel Dupoux. 2015. A deep scattering spectrum - deep siamese network pipeline for unsupervised acoustic modeling. In *IEEE International Conference on Acoustics, Speech and Signal Processing*.

Will Y Zou, Richard Socher, Daniel M Cer, and Christopher D Manning. 2013. Bilingual word embeddings for phrase-based machine translation. In *EMNLP*, pages 1393–1398.

A Two-stage Approach for Extending Event Detection to New Types via Neural Networks

Thien Huu Nguyen, Lisheng Fu, Kyunghyun Cho and Ralph Grishman
Computer Science Department, New York University, New York, NY 10003, USA
thien@cs.nyu.edu lisheng@cs.nyu.edu
kyunghyun.cho@nyu.edu grishman@cs.nyu.edu

Abstract

We study the event detection problem in the new type extension setting. In particular, our task involves identifying the event instances of a target type that is only specified by a small set of seed instances in text. We want to exploit the large amount of training data available for the other event types to improve the performance of this task. We compare the convolutional neural network model and the feature-based method in this type extension setting to investigate their effectiveness. In addition, we propose a two-stage training algorithm for neural networks that effectively transfers knowledge from the other event types to the target type. The experimental results show that the proposed algorithm outperforms strong baselines for this task.

1 Introduction

Event detection (ED) is an important task of information extraction that seeks to locate instances of events with some types in text. Each event mention is associated with a phrase, the event trigger[1], which evokes that event. Our task, more precisely stated, involves identifying event triggers of some types of interest. For instance, in the sentence "*A cameramen was shot in Texas today*", an ED system should be able to recognize the word "*shot*" as a trigger for the event "*Attack*". ED is a crucial component in the overall task of event extraction, which also involves event argument discovery.

There have been two major approaches to ED in the literature. The first approach extensively leverages linguistic analysis and knowledge resources to capture the *discrete* structures for ED, focusing on the combination of various properties such as lexicon, syntax, and gazetteers. This is called the feature-based approach that has dominated the ED research in the last decade (Ji and Grishman, 2008; Gupta and Ji, 2009; Liao and Grishman, 2011; McClosky et al., 2011; Riedel and McCallum, 2011; Li et al., 2013; Venugopal et al., 2014). The second approach, on the other hand, is proposed very recently and uses convolutional neural networks (CNN) to exploit the *continuous* representations of words. These continuous representations have been shown to effectively capture the underlying structures of a sentence, thereby significantly improving the performance for ED (Nguyen and Grishman, 2015; Chen et al., 2015).

The previous research has mainly focused on building an ED system in a supervised setting. The performance of such systems strongly depends on a sufficient amount of labeled instances for each event type in the training data. Unfortunately, this setting does not reflect the real world situation very well. In practice, we often have a large amount of training data for some old event types but are interested in extracting instances of a new event type. The new event type is only specified by a small set of seed instances provided by clients (the event type extension setting). How can we effectively leverage the training data of old event types to facilitate the extraction of the new event type?

Inspired by the work on transfer learning and domain adaptation (Blitzer et al., 2006; Jiang and Zhai, 2007; Daume III, 2007; Jiang, 2009), in this paper, we systematically evaluate the representative methods (i.e, the feature based model and the CNN model) for ED to gain an insight into which kind of method performs better in the new extension setting. In addition, we propose a two-stage algorithm to train a CNN model that effectively learns and transfers the knowledge from the old event types for the extraction of the target type.

---

[1]most often a single verb or nominalization

Proceedings of the 1st Workshop on Representation Learning for NLP, pages 158–165,
Berlin, Germany, August 11th, 2016. ©2016 Association for Computational Linguistics

The experimental results show that this two-stage algorithm significantly outperforms the traditional methods in the type extension setting for ED and demonstrates the benefit of CNN in transfer learning. To our knowledge, this is the first work on the type extension setting as well as on transferring knowledge with neural networks for ED of natural language processing.

2   Task Definition

The event type extension setting in this work is as follow. We are given a document set D annotated for a large set D_A of trigger words (positive instances) of some event types (the *auxiliary* types, denoted by A). However, we are interested in extracting trigger words of a new event type T (the *target* type, $T \notin A$) that is only specified by a small annotated set D_T of positive instances (the seeds) in D. Note that while D_A involves all the positive instances of the auxiliary types, D_T might only be partial and not necessarily include all the trigger words of type T in D.

Also, we call D_N the set of the negative instances generated from D under this setting (to be discussed in more details later). In general, D_N might contains unannotated trigger words of T (false negatives), making this task more challenging. Eventually, our goal is to *learn an event detector for T, leveraging the training data D_T, D_A and D_N for both the target and auxiliary types.* Note that our work is related to Jiang (2009) who studies the relation type extension problem.

3   Models for Event Detection

In this section, we first present the representative approaches for ED. The two-stage algorithm will be discussed in the next section.

We treat the event detection problem for the target type T as a binary classification problem. For every token in a given sentence, we want to predict if the current token is an event trigger of type T or not? The current token along with its context in the sentence constitute an event trigger candidate or an example in the binary classification terms.

3.1   The Feature-based Model

In the feature-based model (denoted by FET), the event trigger candidates are first transformed into rich feature vectors to encapsulate linguistically useful properties for ED. These vectors are then fed into a statistical classifier such as maximum entropy (MaxEnt) and classified as the type T or not. In this work, we employ the feature set for ED from (Li et al., 2013), which is the state-of-the-art FET.

3.2   The Convolutional Neural Networks

In a CNN for ED, we limit the context of the trigger candidates to a fixed window size by trimming longer sentences and padding shorter sentences with a special token when necessary. Let $2w + 1$ be the fixed window size, and $x = [x_{-w}, x_{-w+1}, \ldots, x_0, \ldots, x_{w-1}, x_w]$ be some trigger candidate where the current token is positioned in the middle of the window (token x_0). Before entering CNN, each token x_i is transformed into a real-valued vector $\mathbf{x}_i$ by concatenating the continuous look-up vectors from the following tables:

1.   Word Embedding Table E (Turian et al., 2010; Mikolov et al., 2013a; Mikolov et al., 2013b).

2.   Position Embedding Table: to embed the relative distance i of x_i to the current token x_0.

3.   Entity Type Embedding Table: to capture the entity type information for each token. Following Nguyen and Grishman (2015), we assign the entity type labels to each token using the heads of the entity mentions in x with the BIO schema.

As a result, the original event trigger candidate x is transformed into a matrix $\mathbf{x} = [\mathbf{x}_{-w}, \mathbf{x}_{-w+1}, \ldots, \mathbf{x}_0, \ldots, \mathbf{x}_{w-1}, \mathbf{x}_w]$. This matrix will serve as the input for CNN.

For CNN, the matrix $\mathbf{x}$ is first passed through a convolution layer and then a max pooling layer to compute the global representation vector R_C for the trigger candidate x (Nguyen and Grishman, 2015). In addition, we obtain the local representation vector R_L by concatenating the embedding vectors of the words in a window size $2d + 1$ of x_0, motivated by the models in Chen et al. (2015):

$$R_L = [E[x_{-d}], \ldots, E[x_0], \ldots, E[x_d]]$$

Finally, the concatenation of the global and local vectors R_C and R_L is used as the input for a feed-forward neural network with a softmax layer in the end to perform trigger identification for T. Note that our CNN model is similar to (Nguyen and Grishman, 2015) and applies multiple window sizes for the feature maps in the convolution layer.

4 Event Type Extension Systems

4.1 The Baseline Systems

For each of the two models presented above (i.e, FET and CNN), we have two baseline mechanisms to train an event detector for T (Jiang, 2009). In the first baseline (denoted by TARGET), we use the small instance set D_T of the target type T together with the negative instances in D_N to train a binary classifier for T. In the second baseline (denoted by UNION), we combine the positive instances in both D_T and D_A as well as the negative instances in D_N to train a binary classifier for T.

Eventually, we have 4 baseline systems corresponding to the two choices of models (i.e, FET, CNN) and the two choices of the training mechanisms (i.e, TARGET, UNION). We denote these four baselines by: FET-TARGET, FET-UNION, CNN-TARGET, and CNN-UNION.

4.2 Hypothesis About the Baselines

The underlying assumption of transfer learning for type extension is the existence of the general features that are effective for prediction across different types (Jiang, 2009). The performance of a model for a given target type, thus, depends on two factors: (i) how well the model identifies and quantifies general features, and (ii) how effectively the model transfers the knowledge about the general features and adapt it to the target type.

Hypothesis: the UNION training mechanism is more effective than TARGET when the number of seed instances of the target type is small. The reason originates from the inclusion of the training data D_A of the auxiliary types in UNION that would provide more evidences to estimate the importance of the general features better (factor (i)).

4.3 The Two-stage Algorithm

Although UNION can help to learn the general features, its major limitation lies in the lack of the directing mechanisms to make the model specific to the target type (factor (ii)). Essentially, UNION treats the positive instances of the target and auxiliary types similarly, making it more about a general purpose event detector rather than a specific detector for the target type. Therefore, we propose to consider the positive instances of the target D_T and the auxiliary types D_A in two separate stages.

In the first stage, a large amount of the training data D_A of the auxiliary types are used by a CNN to learn the general feature extractors across event types. In the second stage, the seed instances of the target type in D_T are used to adapt the models to the target type. In order to transfer the knowledge from the auxiliary types to the target type between these two stages, we propose to utilize a CNN that facilitates the transferring process via the weight initialization. The two-stage algorithm (CNN-2-STAGE) is presented below.

Algorithm 1: CNN-2-STAGE

Input : D_T, D_A and D_N
Output: An event detector for T

1   Stage I: Train a CNN model on $D_A \cup D_N$ with randomly initialized weight matrices and embedding.
2   Let P be the set of weight matrices and embedding tables after the training process of CNN in stage I.
3   Stage II: Train a CNN on $D_T \cup D_N$ *with the weight matrices and embedding tables initialized by the corresponding elements in P.*
4   Return the CNN model trained in Stage II

Note that similar to stage I of the algorithm and previous work on neural networks (Nguyen and Grishman, 2015; Chen et al., 2015), the weight matrices and embedding tables are also initialized randomly in the training mechanisms UNION and TARGET. The only exception is the word embedding table that is pre-trained on a large corpus for UNION, TARGET as well as the stage I.

All the weight matrices and embedding tables are optimized during training (for UNION, TARGET as well as CNN-2-STAGE) to achieve the optimal state. This is especially important in Stage II of CNN-2-STAGE as it helps to adapt the general feature extractors in Stage I to the target type T.

5 Training

Following Nguyen and Grishman (2015), we train the NN models using stochastic gradient descent with shuffled mini-batches, the AdaDelta update rule, back-propagation and dropout. Finally, we rescale the weights whose l_2-norms exceed a predefined threshold.

6 Experiments

6.1 Parameters and Resources

For all the experiments below, we utilize the pre-trained word embeddings `word2vec` (300 dimensions) from Mikolov et al. (2013a) to initialize the word embedding table. The parameters for CNN and training the network are inherited from the previous studies, i.e, the fixed window size $w = 15$, the window size set for feature maps

$= \{2, 3, 4, 5\}$, 150 feature maps for each window size, 50 dimensions for all the embedding tables (except the word embedding table), the dropout rate $= 0.5$, the mini-batch size $= 50$, the hyper-parameter for the l_2 norms $= 3$ and the window for local context $d = 5$ (Nguyen and Grishman, 2015; Chen et al., 2015).

6.2 Dataset and Settings

Following the previous work (Li et al., 2013; Chen et al., 2015; Nguyen and Grishman, 2015), we consider the ED task of the 2005 Automatic Context Extraction (ACE) evaluation that annotates 8 event types and 33 event subtypes [2]. As the numbers of event mentions (triggers) for each subtype in ACE are small, in this work, we focus on the extraction of the event types: *"Life"*, *"Movement"*, *"Transaction"*, *"Business"*, *"Conflict"*, *"Contact"*, *"Personell"*, and *"Justice"*. We remove the event triggers of types *"Transaction"* and *"Business"* due to their small numbers of occurrences, resulting in the dataset with six remaining event types (denoted from 1 to 6).

In the experiments, we use the same data split in Li et al. (2013) with 40 newswire documents as a test set, 30 other documents as a development set and the 529 remaining documents as a training set. Note that the training documents correspond to our original dataset D above. Let P_i be the positive instance set of the type i in D ($i = 1$ to 6).

We take each event type i as the target type T and treat the other 5 types as the auxiliary types, constituting 6 sets of experiments. In each set of experiments for a target type i (T), we randomly select S positive instances of T for the seed set D_T ($S = |D_T|$) and *treat the remaining target instances $P_i \setminus D_T$ as negative*. Note that this essentially introduces false negatives into the training data and makes the task more challenging.

In order to deal with false negatives, we remove all the sentences that do not contain any events in the original dataset D. In this way, we remove a large number of true negatives along with a fraction of the false negatives, leading to the reduced dataset D'. We do the experiments on D' with:

$$D_A = \bigcup_{j=1(j \neq i)}^{6} P_j$$

$$D_N = D' \setminus D_T \setminus D_A$$

<hr>

[2] https://www.ldc.upenn.edu/sites/www.ldc.upenn.edu/files/english-events-guidelines-v5.4.3.pdf

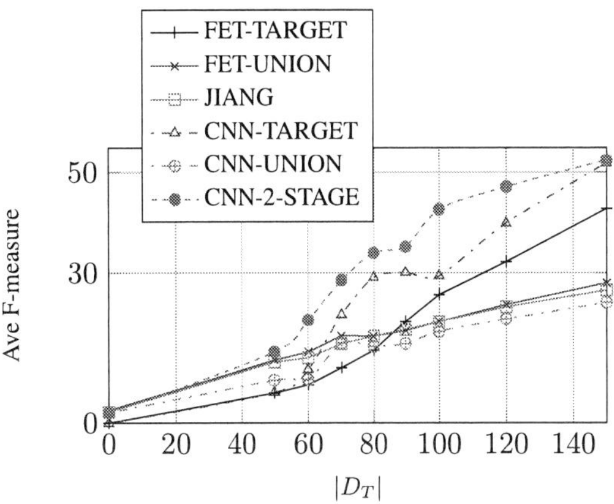

Figure 1: Average F measures vs $|D_T|$.

We note that (Jiang, 2009) uses a different setting in training where she removes all the remaining target instances $P_i \setminus D_T$ directly. In our opinion, this is unrealistic as it assumes the label of the instances in $P_i \setminus D_T$ while we are only provided with the label of the seed set D_T in practice.

Finally, similar to (Jiang, 2009), we remove the positive instances of the auxiliary event types from the test set to concentrate on the classification accuracy for the target type. We also remove all the positive instances of the target type in the development set to make it more realistic.

6.3 Evaluation

This section compares the four baseline models in Section 4.1 with the proposed two-stage model CNN-2-STAGE. For completeness, we also evaluate the transfer learning model in Jiang (2009), adapted to the event type extension task (called JIANG). For JIANG, we apply the automatic feature separation method as the general syntactic patterns and type constraints for relation in Jiang (2009) are not applicable to our ED task.

For each described model, we perform six sets of experiments in Section 6.2, where the number of seed instances $|D_T|$ is varied from 0 to 150. We then report the *average F-scores* of the six experiment sets for each value of S. Figure 1 shows the curves.

Assuming the same kind of model (i.e, either FET or CNN), we see that UNION is better than TARGET when $|D_T|$ is small, confirming our hypothesis in Section 4.2. This demonstrates the benefit of UNION and the training data D_A of the auxiliary types when there are not enough training

| Target | FET | FET | JIANG | CNN | CNN | CNN |
Type	TARGET	UNION		TARGET	UNION	2-STAGE
Movement	**21.8**	9.2	9.6	4.1	4.0	19.7
Personnel	19.4	15.8	17.3	27.3	16.4	**40.5**
Conflict	12.8	18.0	17.9	12.8	29.8	**43.0**
Contact	45.4	35.7	34.6	**62.5**	19.2	54.6
Life	29.8	21.8	22.5	22.2	24.7	**50.0**
Justice	24.6	20.9	19.4	47.4	15.3	**48.0**
Average	25.6	20.2	20.2	29.4	18.2	**42.6**

Table 1: System Performance

Event Type	Examples
Personnel	*Georgia **fired** football coach Jim Donnan Monday after a disappointing 7-4 season* . . . *The bad doctors are **removed** from the practice of medicine.*
Conflict	*U.S. forces continued to **bomb** Fallujah.* *Israel retaliated with rocket **attacks** and terrorists **blew** a hole in a United States warship in Yemen.* *Protesters **rallied** on the White House lawn.*
Life	*. . . and two Israeli soldiers were **wounded**, one critically.* *Witnesses said the soldiers responded by firing tear gas and rubber bullets, which led to ten demonstrators being **injured**.* *John Hinckley attempted to **assassinate** Ronald Reagan.*
Justice	*Since May, Russia has **jailed** over 20 suspected terrorists without a trial.* *A judicial source said today, Friday, that five Croatians were **arrested** last Tuesday during an operation . . .*

Table 2: Examples for the trigger words with the latent semantic. The trigger words are underlined.

instances for T. However, when we are provided with more seed instances for the target type (i.e, $|D_T|$ becomes larger), TARGET turns out to be significantly better than UNION.

We also observe that CNN outperforms FET in the TARGET mechanism. This is consistent with the previous studies for ED (Nguyen and Grishman, 2015). However, in the UNION mechanism, CNN is less effective than FET, suggesting that UNION is not a good mechanism to transfer knowledge in CNN.

We do not see much performance improvement of JIANG over FET-UNION. This can be explained by the lack of explicit linguistic guidance (i.e, the syntactic patterns and type constraints) for the general features in the event extension task that are crucial to the success of the model in Jiang (2009).

Finally and most importantly, we see that the two-stage model CNN-2-STAGE outperforms all the compared models regardless of $|D_T|$. This is significant when $|D_T|$ is greater than 50. These results suggest the effectiveness of the two-stage training algorithm on transferring knowledge from the auxiliary types to the target type for CNN.

6.4 Analysis

In order to further understand the systems on the separate event types, Table 1 presents the performance of the compared systems for the six experiment sets in Section 6.2 (corresponding to the 6 different choices of the event target type T in the dataset) when S is set to 100.

One of the most important observations from the table is that CNN-2-STAGE is significantly better than JIANG, CNN-TARGET and CNN-UNION on five target types (i.e, $Y = \{Movement, Personnel, Conflict, Life, Justice\}$)[3] and only worse than CNN-TARGET on the *Contact* type. This raises a question on the distinction between *Contact* and the other event types in Y that affects the transferring effectiveness of CNN-2-STAGE. Also, what is the common feature of the event types in Y that helps CNN-2-STAGE successfully transfers knowledge between them?

The key insight of our system output analysis is the shared latent semantic among a large por-

---

[3] Although it is less pronounced for *Justice*

Even Type	Event Subtypes	Most Frequent Triggers
Contact	*Meet, Phone-Write*	*meeting, talks, meet, call, summit, meetings, met, letters, talked, conference*
Movement	*Transport*	*go, come, arrived, get, trip, leave, went, moving, moved, take*
Personnel	*Start-Position, End-Position, Nominate, Elect*	*election, elections, former, elected, appointed, resigned, fired, retired, won, leaving*
Conflict	*Attack, Demonstrate*	*war, attack, fighting, attacks, fire, bombing, fight, hit, combat, shot*
Life	*Be-Born, Marry, Divorce, Injure, Die*	*killed, death, died, suicide, injured, dead, killing, divorce, married, die*
Justice	*Arrest-Jail, Release-Parole, Trial-Hearing, Charge-Indict, Sue, Convict, Sentence, Fine, Execute, Extradite, Acquit, Appeal, Pardon*	*trial, convicted, sentence, charges, arrested, appeal, sentenced, charged, sued, parole*

Table 3: Event types, subtypes and the most frequent trigger words.

tion of trigger words of the four event types in $Y \setminus \{Movement\}$. In particular, all the four event types in $Y \setminus \{Movement\}$ includes trigger words that induce some level of conflict between their subjects and objects. These conflicts are often manifested by some physical and irritating actions between the two engaged parties. Some examples of the trigger words with the latent semantic for the event types in $Y \setminus \{Movement\}$ are given in Table 2[4]. This latent semantic is first captured by word embeddings and CNN in Stage I of CNN-2-STAGE, and then transferred to the target type in Stage II. The feature-based transfer learning systems like JIANG, on the other hand, cannot encode such latent semantics effectively as they rely on the discrete features with the symbolic representation of words.

In the ACE 2005 corpus, the event type *Movement* only has one subtype of *Transport* which mainly focuses on the transportation of weapons, vehicles or people. The context of the trigger words of the subtype *Transport* often involves the military or struggling objects such as soldiers, Iraq, forces etc. These context words are similar to those of the trigger words of the types *Conflict* and *Life*. As a result, the CNN-2-STAGE algorithm can learn these general features from the trigger words of *Conflict* and *Life*, and then transfer them to improve the extraction of *Movement*. We show some examples of *Movement* below:

1. *After today's air strikes, 13 Iraqi soldiers **abandoned** their posts and surrendered to Kurdish fighters.*

2. *The convoy was **escorted** by U.S. soldiers.*

3. *Israeli forces **moved** into Hebron's Al-Sheikh district where his family lived ...*

Finally, regarding the event type *Contact*, it occurs when two or more entities engage in discussion either directly or remotely[5]. The purpose of such discussions are often about information or opinion exchange rather than a mean to express discussions or conflicts with irritating actions (as the event types in Y do). This divergence between *Contact* and Y leads to the poor quality of the general features learnt by the transfer learning methods (i.e, JIANG and CNN-2-STAGE), eventually degrading their performances. Some examples of the *Contact* event type are given below:

1. *People can **communicate** with international friends without the hefty phone bills.*

2. *I'm chewing gum and **talking** on the phone while writing this note.*

3. *Mr. Erekat is due to travel to Washington to **meet** with US Secretary of State Madeleine Albright and other US officials ...*

In order to further demonstrate the difference between *Contact* and the other event types, Table 3 enumerates the event subtypes and the most frequent trigger words for each event. The event subtypes in Table 3 can be considered as the concepts or topics covered by the corresponding event types in the ACE 2005 corpus. As we can see from the

---

[4]Taken from the ACE 2005 Annotation Guideline

[5]Defined by the annotation guideline.

table, the *Meet* and *Phone-Write* subtypes or topics of *Contact* are quite separate from those of the other types.

7 Related Work

Early research on event extraction has primarily focused on local sentence-level representations in a pipelined architecture (Grishman et al., 2005; Ahn, 2006). Afterward, higher level features have been found to improve the performance (Ji and Grishman, 2008; Gupta and Ji, 2009; Patwardhan and Riloff, 2009; Liao and Grishman, 2010; Liao and Grishman, 2011; Hong et al., 2011; McClosky et al., 2011; Huang and Riloff, 2012; Li et al., 2013). Some recent research has proposed joint models for EE, including the methods based on Markov Logic Networks (Riedel et al., 2009; Poon and Vanderwende, 2010; Venugopal et al., 2014), structured perceptron (Li et al., 2013; Li et al., 2014b), and dual decomposition (Riedel et al. (2009; 2011b)).

The application of neural networks to EE is very recent. In particular, Zhou et al. (2014) and Boros et al. (2014) use neural networks to learn word embeddings from a corpus of specific domains and then directly utilize these embeddings as features in statistical classifiers. Chen et al. (2015) apply dynamic multi-pooling CNNs for EE in a pipelined framework, while Nguyen et al. (2016) propose joint event extraction using recurrent neural networks.

Finally, domain adaptation and transfer learning have been studied extensively for various NLP tasks, including part of speech tagging (Blitzer et al., 2006), name tagging (Daume III, 2007), parsing (McClosky et al., 2010), relation extraction (Plank and Moschitti, 2013; Nguyen and Grishman, 2014; Nguyen et al., 2015a), to name a few. For event extraction, Miwa et al. (2013) study instance weighting and stacking models while Riedel and McCallum (2011b) examine joint models with domain adaptation. However, none of them studies the new type extension setting for ED using neural networks like we do.

8 Conclusion

We systematically evaluate the ED models on the new type extension setting. A two-stage algorithm to train the CNN model and transfer knowledge is introduced, yielding the state-of-the-art performance for the extension task. In the future, we plan to apply the two-stage algorithm to other tasks such as relation extension to further verify its effectiveness.

References

David Ahn. 2006. The stages of event extraction. In *Proceedings of the Workshop on Annotating and Reasoning about Time and Events*.

John Blitzer, Ryan McDonald, and Fernando Pereira. 2006. Domain adaptation with structural correspondence learning. In *EMNLP*.

Emanuela Boros, Romaric Besançon, Olivier Ferret, and Brigitte Grau. 2014. Event role extraction using domain-relevant word representations. In *EMNLP*.

Yubo Chen, Liheng Xu, Kang Liu, Daojian Zeng, and Jun Zhao. 2015. Event extraction via dynamic multi-pooling convolutional neural networks. In *ACL-IJCNLP*.

Hal Daume III. 2007. Frustratingly easy domain adaptation. In *ACL*.

Ralph Grishman, David Westbrook, and Adam Meyers. 2005. Nyus english ace 2005 system description. In *ACE 2005 Evaluation Workshop*.

Prashant Gupta and Heng Ji. 2009. Predicting unknown time arguments based on cross-event propagation. In *ACL-IJCNLP*.

Yu Hong, Jianfeng Zhang, Bin Ma, Jianmin Yao, Guodong Zhou, and Qiaoming Zhu. 2011. Using cross-entity inference to improve event extraction. In *ACL*.

Ruihong Huang and Ellen Riloff. 2012. Modeling textual cohesion for event extraction. In *AAAI*.

Heng Ji and Ralph Grishman. 2008. Refining event extraction through cross-document inference. In *ACL*.

Jing Jiang and ChengXiang Zhai. 2007. A two-stage approach to domain adaptation for statistical classifiers. In *CIKM*.

Jing Jiang. 2009. Multi-task transfer learning for weakly-supervised relation extraction. In *ACL-IJCNLP*.

Qi Li, Heng Ji, and Liang Huang. 2013. Joint event extraction via structured prediction with global features. In *ACL*.

Qi Li, Heng Ji, Yu Hong, and Sujian Li. 2014b. Constructing information networks using one single model. In *EMNLP*.

Shasha Liao and Ralph Grishman. 2010. Using document level cross-event inference to improve event extraction. In *ACL*.

Shasha Liao and Ralph Grishman. 2011. Acquiring topic features to improve event extraction: in pre-selected and balanced collections. In *RANLP*.

David McClosky, Eugene Charniak, , and Mark Johnson. 2010. Automatic domain adaptation for parsing. In *NAACL-HLT*.

David McClosky, Mihai Surdeanu, and Christopher Manning. 2011. Event extraction as dependency parsing. In *BioNLP Shared Task Workshop*.

Tomas Mikolov, Kai Chen, Greg Corrado, and Jeffrey Dean. 2013a. Efficient estimation of word representations in vector space. In *ICLR*.

Tomas Mikolov, Ilya Sutskever, Kai Chen, Greg Corrado, and Jeffrey Dean. 2013b. Distributed representations of words and phrases and their compositionality. In *NIPS*.

Makoto Miwa, Paul Thompson, and Sophia Ananiadou. 2013. Boosting automatic event extraction from the literature using domain adaptation and coreference resolution. In *Bioinformatics*.

Thien Huu Nguyen and Ralph Grishman. 2014. Employing word representations and regularization for domain adaptation of relation extraction. In *ACL*.

Thien Huu Nguyen and Ralph Grishman. 2015. Event detection and domain adaptation with convolutional neural networks. In *ACL-IJCNLP*.

Thien Huu Nguyen, Barbara Plank, and Ralph Grishman. 2015a. Semantic representations for domain adaptation: A case study on the tree kernel-based method for relation extraction. In *ACL-IJCNLP*.

Thien Huu Nguyen, Kyunghyun Cho, and Ralph Grishman. 2016. Joint event extraction via recurrent neural networks. In *NAACL-HLT*.

Siddharth Patwardhan and Ellen Riloff. 2009. A unified model of phrasal and sentential evidence for information extraction. In *EMNLP*.

Barbara Plank and Alessandro Moschitti. 2013. Embedding semantic similarity in tree kernels for domain adaptation of relation extraction. In *ACL*.

Hoifung Poon and Lucy Vanderwende. 2010. Joint inference for knowledge extraction from biomedical literature. In *NAACL-HLT*.

Sebastian Riedel and Andrew McCallum. 2011. Fast and robust joint models for biomedical event extraction. In *EMNLP*.

Sebastian Riedel and Andrew McCallum. 2011b. Robust biomedical event extraction with dual decomposition and minimal domain adaptation. In *BioNLP Shared Task 2011 Workshop*.

Sebastian Riedel, Hong-Woo Chun, Toshihisa Takagi, and Jun'ichi Tsujii. 2009. A markov logic approach to bio-molecular event extraction. In *BioNLP 2009 Workshop*.

Joseph Turian, Lev-Arie Ratinov, and Yoshua Bengio. 2010. Word representations: A simple and general method for semi-supervised learning. In *ACL*.

Deepak Venugopal, Chen Chen, Vibhav Gogate, and Vincent Ng. 2014. Relieving the computational bottleneck: Joint inference for event extraction with high-dimensional features. In *EMNLP*.

Deyu Zhou, Dayou Zhong, and Yulan He. 2014. Event trigger identification for biomedical events extraction using domain knowledge. In *Bioinformatics Journal*.

Parameterized context windows in Random Indexing

Tobias Norlund
Schibsted Products and Technology
Västra Järnvgsgatan 21
111 64 Stockholm
Sweden
tobias.norlund@schibsted.com

David Nilsson
Nepa
Maria Skolgata 83
118 53 Stockholm
Sweden
david.nilsson@nepa.com

Magnus Sahlgren
Gavagai
Slussplan 9
111 30 Stockholm
Sweden
magnus.sahlgren@gavagai.se

Abstract

This paper introduces a parameterization for word embeddings produced by the Random Indexing framework. The parameterization introduces position specific weights in the context windows, and the approach is shown to improve the performance in both word similarity and sentiment classification tasks. We also demonstrate the relation between Random Indexing and Convolutional Neural Networks.

1 Introduction

Quantifying the importance of contextual information for semantic representation is the goal of *distributional semantics*, in which contextual information is used to quantify semantic similarities between words (Turney and Pantel, 2010). However, standard practice in distributional semantics is to weight the importance of context items based on either its frequency (Sahlgren et al., 2016), its distance to the focus word (Lund et al., 1995), or its global co-occurrence statistics (Niwa and Nitta, 1994). Thus far, there has not been much work on applying machine learning to this in order to select useful context items for distributional semantics.

The idea with the proposed parameterization is to weight the items in the context window based on their usefulness for accomplishing some specific task, such as sentiment classification or word similarity rating. In this paper, we introduce a simple parameterization for the Random Indexing processing model. We first show that Random Indexing can be formulated in terms of a convolution, in order to situate the framework in the context of neural networks. We then introduce a simple parameterization of the positions on the context windows, and we show that it improves the

performance of the embeddings in some word similarity and sentiment classification tasks. [1]

2 Notation

Using a vocabulary $\mathcal{V}$ of words w_i for $i = 1, \ldots, |\mathcal{V}|$, we seek word embeddings $\mathbf{v}_i \in \mathbb{R}^d$ by collecting statistics from a corpus $\mathcal{C} = \{w_1, \ldots, w_t, \ldots, w_N\}$. We will interchangeably mix subscripts i and t of words and embeddings to index the vocabulary and corpus respectively.

3 Random Indexing as Convolution

Random Indexing (RI) (Kanerva et al., 2000; Kanerva, 2009) is a distributional semantic model that updates the embedding vectors $\mathbf{v}_*$ in an online fashion by summing the sparse random vectors $\mathbf{e}_*$ that represent the context items (these vectors are called *random index vectors* and act as unique identifiers for the context items, words in this case):

$$\mathbf{v}_t \leftarrow \mathbf{v}_t + \sum_{\substack{l=-k \\ l \neq 0}}^{k} h(w_{t+l})\mathbf{e}_{t+l} \qquad (1)$$

k is the context window size and $h(w)$ some weight that quantifies the importance of the context item (the standard setting is $h(w) = 1$ for all w). Here $\mathbf{e}_{t+l}$ is the random index vector to corpus item w_{t+l}.

Equation (1) describes the update rule of RI and the final embeddings $\mathbf{v}_i$ can be expressed as:

$$\mathbf{v}_i = \sum_{\substack{l=-k \\ l \neq 0}}^{k} \sum_{\substack{t=1 \\ w_t=w_i}}^{N} h(w_{t+l})\mathbf{e}_{t+l} \qquad (2)$$

To establish the equivalence between RI and convolution, we can reformulate the update rule

---

[1]The code is available at: http://github.com/TobiasNorlund/Attention_RI

Proceedings of the 1st Workshop on Representation Learning for NLP, pages 166–173,
Berlin, Germany, August 11th, 2016. ©2016 Association for Computational Linguistics

in Equation (1) as follows; let $\mathbf{h} \in \mathbb{R}^{(2k+1) \times d}$ be a filter function where

$$h_{lj} = \begin{cases} 1, & \forall (l,j) \in \{(0, \frac{d}{2}), \ldots, (k-1, \frac{d}{2}), (k+1, \frac{d}{2}), \ldots, (2k, \frac{d}{2})\} \\ 0, & \text{else} \end{cases}$$

Furthermore, let $\mathbf{S} \in \mathbb{R}^{N \times d}$ be a matrix of stacked sparse random vectors $\mathbf{e}_t$. Now, if we use $\mathbf{h}$ and $\mathbf{S}$, we can rewrite the second term of the random indexing update rule in Equation (1):

$$\mathbf{Z}_{tv} = \sum_{l=0}^{2k} \sum_{j=0}^{d} (\mathbf{e}_{t-l+k})_{v-j+d} \mathbf{h}_{lj}. \tag{3}$$

Equation (3) is a 2D discrete convolution between $\mathbf{S}$ and $\mathbf{h}$, hence:

$$\mathbf{Z}_{tv} = (\mathbf{S} * \mathbf{h})[t, v] = \sum_{l=0}^{2k} \sum_{j=0}^{d} (\mathbf{e}_{t-l+k})_{v-j+d} \mathbf{h}_{lj}. \tag{4}$$

Because $\mathbf{h}$ has been defined with zeros everywhere except for column $\frac{d}{2}$, Equation (4) can been seen as a 1D convolution over each column vector in $\mathbf{S}$,

$$\mathbf{Z}_{tv} = (\mathbf{S}_v^T * \mathbf{h}_{\frac{d}{2}}^T)[t] = \sum_{l=0}^{2k} (\mathbf{e}_{t-l+k})_v \mathbf{h}_{t\frac{d}{2}}. \tag{5}$$

4 Dealing with Redundant Features

Since word embeddings (produced by RI or some other distributional model) are constructed unsupervised by collecting co-occurrence information from a large corpus, it is likely that the resulting embeddings are very general, which may lower the expressiveness of the embeddings if they are going to be used in a very specific domain. Take the example of training a text categorization classifier within a financial context; corpus occurrences of the words "bank" and "stock" in the senses of LARGE COLLECTION and INVENTORY will likely not provide useful information for the embeddings in this domain. In word embeddings, different senses are represented by co-occurrences with different context items (Cuba Gyllensten and Sahlgren, 2015). We refer to context items that are less useful for a specific task as *redundant features* of the embeddings.

Unfortunately, it is not, in the general case, possible to know a priori which context items will be useful to construct embeddings for a particular task. Such context (i.e. feature) selection instead needs to be performed jointly with training the classifier. When backpropagation is used as optimization strategy of the classifier, one can also

treat the word embeddings as parameters to update. It is straightforward to take the derivatives of the objective function with respect to the input and apply Stochastic Gradient Descent (SGD) updates just as for the model parameters. This strategy is well known (Zhang and Wallace, 2015), and will be referred to as SGD Random Indexing (SGD-RI).

5 Parameterization of context window

Another strategy is to parameterize the word embeddings, and to optimize those parameters jointly with the task using backpropagation. The RI algorithm, as defined in (Sahlgren et al., 2016), weights the importance of context items based on their relative frequency according to Equation (6):

$$h(w_t) = \exp\left(-c \cdot \frac{f(w_t)}{|\mathcal{V}|}\right) \tag{6}$$

where c is a constant, $f(w_t)$ is the corpus frequency of item w_t, and $|\mathcal{V}|$ is the size of the vocabulary (i.e. the number of unique words seen thus far).

We would however like to parameterize context items not only depending on relative frequency but also on their usefulness for the specific task at hand. To describe the suggested parametrization, recall the Random Indexing algorithm in Equation (1) where we look at each word and its context in the corpus in a streaming fashion, and construct embedding vectors by summing the index vectors of all words occurring in the context. A fairly obvious refinement of this algorithm would be to parameterize the relative positions within the context window depending on their usefulness for the task at hand. Equation (7) formalizes the parameterization by introducing an additional factor to the weighting scheme:

$$h(w_{t+l}) = \theta_l^{w_t} \exp\left(-c \cdot \frac{f(w_t)}{|\mathcal{V}|}\right) \tag{7}$$

Inserting this parameterization into the update rule in Equation (1), we get:

$$\mathbf{v}_t \leftarrow \mathbf{v}_t + \sum_{\substack{l=-k \\ l \neq 0}}^{k} \theta_l^{w_t} \exp\left(-c \cdot \frac{f(w_{t+l})}{|\mathcal{V}|}\right) \mathbf{e}_{t+l} \tag{8}$$

which is equivalent to:

$$\mathbf{v}_i = \sum_{\substack{l=-k \\ l \neq 0}}^{k} \sum_{\substack{t=1 \\ w_t = w_i}}^{N} \theta_l^{w_t} \exp\left(-c \cdot \frac{f(w_{t+l})}{|\mathcal{V}|}\right) \mathbf{e}_{t+l} \tag{9}$$

By careful inspection, the $\theta_l^{w_t}$ can be moved outside the inner sum, while swapping the subscript to i since $w_t = w_i$:

$$\mathbf{v}_i = \sum_{\substack{l=-k \\ l \neq 0}}^{k} \theta_l^{w_i} \underbrace{\sum_{\substack{t=1 \\ w_t = w_i}}^{N} \exp\left(-c \cdot \frac{f(w_{t+l})}{|\mathcal{V}|}\right) \mathbf{e}_{t+l}}_{\tilde{\mathbf{v}}_i^l} \tag{10}$$

The rewrite now allows the inner sum to be calculated before fitting the $\theta_l^{w_i}$s which makes the algorithm much more efficient. In practice, this means we aggregate an embedding vector $\tilde{\mathbf{v}}_i^l$ *for each relative window position l, for each word w_i.* Stacking these $2k$ context vectors into a matrix $\mathbf{V}_i$ and collecting the $\theta_l^{w_i}$s in a vector yields:

$$\mathbf{V}_i = \begin{bmatrix} \tilde{\mathbf{v}}_i^{-k} & \cdots & \tilde{\mathbf{v}}_i^{-1} & \tilde{\mathbf{v}}_i^{+1} & \cdots & \tilde{\mathbf{v}}_i^{+k} \end{bmatrix} \tag{11}$$

$$\theta_i = \begin{bmatrix} \theta_{-k}^{w_i} \\ \vdots \\ \theta_{-1}^{w_i} \\ \theta_{+1}^{w_i} \\ \vdots \\ \theta_{+k}^{w_i} \end{bmatrix} \tag{12}$$

Equation (10) can now be rewritten as a matrix vector multiplication:

$$\mathbf{v}_i = \mathbf{V}_i \theta_i. \tag{13}$$

In other words, this suggests instead of aggregating embedding vectors $\mathbf{v}_i$ according to (9), to aggregate matrices $\mathbf{V}_i$ upon parsing the corpus. The embedding vectors are then calculated as a multiplication with a parameter vector θ_i according to (13). Note that when $\theta_i = \mathbf{1}$ you recover the vanilla Random Indexing embeddings.

We will refer to this strategy as Parameterized Random Indexing (PAR-RI).

6 Example: Word Similarity

To exemplify the effectiveness of the proposed parameterization, we use the SimLex-999 (Hill et al., 2015) test in order to see how much the Spearman rank correlation can be improved by fitting the θ_is such that cosine similarity between the embedding vectors correspond to the similarity ratings. Formally, we seek to minimize the following objective function:

$$\min_{\theta_*} \sum_{(w_i, w_j) \in \mathcal{S}} \underbrace{\frac{1}{2}\left(\cos \alpha_{ij} - s(w_i, w_j)\right)^2}_{f(w_i, w_j)} \tag{14}$$

where $(w_i, w_j) \in \mathcal{S}$ corresponds to each word pair in SimLex. $s(w_i, w_j)$ is the SimLex similarity score for the word pair (scaled to $[0,1]$) and $\cos \alpha_{ij}$ is the cosine similarity between the word's corresponding vectors:

$$\alpha_{ij} = \frac{\mathbf{v}_i^T \mathbf{v}_j}{\|\mathbf{v}_i\|_2 \|\mathbf{v}_j\|_2} \tag{15}$$

where $\mathbf{v}_i$ and $\mathbf{v}_j$ are w_i and w_j's corresponding word vectors, calculated as in equation (13). Since this is a non-convex problem, SGD is applied as optimization strategy. Calculating the gradient of f with respect to θ_i and θ_j is straightforward:

$$\frac{\delta f}{\delta \theta_i} = (\cos \alpha_{ij} - s(w_i, w_j)) \frac{\delta \cos \alpha_{ij}}{\delta \theta_i} \tag{16}$$

$$\frac{\delta f}{\delta \theta_j} = (\cos \alpha_{ij} - s(w_i, w_j)) \frac{\delta \cos \alpha_{ij}}{\delta \theta_j}. \tag{17}$$

Applying the chain rule, the gradient of $\cos \alpha_{ij}$ becomes:

$$\frac{\delta \cos \alpha_{ij}}{\delta \theta_i} = \frac{\delta \cos \alpha_{ij}}{\delta \mathbf{v}_i} \frac{\delta \mathbf{v}_i}{\delta \theta_i}$$

$$\frac{\delta \cos \alpha_{ij}}{\delta \mathbf{v}_i} = \frac{\mathbf{v}_j \|\mathbf{v}_i\|_2 - \mathbf{v}_i \frac{\mathbf{v}_i^T \mathbf{v}_j}{\|\mathbf{v}_i\|_2}}{\|\mathbf{v}_i\|_2^2 \|\mathbf{v}_j\|_2} \tag{18}$$

$$\frac{\delta \mathbf{v}_i}{\delta \theta_i} = \mathbf{V}_i.$$

The expression for $\frac{\delta \cos \alpha_{ij}}{\delta \theta_j}$ is the same, but with the subscripts interchanged. We now apply SGD to optimize the θ_is iteratively using the following update rules:

$$\theta_i^{(t+1)} = \theta_i^t - \eta \frac{\delta f}{\delta \theta_i}$$

$$\theta_j^{(t+1)} = \theta_j^t - \eta \frac{\delta f}{\delta \theta_j}. \tag{19}$$

This procedure is performed using $\mathbf{V}_*$ matrices generated from a dump of Wikipedia with the Random Indexing hyper-parameters listed in Table 1. The $\boldsymbol{\theta}_i$s are initialized to one-vectors ($\boldsymbol{\theta}_* = \mathbf{1}$) and updated according to equation (19) with a learning rate $\eta = 1.0$ until convergence.

Table 1: Hyper-parameters for PAR-RI.

Parameter	Value	Description
d	2,000	Dimensionality
k	10	Window size
c	60	Constant in frequency weight
ϵ	10	Non-zero elements in index vectors randomly drawn from $\{-1, +1\}$

The results are summarized in Table 2. We can see that the Spearman correlation is drastically improved with the optimized $\boldsymbol{\theta}_i$s. This experiment can be seen as, for each word w_i, finding a linear combination in the column space of $\mathbf{V}_i$ that optimizes the cosine similarity of the word vectors to match the SimLex similarity scores. It is remarkable that optimizing the $\boldsymbol{\theta}_i$s in the relatively small 20-dimensional ($\mathbf{R}^{2k}$) subspaces of the full word space ($\mathbf{R}^{2000}$) yields such a big improvement.

Table 2: Results of the SimLex experiment.

	Avg. error	Spearman
Initial $\boldsymbol{\theta}_i$s ($\boldsymbol{\theta}_* = \mathbf{1}$)	0.28	0.21
Optimized $\boldsymbol{\theta}_i$s	0.19	**0.62**

7 Example: Sentiment Classification

The improvements reported in the previous section should motivate the parameterization to be viable for improving the performance in text classification as well. In this section, we parameterize the embeddings for sentiment classification using two standard benchmarks; the Pang and Lee Sentence Polarity Dataset v1.0 (PL05) (Pang and Lee, 2005) and the Stanford Sentiment Treebank (SST) (Socher et al., 2013). The PL05 data consists of 10,662 short movie reviews that are classified as either positive or negative. Experiments using this dataset are split into 25% test and 75% train/validation sets and evaluated by 5-fold cross validation on the training/validation set. We make two consecutive runs, in total 10 trainings, and report their maximum, minimum and mean accuracy as well as their standard deviation. The SST data is an extension of PL05 with train/validation/test splits provided. The dataset also provides fine-grained labels (very positive, positive, neutral, negative, very negative). In this study we have however omitted the neutral labels and treated it as a binary classification problem by merging the very positive, positive, very negative and negative classes into two. We report the maximum, minimum and mean accuracy as well as the standard deviation of 10 consecutive runs using the provided train/val/test splits.

We use two different classifiers in these experiments. The first is a standard neural network (referred to as MLP for Multi-Layer Perceptron) (Rumelhart et al., 1986) with one hidden layer of 120 nodes with sigmoid activations and one sigmoid output unit. All word vectors are normalized to an l_2 norm of 1 and naively summed to produce document vectors. The weights in the neural network are also l_2 regularized with a constant factor of $\lambda = 0.001$. The second classifier is the model proposed by Kim (2014) which implements a Convolutional Neural Network (CNN). The hyper-parameters used are listed in table 3. Like the MLP model, the word embeddings are also normalized to unit length.

Table 3: Hyper-parameters for CNN.

Parameter	Value	Description
n	300	Number of filters, 100 of height 3,4,5 respectively
p	0.5	Dropout rate
s	3	Filter max l_2-norm

As comparison with the different RI-based embeddings (RI, SGD-RI, and PAR-RI), we also include results using embeddings produced with SGNS (Mikolov et al., 2013) and GloVe (Pennington et al., 2014), both with 300-dimensional vectors and a window size of 2. We also include results using embeddings randomly sampled from a uniform $U(-0.25, 0.25)$ distribution (RAND). All word embeddings (except for the RAND vectors) are pre-trained (unsupervised) on a dump of Wikipedia. We list all hyper-parameters for RI, SGNS and GloVe in table 4, 5 and 6

Table 4: Hyper-parameters for RI

Parameter	Value	Description
d	2,000	Dimensionality
k	2	Window size
c	60	Constant
ϵ	10	# non-zero elements in index vectors randomly drawn from $\{-1, +1\}$

The results of all experiments are shown in ta-

Table 5: Hyper-parameters for SGNS

Parameter	Value	Description
d	300	Dimensionality
k	2	Window size
negative	5	Number of negative samples per positive
down sampling	no	No down sampling is applied
α	0.025	Initial learning rate
iter	5	Number of iterations

Table 6: Hyper-parameters for GloVe

Parameter	Value	Description
d	300	Dimensionality
k	2	Window size
iter	15	Number of training iterations
x-max	10	Cutoff in weighting function
α	0.75	Constant in exponent of weighting function
η	0.05	Initial learning rate

ble 7 (next page).[2] Comparing the various embeddings, it is obvious that the performance differences are very small, and thus not likely to be of any significant practical importance. This is especially true for the MLP experiments where the variances reach over two points in many cases. On the other hand, all embeddings outperform the randomized RAND vectors, which demonstrates that classification performance is improved when the model can take semantic information into account. The best performing embedding for the MLP classifier is PAR-RI, while SGNS performs better using the CNN model. The GloVe embeddings, despite their theoretical similarities to the SGNS embeddings (Suzuki and Nagata, 2015), consistently underperform both in comparison with SGNS and PAR-RI (and, in the case of the MLP classifier, also the SGD-RI embeddings). This is in contrast to the experiments performed by (Zhang and Wallace, 2015) where the difference was minor.

Comparing the PAR-RI embeddings with SGD-RI and standard RI, it seems PAR-RI performs well, with the highest mean accuracy on the SST dataset, using the MLP model. SGD-RI improves the results compared to the standard RI embeddings for the MLP model, but not for the CNN model. Updating of the SGNS embeddings just like SGD-RI for the CNN have also been studied in Zhang and Wallace (2015), who report a performance boost of about $\sim$0.8%. This also contrasts to our results with SGD-RI using the CNN model,

which instead decrease the performance compared to standard RI. This could be due to the RI embeddings being more high dimensional than SGNS, yielding a larger and harder parameter space to optimize.

Comparing our results to other reported results in the literature, Kim (2014) and Zhang and Wallace (2015) manage to push the boundaries up to 80.10 for the PL05 data, and up to 84.88 for the SST data using SGNS embeddings pre-trained on a much larger 100 billion tokens Google News dataset. We believe this somewhat increased performance is partly due to the bigger dataset. Another factor could also be that the language style in news articles is more similar to the movie reviews compared to Wikipedia, arguably yielding better-suited embeddings.

8   Optimized Context Profiles

When the PAR-RI parametrization was proposed, the hypothesis was that certain relative positions in the context windows would be more important in describing the context of a word than others. The results in the two previous sections demonstrate that the proposed parameterization is able to improve the embeddings in both a word similarity task, and (to a lesser extent) a sentiment classification task. This indicates that the parameterization is actually able to find useful context profiles for terms used in the various test settings. In this section, we exemplify the kinds of context profiles learned when trained for the sentiment classification task.

Figure 1 (on page 7) shows the learned weights per context window position for four different adjectives (top row), four different determiners (middle row), and four different nouns (bottom row). The parameterization obviously has a larger effect for some words than for others; as an example, the windows for "good" and "bad" is much more parameterized than the windows for "reliable" and "positive", and the windows for the determiners are in general much more parameterized than the windows for nouns. It is interesting to note that there is a small tendency that the windows for the adjectives have a higher weight in the +1 position, which is consistent with a linguistic analysis of adjectives as qualifiers of succeeding nouns. By contrast, the window positions for the determiners seem to have a higher weight in the positions just preceding the focus word, while the windows for

---

[2]Since our focus in this paper is the effect of the word embeddings, we will not comment further on the performance differences between the MLP and CNN classifiers.

Table 7: Experiment results. Mean accuracies in %. The parentheses contain the maximum achieved accuracy, the standard deviation and the minimum achieved accuracy of the consecutive runs

Emb + Model	PL05	SST
RAND MLP	68.23 (↑ 69.58, ±0.98, ↓ 66.32)	69.89 (↑ 71.11, ±0.83, ↓ 68.64)
RI MLP	72.45 (↑ **74.91**, ±2.99, ↓ 66.54)	75.13 (↑ 77.98, ±2.54, ↓ 73.75)
SGD-RI MLP	73.62 (↑ 74.16, ±0.77, ↓ 71.42)	77.91 (↑ 78.80, ±0.82, ↓ 76.11)
ATT-RI MLP	72.45 (↑ 74.83, ±2.20, ↓ 68.90)	**78.03** (↑ **79.63**, ±1.60, ↓ 74.46)
SGNS MLP	**73.84** (↑ 74.76, ±1.14, ↓ 71.57)	77.27 (↑ 79.57, ±3.13, ↓ 70.02)
GLOVE MLP	71.29 (↑ 73.67, ±1.67, ↓ 68.60)	76.26 (↑ 77.32, ±1.66, ↓ 71.61)
RAND CNN	72.12 (↑ 72.91, ±0.50, ↓ 71.28)	76.99 (↑ 77.94, ±0.76, ↓ 75.50)
RI CNN	76.18 (↑ 76.60, ±0.35, ↓ 75.51)	81.83 (↑ 82.72, ±0.39, ↓ 81.39)
SGD-RI CNN	75.67 (↑ 76.26, ±0.63, ↓ 74.22)	81.31 (↑ 81.89, ±0.38, ↓ 80.78)
ATT-RI CNN	77.55 (↑ 78.08, ±0.31, ↓ 77.09)	81.77 (↑ 82.64, ±0.60, ↓ 80.66)
SGNS CNN	**77.92** (↑ **78.34**, ±0.24, ↓ 77.55)	**83.44** (↑ **84.00**, ±0.51, ↓ 82.00)
GLOVE CNN	77.35 (↑ 77.77, ±0.34, ↓ 76.79)	81.56 (↑ 82.06, ±0.34, ↓ 80.78)

nouns seem to have very small parameterization. It thus seems as if the parameterization is able to learn slightly different window profiles for different parts of speech.

As noted in the introduction, is is common practice in distributional semantics to weight the context windows by the distance to the focus word. If this is an optimal strategy, we should see a bell-like curve leaning to zero at the edges. Such a shape is partially present for some of the words, for example in "and", "of", "good" and "bad", but for most words, the weights are almost unchanged. We believe this could be due to the vanishing gradient problem where the gradient seems to vanish deeper down the model. In addition, the less common the word is in the training set, the less it is updated. Another interesting aspect of the learned weights is that by inspecting the l_1 norm of the weight vectors, we get a hint of the words' relative importance for the given task. We can see that the l_1 norm for the words "good" and "bad" are larger than for "the" and "of", which feels natural for the sentiment classification task.

9 Conclusion

This paper has introduced a simple parameterization for the RI framework, which has also been derived in terms of convolution. It parameterizes the positions in the context windows and optimizes with respect to the performance of the embeddings in some given task, such as word similarity or text classification. Our experiments show that the proposed PAR-RI model is able to improve the performance of the embeddings in many cases, and that the results are competitive in comparison with other well-known embeddings. The idea of parameterizing the window positions could also be applied to other distributional semantic models, such as SGNS.

We note that all embeddings used in the sentiment classification task produce very similar results. This indicates that in practice, the word embeddings included in this paper are more or less equivalent. It is therefore doubtful whether it is possible to draw any conclusions based on these results regarding the question whether any single embedding is superior to the others in the general case.

The examples of context profiles provided as examples of the parameterization shows some interesting effects. However, training the position-dependent weights is non-trivial, and one could probably think of better initializations of the weights than just one-vectors, for example using a bell-like shape. The vanishing gradient problem would however remain, and the weights for uncommon words will not change significantly.

The conclusion of the experiments using SGD-RI is that updating the embeddings jointly with the classification model using SGD does not necessarily improve generalization. This is in fact not so strange. Moving around only a subset of the words (i.e. the words present in the training set), while leaving the rest untouched produces an inconsistent space with undefined distributional properties between updated and non-updated embeddings. It could therefore be an idea to use randomized embeddings for all words not present in the training

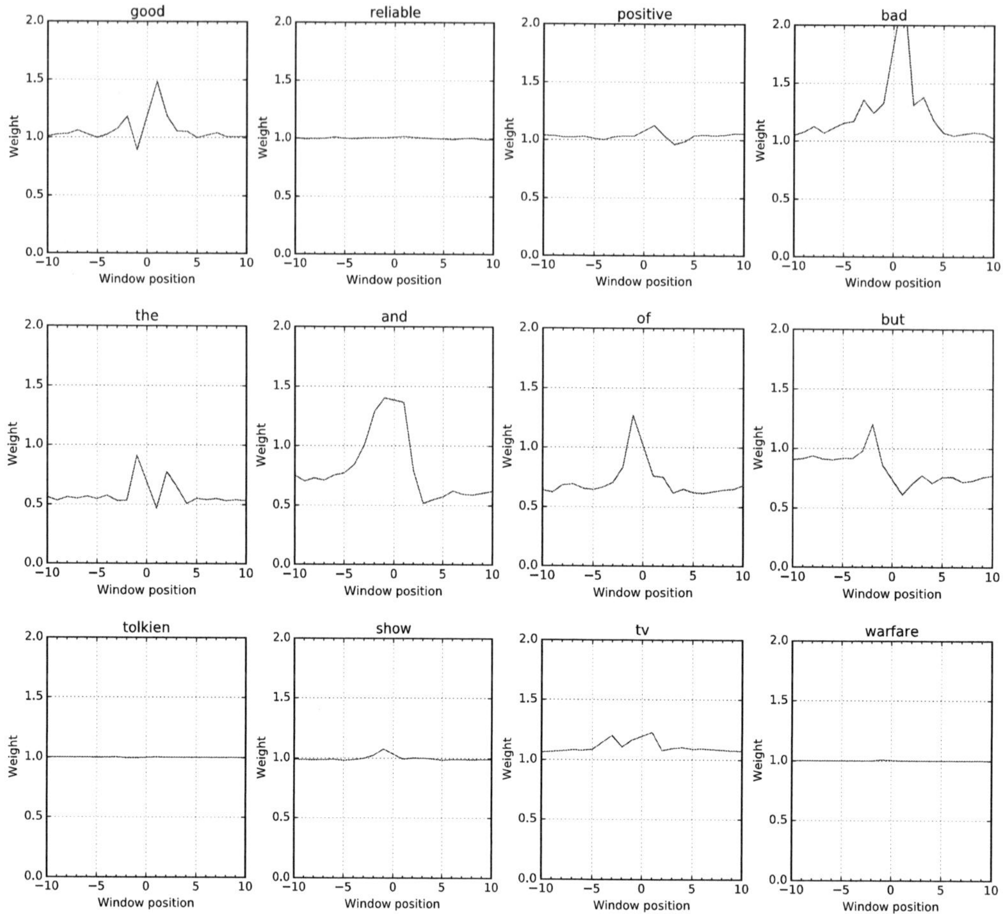

Figure 1: The learned weights for four adjectives (top row), four determiners (middle row), and four nouns (bottom row).

set because they then can be regarded as approximately orthogonal, and thus should not interfere with the semantic structure.

References

Amaru Cuba Gyllensten and Magnus Sahlgren. 2015. Navigating the semantic horizon using relative neighborhood graphs. In *Proceedings of EMNLP*, pages 2451–2460.

Felix Hill, Roi Reichart, and Anna Korhonen. 2015. Simlex-999: Evaluating semantic models with (genuine) similarity estimation. *Computational Linguistics*, 41(4):665–695.

Pentti Kanerva, Jan Kristofersson, and Anders Holst. 2000. Random Indexing of text samples for Latent Semantic Analysis. In *Proceedings of CogSci*, page 1036.

Pentti Kanerva. 2009. Hyperdimensional computing. *Cognitive Computation*, 1(2):139–159.

Yoon Kim. 2014. Convolutional neural networks for sentence classification. In *Proceedings of the 2014 Conference on Empirical Methods in Natural Language Processing (EMNLP)*, pages 1746–1751, Doha, Qatar, October. Association for Computational Linguistics.

Kevin Lund, Curt Burgess, and Ruth A. Atchley. 1995. Semantic and associative priming in high-dimensional semantic space. In *Proceedings of the 17th Annual Conference of the Cognitive Science Society*, pages 660–665. Hillsdale, NJ: Erlbaum.

Tomas Mikolov, Kai Chen, Greg Corrado, and Jeffrey Dean. 2013. Efficient estimation of word representations in vector space. *CoRR*, abs/1301.3781.

Yoshiki Niwa and Yoshihiko Nitta. 1994. Co-occurrence vectors from corpora vs. distance vectors from dictionaries. In *Proceedings of the 15th Conference on Computational Linguistics - Volume*

1, COLING '94, pages 304–309, Stroudsburg, PA, USA. Association for Computational Linguistics.

Bo Pang and Lillian Lee. 2005. Seeing stars: Exploiting class relationships for sentiment categorization with respect to rating scales. In *Proceedings of ACL*, pages 115–124.

Jeffrey Pennington, Richard Socher, and Christopher D. Manning. 2014. Glove: Global vectors for word representation. In *Proceedings of the 2014 Conference on Empirical Methods in Natural Language Processing (EMNLP 2014)*, pages 1532–1543.

David E. Rumelhart, Geoffrey E. Hinton, and Ronald J. Williams. 1986. Parallel distributed processing: Explorations in the microstructure of cognition, vol. 1. chapter Learning Internal Representations by Error Propagation, pages 318–362. MIT Press, Cambridge, MA, USA.

Magnus Sahlgren, Amaru Cuba Gyllensten, Fredrik Espinoza, Ola Hamfors, Anders Holst, Jussi Karlgren, Fredrik Olsson, Per Persson, and Akshay Viswanathan. 2016. The Gavagai Living Lexicon. In *Proceedings of LREC*.

Richard Socher, Alex Perelygin, Jean Y. Wu, Jason Chuang, Christopher D. Manning, Andrew Y. Ng, and Christopher Potts. 2013. Recursive deep models for semantic compositionality over a sentiment treebank. In *Proceedings of the conference on empirical methods in natural language processing (EMNLP)*, volume 1631, page 1642. Citeseer.

Jun Suzuki and Masaaki Nagata. 2015. A unified learning framework of skip-grams and global vectors. In *Proceedings of the 53rd Annual Meeting of the Association for Computational Linguistics and the 7th International Joint Conference on Natural Language Processing (Volume 2: Short Papers)*, pages 186–191, Beijing, China, July. Association for Computational Linguistics.

Peter D. Turney and Patrick Pantel. 2010. From frequency to meaning: Vector space models of semantics. *Journal of Artificial Intelligence Research*, 37(1):141–188, January.

Ye Zhang and Byron Wallace. 2015. A sensitivity analysis of (and practitioners' guide to) convolutional neural networks for sentence classification. *CoRR*, abs/1510.03820.

Making Sense of Word Embeddings

Maria Pelevina[1], Nikolay Arefyev[2], Chris Biemann[1] and Alexander Panchenko[1]

[1]Technische Universität Darmstadt, LT Group, Computer Science Department, Germany
[2]Moscow State University, Faculty of Computational Mathematics and Cybernetics, Russia
`panchenko@lt.informatik.tu-darmstadt.de`

Abstract

We present a simple yet effective approach for learning word sense embeddings. In contrast to existing techniques, which either directly learn sense representations from corpora or rely on sense inventories from lexical resources, our approach can induce a sense inventory from existing word embeddings via clustering of ego-networks of related words. An integrated WSD mechanism enables labeling of words in context with learned sense vectors, which gives rise to downstream applications. Experiments show that the performance of our method is comparable to state-of-the-art unsupervised WSD systems.

1 Introduction

Term representations in the form of dense vectors are useful for many natural language processing applications. First of all, they enable the computation of semantically related words. Besides, they can be used to represent other linguistic units, such as phrases and short texts, reducing the inherent sparsity of traditional vector-space representations (Salton et al., 1975).

One limitation of most word vector models, including sparse (Baroni and Lenci, 2010) and dense (Mikolov et al., 2013) representations, is that they conflate all senses of a word into a single vector. Several architectures for learning multi-prototype embeddings were proposed that try to address this shortcoming (Huang et al., 2012; Tian et al., 2014; Neelakantan et al., 2014; Nieto Piña and Johansson, 2015; Bartunov et al., 2016). Li and Jurafsky (2015) provide indications that such sense vectors improve the performance of text pro-

cessing applications, such as part-of-speech tagging and semantic relation identification.

The contribution of this paper is a novel method for learning word sense vectors. In contrast to previously proposed methods, our approach relies on existing single-prototype word embeddings, transforming them to sense vectors via ego-network clustering. An ego network consists of a single node (ego) together with the nodes they are connected to (alters) and all the edges among those alters. Our method is fitted with a word sense disambiguation (WSD) mechanism, and thus words in context can be mapped to these sense representations. An advantage of our method is that one can use existing word embeddings and/or existing word sense inventories to build sense embeddings. Experiments show that our approach performs comparably to state-of-the-art unsupervised WSD systems.

2 Related Work

Our method learns multi-prototype word embeddings and applies them to WSD. Below we briefly review both strains of research.

2.1 Multi-Prototype Word Vector Spaces

In his pioneering work, Schütze (1998) induced sparse sense vectors by clustering context vectors using the EM algorithm. This approach is fitted with a similarity-based WSD mechanism. Later, Reisinger and Mooney (2010) presented a multi-prototype vector space. Sparse TF-IDF vectors are clustered using a parametric method fixing the same number of senses for all words. Sense vectors are centroids of the clusters.

While most dense word vector models represent a word with a single vector and thus conflate senses (Mikolov et al., 2013; Pennington et al., 2014), there are several approaches that produce word sense embeddings. Huang et al. (2012) learn

Proceedings of the 1st Workshop on Representation Learning for NLP, pages 174–183,
Berlin, Germany, August 11th, 2016. ©2016 Association for Computational Linguistics

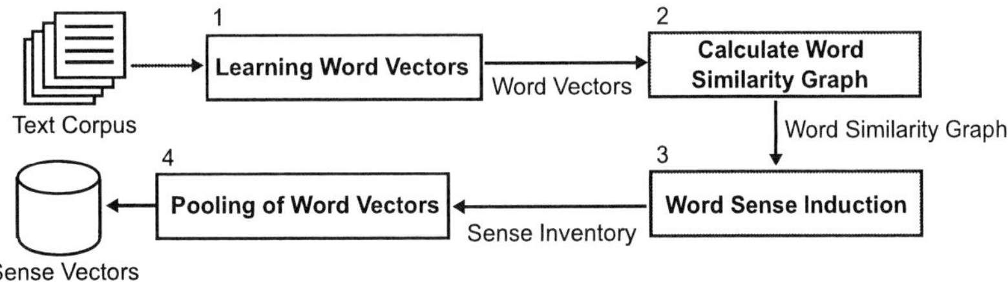

Figure 1: Schema of the word sense embeddings learning method.

dense vector spaces with neural networks. First, contexts are represented with word embeddings and clustered. Second, word occurrences are re-labeled in the corpus according to the cluster they belong to. Finally, embeddings are re-trained on this sense-labeled terms. Tian et al. (2014) introduced a probabilistic extension of the Skip-gram model (Mikolov et al., 2013) that learns multiple sense-aware prototypes weighted by their prior probability. These models use parametric clustering algorithms that produce a fixed number of senses per word.

Neelakantan et al. (2014) proposed a multi-sense extension of the Skip-gram model that was the first one to learn the number of senses by itself. During training, a new sense vector is allocated if the current context's similarity to existing senses is below some threshold. Li and Jurafsky (2015) use a similar idea by integrating the Chinese Restaurant Process into the Skip-gram model. All mentioned above sense embeddings were evaluated on the contextual word similarity task, each one improving upon previous models.

Nieto and Johansson (2015) presented another multi-prototype modification of the Skip-gram model. Their approach outperforms that of Neelakantan et al. (2014), but requires as an input the number of senses for each word.

Li and Jurafsky (2015) show that sense embeddings can significantly improve the performance of part-of-speech tagging, semantic relation identification and semantic relatedness tasks, but yield no improvement for named entity recognition and sentiment analysis.

Bartunov et al. (2016) introduced AdaGram, a non-parametric method for learning sense embeddings based on a Bayesian extension of the Skip-gram model. The granularity of learned sense embeddings is controlled by the parameter α. Comparisons of their approach to (Neelakantan et al., 2014) on three SemEval word sense induction and

disambiguation datasets show the advantage of their method. For this reason, we use AdaGram as a representative of the state-of-the-art methods in our experiments.

Several approaches rely on a knowledge base (KB) to provide sense information. Bordes et al. (2011) propose a general method to represent entities of any KB as a dense vector. Such representation helps to integrate KBs into NLP systems. Another approach that uses sense inventories of knowledge bases was presented by Camacho-Collados et al. (2015). Rothe and Schütze (2015) combined word embeddings on the basis of Word-Net synsets to obtain sense embeddings. The approach is evaluated on lexical sample tasks by adding synset embeddings as features to an existing WSD system. They used a weighted pooling similar to the one we use, but their method is not able to find new senses in a corpus. Finally, Nieto Piña and Johansson (2016) used random walks on the Swedish Wordnet to generate training data for the Skip-gram model.

2.2 Word Sense Disambiguation (WSD)

Many different designs of WSD systems were proposed, see (Agirre and Edmonds, 2007; Navigli, 2009). Supervised approaches use an explicitly sense-labeled training corpus to construct a model, usually building one model per target word (Lee and Ng, 2002; Klein et al., 2002). These approaches demonstrate top performance in competitions, but require considerable amounts of sense-labeled examples.

Knowledge-based approaches do not learn a model per target, but rather derive sense representation from information available in a lexical resource, such as WordNet. Examples of such system include (Lesk, 1986; Banerjee and Pedersen, 2002; Pedersen et al., 2005; Moro et al., 2014)

Unsupervised WSD approaches rely neither on hand-annotated sense-labeled corpora, nor on

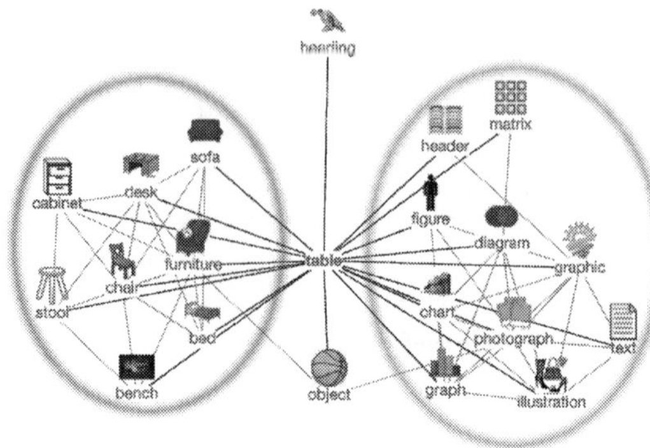

Figure 2: Visualization of the ego-network of "table" with furniture and data sense clusters. Note that the target "table" is excluded from clustering.

handcrafted lexical resources. Instead, they automatically induce a sense inventory from raw corpora. Such unsupervised sense induction methods fall into two categories: context clustering, such as (Pedersen and Bruce, 1997; Schütze, 1998; Reisinger and Mooney, 2010; Neelakantan et al., 2014; Bartunov et al., 2016) and word (ego-network) clustering, such as (Lin, 1998; Pantel and Lin, 2002; Widdows and Dorow, 2002; Biemann, 2006; Hope and Keller, 2013). Unsupervised methods use disambiguation clues from the induced sense inventory for word disambiguation. Usually, the WSD procedure is determined by the design of sense inventory. It might be the highest overlap between the instance's context words and the words of the sense cluster, as in (Hope and Keller, 2013) or the smallest distance between context words and sense hubs in graph sense representation, as in (Véronis, 2004).

3 Learning Word Sense Embeddings

Our method consists of the four main stages depicted in Figure 1: (1) learning word embeddings; (2) building a graph of nearest neighbours based on vector similarities; (3) induction of word senses using ego-network clustering; and (4) aggregation of word vectors with respect to the induced senses.

Our method can use existing word embeddings, sense inventories and word similarity graphs. To demonstrate such use-cases and to study the performance of the method in different settings, as variants of the complete pipeline presented in Figure 1, we experiment with two additional setups. First, we use an alternative approach to compute the word similarity graph, which relies on dependency features and is expected to provide more accurate similarities (therefore, the stage (2) is changed). Second, we use a sense inventory constructed using crowdsourcing (thus, stages (2) and (3) are skipped). Below we describe each of the stages of our method in detail.

3.1 Learning Word Vectors

To learn word vectors, we use the *word2vec* toolkit (Mikolov et al., 2013), namely we train CBOW word embeddings with 100 or 300 dimensions, context window size of 3 and minimum word frequency of 5. We selected these parameters according to prior evaluations, e.g. (Baroni et al., 2014), and tested them on the development dataset (see Section 5.1). Initial experiments showed that this configuration is superior to others, e.g. the Skip-gram model, with respect to WSD performance.

For training, we modified the standard implementation of *word2vec*[1] so that it also saves context vectors needed for one of our WSD approaches. For experiments, we use two commonly used corpora for training distributional models: Wikipedia[2] and ukWaC (Ferraresi et al., 2008).

3.2 Calculating Word Similarity Graph

At this step, we build a graph of word similarities, such as (table, desk, 0.78). For each word we retrieve its 200 nearest neighbours. This number is motivated by prior studies (Biemann and Riedl, 2013; Panchenko, 2013): as observed, only few words have more strongly semantically related words. This graph is computed either based on word embeddings learned during the previous step or using semantic similarities provided by the *JoBimText* framework (Biemann and Riedl, 2013).

Similarities using word2vec (w2v). In this case, nearest neighbours of a term are terms with the highest cosine similarity of their respective vectors. For scalability reasons, we perform similarity computations via block matrix multiplications, using blocks of 1000 vectors.

Similarities using JoBimText (JBT). In this unsupervised approach, every word is represented

---

[1] https://code.google.com/p/word2vec
[2] We used an English Wikipedia dump of October 2015: http://panchenko.me/data/joint/corpora/en59g/wikipedia.txt.gz

as a bag of sparse dependency-based features extracted using the Malt parser and collapsed using an approach similar to (Ruppert et al., 2015). Features are normalized using the LMI score (Church and Hanks, 1990) and further pruned down according to the recommended defaults: we keep 1000 features per word and 1000 words per feature. Similarity of two words is equal to the number of common features.

Multiple alternatives exist for computation of semantic relatedness (Zhang et al., 2013). JBT has two advantages in our case: (1) accurate estimation of word similarities based on dependency features; (2) efficient computation of nearest neighbours for all words in a corpus. Besides, we observed that nearest neighbours of word embeddings often tend to belong to the dominant sense, even if minor senses have significant support in the training corpus. We wanted to test if the same problem remains for a principally different method for similarity computation.

Algorithm 1: Word sense induction.

input : T – word similarity graph, N –
ego-network size, n – ego-network
connectivity, k – minimum cluster size
output: for each term $t \in T$, a clustering S_t of its
N most similar terms

foreach $t \in T$ **do**
  $V \leftarrow N$ most similar terms of t from T
  $G \leftarrow$ graph with V as nodes and no edges E

  foreach $v \in V$ **do**
    $V' \leftarrow n$ most similar terms of v from T
    foreach $v' \in V'$ **do**
      if $v' \in V$ **then** add edge (v, v') to E
    end
  end
  $S_t \leftarrow \texttt{ChineseWhispers}(G)$
  $S_t \leftarrow \{s \in S_t : |s| \geq k\}$
end

3.3 Word Sense Induction

We induce a sense inventory using a method similarly to (Pantel and Lin, 2002) and (Biemann, 2006). A word sense is represented by a word cluster. For instance the cluster "chair, bed, bench, stool, sofa, desk, cabinet" can represent the sense "table (furniture)". To induce senses, first we construct an ego-network G of a word t and then perform graph clustering of this network. The iden-

Vector	Nearest Neighbours
table	tray, bottom, diagram, bucket, brackets, stack, basket, list, parenthesis, cup, trays, pile, play-field, bracket, pot, drop-down, cue, plate
table#0	leftmost#0, column#1, randomly#0, tableau#1, top-left0, indent#1, bracket#3, pointer#0, footer#1, cursor#1, diagram#0, grid#0
table#1	pile#1, stool#1, tray#0, basket#0, bowl#1, bucket#0, box#0, cage#0, saucer#3, mirror#1, birdcage#0, hole#0, pan#1, lid#0

Table 1: Neighbours of the word "table" and its senses produced by our method. The neighbours of the initial vector belong to both senses, while those of sense vectors are sense-specific.

tified clusters are interpreted as senses (see Table 2). Words referring to the same sense tend to be tightly connected, while having fewer connections to words referring to different senses.

The sense induction presented in Algorithm 1 processes one word t of the word similarity graph T per iteration. First, we retrieve nodes V of the ego-network G: these are the N most similar words of t according to T. The target word t itself is not part of the ego-network. Second, we connect the nodes in G to their n most similar words from T. Finally, the ego-network is clustered with the Chinese Whispers algorithm (Biemann, 2006). This method is parameter free, thus we make no assumptions about the number of word senses.

The sense induction algorithm has three meta-parameters: the ego-network size (N) of the target ego word t; the ego-network connectivity (n) is the maximum number of connections the neighbour v is allowed to have within the ego-network; the minimum size of the cluster k. The n parameter regulates the granularity of the inventory. In our experiments, we set the N to 200, n to 50, 100 or 200 and k to 5 or 15 to obtain different granulates, cf. (Biemann, 2010).

Each word in a sense cluster has a weight which is equal to the similarity score between this word and the ambiguous word t.

3.4 Pooling of Word Vectors

At this stage, we calculate sense embeddings for each sense in the induced inventory. We assume that a word sense is a composition of words that represent the sense. We define a sense vector as a function of word vectors representing cluster items. Let W be a set of all words in the training corpus and let $S_i = \{w_1, \ldots, w_n\} \subseteq W$ be

	TWSI	JBT	w2v
table (furniture)	counter, console, bench, dinner table, dining table, desk, surface, bar, board	chair, room, desk, pulpit, couch, furniture, fireplace, bench, door, box, railing, tray	tray, bottom, bucket, basket, cup, pile, bracket, pot, cue, plate, jar, platter, ladder
table (data)	chart, list, index, graph, columned list, tabulation, standings, diagram, ranking	procedure, system, datum, process, mechanism, tool, method, database, calculation, scheme	diagram, brackets, stack, list, parenthesis, playfield, dropdown, cube, hash, results, tab
table (negotiations)	surface, counter, console, bargaining table, platform, negotiable, machine plate, level	—	—
table (geo)	level, plateau, plain, flatland, saturation level, water table, geographical level, water level	—	—

Table 2: Word sense clusters from inventories derived from the Wikipedia corpus via crowdsourcing (TWSI), JoBimText (JBT) and word embeddings (w2v). The sense labels are introduced for readability.

a sense cluster obtained during the previous step. Consider a function $vec_w : W \rightarrow \mathbb{R}^m$ that maps words to their vectors and a function $\gamma_i : W \rightarrow \mathbb{R}$ that maps cluster words to their weight in the cluster S_i. We experimented with two ways to calculate sense vectors: unweighted average of word vectors:

$$\mathbf{s}_i = \frac{\sum_{k=1}^{n} vec_w(w_k)}{n};$$

and weighted average of word vectors:

$$\mathbf{s}_i = \frac{\sum_{k=1}^{n} \gamma_i(w_k) vec_w(w_k)}{\sum_{k=1}^{n} \gamma_i(w_k)}.$$

Table 1 provides an example of weighted pooling results. While the original neighbours of the word "table" contain words related to both furniture and data, the neighbours of the sense vectors are either related to furniture or data, but not to both at the same time. Besides, each neighbour of a sense vector has a sense identifier as we calculate cosine between sense vectors, not word vectors.

4   Word Sense Disambiguation

This section describes how sense vectors are used to disambiguate a word in a context.

Given a target word w and its context words $C = \{c_1, \ldots, c_k\}$, we first map w to a set of its sense vectors according to the inventory: $S = \{\mathbf{s}_1, \ldots, \mathbf{s}_n\}$. We use two strategies to choose a correct sense taking vectors for context words either from the matrix of context embeddings or from the matrix of word vectors. The first one is based on sense probability in given context:

$$s^* = \arg\max_i P(C|\mathbf{s}_i) = \arg\max_i \frac{1}{1 + e^{-\mathbf{c}_c \cdot \mathbf{s}_i}},$$

where $\bar{\mathbf{c}}_c$ is the mean of context embeddings: $k^{-1} \sum_{i=1}^{k} vec_c(c_i)$ and functions $vec_c : W \rightarrow \mathbb{R}^m$ map context words to context embeddings. Using the mean of context embeddings to calculate sense probability is natural with the CBOW because this model optimises exactly the same mean to have high scalar product with word embeddings for words occurred in context and low scalar product for random words (Mikolov et al., 2013).

The second disambiguation strategy is based on similarity between sense and context:

$$s^* = \arg\max_i sim(\mathbf{s}_i, C) = \arg\max_i \frac{\bar{\mathbf{c}}_w \cdot \mathbf{s}_i}{\|\bar{\mathbf{c}}_w\| \cdot \|\mathbf{s}_i\|},$$

where $\bar{\mathbf{c}}_w$ is the mean of word embeddings: $k^{-1} \sum_{i=1}^{k} vec_w(c_i)$. The latter method uses only word vectors (vec_w) and require no context vectors (vec_c). This is practical, as the standard implementation of *word2vec* does not save context embeddings and thus most pre-computed models provide only word vectors.

To improve WSD performance we also apply context filtering. Typically, only several words in context are relevant for sense disambiguation, like "chairs" and "kitchen" are for "table" in "They bought a table and chairs for kitchen." For each word c_j in context $C = \{c_1, \ldots, c_k\}$ we calculate a score that quantifies how well it discriminates the senses:

$$\max_i f(\mathbf{s}_i, c_j) - \min_i f(\mathbf{s}_i, c_j),$$

where $\mathbf{s}_i$ iterates over senses of the ambiguous word and f is one of our disambiguation strategies: either $P(c_j|\mathbf{s}_i)$ or $sim(\mathbf{s}_i, c_j)$. The p most discriminative context words are used for disambiguation.

	Full TWSI		Balanced TWSI	
	w2v	JBT	w2v	JBT
no filter	0.676	0.669	0.383	0.397
filter, $p = 5$	0.679	0.674	0.386	0.403
filter, $p = 3$	0.681	0.676	0.387	0.409
filter, $p = 2$	**0.683**	**0.678**	**0.389**	**0.410**
filter, $p = 1$	**0.683**	0.676	**0.390**	**0.410**

Table 4: Influence of context filtering on disambiguation in terms of F-score. The models were trained on Wikipedia corpus; the w2v is based on weighted pooling and similarity-based disambiguation. All differences between filtered and unfiltered models are significant ($p < 0.05$).

5 Experiments

We evaluate our method on two complementary datasets: (1) a crowdsourced collection of sense-labeled contexts; and (2) a commonly used SemEval dataset.

5.1 Evaluation on TWSI

The goal of this evaluation is to test different configurations of our approach on a large-scale dataset, i.e. it is used for development purposes.

Dataset. This test collection is based on a large-scale crowdsourced resource by Biemann (2012) that comprises 1,012 frequent nouns with average polysemy of 2.26 senses per word. For these nouns the dataset provides 145,140 annotated sentences sampled from Wikipedia. Besides, it is accompanied by an explicit sense inventory, where each sense is represented with a list of words that can substitute target noun in a given sentence.

The sense distribution across sentences in the dataset is skewed, resulting in 79% of contexts assigned to the most frequent senses. Therefore, in addition to the full TWSI dataset, we also use a balanced subset that has no bias towards the Most Frequent Sense (MFS). This dataset features 6,165 contexts with five contexts per sense excluding monosemous words.

Evaluation metrics. To compute WSD performance, we create an explicit mapping between the system-provided sense inventory and the TWSI senses: senses are represented as bag of words vectors, which are compared using cosine similarity. Every induced sense gets assigned to at most one TWSI sense. Once the mapping is completed, we can calculate precision and recall of sense prediction with respect to the original TWSI labeling.

Performance of a disambiguation model depends on quality of the sense mapping. These baselines facilitate interpretation of results:

- **Upper bound of the induced inventory** selects the correct sense for the context, but only if the mapping exist for this sense.
- **MFS of the TWSI inventory** assigns the most frequent sense in the TWSI dataset.
- **MFS of the induced inventory** assigns the identifier of the largest sense cluster.
- **Random sense baseline** of the TWSI and induced sense inventories.

Discussion of results. Table 2 presents examples of the senses induced via clustering of nearest neighbours generated by word embeddings (w2v) and JBT as compared to the inventory produced via crowdsourcing (TWSI). The TWSI contains more senses (2.26 on average), while induced ones have less senses (1.56 and 1.64, respectively). The senses in the table are arranged in the way they are mapped to TWSI during evaluation.

Table 3 illustrates how the granularity of the inventory influences WSD performance. The more granular the sense inventory, the better the match between the TWSI and the induced inventory can be established (mind that we map every induced sense to at most one TWSI sense). Therefore, the upper bound of WSD performance is maximal for the most fine-grained inventories.

However, the relation of actual WSD performance to granularity is inverse: the lower the number of senses, the higher the WSD performance (in the limit, we converge to the strong MFS baseline). We select a coarse-grained inventory for our further experiments (n=200, $k = 15$).

Table 4 illustrates the fact that using context filtering positively impacts disambiguation performance, reaching optimal characteristics when two context words are used.

Finally, Figure 3 presents results of our experiments on the full and sense-balanced TWSI datasets. First of all, our models significantly outperform random sense baseline of both TWSI and induced inventories. Secondly, we observe that pooling vectors using similarity scores as weights is better than unweighted pooling. Indeed, some clusters may contain irrelevant words and thus their contribution should be discounted. Third, we observe that using similarity-based disambiguation mechanism yields better results as compared

Inventory	#Senses	Upper-bound of Inventory			Probability-based WSD		
		Prec.	Recall	F-score	Prec.	Recall	F-score
TWSI	2.26	1.000	1.000	1.000	0.484	0.483	0.484
w2v wiki, $k = 15$	1.56	1.000	0.479	0.648	0.367	0.366	0.366
JBT wiki, $n = 200, k = 15$	1.64	1.000	0.488	0.656	**0.383**	**0.383**	**0.383**
JBT ukWaC, $n = 200, k = 15$	1.89	1.000	0.526	0.690	0.360	0.360	0.360
JBT wiki, $n = 200, k = 5$	2.55	1.000	0.598	0.748	0.338	0.338	0.338
JBT wiki, $n = 100, k = 5$	3.59	1.000	0.671	0.803	0.305	0.305	0.305
JBT wiki, $n = 50, k = 5$	5.13	**1.000**	**0.724**	**0.840**	0.275	0.275	0.275

Table 3: Upper-bound and actual value of the WSD performance on the sense-balanced TWSI dataset, function of sense inventory used for unweighted pooling of word vectors.

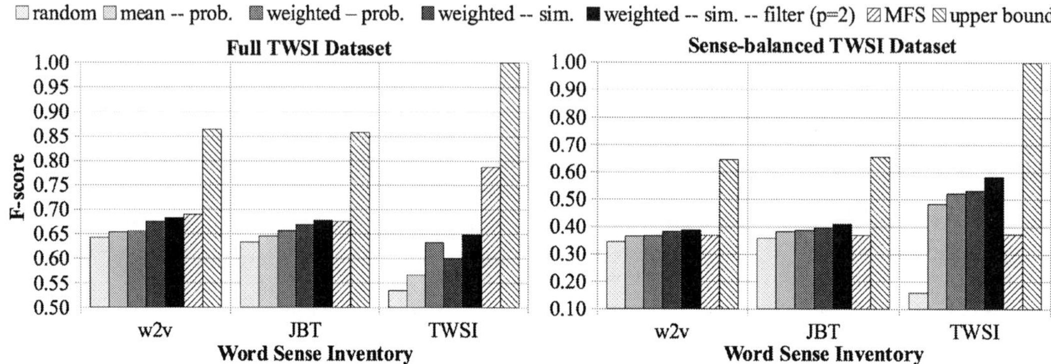

Figure 3: WSD performance of our method trained on the Wikipedia corpus on the full (on the left) and on the sense-balanced (on the right) TWSI dataset. The w2v models are based on the CBOW with 300 dimensions and context window size 3. The JBT models are computed using the Malt parser.

to the mechanism based on probabilities. Indeed, cosine similarity between embeddings proved to be useful for semantic relatedness, yielding state-of-the-art results (Baroni et al., 2014), while there is less evidence about successful use-cases of the CBOW as a language model.

Fourth, we confirm our observation that filtering context words positively impacts WSD performance. Finally, we note that models based on JBT- and w2v-induced sense inventories yield comparable results. However, the JBT inventory shows higher performance (0.410 vs 0.390) on the balanced TWSI, indicating the importance of a precise sense inventory. Finally, using the "gold" TWSI inventory significantly improves the performance on the balanced dataset outperforming models based on induced inventories.

5.2 Evaluation on SemEval-2013 Task 13

The goal of this evaluation is to compare the performance of our method to state-of-the-art unsupervised WSD systems.

Dataset. The SemEval-2013 task 13 "Word Sense Induction for Graded and Non-Graded Senses" (Jurgens and Klapaftis, 2013) provides 20 nouns, 20 verbs and 10 adjectives in WordNet-sense-tagged contexts. It contains 20-100 contexts per word, and 4,664 contexts in total, which were drawn from the Open American National Corpus. Participants were asked to cluster these 4,664 instances into groups, with each group corresponding to a distinct word sense.

Evaluation metrics. Performance is measured with three measures that require a mapping of sense inventories (Jaccard Index, Tau and WNDCG) and two cluster comparison measures (Fuzzy NMI and Fuzzy B-Cubed).

Discussion of results. We compare our approach to SemEval participants and the AdaGram sense embeddings. The *AI-KU* system (Baskaya et al., 2013) directly clusters test contexts using the k-means algorithm based on lexical substitution features. The *Unimelb* system (Lau et al., 2013) uses a hierarchical topic model to induce and dis-

Model		Supervised Evaluation			Clustering Evaluation	
		Jacc. Ind.	**Tau**	**WNDCG**	**F.NMI**	**F.B-Cubed**
Baselines	One sense for all	0.171	0.627	0.302	0.000	0.631
	One sense per instance	0.000	0.953	0.000	0.072	0.000
	Most Frequent Sense (MFS)	0.579	0.583	0.431	–	–
SemEval	AI-KU (add1000)	0.176	0.609	0.205	0.033	0.317
	AI-KU	0.176	0.619	0.393	0.066	0.382
	AI-KU (remove5-add1000)	0.228	0.654	0.330	0.040	0.463
	Unimelb (5p)	0.198	0.623	0.374	0.056	0.475
	Unimelb (50k)	0.198	0.633	0.384	0.060	0.494
	UoS (#WN senses)	0.171	0.600	0.298	0.046	0.186
	UoS (top-3)	0.220	0.637	0.370	0.044	0.451
	La Sapienza (1)	0.131	0.544	0.332	–	–
	La Sapienza (2)	0.131	0.535	0.394	–	–
Sense emb.	AdaGram, $\alpha = 0.05$, 100 dim. vectors	0.274	0.644	0.318	0.058	0.470
Our models	w2v – weighted – sim. – filter ($p = 2$)	0.197	0.615	0.291	0.011	0.615
	w2v – weighted – sim. – filter ($p = 2$): nouns	0.179	0.626	0.304	0.011	0.623
	JBT – weighted – sim. – filter ($p = 2$)	0.205	0.624	0.291	0.017	0.598
	JBT – weighted – sim. – filter ($p = 2$): nouns	0.198	0.643	0.310	0.031	0.595
	TWSI – weighted – sim. – filter ($p = 2$): nouns	0.215	0.651	0.318	0.030	0.573

Table 5: The best configurations of our method selected on the TWSI dataset on the SemEval 2013 Task 13 dataset. The w2v-based methods rely on the CBOW model with 100 dimensions and context window size 3. The JBT similarities were computed using the Malt parser. All systems were trained on the ukWaC corpus.

ambiguate word senses. The *UoS* system (Hope and Keller, 2013) is most similar to our approach: to induce senses it builds an ego-network of a word using dependency relations, which is subsequently clustered using a simple graph clustering algorithm. The *La Sapienza* system (Agirre and Soroa, 2009), relies on WordNet to get word senses and perform disambiguation.

Table 5 shows a comparative evaluation of our method on the SemEval dataset. Like above, dependency-based (JBT) word similarities yield slightly better results than word embedding similarity (w2v) for inventory induction. In addition to these two configurations, we also built a model based on the TWSI sense inventory (only for nouns as the TWSI contains nouns only). This model significantly outperforms both JBT- and w2v-based models, thus precise sense inventories greatly influence WSD performance.

As one may observe, performance of the best configurations of our method is comparable to the top-ranked SemEval participants, but is not systematically exceeding their results. AdaGram sometimes outperforms our method, sometimes it is on par, depending on the metric. We interpret these results as an indication of comparability of our method to state-of-the-art approaches.

Finally, note that none of the unsupervised WSD methods discussed in this paper, includ-

ing the top-ranked SemEval submissions and Ada-Gram, were able to beat the most frequent sense baselines of the respective datasets (with the exception of the balanced version of TWSI). Similar results are observed for other unsupervised WSD methods (Nieto Piña and Johansson, 2016).

6 Conclusion

We presented a novel approach for learning of multi-prototype word embeddings. In contrast to existing approaches that learn sense embeddings directly from the corpus, our approach can operate on existing word embeddings. It can either induce or reuse a word sense inventory. Experiments on two datasets, including a SemEval challenge on word sense induction and disambiguation, show that our approach performs comparably to the state of the art.

An implementation of our method with several pre-trained models is available online.[3]

Acknowledgments

We acknowledge the support of the Deutsche Forschungsgemeinschaft (DFG) foundation under the project "JOIN-T: Joining Ontologies and Semantics Induced from Text".

---

[3] `https://github.com/tudarmstadt-lt/sensegram`

References

Eneko Agirre and Philip Edmonds. 2007. *Word sense disambiguation: Algorithms and applications*, volume 33. Springer Science & Business Media.

Eneko Agirre and Aitor Soroa. 2009. Personalizing PageRank for Word Sense Disambiguation. In *Proceedings of the 12th Conference of the European Chapter of the ACL*, pages 33–41, Athens, Greece.

Satanjeev Banerjee and Ted Pedersen. 2002. An adapted Lesk algorithm for word sense disambiguation using WordNet. In *Proceedings of the Third International Conference on Intelligent Text Processing and Computational Linguistics*, pages 136–145, Mexico City, Mexico.

Marco Baroni and Alessandro Lenci. 2010. Distributional memory: A general framework for corpus-based semantics. *Computational Linguistics*, 36(4):673–721.

Marco Baroni, Georgiana Dinu, and Germán Kruszewski. 2014. Don't count, predict! a systematic comparison of context-counting vs. context-predicting semantic vectors. In *Proceedings of the 52nd Annual Meeting of the Association for Computational Linguistics*, pages 238–247, Baltimore, Maryland. Association for Computational Linguistics.

Sergey Bartunov, Dmitry Kondrashkin, Anton Osokin, and Dmitry Vetrov. 2016. Breaking sticks and ambiguities with adaptive skip-gram. In *Proceedings of the International Conference on Artificial Intelligence and Statistics (AISTATS)*.

Osman Baskaya, Enis Sert, Volkan Cirik, and Deniz Yuret. 2013. AI-KU: Using Substitute Vectors and Co-Occurrence Modeling for Word Sense Induction and Disambiguation. In *Second Joint Conference on Lexical and Computational Semantics (*SEM): SemEval 2013)*, volume 2, pages 300–306, Atlanta, Georgia, USA.

Chris Biemann and Martin Riedl. 2013. Text: Now in 2D! a framework for lexical expansion with contextual similarity. *Journal of Language Modelling*, 1(1):55–95.

Chris Biemann. 2006. Chinese Whispers: An Efficient Graph Clustering Algorithm and Its Application to Natural Language Processing Problems. In *Proceedings of the First Workshop on Graph Based Methods for Natural Language Processing*, pages 73–80, New York City, USA.

Chris Biemann. 2010. Co-occurrence cluster features for lexical substitutions in context. In *Proceedings of the 5th Workshop on TextGraphs in conjunction with ACL 2010*, Uppsala, Sweden.

Chris Biemann. 2012. Turk Bootstrap Word Sense Inventory 2.0: A Large-Scale Resource for Lexical Substitution. In *Proceedings of the 8th International Conference on Language Resources and Evaluation*, pages 4038–4042, Istanbul, Turkey.

Antoine Bordes, Weston Jason, Ronan Collobert, and Yoshua Bengio. 2011. Learning structured embeddings of knowledge bases. In *Proc. AAAI*, San Francisco, CA, USA.

José Camacho-Collados, Mohammad Taher Pilehvar, and Roberto Navigli. 2015. A unified multilingual semantic representation of concepts. In *Proceedings of the Association for Computational Linguistics*, pages 741–751, Beijing, China.

Kenneth Ward Church and Patrick Hanks. 1990. Word association norms, mutual information, and lexicography. *Computational linguistics*, 16(1):22–29.

Adriano Ferraresi, Eros Zanchetta, Marco Baroni, and Silvia Bernardini. 2008. Introducing and evaluating ukwac, a very large web-derived corpus of english. In *Proceedings of the 4th Web as Corpus Workshop (WAC-4) Can we beat Google*, pages 47–54.

David Hope and Bill Keller. 2013. MaxMax: A Graph-based Soft Clustering Algorithm Applied to Word Sense Induction. In *Proceedings of the 14th International Conference on Computational Linguistics and Intelligent Text Processing - Volume Part I*, pages 368–381, Samos, Greece. Springer-Verlag.

Eric H. Huang, Richard Socher, Christopher D. Manning, and Andrew Y. Ng. 2012. Improving word representations via global context and multiple word prototypes. In *Proceedings of the ACL*, pages 873–882, Jeju Island, Korea.

David Jurgens and Ioannis Klapaftis. 2013. Semeval-2013 task 13: Word sense induction for graded and non-graded senses. In *Proceedings of the Seventh International Workshop on Semantic Evaluation (SemEval 2013)*, volume 2, pages 290–299, Atlanta, Georgia, USA.

Dan Klein, Kristina Toutanova, H. Tolga Ilhan, Sepandar D. Kamvar, and Christopher D. Manning. 2002. Combining Heterogeneous Classifiers for Word-Sense Disambiguation. In *Proceedings of the ACL-02 Workshop on Word Sense Disambiguation: Recent Successes and Future Directions*, volume 8, pages 74–80, Philadelphia, PA.

Jey Han Lau, Paul Cook, and Timothy Baldwin. 2013. unimelb: Topic Modelling-based Word Sense Induction. In *Second Joint Conference on Lexical and Computational Semantics (*SEM): SemEval 2013)*, volume 2, pages 307–311, Atlanta, Georgia, USA.

Yoong Keok Lee and Hwee Tou Ng. 2002. An empirical evaluation of knowledge sources and learning algorithms for word sense disambiguation. In *Proceedings of the Empirical Methods in Natural Language Processing*, volume 10, pages 41–48, Philadelphia, PA.

Michael Lesk. 1986. Automatic Sense Disambiguation Using Machine Readable Dictionaries: How to Tell a Pine Cone from an Ice Cream Cone. In *Proceedings of the 5th International Conference on Systems Documentation*, pages 24–26, Toronto, ON, Canada. ACM.

Jiwei Li and Dan Jurafsky. 2015. Do multi-sense embeddings improve natural language understanding? In *Conference on Empirical Methods in Natural Language Processing, EMNLP'2015*, pages 1722–1732, Lisboa, Portugal.

Dekang Lin. 1998. An information-theoretic definition of similarity. In *Proceedings of ICML*, volume 98, pages 296–304, Madison, WI, USA.

Tomas Mikolov, Kai Chen, Greg Corrado, and Jeffrey Dean. 2013. Efficient estimation of word representations in vector space. In *Workshop at International Conference on Learning Representations (ICLR).*, pages 1310–1318, Scottsdale, AZ, USA.

Andrea Moro, Alessandro Raganato, and Roberto Navigli. 2014. Entity linking meets word sense disambiguation: a unified approach. *Transactions of the Association for Computational Linguistics*, 2:231–244.

Roberto Navigli. 2009. Word sense disambiguation: A survey. *ACM Computing Surveys (CSUR)*, 41(2):10.

Arvind Neelakantan, Jeevan Shankar, Alexandre Passos, and Andrew McCallum. 2014. Efficient non-parametric estimation of multiple embeddings per word in vector space. In *Conference on Empirical Methods in Natural Language Processing (EMNLP)*, pages 1059–1069, Doha, Qatar.

Luis Nieto Piña and Richard Johansson. 2015. A simple and efficient method to generate word sense representations. In *Proceedings of the International Conference Recent Advances in Natural Language Processing*, Hissar, Bulgaria, September.

Luis Nieto Piña and Richard Johansson. 2016. Embedding senses for efficient graph-based word sense disambiguation. In *Proceedings of TextGraphs-10, Proceedings of the Human Language Technology Conference of the NAACL*, San Diego, United States.

Alexander Panchenko. 2013. *Similarity measures for semantic relation extraction*. Ph.D. thesis, Université catholique de Louvain, Louvain-la-Neuve, Belgium.

Patrick Pantel and Dekang Lin. 2002. Discovering word senses from text. In *Proceedings of the eighth ACM SIGKDD international conference on Knowledge discovery and data mining*, pages 613–619. ACM.

Ted Pedersen and Rebecca Bruce. 1997. Distinguishing word senses in untagged text. In *Proceedings of the Second Conference on Empirical Methods in Natural Language Processing*, pages 197–207, Providence, RI.

Ted Pedersen, Satanjeev Banerjee, and Siddharth Patwardhan. 2005. Maximizing semantic relatedness to perform word sense disambiguation. *University of Minnesota supercomputing institute research report UMSI*, 25:2005.

Jeffrey Pennington, Richard Socher, and Christopher Manning. 2014. Glove: Global vectors for word representation. In *Proceedings of the Empirical Methods in Natural Language Processing (EMNLP)*, pages 1532–1543, Doha, Qatar.

Joseph Reisinger and Raymond J. Mooney. 2010. Multi-prototype vector-space models of word meaning. In *Human Language Technologies: The 2010 Annual Conference of the North American Chapter of the Association for Computational Linguistics*, pages 109–117, Los Angeles, California.

Sascha Rothe and Hinrich Schütze. 2015. Autoextend: Extending word embeddings to embeddings for synsets and lexemes. In *Proceedings of the Association for Computational Linguistics*, pages 1793–1803, Beijing, China. Association for Computational Linguistics.

Eugen Ruppert, Jonas Klesy, Martin Riedl, and Chris Biemann. 2015. Rule-based dependency parse collapsing and propagation for german and english. In *Proceedings of the GSCL 2015*, pages 58–66, Duisburg, Germany.

Gerard Salton, Anita Wong, and Chung-Shu Yang. 1975. A vector space model for automatic indexing. *Communications of the ACM*, 18(11):613–620.

Hinrich Schütze. 1998. Automatic word sense discrimination. *Computational linguistics*, 24(1):97–123.

Fei Tian, Hanjun Dai, Jiang Bian, Bin Gao, Rui Zhang, Enhong Chen, and Tie-Yan Liu. 2014. A probabilistic model for learning multi-prototype word embeddings. In *COLING*, pages 151–160, Dublin, Ireland.

Jean Véronis. 2004. HyperLex: Lexical cartography for information retrieval. *Computer Speech and Language*, 18:223–252.

Dominic Widdows and Beate Dorow. 2002. A graph model for unsupervised lexical acquisition. In *Proceedings of the 19th international conference on Computational linguistics*, pages 1–7, Taipei, Taiwan.

Ziqi Zhang, Anna Lisa Gentile, and Fabio Ciravegna. 2013. Recent advances in methods of lexical semantic relatedness–a survey. *Natural Language Engineering*, 19(04):411–479.

Pair Distance Distribution:
a Model of Semantic Representation

Yonatan Ramni   **Oded Maimon**   **Evgeni Khmelnitsky**

Department of Industrial Engineering

Tel-Aviv University

Tel-Aviv, Israel

{yona5;maimon;xmel}@post.tau.ac.il

Abstract

We introduce PDD (Pair Distance Distribution), a novel corpus-based model of semantic representation. Most corpus-based models are VSMs (Vector Space Models), which while being successful, suffer from both practical and theoretical shortcomings. VSM models produce very large, sparse matrices, and dimensionality reduction is usually performed, leading to high computational complexity, and obscuring the meaning of the dimensions. Similarity in VSMs is constrained to be both symmetric and transitive, contrary to evidence from human subject tests. PDD is feature-based, created automatically from corpora without producing large, sparse matrices. The dimensions along which words are compared are meaningful, enabling better understanding of the model and providing an explanation as to how any two words are similar. Similarity is neither symmetric nor transitive. The model achieved accuracy of 97.6% on a published semantic similarity test.

1 Introduction

Semantic representation models are described by Mitchell and Lapata (2008) as belonging to one of three families, semantic networks, feature-based models and semantic spaces. Briefly, semantic networks represent words as nodes in a graph and the semantic relations between them as edges, and similarity between words is represented by the path length between them. Edges may represent a variety of different relations. Feature-based models assign a list of discrete features to each word, and similarity of words is obtained from the commonalities and differences of their feature sets. As indicated by Mitchell and Lapata (2008), semantic networks and feature-based models are often manually created by modelers, so that an effort is required to produce them, and the results are subjective.

Semantic spaces, also named DSMs (distributional semantic models) by Baroni and Lenci (2010), rely on the distributional hypothesis, that words that occur in the same contexts tend to have similar meanings (Harris, 1954). At their most basic form, word co-occurrences in various contexts are used to form feature vectors of words. DSMs are divided by Baroni and Lenci (2010) into unstructured DSMs, where word co-occurrences are counted without regard to the relation between the words, and structured DSMs, where triples of two words and particular syntactic or lexico-syntactic relations between them are counted. Various feature weighting schemes are employed, and a VSM (vector space model) is usually formed using the feature vectors (topic modeling (Griffiths et al., 2007) is a notable exception). Similarities between words are measured by distances between vectors in this multi-dimensional space, usually following a dimensionality reduction. VSMs have been successful in a number of tasks, such as word similarity and word-relation similarity tests. However, VSMs have several shortcomings. Placing all words in a multi-dimensional space, with greater distance between any two words signifying lower similarity between them, implies:

- All words have some similarity with one another.

- For any word, all other words can be ordered by their similarity to the given word.

- All pairs of words can be ordered by their similarity.

- Similarity is symmetric.

Proceedings of the 1st Workshop on Representation Learning for NLP, pages 184–192,
Berlin, Germany, August 11th, 2016. ©2016 Association for Computational Linguistics

- Transitivity - if any two words are both very similar to a third word, they cannot be very dissimilar.

- All instances of a word, whether the word is ambiguous, polysemous, or attains different meanings in different contexts, are mapped to the same position in space.

It is our view that for similarity to exist between two concepts (represented in our case by words), they must have something in common, such as a common dimension along which they have (possibly different) values. With nothing in common, two concepts bear no similarity to one another, which is not the same as having little similarity. As with relatives, some are close relatives of a person, others are more distant relations of his, and yet others are not related to him at all. Furthermore, similarity is ordinal, with numerical values, when given by human subjects, serving as an aid in ranking similarity, as is done with feelings of pain, or happiness. Let's illustrate some limitations of VSMs with examples.

Example 1: is 'bank' more similar to 'embankment' or to 'stock exchange'? 'bank' is ambiguous, so a possible solution would be to map these two different senses independently to different positions in multi-dimensional space, assuming one could automatically disambiguate them.

Example 2: is 'break' more similar to 'interrupt', 'separate', 'breach', 'burst', or 'violate'? 'break' is polysemous, with WordNet[1] listing 59 senses, which are in various degrees related to one another, just for the verb. In this case, it does not seem right to map each sense independently, as they share some meaning.

Example 3: is 'queen' more similar to 'king' or to 'woman'? The court advisers may have one opinion, and the queen's physician another. It depends on context. Similarly for 'man' vs. 'woman' and 'boy', or 'cat' vs. 'stuffed cat' and 'dog'. When VSMs are formed from a corpus, context is given by the corpus for all instances of all words as a package deal, and vectors of words are based on that context.

Example 4: How similar is 'cat' to 'submarine'? If we find nothing in common, there is no similarity, and the question doesn't seem to make sense. As with partially ordered sets, some pairs of words are related to one another, while others are not.

Example 5: Is 'flat' more similar to 'apartment', or 'chair' to 'table'? 'dog' to 'cat' or 'cow' to 'sheep'? 'fork' to 'shirt' or 'stone' to 'computer'? For some questions of this kind we may have a firm opinion, for others we may not be so sure, and some questions don't really make sense. However, a VSM will have definite answers to all questions in the above examples, regardless of sense or context. Moreover, the symmetry and transitivity of similarity imposed by VSMs contradict human similarity judgments (Tversky, 1977). These constraints of VSMs are due to the symmetry and triangle inequality conditions that must be satisfied by any distance function. In addition, Tversky and Hutchinson (1986) show that geometric models impose an upper bound on the number of points that can share the same nearest neighbor, and that particularly for conceptual data (such as categorical ratings or associations of words), values for these exceed those possible in geometric models. It has been suggested by Tversky and Gati (1982) that "similarity may be better characterized as a feature-matching process based on the weighting of common and distinctive features than as a metric-distance function". The model we propose makes use of word co-occurrence in a corpus to build a feature-based model of semantic representation. We use sentence limits as our context window, and measure the distance (counted in the number of intervening words) between pairs of words that co-occur in sentences. It is found that for a word, its mean pmf (probability mass function) of distance with its pair-words (hence termed PDD - pair distance distribution) characterizes it across corpora, and that semantically similar words have a similar mean PDD. Given a word, its features in our model are its pair-words (those that co-occur with it within sentences), together with the frequency of pair occurrence and its PDD. Thus we take into account word order, which is disregarded by 'bag-of-words' models. As no sparse matrices are created, no dimensionality reduction is required. This makes our model scalable both in computation and in storage, but more importantly, the 'dimensions' along which we compare words are the feature words, which are clear and meaningful. This stands in contrast to the dimensions obtained following a dimensionality reduction, the meanings of which often aren't clear. As words are not mapped into high-dimensional spaces, and consequently similarities

---

[1] http://wordnet.princeton.edu

are not measured with distances, the shortcomings of VSMs are avoided. The rest of this paper is structured as follows: Section 2 gives details of the semantic representation model. In section 3, an algorithm for evaluating similarity, based on our model, is presented. In section 4, experiments and their results are presented. Section 5 discusses the scalability of our method, and section 6 concludes the paper.

2   Model Details

Let w_1, w_2 be two distinct word forms (hence referred to as words). Given a corpus of documents C, let S be the collection of all sentences in C in which both w_1, w_2 appear at least once, $S = \{s_1, s_2, \ldots s_N\}$, for a total of N such sentences in S. For each sentence $s_i \in S$, let p_1, p_2 be the positions in the sentence of the words w_1, w_2 respectively. Define the distance between the two words w_1, w_2 in the sentence s_i:

$$d(s_i) = p_2 - p_1 \tag{1}$$

For sentences of maximal length L,

$$|d(s_i)| \leq L - 1, \; d(s_i) \neq 0 \tag{2}$$

As an example, in the sentence "The cat drank some milk", 'cat' and 'milk' are in positions 2 and 5 respectively, and the distance between 'cat' and 'milk' is 3. Define S_j as the collection of sentences s_i in S in which $d(s_i) = j$, and $|S_j|$ as the number of sentences in S_j, then for corpus C and word-pair $\langle w_1, w_2 \rangle$, the probability that the distance between the words (given a sentence containing both words) is j is:

$$pr(d(s_i) = j) = \begin{cases} \dfrac{|S_j|}{N}, & |j| \leq L - 1, j \neq 0 \\ 0, & otherwise \end{cases} \tag{3}$$

where N is the total number of sentences in S, and L is the maximal sentence length. (if either w_1 or w_2 appear more than once in s_i, only the nearest pair is counted). In this manner, the Corpus pmf, termed $PDD_C(w_1, w_2)$, of word-pair $\langle w_1, w_2 \rangle$ distance in corpus C is obtained, for any word-pair. Given S and the position p_1 of word w_1 for each $s_i \in S$, it is also possible to calculate the pmf of position p_2 of w_2 in each sentence s_i, assuming random distribution of p_2. Denoting the length of sentence s_i as l_i, the probability for the

position p_2 of w_2 in the sentence to be k is:

$$pr(p_2 = k) = \begin{cases} \dfrac{1}{l_i - 1}, & 1 \leq k \leq l_i, k \neq p_1 \\ 0, & otherwise \end{cases} \tag{4}$$

From this, it follows that the probability for any distance j between the two words w_1, w_2 in the sentence s_i (given p_1 and assuming random distribution of p_2) is:

$$pr(d(s_i) = j) =$$

$$\begin{cases} 1/(l_i - 1), & 1 - p_1 \leq d(s_i) \leq l_i - p_1, \\ & d(s_i) \neq 0 \\ 0, & otherwise \end{cases} \tag{5}$$

The probability for any particular distance j for the word-pair $\langle w_1, w_2 \rangle$ in any sentence in corpus C, $pr(d(S) = j)$, given that the pair occurs in the sentence, the position p_1 of w_1 in the sentence and assuming random distribution of p_2 may be obtained by averaging the probability for that distance over all sentences $s_i \in S$:

$$pr(d(S) = j) = \frac{1}{N} \sum_i pr(d(s_i) = j) \tag{6}$$

Hence another pmf for word-pair $\langle w_1, w_2 \rangle$ distance in corpus C is obtained. Denote this, the Random PDD, as $PDD_R(w_1, w_2)$. Whereas the Corpus pmf, $PDD_C(w_1, w_2)$, is based on the corpus data, the Random pmf, $PDD_R(w_1, w_2)$, is based on the position of w_1 in sentences where the word-pair occurs and on the sentences' lengths, and assumes random position of w_2 in those sentences. Given a corpus C and a word w_1, denote the set of all sentences in C in which w_1 appears as S_{w_1}. The company of w_1, $Co(w_1)$ are defined as those words which appear in a number of sentences in S_{w_1} above some threshold. Calculating both Corpus and Random pmfs (as outlined above) for each word-pair $\langle w_1, w_i \rangle$, $w_i \in Co(w_1)$, it is now possible to calculate the average Corpus and Random pmfs for w_1 with its companion words, $PDD_C(w_1)$ and $PDD_R(w_1)$ respectively, by averaging the distance probabilities for all companion words weighted by their frequency of occurrence in sentences of S_{w_1},

$$PDD_C(w_1) = \frac{\sum_i (PDD_C(w_1, w_i) \times n(i))}{\sum_i n(i)},$$

$$w_i \in Co(w_1) \tag{7}$$

$$PDD_R(w_1) = \frac{\sum_i (PDD_R(w_1, w_i) \times n(i))}{\sum_i n(i)},$$

$$w_i \in Co(w_1) \tag{8}$$

where $n(i)$ is the number of sentences in which the pair of words $\langle w_1, w_i \rangle$ appears. By using KLD (Kullback-Leibler Divergence) between Corpus and Random pmfs, $D(PDD_C \| PDD_R)$, we can measure the amount of information that is lost when the Random pmf of a word w_1, $PDD_R(w_1)$, is used to approximate its Corpus pmf, $PDD_C(w_1)$, as in the case of rectangular context windows of unstructured DSMs.

$$D\left(PDD_C \| PDD_R\right) =$$

$$\sum_j \left(log\left(\frac{PDD_C(j)}{PDD_R(j)}\right) PDD_C(j) \right),$$

$$1 - L \le j \le L - 1, \ j \neq 0 \tag{9}$$

where j is the distance between w_1 and its company words (all PDDs in eq. 9 are of w_1, which has been omitted for clarity). This statistic is a property of word w_1 in corpus C, which indicates the amount of information contained in the order of the words that are in the context of w_1, above the information that is carried by their mere presence there. It is also possible to calculate the information in any specific position in the context, by replacing the PDD_R value for that position with the PDD_C value, multiplying the remaining probabilities by a suitable factor to keep the sum of probabilities one, and calculating KLD between PDD_C and the amended PDD_R. The difference between this KLD value and the former KLD value indicates the information for that position.

Most previous research on unstructured DSMs has used, in any one study, the same context window for all words in the corpus, as regards window size, position and weights. Even when several different window parameters have been compared,(Bullinaria and Levy, 2007; Levy et al., 1999; Lund and Burgess, 1996; Sahlgren, 2006), each window configuration was used for the whole corpus, and comparison made on basis of the final results. We know of no attempt to test different window configurations for different words. However, there is no evidence to suggest that the same window configuration is the optimal one for all

words. We suggest a scheme that could be useful in determining weighting due to word order. *PPMI* (positive pointwise mutual information), which compares context window co-occurrence frequency with expected frequency, has been successfully used to weight words found in rectangular context windows (Bullinaria and Levy, 2007; Church and Hanks, 1990; Niwa and Nitta, 1994), based on their occurrence regardless of order. In our case, $PDD_R(k)$ represents the chance probability of observing one of a word's company words a distance of k words from it, and $PDD_C(k)$ represents the probability of this occurring in the corpus (given they co-occur in a sentence). We propose the following additional weight, $Wt(k)$, be used for word w_1, for position k words away from it,

$$Wt(k) =$$

$$\begin{cases} log\dfrac{PDD_C(k)}{PDD_R(k)}, & PDD_C(k) > PDD_R(k), \\ 0, & \text{otherwise} \end{cases} \tag{10}$$

where PDD_C is the Corpus pmf of word w_1, and PDD_R is its Random pmf.

3 Similarity Algorithm

Though differences between word PDDs could be used to measure similarity between words, this would lead to some of difficulties associated with VSMs, as in effect we would be measuring distances in a high-dimensional space. By treating a word's company as its features, we can compare two words based on their common pair-words. The algorithm we adopt is as follows:

- For every vocabulary word w_1:

- For every other vocabulary word w_2,:
* Determine words $Co(w_1, w_2)$ that are in the company of both w_1 and w_2,

$$Co(w_1, w_2) = Co(w_1) \cap Co(w_2) \tag{11}$$

* For every $w_f \in Co(w_1, w_2)$, calculate $PDD_C(w_1, w_f)$ and $PDD_C(w_2, w_f)$ using Eq. (3), and determine the difference between w_1 and w_2, based on w_f, as the cosine "distance" between them,

$$d_{w_f}(w_1, w_2) =$$

$$1 - \frac{PDD_C(w_1, w_f) PDD_C(w_2, w_f)}{|PDD_C(w_1, w_f)| |PDD_C(w_2, w_f)|} \tag{12}$$

* For all $w_f \in Co(w_1, w_2)$, sort $d_{w_f}(w_1, w_2)$ in ascending order,

$$D_{w_1,w_2} =$$

$$\left\{ d_{w_{f_1}}(w_1, w_2), d_{w_{f_2}}(w_1, w_2) \ldots \right\} \quad (13)$$

* Set the dissimilarity of w_1 to w_2 to be the sum of the first n elements of D_{w_1,w_2}, (n is an experimentally determined parameter):

$$Diss(w_1, w_2) = \sum_{i=1}^{n} D_{w_1,w_2}(i) \quad (14)$$

w_1 is considered to have no similarity with words w_2 that do not have common pair-words with it.

– Order all vocabulary words that have common pair-words with w_1, by increasing dissimilarity of w_1 to them.

We now have, for each vocabulary word w_1, all other vocabulary words that have common pair-words with w_1, sorted by the dissimilarity of w_1 to them. We define the dissimilarity of w_1 to any other word w_x in this list to be the rank of w_x in this sorted list, not the numerical value $Diss(w_1, w_x)$. The differences used above, in Equation (12), do not take into account the corpus frequency of the words and pairs of words, and are termed unweighted differences. Another possibility is to use weighting that expresses these frequencies. The following weighting has been shown to give good results (see Section 4):

Weighted Difference$_{w_f}(w_1, w_2) =$

$$d_{w_f}(w_1, w_2) \times log\left(\frac{C_f}{C_{1,f}}\right)^d \times log(C_2)^{\frac{d}{2}} \quad (15)$$

where $d_{w_f}(w_1, w_2)$ is the unweighted difference, C_f is the corpus count of w_f, $C_{1,f}$ is the corpus count of co-occurrence of w_1 and w_f in sentences, C_2 is the corpus count of w_2, and d is an experimentally determined parameter. The weighted difference is then used in place of the unweighted difference in the next stages. It will be noted that $log\left(\frac{C_f}{C_{1,f}}\right)$ is non-negative, and increases as the PMI (pointwise mutual information) between w_1 and w_f decreases (the corpus count of w_1 is constant when ordering the similarity of w_1 to all other words, and is therefore omitted), so this term penalizes pair-words with low PMI to w_1. The last term penalizes, in the ordering of all corpus words by similarity of w_1 to them, words w_2 with high corpus frequency. Note that the dissimilarity $Diss(w_1, w_2)$ based on weighted differences is not symmetric with respect to w_1 and w_2. Dissimilarities based on both weighted and unweighted differences do not obey the triangle inequality, so that w_1 may be very similar to both w_2 and w_3, without requiring any minimal similarity between w_2 and w_3. Both dissimilarities also do not restrict the number of words that can share a nearest neighbor - any number of words can have w_1 as the word they are most similar to.

4 Experimental Details

4.1 Computing PDD_C

An initial experiment was carried out on 17,000 medical papers on diseases in eight different, but related, domains. The papers were returned by Google Scholar using search words relating to each domain, downloaded in pdf format and converted to text, to form eight corpora. The texts were tokenized, and lower-cased (using raw surface forms of words means different parts of speech, as well as different senses, are conflated). For vocabulary purpose, the text was filtered for stop words, numbers and any word not beginning with an alphanumeric character, and only words appearing at least 100 times were used. Sentences were delimited, and sentences with a length of over 50 words were discarded. Word-pairs were obtained from the eight corpora, for word-pair distance of up to 25 words, for word-pairs appearing in at least 10 sentences. PDD_C was calculated for all pair words, which ranged in number from 6,300 to 13,700 words for each domain, and a total number of 14,900 unique words, and 2.95 million unique pairs, for all domains combined. Fig. 1 below shows PDD_C for 'effect', 'cell', 'red' and 'show', respectively, for the eight domains superimposed. It may be seen that each word has a characteristic PDD_C across domains, and that different words have a different PDD_C.

4.2 Computing PDD_C and PDD_R

Google Scholar was again used to download articles from journals with the word 'science' in their title. Seven search words were used: 'physics', 'chemistry', 'biology', 'engineering', 'medicine', 'information' and 'environment'. Over 27,000 pdfs were downloaded, and processed as in the previous experiment. Again, only words appear-

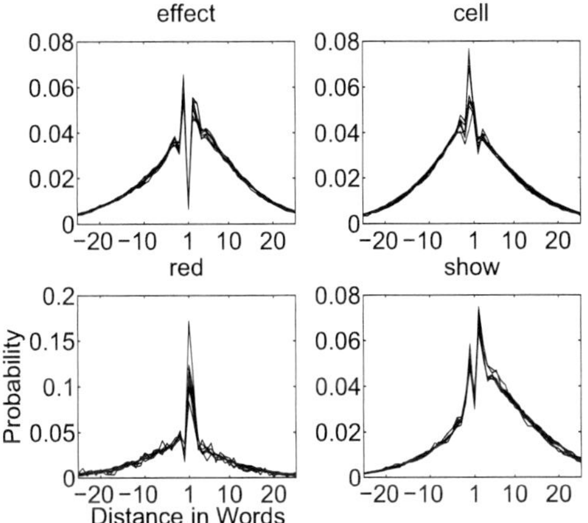

Figure 1: PDD_C for 'effect', 'cell', 'red' and 'show' across eight domains

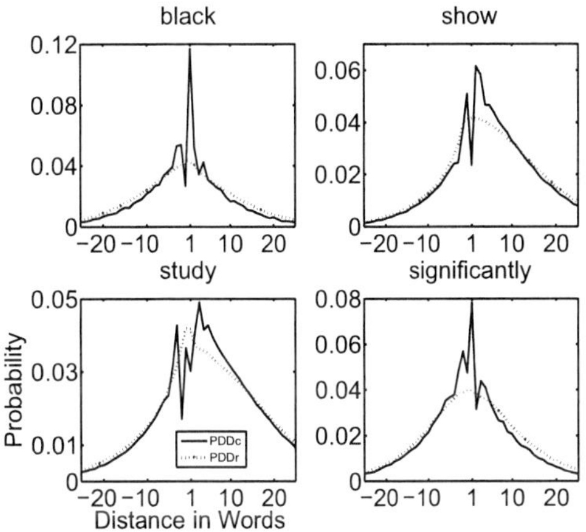

Figure 2: PDD_C and PDD_R for 'black', 'show', 'study', and 'significantly'

ing at least 100 times were used (32,341 words), pair distance of up to 25 words was considered, and PDD_C and PDD_R for all pairs appearing at least 10 times calculated. This resulted in 23,155 words and 3.9 million word pairs. Figure 2 below shows PDD_C and PDD_R for four words, 'black', 'show', 'study' and 'significantly'. The PDD_R of a word is determined by its position in sentences and the length of these sentences. The PDD_C is determined by the usage of the word with its company. It may be seen that as we move in the sentence away from the word, its PDD_C eventually follows its PDD_R from below. This is expected, as a word's company are more likely to be near it (and hence less likely to be farther away) than predicted by random chance, and because not much information is expected to be found in the order of a word's company that is not near it. However, the more interesting part is the one near the word, where the PDD_C and PDD_R differ considerably. Each word has a distinctive pattern, from which we may learn the amount of information in the order of the words around it, as detailed in Section 2. For 'black' and 'significantly', it is the following word that holds the most information, for 'show' it is the second word following, and for 'study' it is the third word following, with positions immediately around it held by company words less often than by chance (presumably because they are held by function words). This behavior is probably affected by each word's most frequent part-of-speech usage in the corpus, for example, 'black' as an adjective is likely to have a related content word following it.

Fig. 3 compares the PDD_C of 10 adjectives, 5 colors ('black', 'red', 'blue', 'white', 'green') and 5 size adjectives ('huge', 'big', 'great', 'large', 'enormous'). The top row shows the five colors and five sizes PDD_C. The bottom row shows on the left the mean color and size PDD_C, and on the right all color and size PDD_C. It may be seen that though color and size PDD_C are similar, they differ, particularly in positions nearest the word. Clustering the ten PDD_C into two clusters, using kmeans clustering and cityblock distance, separates them correctly into colors and sizes. This illustrates that (at least in this case) the PDD_C is related also to their semantic content, and not only to their part-of-speech.

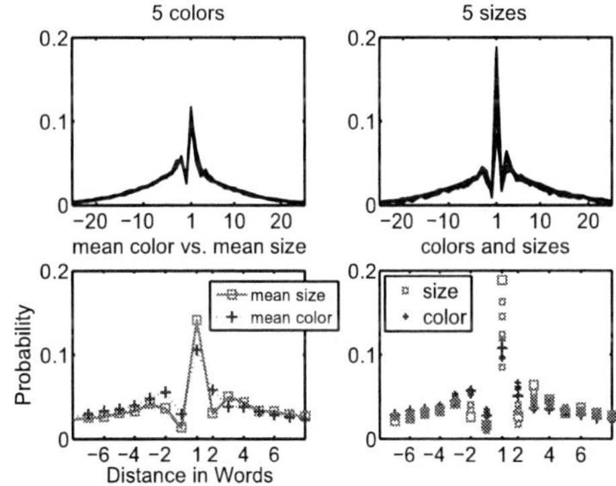

Figure 3: PDD_C Comparison for Color and Size Adjectives

4.3 Computing Weights for Positions in the Context Window

Using eq. 10, weights were calculated for positions in the context window of all words that have pairs. These weights are meant to reflect the information in the order of the words, given that they occur in the window (a fact that by itself carries information). It turns out that these weights differ from one word to another. Fig. 4.3 shows on the top row PDD_C vs. PDD_R for 'red' and 'year'. The bottom row shows the weights calculated for their context windows, together with the weights for another, semantically similar word ('black' and 'day' respectively). Weights not shown are zero. The adjectives get the greatest weight for the following word, and zero weight for the preceding word. The nouns 'year' and 'day' get zero weight for both the preceding and the following words, with 'year' getting the greatest weights for the fourth word preceding and the third word following, and 'day' for the second word preceding and the third word following. The nouns also have weights for wider contexts than the adjectives. This example shows that different words have different optimal context windows, both in width and in weight, as regards the information in word order.

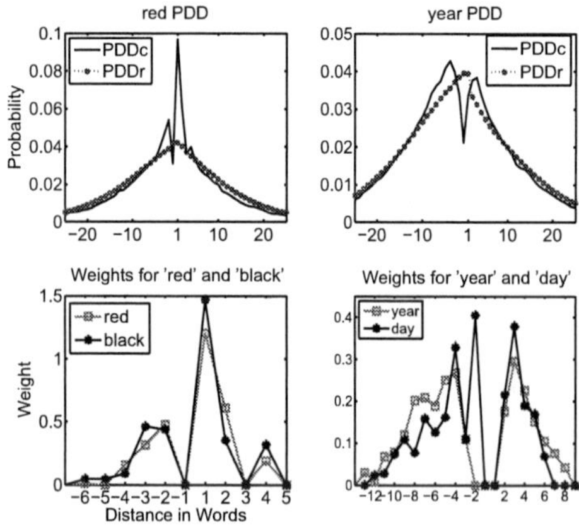

Figure 4: Context Window Weights

4.4 TOEFL Test

In order to increase vocabulary size, the ukWaC corpus[2] holding over a billion words in documents crawled from the internet was used (Baroni et al., 2009). The same processing as in the previous experiments was applied. This resulted in a vocabulary of 136,812 words with a frequency of at least 100 in the corpus. The TOEFL synonym dataset (Landauer and Dumais, 1997) consists of 80 question words, for each of which 4 answer words are given, and the task is to select the answer word most similar to the question word. The test contains 391 unique words, 7 of which were missing in our vocabulary. Three questions had one wrong answer word missing, and these were attempted without the missing word. One question had all but one wrong answer word missing, and was marked as wrong. For each TOEFL word, word-pairs that appear in at least 10 sentences in the corpus were extracted. The method we used to select the correct answer is by ordering the answer words by decreasing similarity of the question word to them as outlined in section 3, and choosing as correct the top word. Cosine distance was used, and values for n, the number of common feature words, from 1 to 50 were evaluated. Both unweighted and weighted differences were calculated. A grid search was performed for the best combination of n and d, and the values of 5 and 3.5 respectively give a result of 86%. However any combination of values for n in the range 3-9 and for d in the range 2-5, give a result of 80% and above. Fig. 5 shows the results with both weighted ($d = 3.5$) and unweighted differences, as a function of the number of feature words used. It will be noticed that with the weighted differences, it takes 3-5 feature words to get optimal results. Better results on the TOEFL test have been achieved by (Rapp, 2003; Han, 2014; Pilehvar et al., 2013; Turney et al., 2003; Bullinaria and Levy, 2012), ranging from 92.5 to 100%. Han (2014) and Turney et al. (2003) are hybrid approaches, combining the results of several methods. Pilehvar et al. (2013) relies on WordNet[3] for sense inventory of words, and uses a substantially different version of the test. Both Bullinaria and Levy (2012) and Rapp (2003), after obtaining a vocabulary from a corpus, artificially introduce into their data out-of-vocabulary TOEFL words, which would not be possible for open-ended questions.

4.5 Distance Test

This experiment uses the same corpus and the same processing as the previous experiment. The

---

[2]http://wacky.sslmit.unibo.it

[3]http://wordnet.princeton.edu

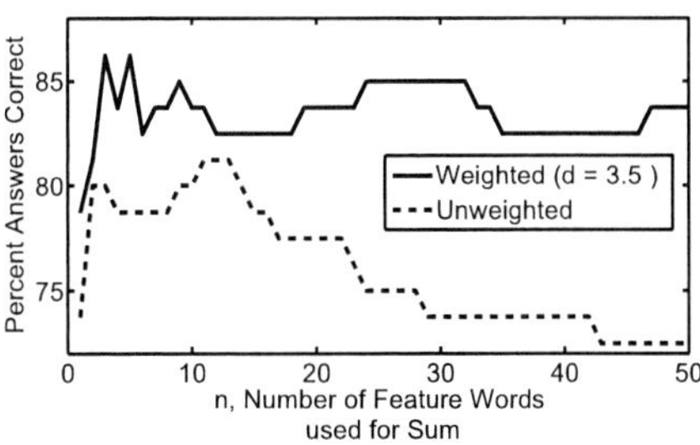

Figure 5: TOEFL Test Results

distance comparison test (Bullinaria and Levy, 2007), for which the data has kindly been made available by the authors on their website, is also similar to the TOEFL test. This test consists of 200 pairs of semantically related words. For each pair, one word is set as the question word. The other pair word, the answer word, is included in a list with 10 additional words, chosen at random from the other pairs. The task is to sort this list in order of decreasing similarity to the question word, and points are awarded according to the position of the answer word in this list (1 point for 1st position, 0.9 for 2nd, etc.). Using the same method as in the previous experiment, results for unweighted and weighted distance ($d = 3$) are shown in fig. 6 below. A value of 97.6% is obtained for this weight, $d{=}3$, and for n with a value of 7 or 8. However any combination of values for d in the range 2-4.5 and n in the range 4-11 yields a result of over 97%.

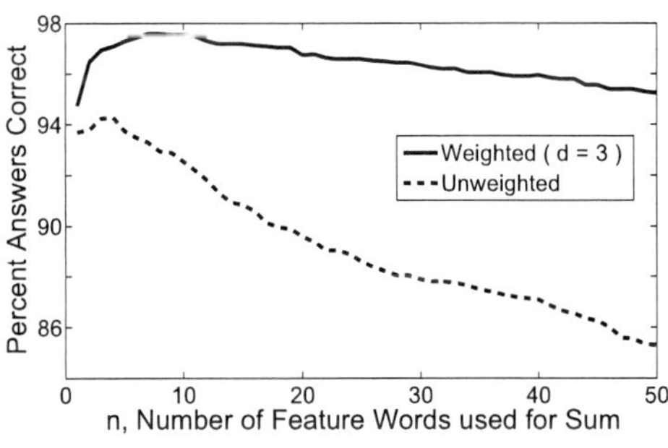

Figure 6: Distance Test Results

5   Scalability

The model size is governed by the number P of distinct word-pairs that occur in sentences of the corpus, which is related to the vocabulary size, V, which in turn depends on N, the number of tokens in the corpus. For the ukWac corpus, $V \sim cN^{0.53}$,

and for pairs with a distance of up to 6 words, that appear at least 5 times, P grows as $N^{0.80}$. This shows that the model size is scalable with corpus size. With p as the maximal pair distance used, the complexity of building the PDD model is bounded by $2pN$, and is therefore $O(N)$, again scalable with corpus size. In order to arrange all vocabulary words V by similarity of a single word w to them, it is necessary to find the best n features each vocabulary word has in common with w, and calculate the similarity based on the sum of differences for the n features. Doing this for all vocabulary words (i.e. arranging all words in order of similarity of every word to them) is governed by C, the number of common features all vocabulary words have with all other vocabulary words. For the ukWac corpus, (again for pairs with a distance of up to 6 words, that appear at least 5 times), C grows as $N^{1.21}$. While this grows faster than corpus size, it is feasible to calculate this for the ukWac corpus. For larger corpora it may be necessary to limit, for each word, the calculation of its similarity to words that have a number of common pair-words with it above some threshold.

6   Discussion and Conclusions

We have presented a novel model of semantic representation, that is scalable and does not suffer from the shortcomings of VSMs. Two words that have no common features are not considered similar, and are not given a similarity value. Similarity is not symmetric, in accordance with human similarity judgments. Similarity is not transitive, so that a given word may be similar to two other words, to each with different senses of the given word, or in different contexts, without necessitating any similarity between the two other words. The features with which the similarity between a pair of words is evaluated are clear and meaningful - the common pair-words. The model makes it possible to select which features of a word to use when evaluating similarity, thus enabling one to take into account different senses and different contexts of a word. The model has been shown to work well on word similarity tasks. Further work could use the model for word disambiguation tasks, as different senses of a word are expected to have different PDDs. The current work has used pair distance distribution, and compared words based on their common features. Future work could use triplet distance distribution, and take into account distinctive word features as well as the common features.

References

Marco Baroni and Alessandro Lenci. 2010. Distributional memory: A general framework for corpus-based semantics. *Computational Linguistics*, 36(4):673–721.

Marco Baroni, Silvia Bernardini, Adriano Ferraresi, and Eros Zanchetta. 2009. The wacky wide web: a collection of very large linguistically processed web-crawled corpora. *Language resources and evaluation*, 43(3):209–226.

John A Bullinaria and Joseph P Levy. 2007. Extracting semantic representations from word co-occurrence statistics: A computational study. *Behavior research methods*, 39(3):510–526.

John A Bullinaria and Joseph P Levy. 2012. Extracting semantic representations from word co-occurrence statistics: stop-lists, stemming, and svd. *Behavior research methods*, 44(3):890–907.

Kenneth Ward Church and Patrick Hanks. 1990. Word association norms, mutual information, and lexicography. *Computational linguistics*, 16(1):22–29.

Thomas L Griffiths, Mark Steyvers, and Joshua B Tenenbaum. 2007. Topics in semantic representation. *Psychological review*, 114(2):211–244.

Lushan Han. 2014. *Schema free querying of semantic data*. Ph.D. thesis, University of Maryland.

Zellig S Harris. 1954. Distributional structure. *Word*, 10(2-3):146–162.

Thomas K Landauer and Susan T Dumais. 1997. A solution to plato's problem: The latent semantic analysis theory of acquisition, induction, and representation of knowledge. *Psychological review*, 104(2):211–240.

Joseph P Levy, John A Bullinaria, and Malti Patel. 1999. Explorations in the derivation of word co-occurrence statistics. *South Pacific Journal of Psychology*, 10(01):99–111.

Kevin Lund and Curt Burgess. 1996. Producing high-dimensional semantic spaces from lexical co-occurrence. *Behavior Research Methods, Instruments, & Computers*, 28(2):203–208.

Jeff Mitchell and Mirella Lapata. 2008. Vector-based models of semantic composition. In *ACL-08: HLT*, pages 236–244.

Yoshiki Niwa and Yoshihiko Nitta. 1994. Co-occurrence vectors from corpora vs. distance vectors from dictionaries. In *Proceedings of the 15th conference on Computational linguistics-Volume 1*, pages 304–309. Association for Computational Linguistics.

Mohammad Taher Pilehvar, David Jurgens, and Roberto Navigli. 2013. Align, disambiguate and walk: A unified approach for measuring semantic similarity. In *Proceedings of the 51st Annual Meeting of the Association for Computational Linguistics*, pages 1341–1351.

Reinhard Rapp. 2003. Word sense discovery based on sense descriptor dissimilarity. In *Proceedings of the ninth machine translation summit*, pages 315–322.

Magnus Sahlgren. 2006. *The Word-Space Model: Using distributional analysis to represent syntagmatic and paradigmatic relations between words in high-dimensional vector spaces*. Ph.D. thesis, Stockholm University.

Peter Turney, Michael L Littman, Jeffrey Bigham, and Victor Shnayder. 2003. Combining independent modules to solve multiple-choice synonym and analogy problems. In *Proceedings of the International Conference on Recent Advances in Natural Language Processing (RANLP-03)*, pages 482–489.

Amos Tversky and Itamar Gati. 1982. Similarity, separability, and the triangle inequality. *Psychological review*, 89(2):123–154.

Amos Tversky and J Hutchinson. 1986. Nearest neighbor analysis of psychological spaces. *Psychological review*, 93(1):3–22.

Amos Tversky. 1977. Features of similarity. *Psychological review*, 84(4):327–352.

Measuring semantic similarity of words using concept networks

Gábor Recski
Research Institute for Linguistics
Hungarian Academy of Sciences
H-1068 Budapest, Benczúr u. 33
recski@mokk.bme.hu

Eszter Iklódi
Dept of Automation and Applied Informatics
Budapest U of Technology and Economics
H-1117 Budapest, Magyar tudósok krt. 2
eszter.iklodi@gmail.com

Katalin Pajkossy
Department of Algebra
Budapest U of Technology and Economics
H-1111 Budapest, Egry J. u. 1
pajkossy@mokk.bme.hu

András Kornai
Institute for Computer Science
Hungarian Academy of Sciences
H-1111 Budapest, Kende u. 13-17
andras@kornai.com

Abstract

We present a state-of-the-art algorithm for measuring the semantic similarity of word pairs using novel combinations of word embeddings, WordNet, and the concept dictionary 4lang. We evaluate our system on the SimLex-999 benchmark data. Our top score of 0.76 is higher than any published system that we are aware of, well beyond the average inter-annotator agreement of 0.67, and close to the 0.78 average correlation between a human rater and the average of all other ratings, suggesting that our system has achieved near-human performance on this benchmark.

0 Introduction

We present a hybrid system for measuring the semantic similarity of word pairs. The system relies both on standard word embeddings, the WordNet database, and features derived from the 4lang concept dictionary, a set of concept graphs built from entries in monolingual dictionaries of English. 4lang-based features improve the performance of systems using only word embeddings and/or WordNet, our top configurations achieve state-of-the-art results on the SimLex-999 data, which has recently become a popular benchmark of word similarity metrics.

In Section 1 we summarize earlier work on measuring word similarity and review the latest results achieved on the SimLex-999 data. Section 2 describes our experimental setup, Sections 2.1 and 2.2 documents the features obtained

using word embeddings and WordNet. In Section 3 we briefly introduce the 4lang resources and the formalism it uses for encoding the meaning of words as directed graphs of concepts, then document our efforts to develop novel 4lang-based similarity features. Besides improving the performance of existing systems for measuring word similarity, the goal of the present project is to examine the potential of 4lang representations in representing non-trivial lexical relationships that are beyond the scope of word embeddings and standard linguistic ontologies.

Section 4 presents our results and provides rough error analysis. Section 5 offers some conclusions and plans for future work. All software presented in this paper is available for download under an MIT license at http://github.com/recski/wordsim.

1 Background

Measuring the semantic similarity of words is a fundamental task in various natural language processing applications. The ability to judge the similarity in meaning of any two linguistic structures reflects on the quality of the representations used. Vector representations (word embeddings) are commonly used as the component encoding (lexical) semantics in virtually all NLP applications. The similarity of word vectors is by far the most common source of information for semantic similarity in state-of-the-art systems, e.g. nearly all top-scoring systems at the 2015 SemEval Task on measuring semantic similarity (Agirre et al., 2015) rely on word embeddings to score sentence pairs (see e.g. (Sultan et al., 2015; Han et al.,

Proceedings of the 1st Workshop on Representation Learning for NLP, pages 193–200,
Berlin, Germany, August 11th, 2016. ©2016 Association for Computational Linguistics

2015)).

Hill et al. (2015) proposed the `SimLex-999` dataset as a benchmark for word similarity, arguing that pre-existing gold standards measure *association*, not similarity, of word pairs; e.g. the words *cup* and *coffee* receive a high score by annotators in the widely used `wordsim353` data (Finkelstein et al., 2002). `SimLex` has since been used to evaluate various algorithms for measuring word similarity. Hill et al. (2015) reports a Spearman correlation of 0.414 achieved by an embedding trained on Wikipedia using `word2vec` (Mikolov et al., 2013). Schwartz et al. (2015) achieves a score of 0.56 using a combination of a standard word2vec-based embedding and the `SP` model, which encodes the cooccurrence of words in *symmetric patterns* such as *X and Y* or *X as well as Y*.

Banjade et al. (2015) combined multiple word embeddings with the word similarity algorithm of (Han et al., 2015) used in a top-scoring SemEval system, and simple features derived from WordNet (Miller, 1995) indicating whether word pairs are synonymous or antonymous. Their top system achieved a correlation of 0.64 on SimLex. The highest score we are aware of is achieved using the `Paragram` embedding (Wieting et al., 2015), a set of vectors obtained by training pre-existing embeddings on word pairs from the Paraphrase Database (Ganitkevitch et al., 2013). The top correlation of 0.69 is measured when using 300-dimension embedding created from the same `GloVe`-vectors that have been introduced in this section (trained on 840 billion tokens). Hyperparameters of this database have been tuned for maximum performance on SimLex, another version tuned for the `WS-353` dataset achieves a correlation of 0.667.

2 Setup

Our system is trained on a variety of real-valued and binary features generated using word embeddings, WordNet, and `4lang` definition graphs. Each class of features will be presented in detail below. We perform support vector regression (with RBF kernel) over all features using the `numpy` library, the model is trained on 900 pairs of the SimLex data and used to obtain scores for the remaining 99 pairs. We compute the Spearman correlation of the output with `SimLex` scores. We evaluate each of our models using tenfold cross-validation and by averaging the ten correlation figures. The changes in performance caused by previously used feature classes are described next, the performance of all major configurations are summarized in Section 4.

2.1 Word embeddings

Features in the first group are based on word vector similarity. For each word pair the cosine similarity of the corresponding two vectors is calculated for all embeddings used. Three sets of word vectors in our experiments were built using the neural models compared by Hill et al. (2015): the `SENNA`[1] (Collobert and Weston, 2008), and `Huang`[2] (Huang et al., 2012) embeddings contain 50-dimension vectors and were downloaded from the authors' webpages. The `word2vec` (Mikolov et al., 2013) vectors are of 300 dimensions and were trained on the Google News dataset[3].

We extend this set of models with `GloVe` vectors[4] (Pennington et al., 2014), trained on 840 billion tokens of Common Crawl data[5], and the two word embeddings mentioned in Section 1 that have recently been evaluated on the `SimLex` dataset: the 500-dimension `SP` model[6] (Schwartz et al., 2015) (see Section 1) and the 300-dimension `Paragram` vectors[7] (Wieting et al., 2015). The model trained on 6 features corresponding to the 6 embeddings mentioned achieves a Spearman correlation of 0.72, the performance of individual embeddings is listed in Table 1.

2.2 Wordnet

Another group of features are derived using WordNet (Miller, 1995). WordNet-based metrics proved to be useful in the Semeval-system of Han et al. (2013), who used these metrics for calculating a boost of word similarity scores. The top system of Banjade et al. (2015) also includes a subset of these features. We chose to use four of these metrics as binary features in our system;

---

[1] `http://ronan.collobert.com/senna/`
[2] `http://www.socher.org`
[3] `https://code.google.com/archive/p/word2vec/`
[4] `http://nlp.stanford.edu/projects/glove/`
[5] `https://commoncrawl.org/`
[6] `http://www.cs.huji.ac.il/~roys02/papers/sp_embeddings/sp_embeddings.html`
[7] `http://ttic.uchicago.edu/~wieting/`

System	Spearman's ρ
Huang	0.14
SENNA	0.27
GloVe	0.40
Word2Vec	0.44
SP	0.50
Paragram	0.68
6 embeddings	**0.72**

Table 1: Performance of word embeddings on `SimLex`

these indicate whether one word is a direct or two-link hypernym of the other, whether the two are derivationally related, and whether one word appears frequently in the glosses of the other (and its direct hypernym and its direct hyponyms). Each of these features improved our system independently, adding all of them brought the system's performance to 0.73. A model trained on the 4 `WordNet`-based features alone achieves a correlation of 0.33.

3 4lang

The `4lang` theory of semantics was introduced and motivated in Kornai (2010) and Kornai (2012). The name refers to the initial concept dictionary, which had bindings in four languages, representative samples of the major language families spoken in Europe; Germanic (English), Slavic (Polish), Romance (Latin), and Finno-Ugric (Hungarian). Today, bindings exist in over 40 languages (Ács et al., 2013). We only present a bird's-eye view here, and refer the reader to the book-length presentation (Kornai, in preparation) for details. In brief, `4lang` is an algebraic (symbolic) system that puts the emphasis on lexical definitions at the word and sub-word level, and on valency (slot-filling) on the phrase and sentence level. Paragraphs and yet higher (discourse) units are not well worked out, but these play no role in any of the approaches to analogy and similarity that we are aware of.

Historically, `4lang` falls in the AI/KR tradition, following on the work of Quillian (1969), Schank (1975), and more recently Banarescu et al. (2013). Linguistically, it is closest to Wierzbicka (1972), Goddard (2002) and to modern theories of case grammar and linking theory (see Butt (2006)

for a summary). Computationally, `4lang` is in the finite state tradition (Koskenniemi, 1983), except it relies on an extension of finite state automata (FSA) introduced by Eilenberg (1974) to *machines*.

In addition to the usual state machine (where letters of the alphabet correspond to directed edges running between the states), an Eilenberg machine will also have a *base set X*, with each letter of the alphabet corresponding to a binary relation over X. As the machine consumes letters one by one, the corresponding relations are composed. How this mechanism can be used to account for slot-filling in a variable-free setting is described in Kornai (2010).

Central to the goals of the current paper is the structure of X. As a first approximation, X can be thought of as a hypergraph, where each hypernode is a lexeme (for a total of about 10^5 such hypernodes), and hyperedges run from (hyper)node a to b if b appears in the definition of a. Since the definition of `fox` includes the word `clever`, we have a link from `fox` to `clever`, but not conversely, since the definition of `clever` does not refer to `fox`. Edges are of three types: 0, corresponding both to attribution and IS_A relations; 1, corresponding to grammatical subjects; and 2, corresponding to grammatical objects. Indirect objects are handled by the decomposition methods pioneered in generative semantics, without recourse to a '3' link type (Kornai, 2012).

Each lexeme is a small Eilenberg machine, with only a few states in its FSA, so the state space X of the entire lexicon is best viewed as a large graph with about 10^6 states (assuming 10 states per hypernode). This base set is shared across the individual machines and functions analogously to the *blackboard* long familiar from AI (Nii, 1986). The primary purpose of the machine apparatus is to formalize the classical distributed model of semantic interpretation, spreading activation (Collins and Loftus, 1975; Nemeskey et al., 2013), by a series of changes in the hypernode activation levels, described by the relations on X. Manual grammar writing in this style can lead to very high precision high recall grammars (Karlsson et al., 1995; Tapanainen and Järvinen, 1997), but for now we rely on the Stanford Parser (Chen and Manning, 2014) to produce the dependency structures that we process into simplified

`4lang` representations (ordinary edge-colored directed graphs rather than hypergraphs) we call definition graphs and describe briefly in Section 3.1.

We derive several similarity features from pairs of definition graphs built using the `4lang` library[8]. Words that are not part of the manually built `4lang` dictionary[9] are defined by graphs built from entries in monolingual dictionaries of English using the Stanford Dependency Parser and a small hand-written mapping from dependency relations to `4lang` connections (see Recski (2016) for details). The set of all words used in definitions of the Longman Dictionary of Contemporary English (Bullon, 2003), also known as the Longman Defining Vocabulary (LDV), is included in the ca. 3000 words that are defined manually in the `4lang` dictionary. Recski and Ács (2015) used a word similarity metric based on `4lang` graphs in their best STS submission, their findings served as our starting point when defining features over pairs of `4lang` graphs.

3.1 The formalism

For the purposes of word similarity calculations we find it expedient to abstract away from some of the hypergraph/machine aspects of `4lang` discussed above and represent the meaning of both words and utterances as directed graphs, similarly to the Abstract Meaning Representations (AMRs) of Banarescu et al. (2013). Nodes correspond to language-independent concepts, edges may have one of three labels (0, 1, 2). 0-edges represent attribution (dog $\xrightarrow{0}$ friendly), the IS_A relation (hypernymy) (dog $\xrightarrow{0}$ animal), and unary predication (dog $\xrightarrow{0}$ bark). Since concepts do not have grammatical categories, phrases like *water freezes* and *frozen water* would both be represented as water $\xrightarrow{0}$ freeze. 1- and 2-edges connect binary predicates to their arguments, e.g. cat $\xleftarrow{1}$ catch $\xrightarrow{2}$ mouse). The meaning of each `4lang` concept is represented as a `4lang` graph over other concepts, e.g. the concept `bird` is defined by the graph in Figure 1.

3.2 Graph-based features

We experimented with various features over pairs of `4lang` graphs as a source of word

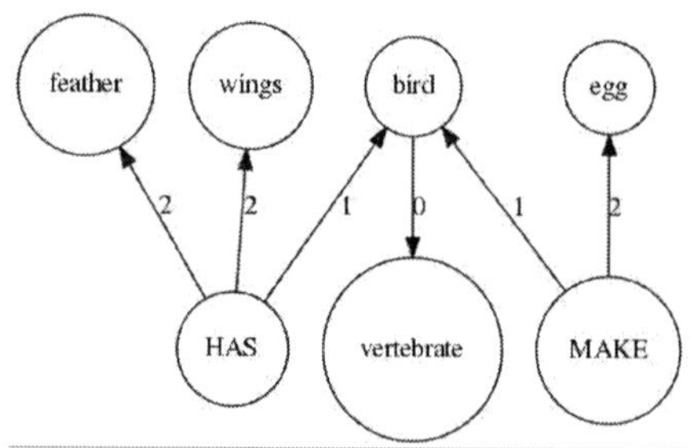

Figure 1: 4lang definition of `bird`.

similarity. The simple metric defined by Recski and Ács (2015) is based on the intuition that similar concepts will overlap in the elementary configurations they take part in: they might share a 0-neighbor, e.g. `train` $\xrightarrow{0}$ `vehicle` $\xleftarrow{0}$ `car`, or they might be on the same path of 1- and 2-edges, e.g. `park` $\xleftarrow{1}$ IN $\xrightarrow{2}$ `town` and `street` $\xleftarrow{1}$ IN $\xrightarrow{2}$ `town`. The metric used by Recski and Ács (2015) defines the sets of *predicates* of each concept based on this intuition: given the example definition of *bird* in Figure 1, predicates of the concept `bird` ($P(\text{bird})$) are {vertebrate; (HAS, feather); (HAS, wing); (MAKE, egg)}. Predicates are also inherited via paths of 0-edges, e.g. (HAS, wing) will be a predicate of all concepts for which $\xrightarrow{0}$ `bird` holds.

Our first feature extracted for each word pair is the Jaccard similarity of the sets of predicates of each concept, i.e.

$$S(w_1, w_2) = \frac{|P(w_1) \cap P(w_2)|}{|P(w_1) \cup P(w_2)|}$$

A second similar feature takes into account all nodes accessible from each concept in its definition graph. Recski and Ács (2015) observe that this allows us to capture minor similarities between concepts, e.g. the definitions of `casualty` and `army` do not share predicates but do have a common node `war` (see Figure 2).

Based on boosting factors in the original metric we also generated three binary features. The `links_contain` feature is true iff either concept is contained in a predicate of the other, `nodes_contain` holds iff either concept is included in the other's definition graph, and `0_connected` is true if the two nodes are connected by a path of 0-edges in either definition

---

[8]http://www.github.com/kornai/4lang
[9]http://hlt.bme.hu/en/resources/4lang_dict

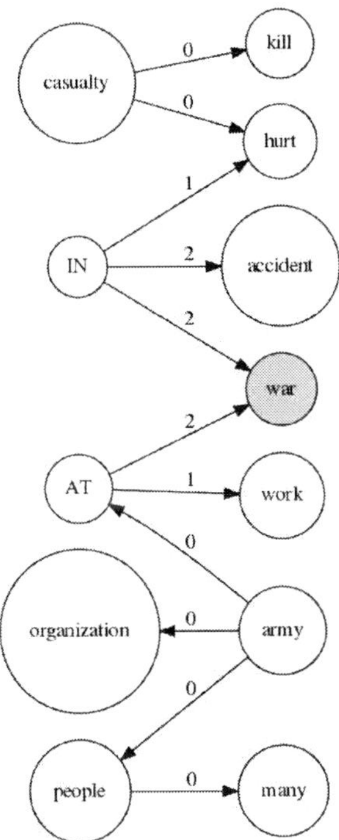

Figure 2: Overlap in the definitions of `casualty` (built from LDOCE) and `army` (defined in `4lang`)

feature	definition
links_jaccard	$J(P(w_1), P(w_2))$
nodes_jaccard	$J(N(w_1), N(w_2))$
links_contain	iff $w_1 \in P(w_2)$ or $w_2 \in P(w_1)$
nodes_contain	iff $w_1 \in N(w_2)$ or $w_2 \in N(w_1)$
0_connected	iff w_1 and w_2 are on a path of 0-edges

Table 2: `4lang` word similarity features

graph. All features are listed in Table 2.

The `dict_to_4lang` module used to build graphs from dictionary definitions allowed us to perform *expansion* on each graph, which involves adjoining the definition graphs of all words to the initial graph; an example is show in Figure 3.

Using only these features in initial experiments resulted in many "false positives": pairs of antonyms in SimLex were often assigned high similarity scores because this feature set is not sensitive to the `4lang` nodes LACK, representing negation (dumb $\xrightarrow{0}$ intelligent $\xrightarrow{0}$ LACK), and BEFORE, indicating that something was only true in the past (forget $\xrightarrow{0}$ know $\xrightarrow{0}$ before),

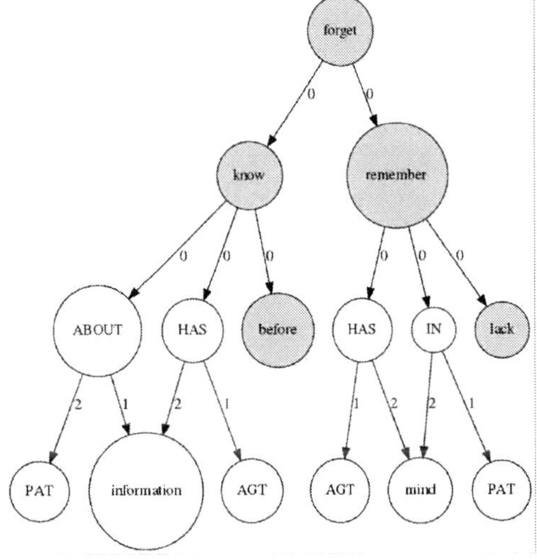

Figure 3: Expanded `4lang` definition of `forget`. Nodes of the unexpanded graph are shown in gray.

We attempt to model the effect of these nodes in two ways. First, we implement the `is_antonym` feature, a binary set to true if one word is within the scope (i.e. 0-connected to) an instance of either `lack` or `before` in the other word's graph. Next, we transform the input graphs of remaining features so that all nodes within the scope of `lack` or `before` are prefixed by `lack_` and are not considered identical with their non-negated counterparts when computing each of the features in Table 2. An example of such a transformation is shown in Figure 4.

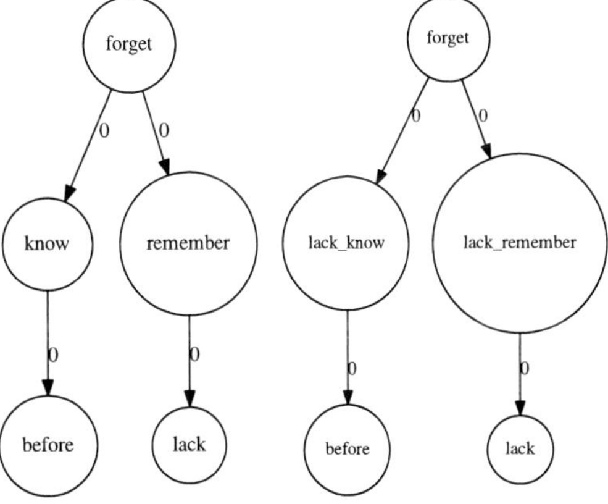

Figure 4: `4lang` definition of *forget* and its modified version

Early experiments show that a system trained on `4lang`-based features only can achieve a Pearson correlation in the range of $0.32 - 0.34$ on the SimLex data, this was increased to 0.38 by the handling of `LACK` and `BEFORE` described above. This score is competitive with some word embeddings, but well below the $0.58 - 0.68$ range achieved by the state-of-the-art vector-based systems cited in Section 1 and reproduced in Section 2.1.

After testing `4lang` features' impact on purely vector-based configurations we came to the conclusion that the only `4lang`-based features that improve their performance significantly are `0-connected` and `is_antonym`. Adding these two features to the vector-based system brings correlation to 0.76.

4 Results

Performance of our main configurations is presented in Table 3. The system relying on word embeddings achieves a Spearman correlation of 0.72. `WordNet` and `4lang` features both improve the vector-based system, combining all three feature classes yields our top correlation of 0.76, higher than any previously published results. Since the average correlation between a human rater and the average of all other raters is 0.78, this figure suggests that our system has achieved near-human performance on this benchmark.

System	Spearman's ρ
embeddings	0.72
embeddings+wordnet	0.73
embeddings+4lang	0.75
embeddings+wordnet+4lang	**0.76**

Table 3: Performance of major configurations on `SimLex`

For the purposes of error analysis we sorted word pairs by the difference between gold similarity values from `SimLex` and the output of our top-scoring model. The top of this list is clearly dominated by two error classes. The largest group consists of (near-)synonyms that have not been identified as related by our model, Table 4 shows the top 5 word pairs from this category. The second error group contains word pairs that have been falsely rewarded for being associated, but not similar by

the definition used when creating the SimLex data. Table 5 shows the top 5 word pairs of this error class. This second error class is an indication of a well-known shortcoming of word similarity models: (Hill et al., 2015) observes that similarity of vectors in word embeddings tend to encode association (or *relatedness*) rather than the similarity of concepts.

word1	word2	output	gold	diff
bubble	*suds*	2.97	8.57	5.59
dense	*dumb*	1.71	7.27	5.56
cop	*sheriff*	3.50	9.05	5.55
alcohol	*gin*	3.43	8.65	5.22
rationalize	*think*	3.50	8.25	4.75

Table 4: Top 5 "false negative" errors

word1	word2	output	gold	diff
girl	*maid*	7.72	2.93	-4.79
happiness	*luck*	6.59	2.38	-4.21
crazy	*sick*	7.49	3.57	-3.92
arm	*leg*	6.74	2.88	-3.86
breakfast	*supper*	8.01	4.40	-3.61

Table 5: Top 5 "false positive" errors

Since our main purpose was to experiment with `4lang` representations and identify its shortcomings, we examined `4lang` graphs of top erroneous word pairs. As expected, the value of the `0-connected` feature was -1 for each "false negative" pair, i.e. word pairs such as those in Table 4 were not on the same path of 0-edges. In most cases this is due to the current lack of simple inferencing on `4lang` representations. For example, `suds` are defined in LDOCE as *the mass of bubbles formed on the top of water with soap in it*, yet the resulting `4lang` subgraph bubble $\xleftarrow{1}$ HAS $\xrightarrow{2}$ mass $\xleftarrow{0}$ suds will not trigger any mechanism that would derive suds $\xrightarrow{0}$ bubble. Inference will also be responsible for deriving all uses of polysemous words, the `4lang` representation of `dense` is therefore built from its first definition in LDOCE: *made of or containing a lot of things or people that are very close together*. A method of inference that will relate this definition with that of `dumb` is clearly out of reach. Better short-term results could be obtained by using all definitions in a dictionary to build `4lang` representations, for `dense` this would include its third definition: *not able to understand things easily.*

Other shortcomings of `4lang` representations are of a more technical nature, e.g. the lemmatizer used to map words of definitions to concepts failed to map *alcoholic* to `alcohol` in the definition of `gin`: *a strong alcoholic drink made mainly from grain.* Yet other errors could be addressed by rewarding the overlap between two representations, e.g. that the graphs for `cop` and `sheriff` both contain $\xrightarrow{0}$ `officer`.

5 Conclusions, future work

The purpose of experimenting with `4lang`-based features was to gain a better understanding of how `4lang` may implicitly encode semantic relations that are difficult to model with standard tools such as word embeddings or WordNet. We found that simple features describing the relation between two concepts in `4lang` improve vector-based systems significantly. Since less explicit relationships may be encoded by more distant relationships in the network of `4lang` concepts, in the future we plan to examine portions of this network larger than the union of two (expanded) definition graphs. Errors made by `4lang`-based systems also indicate that a more sophisticated form of lexical inference on `4lang` graphs may be necessary to establish the more distant connections between pairs of concepts. In the near future we plan to experiment with features defined on larger `4lang` networks. We also plan to extend our system to include the task of measuring phrase similarity, which can also be pursued using supervised learning given new resources such as the `Annotated-PPDB` and `ML-Paraphrase` datasets introduced by (Wieting et al., 2015).

References

Judit Ács, Katalin Pajkossy, and András Kornai. 2013. Building basic vocabulary across 40 languages. In *Proceedings of the Sixth Workshop on Building and Using Comparable Corpora*, pages 52–58, Sofia, Bulgaria. ACL.

Eneko Agirre, Carmen Banea, Claire Cardie, Daniel Cer, Mona Diab, Aitor Gonzalez-Agirre, Weiwei Guo, Iñigo Lopez-Gazpio, Montse Maritxalar, Rada Mihalcea, German Rigau, Larraitz Uria, and Janyce Wiebe. 2015. SemEval-2015 Task 2: Semantic Textual Similarity, English, Spanish and Pilot on Interpretability. In *Proceedings of the 9th International Workshop on Semantic Evaluation (SemEval 2015)*, Denver, CO, U.S.A.

Laura Banarescu, Claire Bonial, Shu Cai, Madalina Georgescu, Kira Griffitt, Ulf Hermjakob, Kevin Knight, Philipp Koehn, Martha Palmer, and Nathan Schneider. 2013. Abstract meaning representation for sembanking. In *Proceedings of the 7th Linguistic Annotation Workshop and Interoperability with Discourse*, pages 178–186, Sofia, Bulgaria. Association for Computational Linguistics.

Rajendra Banjade, Nabin Maharjan, Nobal B. Niraula, Vasile Rus, and Dipesh Gautam. 2015. Lemon and tea are not similar: Measuring word-to-word similarity by combining different methods. In Alexander Gelbukh, editor, *Proc. CICLING15*, pages 335–346. Springer.

Stephen Bullon. 2003. *Longman Dictionary of Contemporary English 4*. Longman.

Miriam Butt. 2006. *Theories of Case*. Cambridge University Press.

Danqi Chen and Christopher D Manning. 2014. A fast and accurate dependency parser using neural networks. In *EMNLP*, pages 740–750.

A.M. Collins and E.F. Loftus. 1975. A spreading-activation theory of semantic processing. *Psychological Review*, 82:407–428.

Ronan Collobert and Jason Weston. 2008. A unified architecture for natural language processing: Deep neural networks with multitask learning. In *Proceedings of the 25th International Conference on Machine Learning*, ICML '08, pages 160–167, New York, NY, USA. ACM.

Samuel Eilenberg. 1974. *Automata, Languages, and Machines*, volume A. Academic Press.

Lev Finkelstein, Evgeniy Gabrilovich, Yossi Matias, Ehud Rivlin, Zach Solan, Gadi Wolfman, , and Eytan Ruppin. 2002. Placing search in context: The concept revisited. *ACM Transactions on Information Systems*, 20(1):116–131, January.

Juri Ganitkevitch, Benjamin Van Durme, and Chris Callison-Burch. 2013. Ppdb: The paraphrase database. In *HLT-NAACL*, pages 758–764.

Cliff Goddard. 2002. The search for the shared semantic core of all languages. In Cliff Goddard and Anna Wierzbicka, editors, *Meaning and Universal Grammar – Theory and Empirical Findings*, volume 1, pages 5–40. Benjamins.

Lushan Han, Abhay Kashyap, Tim Finin, James Mayfield, and Jonathan Weese. 2013.

UMBC_EBIQUITY-CORE: Semantic textual similarity systems. In *Proceedings of the 2nd Joint Conference on Lexical and Computational Semantics*, pages 44–52.

Lushan Han, Justin Martineau, Doreen Cheng, and Christopher Thomas. 2015. Samsung: Align-and-Differentiate Approach to Semantic Textual Similarity. In *Proceedings of the 9th International Workshop on Semantic Evaluation (SemEval 2015)*, pages 172–177, Denver, Colorado. Association for Computational Linguistics.

Felix Hill, Roi Reichart, and Anna Korhonen. 2015. Simlex-999: Evaluating semantic models with (genuine) similarity estimation. *Computational Linguistics*.

Eric H. Huang, Richard Socher, Christopher D. Manning, and Andrew Y. Ng. 2012. Improving word representations via global context and multiple word prototypes. In *Proceedings of the 50th Annual Meeting of the Association for Computational Linguistics: Long Papers - Volume 1*, ACL '12, pages 873–882, Stroudsburg, PA, USA. Association for Computational Linguistics.

Fred Karlsson, Atro Voutilainen, Juha Heikkila, and Arto Anttila. 1995. *Contraint Grammar, A Language-Independent System for Parsing Unrestricted Text*. Mouton de Gruyter, Berlin, New-York.

András Kornai. 2010. The algebra of lexical semantics. In Christian Ebert, Gerhard Jäger, and Jens Michaelis, editors, *Proceedings of the 11th Mathematics of Language Workshop*, LNAI 6149, pages 174–199. Springer.

András Kornai. 2012. Eliminating ditransitives. In Ph. de Groote and M-J Nederhof, editors, *Revised and Selected Papers from the 15th and 16th Formal Grammar Conferences*, LNCS 7395, pages 243–261. Springer.

András Kornai. in preparation. *Semantics*. `http://kornai.com/Drafts/sem.pdf`.

Kimmo Koskenniemi. 1983. *Two-Level Morphology: A General Computational Model for Word-Form Recognition and Production*. PhD thesis, University of Helsinki.

Tomas Mikolov, Kai Chen, Greg Corrado, and Jeffrey Dean. 2013. Efficient estimation of word representations in vector space. In Y. Bengio and Y. LeCun, editors, *Proceedings of the ICLR 2013*.

George A. Miller. 1995. Wordnet: a lexical database for English. *Communications of the ACM*, 38(11):39–41.

Dávid Nemeskey, Gábor Recski, Márton Makrai, Attila Zséder, and András Kornai. 2013. Spreading activation in language understanding. In *Proc. CSIT 2013*, pages 140–143, Yerevan, Armenia. Springer.

H. Penny Nii. 1986. Blackboard application systems, blackboard systems and a knowledge engineering perspective. *AI Magazine*, 7(3):82–110.

Jeffrey Pennington, Richard Socher, and Christopher Manning. 2014. Glove: Global vectors for word representation. In *Conference on Empirical Methods in Natural Language Processing (EMNLP 2014)*.

M. Ross Quillian. 1969. The teachable language comprehender. *Communications of the ACM*, 12:459–476.

Gábor Recski and Judit Ács. 2015. MathLingBudapest: Concept networks for semantic similarity. In *Proceedings of the 9th International Workshop on Semantic Evaluation (SemEval 2015)*, pages 543–547, Denver, Colorado. Association for Computational Linguistics.

Gábor Recski. 2016. Building concept graphs from monolingual dictionary entries. In Nicoletta Calzolari, Khalid Choukri, Thierry Declerck, Marko Grobelnik, Bente Maegaard, Joseph Mariani, Asuncion Moreno, Jan Odijk, and Stelios Piperidis, editors, *Proceedings of the Tenth International Conference on Language Resources and Evaluation (LREC 2016)*, Portorož, Slovenia. European Language Resources Association (ELRA).

Roger C. Schank. 1975. *Conceptual Information Processing*. North-Holland.

Roy Schwartz, Roi Reichart, and Ari Rappoport. 2015. Symmetric pattern based word embeddings for improved word similarity prediction. *CoNLL 2015*, page 258.

Md Arafat Sultan, Steven Bethard, and Tamara Sumner. 2015. DLS@CU: Sentence similarity from word alignment and semantic vector composition. In *Proceedings of the 9th International Workshop on Semantic Evaluation (SemEval 2015)*, pages 148–153, Denver, Colorado. Association for Computational Linguistics.

Pasi Tapanainen and Timo Järvinen. 1997. A non-projective dependency parser. In *Proceedings of the 5th Conference on Applied Natural Language Processing*, pages 64–71.

Anna Wierzbicka. 1972. *Semantic Primitives*. Athenäum, Frankfurt.

John Wieting, Mohit Bansal, Kevin Gimpel, Karen Livescu, and Dan Roth. 2015. From paraphrase database to compositional paraphrase model and back. *TACL*, 3:345–358.

Using Embedding Masks for Word Categorization

Stefan Ruseti, Traian Rebedea and **Stefan Trausan-Matu**
University Politehnica of Bucharest
{stefan.ruseti, traian.rebedea, stefan.trausan}@cs.pub.ro

Abstract

Word embeddings are widely used nowadays for many NLP tasks. They reduce the dimensionality of the vocabulary space, but most importantly they should capture (part of) the meaning of words. The new vector space used by the embeddings allows computation of semantic distances between words, while some word embeddings also permit simple vector operations (e.g. summation, difference) resembling analogical reasoning. This paper proposes a new operation on word embeddings aimed to capturing categorical information by first learning and then applying an embedding mask for each analyzed category. Thus, we conducted a series of experiments related to categorization of words based on their embeddings. Several classical approaches were compared together with the one introduced in the paper which uses different embedding masks learnt for each category.

1 Introduction

The idea of using vector representations of words for various natural language processing (NLP) and machine learning tasks has become more and more popular in the last years. Most of these representations are based on the idea that the meaning of a word can be determined by the context in which each word is used.

Sometimes, additional information about the words is available or can be computed and this might be used along with the embedding for each word. This information may consist of relations between words (e.g. syntactic dependencies), part of speech (POS) tags, word categories, word senses, etc.

In this paper, we propose to encode this extra information in the form of a vector mask that can be applied on the word embedding before being used as an input by any classifier, such as a neural network, or before computing any semantic distance between the word embeddings. We explore the possibility of using vector masks for assigning WordNet (Miller, 1995) categories to words. We define a word category as one of the top concepts in the WordNet taxonomy as will be later explained in more detail. Using the trained masks for a subset of words, we then test whether they improve the accuracy of determining the correct category for new words that are not part of the training corpus.

2 Related Work

Distributed words' embeddings based on word co-occurrences can be computed using various mechanisms and theories. Some of them employ algebraic decompositions of the original vector space, others use mixture models to compute a distribution of words in topics from a large collection of texts, while newer methods make use of neural embeddings to train word representations on even larger corpora of texts than the previous models. All the methods described in this section are completely unsupervised and are based on the frequency of words in documents and their co-occurrences.

Latent Semantic Analysis (LSA) (Landauer and Dumais, 1997) is a commonly used vector representation for words. The word vectors are obtained through a Singular Value Decomposition (SVD). The main reasoning behind LSA is that the decomposed space can generalize the relationships between words and documents existing in the original term-document matrix and will remove noisy features. While SVD is generally used for LSA,

Proceedings of the 1st Workshop on Representation Learning for NLP, pages 201–205,
Berlin, Germany, August 11th, 2016. ©2016 Association for Computational Linguistics

other matrix factorizations such as Non-negative Matrix Factorization (Lee et al., 2010) have been successfully employed for various tasks.

A newer approach which can also be used for computing embeddings is Latent Dirichlet Allocation (LDA) (Blei et al., 2003). This model assumes that each document is a mixture of topics and each topic is defined as a distribution over the words in the corpus. Although LDA is mainly used for topic modelling, it can also be employed for computing word embeddings, which are represented by the probabilities that each word is included in a topic.

One of the most recent and popular models for training word embeddings is Word2Vec (Mikolov et al., 2013a) which makes use of neural embedding models. The word representations are computed by a neural network that predicts the probabilities of a word occuring in a context window. Levy and Goldberg (2014) showed that this model performs, in fact, a factorization of a word-context matrix. The main advantage of this model over other similar ones is the fact that it can be trained on much larger texts, which could produce better embeddings.

GloVe (Pennington et al., 2014) is a word representation model based on the global word co-occurrence matrix which is reduced to a lower-dimensional representation after normalization and log-smoothing. The model achieves better results than Word2Vec, at least for the word analogy, word similarity and named entity recognition tasks presented in the paper (Pennington et al., 2014).

Recent work was also focused on improving given vector representations. Usually, the vectors are computed with an unsupervised method and a post-processing step is applied on the final vectors that do not depend on the representation model. Mrki et al. (2016) use pairs of synonyms and antonyms to bring words closer or apart, while keeping as much of the original topology as possible. A similar method, that uses WordNet relations between words, was proposed by Faruqui et al. (2014).

Tsubaki et al. (2013) proposed a method of improving vectors in the training step. For each word and syntactic relations, a group of frequent words was computed. Based on them, the representation of a word can be projected in another space depending on the words connected to it.

All representations presented so far learn, for simplicity, only one embedding vector per word. Neelakantan et al. (2014) propose a Multi-Sense Skip-gram that learns different representations for each sense of a word. The advantage over other multi-sense representations is the fact that sense discrimination and embedding learning are performed in the same step.

3 Problem Description

In our approach we considered WordNet for extracting word categories. WordNet contains sets of synonym words (synsets) with various linguistic relations between them. In our case, the important relations are hyponymy and hypernymy, which describe specializations/generalizations between concepts. These relations form a tree, with "entity" as the top concept in the case of nouns.

Our experiment starts from the assumption that word embeddings should partially capture the hypernym/hyponym relations from Wordnet. To test this supposition, we decided to split the nouns synset tree into several top-level subtrees rooted in concepts who subsum a somehow similar size set of words. These top-level concepts denote the word categories. We opted to use only a small number of categories, because of their hierarchical structure of the tree. In order to determine a balanced set of categories, a top-down approach was used where a candidate concept for a category was split if its subtree contained too many words or if it had more than one child containing most of the words in that subtree.

One of the problems that we encountered was the fact that there is a many-to-many relation between words and synsets. Since the hierarchy was based on synsets and the embeddings are computed on words, a simply greedy approach was chosen by taking the first word for each synset.

In the filtering process, which established the initial balanced categories for our experiment, we kept only the synsets corresponding to single word lemmas that had a corresponding vector in our pre-trained Word2Vec representations.

After computing the mapping between words and categories, a corpus was built in order to test the hypothesis that embeddings can be used to determine the category of a word. The generated dataset consists of triples of the form $(word, category, result)$, where $result$ is 1 when the first synset of the $word$ is part of $category$ and 0 otherwise. For simplicity, the number of positive and negative examples in the dataset is equal.

4 Vector Operations and Masks for Word Embeddings

We start from the more complex assumption that two adjacent words in a sentence should have a combined meaning depending on their individual senses and the type of syntactical dependency between them. If a mathematical function may be learned for each dependency type, then the meaning of the sentence may be recursively computed by combining embeddings two by two.

The word embeddings computed using the skip-gram method presents another interesting feature. Mikolov et al. (2013b) showed that vectors can be combined to resemble analogies. A famous example is $"King - Man + Woman = Queen"$, where the operations are applied on the corresponding vectors of each word, and the closest vector to the result is the one corresponding to the word *Queen*. We hope to detect other relations between words, relations that could be expressed by more complicated mathematical functions in the embedding space.

Assuming that we use word embeddings of size d, we have to find a function that combines the two vectors and the dependency to produce another vector of size d. Considering that the dependency also uses some embedding, of size d', the function to generate the combined embedding can be expressed like $W_{d,2d+d'} * [w_1; w_2; dep]$. The problem with this representation is that it cannot capture relations similar to $w_1 - w_2$ which exist in the vector space. Thus the dependency should not be added as a distinct feature, but rather define how the two embeddings are combined.

The simplest solution is to consider different networks for each dependency type. This would allow us to represent any function between the words, but requires a very large number of weights. This might not be possible due to the limited training examples and because some dependency types are too rare.

In order to decrease the number of required weights, the dependency can be represented as a mask. The mask can be applied as a point-wise multiplication with the $[w_1; w_2]$ vector, which allows learning transformations like $w_1 - w_2$.

In a first experiment, we decided to test the vector masks on the word categorization dataset. The assumption is that some part of the representation of words in the same category might be common, while the other corresponds to specific context for each word. This means that two words can become closer in the vector space by neutralizing the specific dimensions for that category. In order to do this, we computed an embedding for each category in the dataset having the same size with the word embeddings. These category embeddings are used as a mask, multiplying them pointwise with a word embedding. This operation is actually a scaling in the word embedding space which should cluster the words from the same category.

5 Experiments

The solutions below were tested in similar conditions on the generated dataset. A brief description of each method was added when needed. Most of the models (Support Vector Machines - SVM, random forest and logistic regression) were developed in Weka [1], while the neural networks were implemented in Tensorflow[2].

Cosine Similarity

A common way of comparing embeddings is using the cosine similarity. A threshold can be used as a boundary between positive and negative examples. For word categorization, the best threshold was chosen based on the training set.

Multilayer Perceptron (MLP)

The network consists of one hidden layer with 100 neurons and an softmax output layer with 2 neurons representing the probabilities for the two classes. The tanh activation function was used and a dropout with probability 0.4 on the hidden layer was added to reduce the effect of overfitting. For training, we opted for cross-entropy loss function and Adagrad Optimizer for 500 epochs.

Cosine with Vector Mask

Given a word and a category, the embedding of the category is applied as pointwise multiplication both to the embedding of the word and the word depicting the category. The resulting vectors are then compared using cosine. The following loss function was used during training the vector masks:

$$max((y - y')^2 - 0.25, 0) + \alpha * \sqrt{\frac{\sum_w w^2}{noweights}} \quad (1)$$

, where:

[1] http://www.cs.waikato.ac.nz/ml/weka/
[2] https://www.tensorflow.org/

- y the output of the network (the cosine similarity between vectors, normalized to 0-1)

- y$'$ the target value (0 for negative and 1 for positive examples)

- w a parameter from the network (a value in the category embedding matrix)

The first term tries to achieve a maximum 0.5 difference between the output and the target value, while the second term is a regularizer to avoid overfitting.

Mask + MLP

This network combines the mask embeddings with the same MLP described earlier. First, the word and category embeddings are transformed by applying the mask. The resulting vectors are used as inputs for the MLP.

6 Results

The described methods are compared on the generated dataset for word categorization based on WordNet. The accuracy scores from Table 1 were obtained using 10-fold cross-validation.

Method	Accuracy (%)
Cosine	60.59
SVM	59.69
Logistic regression	60.12
Random forest	77.79
MLP	83.00
Mask + cosine	77.00
Mask + MLP	**85.50**

Table 1: Accuracy of the compared methods.

The poor results obtained by the SVM are not very surprising. While the words from the same category might be grouped together in the Word2Vec embedding space, the training examples consisted in pairs of words and categories. Positive pairs have no reason to be close to each other, meaning that the positive and negative examples are not linearly separable in this case.

Comparing cosine similarity with the mask-cosine method, an important improvement of 27% can be observed. This demonstrates that scaling both the word and its category will make them closer, while scaling a word and a different category will make them more distant. This means that each mask successfully minimizes the effect

of dimensions in the space that are not related to the given category.

It was also expected that the mask+MLP approach to work better than a simple MLP because the first one has more parameters. In our experiments, the improvement was not impressive (about 3%), but we observed a much faster training rate. While the MLP needed 500 epochs to reach this accuracy, the version with masks achieved the same performance in 50 epochs. The masks accelerate training, but also have a tendency to quickly over-fit on the training data.

7 Conclusion

Mask embeddings proved to be useful for the proposed word categorization task. Although this is an artificial task (the category of each word is already known from WordNet), the method can be applied in other scenarios. The results show that such masks can learn which dimensions are important in a given situation. Also, the masks can be learnt much faster than a regular fully-connected layer.

An alternative for masks would be the use of different networks for each category. This solution is more general than the method proposed in this paper which uses embeddings masks and MLP; for this reason they will have more parameters than the Mask+MLP technique. Further testing is needed on this subject, but masks seem a viable solution for limiting the number of parameters of a network, which can be crucial when dealing with small datasets.

References

David M. Blei, Andrew Y. Ng, and Michael I. Jordan. 2003. Latent dirichlet allocation. *The Journal of Machine Learning Research*, 3:993–1022, mar.

Manaal Faruqui, Jesse Dodge, Sujay K. Jauhar, Chris Dyer, Eduard Hovy, and Noah A. Smith. 2014. Retrofitting Word Vectors to Semantic Lexicons. nov.

Thomas K Landauer and Susan T. Dumais. 1997. A solution to Plato ' s problem: The Latent Semantic Analysis Theory of Acquisition, Induction, and Representation of Knowledge. *Psychological Review*, 104(2):211–240.

Hyekyoung Lee, Jiho Yoo, and Seungjin Choi. 2010. Semi-Supervised Nonnegative Matrix Factorization. *IEEE Signal Processing Letters*, 17(1):4–7, jan.

Omer Levy and Yoav Goldberg. 2014. Neural Word Embedding as Implicit Matrix Factorization. In *Advances in Neural Information Processing Systems*, pages 2177–2185.

Tomas Mikolov, Greg Corrado, Kai Chen, and Jeffrey Dean. 2013a. Efficient Estimation of Word Representations in Vector Space. *Proceedings of the International Conference on Learning Representations (ICLR 2013)*, pages 1–12.

Tomas Mikolov, Wen-tau Yih, and Geoffrey Zweig. 2013b. Linguistic regularities in continuous space word representations. *Proceedings of NAACL-HLT*, (June):746–751.

George A. Miller. 1995. WordNet: a lexical database for English. *Communications of the ACM*, 38(11):39–41, nov.

Nikola Mrkšić, Diarmuid Ó Séaghdha, Blaise Thomson, Milica Gašić, Lina Rojas-Barahona, Pei-Hao Su, David Vandyke, Tsung-Hsien Wen, and Steve Young. 2016. Counter-fitting Word Vectors to Linguistic Constraints. mar.

Arvind Neelakantan, Jeevan Shankar, Alexandre Passos, and Andrew Mccallum. 2014. Efficient Nonparametric Estimation of Multiple Embeddings per Word in Vector Space. *Emnlp-2014*, pages 1059–1069.

Jeffrey Pennington, Richard Socher, and Christopher D Manning. 2014. GloVe: Global Vectors for Word Representation. *Proceedings of the 2014 Conference on Empirical Methods in Natural Language Processing*, pages 1532–1543.

Masashi Tsubaki, Kevin Duh, Masashi Shimbo, and Yuji Matsumoto. 2013. Modeling and Learning Semantic Co-Compositionality through Prototype Projections and Neural Networks. In *EMNLP*, pages 130–140.

Sparsifying Word Representations for Deep Unordered Sentence Modeling

Prasanna Sattigeri
IBM T. J. Watson Research Center
Yorktown Heights, NY
psattig@us.ibm.com

Jayaraman J. Thiagarajan
Lawrence Livermore National Laboratory
Livermore, CA
jayaramanthi1@llnl.gov

Abstract

Sparsity often leads to efficient and interpretable representations for data. In this paper, we introduce an architecture to infer the appropriate sparsity pattern for the word embeddings while learning the sentence composition in a deep network. The proposed approach produces competitive results in sentiment and topic classification tasks with high degree of sparsity. It is computationally cheaper to compute sparse word representations than existing approaches. The imposed sparsity is directly controlled by the task considered and leads to more interpretability.

1 Introduction

The recent surge in representation learning has resulted in remarkable advances in a variety of applications including computer vision and speech processing. In the context of natural language processing, much effort has been focused on constructing vector space representations for words through neural language models (Mikolov et al., 2013; Pennington et al., 2014) and designing appropriate composition functions to apply word embeddings for modeling sentences or documents. By design, the goal of neural word embedding approaches is to build *dense* vector representations that capture syntactic and semantic similarities in data (e.g., beautiful, and attractive have similar meanings, as opposed to ugly, and repulsive), that the classic categorical representation of words as indices of a vocabulary fails to capture.

The composition function based on these embeddings can be either unordered (e.g. average of the word representations) or syntactic, wherein the word order is explicity modeled (Socher et al., 2013a; Sutskever et al., 2011; Bowman, 2013).

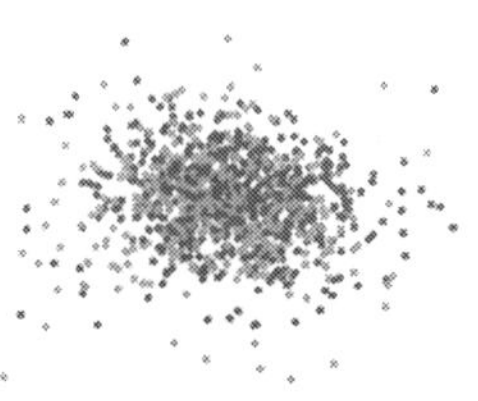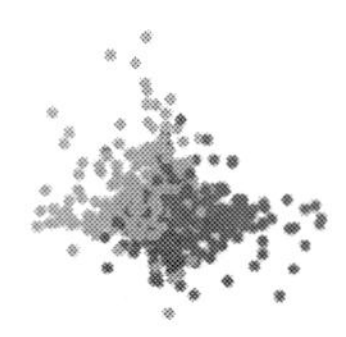

(a) Original word vectors.   (b) Sparsified word vectors.

Figure 1: t-SNE embedding of the sentence representations obtained as the average of word vectors for a random set of 1000 sentences from the SUBJ dataset.

While the former class of approaches results in simple architectures that are easily scalable, the latter can provide richer models with much severe computational complexity during training. Furthermore, the input word vectors are often fine-tuned during the training phase to improve the sentence (or document) classification performance. However, this can lead to severe overfitting and hence regularization strategies such as *word-dropout* are used (Iyyer et al., 2015) and in other cases the original word vectors are augmented to the input as a *static* channel (Kim, 2014; Zhang and Wallace, 2015).

Alternately, approaches that build word representations using different forms of regularization inspired by the linguistic study of word meanings have been effective in modeling sentences. For example, *sparsity* regularization can be been used to construct distributed representations (Eisenstein et al., 2011) that capture some of the crucial lexical semantics largely based on familiar, discrete classes (e.g., supersenses) and relations (e.g., synonymy and hypernymy).

Instead of employing sparsity to regularize word embeddings, we propose to infer appropriate sparsity patterns for pre-learned word vectors

206

Proceedings of the 1st Workshop on Representation Learning for NLP, pages 206–214,
Berlin, Germany, August 11th, 2016. ©2016 Association for Computational Linguistics

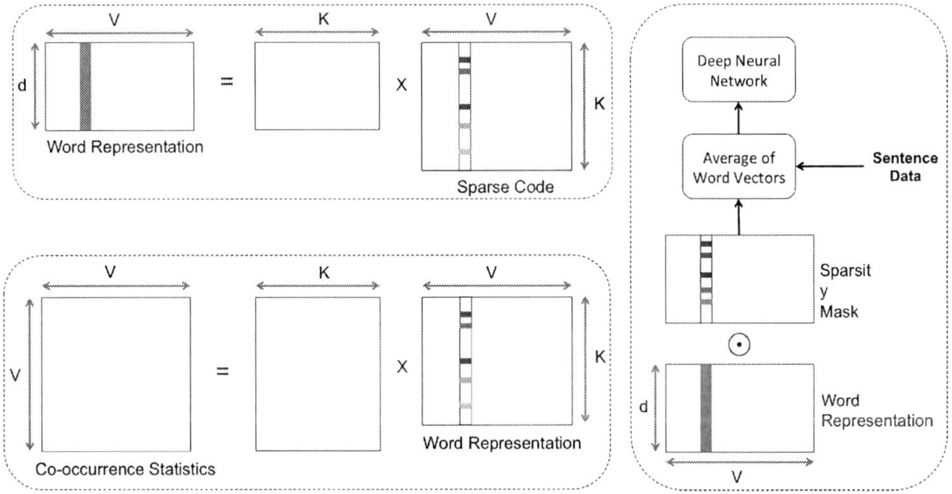

Figure 2: Sparsity has been commonly used to regularize word embeddings in order to effectively govern the relationship between word dimensions and provide interpretable representations. Examples include the approaches in (Yogatama et al., 2015) (left-top) and (Faruqui et al., 2015) (left-bottom). In contrary, we propose to infer sparsity patterns for pre-learned word embeddings in order to preserve only the key semantics required for the sentence classification task (right).

to improve the discrimination of sentence representations. In particular, we consider a unordered composition setting, similar to (Iyyer et al., 2015), wherein the sentence representation is obtained as the average of the words. Intuitively, sparsity is imposed to govern the relationship between word dimensions to capture only the semantics crucial to the particular task considered. For example, in a sentiment analysis task, opposite relationships between adjectives such as beautiful and ugly are more important than gender relationships such as king and queen. Surprisingly, without any additional regularization such as word-dropout or static channel of word vectors, the proposed approach produces competitive results in sentiment and topic classification tasks with high degree of sparsity. While it is cheaper to compute sparse word representations than existing approaches (Faruqui et al., 2015; Yogatama et al., 2015) the imposed sparsity is not merely based on the semantics of the space of words, but directly controlled by the task considered. Furthermore, by automatically learning sparsity masks that preserve only the semantic relationships appropriate for the task at hand, the resulting sentence models are highly discriminative. For example, in Figures 6(a) and 6(b), we show the sentence representations (word averaging) obtained using the original Glove word embeddings and the proposed approach.

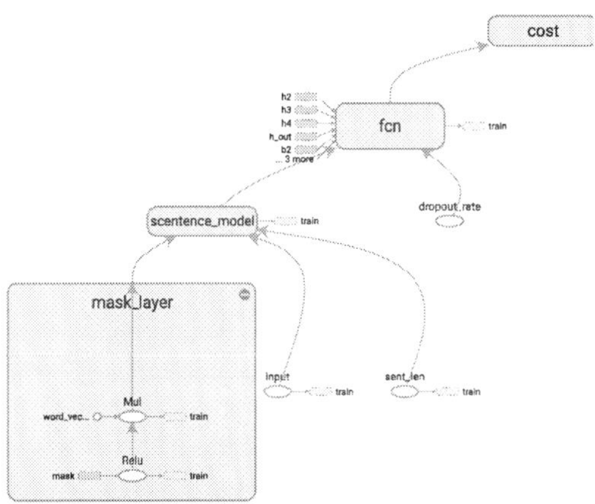

Figure 3: Tensorflow architecture for the proposed approach of sparsifying word embeddings based on labeled sentence data.

proach.

2 Sparsity in Word Embeddings

Though neural word representations are highly effective in enabling inference of complex semantic relationships between words, the interpretability of the word dimensions themselves is highly opaque. Hence, there is a disconnect between such dense representations and the word representa-

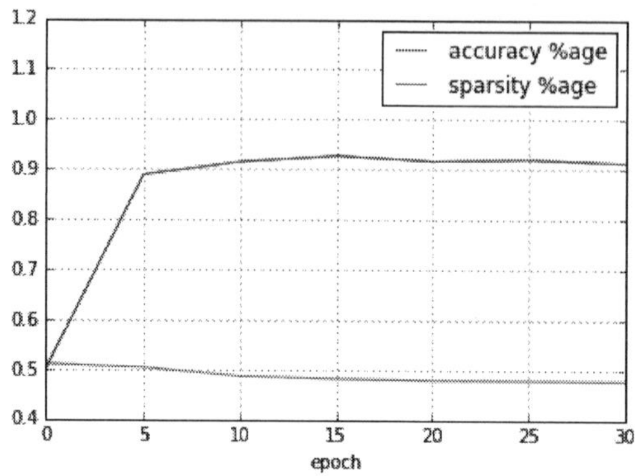

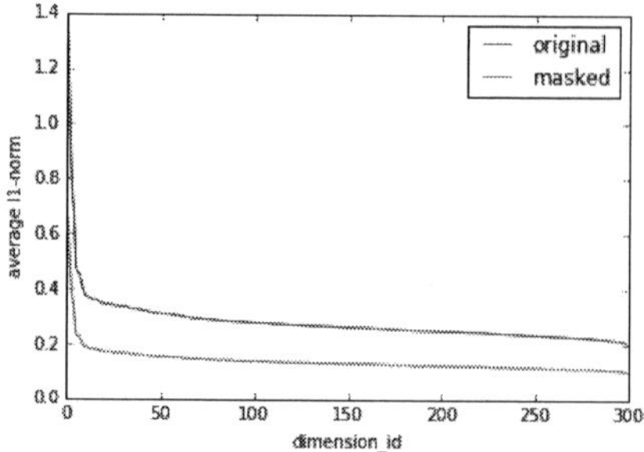

(a) Average ℓ_1 norm per dimension

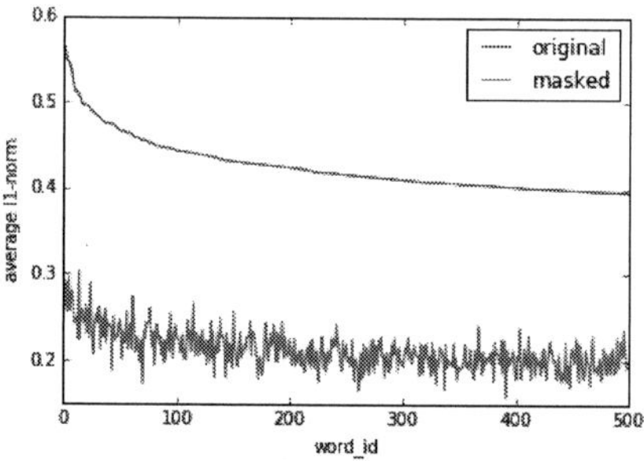

(b) Average ℓ_1 norm for the top 500 words based with the largest ℓ_1 norm in the original word vector space.

Figure 5: Measuring changes in the original dense word vectors and word vectors sparsified using mask inferred from the newswire dataset.

Figure 4: Convergence behavior of the proposed approach on the SUBJ dataset - Both the %Sparsity of the inferred mask and the testing accuracy are shown. Interestingly, only less than 50% of the entries are retained.

tions typically found in lexical semantics, wherein each word can be represented sparsely in terms of an extensive set of discrete classes. For example, the word *apple* can be sparsely represented in terms of discrete concepts such as *fruit, edible food, red* etc. In contrast, learned word representations such as the Word2vec produces dense vectors, where the word dimensions that actually reveal a particular semantic relationship are not transparent. This motivated NLP researchers to explicitly impose sparsity into the word embedding inference. Sparse modeling with an overcomplete set of features is well known to produce simple, interpretable representations, while retaining the approximation power of dense models. Authors in (Andreas and Klein, 2014), use the creation of a word such as *northeast* from words north and east to illustrate that linguistic descriptors orient along a sparse set of perceptual basis. In the context of nlp tasks, it has been showed that sparse codes inferred from the pre-learned word embeddings (Figure 2) are more interpretable and hence sparsity can be used to govern relationships between word dimensions (Fyshe et al., 2014; Faruqui et al., 2015). Since sparsity can reveal the word dimensions pertinent to specific semantics, the resulting sparse representations were more effective in sentence classification. Similarly Chang et.al. found that sparse word vectors performed better in the behavioral task used to quantify interpretability (Chang et al., 2009). Furthermore, in (Yogatama and Smith, 2014), the authors ad-

vocate several sparsity based structural regularization schemes as a more suitable inductive bias and show improvements over dense representations several NLP tasks. In addition to the inherent computational complexity, an important downside of these approaches is that sparsity is merely used to regularize the word embeddings and hence cannot directly improve the discrimination of sentence representations constructed using these word vectors.

A striking similarity between all existing approaches for learning sparse word embeddings is that they aim to make the word dimensions corresponding to different semantic groups disjoint. However, given the large range of potential semantic relationships, it becomes computationally challenging to infer sparse representations that can discriminate all of them. This challenge is even more severe when word embeddings are applied to NLP tasks such as sentence classification. This motivates the need to infer the appropriate sparsity patterns for word embeddings such that they can easily discriminate the semantic concepts crucial for

Model	SST-fine	IMDB	SUBJ	Reuters
CNN-MC (Kim, 2014)	47.4	–	93.2	–
F-Dropout (Wang and Manning, 2013)	–	91.1	**93.6**	–
TreeLSTM (Tai et al., 2015)	**50.6**	–	–	–
PVEC (Le and Mikolov, 2014)	48.7	**92.6**	–	–
DAN + Word-Drop (Iyyer et al., 2015)	46.9	89.4	92.4	72.6
DAN + Sparsity-Mask	47.4	91.1	92.9	**73.7**
DAN + Binary-Mask	47.2	88.7	92.4	72.1

Table 1: Sentence classification performance of the proposed approach in comparison to other methods. In addition to outperforming the deep averaging architecture, our approach achieves competitive performances in comparison to state-of-the-art syntactic sentence classification methods.

Word / NNs	Sentiment Mask	Newswire Mask	Original
uncomfortable	uneasy, enough, terribly, hence	renovations, racket, contingent, competing	awkward, uneasy, unpleasant, bothered
president	being, concerned, nothing, then	between, growth, bank, earnings	vice, chief, executive, former

Table 2: Neighborhood of words obtained with two different sparsity masks: (a) sentiment mask from the SST dataset, (b) Newswire mask from the Reuters newswire dataset. In addition, we show the neighbors identified using the original word embeddings.

the NLP task at hand. Such a task-driven approach has two important advantages: (a) By inferring sparsity patterns specific to the task/dataset there is improved discrimination, (b) We can circumvent the computationally intensive sparse learning by adding this as a layer into the traditional deep learning architectures used for sentence classification. In the rest of paper, we describe our approach to couple the process of sparsifying word embeddings in deep undordered sentence classification framework similar to (Iyyer et al., 2015).

3 Proposed Approach

The proposed architecture shown in Figure 2(right) aims to infer a sparsity mask for the word embeddings using a deep unordered composition network (Iyyer et al., 2015). Note that, the sentence modeling corresponds to simply averaging the word vectors in that sentence. Let the word vectors be denoted by a matrix $\mathbf{W} \in R^{V,d}$. In our architecture, we introduce the sparsity mask M which is applied to the word vector matrix W as an element-wise product. The mask is a real valued matrix which is passed through $Relu$ non-linear activation to transform into a sparse mask with non-negative entries. This mask is applied in a multiplicative manner on W to obtain the masked word vector matrix $\hat{W} = W \odot Relu(M)$ and is

optimized such that the sentence-level classification performance is maximized. We also consider a variant of this architecture, wherein the entries are thresholded to discrete values 0 or 1 based on the sign of entries in the real valued mask.

For all analysis and results reported in this paper, we used the pre-trained $300-$dimensional *Glove* (Pennington et al., 2014) word vectors. As described earlier, a sentence level representation is created by averaging the word vectors corresponding to the constituent words. This 300-dimensional representation is then passed through a series of fully connected layers and finally a softmax layer for prediction of labels. In contrast to the architecture in (Iyyer et al., 2015) no word-dropout regularization is used. Apart form the standard cross-entropy loss with a weight-decay regularization, we also include a term in the loss function to minimize the ℓ_1-norm of the mask to explicitly enforce sparsity on the latter. We implemented the architectures for both the real mask and binary mask versions using Tensorflow and Figure 3 shows the masking operation in detail using the tensorboard network architecture. visualizer.

The fully-connected deep network (FCN) on top of the sentence model is maintained the same for all datasets. The FCN is made up of three non-

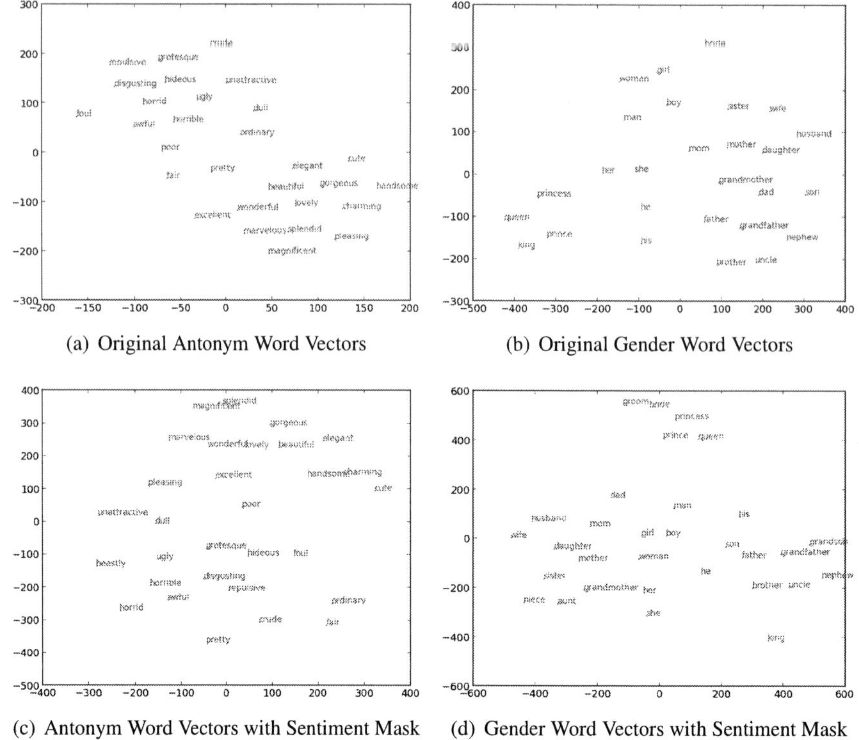

(a) Original Antonym Word Vectors   (b) Original Gender Word Vectors

(c) Antonym Word Vectors with Sentiment Mask   (d) Gender Word Vectors with Sentiment Mask

Figure 6: t-SNE plots of original and sparsified word vectors illustrating the ability of the learned mask to retain only semantic relationships relevant to the task at hand.

linear layers followed by the soft-max layer. The non-linear layer consisted of a linear transformation followed by the ReLu unit. The hidden layers have a constant dimension of 300 and dropout is applied at each of these layers. The same hyperparameters were used across all datasets. Adam optimizer was used with learning rate set to $1e-4$ and the dropout out rate was set 0.5. The ℓ_2 regularization parameter for weight-decay was set to $1e-4$.. The weights of the FCN layers were initialized randomly from uniform distribution $[-1, 1]$ and scaled with a factor of 0.08. 10-fold CV was applied to datasets with no explicit train/test splits.

4   Experiments and Results

We evaluated the proposed approaches using a set of commonly used text classification datasets both at the sentence level and the document level. We report the performance of the proposed architecture with respect to the classification task pertaining to each dataset. This is followed up by investigation of the properties of the sparsified word vectors. For all classification performance compar-

isons we used the vanilla DAN with word-dropout regularization (Iyyer et al., 2015), and the proposed DAN + sparsity mask and DAN + binary mask variants.

Datasets:

- IMDB (document level): This dataset (Maas et al., 2011) consists of 50,000 labeled instances of movie reviews taken form the movie review site, IMDB. Each review can be made up of several sentences and is labeled as either positive or negative. The dataset also provides a balanced split of 25,000 instances for training and 25,000 instances for testing.

- SST-fine (sentence level): This sentence level dataset was created by (Pang and Lee, 2005) and extended by (Socher et al., 2013b). The sentences are taken from movie review site, Rotten Tomatoes (RT). In our experiments, we use the fine-grain labels for the classification task. The dataset provides three set for training, validation and testing with each containing and, respectively. Note that, sev-

| original: fanatically, stylings, melding, inimitable, ardently |
| masked: whole-heartedly, uncompromising, rosily, principled, hard-driving |
| original: post-camp, larceny, family-friendly, light-years, matchmaking |
| masked: post-camp, family-friendly, voyages, four-star, cabins |
| original: ballot, ontiveros, candidate, nomination, badge |
| masked: candidate, nomination, laziest, vote, voting |
| original: 95, shave, grad, veggietales, colgate |
| masked: shave, grad, veggietales, colgate, golf |

Table 3: Words in the newswire dataset with largest coefficient along a random dimension of word vectors. Each row belongs to different dimension.

Original	blinddate, micro-device, bible-study, greenfingers, fever-pitched, bogosian, darabont, navona, 66-day, murri
Masked	screenplay, cinematic, entertaining, fascinating, movie, daughter, he, micro-device, secret, discovers

Table 4: Demonstration of the discriminative power of sparsified word embeddings - Words with largest ℓ_1-norm in the SUBJ dataset. The words colored in blue occur most commonly found in sentences from the subjective class while words marked in red occur commonly in objective sentences.

eral existing syntactic approaches also utilize the phrase level labels by augmenting them to the training set. However, we evaluate the three DAN architectures without the phrase-level labels.

- SUBJ (sentence level): This dataset called as the Subjective dataset (Pang and Lee, 2004) involves classifying a sentence as either being subjective or objective. This dataset provides 10,000 instances in total and contain separate validation/test set.

- Reuters (document level): This dataset comprises of 11228 newswires from Reuters. The task is to classify the newswires into one of the given 46 topics. There is no standard train/test split for this dataset.

The classification performance on these datasets is reported in table 1. As it can be observed, the sparsified word vectors ourperform the conventional word embeddings with the DAN architecture and perform competitively with respect to state-of-the-art syntactic methods. Investigating the properties of the masked work vectors and comparing them to original work vectors can shed some light on the behavior of the sparsification procedure. Figure 5(a) shows the mean ℓ_1-norm of each dimension of the word vector across all the words in the vocabulary for the SST sentiment classification dataset. The dimensions are ordered by their ℓ_1-norm in the original word vector space. The general behavior remains the same, however with an overall reduction in norm that can be attributed to the sparsity in the masked word vectors. Similar analysis can be performed with respect to words instead of each word vector dimensions. In figure 5(b), the blue line corresponds to ℓ_1-norm of the top 500 words ordered by the norm. The norm for the same words in the masked space is shown in red, which indicates that the mask is word-specific and can tune the entries as suited for the task in hand.

Analysis of task-specific mask: To understand the effect of the task-specific mask, we study the similarity of words and compare them in the original word vector space and the sparsified word vector spaces. Table 4 shows a couple of example neighborhoods of words in these spaces. Subjectively, we can see that the word vector semantic space is modified such that word neighborhoods that are more important for the task are preserved and enhanced. We can draw similar inferences by looking at the t-SNE (Van der Maaten and Hinton, 2008; Faruqui and Dyer, 2014) plots as seen in figure 6.

Another approach is to investigate the individual dimensions of word vector and how the mask affects their behavior is isolation. In table 3, we show the top words for 4 random dimensions

original: officials, he, government, who, political
masked: she, he, local, until, decision
original: societal, well-defined, physiological, mechanisms, perceptible
masked: predictable, least, familial, elements, unconditional
original: wanna, song, lil, bitch, gonna
masked: movies, laugh, fans, moments, wit
original: voltage, layer, cells, surface, battery
masked: easy, i, velocity, provides, functions
original: goldie, knowles, hailey, dick, dildo
masked: rachel, peter, patricia, alex, johnny

Table 5: Words from SUBJ dataset with largest coefficient along the top-5 dimensions (in terms of ℓ_1-norm) of word vectors.

of the original word vectors and the corresponding dimensions from the masked counterparts obtained from the SST-fine sentiment classification task. The top words are obtained by sorting the absolute value of the words along each of those dimensions. Since, there is a direct correspondence between original and masked word vector dimensions, we can directly compare them. The examples in table 3 show that mask improves the semantic consistency and hence improves interpretation of individual dimensions. Similar analysis is carried our for the SUBJ dataset and the results are reported in Table 5

Finally, we use the SUBJ dataset to demonstrate the discriminative power of sparsified word embeddings in sentence classification. The words with the largest ℓ_1-norm in the masked vector space in Table 4 reveal that the sparsity mask identifies a set of words crucial for discriminating the two classes. Finally, we consider an example sentence in each of the two classes and show the average ℓ_1 norms for words in the sentences in Figure 7. As it can be observed, words such as *emotional* and *material* are crucial to identifying the subjective nature of the sentence while words such as $125 - year$ which has prominence in the original word vector space has no relevance.

5 Conclusions

We have described an architecture that performs fine tuning of the word vectors in a classification setup while promoting sparsity in them. The resulting network achieves competitive results on several text classification datasets. This approach of inducing sparsity is computationally much cheaper than the traditional sparse models. The fine-tuned word vectors are also shown to be more interpretable, task specific and in process enhance the effectiveness of architectures based on simple unordered composition model. Also, the resulting word vectors posses improved discriminatory power suggesting that the use of this method as a pre-processing step can potentially lead to improved performance in other tasks which utilize word vectors.

References

Jacob Andreas and Dan Klein. 2014. Grounding language with points and paths in continuous spaces. In *CoNLL*, pages 58–67.

Samuel R Bowman. 2013. Can recursive neural tensor networks learn logical reasoning? *arXiv preprint arXiv:1312.6192*.

Jonathan Chang, Sean Gerrish, Chong Wang, Jordan L Boyd-Graber, and David M Blei. 2009. Reading tea leaves: How humans interpret topic models. In *Advances in neural information processing systems*, pages 288–296.

Jacob Eisenstein, Noah A Smith, and Eric P Xing. 2011. Discovering sociolinguistic associations with structured sparsity. In *Proceedings of the 49th Annual Meeting of the Association for Computational Linguistics: Human Language Technologies-Volume 1*, pages 1365–1374. Association for Computational Linguistics.

Manaal Faruqui and Chris Dyer. 2014. Community evaluation and exchange of word vectors at word-vectors.org. In *Proceedings of the 52nd Annual Meeting of the Association for Computational Linguistics: System Demonstrations*, Baltimore, USA, June. Association for Computational Linguistics.

Manaal Faruqui, Yulia Tsvetkov, Dani Yogatama, Chris Dyer, and Noah Smith. 2015. Sparse overcomplete word vector representations. *arXiv preprint arXiv:1506.02004*.

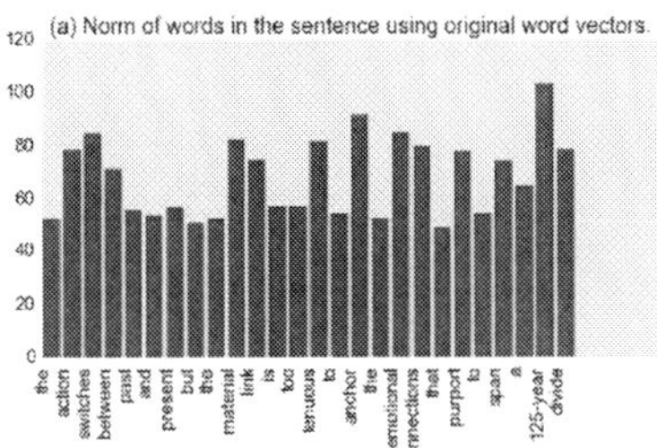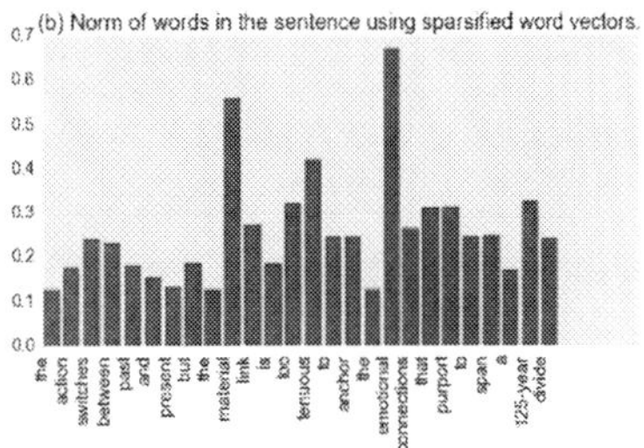

SUBJECTIVE: The action switches between past and present but the material link is too tenuous to anchor the emotional connections that purport to span a 125-year divide.

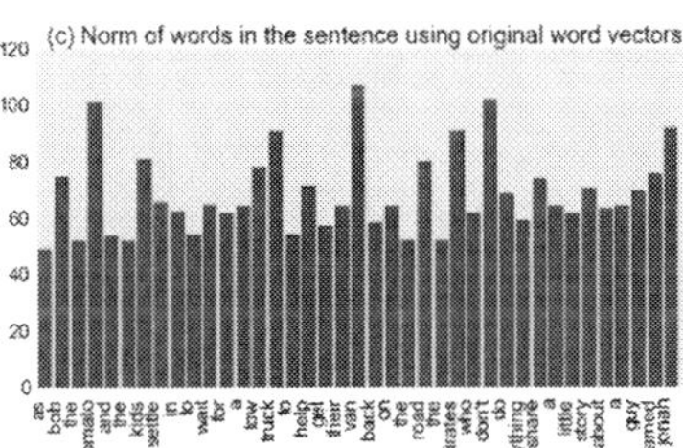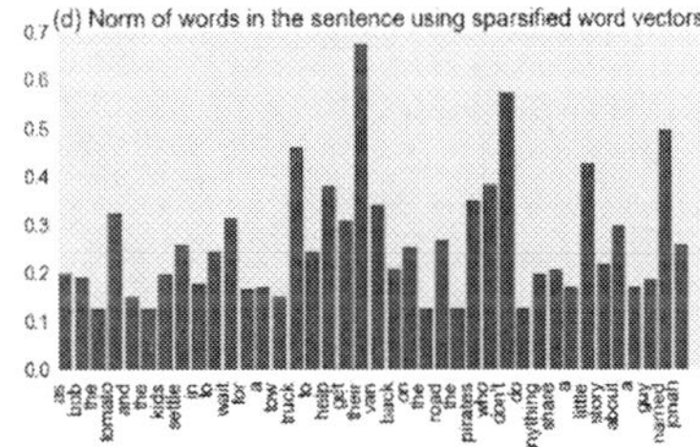

OBJECTIVE: As bob the tomato and the kids settle in to wait for a tow truck to help get their van back on the road the pirates who don't do anything share a little story about a guy named Jonah

Figure 7: An example from the SUBJ dataset demonstrating the ability of the proposed sparisification to choose words that easily discriminate the two classes.

Alona Fyshe, Partha P Talukdar, Brian Murphy, and Tom M Mitchell. 2014. Interpretable semantic vectors from a joint model of brain-and text-based meaning. In *Proceedings of the conference. Association for Computational Linguistics. Meeting*, volume 2014, page 489. NIH Public Access.

Mohit Iyyer, Varun Manjunatha, Jordan Boyd-Graber, and Hal Daumé III. 2015. Deep unordered composition rivals syntactic methods for text classification. In *Proceedings of the 53rd Annual Meeting of the Association for Computational Linguistics and the 7th International Joint Conference on Natural Language Processing*, volume 1, pages 1681–1691.

Yoon Kim. 2014. Convolutional neural networks for sentence classification. *arXiv preprint arXiv:1408.5882*.

Quoc V Le and Tomas Mikolov. 2014. Distributed representations of sentences and documents. *arXiv preprint arXiv:1405.4053*.

Andrew L Maas, Raymond E Daly, Peter T Pham, Dan Huang, Andrew Y Ng, and Christopher Potts. 2011. Learning word vectors for sentiment analysis. In *Proceedings of the 49th Annual Meeting of the Association for Computational Linguistics: Human Language Technologies-Volume 1*, pages 142–150. Association for Computational Linguistics.

Tomas Mikolov, Ilya Sutskever, Kai Chen, Greg S Corrado, and Jeff Dean. 2013. Distributed representa-

tions of words and phrases and their compositionality. In *Advances in neural information processing systems*, pages 3111–3119.

Bo Pang and Lillian Lee. 2004. A sentimental education: Sentiment analysis using subjectivity summarization based on minimum cuts. In *Proceedings of the 42nd annual meeting on Association for Computational Linguistics*, page 271. Association for Computational Linguistics.

Bo Pang and Lillian Lee. 2005. Seeing stars: Exploiting class relationships for sentiment categorization with respect to rating scales. In *Proceedings of the 43rd Annual Meeting on Association for Computational Linguistics*, pages 115–124. Association for Computational Linguistics.

Jeffrey Pennington, Richard Socher, and Christopher D Manning. 2014. Glove: Global vectors for word representation. In *EMNLP*, volume 14, pages 1532–1543.

Richard Socher, Danqi Chen, Christopher D Manning, and Andrew Ng. 2013a. Reasoning with neural tensor networks for knowledge base completion. In *Advances in Neural Information Processing Systems*, pages 926–934.

Richard Socher, Alex Perelygin, Jean Y Wu, Jason Chuang, Christopher D Manning, Andrew Y Ng, and Christopher Potts. 2013b. Recursive deep models for semantic compositionality over a sentiment treebank. In *Proceedings of the conference on empirical methods in natural language processing (EMNLP)*, volume 1631, page 1642. Citeseer.

Ilya Sutskever, James Martens, and Geoffrey E Hinton. 2011. Generating text with recurrent neural networks. In *Proceedings of the 28th International Conference on Machine Learning (ICML-11)*, pages 1017–1024.

Kai Sheng Tai, Richard Socher, and Christopher D Manning. 2015. Improved semantic representations from tree-structured long short-term memory networks. *arXiv preprint arXiv:1503.00075*.

Laurens Van der Maaten and Geoffrey Hinton. 2008. Visualizing data using t-sne. *Journal of Machine Learning Research*, 9(2579-2605):85.

Sida Wang and Christopher Manning. 2013. Fast dropout training. In *Proceedings of the 30th International Conference on Machine Learning*, pages 118–126.

Dani Yogatama and Noah A Smith. 2014. Linguistic structured sparsity in text categorization.

Dani Yogatama, Manaal Faruqui, Chris Dyer, and Noah Smith. 2015. Learning word representations with hierarchical sparse coding. In *Proceedings of the 32nd International Conference on Machine Learning (ICML-15)*, pages 87–96.

Ye Zhang and Byron Wallace. 2015. A sensitivity analysis of (and practitioners' guide to) convolutional neural networks for sentence classification. *arXiv preprint arXiv:1510.03820*.

Why "Blow Out"? A Structural Analysis of the Movie Dialog Dataset

Richard Searle
Eccentric Data, Cambridge
richard@eccentricdata.com

Megan Bingham-Walker
Eccentric Data, Cambridge
megan@eccentricdata.com

Abstract

A long-term goal of machine learning is to build an intelligent dialogue agent that is capable of learning associations within data and using them to understand and answer questions and make relevant recommendations. The Facebook Movie Dialog Dataset (MDD) was recently proposed in Dodge et al. (2016) to evaluate the comparative performance of dialogue agent systems. However, a structural analysis of the data for the recommendation tasks suggests that there may be some flaws in the design of the dataset.

1 Introduction

There has been a recent upsurge of commercial interest in the development of intelligent dialogue systems to answer questions, provide personalized recommendations and deliver services across a range of different domains. Some of the challenges that an intelligent dialogue agent will need to overcome in order to fulfill these objectives are: to be able to learn incrementally from heteregenous sources; to be able to adapt to changes in context; and to hold information in a long-term structured memory for rapid recall (Bordes et al., 2015).

Facebook recently proposed the Movie Dialog dataset (MDD) in Dodge et al. (2016) to encourage new research on this topic by providing a benchmark to evaluate the specific strengths and weaknesses of such systems. The MDD is part of the bAbI project of research into methods for automatic text understanding and reasoning (Weston et al., 2015). The MDD supports four question answering tasks featuring information retrieval and movie recommendation.

We had already developed an efficient, structural approach to incrementally learn clusters of associated products from high-dimensional, time-series data, for marketing personalized structured products to the clients of a financial services company. A structured product is an investment product that comprises a basket of underlying financial instruments, for example, equities, debt issuance, commodities, currencies or a combination of globally traded securities. In this case, the sparse hyper-dynamic nature of the product combinations and customer preferences necessitated an automated, algorithmic ranking metric. User preferences are conditioned with respect to the characteristics of a particular product offer, whereas individual products are a function of their underlying components. This decoupling of user preferences from the attributes of the structured product proves problematic when trying to identify an affinity between discrete users and potential product offers using techniques such as latent factorization.

Since our prior work constituted a generic, unsupervised approach, we were curious to see how it could perform against recommendation tasks in other domains and whether the structural model could be extended to act as a long-term memory for question answering.

One of the benefits of a structural approach, encompassing graphical learning representation, is that it is possible to track the reasons why certain recommendations are made, which can be beneficial to users (Tintarev and Masthoff, 2007) and enables accurate evaluation of the performance of the system. We report results from the application of a dynamic structural model as a contextual memory for Task 2 and Task 3, as defined in Dodge et al. (2016). Analysis of our findings reveals a possible flaw in the design of the Facebook Movie Dialog Dataset which may explain the results obtained by our method and those previously

Proceedings of the 1st Workshop on Representation Learning for NLP, pages 215–221,
Berlin, Germany, August 11th, 2016. ©2016 Association for Computational Linguistics

reported by Dodge et al. (2016).

2 Recommendation Tasks

2.1 Task 2 - Undirected recommendations

Task 2 aims to test whether an intelligent dialogue agent is able to make valid personalized recommendations for a user.

Dodge et al. (2016) selected ∼11k movies from the MovieLens dataset. They randomly sampled ∼110k users and for each of these users selected 1-8 movies that the user had rated 5. A statement was generated to express the user's opinion of these movies from a template, and this forms the statement input text (see Table 1 below). From the list of other movies that the same user had also rated 5, they randomly selected one to be the target answer representing a valid recommendation based on the composition of the basket of movies in the statement.

Statement
Gentlemen of Fortune, Revanche,
Eternal Sunshine of the Spotless Mind,
Prometheus, Fanny and Alexander, The Hurt
Locker, and 127 Hours are films I really like.
Would you recommend something to watch?
Answer
Blow Out

Table 1: Task 2 Example.

Data from ∼110k users was sampled multiple times to generate 1M training samples, data from ∼1k users was used to generate 10k development samples and data from a further ∼1k users was used to generate 10k test samples.

An important aspect of the MDD defined by Dodge et al. (2016) is that the number of users in each dataset is expanded by a factor of ∼10 through random sampling with replacement. The resultant datasets do not, however, identify unique users and, thus, preferred aggregations of movies by user. This characteristic of the MDD prevents user profiling and restricts the selection of recommended movies in Task 2 and Task 3 to a probabilistic similarity measure.

2.2 Task 3 - QA and contextual recommendations

Task 3 evaluates a short three-stage dialogue involving a combination of QA and recommendations that draws on additional contextual information. The first question is in the same format as Task 2, with the addition of a selection criterion - the writer and director Brian De Palma, in the example shown in Table 2. The second question is a factoid question about the response to the first question. The third question is a request for a follow-up recommendation, which refers to the context provided in the first question and a secondary contextual criterion defined by the statement in question 3 (see Table 2 below).

Statement 1
Gentlemen of Fortune, Revanche,
Eternal Sunshine of the Spotless Mind,
Prometheus, Fanny and Alexander, The Hurt
Locker, and 127 Hours are films I really like.
I'm looking for a Brian De Palma movie.
Answer 1
Blow Out
Statement 2
Who does that star?
Answer 2
John Travolta, John Lithgow,
Nancy Allen, Dennis Franz
Statement 3
I prefer Robert De Niro movies.
Can you suggest an alternative?
Answer 3
Hi, Mom!

Table 2: Task 3 Example.

3 Related Work

A network-based representational model has been demonstrated to be an accurate and efficient method for information retrieval, inference and reasoning for question answering (Berant et al., 2013; Berant et al., 2014; Hixon et al., 2015; Guu et al., 2015). Recent research has demonstrated some success in learning undirected graphical structural models from data (Lake and Tenenbaum, 2010; Mao et al., 2015) and it has also been shown that associations in data, intrinsic to a network-based architecture, form an important element of human learning (Spelke and Kinzler, 2007; Gershman, 2015).

We sought to augment a structural network-based representation of entities (in this case movies) and their attribute features by using the training data to learn statistical relationships between the entities from their recommendation histories. This form of relationship learning is consistent with the treatment of each sample as a unique user outcome and enables a top-k for k = number of hits (@100 for Task 2 and @10 for Task 3) ranking of the distance metrics between movie titles. The resultant ranking is used to assess the prediction accuracy of the recommendations made by the system.

4 Methodology

It is possible to conceive two primitive methods for recommending a movie based on the sample training data:

1. recommendation according to user movie preferences, by movie attribute (commonly achieved through the use of techniques such as latent matrix factorization), and

2. recommendation according to movie similarity, by movie attribute or user co-preference (as defined by a probabilistic distance measure between items or attribute features).

Since unique user data was lost in the construction of the MDD, it is not possible to associate movies with communities of users, which is a technique that we have found to aid both computational efficiency and accuracy of personalized user profiling in financial services. Instead, recommendations must be generated from either the similarity of movie attributes or the frequency of users co-rating movies as a 5. We will show that the latter method is the only viable approach to selection of a candidate recommendation using the MDD. Dodge et al. (2016) do not disclose the basis for their calculation of discrete and cumulative accuracy for Task 3 and the example data, shown in Table 1 and Table 2, does not discriminate between films with identical titles (e.g. versions of "20,000 Leagues Under the Sea" were released in 1916, 1954, and 1997). Consequently, we report accuracy of recommendation based on hits@100 or hits@10 with respect to correct identification of the movie title only. In Task 3, question 2 refers to a specific movie and for this task element we report the accuracy of our system under the assumption that a unique film was recommended with additional discriminatory training data (i.e. a hits@1 selection with a definitive release year, e.g. "20,000 Leagues Under the Sea" + 1954). Since,

Task 3, question 2 cannot be accurately answered without a definitive answer to question 1, we do not report a mean accuracy as we consider this to be a misleading representation of the effective accuracy of a system over the task. Instead, we report the cumulative accuracy, α_{T3}, over Task 3 given by the formula:

$$\alpha_{T3} = (P(\alpha_{Q1}) * P(\alpha_{Q2})) * P(\alpha_{Q3}) \qquad (1)$$

The cumulative accuracy α_{T3} is shown in Table 3 for our structural approach and is applied to the results reported by Dodge et al. (2016). We suggest that the cumulative accuracy α_{T3} represents a more realistic evaluation of the predicted accuracy of system responses in a dialog exchange of the type characterizing Task 3, whereby the success of a system is governed by the conditional probability introduced by the question sequence.

5 Building the Structural Model

Algorithm 1 below illustrates how the structural model is built from the movie knowledge base, training and development data. The variable b is defined as the movies in the basket of movies in the statement. The variable r is the recommended movie in the answer.

Algorithm 1 Building Structural Model

1: **procedure** CREATEGRAPH(K)
2:     *load movie knowledge base*
3:     **for** movie in knowledge base **do**
4:         $K \leftarrow$ add node movie
5:         $K \leftarrow$ add movie attributes
6:     *load task training data as d*
7:     **for** task in MDD tasks **do**
8:         **for** user in d **do**
9:             **for** b in basket and r in rec **do**
10:               $K \leftarrow$ add edge(b, r)
11:               $K \leftarrow$ count users, freq rec
12:             **for** edge in K **do**
13:               distance metric m(b, r)
14:     *freeze system memory K for testing*

Algorithm 2 below provides a workflow for how a prediction is generated from the test data for Tasks 2 and 3. In accordance with the experimental protocols, Task 2 top-k is reported for hits@100 and Task 3 top-k is reported for hits@10.

On completion of training and development cycles, the structural model comprising the system

Algorithm 2 Recommend using item similarity
1: **procedure** MAKEREC(basket, criteria)
2:     *load task test data as sample*
3:     **for** s in sample **do**
4:         **for** b in basket and c in candidates **do**
5:            $rec[s] = \text{edge}(b,c)$ if $c[crit]$=True
6:         **for** r in rec[s] **do**
7:            $rec \in rec[s]$ if metric $e[m]$ in top-k

memory is frozen. However, in practice, the system memory should continuously update to reflect user feedback on the recommended movies, a capability that is embedded in our dynamic model but not applied here. Such a capability is consistent with some of the challenges that an intelligent dialogue agent will need to overcome, as noted by Bordes et al. (2015).

6   Results and Analysis

We report our results in conjunction with those reported in Dodge et al. (2016) in Table 3.

Our graphical model renders the information retrieval Task 3, question 2 and Task 1 trivial, subject to valid data being held in the long-term memory. Following initial concern regarding the accuracy of our system, we are satisfied that our structural approach produces a valid model as a basis for movie recommendations using the statistical relationships encoded within the graph. This begs the question as to why the recommendation accuracy of our system and those produced by the method of Dodge et al. (2016) is so low?

Dodge et al. (2016) suggests that the reason why results for Task 2 are lower than for the information retrieval Task 1 and comparable Task 3, question 2 is due to missing labels, as a consequence of the sampling methodology they describe. We contend, however, that the basis of recommendation imposed by the MDD is flawed and that the frequency of occurrence of movies established by the effective 1M user population generates super-nodes that penalize valid answers with sparse structural association. Furthermore, our structural model of the MDD enables detailed analysis of the causes of recommendation error, as shown in Table 6 in the Appendix. Examination of the statistical relationships between answer recommendations and the statement basket of movies reveals that in many cases the sparse association and characteristic attributes of the answer provides

no statistical basis for its inclusion as a recommendation in preference to other candidate films.

We consider that the MDD construction of the basket-recommendation relationship by arbitrary selection of films rated 5 by a user does not indicate the suitability of the proposed answer as a recommendation, hence the title of our paper. For the Task 3 example shown in Table 1, the movie "Blow Out" was not rated 5 by any user that also rated the basket movies 5. For the example in Table 2, "Blow Out" could not, therefore, be recommended by our system without recourse to joint training and is included within the "No association" error for Task 3 in Table 6.

For Task 2, "Blow Out" is associated with three of the basket films; "Eternal Sunshine of the Spotless Mind" (ESSM), "Fanny and Alexander" (FA), and "The Hurt Locker" (THL). However, as shown in Table 5, the sparse association of "Blow Out" with the basket films excludes it from the top-k for $k = 100$ strongest recommendations as the similarity metric for "Blow Out" falls below the minimum threshold for the top-k recommendations. The weak similarity metric generated between "Blow Out" and the basket movies is a product of the disparity between the number of users rating the basket movie as 5 and the fact that only 158 users rated "Blow Out" as 5.

Importantly, the genre information in Table 4 also illustrates that criteria-based association of recommendations is prevented by the heterogeneous nature of the MDD basket compositions. We evaluated this approach in the development of our system, but found reduced correlation of movies when compared to the use of frequency of user rating as the basis for a valid distance metric.

Furthermore, where the correct answer is identified by the system as a potential candidate, the imposition of a statistically valid top-k ranking excludes the majority of answers in favour of super-nodes that feature more prominently within films rated 5 by all users. The distribution of these dominant movie titles suggests a causal link between the reported accuracy of our system and those described by Dodge et al. (2016). The improvement shown in the results of Dodge et al. (2016) over our own may be attributable to the difference between our, definitive, structural method, and the alternative, parametric methods described in their research.

We consider that the hash lookup employed by

Methods	Recs Task	QA+Recs	QA+Recs	QA+Recs	QA+Recs
	Task 2	Task 3	Task 3	Task 3	Task 3
		Question 1	Question 2	Question 3	Cumulative
	hits@100	hits@10	hits@1	hits@10	
LSTM	27.1	35.3	14.3	9.2	3.2
Supervised Embeddings	29.2	56.7	76.2	38.8	22.0
MemN2N	28.6				
MemN2N (2 hops)		53.4	90.1	88.6	47.3
Structural Model	20.0	46.2	100.0	70.5	32.6

Table 3: Test results for Task 2, benchmarked against Dodge et al. (2016, Table 6) and test results for the individual questions in Task 3 benchmarked against Dodge et al. (2016, Table 9). Results reported as percentage accuracy.

Basket movie	Movies co-rated 5	Users rating movie 5	Users rating "Blow Out" 5	"Blow Out" recommendations	Genre
ESSM	4511	17485	2	1	*unknown*
FA	2160	1801	1	0	Drama
THL	1919	1283	1	0	War

Table 4: Structural association of "Blow Out" with basket movies for Task 2 example shown in Table 1.

Dodge et al. (2016) may introduce the possibility of conflation error by virtue of the inclusion of candidate movie titles on the basis of their semantic or syntactic structure. The embedding of movie titles without recourse to their probabilistic association with the expressed basket of films liked by the user may yield false positives in the case of the MDD, which will augment the evaluated accuracy of a system. In practice, however, the repeatability and accuracy of such a system may prove problematic.

7 Conclusion

Our experience of personalized user profiling in the financial services sector and analysis of the application of our method to the MDD tasks suggests that a combination of different methods may represent the most efficient path to effective, contextual personalized recommendations. In particular, the use of parametric candidate selection and relaxation of the strict statistical association required for candidate films helps to overcome issues of dominance in sparse, high-dimensional datasets. Critical factors in the success of both supervised and unsupervised approaches to recommendation are, however, the primacy and individual characteristics of the user and distinct user communities that support latent factorization methods. We believe that a simple reconfiguration of the MDD to reflect these characteristics would enable a more informative analysis of competing methods and technologies and thus contribute to fulfilling the objectives for intelligent dialog agents as set out by Bordes et al. (2015).

References

Jonathan Berant, Andrew Chou, Roy Frostig, and Percy Liang. 2013. Semantic Parsing on Freebase from Question-Answer Pairs. In *2013 Conference on Empirical Methods in Natural Language Processing*, pages 1533–1544, Seattle. Association for Computational Linguistics.

Jonathan Berant, Vivek Srikumar, Pei-Chun Chen, Brad Huang, Christopher D. Manning, Abby Vander Linden, Brittany Harding, and Peter Clark. 2014. Modeling Biological Processes for Reading Comprehension. In *2014 Conference on Empirical Methods in Natural Language Processing*, pages 1499–1510, Doha. Association for Computational Linguistics.

Antoine Bordes, Jason Weston, Sumit Chopra, Tomas Mikolov, Arman Joulin, and Léon Bottou. 2015. Artificial Tasks for Artificial Intelligence. In *2015 International Conference on Learning Representations*, San Diego.

Jesse Dodge, Andreea Gane, Xiang Zhang, Antoine Bordes, Sumit Chopra, Alexander Miller, Arthur Szlam, and Jason Weston. 2016. Evaluating Prerequisite Qualities for Learning End-to-End Dialog Systems. In *2016 International Conference on Learning Representations*, San Juan.

Basket movie	"Blow Out" similarity metric	"Blow Out" Pr(recommended by basket movie)	"Blow Out" Pr(same user rating 5)
ESSM	0.00011	0.01351	0.01266
FA	0.00051	0	0.00633
THL	0.00694	0	0.00632
k rank min. threshold for hits@$k = 100$	0.00980	0.3	0.25
k rank	3906	2911	3088

Table 5: k rank of "Blow Out" for example basket of movies for Task 2 example shown in Table 1 (similarity metric and probabilistic k^{th} rank from $K = 5235$ candidate movies shown).

Samuel J. Gershman. 2015. A Unifying Probabilistic View of Associative Learning. *PLoS Computational Biology*, 11(11):e1004567.

Kelvin Guu, John Miller, and Percy Liang. 2015. Traversing Knowledge Graphs in Vector Space. In *2015 Conference on Empirical Methods in Natural Language Processing*, pages 318–327, Lisbon. Association for Computational Linguistics.

Ben Hixon, Peter Clark, and Hannaneh Hajishirzi. 2015. Learning Knowledge Graphs for Question Answering through Conversational Dialog. In *Human Language Technologies: The 2015 Annual Conference of the North American Chapter of the ACL*, pages 851–861, Denver. Association for Computational Linguistics.

Brenden Lake and Joshua Tenenbaum. 2010. Discovering Structure by Learning Sparse Graphs. In *Cognition in Flux: Proceedings of the 32nd Cognitive Science Conference*, pages 778–783, Portland. Cognitive Science Society.

Qi Mao, Li Wang, Ivor W. Tsang, and Yijun Sun. 2015. A Novel Regularized Principal Graph Learning Framework on Explicit Graph Representation. *arXiv preprint arXiv:1512.02752*.

Elizabeth S. Spelke and Katherine D. Kinzler. 2007. Core knowledge. *Developmental Science*, 10(1):89–96.

Nava Tintarev and Judith Masthoff. 2007. A Survey of Explanations in Recommender Systems. In *WPRSIUI Associated with ICDE'07*, pages 801–810. IEEE.

Jason Weston, Antoine Bordes, Sumit Chopra, Alexander M. Rush, Bart van Merriënboer, Armand Joulin, and Tomas Mikolov. 2015. Towards AI-Complete Question Answering: A Set of Prerequisite Toy Tasks. In *2016 International Conference on Learning Representations*, San Juan.

A Test Data and Discussion

Table 6 below provides details of the test results obtained for Task 2 and Task 3 using the MDD and test protocol defined by Dodge et al. (2016). We identified three principal causes of error:

1. the absence of an association between basket movies and the answer movie, due to no common user rating a basket film and an answer film 5;

2. low k rank of the answer film excluding it from the top-k for $k = 100$ or $k = 10$ recommendations for the basket of movies liked by a user;

3. for Task 3; the absence of a selection criterion from the answer film, thereby excluding its inclusion in the list of possible candidate recommendations. This is consistent with the observation made by Dodge et al. (2016) regarding potential errors due to missing labels.

Using the movie knowledge base as a long-term memory, we discern 17,928 unique movies and construct >3M edges within our structural model for both Task 2 and Task 3.

We did not apply joint training over the tasks but note that this would yield an improvement in the results by reducing errors due to absence of association, as illustrated by Table 4 since "Blow Out" is only connected to "Eternal Sunshine of the Spotless Mind" for Task 2 and is not connected to any of the basket movies for the Task 3 example shown in Table 2.

Table 6 indicates that the vast majority of errors are attributable to the low statistical association between basket films, compositions of basket films, and the hypothesized recommendations generated by random selection from specific

	Recs Task	**QA+Recs**	**QA+Recs**	**QA+Recs**
	Task 2	Task 3	Task 3	Task 3
		Question 1	Question 2	Question 3
	hits@100	hits@10	hits@1	hits@10
Test samples	10000	4915	4915	4470
Correct answers	1996	2269	4915	3153
Errors:				
Total	8004	2646	0	1317
No association	232	146	0	716
Low k rank	7772	2428	0	532
Accuracy (%)	20.0	46.2	100.0	70.5

Table 6: Test results breakdown for Tasks 2 and 3.

users' movie ratings. We contend that it is the underlying methodology behind the construction of the MDD that leads to the poor accuracy reported in Table 6 and not the intrinsic design of our system.

We attribute the improved results of Dodge et al. (2016) shown in Table 3 to the inclusion of answer recommendations on the basis of parametric affinity with the basket movie titles, rather than their statistical relevance as a potential user selection.

This may occur through the conflation of movie titles with independent basket-answer instances on account of words within their titles or characteristic attributes. Although we explored alternative methods for defining a statistical association based on the propinquity of movie attributes or attribute ranking, we were unable to identify a rigorous methodology that improved our reported accuracy for either Task 2 or Task 3.

Learning Word Importance with the Neural Bag-of-Words Model

Imran Sheikh[*+], **Irina Illina**[*], **Dominique Fohr**[*], **Georges Linarès**[+]

[*]Université de Lorraine, LORIA, UMR 7503, Vandoeuvre-lès-Nancy, F-54506, France
[*]Inria, Villers-lès-Nancy, F-54600, France
[*]CNRS, LORIA, UMR 7503, Vandoeuvre-lès-Nancy, F-54506, France
[+]Laboratoire Informatique d'Avignon, University of Avignon
{imran.sheikh, irina.illina, dominique.fohr}@loria.fr
georges.linares@univ-avignon.fr

Abstract

The *Neural Bag-of-Words* (NBOW) model performs classification with an average of the input word vectors and achieves an impressive performance. While the NBOW model learns word vectors targeted for the classification task it does not explicitly model *which words are important for given task*. In this paper we propose an improved NBOW model with this ability to learn task specific word importance weights. The word importance weights are learned by introducing a new weighted sum composition of the word vectors. With experiments on standard topic and sentiment classification tasks, we show that (a) our proposed model learns meaningful word importance for a given task (b) our model gives best accuracies among the BOW approaches. We also show that the learned word importance weights are comparable to tf-idf based word weights when used as features in a BOW SVM classifier.

1 Introduction

A Bag-of-Words *BOW* represents text (a sentence, paragraph or a document) as a vector of word features. Traditional BOW methods have used word occurrence frequency and variants of *TermFrequency-InverseDocumentFrequency* (tf-idf) as the word feature (Manning et al., 2008). Development in neural network and deep learning based language processing has led to the development of more powerful continuous vector representation of words (Bengio et al., 2003; Collobert and Weston, 2008; Turian et al., 2010; Mikolov et al., 2013b). It was shown that these predictive word vector representations capture syntactic and/or semantic characteristics

of words and their surrounding context (Mikolov et al., 2013a; Pennington et al., 2014), and that they outperform the count based word (vector) representations (Baroni et al., 2014).

Many approaches in text classification are now driven by models built on word vectors. Earlier works proposed models which learned word vectors targeted for the classification task (Maas et al., 2011). In more recent works, text classification is performed with compositional representations learned with neural networks or by training the network specifically for text classification (Goldberg, 2015). One such network is the *Neural Bag-of-Words* (NBOW) model (Kalchbrenner et al., 2014; Iyyer et al., 2015). The NBOW model takes an average of the word vectors in the input text and performs classification with a logistic regression layer. Essentially the NBOW model is a fully connected feed forward network with BOW input. The averaging operation can be attributed to the absence of non-linearity at the hidden layer and the BOW inputs where words are set to 1 (or number of occurrences of that word) and 0. While the NBOW model learns word vectors targeted for the classification task, it does not explicitly model *which words are important for given task*. In this paper, we propose an improved NBOW model which learns these task specific word importance weights. We replace the average with a weighted sum, where the weights applied to each word (vector) are learned during the training of the model. With experiments on sentiment and topic classification tasks, we will show that our proposed model learns meaningful word importance weights and it can perform better than the NBOW model.

The rest of the paper is organised as follows. First in Section 2 we discuss about the related works. In Section 3 we briefly introduce the NBOW model and present our proposed

Proceedings of the 1st Workshop on Representation Learning for NLP, pages 222–229,
Berlin, Germany, August 11th, 2016. ©2016 Association for Computational Linguistics

model, termed as the *Neural Bag-of-Weighted-Words* (NBOW2) model, in Section 4. In Section 5 we give details about the experiment setup and the tasks used in our experiments. Section 6 presents a discussion on the word importance weights learned and the classification performance achieved by the proposed NBOW2 model, followed by the conclusion in Section 7.

2 Related Work

A variety of neural network architectures have been proposed for different language processing tasks. In context of text classification, fully connected feed forward networks (Le and Mikolov, 2014; Iyyer et al., 2015; Nam et al., 2014), *Convolutional Neural Networks* (CNN) (Kim, 2014; Johnson and Zhang, 2015; Wang et al., 2015) and also *Recurrent/Recursive Neural Networks* (RNN) (Socher et al., 2013; Hermann and Blunsom, 2013; Dong et al., 2014; Tai et al., 2015; Dai and Le, 2015) have been used. On one hand, the approaches based on CNN and RNN capture rich compositional information, and have been outperforming the state-of-the-art results, on the other hand they are computationally intensive and may require careful hyper-parameter selection and/or regularisation (Zhang and Wallace, 2015; Dai and Le, 2015). We focus our study to the NBOW model which gives an impressive performance in text classification, not far below the state-of-the-art CNN and RNN systems. We propose an improved NBOW model which learns these task specific word importance weights.

Word weights based on variants of word occurrence frequency or tf-idf have been commonly used and studied in literature (Manning et al., 2008; Paltoglou and Thelwall, 2010; Quan et al., 2011). Supervised weighting schemes for adjusting tf-idf for text classification have been proposed earlier (Kim and Zhang, 2014; Deng et al., 2014; Mammadov et al., 2011; Lan et al., 2006). Use of a small number of important words against all the words in the text was studied by Islam(2015) for the task of text relatedness using Latent Semantic Analysis and Google Trigram Model. Our work is in line with recent approaches of text processing with neural networks and learns word importance weights along with the word vectors.

We found that the works by Ling (2015) and Li (2014) are most related to our proposed method. Ling (2015) proposes position based weights to improve word vectors learned by the *Continuous Bag-Of-Words* (CBOW) model (Mikolov et al., 2013a). Li (2014) proposes *Weighted Neural Network* (WNN) for training RNNs which learn compositional representation of text with a parse tree. The WNN weighs how much one specific node contributes to the higher-level representation. Also related are works on learning to pay attention in a sequence of input, as applied in text (Bahdanau et al., 2014) as well as speech (Chan et al., 2015), image (Xu et al., 2015) and protein sequence analysis (Sønderby et al., 2015). The model with convolutional-pooling structures presented by Gao (2014) is also shown to capture keywords in text.

3 Neural Bag-of-Words (NBOW) model

The Neural Bag-of-Words (NBOW) model (Kalchbrenner et al., 2014; Iyyer et al., 2015) is a fully connected network which maps text X, a sequence of words, to one of k output labels. The NBOW model has d dimensional word vectors for each word in the chosen task vocabulary. For the words $w \in X$, corresponding word vectors v_w are looked up and a hidden vector representation z is obtained as an average of the input word vectors

$$z = \frac{1}{|X|} \sum_{w \in X} v_w \tag{1}$$

The average vector z is then fed to a fully connected layer to estimate probabilities for the output labels as:

$$\hat{y} = softmax(W_l\,z + b) \tag{2}$$

where W_l is $k \times d$ matrix, b is a bias vector and $softmax(q) = exp(q)/\sum_{j=1}^{k} exp(q_j)$. For text classification tasks, the NBOW model is trained to minimise the categorical cross-entropy loss (Goldberg, 2015) using a stochastic gradient descent algorithm. Additional fully connected layers can be added into the NBOW model to form Deep Averaging Networks (DAN) (Iyyer et al., 2015).

4 Proposed model: Neural Bag-of-Weighted-Words (NBOW2)

While the NBOW model learns word vectors specialised for the classification task, it lacks to *explicitly* model and provide the information that certain words are more important than the others in the given classification task. While tf-idf weights capture word importance weights over a given corpus and can be used at the input of the NBOW model, we are interested in letting the model learn the word importance weights which are task specific. We thus propose the NBOW2 model, with the motivation to enable the NBOW model to provide task specific word importance weights.

It is easy to realise that the NBOW model is essentially a fully connected feed forward network with a BOW input vector. The absence of non-linearity at the hidden layer and the BOW inputs where words are set to 1 and 0, results into a sum of the word vectors. However average of word vectors is used as it gives a better performance compared to a sum. To learn the word importance weights, we form a weighted sum composition of the text X as follows:

$$z = \frac{1}{|X|} \sum_{w \in X} \alpha_w \, v_w \qquad (3)$$

where α_w are the scalar word importance weights for each word $w \in X$. Learning task specific word vectors with Equation 3 ensures that words which drive the classification task are given higher importance or α_w values (see example in Figure 1).

α_w are obtained by introducing a vector a in the model, and are calculated as follows:

$$\alpha_w = f(v_w \cdot a) \qquad (4)$$

where $v_w \cdot a$ represents a dot product between input word vector v_w and vector a; and f scales the importance weights to range $[0, 1]$. Equation 4, which makes the scalar word importance weight α_w a function of the distance of the word w from a in the context space, ensures that calculation of word importance takes into account the contextual word similarities and that it is not biased by the frequency of occurrence of words in the training corpus.

For f common activation functions including softmax, sigmoid and also hyperbolic tangent can be used. From our experiments we found that the sigmoid function $f(t) = (1 + e^{-t})^{-1}$ is a better choice in terms of model convergence and accuracy. However, it must be noted the softmax f could be more interesting in certain tasks because (a) the importance of a word (α_w) in an input document will be dependent not only on the distance of this word from vector a but also on that of the other words in the given input document (b) being a max function the softamax f will bias the

composition of input document context vector z (in Equation 3) to only a handful of input words.

To summarise the as compared to the NBOW model, the NBOW2 model will include one additional vector (a). This vector is randomly initialised before training and learned along with the word vectors and other model parameters. The model training, with stochastic gradient descent, and classification (with a forward pass) both will use Equations 3 and 4, along with the output class probability estimates $\hat{y} = softmax(W_l \, z + b)$ similar to the NBOW model.

5 Experiment Setup

To analyse the working and performance of our proposed NBOW2 model, we consider two common tasks: (a) binary sentiment classification on IMDB (Maas et al., 2011) and Rotten Tomatoes movie review dataset (Pang and Lee, 2005) (b) topic classification of 20 Newsgroup dataset. We make available the source code used in our experiments[1].

5.1 Sentiment Analysis

For the IMDB task we use the original dataset[2] with 25000 train and 25000 test movie reviews. For Rotten Tomatoes (RT) we obtained the v1.0 dataset[3] and we do 10-fold cross-validation over the balanced binary dataset of 10,662 sentences. In both IMDB and RT tasks, model training parameters[4] for NBOW2 are kept similar to those chosen for NBOW by Iyyer (2015) after cross validation. For NBOW and NBOW2 models '-RAND' suffix will denote random word vector initialisation and no suffix is initialisation with publicly available 300-d GloVe vectors trained over the Common Crawl (Pennington et al., 2014)[5].

5.2 20 Newsgroup Topic Classification

We use the 'bydate' train/test splits, cleaned and made available by Cardoso (2007)[6]. There are 11,293 documents in the original training set and 7,528 in the test set. For training the NBOW and NBOW2 models, we randomly extract 15%

---

[1]Source code available at the url https://github.com/mranahmd/nbow2-text-class

[2]http://ai.stanford.edu/ amaas/data/sentiment/

[3]https://www.cs.cornell.edu/people/pabo/movie-review-data/

[4]word vector size 300, word dropout probability 0.3, L2 regularisation weight 1e-5

[5]http://nlp.stanford.edu/projects/glove/

[6]http://web.ist.utl.pt/acardoso/datasets/

of the original train set as the validation set and use remaining 85% as the final training set. Training was performed with the ADADELTA (Zeiler, 2012) gradient descent algorithm. L2 regularisation weight of 1e-5 was applied to all parameters. Further, to add robustness, we applied 75%[7] word dropout (Iyyer et al., 2015; Dai and Le, 2015). Additionally we use early stopping when the validation error starts to increase. Similar to the sentiment analysis experiments '-RAND' suffix will denote random word vector initialisation and no suffix is initialisation with 300-d GloVe.

6 Analysis and Discussion

6.1 Word importance weights learned by the NBOW2 model

We perform an analysis of the word importance weights learned by the NBOW2 model by presenting some qualitative and quantitative results.

6.1.1 Visualisation of word vectors from the RT sentiment analysis task

We visually examine the word vectors learned by the NBOW and NBOW2 models. To visualise word vectors they can be projected into a two dimensional space using the *t-Distributed Stochastic Neighbour Embedding* (t-SNE) technique (van der Maaten and Hinton, 2008). Figure 1 shows the two dimensional t-SNE visualisations of word vectors learned by the NBOW and NBOW2 models. Figure 1a shows a plot of the word vectors learned by the NBOW model and Figure 1b shows a plot of the word vectors learned by the NBOW model. Additionally in Figure 1b each word is given a colour based on the word importance assigned to it by the NBOW2 model.

From Figure 1a we can see that NBOW model tries to separate the words in the word vector space. According to the word examples labelled in Figure 1a the words appear to be grouped into regions corresponding to positive and negative sentiments of the RT movie review task. Similarly the NBOW2 model also learns to separate the words into regions of positive and negative sentiments as shown, by the same word examples, in Figure 1b. If we examine the word importance assigned by the NBOW2 model, indicated by colours in Figure 1b, it is evident that the NBOW2 model also learns to separate words based on their importance

weights. To support this statement we show additional word examples labelled in different regions in Figure 1b. For instance the words *a, on, it, for, there* are not so important[8] for the RT sentiment classification task and are present together in region of lowest word importance. The words *staid, inflated, softens* can contribute to (negative) polarity of the reviews and hence have relatively higher importance weights (and are present together near the negative sentiment region in the word vector space).

To further verify our claim that, in comparison to the NBOW model, the NBOW2 model is able to distinguish words based on their importance we show Figure 1c. Figure 1c shows the word vectors learned by the NBOW model (same as in Figure 1a) but it depicts each word with (a colour based on) word importance weight learned by the NBOW2 model. It can be seen in Figure 1c that the NBOW model does not separate/group words based on word importance, even if we restrict only to the example words *a, on, it, for, there*.

6.1.2 Word importance weights v/s Tf-Idf weights as classification features

In this analysis, we compare the word importance weights learned by the NBOW2 model with tf-idf weights and other word weight features proposed in the previous works. For this comparison, an SVM classifier is used for the IMDB and RT binary classification tasks. Each train/test document is represented as a sparse BOW feature vector in which each word feature is only the word weight. For NBOW2 model it is the scalar word importance weight learned by the model. We compare it with (a) classical tf-idf weights (b) credibility adjusted tf-idf (cred-tf-idf) weights proposed by Kim (2014) (c) binary cosine-normalised weights (bnc) and binary delta-smoothed-idf cosine-normalised (bΔ'c) weights used by Maas (2011) (d) the Naive-Bayes SVM (NBSVM) method proposed by Wang (2012). Tf-idf, bnc and bΔ'c word weights are task independent word weights but cred-tf-idf and NBSVM are built based on the class/task information. It should be noted that some of these methods/features have been the earlier state-of-the-art results for IMDB and RT tasks.

The classification accuracies obtained by the SVM classifiers are reported in Table 1. The tf-

---

[7]choice based on accuracy on validation set

[8]from a BOW sentiment classification perspective; for other approaches or text analysis they might be essential

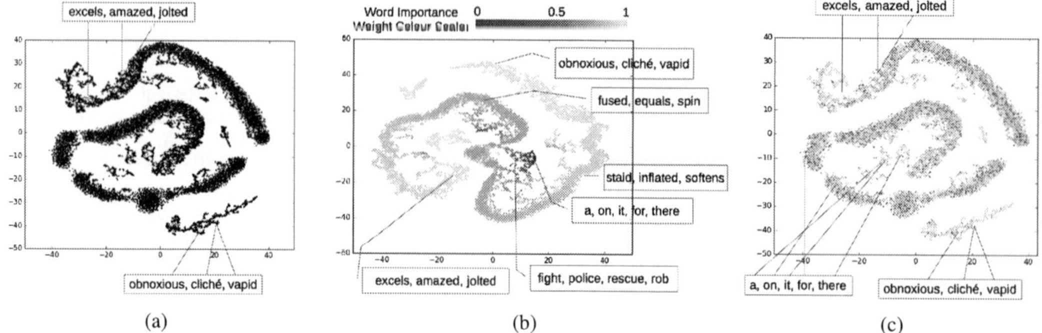

Figure 1: Visualisation of word vectors learned by the NBOW and NBOW2 models in the RT task. Word vectors are reduced to 2 dimension using t-SNE technique and shown in each plot. Plot (a) represents word vectors from the NBOW model, (b) represents words from NBOW2 model, with colours indicating the word importance weights learned by the NBOW2 model, (c) represents word vectors from the NBOW model as in (a) but depicts each word with word importance weight learned by the NBOW2 model.

Features for SVM Classifier	IMDB	RT
bnc (Maas et al., 2011)	87.8	-
b∆'c (Maas et al., 2011)	88.2	-
tf-idf-uni (Kim and Zhang, 2014)	88.6	77.1
cred-tf-idf-uni (Kim and Zhang, 2014)	88.8	77.5
NBSVM-uni (Wang and Manning, 2012)	88.3	78.1
NBOW2-RAND Word Importance Weights	88.2	76.7
NBOW2 Word Importance Weights	88.3	76.3

Table 1: Classification accuracy obtained for the IMDB and Rotten Tomatoes (RT) movie reviews sentiment classification task by training an SVM classifier on different word weights as features. (For IMDB 0.1% corresponds to 25 test documents. For RT 1% is about 10 test sentences.)

idf, cred-tf-id and NBSVM methods are denoted with a '-uni' suffix in Table 1 following the notation used by Kim (2014) . For the SVM classifier on 25k full length documents of IMDB task, the NBOW2 model weights are as good as NBSVM and b∆'c and better than bnc. But they do not perform as good as tf-idf weights. Whereas for the RT task with 1066 test sentences, the NBOW2 model word weights achieve accuracy closer to tf-idf variants.

6.2 NBOW2 model Classification Performance

After the discussion on the word importance weights learnt by the NBOW2 model we compare the classification results obtained with our NBOW2 model. We compare the NBOW2 model classification accuracy to that obtained from the NBOW model (Iyyer et al., 2015),

Model	IMDB	RT
NBOW-RAND (Iyyer et al., 2015)	88.9	76.2
NBOW (Iyyer et al., 2015)	89.0	79.0
NBOW2-RAND	88.7	78.2
NBOW2	**89.1**	**80.5**
NBSVM-uni (Wang and Manning, 2012)	88.3	78.1
NBSVM-bi (Wang and Manning, 2012)	91.2	79.4
CNN-MC (Kim, 2014)	-	81.1
CNN-non-static (Kim, 2014)	-	**81.5**
s2-bown-CNN (Johnson and Zhang, 2015)	92.3	-
SA-LSTM (Dai and Le, 2015)	**92.8**	**83.3**
LM-LSTM (Dai and Le, 2015)	92.4	78.3

Table 2: IMDB and Rotten Tomatoes (RT) movie reviews binary classification accuracy. First group lists BOW methods; including different initialisations of NBOW and NBOW2 (this work). The next group shows best reported results with bi-gram BOW and CNN methods, followed by LSTM RNN. Best method in each group is shown in bold. (For IMDB 0.1% corresponds to 25 test documents. For RT 1% is about 10 test sentences.)

BOW approaches based on Restricted Boltzmann Machines (RBM) and Support Vector Machines (SVM) and more complex approaches based on RNN, CNN. It must be noted that the CNN and RNN based approaches operate on rich word sequence information and have been shown to perform better than BOW approaches on these tasks.

Table 2 compares the classification accuracy of the NBOW2 model on IMDB and Rotten Tomatoes (RT) movie reviews binary classification tasks. Table 3 compares the classification accuracy on 20 Newsgroup topic classification. Results in Table 2 and 3 indicate that the NBOW2 model

Model	Accuracy (%)
NBOW-RAND	83.2
NBOW	83.2
NBOW2-RAND	82.7
NBOW2	**83.4**
RBM-MLP (Dauphin and Bengio, 2013)	79.5
SVM + BoW (Cardoso-Cachopo, 2007)	82.8
SA-LSTM (Dai and Le, 2015)	84.4
LM-LSTM (Dai and Le, 2015)	**84.7**

Table 3: 20 Newsgroup topic classification accuracy. First group lists BOW methods; including different initialisations of NBOW (Iyyer et al., 2015) and NBOW2 (this work). The second group shows best reported results with LSTM RNN. Best method in each group is shown in bold. (0.2% corresponds to about 15 test set documents.)

gives best accuracy among the BOW approaches. For IMDB and newsgroup task, the accuracy of NBOW2 model is closer to that of NBOW (not statistically significant for the 20 Newsgroup). It is also evident that for RT and newsgroup classification, the performance of NBOW2 is not far from CNN and LSTM methods. For further analysis we also trained the NBOW2 model by simply using fixed tf-idf weights in Equation 3. This gave 87.6% and 79.4% accuracy for IMDB and RT task. Thus we can state that the word importance weights of the NBOW2 model are themselves informative.

7 Conclusion and Future Work

We proposed a novel extension to the NBOW model, which enables the model to learn task specific word importance. With experiments and analysis on sentiment and topic classification tasks, we showed that our proposed NBOW2 model learns meaningful word importance weights. We showed that the NBOW2 model gives the best accuracy among the BOW approaches and it can outperform the NBOW model. This motivates us to explore extensions to the model, including (a) class-specific vectors a_q, instead of a single vector a, to obtain class-specific word importance (b) document context specific word importance weights.

References

Dzmitry Bahdanau, Kyunghyun Cho, and Yoshua Bengio. 2014. Neural machine translation by jointly learning to align and translate. In *ICLR 2015*.

Marco Baroni, Georgiana Dinu, and Germán Kruszewski. 2014. Don't count, predict! a systematic comparison of context-counting vs. context-predicting semantic vectors. In *Proceedings of the 52nd Annual Meeting of the Association for Computational Linguistics (Volume 1: Long Papers)*, pages 238–247, Baltimore, Maryland, June. Association for Computational Linguistics.

Yoshua Bengio, Réjean Ducharme, Pascal Vincent, and Christian Janvin. 2003. A neural probabilistic language model. *J. Mach. Learn. Res.*, 3:1137–1155, March.

Ana Cardoso-Cachopo. 2007. Improving Methods for Single-label Text Categorization. PdD Thesis, Instituto Superior Tecnico, Universidade Tecnica de Lisboa.

William Chan, Navdeep Jaitly, Quoc V. Le, and Oriol Vinyals. 2015. Listen, attend and spell. *CoRR*, abs/1508.01211.

Ronan Collobert and Jason Weston. 2008. A unified architecture for natural language processing: Deep neural networks with multitask learning. In *Proceedings of the 25th International Conference on Machine Learning*, ICML '08, pages 160–167, New York, NY, USA. ACM.

Andrew M Dai and Quoc V Le. 2015. Semi-supervised sequence learning. In C. Cortes, N. D. Lawrence, D. D. Lee, M. Sugiyama, and R. Garnett, editors, *Advances in Neural Information Processing Systems 28*, pages 3061–3069. Curran Associates, Inc.

Yann Dauphin and Yoshua Bengio. 2013. Stochastic ratio matching of rbms for sparse high-dimensional inputs. In C. J. C. Burges, L. Bottou, M. Welling, Z. Ghahramani, and K. Q. Weinberger, editors, *Advances in Neural Information Processing Systems 26*, pages 1340–1348. Curran Associates, Inc.

Zhi-Hong Deng, Kun-Hu Luo, and Hong-Liang Yu. 2014. A study of supervised term weighting scheme for sentiment analysis. *Expert Syst. Appl.*, 41(7):3506–3513, June.

Li Dong, Furu Wei, Chuanqi Tan, Duyu Tang, Ming Zhou, and Ke Xu. 2014. Adaptive recursive neural network for target-dependent twitter sentiment classification. In *Proceedings of the 52nd Annual Meeting of the Association for Computational Linguistics, ACL 2014, June 22-27, 2014, Baltimore, MD, USA, Volume 2: Short Papers*, pages 49–54.

Jianfeng Gao, Patrick Pantel, Michael Gamon, Xiaodong He, and Li Deng. 2014. Modeling interestingness with deep neural networks. In *Proceedings of the 2014 Conference on Empirical Methods in Natural Language Processing (EMNLP)*, pages 2–13, Doha, Qatar, October. Association for Computational Linguistics.

Yoav Goldberg. 2015. A primer on neural network models for natural language processing. *CoRR*, abs/1510.00726.

Karl Moritz Hermann and Phil Blunsom. 2013. The Role of Syntax in Vector Space Models of Compositional Semantics. In *Proceedings of ACL*, August.

Aminul Islam, Evangelos Milios, and Vlado Kešelj, 2015. *Text, Speech, and Dialogue: 18th International Conference, TSD 2015, Pilsen,Czech Republic, September 14-17, 2015, Proceedings*, chapter Do Important Words in Bag-of-Words Model of Text Relatedness Help?, pages 569–577. Springer International Publishing, Cham.

Mohit Iyyer, Varun Manjunatha, Jordan Boyd-Graber, and Hal Daumé III. 2015. Deep unordered composition rivals syntactic methods for text classification. In *Proceedings of the 53rd Annual Meeting of the Association for Computational Linguistics and the 7th International Joint Conference on Natural Language Processing (Volume 1: Long Papers)*, pages 1681–1691, Beijing, China, July. Association for Computational Linguistics.

Rie Johnson and Tong Zhang. 2015. Effective use of word order for text categorization with convolutional neural networks. In *Proceedings of the 2015 Conference of the North American Chapter of the Association for Computational Linguistics: Human Language Technologies*, pages 103–112, Denver, Colorado, May–June. Association for Computational Linguistics.

Nal Kalchbrenner, Edward Grefenstette, and Phil Blunsom. 2014. A convolutional neural network for modelling sentences. In *Proceedings of the 52nd Annual Meeting of the Association for Computational Linguistics (Volume 1: Long Papers)*, pages 655–665, Baltimore, Maryland, June. Association for Computational Linguistics.

Yoon Kim and Owen Zhang. 2014. Credibility adjusted term frequency: A supervised term weighting scheme for sentiment analysis and text classification. In *Proceedings of the 5th Workshop on Computational Approaches to Subjectivity, Sentiment and Social Media Analysis*, pages 79–83, Baltimore, Maryland, June. Association for Computational Linguistics.

Yoon Kim. 2014. Convolutional neural networks for sentence classification. In *Proceedings of the 2014 Conference on Empirical Methods in Natural Language Processing (EMNLP)*, pages 1746–1751, Doha, Qatar, October. Association for Computational Linguistics.

Man Lan, Chew-Lim Tan, and Hwee-Boon Low. 2006. Proposing a new term weighting scheme for text categorization. In *Proceedings of the 21st National Conference on Artificial Intelligence - Volume 1*, AAAI'06, pages 763–768. AAAI Press.

Quoc V. Le and Tomas Mikolov. 2014. Distributed representations of sentences and documents. In *Proceedings of the 31th International Conference on Machine Learning, ICML 2014, Beijing, China, 21-26 June 2014*, pages 1188–1196.

Jiwei Li. 2014. Feature weight tuning for recursive neural networks. *CoRR*, abs/1412.3714.

Wang Ling, Yulia Tsvetkov, Silvio Amir, Ramon Fermandez, Chris Dyer, Alan W Black, Isabel Trancoso, and Chu-Cheng Lin. 2015. Not all contexts are created equal: Better word representations with variable attention. In *Proceedings of the 2015 Conference on Empirical Methods in Natural Language Processing*, pages 1367–1372, Lisbon, Portugal, September. Association for Computational Linguistics.

Andrew L. Maas, Raymond E. Daly, Peter T. Pham, Dan Huang, Andrew Y. Ng, and Christopher Potts. 2011. Learning word vectors for sentiment analysis. In *Proceedings of the 49th Annual Meeting of the Association for Computational Linguistics: Human Language Technologies - Volume 1*, HLT '11, pages 142–150, Stroudsburg, PA, USA. Association for Computational Linguistics.

Musa Mammadov, John Yearwood, and Lei Zhao, 2011. *AI 2010: Advances in Artificial Intelligence: 23rd Australasian Joint Conference, Adelaide, Australia, December 7-10, 2010. Proceedings*, chapter A New Supervised Term Ranking Method for Text Categorization, pages 102–111. Springer Berlin Heidelberg, Berlin, Heidelberg.

Christopher D. Manning, Prabhakar Raghavan, and Hinrich Schütze, 2008. *Introduction to Information Retrieval*, chapter Scoring, term weighting, and the vector space model. Cambridge University Press, New York, NY, USA.

Tomas Mikolov, Kai Chen, Greg Corrado, and Jeffrey Dean. 2013a. Efficient estimation of word representations in vector space. *CoRR*, abs/1301.3781.

Tomas Mikolov, Wen-tau Yih, and Geoffrey Zweig. 2013b. Linguistic regularities in continuous space word representations. In *Proceedings of the 2013 Conference of the North American Chapter of the Association for Computational Linguistics: Human Language Technologies*, pages 746–751, Atlanta, Georgia, June. Association for Computational Linguistics.

Jinseok Nam, Jungi Kim, Eneldo Loza Mencía, Iryna Gurevych, and Johannes Fürnkranz. 2014. Large-scale multi-label text classification - revisiting neural networks. In Toon Calders, Floriana Esposito, Eyke Hüllermeier, and Rosa Meo, editors, *Proceedings of the European Conference on Machine Learning and Principles and Practice of Knowledge Discovery in Databases (ECML-PKDD-14), Part 2*, volume 8725 of *Lecture Notes in Computer Science*, pages 437–452. Springer Berlin Heidelberg, September.

Georgios Paltoglou and Mike Thelwall. 2010. A study of information retrieval weighting schemes for sentiment analysis. In *Proceedings of the 48th Annual Meeting of the Association for Computational Linguistics*, ACL '10, pages 1386–1395, Stroudsburg, PA, USA. Association for Computational Linguistics.

Bo Pang and Lillian Lee. 2005. Seeing stars: Exploiting class relationships for sentiment categorization with respect to rating scales. In *Proceedings of the 43rd Annual Meeting on Association for Computational Linguistics*, ACL '05, pages 115–124, Stroudsburg, PA, USA. Association for Computational Linguistics.

Jeffrey Pennington, Richard Socher, and Christopher Manning. 2014. Glove: Global vectors for word representation. In *Proceedings of the 2014 Conference on Empirical Methods in Natural Language Processing (EMNLP)*, pages 1532–1543, Doha, Qatar, October. Association for Computational Linguistics.

Xiaojun Quan, Wenyin Liu, and Bite Qiu. 2011. Term weighting schemes for question categorization. *IEEE Transactions on Pattern Analysis and Machine Intelligence*, 33(5):1009–1021.

Richard Socher, Alex Perelygin, Jean Wu, Jason Chuang, Christopher D. Manning, Andrew Y. Ng, and Christopher Potts. 2013. Recursive deep models for semantic compositionality over a sentiment treebank. In *Proceedings of the 2013 Conference on Empirical Methods in Natural Language Processing*, pages 1631–1642, Stroudsburg, PA, October. Association for Computational Linguistics.

Søren Kaae Sønderby, Casper Kaae Sønderby, Henrik Nielsen, and Ole Winther, 2015. *Algorithms for Computational Biology: Second International Conference, AlCoB 2015, Mexico City, Mexico, August 4-5, 2015, Proceedings*, chapter Convolutional LSTM Networks for Subcellular Localization of Proteins, pages 68–80. Springer International Publishing, Cham.

Kai Sheng Tai, Richard Socher, and Christopher D. Manning. 2015. Improved semantic representations from tree-structured long short-term memory networks. In *Proceedings of the 53rd Annual Meeting of the Association for Computational Linguistics and the 7th International Joint Conference on Natural Language Processing (Volume 1: Long Papers)*, pages 1556–1566, Beijing, China, July. Association for Computational Linguistics.

Joseph Turian, Lev Ratinov, and Yoshua Bengio. 2010. Word representations: A simple and general method for semi-supervised learning. In *Proceedings of the 48th Annual Meeting of the Association for Computational Linguistics*, ACL '10, pages 384–394, Stroudsburg, PA, USA. Association for Computational Linguistics.

Laurens van der Maaten and Geoffrey E. Hinton. 2008. Visualizing high-dimensional data using t-sne. *Journal of Machine Learning Research*, 9:2579–2605.

Sida Wang and Christopher D. Manning. 2012. Baselines and bigrams: Simple, good sentiment and topic classification. In *Proceedings of the 50th Annual Meeting of the Association for Computational Linguistics: Short Papers - Volume 2*, ACL '12, pages 90–94, Stroudsburg, PA, USA. Association for Computational Linguistics.

Peng Wang, Jiaming Xu, Bo Xu, Chenglin Liu, Heng Zhang, Fangyuan Wang, and Hongwei Hao. 2015. Semantic clustering and convolutional neural network for short text categorization. In *Proceedings of the 53rd Annual Meeting of the Association for Computational Linguistics and the 7th International Joint Conference on Natural Language Processing (Volume 2: Short Papers)*, pages 352–357, Beijing, China, July. Association for Computational Linguistics.

Kelvin Xu, Jimmy Ba, Ryan Kiros, Kyunghyun Cho, Aaron C. Courville, Ruslan Salakhutdinov, Richard S. Zemel, and Yoshua Bengio. 2015. Show, attend and tell: Neural image caption generation with visual attention. In *Proceedings of the 32nd International Conference on Machine Learning, ICML 2015, Lille, France, 6-11 July 2015*, pages 2048–2057.

Matthew D. Zeiler. 2012. ADADELTA: an adaptive learning rate method. *CoRR*, abs/1212.5701.

Ye Zhang and Byron Wallace. 2015. A sensitivity analysis of (and practitioners' guide to) convolutional neural networks for sentence classification. *CoRR*, abs/1510.03820.

A Vector Model for Type-Theoretical Semantics

Konstantin Sokolov

Peter the Great Polytechnic University, St. Petersburg, Russia

sokolov@dcn.icc.spbstu.ru

Abstract

Vector models of distributional semantics can be viewed as a geometric interpretation of a fragment of dependent type theory. By extending to a bigger fragment to include the dependent product we achieve a significant increase in expressive power of vector models, which allows for an implementation of contextual adaptation of word meanings in the compositional setting.

1 Introduction

In this paper we discuss a possibility of reconciling two distinct threads of research in computational lexical semantics, namely distributional semantics (Lenci, 2008; Baroni et al., 2014) and formal semantics based on dependent type theory (Ranta, 1994; Luo, 2012). Although both approaches focus on related problems of lexical semantics and composition, it is hard to combine them in a unified framework because of differences in computational techniques they employ. However, their theoretical foundations are compatible and it is possible to incorporate vector space models into a computational framework based on dependent type theory. The extensions of existing vector representations required for this task are motivated by the geometric interpretation of type theory.

The reason why such extensions are necessary is the limitations of the function application model of compositionality. In formal semantics compositionality is traditionally modeled as an application of one logical form to another, technically realized as a reduction of concatenated logical forms expressed in a variant of typed lambda calculus (Montague, 1975). In distributional semantics this approach is retained, although lambda terms are substituted with vectors and tensors of various ranks (Baroni et al., 2014). This model of compositionality has difficulties with the compositional treatment of certain common types of natural language expressions, that require context-dependence of terms and a non-trivial machanism of meaning adaptation. Paradigmatic examples of such linguistic phenomena are logical polysemy and co-predication, which received formal treatment in the works of Pustejovsky (1995) and are among the central problems of type-theoretical semantics (Cooper, 2005; Asher, 2011; Luo, 2012).

The problems related to logical polysemy include cases where an intended aspect of meaning of an argument requires an adaptation of a predicate which is applied to it and vice versa. Consider the case of an adjective applied to a noun in *red apple*, *red watermelon* and *red crystal* (Lahav, 1989). In these examples a notion of "redness" is different for each of the arguments. A red apple is red when most of its surface is red, a watermelon is red inside, a crystal is red entirely. It is possible to characterize a watermelon as being ripe by saying that it is red, which is not the case for a crystal. As a result, an adaptation of a predicate is needed to properly account for the meaning variations in all these cases. Similarly, an argument can have multiple aspects of meaning selected by various predicates. In *heavy book* and *boring book* a book is treated as either a physical object or an information content. Both aspects clearly correspond to different sets of properties, which are taken into account by the predicates and reflect in the systemic organization of the lexicon, e. g. hypernym relations between synsets or relations between word classes (Hanks, 1996). Words both in argument and predicate positions can demonstrate capability of contextual meaning adaptation, sometimes even simultaneously, like in *red book*. Such cases violate the direction of application of a

Proceedings of the 1st Workshop on Representation Learning for NLP, pages 230–238,
Berlin, Germany, August 11th, 2016. ©2016 Association for Computational Linguistics

predicate and are problematic for the function application model of composition.

Another violation occurs in cases of co-predication, which takes place when two or more predicates make use of conflicting meaning aspects of an argument, leading to the necessity to assign at least two incompatible meaning representations (e. g. types) to a single word. The "lunch sentence" proposed by Pustejovsky (1995) is a classic example:

A lunch was delicious but took forever.

Notwithstanding these obstacles, we find that the function application model of composition can in fact be made compatible with context-dependent meaning alternations. An extension required for this task follows naturally from an identification of basic operations of composition in vector models and computation rules in type theory. The resulting model can in turn be given an intuitive geometric interpretation, that greatly clarifies the options for its computational implementation. Recent developments in type theory made clear a tight connection between computation and geometry (Univalent Foundations Program, 2013). In the following sections we give a sketch of a method of incorporating semantic vector spaces within a type-theoretical framework of Luo by interpreting primitive types as vector spaces, dependent types as fibers of a vector bundle and so forth. Currently we limit ourselves to the dependent product type, leaving an analysis of the dependent sum and dot types for later. However, we give some general remarks as to how these important constructs might be implemented in our setting.

2   Related Work

In this section we give an overview of the general framework of composition currently adopted in distributional semantic, followed by a brief discussion of type-theoretical semantics.

2.1   Compositional Vector Models

Lack of support for compositionality remains a serious limitation of distributional semantics, although many techniques were proposed to enable compositional treatment of vector representations. These proposals include methods based on vector addition and multiplication (Mitchell and Lapata, 2010), tensor operations (Smolensky, 1990; Widows, 2008), linear maps (Baroni et al., 2014; Coecke et al., 2010), tensor decomposition (Van de Cruys et al., 2013), co-composition based on vector space projections (Tsubaki et al., 2013), simultaneous processing of meaning and composition in neural embeddings (Socher et al., 2013; Pennington et al., 2014) and more. There is an evident tradeoff between expressiveness and computational properties of the compositional vector models. Simple additive and multiplicative models cannot capture important properties of composition in natural language, such as its non-commutative character, relation to syntax, polysemy and contextual meaning adaptation. Complex models generally make use of tensors of various ranks to represent different word types and linear maps that operate on them and in principle are better suited for compositional analysis. However, the actual implementations are very difficult to train and to date no methods of training such models on a large scale were proposed.

Although commutative (vector mixture) methods of composition are easier to implement, non-commutativity is dictated by both linguistic properties and the properties of vector representations. In the analysis of adjective-noun pairs Baroni and Zamparelli (2010) used an asymmetric function application model of compositionality, where an adjective is represented as a matrix applied to a noun vector to produce a new vector. This approach turned into a large research program of compositional distributional semantics (Baroni et al., 2014), which is currently widely accepted.

A similar program was proposed earlier by Coecke et al. (2010), where category theory was used to devise a method of validating paths of composition accross multiple vector spaces specific for various word types in order to arrive to a distinguished "sentence" space, where comparison of the meanings of sentences could be performed. The composition here is modeled on the basis of a linear map sending a tensor product of meaning representations of words (i. e. their superposition) to a vector in the sentence space. The particular structure of this linear map is determined by the sentence structure explicated as a reduction in the pregroup grammar formalism. Since linear maps $V \to W$ are actually in a bijective correspondence with vectors in a tensor product space $V \otimes W$, the actual procedure of computation of the sentence meaning consists in "carving out" the right sequence of function applications from the space of all possible reduction paths. The model of composition here is slightly different, but it does not diverge too much from Baroni's proposal. Under the aforementioned bijection a transitive verb can also be viewed as a function applied to the meaning representations of its participants to produce a vector in the sentence space.

Contextual variation of meaning in relation to word sense disambiguation and semantic similarity has been investigated almost since inception of the field (Schütze, 1998; Thater et al., 2010; Thater et al., 2011). However, disambiguation is different from composition (Kartsaklis et al., 2013). Attempts to give an analysis of logical polysemy and contextual adaptation in the compositional setting are limited (Erk and Padó, 2008; Tsubaki et al., 2013).

2.2 Type-Theoretical Semantics

Type-theoretical semantics is an approach to modeling semantics of natural language initiated by Ranta (1994) and heavily influenced by Pustejovsky's Generative Lexicon (Pustejovsky, 1991; Pustejovsky, 1995). It proved capable of giving a convincing analysis of logical polysemy, copredication and systemic organization of the lexicon modeled as subtyping. Although it belongs roughly in the tradition of Montague Grammar (Montague, 1975), it diverges from formal semantics in a number of ways. The distinction between a formal meaning representation and its interpretation in a model is not present. Meaning representations are type expressions and their justification is achieved by an effective computational process. As a consequence, type-theoretical meaning representations have a strong connection with computability due to the Curry-Howard correspondence. Unlike in Montague Grammar, in type-theoretical semantics words are not treated as atomic entities. Instead, their meaning is analysed on the basis of argument-predicate structures. The meaning of a predicate is represented as a function type, which incorporates types of its arguments to the effect similar to selectional restrictions in the study of verb classes (Levin, 1993). Explication of a word meaning through argument type restrictions, i. e. constraints on co-occurence, leads to a duality between argument-predicate structure and lexical meaning (Pustejovsky, 2013). To our view, this notion of duality is closely related to the dis-

tibutional hypothesis of Z. Harris and justifies an attempt to give a unified treatment of lexical semantics based on both theories.

Current proposals are targeted at developing a formal system that would incorporate words as either terms of a certain type or as types themselves and provide a set of type formation, introduction, elimination and computation rules to be used in derivations. Traditional formal semantics is based on the simply typed lambda calculus à la Church and is given a set-theoretical interpretation. A type-theoretical formalism proposed by Asher and Pustejovsky (2006) builds on a type theory which is close to that used in formal semantics. The distinction between terms and types is retained, a subtyping relation is inherited from the Generative Lexicon and is modeled on the basis of a subsumption relation. In (Asher, 2011) a conflict between subsumptive subtyping and an intended interpretation of dot types is resolved by modifications of the interpertation procedure, which is based on a category-theoretic interpretation in a topos. Other systems (Cooper, 2005; Mery et al., 2007; Luo, 2012) are based on Martin-Löf's dependent type theory, where the boundary between terms and types is blurred. The framework of dependent type semantics (Luo, 2012) makes use of a special mechanism of coercive subtyping, which will be characterized in the next section.

An obvious limitation of type-theoretical semantics is that to date no method of large scale building of such representations on the basis of real-world data has been given, which greatly hinders empirical evaluation. A possible way to overcome this limitation is to adapt logical form learning techniques developed for other types of symbolic semantic representation (Zettlemoyer and Collins, 2012; Liang and Potts, 2015).

3 Formal Background

In this section we give a motivation for the use of dependent types in formal semantics, followed by a brief overview of the coercive subtyping framework of Luo as applied to natural language expressions. The notion of a vector bundle plays a crucial role in our interpretation, so we also give here the definition.

3.1 Dependent Type Theory

Martin-Löf's type theory can be viewed as a formal system of deduction. When used as a metalanguage, a type theory can incorporate both rules of formation of logical statements and deduction rules of a logical system. The basic elements of a formal system of type theory are judgements of various forms. A judgement that proposition A is true is written A *true*, $a : A$ is a judgement saying that a is an element of type A, a judgement $a = b : A$ says that a and b are equal objects of type A. Besides simple judgements of the forms given above there are hypothetical judgements that depend on another judgements, e. g. $f(a) : B$ $(a : A)$ says that an object $f(a)$ is of type B given that a is an object of type A. With hypothetical judgements and a number of deduction rules which can bind hypotheses it is possible to construct a derivation of a particular judgement, which does not depend on any hypothesis, i. e. a derivation in a system of natural deduction for judgements. Such a system can be presented in two forms, the so called Prawitz and Gentzen style natural deduction, the latter uses sequents, i. e. expressions involving typing contexts and a turnstile.

As a short example, consider the introduction and elimination rules for conjunction implemented inside a metalanguage of type theory (Gentzen style):

$$\frac{\Gamma \vdash A\ true \qquad \Gamma \vdash B\ true}{\Gamma \vdash A \wedge B\ true}\ I_\wedge$$

$$\frac{\Gamma \vdash A \wedge B\ true}{\Gamma \vdash A\ true}\ E_\wedge \qquad \frac{\Gamma \vdash A \wedge B\ true}{\Gamma \vdash B\ true}\ E_\wedge$$

Since all components of a logical system are immersed in the same metalanguage, it is possible to extend the language by allowing types to depend on terms of another types, which significantly raises expressivity. A dependent type is written $A(x)$, and two special type expressions are introduced, the dependent product type $\Pi(x : A)B(x)$ and the dependent sum type $\Sigma(x : A)B(x)$. When there is no actual dependency of $B(x)$ on the elements of A, the product type simplifies to a function type $A \rightarrow B$, and the sum type to a direct product $A \times B$.

To establish an equality of two terms of a type it is necessary to reduce each of them to their corresponding canonical objects. Then an equality judgement is justified by the syntactic equivalence of canonical objects. As an example, consider an inductive type for natural numbers $\mathbb{N}$, which has two type constructors $0 : \mathbb{N}$ and $succ(n) : \mathbb{N}$ $(n : \mathbb{N})$. To prove $1 + 1 = 2 : \mathbb{N}$ both sides of the equality are reduced to the form $succ(succ(0))$.

The rules used for reducing an object to its canonical form are called computation rules, reduction itself is often called computation.

Types and propositions are identified. For instance, in the judgement A *true* a symbol A is treated as a proposition assumed to be true, whereas in $a : A$ it is treated as a type. Under such identification an object of type A is treated as an evidence (a proof object) that proposition A is true. To prove A is to construct an object of type A using the rules of the system. That justifies the possibility to use type theory for formal semantics, since to say that a proposition is provable is to say that its truth conditions are satisfied (Ranta, 1994).

One of the main obstacles to applying dependent type theory to the task of modeling lexical semantics is that the subtyping relation, which naturally represents hypernym relations between concepts and is traditionally modeled as subsumption (Pustejovsky, 1995), is incompatible with the notion of canonical object (Luo et al., 2013). For example, the subsumptive subtyping justifies inferences of the form

$$\frac{\Gamma \vdash a : A \qquad \Gamma \vdash A < B}{\Gamma \vdash a : B}$$

In case of dependent types, an inference like

$$\frac{\Gamma \vdash a : List(A) \qquad \Gamma \vdash A < B}{\Gamma \vdash a : List(B)}$$

is incorrect. To justify that we would need to reduce both $a : List(A)$ and $a : List(B)$ to the same canonical representation, which is impossible to do since canonical objects of these two types are built with different sets of type constructors.

To solve this Luo (2012) proposed a mechanism of type coercions, which allows for the substitution of a term of a subtype in a context where a term of its supertype is required. The actual coercion is achieved by applying a coercion function to the term. A coercion judgement of the form $\Gamma \vdash A <_c B : Type$ states that objects of the form $c(a)$, where a is an object of type A and c is a coercion function, can be used in contexts where objects of type B are expected. By using such a mechanism it becomes possible to justify relations between predicates such as $[\![human]\!] \rightarrow [\![book]\!] \rightarrow Prop < [\![man]\!] \rightarrow \Sigma([\![book]\!], [\![heavy]\!]) \rightarrow Prop$ by declaring coercions $[\![man]\!] <_{c_1} [\![human]\!]$ and $\Sigma(A, B) <_{p_1} A$. The resulting subtyping is contravariant in arguments as is usually expected. Coercive subtyping is a conservative extension (in the weak sense) of dependent type theory, s. (Luo et al., 2013) for details.

3.2 Vector Bundles

Intuitively, a vector bundle is a set of vector spaces parameterized by points of some topological space. Formal definitions follow (Luke and Mishchenko, 2013).

A vector bundle is a continuous map $p : E \to B$ s.t. $p^{-1}(b)$ is a vector space for each $b \in B$. Additionally, there is an open cover $\{U_\alpha\}$ of B and for each U_α there exists a homeomorphism $h_\alpha : p^{-1}(U_\alpha) \to U_\alpha \times \mathbb{R}^k$ s.t. $h_\alpha(p^{-1}(b))$ is a vector space isomorphic to $\{b\} \times \mathbb{R}^k$ for each $b \in U_\alpha$. This is called a local trivialization condition. The resulting construct is a locally trivial real vector bundle of rank k (we say vector bundle for short), E is the total space, B is the base space, $p^{-1}(b)$ is a fiber over b.

A pair of trivializations $h_\alpha : p^{-1}(U_\alpha) \to U_\alpha \times \mathbb{R}^k$ and $h_\beta : p^{-1}(U_\beta) \to U_\beta \times \mathbb{R}^k$ induces a map $h_\alpha h_\beta^{-1} : (U_\alpha \cap U_\beta) \times \mathbb{R}^k \to (U_\alpha \cap U_\beta) \times \mathbb{R}^k$ called transition function. Transitions can be thought of as continuous changes of coordinates.

4 Vector Models for Dependent Types

In this section we discuss a geometric interpretation of a dependent type system, resulting from the treatment of types as vector spaces. Such an interpretation provides insights into a possible computational implementation.

4.1 Geometric Interpretation

The usual way to represent words in vector models is to identify them with vectors. In our approach, instead of using vectors as primitive elements, we switch to an equivalence class of vectors w. r. t. multiplication by a scalar. Such a modification does not affect our ability to compute the cosine similarity between primitive elements. We do not identify equivalence classes of vectors with words right away. Instead, it is more convenient to think of a word as a region or a neighbourhood in the space obtained from the initial vector space by the factorization we have just described, cf. (Erk, 2009). We denote that initial vector space A and treat it as a primitive type of our system. This approach allows to make all types and their objects be vector spaces. For example, if $A = \mathbb{R}^2$, then $a : A$ is a one-dimensional linear subspace of A.

Function types are built recursively with an arrow constructor. The simplest possible function type in our system is $A \to A$, objects of this type are linear operators on A. Analogously to the primitive type, we would like to consider equivalence classes of operators as objects of that type.

A dependent product $\Pi(x : A)B(x)$ is interpreted as a vector bundle. Its fibers are vector spaces, parameterized by points of the base space. An easy way to imagine this situation is to consider an orthogonal complement of a one-dimensional subspace in $\mathbb{R}^3$ with the usual scalar multiplication, which is isomorphic to $\mathbb{R}^2$. Then for any one-dimensional subspace in $\mathbb{R}^2$ there is a corresponding orthogonal subspace of dimension two, which is a fiber of a vector bundle $p : E \to B$. A section of a vector bundle is a map $s : U \to E$, where U is an open subset of B, such that $p(s(b)) = b$. We interpret predicates as global sections, which have B as the domain and send every point $b \in B$ to some vector in the fiber $p^{-1}(b)$.

Consider the previous example, where the base space is a two-dimensional euclidean space embedded in $\mathbb{R}^3$ and the fibers are two-dimensional subspaces orthogonal to the lines in the base space. We can view this construct as a real vector bundle of rank two. A global section sends in a continuous manner a vector from the base space to some vector in the plane orthogonal to it.

We summarize corespondences between variuos interpretations in Table 1.

4.2 Computation

The notion of canonical object is central to the dependent type theory. The computation of a canonical representation of an object of some type is achieved by a series of reductions in an order prescribed by the structure of that type. More precisely, application of an object of type $\Pi(x : A)B(x)$ to an object of type A amounts to selecting a point from the "result space" $B(a)$ parameterized by the argument, given a point $a : A$ as an input:

$$\frac{\Gamma \vdash f : \Pi(x : A)B(x) \qquad \Gamma \vdash a : A}{\Gamma \vdash app(f, a, \Pi(x : A)B(x), A) = f(a) : B(a)} \, C_\Pi$$

Elements of the same type are comparable, whereas elements of different types are not. For instance, objects of type $B(x)$, which is the type of a fiber, are not comparable with objects of type A, which is the type of the base. This is exactly

Type theory	Vector model	Geometric interpretation	Linguistic interpretation
element $x\colon A$	a vector in $\mathbb{R}^2$	a point in the base space B	a word
dependent type $A(x)$	a vector space parameterized by $x \in \mathbb{R}^2$	a fiber $p^{-1}(x)$	contextual modifications of words w. r. t a word x
product type $\Pi(x\colon A)B(x)$	linear maps parameterized by vectors in $\mathbb{R}^2$	a vector bundle	a set of predicates adapted to an argument
element $f\colon\Pi(x\colon A)B(x)$	a parameterized linear map	a global section	an adapted predicate

Table 1: Correspondences between interpretations.

where the coercive subtyping shows up. Recall that coercions are formulated in such a way as to make it possible to use an object of some type instead of an object of its supertype in a given context. Also note, that in the framework of Luo coercions are maps. To make things easier, currently we impose a restriction on vector bundles that the dimensionality of fibers be equal to the dimensionality of the base space. Note, that the general definition of a vector bundle does not require that. Then coersions from $B(x)$ to A can be implemented uniformly as trivial maps from fibers to the base, which we normally omit writing down explicitly. Comparing objects of $B(a)$ to objects of $B(b)$, given that a and b are points in the base space, does not require any special arrangements. Coercions in that case are determined by the usual transition functions.

4.3 Implementation

We give an example of the construct for the simplest possible case.

Let $A \approx \mathbb{R}^2$ be a distinguished plane of a three-dimensional euclidean space. Its one-dimensional subspaces are equivalence classes of vectors with respect to multiplication by a scalar. We build a vector bundle $p : E \to A$ with a fiber isomorphic to $\mathbb{R}^2$ and therefore also isomorphic to the base space. It is natural to use an associated projective space instead of $\mathbb{R}^2$, denoted $P(\mathbb{R}^2)$. Projectivization has a number of advantages. Under identification of projective points with rotations of an underlying $\mathbb{R}^2$, it can be seen as a compact Lie group, namely a projective special orthogonal group $PSO(2, \mathbb{R})$. The usual cosine similarity measure for words translates to an additive metric on $P(\mathbb{R}^2)$. In the induced topology the notion of a neighborhood of a word is well-defined. Analogously, switching to an associated projective bundle $P(E)$ allows us to treat fibers in the same manner. As usual, we can represent $P(\mathbb{R}^2)$ as a circle S^1 with opposite points identified, then the projective bundle can be represented as a torus

$S^1 \times S^1$, this time with four antipodal points identified. Care is needed to correctly assign orientations on the fibers.

Sections can be viewed as vector-valued functions defined on the base space. Since in our case the vectors can be obtained by an action of $PSO(2, \mathbb{R})$, a single parameter is sufficient to encode the vectors. This parameter is actually an angle between the zero and the value vectors in the fiber. That allows us to represent each section as a big cirle on a torus and to encode the required value as an angular offset assigned to each point. Such a scalar function must be smooth and periodic to satisfy the properties of a vector bundle, and it suffices to limit its range to $[0, \pi)$, since we sum angles modulo π. The function can be approximated with a square table with entries periodic accross both rows and columns. It is easy to vizualize the scalar function on a torus as a heat map or as a 2D surface over the square, with the height of a point being equal to the value of the function at that point. The periodicity and smoothness requirements suggest that it should be possible to approximate that surface with a partial weighted sum of two-dimesional harmonics.

5 Discussion

A characteristic trait of our model is that both arguments and predicates are treated as entities of a continuous nature. Their co-adaptation turns into a process of evaluation of stability areas where small changes of both the predicate and the argument do not lead to drastic changes in the meaning of a composite expression. This is a property that we pursue by intention and it is reminiscent of multiple examples of zonal reasoning in cognitive linguistics and perception (Stevens, 1972; Gärdenfors, 2004). Symbolic representations are often considered to be incompatible with that type of meaning representations. However, a more expressive formalism like that of dependent type theory makes the boundary less apparent. It is still to be determined whether our model can be given a sound interpretation in terms of cognitive lingusitics.

Early vector models were based on words co-occurence in a corpus and required very high dimensionality of representations (Deerwester et al., 1990; Landauer and Dumais, 1997). Vector coordinates could be interpreted as contextual co-occurence counts or as weights of the latent factors, depending on the model. Later the field was revolutionized by introduction of machine learning techniques, which allowed to approximate low dimensional vector representations (Mikolov et al., 2013; Pennington et al., 2014). It made the problem more tractable, while at the same time it became impossible to interpret single coordinates, as in these approaches the size of the vectors is determined on the basis of the desired accuracy of approximation and not the actual counts. In our model we consider the primitive elements of representation as abstract vectors. We also consider complex mathematical structures such as inverse image and fibration as parts of our representation. As a consequence, it would be incorrect to compare the dimensionality of a local trivialization of a vector bundle with the number of vector components in the previous models. Usually raising the dimensionality of vector representations is used to achieve better approximation and numerical stability of algorithms. Whether it is more appropriate to raise the dimensionality of the model (i. e., the rank of a vector bundle) or the number of harmonics used for approximation to achieve these goals in our case is an open question.

Another way of making the model more expressive is to incorporate other forms of dependent types, which are considered in type theoretical semantics, namely dependent sums and dot types. In the framework of Luo (2012) an adjective-noun pair is treated as an element of a dependent sum $\Sigma(x : A)B(x)$, where a noun is substituted for the x, e. g. a representation for *heavy book* is an object of type $\Sigma(\llbracket book \rrbracket, \llbracket heavy \rrbracket)$. Objects of this type are pairs (a, b), where a is a noun and b is a variant of an adjective adapted to the noun similarly to the way the verbs are adapted to their objects. In the geometric interpretation such a pair is an element of a direct product of the base space and the fiber over a point in the base. Since the elements of A and the elements of $\Sigma(x : A)B(x)$ are not directly comparable, a mechanism of type coercion is required to make such a construct work.

6 Conclusion

In this paper we proposed a geometric interpretation for a fragment of lexical semantics based on dependent type theory. The fragment includes the dependent product, which is the type of functions with a range dependent on the argument, therefore the fragment also includes function types of traditional formal semantics as a special case. The types are interpreted as vector spaces, which makes it possible to treat vector models of distributional semantics as a computational realization of a fragment of type-theoretical semantics. By making extensions suggested by the geometric interpretation, we achieve a significant increase in expressive power of the model while retaining control over its computability. The meaning evaluation technique arising from the geometric interpretation is compositional and allows for an analysis of non-trivial phenomena of logical polysemy and co-predication.

References

Nicholas Asher and James Pustejovsky. 2006. A type composition logic for generative lexicon. *Journal of Cognitive Science*, 6:1–38.

Nicholas Asher. 2011. *Lexical meaning in context: A web of words*. Cambridge University Press.

Marco Baroni and Roberto Zamparelli. 2010. Nouns are vectors, adjectives are matrices: Representing adjective-noun constructions in semantic space. In *Proceedings of the 2010 Conference on Empirical Methods in Natural Language Processing*, pages 1183–1193. Association for Computational Linguistics.

Marco Baroni, Raffaela Bernardi, and Roberto Zamparelli. 2014. Frege in space: A program of compositional distributional semantics. *Linguistic Issues in Language Technology*, 9.

Bob Coecke, Mehrnoosh Sadrzadeh, and Stephen Clark. 2010. Mathematical foundations for distributed compositional model of meaning. *Linguistic Analysis*, 36:345–384.

Robin Cooper. 2005. Records and record types in semantic theory. *Journal of Logic and Computation*, 15(2):99–112.

Scott Deerwester, Susan T. Dumais, George W. Furnas, Thomas K. Landauer, and Richard Harshman. 1990. Indexing by latent semantic analysis. *Journal of the American society for information science*, 41(6):391.

Katrin Erk and Sebastian Padó. 2008. A structured vector space model for word meaning in context. In *Proceedings of the Conference on Empirical Methods in Natural Language Processing*, pages 897–906. Association for Computational Linguistics.

Katrin Erk. 2009. Representing words as regions in vector space. In *Proceedings of the Thirteenth Conference on Computational Natural Language Learning*, pages 57–65. Association for Computational Linguistics.

Peter Gärdenfors. 2004. *Conceptual spaces: The geometry of thought*. MIT press.

Patrick Hanks. 1996. Contextual dependency and lexical sets. *International Journal of Corpus Linguistics*, 1(1):75–98.

Dimitri Kartsaklis, Mehrnoosh Sadrzadeh, and Stephen Pulman. 2013. Separating disambiguation from composition in distributional semantics. In *CoNLL*, pages 114–123.

Ran Lahav. 1989. Against compositionality: the case of adjectives. *Philosophical studies*, 57(3):261–279.

Thomas K. Landauer and Susan T. Dumais. 1997. A solution to Plato's problem: The latent semantic analysis theory of acquisition, induction, and representation of knowledge. *Psychological review*, 104(2):211.

Alessandro Lenci. 2008. Distributional semantics in linguistic and cognitive research. *Italian journal of linguistics*, 20(1):1–31.

Beth Levin. 1993. *English verb classes and alternations: A preliminary investigation*. University of Chicago press.

Percy Liang and Christopher Potts. 2015. Bringing machine learning and compositional semantics together. *Annu. Rev. Linguist.*, 1(1):355–376.

Glenys Luke and Alexander S. Mishchenko. 2013. *Vector bundles and their applications*, volume 447. Springer Science & Business Media.

Zhaohui Luo, Sergei Soloviev, and Tao Xue. 2013. Coercive subtyping: theory and implementation. *Information and Computation*, 223:18–42.

Zhaohui Luo. 2012. Formal semantics in modern type theories with coercive subtyping. *Linguistics and Philosophy*, 35(6):491–513.

Bruno Mery, Christian Bassac, and Christian Retoré. 2007. A montagovian generative lexicon. In *12th conference on Formal Grammar (FG 2007)*. CSLI Publications.

Tomas Mikolov, Ilya Sutskever, Kai Chen, Greg S. Corrado, and Jeff Dean. 2013. Distributed representations of words and phrases and their compositionality. In *Advances in neural information processing systems*, pages 3111–3119.

Jeff Mitchell and Mirella Lapata. 2010. Composition in distributional models of semantics. *Cognitive science*, 34(8):1388–1429.

Richard Montague. 1975. *Formal philosophy*.

Jeffrey Pennington, Richard Socher, and Christopher D. Manning. 2014. Glove: Global vectors for word representation. In *Empirical Methods in Natural Language Processing (EMNLP)*, pages 1532–1543.

James Pustejovsky. 1991. The generative lexicon. *Computational linguistics*, 17(4):409–441.

James Pustejovsky. 1995. *The generative lexicon*. Cambridge MA: MIT Press.

James Pustejovsky. 2013. Type theory and lexical decomposition. In *Advances in generative lexicon theory*, pages 9–38. Springer.

Aarne Ranta. 1994. *Type-theoretical grammar*.

Hinrich Schütze. 1998. Automatic word sense discrimination. *Computational linguistics*, 24(1):97–123.

Paul Smolensky. 1990. Tensor product variable binding and the representation of symbolic structures in connectionist systems. *Artificial intelligence*, 46(1):159–216.

Richard Socher, Alex Perelygin, Jean Y. Wu, Jason Chuang, Christopher D. Manning, Andrew Y. Ng, and Christopher Potts. 2013. Recursive deep models for semantic compositionality over a sentiment treebank. In *Proceedings of the conference on empirical methods in natural language processing (EMNLP)*, volume 1631, page 1642.

Kenneth N. Stevens. 1972. The quantal nature of speech: Evidence from articulatory-acoustic data. *Human communication: A unified view*, pages 51–66.

Stefan Thater, Hagen Fürstenau, and Manfred Pinkal. 2010. Contextualizing semantic representations using syntactically enriched vector models. In *Proceedings of the 48th Annual Meeting of the Association for Computational Linguistics*, pages 948–957. Association for Computational Linguistics.

Stefan Thater, Hagen Fürstenau, and Manfred Pinkal. 2011. Word meaning in context: A simple and effective vector model. In *IJCNLP*, pages 1134–1143.

Masashi Tsubaki, Kevin Duh, Masashi Shimbo, and Yuji Matsumoto. 2013. Modeling and learning semantic co-compositionality through prototype projections and neural networks. In *EMNLP*, pages 130–140.

The Univalent Foundations Program. 2013. *Homotopy Type Theory: Univalent Foundations of Mathematics*. https://homotopytypetheory.org/book, Institute for Advanced Study.

Tim Van de Cruys, Thierry Poibeau, and Anna Korhonen. 2013. A tensor-based factorization model of semantic compositionality. In *Conference of the North American Chapter of the Association of Computational Linguistics (HTL-NAACL)*, pages 1142–1151.

Dominic Widdows. 2008. Semantic vector products: Some initial investigations. In *Second AAAI Symposium on Quantum Interaction*, volume 26.

Luke S. Zettlemoyer and Michael Collins. 2012. Learning to map sentences to logical form: Structured classification with probabilistic categorial grammars. *arXiv preprint arXiv:1207.1420.*

Towards Generalizable Sentence Embeddings

Eleni Triantafillou, Jamie Ryan Kiros, Raquel Urtasun, Richard Zemel
Department of Computer Science
University of Toronto
{eleni, rkiros, urtasun, zemel}@cs.toronto.edu

Abstract

In this work, we evaluate different sentence encoders with emphasis on examining their embedding spaces. Specifically, we hypothesize that a "high-quality" embedding aids in generalization, promoting transfer learning as well as zero-shot and one-shot learning. To investigate this, we modify Skipthought vectors to learn a more generalizable space by exploiting a small amount of supervision. The aim is to introduce an additional notion of similarity in the embeddings, rendering the vectors informative for different tasks requiring less adaptation. Our embeddings capture human intuition on similarity favorably than competing models, while we also show positive indications of transfer from the task of natural language inference to paraphrase detection and paraphrase ranking. Further, our model's behaviour on paraphrase detection when trained with an increasing amount of labelled data is indicative of a generalizable model. Finally, we support our hypothesis on generalizability of our embeddings through inspection of their statistics.

1 Introduction

Natural language is an integral part of numerous applications, such as web search, information retrieval, and automatic text summarization, to name just a few. Therefore, constructing high-quality text representations is very important. In addition, despite having well-established methods to construct word representations, it remains an open problem to capture the semantics of larger pieces of text in a vector that is useful for different tasks with minimal adaptation. In this paper we report

on our efforts towards building such generalizable sentence representations.

Representing a sentence as a vector can be thought of as "embedding" it into a high-dimensional space. Therefore, a meaningful representation relies on a function which sends "related" sentences to neighbouring points in this vector space. There are, however, many possible notions of closeness that may be desirably reflected in the embeddings. For instance, two sentences could be considered similar if they are likely to be found in the same context ("distributional similarity"), or if the second is entailed from the first, or if they are paraphrases of each other.

We hypothesize that an embedding space which adheres to multiple of these notions can host more generalizable vectors. For instance our hypothesis is that in a "generalizable" space, two sentences that are likely to be found in the same context and also entail each other are closer that two other sentences which are also likely to be found in the same context but contradict each other.

Moreover, we believe that "supervised evaluation" of sentence encoders is not informative of the embedding quality: a classifier is trained on top of the sentence embeddings and then the accuracy for the task is computed, and is used as a proxy for the quality of the embeddings. This approach has the disadvantage that it hides the embedding properties due to the extra training which allows to mend its potential shortcomings. We instead focus our attention on directly inspecting the model space.

In this work, we introduce a sentence encoder that is learned by injecting supervised information from the Stanford Natural Language Inference (SNLI) dataset (Bowman et al., 2015) in the commonly used Skipthought embeddings. The aim is to enhance the embeddings with an additional notion of similarity, rendering them more generalizable. We experiment with this model and with

Proceedings of the 1st Workshop on Representation Learning for NLP, pages 239–248,
Berlin, Germany, August 11th, 2016. ©2016 Association for Computational Linguistics

sentence encoders of different training objectives in order to compare both their performance in the commonly used supervised fashion (Kiros et al., 2015; Collobert et al., 2011; Mikolov et al., 2013a; Wieting et al., 2015) for reference, but more importantly their embedding quality. We perform supervised evaluation on paraphrase detection, semantic relatedness, natural language inference and various classification benchmarks. We then evaluate the embeddings through paraphrase ranking, correlation of their similarity notion with human judgements (Hill et al., 2016; Hill et al., 2015; Levy et al., 2015; Baroni et al., 2014), through paraphrase detection with little or no training, and through examination of embedding statistics.

2 Related Work

The Skip-gram model for word embeddings (Mikolov et al., 2013a; Mikolov et al., 2013b), is trained on a text corpus with the objective of predicting the vectors of the surrounding words of a given word, when conditioned on its vector representation. Its success inspired Kiros et al. (2015) to create its sentence analogue, Skipthought vectors, which are trained by predicting the surrounding sentences when conditioned on the current one. Despite this simple objective, Skipthoughts perform remarkably well on various tasks: semantic relatedness, paraphrase detection, image-sentence ranking, and a number of classification benchmarks. In this paper we investigate how we can improve their embedding space through injecting small amounts of supervised information.

Aside from Skipthoughts, there are numerous sentence encoders. (Socher et al., 2013; Yin and Schütze, 2015; Wang and Nyberg, 2015; Socher et al., 2014) create sentence encoders which are optimized for a specific task of interest. On the other hand, methods which aim at constructing "universal" embeddings include (Le and Mikolov, 2014; Socher et al., 2011; Li et al., 2015; Pham et al., 2015). Le and Mikolov (2014) learn paragraph embeddings by predicting sentences within a paragraph when conditioned on its representation, Pham et al. (2015) predict context in all levels of a syntactic tree, whereas Socher et al. (2011) and Li et al. (2015) present autoencoder-type models.

Hill et al. (2016) presented an extensive evaluation of unsupervised sentence encoders. They showed that Bag of Words (BOW) models on av-erage perform on par with non-BOW models. Our results agree with this and we provide a possible explanation through examining the statistics of the datasets used for evaluation. An important distinction between our work and theirs is that Hill et al. (2016) focused on models that were trained in an unsupervised fashion, whereas we also present models finetuned or trained on SNLI for natural language inference.

Wieting et al. (2015) learned "universal" sentence vectors by exploiting a database of paraphrases: they optimize an objective which encourages paraphrases to lie closer to each other in space than to negative examples. Similarly to their work, we also use supervised information to construct informative embeddings, but our supervision comes from the task of natural language inference.

Transfer learning is the process of exploiting knowledge from one task or domain in order to benefit from it for a different ("target") task or domain. This method has enjoyed considerable success in computer vision applications (notably the use of features derived from neural networks trained for object classification such as (Krizhevsky et al., 2012) for other tasks) but is less successful in language applications. Collobert and Weston (2008) perform mutli-task learning on various natural language processing tasks and report a very small gain for each task. Mou et al. (2016) presented negative results on their effort to transfer from the task of natural language inference to paraphrase detection. In this work, we show positive results on transfer from natural language inference to paraphrase detection and to the related task of paraphrase ranking.

3 Models

The success of Skipthoughts verify that predicting the "context" of a sentence is a valuable objective. However, sentences are also a nontrivial function of the words comprising them, so we believe that explicitly capturing their "content" in addition to their "context" can yield more informative embeddings.

Therefore, we experimented with several ways of capturing content, and evaluate the quality of content-only encoders as well as that of an encoder that combines a content with a context objective. The content-only models we use are two autoencoders (AEs): a BOW one which we refer to as "BOW AE", and a Recurrent Neural Netowrk (RNN)-based one, referred to as "RNN AE". BOW AE is the model proposed in (Lauly et al., 2014) which encodes the sentence as a vector that indicates which vocabulary words are present in the sentence, irrespective of their order. The objective is to reconstruct this indicator vector when given a nonlinear function of the sum of the embeddings of the present words according to the indicator. RNN AE, on the other hand, uses an RNN encoder with GRU units to represent the sentence and a similar RNN decoder which is trained to predict the same sentence when conditioned on its encoded representation. We trained these models on the Toronto book corpus (Zhu et al., 2015).

We also made use of the SNLI dataset for the purpose of capturing content, and created 3 "SNLI models": a BOW and an RNN-based "content SNLI" models, which we refer to as "SNLI BOW" and "SNLI RNN", respectively, as well as a finetuned version of Skipthoughts which we argue has encoded a combination of context and content and refer to as "SNLI-finetuned Skipthoughts". These 3 SNLI models are illustrated in Figure 1.

SNLI is comprised of pairs of sentences with a label of "entailment", "contradiction", or "neutral" associated with each pair. Each SNLI model creates the representation of each sentence of the given pair separately (but using the same encoder), and then concatenates the two sentence embeddings, and feeds these into a single hidden layer neural network, with a softmax on top for the three-way classification of SNLI. We backpropagate through the encoder and the word embeddings as well. In the case of SNLI-finetuned Skipthoughts, the encoder is initialized from Skipthoughts, and subsequently finetuned to add "content-based" SNLI information. On the other hand, the encoder of SNLI BOW merely corresponds to the sum of the word embeddings (which are initialized from Skipthought word embeddings and modified during training), while the encoder of SNLI RNN is an RNN which is initialized "from scratch".

An overview of the model space is presented in figure 2.

4   Training Details

The Skipthought model that we compare with in the experiments is the model which is referred to as combine-skip in (Kiros et al., 2015). This

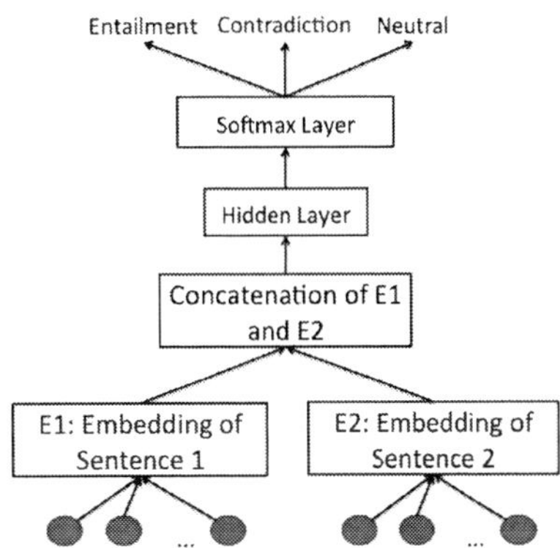

Figure 1: The 3 SNLI models are all formed from the same formulation, illustrated above. For SNLI-finetuned Skipthoughts, E1 and E2 are initialized to the Skipthought Encoder, for SNLI BOW E1 and E2 are the sum of the word embeddings and for SNLI RNN E1 and E2 are an RNN encoder which is initialized from scratch.

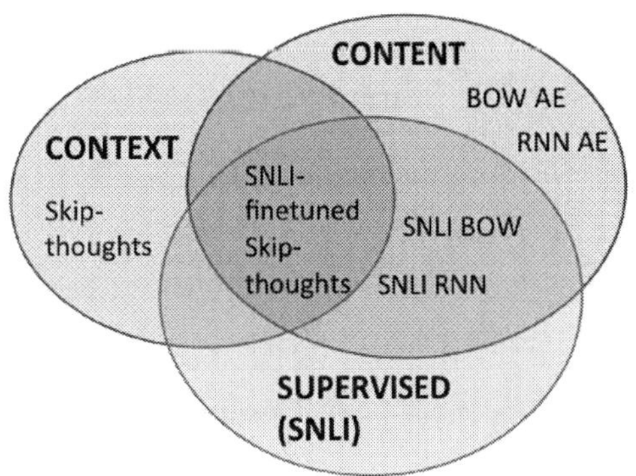

Figure 2: An overview of the models used in the experiments of this paper.

model is created from the combination of two separate encoders: a "uni-directional" and a "bi-directional" one. The uni-directional model is comprised of an RNN encoder with GRU units whose hidden state consists of 4800 dimensions. The bi-directional model is the concatenation of a 1200-dimensional GRU RNN encoder which reads the sentence in forward order (from left to right) and an equally sized GRU RNN encoder which reads the sentence in reverse order. After the separate training of the uni-directional and bi-directional models, their representations are combined for the creation of the 4800-dimensional combine-skip embedding.

In order to fairly compare with the combine-skip model, we have created the analogous SNLI-finetuned Skipthoughts model. The uni-directional and bi-directional Skipthought models were finetuned separately using the architecture mentioned in the previous section (Figure 1) and subsequently combined to yield 4800-dimensional embeddings. This is the model which we refer to as SNLI-finetuned Skipthoughts in the remainder of this paper.

The word embeddings of all 3 SNLI models and the 2 autoencoder models was initialized from the Skipthought word embeddings, which are 620-dimensional. The RNN of SNLI RNN, and the en-coder and decoder RNNs of RNN AE have GRU units and their hidden state is 2400-dimensional. We initialized these recurrent weights with orthog-onal initialization (Saxe et al., 2013). The non-recurrent weights of the hidden and softmax layers for the SNLI models are initialized from a uniform distribution in the range [-0.1, 0.1].

Adam optimizer (Kingma and Ba, 2014) was used for training all of these models.

In the following sections we present our results in two evaluation settings: Firstly, we perform supervised evaluation (Section 5), and then more importantly we directly evaluate the embedding space of the different models (Section 6).

5 Supervised Evaluation

In this section we present results on a number of supervised tasks. These results are obtained by encoding the sentence at hand (or each sentence of the pair when applicable) and using this encod-ing as the features of a logistic regression which is trained for the given task, following the approach in (Kiros et al., 2015). For the tasks involving pairs of sentences, the features that were given to the logistic classifier were computed as follows: the element-wise product and absolute difference between the two sentence embeddings were com-puted and then concatenated, resulting in a 9600-dimensional vector, as was also done in (Kiros et al., 2015). In the next paragraph we briefly de-scribe the tasks that we report experiments on.

Paraphrase detection (MSRP dataset) is the task where given pairs of sentences, the goal is to as-sign a binary label indicating whether the sen-tences of each pair are paraphrases. For seman-tic relatedness we use SICK (Marelli et al., 2014), and the objective is to assign a score of related-ness in the range 1-5 to pairs of sentences. Nat-ural language inference is the task of predicting a label of "entailment", "contradiction", or "neu-tral" for each pair. Note that SNLI is a dataset for this task, but the results we report here are on SICK, which has both relatedness scores as well as these 3-way classifications labels for each pair. TREC is a dataset for (6-way) question-type clas-sification and finally, MR and SUBJ come from a movie review dataset and they are binary classifi-cation tasks for sentiment polarity (MR) and sub-jectivity status (SUBJ).

The results are shown in tables 1, 2, 3, and 4. In all tables, we use the following abbrevi-ations for model names. ST: Skipthoughts, FT-ST: SNLI-FineTuned Skipthoughts, BOW: SNLI-BOW, RNN: SNLI-RNN. Results which outper-form or perform on par with Skipthoughts are shown in bold, since Skipthoughts have shown to perform remarkably well in this supervised evalu-ation setting as demonstrated in detail in (Kiros et al., 2015), and verified in (Hill et al., 2016).

	ST	FT-ST	BOW	RNN	BOW-AE	RNN-AE
test acc	0.73	**0.75**	0.70	0.71	0.71	0.67
test f1	0.82	**0.83**	0.80	0.81	0.80	0.80

Table 1: Results on paraphrase detection (MSRP).

	ST	FT-ST	BOW	RNN	BOW-AE	RNN-AE
test acc	0.80	**0.83**	**0.81**	**0.82**	0.79	0.75

Table 2: Results on natural language inference (SICK). Note that this is the same task as SNLI, but different dataset.

	ST	FT-ST	BOW	RNN	BOW-AE	RNN-AE
test PR	0.84	**0.85**	0.81	0.82	0.79	0.70
test SR	0.78	**0.79**	0.76	0.77	0.72	0.64
test SE	0.30	**0.28**	0.36	0.34	0.39	0.52

Table 3: Results on semantic relatedness (SICK). PR, SR, SE: Pearson, Spearman correlation coeffi-cient and mean squared error, resp. between model scores and human scores.

Overall, the most important observation is that a lot of these results are very comparable, with the reported numbers being within a small range in most cases, despite the very different nature of these models. For example, the fact that SNLI-RNN performs comparably with Skipthoughts on Semantic Relatedness is surprising given their training objectives. Recall that the encoder in SNLI-RNN was initialized from scratch. This fact

	ST	FT-ST	BOW	RNN	BOW-AE	RNN-AE
MR	0.76	**0.79**	**0.76**	0.71	0.75	0.65
SUBJ	0.94	**0.94**	0.93	0.89	0.92	0.86
TREC	0.92	**0.92**	0.86	0.87	0.85	0.82

Table 4: Results on various classification tasks. Each row stores test accuracies of the corresponding dataset.

	ST	FT-ST	BOW	RNN	BOW-AE	RNN-AE
accuracy@1	0.63	0.77	0.87	0.56	**0.90**	0.33
accuracy@10	0.74	0.86	0.93	0.67	**0.96**	0.40
accuracy@100	0.86	0.96	0.99	0.84	**1**	0.54
MRC	93	15	6	97	**2**	455

Table 5: Results on paraphrase ranking. accuracy@k is the proportion of sentences for which the true paraphrase received rank at most k. MRC is the Mean Rank of the Correct paraphrase.

could suggest that SNLI information, when injected into an RNN encoder and fed into a logistic regression classifier, is adequate in order to perform reasonably well on paraphrase detection and semantic relatedness. But we believe that this observation underlines the weakness of this method of evaluation.

The 2% improvment of SNLI-Finetuned Skipthoughts over skipthoughts for paraphrase detection is an indication of transfer from SNLI to MSRP, on which (Mou et al., 2016) presented negative results. Our results on transfer to the related task of paraphrase ranking which also uses MSRP (Section 6.1) are even more encouraging.

Further, on natural language inference all SNLI models (slightly) outperform the non-SNLI ones. This is not surprising given their training objective, and constitutes a less impressive sign of transfer between these two datasets of the same task.

Finally, we note that SNLI-finetuned Skipthoughts perform either better or on par with Skipthoughts on all tasks considered. This shows that the added SNLI information does not hurt Skipthoughts' performance on this evaluation while outperforming it in terms of embedding space quality as demonstrated in the next section, which we argue is more important.

6 Evalutating Embedding Spaces directly

In this section we evaluate the embedding quality directly. We do this firstly through paraphrase ranking, secondly though correlating embedding similarity with human scores, thirdly through paraphrase detection with few or no labelled examples, and finally through examination of the statistics of the embeddings.

6.1 Paraphrase Ranking

Paraphrase ranking is the task of assigning a rank to each sentence from a pool S, representing how likely they are to be paraphrases of a given sentence. To compute the ranks that S_1 assigns to the

sentences, $sim(v_1, v_2)$ is computed $\forall S_2 \neq S_1 \in S$, where sim stands for cosine similarity and v_1 and v_2 are the embeddings of S_1 and S_2, respectively. Ranks are then assigned by sorting these similarities in decreasing order. In this setting, the sentence to which S_1 assigns rank 1 is predicted to be its paraphrase.

For this, we used the sentences from the MSRP dataset, which is comprised of pairs of sentences with a binary label indicating whether or not they are paraphrases. We "break" the pair ties and treat all sentences as members of a large pool, making use of the (binary) labels of MSRP in order to yield the (non-binary) label for this new task. We use both the training and test set of MSRP for this, totalling over 11000 sentences. The evaluation metrics we used are "Mean Rank of the Correct paraphrase", referred to as MRC from now on, and accuracy@k which is the proportion of sentences for which the true paraphrase is contained in the top k ranked sentences.

The results are shown in Table 5. We observe that BOW AE outperforms Skipthoughts by a large margin, with BOW following closely behind. In fact, it is not a coincidence that BOW models perform well on this task. To investigate this effect even further, we created a very simple BOW model which represents the sentence as the sum of its word embeddings, which are randomly generated 620-length vectors. Its performance is shown in Table 6. This model is in no way informative of the semantics, syntax, structure, or any useful property of the sentence whatsoever, and yet it outperforms Skipthoughts for example. This problematic behavior may be due to the fact that sentences in pairs with positive labels in MSRP have a very high word overlap. This suggests that any BOW model has an unfair advantage when evaluated on this dataset. We elaborate on this in the Discussion section, and provide statistics from the datasets to support this hypothesis.

However, the comparison between

Skipthoughts and SNLI-finetuned Skipthoughts here is valuable. The superiority of the latter model constitutes positive results of transfer from SNLI to paraphrase ranking using MSRP, supporting our conjecture regarding the generalizability of the SNLI-finetuned Skipthought space.

	random BOW
accuracy@1	79
accuracy@10	88
accuracy@100	96
MRC	21

Table 6: Very simple baseline for paraphrase ranking. random BOW is no way capturing anything informative about the sentence (see section 5.1 for description). These results suggest that BOW models may have an unfair advantage for MSRP.

6.2 Semantic Relatedness

SICK is comprised of pairs of sentences, each associated with a relatedness score in the range from 1 to 5. In order to directly evaluate the merit of the embeddings in capturing semantics, we used cosine similarity to estimate the relatedness of each pair. These similarity scores were then correlated with the human-annotated scores using Pearson's and Spearman's correlation coefficients and mean squared error. The results are shown in Table 7.

	ST	FT-ST	BOW	RNN	BOW-AE	RNN-AE
test PR	0.50	0.57	0.69	0.62	0.64	0.39
test SR	0.48	0.56	0.65	0.59	0.57	0.39
test SE	1.53	1.10	1.12	0.98	1.21	1.84

Table 7: Results on semantic relatedness (SICK) based on cosine distances. PR, SR, SE: Pearson, Spearman correlation coefficient and mean squared error, resp. between model scores and human scores.

As was the case for the MSRP dataset, we believe that SICK offers an unfair advantage to BOW models, therefore we do not believe that the success of BOW AE and SNLI BOW is necessarily indicative of their quality.

We observe that SNLI-Finetuned Skipthoughts outperform Skipthoughts on this task as well, supporting the conjecture that adding supervision through SNLI has lead to a more informative space. Moreover, the performance of SNLI RNN is impressive, outperforming both Skipthought-based models. Finally, out of the BOW models,

the SNLI one performs better than the AE one. These are indications that SNLI information can aid in inducing a notion of similarity which is compatible with human intuition.

6.3 Towards Zero Shot Paraphrase Detection

We claimed earlier that learning an informative embedding space would facilitate zero-shot and one-shot learning applications. The aim of this section is to investigate whether SNLI-finetuned Skipthoughts are a more appropriate model for this purpose than the other models we explored.

By zero-shot paraphrase detection, we refer to the task of predicting a binary label for the "paraphrase status" of a pair of sentences without performing any training for this task. This amounts to choosing a threshold so that a pair is classified positively if and only if the similarity of its sentence embeddings surpasses this threshold. Since the choice of such a threshold is not obvious, we present the precision-recall curve in Figure 3 which corresponds to multiple thresholds.

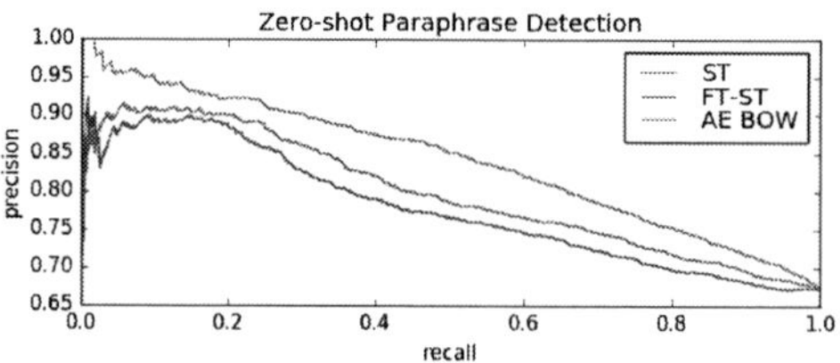

Figure 3: Precision-Recall curve for zero-shot paraphrase detection. (FT-)ST stands for (SNLI-Finetuned) Skipthoughts.

In figure 3 we have included the best-performing model for this task for reference, which is BOW AE, but we are more interested in the comparison between Skipthoughts and SNLI-Finetuned Skipthoughts. This is because we believe that the success of BOW AE on this task does not necessarily reflect its merit as a sentence encoder, as we elaborate on in the Discussion section.

The superior performance of SNLI-finetuned Skipthoughts in Figure 3 advocates for the generalizability of the former model since it requires less adaptation for paraphrase detection compared to Skipthoughts.

It is also interesting to investigate the behavior of our models when given various amounts of training data for the task of paraphrase detection.

For this, we plot in Figure 4 how the test set accuracy increases as more data is fed into the models.

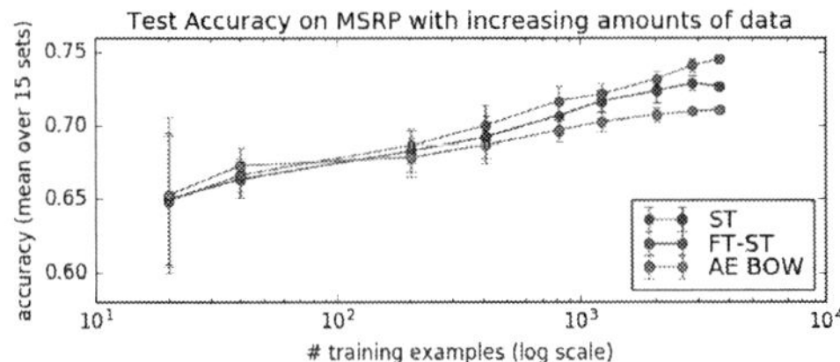

Figure 4: Test accuracy when an increasing amount of data was used for training. (FT-)ST stands for (SNLI-Finetuned) Skipthoughts.

We notice that AE BOW is less "data hungry" in that its performance ceases to increase significantly with the increase of data. SNLI-Finetuned Skipthoughts reach higher accuracy than Skipthoughts when given the same amount of data, supporting its aptness for one shot learning.

Figure 4 justifies the fact that Skipthought-based models outperform BOW AE in the supervised evaluation setting even though these roles are reversed in the zero-shot setting of Section 5. In particular, it appears that BOW AE is less capable of taking advantage of training data to improve its quality.

6.4 Diving into Embedding Space

In this section, we use the sentences from MSRP and examine their relationships in model space. The histograms in Figure 5 show the distribution of the pairwise-similarity for these sentences in Skipthought and SNLI-Finetuned Skipthought spaces.

Crucially, we observe that in Skipthought space, pairwise sentence similarities are significantly higher than in its SNLI-Finetuned variant, and there is less variation. This behavior can be attributed to their training objective. In particular, two sentences are neighbours in this space if they are likely to be found in the same contexts, resulting to sentences such as "I love sushi", "I really really like sushi" and "I hate sushi" to be possibly equidistant neighbours.

On the other hand, the histogram for SNLI-Finetuned Skipthoughts contains more variation, which we conjecture is due to the fact that a second notion of relatedness is introduced, which pushes sentences with contradictory meanings further away from each other, in order to keep sentences which entail each other close.

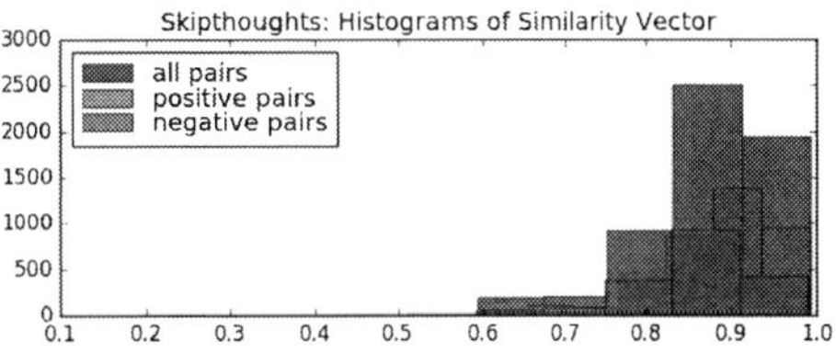

(a) Skipthought Space

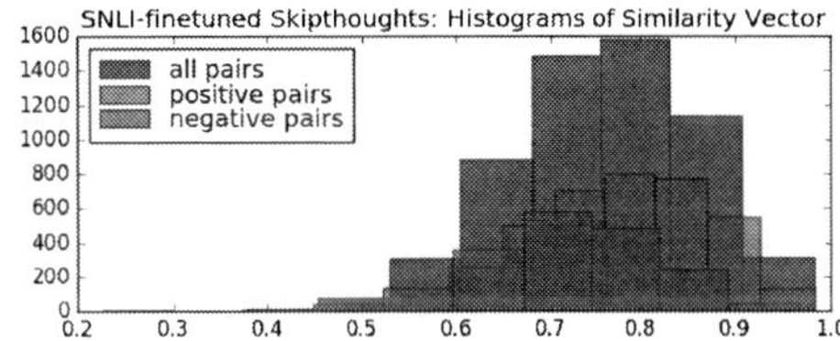

(b) SNLI-Finetuned Skipthought Space

Figure 5: Distribution of Pairwise Similarities in Embedding Space (best viewed in color). Green and red denote positive and negative pairs, respectively.

Moreover, it is of interest to examine the red and green histograms, corresponding to the distributions of pair-wise similarities for positively and negatively labelled pairs, respectively. In both cases the similarity for green tends to be higher than that for red, as desired. However, in the case of SNLI-Finetuned Skipthoughts this separation is more prominent, possibly justifying the better performance shown in the precision recall curve in Figure 3.

7 Discussion

In this section we discuss a limitation of the datasets used for evaluation. Specifically, both MSRP and SICK have a high mean proportion of common words between the two sentences of the pairs. Further, this average is significantly higher for "positive pairs" (ie. labelled as paraphrases in the case of MSRP, or assigned a high human relatedness score, for the case of SICK), than it is for "negative" pairs. Figure 6 shows the histograms for the distribution of word overlap between pairs of sentences from these datasets, where word overlap for a pair is the proportion of words that are common between its two sentences.

Therefore, it may be inappropriate to draw conclusions on the quality of BOW models merely from their superior performance on these datasets. For example, models like the baseline in Table 6 are not expected to generalize to other tasks. We

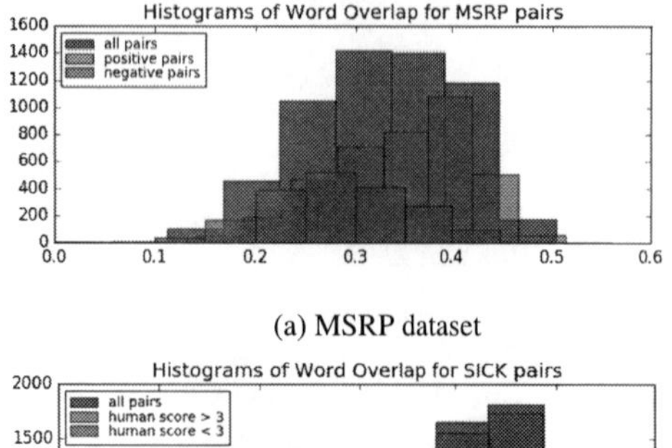

(a) MSRP dataset

(b) SICK dataset

Figure 6: Distribution of Pairwise Word Overlap in MSRP and SICK (best viewed in color)

Group 1
- There is steam coming out of my soup
- My tongue got burned when I tasted my soup
- I just heated up my soup

Group 2
- My soup is very cold
- My tongue did not get burned when I tasted my soup
- My soup is not hot anymore

Figure 7: Our small dataset for evaluating how well the encoders have captured "latent" relatedness (which does not rely on common word identification)

remind the reader that this model represents a sentence as a sum of its word embeddings, which are randomly-generated vectors. We do not expect this to capture any meaningful aspects of sentences, but yet it performs well in this setting. On the other hand, more complicated models like Skipthoughts, SNLI-finetuned Skipthoughts, SNLI RNN, and RNN AE attempt to capture a "latent" notion of relatedness, which does not rely on identifying common words. These models are unfairly penalized in this setting, rendering comparisons between these and BOW models irrelevant.

However, we believe that comparisons between models from within this "more complicated" group are still valid. For example, it is appropriate to compare Skipthoughts with SNLI-Finetuned Skipthoughts on these datasets: they both make the same effort to capture the more abstract sense of relatedness, and are in this sense equally penalized when evaluated on these datasets.

The histograms in Figure 6 underline the need for creation of high-quality datasets to evaluate a model's understanding of "latent" relatedness. For this, we have put together a small number of sentences, grouped into two semantically contradictory groups, as shown in Figure 7. Each model was used to compute the similarities of all pairs and assign ranks in the same way as for paraphrase ranking. The aim is to assign lower ranks (higher similarities) to sentences from the same group as the current sentence, than to sentences from the contradictory group.

The results for the ranks and corresponding similarities that sentence "My soup is not hot anymore" assigns to the rest of the sentences are displayed in Table 8.

SNLI-Skipthoughts, SNLI BOW, SNLI RNN and BOW AE all assign the two highest ranks to the remaining sentences of Group 2, as desired. This means that they all have perfect average precision, outperforming Skipthoughts. However, it is more important to examine the "closeness" of these sentences in space (columns "sim" of Table 8). BOW AE, for example, produces a perfect ranking but sentences with ranks 2, 3 and 4 have approximately equal similarity with the "reference" sentence, casting doubts on the quality of the embeddings.

With this in mind, maybe the best performing method for this small group of sentences is SNLI RNN: the similarities between sentences of Group 2 with the reference sentence are much higher than those between Group 1 sentences and the reference sentence. Specifically, there is a gap of 13% between the lowest similarity with a Group 2 sentence and the highest with a Group 1 sentence. SNLI BOW is second best according to this metric, followed by SNLI-Skipthoughts.

This dataset is far too small to draw confident conclusions from but these results may serve as a preliminary indication of the benefit of SNLI information for separating semantically contradictory sentences and understanding "latent" relatedness.

8 Conclusion

In conclusion, we have exploited supervised information from SNLI to enrich the model

Skipthoughts		SNLI-Skipthoughts		SNLI BOW		SNLI RNN		BOW AE	
sim	Sentence	*sim*	Sentence	*sim*	Sentence	*sim*	Sentence	*sim*	Sentence
0.61	**My soup is very cold**	0.48	**My soup is very cold**	0.59	**My tongue did not get burned ...**	0.51	**My tongue did not get burned ...**	0.51	**My soup is very cold**
0.43	There is steam ...	0.32	**My tongue did not get burned ...**	0.45	**My soup is very cold**	0.47	**My soup is very cold**	0.35	**My tongue did not get burned ...**
0.39	I just heated ...	0.29	I just heated ...	0.39	My tongue got burned ...	0.34	My tongue got burned ...	0.35	I just heated ...
0.39	**My tongue did not get burned ...**	0.29	There is steam ...	0.37	I just heated ...	0.30	I just heated ...	0.35	There is steam ...
0.38	My tongue got burned ...	0.28	My tongue got burned ...	0.32	There is steam ...	0.28	There is steam ...	0.31	My tongue got burned ...

Table 8: Results of the ranking task for the reference sentence **My soup is not hot anymore**. *sim* refers to the similarity between the reference sentence and the sentence of the corresponding row in embedding space. Sentences which are "relevant" to this one (**Group 2**), and thus should receive lower ranks, are shown in bold.

space of Skipthoughts, inducing SNLI-Finetuned Skipthoughts. Aside from performing better or on par with Skipthoughts on the supervised evaluations, this model exhibits properties of a superior embedding space. We report results on transfer from SNLI to MSRP in Table 1, and more encouraging results from SNLI to paraphrase ranking in Table 5. We also showed that SNLI-induced embedding spaces capture human intuition about relatedness favorably to other models. Finally, SNLI-finetuned Skipthoughts perform better than its competitors when few or no labelled examples are available for paraphrase detection.

References

Marco Baroni, Georgiana Dinu, and Germán Kruszewski. 2014. Don't count, predict! a systematic comparison of context-counting vs. context-predicting semantic vectors. In *ACL (1)*, pages 238–247.

Samuel R Bowman, Gabor Angeli, Christopher Potts, and Christopher D Manning. 2015. A large annotated corpus for learning natural language inference. *arXiv preprint arXiv:1508.05326*.

Ronan Collobert and Jason Weston. 2008. A unified architecture for natural language processing: Deep neural networks with multitask learning. In *Proceedings of the 25th international conference on Machine learning*, pages 160–167. ACM.

Ronan Collobert, Jason Weston, Léon Bottou, Michael Karlen, Koray Kavukcuoglu, and Pavel Kuksa. 2011. Natural language processing (almost) from scratch. *The Journal of Machine Learning Research*, 12:2493–2537.

Felix Hill, Kyunghyun Cho, Anna Korhonen, and Yoshua Bengio. 2015. Learning to understand phrases by embedding the dictionary. *arXiv preprint arXiv:1504.00548*.

Felix Hill, Kyunghyun Cho, and Anna Korhonen. 2016. Learning distributed representations of sentences from unlabelled data. *arXiv preprint arXiv:1602.03483*.

Diederik Kingma and Jimmy Ba. 2014. Adam: A method for stochastic optimization. *arXiv preprint arXiv:1412.6980*.

Ryan Kiros, Yukun Zhu, Ruslan R Salakhutdinov, Richard Zemel, Raquel Urtasun, Antonio Torralba, and Sanja Fidler. 2015. Skip-thought vectors. In *Advances in Neural Information Processing Systems*, pages 3276–3284.

Alex Krizhevsky, Ilya Sutskever, and Geoffrey E Hinton. 2012. Imagenet classification with deep convolutional neural networks. In *Advances in neural information processing systems*, pages 1097–1105.

Stanislas Lauly, Hugo Larochelle, Mitesh Khapra, Balaraman Ravindran, Vikas C Raykar, and Amrita Saha. 2014. An autoencoder approach to learning bilingual word representations. In *Advances in Neural Information Processing Systems*, pages 1853–1861.

Quoc V Le and Tomas Mikolov. 2014. Distributed representations of sentences and documents. *arXiv preprint arXiv:1405.4053*.

Omer Levy, Yoav Goldberg, and Ido Dagan. 2015. Improving distributional similarity with lessons learned from word embeddings. *Transactions of the Association for Computational Linguistics*, 3:211–225.

Jiwei Li, Minh-Thang Luong, and Dan Jurafsky. 2015. A hierarchical neural autoencoder for paragraphs and documents. *arXiv preprint arXiv:1506.01057*.

Marco Marelli, Luisa Bentivogli, Marco Baroni, Raffaella Bernardi, Stefano Menini, and Roberto Zamparelli. 2014. Semeval-2014 task 1: Evaluation of compositional distributional semantic models on full sentences through semantic relatedness and textual entailment. *SemEval-2014*.

Tomas Mikolov, Kai Chen, Greg Corrado, and Jeffrey Dean. 2013a. Efficient estimation of word representations in vector space. *arXiv preprint arXiv:1301.3781*.

Tomas Mikolov, Ilya Sutskever, Kai Chen, Greg S Corrado, and Jeff Dean. 2013b. Distributed representations of words and phrases and their compositionality. In *Advances in neural information processing systems*, pages 3111–3119.

Lili Mou, Zhao Meng, Rui Yan, Ge Li, Yan Xu, Lu Zhang, and Zhi Jin. 2016. How transferable are neural networks in nlp applications? *arXiv preprint arXiv:1603.06111*.

Nghia The Pham, Germán Kruszewski, Angeliki Lazaridou, and Marco Baroni. 2015. Jointly optimizing word representations for lexical and sentential tasks with the c-phrase model. In *Proceedings of ALC*.

Andrew M Saxe, James L McClelland, and Surya Ganguli. 2013. Exact solutions to the nonlinear dynamics of learning in deep linear neural networks. *arXiv preprint arXiv:1312.6120*.

Richard Socher, Eric H Huang, Jeffrey Pennin, Christopher D Manning, and Andrew Y Ng. 2011. Dynamic pooling and unfolding recursive autoencoders for paraphrase detection. In *Advances in Neural Information Processing Systems*, pages 801–809.

Richard Socher, Alex Perelygin, Jean Y Wu, Jason Chuang, Christopher D Manning, Andrew Y Ng, and Christopher Potts. 2013. Recursive deep models for semantic compositionality over a sentiment treebank. In *Proceedings of the conference on empirical methods in natural language processing (EMNLP)*, volume 1631, page 1642. Citeseer.

Richard Socher, Andrej Karpathy, Quoc V Le, Christopher D Manning, and Andrew Y Ng. 2014. Grounded compositional semantics for finding and describing images with sentences. *Transactions of the Association for Computational Linguistics*, 2:207–218.

Di Wang and Eric Nyberg. 2015. A long short-term memory model for answer sentence selection in question answering. *ACL, July*.

John Wieting, Mohit Bansal, Kevin Gimpel, and Karen Livescu. 2015. Towards universal paraphrastic sentence embeddings. *arXiv preprint arXiv:1511.08198*.

Wenpeng Yin and Hinrich Schütze. 2015. Convolutional neural network for paraphrase identification. In *Proceedings of the 2015 Conference of the North American Chapter of the Association for Computational Linguistics: Human Language Technologies*, pages 901–911.

Yukun Zhu, Ryan Kiros, Rich Zemel, Ruslan Salakhutdinov, Raquel Urtasun, Antonio Torralba, and Sanja Fidler. 2015. Aligning books and movies: Towards story-like visual explanations by watching movies and reading books. In *Proceedings of the IEEE International Conference on Computer Vision*, pages 19–27.

Domain Adaptation for Neural Networks by Parameter Augmentation

Yusuke Watanabe
SONY
1-7-1 Konan Minato-ku,
Tokyo, Japan
YusukeB.Watanabe@jp.sony.com

Kazuma Hashimoto, Yoshimasa Tsuruoka
University of Tokyo
7-3-1 Hongo, Bunkyo-ku,
Tokyo, Japan
hassy@logos.t.u-tokyo.ac.jp
tsuruoka@logos.t.u-tokyo.ac.jp

Abstract

We propose a simple domain adaptation method for neural networks in a supervised setting. Supervised domain adaptation is a way of improving the generalization performance on the target domain by using the source domain dataset, assuming that both of the datasets are labeled. Recently, recurrent neural networks have been shown to be successful on a variety of NLP tasks such as caption generation; however, the existing domain adaptation techniques are limited to (1) tune the model parameters by the target dataset after the training by the source dataset, or (2) design the network to have dual output, one for the source domain and the other for the target domain. Reformulating the idea of the domain adaptation technique proposed by Daumé (2007), we propose a simple domain adaptation method, which can be applied to neural networks trained with a cross-entropy loss. On captioning datasets, we show performance improvements over other domain adaptation methods.

1 Introduction

Domain adaptation is a machine learning paradigm that aims at improving the generalization performance of a new (target) domain by using a dataset from the original (source) domain. Suppose that, as the source domain dataset, we have a captioning corpus, consisting of images of daily lives and each image has captions. Suppose also that we would like to generate captions for exotic cuisine, which are rare in the corpus. It is usually very costly to make a new corpus for the target domain, i.e., taking and captioning those images. The research question here is how we can leverage the source domain dataset to improve the performance on the target domain.

As described by Daumé (2007), there are mainly two settings of domain adaptation: fully supervised and semi-supervised. Our focus is the supervised setting, where both of the source and target domain datasets are labeled. We would like to use the label information of the source domain to improve the performance on the target domain.

Recently, Recurrent Neural Networks (RNNs) have been successfully applied to various tasks in the field of natural language processing (NLP), including language modeling (Mikolov et al., 2010), caption generation (Vinyals et al., 2015b) and parsing (Vinyals et al., 2015a).

For neural networks, there are two standard methods for supervised domain adaptation (Mou et al., 2016). The first method is *fine tuning*: we first train the model with the source dataset and then tune it with the target domain dataset (Venugopalan et al., 2015; Kim, 2014). Since the objective function of neural network training is non-convex, the performance of the trained model can depend on the initialization of the parameters. This is in contrast with the convex methods such as Support Vector Machines (SVMs). We expect that the first training gives a good initialization of the parameters, and therefore the latter training gives a good generalization even if the target domain dataset is small. The downside of this approach is the lack of the optimization objective.

The other method is to design the neural network so that it has two outputs. The first output is trained with the source dataset and the other output is trained with the target dataset, where the input part is shared among the domains. We call this method *dual outputs*. This type of network architecture has been successfully applied to multitask learning in NLP such as part-of-speech tag-

Proceedings of the 1st Workshop on Representation Learning for NLP, pages 249–257,
Berlin, Germany, August 11th, 2016. ©2016 Association for Computational Linguistics

ging and named-entity recognition (Collobert et al., 2011; Yang et al., 2016).

In the NLP community, there has been a large body of previous work on domain adaptation. One of the state-of-the-art methods for the supervised domain adaptation is *feature augmentation* (Daumé, 2007). The central idea of this method is to augment the original features/parameters in order to model the source specific, target specific and general behaviors of the data. However, it is not straight-forward to apply it to neural network models in which the cost function has a form of log probabilities.

In this paper, we propose a new domain adaptation method for neural networks. We reformulate the method of Daumé (2007) and derive an objective function using convexity of the loss function. From a high-level perspective, this method shares the idea of feature augmentation. We use redundant parameters for the source, target and general domains, where the general parameters are tuned to model the common characteristics of the datasets and the source/target parameters are tuned for domain specific aspects.

In the latter part of this paper, we apply our domain adaptation method to a neural captioning model and show performance improvement over other standard methods on several datasets and metrics. In the datasets, the source and target have different word distributions, and thus adaptation of output parameters is important. We augment the output parameters to facilitate adaptation. Although we use captioning models in the experiments, our method can be applied to any neural networks trained with a cross-entropy loss.

2   Related Work

There are several recent studies applying domain adaptation methods to deep neural networks. However, few studies have focused on improving the fine tuning and dual outputs methods in the supervised setting.

Sun et al. (2015) have proposed an unsupervised domain adaptation method and apply it to the features from deep neural networks. Their idea is to minimize the domain shift by aligning the second-order statistics of source and target distributions. In our setting, it is not necessarily true that there is a correspondence between the source and target input distributions, and therefore we cannot expect their method to work well.

Wen et al. (2016) have proposed a procedure to generate natural language for multiple domains of spoken dialogue systems. They improve the fine tuning method by pre-trainig with synthesized data. However, the synthesis protocol is only applicable to the spoken dialogue system. In this paper, we focus on domain adaptation methods which can be applied without dataset-specific tricks.

Yang et al. (2016) have conducted a series of experiments to investigate the transferability of neural networks for NLP. They compare the performance of two transfer methods called `INIT` and `MULT`, which correspond to the fine tuning and dual outputs methods in our terms. They conclude that `MULT` is slightly better than or comparable to `INIT`; this is consistent with our experiments shown in section 5. Although they obtain little improvement by transferring the output parameters, we achieve significant improvement by augmenting parameters in the output layers.

3   Domain adaptation and language generation

We start with the basic notations and formalization for domain adaptation. Let $\mathcal{X}$ be the set of inputs and $\mathcal{Y}$ be the outputs. We have a source domain dataset D^s, which is sampled from some distribution $\mathcal{D}^s$. Also, we have a target domain dataset D^t, which is sampled from another distribution $\mathcal{D}^t$. Since we are considering supervised settings, each element of the datasets has a form of input output pair (x, y). The goal of domain adaptation is to learn a function $f : \mathcal{X} \to \mathcal{Y}$ that models the input-output relation of D^t. We implicitly assume that there is a connection between the source and target distributions and thus can leverage the information of the source domain dataset. In the case of image caption generation, the input x is an image (or the feature vector of an image) and y is the caption (a sequence of words).

In language generation tasks, a sequence of words is generated from an input x. A state-of-the-art model for language generation is LSTM (Long Short Term Memory) initialized by a context vector computed by the input (Vinyals et al., 2015b). LSTM is a particular form of recurrent neural network, which has three gates and a memory cell. For each time step t, the vectors c_t and h_t are computed from u_t, c_{t-1} and h_{t-1} by the fol-

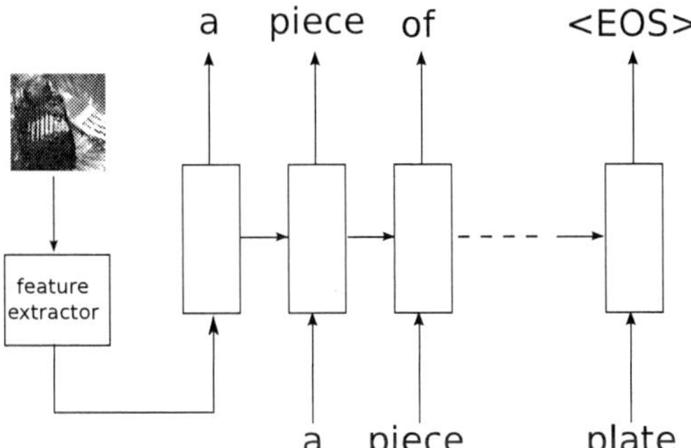

Figure 1: A schematic view of the LSTM captioning model. The first input to the LSTM is an image feature. Then a sentence "*a piece of chocolate cake that is on a glass plate*" is generated. The generation process ends with the EOS symbol.

lowing equations:

$$i = \sigma(W_{ix}u_t + W_{ih}h_{t-1})$$
$$f = \sigma(W_{fx}u_t + W_{fh}h_{t-1})$$
$$o = \sigma(W_{ox}u_t + W_{oh}h_{t-1})$$
$$g = \tanh(W_{gx}u_t + W_{gh}h_{t-1})$$
$$c_t = f \odot c_{t-1} + i \odot g$$
$$h_t = o \odot \tanh(c_t),$$

where σ is the sigmoid function and $\odot$ is the element-wise product. Note that all the vectors in the equations have the same dimension n, called the cell size. The probability of the output word at the t-th step, y_t, is computed by

$$p(y_t|y_1, \ldots, y_{t-1}, x) = \text{Softmax}(Wh_t), \quad (1)$$

where W is a matrix with a size of vocabulary size times n. We call this matrix as the parameter of the *output layer*. The input u_t is given by the word embedding of y_{t-1}.

To generate a caption, we first compute feature vectors of the image, and put it into the beginning of the LSTM as

$$u_0 = W_0\text{CNN}(x), \quad (2)$$

where W_0 is a tunable parameter matrix and CNN is a feature extractor usually given by a convolutional neural network. Output words, y_t, are selected in order and each caption ends with special symbol <EOS>. The process is illustrated in Figure 1. Note that the cost function for the generated caption is

$$\log p(y|x) = \sum_t \log p(y_t|y_1, \ldots, y_{t-1}, x),$$

where the conditional distributions are given by Eq. (1). The parameters of the model are optimized to minimize the cost on the training dataset. We also note that there are extensions of the models with attentions (Xu et al., 2015; Bahdanau et al., 2015), but the forms of the cost functions are the same.

4 Domain adaptation for language generation

In this section, we review standard domain adaptation techniques which are applicable to the neural language generation. The performance of these methods is compared in the next section.

4.1 Standard and baseline methods

A trivial method of domain adaptation is simply ignoring the source dataset, and train the model using only the target dataset. This method is hereafter denoted by TGTONLY. This is a baseline and any meaningful method must beat it.

Another trivial method is SRCONLY, where only the source dataset is used for the training. Typically, the source dataset is bigger than that of the target, and this method sometimes works better than TGTONLY.

Another method is ALL, in which the source and target datasets are combined and used for the training. Although this method uses all the data, the training criteria enforce the model to perform well on both of the domains, and therefore the performance on the target domain is not necessarily high. [1]

An approach widely used in the neural network community is FINETUNE. We first train the model with the source dataset and then it is used as the initial parameters for training the model with target dataset. The training process is stopped in reference to the development set in order to avoid over-fitting. We could extend this method by posing a regularization term (e.g. l_2 regularization) in order not to deviate from the pre-trained parameter. In the latter experiments, however, we do not pursue this direction because we found no performance gain. Note that it is hard to control the scales of the regularization for each part of the neural net because there are many parameters hav-

---

[1] As a variant of this method, we can weight the samples in each domain. This is a kind of interpolation between TGTONLY, ALL and SRCONLY. We do not consider this method in the latter experiments because we observe little improvement over ALL.

ing different roles.

Another common approach for neural domain adaptation is DUAL. In this method, the output of the network is "dualized". In other words, we use different parameters W in Eq. (1) for the source and target domains. For the source dataset, the model is trained with the first output and the second for the target dataset. The rest of the parameters are shared among the domains. This type of network design is often used for multi-task learning.

4.2 Revisiting the feature augmentation method

Before proceeding to our new method, we describe the feature augmentation method (Daumé, 2007) from our perspective. let us start with the feature augmentation method.

Here we consider the domain adaptation of a binary classification problem. Suppose that we train SVM models for the source and target domains separately. The objective functions have the form of

$$\frac{1}{n_s} \sum_{(x,y)\in\mathcal{D}_s} \max(0, 1 - y(w_s^T \Phi(x))) + \lambda\|w_s\|^2$$

$$\frac{1}{n_t} \sum_{(x,y)\in\mathcal{D}_t} \max(0, 1 - y(w_t^T \Phi(x))) + \lambda\|w_t\|^2,$$

where $\Phi(x)$ is the feature vector and w_s, w_t are the SVM parameters. In the feature augmentation method, the parameters are decomposed to $w_s = \theta_g + \theta_s$ and $w_t = \theta_g + \theta_t$. The optimization objective is different from the sum of the above functions:

$$\frac{1}{n_s} \sum_{(x,y)\in\mathcal{D}_s} \max(0, 1 - y(w_s^T \Phi(x)))$$

$$+ \lambda(\|\theta_g\|^2 + \|\theta_s\|^2)$$

$$+ \frac{1}{n_t} \sum_{(x,y)\in\mathcal{D}_t} \max(0, 1 - y(w_t^T \Phi(x)))$$

$$+ \lambda(\|\theta_g\|^2 + \|\theta_t\|^2),$$

where the quadratic regularization terms $\|\theta_g + \theta_s\|^2$ and $\|\theta_g + \theta_t\|^2$ are changed to $\|\theta_g\|^2 + \|\theta_s\|^2$ and $\|\theta_g\|^2 + \|\theta_t\|^2$, respectively. Since the parameters θ_g are shared, we cannot optimize the problems separately.

This change of the objective function can be un-

derstood as adding additional regularization terms

$$2(\|\theta_g\|^2 + \|\theta_t\|^2) - \|\theta_g + \theta_t\|^2,$$
$$2(\|\theta_g\|^2 + \|\theta_s\|^2) - \|\theta_g + \theta_s\|^2.$$

We can easily see that those are equal to $\|\theta_g - \theta_t\|^2$ and $\|\theta_g - \theta_s\|^2$, respectively and thus this additional regularization enforces θ_g and θ_t (and also θ_g and θ_s) not to be far away. This is how the feature augmentation method shares the domain information between the parameters w_s and w_t.

4.3 Proposed method

Although the above formalization is for an SVM, which has the quadratic cost of parameters, we can apply the idea to the log probability case.

In the case of RNN language generation, the loss function of each output is a cross entropy applied to the softmax output

$$-\log p_s(y|y_1, \ldots, y_{t-1}, x)$$
$$= -w_{s,y}^T h + \log Z(w_s; h), \qquad (3)$$

where Z is the partition function and h is the hidden state of the LSTM computed by $y_0, \ldots, y_{t-1}$ and x. Again we decompose the word output parameter as $w_s = \theta_g + \theta_s$. Since $\log Z$ is convex with respect to w_s, we can easily show that the Eq. (3) is bounded above by

$$-\theta_{g,y}^T h + \frac{1}{2} \log Z(2\theta_g; x)$$

$$-\theta_{s,y}^T h + \frac{1}{2} \log Z(2\theta_s; x).$$

The equality holds if and only if $\theta_g = \theta_s$. Therefore, optimizing this upper-bound effectively enforces the parameters to be close as well as reducing the cost.

The exact same story can be applied to the target parameter $w_t = \theta_g + \theta_t$. We combine the source and target cost functions and optimize the sum of the above upper-bounds. Then the derived objective function is

$$\frac{1}{n_s} \sum_{(x,y)\in\mathcal{D}_s} [-\theta_{g,y}^T h + \frac{1}{2} \log Z(2\theta_g; x)$$

$$-\theta_{s,y}^T h + \frac{1}{2} \log Z(2\theta_s; x)]$$

$$+\frac{1}{n_t} \sum_{(x,y)\in\mathcal{D}_t} [-\theta_{g,y}^T h + \frac{1}{2} \log Z(2\theta_g; x)$$

$$-\theta_{t,y}^T h + \frac{1}{2} \log Z(2\theta_t; x)].$$

Algorithm 1: Proposed Method
1 **while** True **do**
2   Select a minibatch of data from source or target dataset
3   **if** *source* **then**
4   Optimize $\ell(\theta_g) + \ell(\theta_s)$ with respect to $\theta_g, \theta_s, \theta_h$ for the minibatch
5   **end**
6   **else**
7   Optimize $\ell(\theta_g) + \ell(\theta_t)$ with respect to $\theta_g, \theta_t, \theta_h$ for the minibatch
8   **end**
9   **if** *development error increases* **then**
10   break;
11   **end**
12 **end**
13 Compute $w_t = \theta_g + \theta_t$ and $w_s = \theta_g + \theta_s$. Use these parameters as the output parameters for each domain.

If we work with the sum of the source and target versions of Eq. (3), the method is actually the same as DUAL because the parameters θ_g is completely redundant. The difference between this objetive and the proposed upper bound works as a regularization term, which results in a good generalization performance.

Although our formulation has the unique objective, there are three types of cross entropy loss terms given by θ_g, θ_s and θ_t. We denote them by $\ell(\theta_g), \ell(\theta_s)$ and $\ell(\theta_t)$, respectively. For the source data, the sum of general and source loss terms is optimized, and for the target dataset the sum of general and target loss terms is optimized.

The proposed algorithm is summarized in Algorithm 1. Note that θ_h is the parameters of the LSTM except for the output part. In one epoch of the training, we use all data once. We can combine any parameter update methods for neural network training such as Adam (Kingma and Ba, 2015).

5   Experiments

We have conducted domain adaptation experiments on the following three datasets. The first experiment focuses on the situation where the domain adaptation is useful. The second experiment show the benefit of domain adaptation for both directions: from source to target and target to source. The third experiment shows an improvement in another metric. Although our method is applicable to any neural network with a cross entropy loss, all the experiments use caption generation models because it is one of the most successful neural network applications in NLP.

5.1   Adaptation to food domain captioning

This experiment highlights a typical scenario in which domain adaptation is useful. Suppose that we have a large dataset of captioned images, which are taken from daily lives, but we would like to generate high quality captions for more specialized domain images such as minor sports and exotic food. However, captioned images for those domains are quite limited due to the annotation cost. We use domain adaptation methods to improve the captions of the target domain.

To simulate the scenario, we split the Microsoft COCO dataset into food and non-food domain datasets. The MS COCO dataset contains approximately 80K images for training and 40K images for validation; each image has 5 captions (Lin et al., 2014). The dataset contains images of diverse categories, including animals, indoor scenes, sports, and foods. We selected the "food category" data by scoring the captions according to how much those are related to the food category. The score is computed based on wordnet similarities (Miller, 1995). The training and validation datasets are split by the score with the same threshold. Consequently, the food dataset has 3,806 images for training and 1,775 for validation. The non-food dataset has 78,976 images for training and 38,749 for validation.

The selected pictures from the food domain are typically a close-up of foods or people eating some foods. Table 1 shows some captions from the food and non-food domain datasets. Table 2 shows the top twenty frequent words in the two datasets except for the stop words. We observe that the frequent words are largely different, but still there are some words common in both datasets.

To model the image captaining, we use LSTMs as described in the previous section. The image features are computed by the trained GoogLeNet and all the LSTMs have a single layer with 300 hidden units (Szegedy et al., 2015). We use a standard optimization method, Adam (Kingma and Ba, 2015) with hyper parameters $\alpha = 0.001$, $\beta_1 = 0.9$ and $\beta_2 = 0.999$. We stop the training based on the loss on the development set. After the training we generate captions by beam search, where the size of the beam is 5. These settings are

| | Closeup of bins of food that include broccoli and bread. |
| A woman sitting in front of a table with a plate of food. |
| A large pizza covered in cheese and toppings. |
| People shopping in an open market for vegetables. |
| A purse sits at the foot of one of the large beds. |
| A large television screen in a large room. |

Table 1: Examples of annotated captions from food domain dataset (top) and non-food dataset (bottom).

| food | food, plate, table, pizza, sitting, man, white, two, eating, people, sandwich, woman, next, plates, vegetables, cheese, bowl, |
| non-food | man, sitting, two, standing, people, next, white, woman, street, holding, person, table, large, down, top, group, field, tennis, small, near, |

Table 2: Top twenty frequent words from the food/non-food datasets.

the same in the latter experiments.

We compare the proposed method with other baseline methods. For all the methods, we use Adam with the same hyper parameters. In FINE-TUNE, we did not freeze any parameters during the target training. In DUAL, all samples in source and target datasets are weighted equally.

We evaluated the performance of the domain adaptation methods by the qualities of the generated captions. We used BLEU, METOR and CIDEr scores for the evaluation. The results are summarized in Table 3. [2] We see that the proposed method improves in most of the metrics. The baseline methods SRCONLY and TGTONLY are worse than other methods, because they use limited data for the training. Note that the CIDEr scores correlate with human evaluations better than BLEU and METOR scores (Vedantam et al., 2015).

Generated captions for sample images are shown in Table 4. In the first example, ALL fails to identify the chocolate cake because there are birds in the source dataset which somehow look similar to chocolate cake. We argue that PROPOSED learns birds by the source parameters and chocolate cakes by the target parameters, and thus succeeded in generating appropriate captions.

5.2 Adaptation between MS COCO and Flickr30K

In this experiment, we explore the benefit of adaptation from both sides of the domains. Flickr30K

	B1	B2	B3	B4	M	C
SRCONLY	60.4	42.3	30.6	21.2	19.4	36.4
TGTONLY	63.0	45.5	33.0	24.0	20.9	35.8
ALL	61.0	45.1	32.7	23.7	20.2	39.9
FINETUNE	61.9	45.8	33.6	24.6	21.5	39.8
DUAL	**63.3**	46.3	33.7	**24.7**	21.2	40.7
PROPOSED	63.2	**46.8**	**34.0**	**24.7**	**21.7**	**42.8**

Table 3: Results of the domain adaptation to the food dataset. The evaluation metrics are BLEU, METOR and CIDEr. The proposed method is the best in most of the metrics.

	B1	B2	B3	B4	M	C
SRCONLY	50.8	30.5	18.6	11.5	12.9	16.0
TGTONLY	52.8	34.6	22.8	15.3	15.7	22.5
ALL	52.6	34.4	22.5	14.8	15.6	23.1
FINETUNE	55.2	36.6	24.3	16.3	16.0	26.2
DUAL	56.0	36.9	24.1	16.0	15.9	25.8
PROPOSED	**56.7**	**37.8**	**25.5**	**17.4**	**16.1**	**27.9**

Table 5: Domain adaptation from MSCOCO to Flickr30K dataset.

is another captioning dataset, consisting of 30K images, and each image has five captions (Young et al., 2014). Although the formats of the datasets are almost the same, the model trained by the MS COCO dataset does not work well for the Flickr 30K dataset and vice versa. The word distributions of the captions are considerably different. If we ignore words with less than 30 counts, MS COCO has 3,655 words and Flicker30K has 2732 words; and only 1,486 words are shared. Also, the average lengths of captions are different. The average length of captions in Flickr30K is 12.3 while that of MS COCO is 10.5.

The first result is the domain adaptation from MS COCO to Flickr30K, summarized in Table 5. Again, we observe that the proposed method achieves the best score among the other methods. The difference between ALL and FINETUNE is bigger than in the previous setting because two datasets have different captions even for similar images. The scores of FINETUNE and DUAL are at almost the same level.

The second result is the domain adaptation from Flickr30K to MS COCO shown in Table 6. This may not be a typical situation because the number of samples in the target domain is larger than that of the source domain. The SRCONLY model is trained only with Flickr30K and tested on the MS COCO dataset. We observe that FINETUNE gives little benefit over TGTONLY, which implies that

---

coco-caption to compute BLEU, METEOR and CIDEr scores.

	True Caption	A piece of chocolate cake that is on a glass plate.
	SRCONLY	a bird sitting on top of a tree branch
	TGTONLY	a piece of chocolate cake sitting on a white plate
	ALL	a close up of a bird on a tree branch
	FINETUNE	a close up of a plate of food on a plate
	DUAL	a close up of a plate of food
	PROPOSED	**a close up of a piece of chocolate cake on a plate**
	True Caption	The woman with a sandwich on her plate is drinking from a wine glass.
	SRCONLY	a woman holding a cake on a table
	TGTONLY	a woman is eating a slice of pizza
	ALL	a person holding a cake on a plate with a fork
	FINETUNE	a close up of a plate of food on a table
	DUAL	a group of people sitting at a table eating food
	PROPOSED	**a woman sitting at a table with a plate of food**

Table 4: Examples of generated captions for food dataset images.

	B1	B2	B3	B4	M	C
SRCONLY	44.0	25.1	14.1	8.6	13.5	15.5
TGTONLY	64.0	45.9	32.6	23.2	21.0	70.2
ALL	63.0	44.9	31.4	22.2	21.0	67.4
FINETUNE	63.6	45.7	32.7	**23.5**	20.9	70.5
DUAL	**65.0**	**46.6**	32.8	23.1	21.0	70.3
PROPOSED	64.3	46.5	**33.0**	23.4	**21.1**	**71.0**

Table 6: Domain adaptation from Flickr30K to MSCOCO dataset.

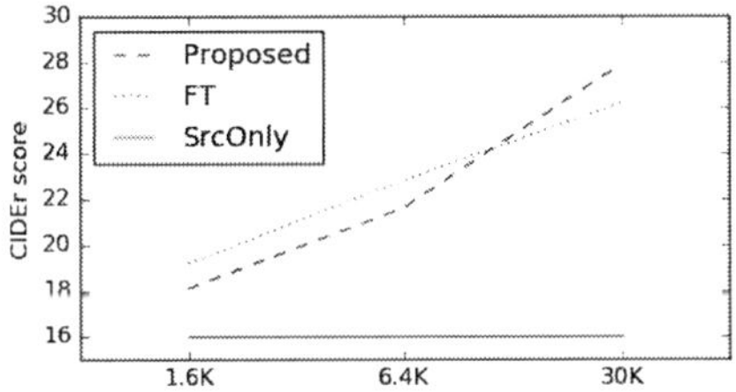

Figure 2: Comparison of CIDEr score of FINE-TUNE and PROPOSED

the difference of the initial parameters has little effect in this case. Also, DUAL gives little benefit over TGTONLY, meaning that the parameter sharing except for the output layer is not important in this case. Note that the CIDEr score of PROPOSED is slightly improved.

Figure 2 shows the comparison of FINETUNE and PROPOSED, changing the number of the Flickr samples to 1600, 6400 and 30K. We observe that FINETUNE works relatively well when the target domain dataset is small.

5.3 Answer sentence selection

In this experiment, we use the captioning model as an affinity measure of images and sentences. TOEIC part 1 test consists of four-choice questions for English learners. The correct choice is the sentence that best describes the shown image. Questions are not easy because there are confusing keywords in wrong choices. An example of the question is shown in Table 7. We downloaded 610 questions from `http://www.english-test.net/toeic/listening/`.

Our approach here is to select the most probable choice given the image by captioning models. We train captioning models with the images and correct answers from the training set. Since the TOEIC dataset is small, domain adaptation can give a large benefit. We compared the domain adaptation methods by the percentage of correct answers. The source dataset is 40K samples from MS COCO and the target dataset is the TOEIC dataset. We split the TOEIC dataset to 400 samples for training and 210 samples for testing.

The percentages of correct answers for each method are summarized in Table 8. Since the questions have four choices, all methods should perform better than 25%. TGTONLY is close to the baseline because the model is trained with only 400 samples. As in the previous experiments, FINETUNE and DUAL are better than ALL and PROPOSED is better than the other methods.

Table 7: A sample question from TOEIC part 1 test. The correct answer is (C).

	correct answer
SRCONLY	29.1%
TGTONLY	28.1%
ALL	31.0%
FINETUNE	33.3%
DUAL	33.3%
PROPOSED	**35.7%**

Table 8: Domain adaptation to TOEIC dataset.

6 Conclusion and Future Work

We have proposed a new method for supervised domain adaptation of neural networks. On captioning datasets, we have shown that the method outperforms other standard adaptation methods applicable to neural networks.

The proposed method only decomposes the output word parameters, where other parameters, such as word embedding, are completely shared across the domains. Augmentation of parameters in the other part of the network would be an interesting direction of future work.

References

Dzmitry Bahdanau, Kyunghyun Cho, and Yoshua Bengio. 2015. Neural machine translation by jointly learning to align and translate. In *Proceedings of the 3rd International Conference on Learning Representations (ICLR)*.

R Collobert, Jason Weston, and L Bottou. 2011. Natural language processing (almost) from scratch. *Journal of Machine Learning Research*, 12:2493–2537.

Hal Daumé, III. 2007. Frustratingly easy domain adaptation. In *Proceedings of the 45th Annual Meeting of the Association of Computational Linguistics (ACL)*, pages 256–263.

Yoon Kim. 2014. Convolutional neural networks for sentence classification. In *Proceedings of the 2014 Conference on Empirical Methods in Natural Language Processing (EMNLP)*, pages 1746–1751.

Diederik Kingma and Jimmy Ba. 2015. Adam: A method for stochastic optimization. In *Proceed-ings of the 3rd International Conference on Learning Representations (ICLR)*.

Tsung-Yi Lin, Michael Maire, Serge Belongie, James Hays, Pietro Perona, Deva Ramanan, Piotr Dollár, and C Lawrence Zitnick. 2014. Microsoft coco: Common objects in context. In *Proceedings of the European Conference on Computer Vision (ECCV)*, pages 740–755.

Tomas Mikolov, Martin Karafiát, Lukas Burget, Jan Cernocký, and Sanjeev Khudanpur. 2010. Recurrent neural network based language model. In *INTERSPEECH*, volume 2, page 3.

Gerge A. Miller. 1995. Wordnet: a lexical database for english. *Communications of The ACM*, 38(11):39–41.

Lili Mou, Zhao Meng, Rui Yan, Ge Li, Yan Xu, Lu Zhang, and Zhi Jin. 2016. How transferable are neural networks in nlp applications? *arXiv preprint arXiv:1603.06111*.

Baochen Sun, Jiashi Feng, and Kate Saenko. 2015. Return of frustratingly easy domain adaptation. In *Proceedings of the 29th AAAI Conference on Artificial Intelligence*.

Christian Szegedy, Wei Liu, Yangqing Jia, Pierre Sermanet, Scott Reed, Dragomir Anguelov, Dumitru Erhan, Vincent Vanhoucke, and Andrew Rabinovich. 2015. Going deeper with convolutions. In *Proceedings of the IEEE Conference on Computer Vision and Pattern Recognition (CVPR)*, pages 1–9.

Ramakrishna Vedantam, C Lawrence Zitnick, and Devi Parikh. 2015. Cider: Consensus-based image description evaluation. In *Proceedings of the IEEE Conference on Computer Vision and Pattern Recognition (CVPR)*, pages 4566–4575.

Subhashini Venugopalan, Huijuan Xu, Jeff Donahue, Marcus Rohrbach, Raymond Mooney, and Kate Saenko. 2015. Translating videos to natural language using deep recurrent neural networks. In *Proceedings of the 2015 Conference of the North American Chapter of the Association for Computational Linguistics: Human Language Technologies (NAACL-HLT)*, pages 1494–1504.

Oriol Vinyals, Łukasz Kaiser, Terry Koo, Slav Petrov, Ilya Sutskever, and Geoffrey Hinton. 2015a. Grammar as a foreign language. In *Advances in Neu-*

ral Information Processing Systems 28 (NIPS 2015), pages 2755–2763.

Oriol Vinyals, Alexander Toshev, Samy Bengio, and Dumitru Erhan. 2015b. Show and tell: A neural image caption generator. In *Proceedings of the IEEE Conference on Computer Vision and Pattern Recognition (CVPR)*, pages 3156–3164.

Tsung-Hsien Wen, Milica Gasic, Nikola Mrksic, Lina M Rojas-Barahona, Pei-Hao Su, David Vandyke, and Steve Young. 2016. Multi-domain neural network language generation for spoken dialogue systems. *arXiv preprint arXiv:1603.01232*.

Kelvin Xu, Jimmy Ba, Ryan Kiros, Aaron Courville, Ruslan Salakhutdinov, Richard Zemel, and Yoshua Bengio. 2015. Show, attend and tell: Neural image caption generation with visual attention. In *Proceedings of the 32nd International Conference on Machine Learning (ICML)*.

Zhilin Yang, Ruslan Salakhutdinov, and William Cohen. 2016. Multi-task cross-lingual sequence tagging from scratch. *arXiv preprint arXiv:1603.06270*.

Peter Young, Alice Lai, Micah Hodosh, and Julia Hockenmaier. 2014. From image descriptions to visual denotations: New similarity metrics for semantic inference over event descriptions. *Transactions of the Association for Computational Linguistics (TACL)*, 2:67–78.

Neural Associative Memory for Dual-Sequence Modeling

Dirk Weissenborn
Language Technology Lab, DFKI
Alt-Moabit 91c
Berlin, Germany
dirk.weissenborn@dfki.de

Abstract

Many important NLP problems can be posed as dual-sequence or sequence-to-sequence modeling tasks. Recent advances in building end-to-end neural architectures have been highly successful in solving such tasks. In this work we propose a new architecture for dual-sequence modeling that is based on associative memory. We derive AM-RNNs, a recurrent associative memory (AM) which augments generic recurrent neural networks (RNN). This architecture is extended to the Dual AM-RNN which operates on two AMs at once. Our models achieve very competitive results on textual entailment. A qualitative analysis demonstrates that long range dependencies between source and target-sequence can be bridged effectively using Dual AM-RNNs. However, an initial experiment on auto-encoding reveals that these benefits are not exploited by the system when learning to solve sequence-to-sequence tasks which indicates that additional supervision or regularization is needed.

1 Introduction

Dual-sequence modeling and sequence-to-sequence modeling are important paradigms that are used in many applications involving natural language, including machine translation (Bahdanau et al., 2015; Sutskever et al., 2014), recognizing textual entailment (Cheng et al., 2016; Rocktäschel et al., 2016; Wang and Jiang, 2016), auto-encoding (Li et al., 2015), syntactical parsing (Vinyals et al., 2015) or document-level question answering (Hermann et al., 2015). We might even argue that most, if not all, NLP problems can (at least partially) be modeled by this paradigm (Li and Hovy, 2015). These models operate on two distinct sequences, the source and the target sequence. Some tasks require the generation of the target based on the source (sequence-to-sequence modeling), e.g., machine translation, whereas other tasks involve making predictions about a given source and target sequence (dual-sequence modeling), e.g., recognizing textual entailment. Existing state-of-the-art, end-to-end differentiable models for both tasks exploit the same architectural ideas.

The ability of such models to carry information over long distances is a key enabling factor for their performance. Typically this can be achieved by employing *recurrent neural networks* (RNN) that convey information over time through an internal memory state. Most famous is the LSTM (Hochreiter and Schmidhuber, 1997) that accumulates information at every time step additively into its memory state, which avoids the problem of vanishing gradients that hindered previous RNN architectures from learning long range dependencies. For example, Sutskever et al. (2014) connected two LSTMs conditionally for machine translation where the memory state after processing the source was used as initialization for the memory state of the target LSTM. This very simple architecture achieved competitive results compared to existing, very elaborate and feature-rich models. However, learning the inherent long range dependencies between source and target requires extensive training on large datasets. Bahdanau et al. (2015) proposed an architecture that resolved this issue by allowing the model to *attend* over all positions in the source sentence when predicting the target sentence, which enabled the model to automatically learn alignments of words and phrases of the source with the target sentence. The important difference is that previous long range

Proceedings of the 1st Workshop on Representation Learning for NLP, pages 258–266,
Berlin, Germany, August 11th, 2016. ©2016 Association for Computational Linguistics

dependencies could be bridged directly via attention. However, this architecture requires a larger number of operations that scales with the product of the lengths of the source- and target sequence and a memory that scales with the length of the source sequence.

In this work we introduce a novel architecture for dual-sequence modeling that is based on *associative memories* (AM). AMs are fixed sized memory arrays used to read and write content via an associated keys. Holographic Reduced Representations (HRR) (Plate, 1995)) enable the robust and efficient retrieval of previously written content from redundant memory arrays. Our approach is inspired by the works of Danihelka et al. (2016) who recently demonstrated the benefits of exchanging the memory cell of an LSTM with an associative memory on various sequence modeling tasks. In contrast to their architecture which directly adapts the LSTM architecture we propose an augmentation to generic RNNs (*AM-RNNs*, §3.2). Similar in spirit to *Neural Turing Machines* (Graves et al., 2014) we decouple the AM from the RNN and restrict the interaction with the AM to read and write operations which we believe to be important. Based on this architecture we derive the *Dual AM-RNN* (§4) that operates on two associative memories simultaneously for dual-sequence modeling. We conduct experiments on the task of recognizing textual entailment (§5). Our results and qualitative analysis demonstrate that AMs can be used to bridge long range dependencies similar to the attention mechanism while preserving the computational benefits of conveying information through a single, fixed-size memory state. Finally, an initial inspection into sequence-to-sequence modeling with Dual AM-RNNs shows that there are open problems that need to be resolved to make this approach applicable to these kinds of tasks.

A TensorFlow (Abadi et al., 2015) implementation of (Dual)-AM RNNs can be found at `https://github.com/dirkweissenborn/dual_am_rnn`.

2   Related Work

Augmenting RNNs by the use of memory is not novel. Graves et al. (2014) introduced Neural Turing Machines which augment RNNs with external memory that can be written to and read from. It contains a predefined number of slots to write

content to. This form of memory is addressable via content or position shifts. Neural Turing Machines inspired subsequent work on using different kinds of external memory, like queues or stacks (Grefenstette et al., 2015). Operations on these memories are calculated via a recurrent controller which is decoupled from the memory whereas AM-RNNs apply the RNN *cell*-function directly upon the content of the associative memory.

Danihelka et al. (2016) introduced Associative LSTMs which extends standard LSTMs directly by reading and writing operations on an associative memory. This architecture is closely related to ours. However, there are crucial differences that are due to the fact that we decouple the associative array from the original *cell*-function. Danihelka et al. (2016) directly include operations on the AM in the definition of their Associative LSTM. This might cause problems, since some operations, e.g., *forget*, are directly applied to the entire memory array although this can affect all elements stored in the memory. We believe that only reading and writing operations with respect to a calculated key should be performed on the associative memory. Further operations should therefore only be applied on the stored elements.

Neural attention is another important mechanism that realizes a form of content addressable memory. Most famously it has been applied to machine translation (MT) where attention models automatically learn soft word alignments between source and translation (Bahdanau et al., 2015). Attention requires memory that stores states of its individual entries, separately, e.g., states for every word in the source sentence of MT or textual entailment (Rocktäschel et al., 2016), or entire sentence states as in Sukhbaatar et al. (2015) which is an end-to-end memory network (Weston et al., 2015) for question answering. Attention weights are computed based on a provided input and the stored elements. The thereby weighted memory states are summed and the result is retrieved to be used as input to a down-stream neural network. Architectures based on attention require a larger amount of memory and a larger number of operations which scales with the usually dynamically growing memory. In contrast to attention Dual AM-RNNs utilize fixed size memories and a constant number of operations.

AM-RNNs also have an interesting connection to LSTM-Networks (Cheng et al., 2016) which recently demonstrated impressive results on various text modeling tasks. LSTM-Networks (LSTMN) select a previous hidden state via attention on a memory tape of past states (intra-attention) opposed to using the hidden state of the previous time step. The same idea is implicitly present in our architecture by retrieving a previous state via a computed key from the associative memory (Equation (6)). The main difference lies in the used memory architecture. We use a fixed size memory array in contrast to a dynamically growing memory tape which requires growing computational and memory resources. The drawback of our approach, however, is the potential loss of explicit memories due to retrieval noise or overwriting.

3 Associative Memory RNN

3.1 Redundant Associative Memory

In the following, we use the terminology of Danihelka et al. (2016) to introduce Redundant Associative Memories and Holographic Reduced Representations (HRR) (Plate, 1995). HRRs provide a mechanism to encode an item x with a key r that can be written to a fixed size memory array m and that can be retrieved from m via r.

In HRR, keys r and values x refer to complex vectors that consist of a *real* and *imaginary* part: $r = r_{re} + i \cdot r_{im}$, $x = x_{re} + i \cdot x_{im}$, where i is the imaginary unit. We represent these complex vectors as concatenations of their respective real and imaginary parts, e.g., $r = [r_{re}; r_{im}]$. The encoding- and retrieval-operation proposed by Plate (1995) and utilized by Danihelka et al. (2016) is the complex multiplication (Equation (1)) of a key r with its value x (*encoding*), and the complex conjugate of the key $\overline{r} = r_{re} - i \cdot r_{im}$ with the memory (*retrieval*), respectively. Note, that this requires the modulus of the key to be equal to one, i.e., $\sqrt{r_{re} \odot r_{re} + r_{im} \odot r_{im}} = 1$, such that $\overline{r} = r^{-1}$. Consider a single memory array m containing N elements x_k with respective keys r_k (Equation (2)).

$$r \circledast x = \begin{bmatrix} r_{re} \odot x_{re} - r_{im} \odot x_{im} \\ r_{re} \odot x_{im} + r_{im} \odot x_{re} \end{bmatrix} \quad (1)$$

$$m = \sum_{k=1}^{N} r_k \circledast x_k \quad (2)$$

We retrieve an element x_k by multiplying $\overline{r_k}$

with m (Equation (3)).

$$\tilde{x}_k = \overline{r_k} \circledast m = \sum_{k'=1}^{N} \overline{r_k} \circledast r_{k'} \circledast x_{k'}$$

$$= x_k + \sum_{k'=1 \neq k}^{N} \overline{r_k} \circledast r_{k'} \circledast x_{k'}$$

$$= x_k + noise \quad (3)$$

To reduce noise Danihelka et al. (2016) introduce permuted, redundant copies m_s of m (Equation (4)). This results in uncorrelated retrieval noises which effectively reduces the overall retrieval noise when computing their mean. Consider N_c permutations represented by permutation matrices P_s. The retrieval equation becomes the following.

$$m_s = \sum_{k=1}^{N} (P_s r_k) \circledast x_k \quad (4)$$

$$\tilde{x}_k = \frac{1}{N_c} \sum_{s=1}^{N_c} \sum_{k'=1}^{N} (P_s \overline{r_k}) \circledast m_s$$

$$= x_k + \sum_{k'=1 \neq k}^{N} x_{k'} \circledast \frac{1}{N_c} \sum_{s=1}^{N_c} P_s(\overline{r_k} \circledast r_{k'})$$

$$= x_k + noise$$

The resulting retrieval noise becomes smaller because the mean of the permuted, complex key products tends towards zero with increasing N_c if the key dimensions are uncorrelated (see Danihelka et al. (2016) for more information).

3.2 Augmenting RNNs with Associative Memory

A recurrent neural network (RNN) can be defined by a parametrized *cell*-function $f_\theta : \mathbb{R}^N \times \mathbb{R}^M \to \mathbb{R}^M \times \mathbb{R}^H$ that is recurrently applied to an input sequence $X = (x_1, ..., x_T)$. At each time step t it emits an output h_t and a state s_t, that is used as additional input in the following time step (Equation (5)).

$$f_\theta(x_t, s_{t-1}) = (s_t, h_t)$$
$$x \in \mathbb{R}^N, s \in \mathbb{R}^M, h \in \mathbb{R}^H \quad (5)$$

In this work we augment RNNs, or more specifically their *cell*-function f_θ, with associative memory to form *Associative Memory RNNs* (AM-RNN) $\tilde{f}_\theta$ as follows. Let $s_t = [c_t; n_t]$ be the concatenation of a memory state c_t and, optionally, some remainder n_t that might additionally be used in f, e.g., the output of an LSTM. For brevity, we neglect n_t in the following, and thus $s_t = c_t$. At first, we compute a key given the previous output and the current input, which is in turn used to read from the associative memory array m to retrieve a memory state s for the specified key (Equation (6)).

$$r_t = \text{bound}\left(W_r \begin{bmatrix} x_t \\ h_{t-1} \end{bmatrix}\right)$$

$$s_{t-1} = \overline{r_t} \circledast m_{t-1} \qquad (6)$$

The bound-operation (Danihelka et al., 2016) (Equation (7)) guarantees that the modulus of r_t is not greater than 1. This is an important necessity as mentioned in § 3.1.

$$\text{bound}(r') = \begin{bmatrix} r'_{re} \oslash d \\ r'_{im} \oslash d \end{bmatrix} \qquad (7)$$

$$d = \max\left(1, \sqrt{r'_{re} \odot r'_{re} + r'_{im} \odot r'_{im}}\right)$$

Next, we apply the original *cell*-function f_θ to the retrieved memory state (Equation (8)) and the concatenation of the current input and last output which serves as input to the internal RNN. We update the associative memory array with the updated state using the conjugate key of the retrieval key (Equation (9)).

$$s_t, h_t = f_\theta\left(\begin{bmatrix} x_t \\ h_{t-1} \end{bmatrix}, s_{t-1}\right) \qquad (8)$$

$$m_t = m_{t-1} + r_t \circledast (s_t - s_{t-1})$$

$$\tilde{f}_\theta(x_t, m_{t-1}) = (m_t, h_t) \qquad (9)$$

The entire computation workflow is illustrated in Figure 1a.

4 Associative Memory RNNs for Dual Sequence Modeling

Important NLP tasks such as machine translation (MT) or detecting textual entailment (TE) involve two distinct sequences as input, a source- and a target sequence. In MT a system predicts the target sequence based on the source whereas in TE source and target are given and an entailment-class should be predicted. Recently, both tasks were successfully modelled using an attention mechanism that can attend over positions in the source

sentence at any time step in the target sentence (Bahdanau et al., 2015; Rocktäschel et al., 2016; Cheng et al., 2016). These models are able to learn important task specific correlations between words or phrases of the two sentences, like word/phrase translation, or word-/phrase-level entailment or contradiction. The success of these models is mainly due to the fact that long range dependencies can be bridged directly via attention, instead of keeping information over long distances in a memory state that can get overwritten.

The same can be achieved through associative memory. Given the correct key a state that was written at any time step in the source sentence can be retrieved from an AM with minor noise that can efficiently be reduced by redundancy. Therefore, AMs can bridge long range dependencies and can therefore be used as an alternative to attention. The trade-off for using an AM is that memorized states cannot be used for their retrieval. However, the retrieval operation is constant in time and memory whereas the computational and memory complexity of attention based architectures grow linearly with the length of the source sequence.

We propose two different architectures for solving dual sequence problems. Both approaches use at least one AM-RNN for processing the source and another for the target sequence. The first approach reads the source sequence $X = (x_1, ..., x_{T_x})$ and uses the final associative memory array $m^x(:= m^x_{T_x})$ to initialize the memory array $m^y_0 = m^x$ of the AM-RNN that processes the target sequence $Y = (y_1, ..., y_{T_y})$. Note that this is basically the the conditional encoding architecture of Rocktäschel et al. (2016).

The second approach uses the final AM array of the source sequence m^x in addition to an independent target AM array m^y_t. At each time step t the *Dual AM-RNN* computes another key r'_t that is used to read from m^x and feeds the retrieved value as additional input to y_t to the inner RNN of the target AM-RNN. These changes are reflected in the Equation (10) (compared to Equation (8))

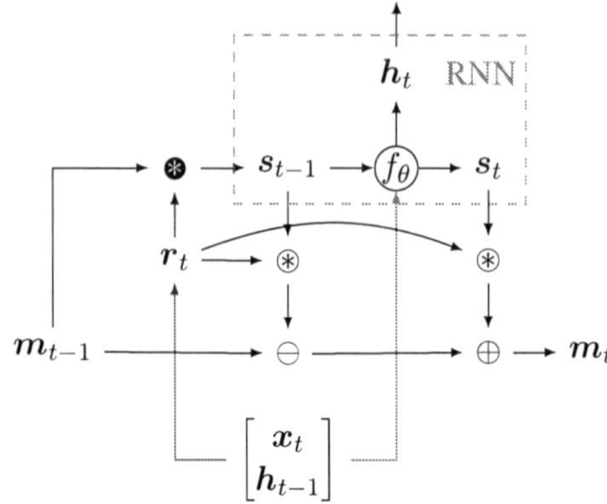

(a) Illustration of AM-RNN for input x_t at time step t.

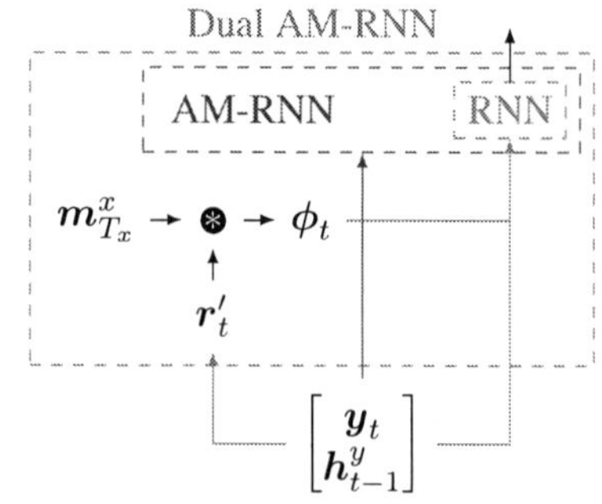

(b) Illustration of a Dual AM-RNN that extends the AM-RNN with the utilization of the final memory array $m^x_{T_x}$ of source sequence X.

Figure 1: Illustration of the computation workflow in AM-RNNs and Dual AM-RNNs. $\circledast$ refers to the complex multiplication with the (complex) conjugate of r'_t and can be interpreted as the retrieval operation. Similarly, $\circledast$ can be interpreted as the encoding operation.

and illustrated in Figure 1b.

$$r'_t = \text{bound}\left(W_{r'}\begin{bmatrix} y_t \\ h^y_{t-1} \end{bmatrix}\right)$$

$$\phi_t = \overline{r'_t} \circledast m^x$$

$$s_t, h^y_t = f_\theta\left(\begin{bmatrix} y_t \\ h^y_{t-1} \\ \phi_t \end{bmatrix}, s_{t-1}\right) \qquad (10)$$

5 Experiments

5.1 Setup

Dataset We conducted experiments on the Stanford Natural Language Inference (SNLI) Corpus (Bowman et al., 2015) that consists of roughly 500k sentence pairs (premise-hypothesis). They are annotated with textual entailment labels. The task is to predict whether a premise *entails*, *contradicts* or is *neutral* to a given hypothesis.

Training We perform mini-batch ($B = 50$) stochastic gradient descent using ADAM (Kingma and Ba, 2015) with $\beta_1 = 0$, $\beta_2 = 0.999$ and an initial learning rate of 10^{-3} for small models ($H \approx 100$) and 10^{-4} ($H = 500$) for our large model. The learning rate was halved whenever accuracy dropped over the period of one epoch. Performance on the development set was checked every 1000 mini-batches and the best model is used for testing. We employ dropout with a probability of 0.1 or 0.2 for the small and large models,

respectively. Following Cheng et al. (2016), word embeddings are initialized with `Glove` (Pennington et al., 2014) or randomly for unknown words. `Glove` initialized embeddings are tuned only after an initial epoch through the training set.

Model In this experiment we compare the traditional GRU with the (Dual) AM-GRU using conditional encoding (Rocktäschel et al., 2016) using shared parameters between source and target RNNs. Associative memory is implemented with 8 redundant memory copies. For the Dual AM-GRU we define $r'_t = r_t$ (see § 4), i.e., we use the same key for interacting with the premise and hypothesis associative memory array while processing the hypothesis. The rationale behind this is that we want to retrieve text passages from the premise that are similar to text passages of the target sequence.

All of our models consist of 2 layers with a GRU as top-layer which is intended to summarize outputs of the bottom layer. The bottom layer corresponds to our different architectures. We concatenate the final output of the premise and hypothesis together with their absolute difference to form the final representation that is used as input to a two-layer perceptron with rectifier-activations for classification.

5.2 Results

The results are presented in Table 1. They long range that the H=100-dimensional Dual AM-

Model	$H/|\theta_{-E}|$	Accuracy
LSTM (Rocktäschel et al., 2016)	116/252k	80.9
LSTM shared (Rocktäschel et al., 2016)	159/252k	81.4
LSTM-Attention (Rocktäschel et al., 2016)	100/252k	**83.5**
GRU shared	126/321k	81.9
AM-GRU shared	108/329k	82.9
Dual AM-GRU shared	100/321k	**84.4**
Dual AM-GRU shared	500/5.6m	<u>85.4</u>
LSTM Network (Cheng et al., 2016)	450/3.4m	**86.3**

Table 1: Accuracies of different RNN-based architectures on SNLI dataset. We also report the respective hidden dimension H and number of parameters $|\theta_{-E}|$ for each architecture without taking word embeddings E into account.

GRU and conditional AM-GRU outperform our baseline GRU system significantly. Especially the Dual AM-GRU does very well on this task achieving 84.4% accuracy, which shows that it is important to utilize the associative memory of the premise separately for reading only. Most notably is that it achieves even better results than a comparable LSTM architecture with two-way attention between all premise and hypothesis words (LSTM-Attention). This indicates that our Dual AM-GRU architecture is at least able to perform similar or even better than an attention-based model in this setup.

We investigated this finding qualitatively from sampled examples by plotting heatmaps of cosine similarities between the content that has been written to memory at every time step in the premise and what has been retrieved from it while the Dual AM-GRU processes the hypothesis. Random examples are shown in Figure 2, where we can see that the Dual AM-GRU is indeed able to retrieve the content from the premise memory that is most related with the respective hypothesis words, thus allowing to bridge important long-range dependencies for solving this task similar to attention. We observe that content for related words and phrases is retrieved from the premise memory when processing the hypothesis, e.g., "play" and "video game" or "artist" and "sculptor".

Increasing the size of the hidden dimension to 500 improves accuracy by another percentage point. The recently proposed LSTM Network achieves slightly better results. However, its number of operations scales with the square of the summed source and target sequence, which is even larger than traditional attention.

5.3 Sequence-to-Sequence Modeling

End-to-end differentiable sequence-to-sequence models consist of an encoder that encodes the source sequence and a decoder which produces the target sequence based on the encoded source. In a preliminary experiment we applied the Dual AM-GRU without shared parameters to the task of auto-encoding where source- and target sequence are the same. Intuitively we would like the AM-GRU to write phrase-level information with different keys to the associative memory. However, we found that the encoder AM-GRU learned very quickly to write everything with the same key to memory, which makes it work very similar to a standard RNN based encoder-decoder architecture where the encoder state is simply used to initialize the decoder state.

This finding is illustrated in Figure 3. The presented heatmap shows similarities between content that has been retrieved while predicting the target sequence and what has been written by the encoder to memory. We observe that the similarities between retrieved content and written content are horizontally slightly increasing, i.e., towards the end of the encoded source sentence. This indicates that the encoder overwrites the the associative memory while processing the source with the same key.

5.4 Discussion

Our experiments on entailment show that the idea of using associative memory to bridge long term dependencies for dual-sequence modeling can work very well. However, this architecture is

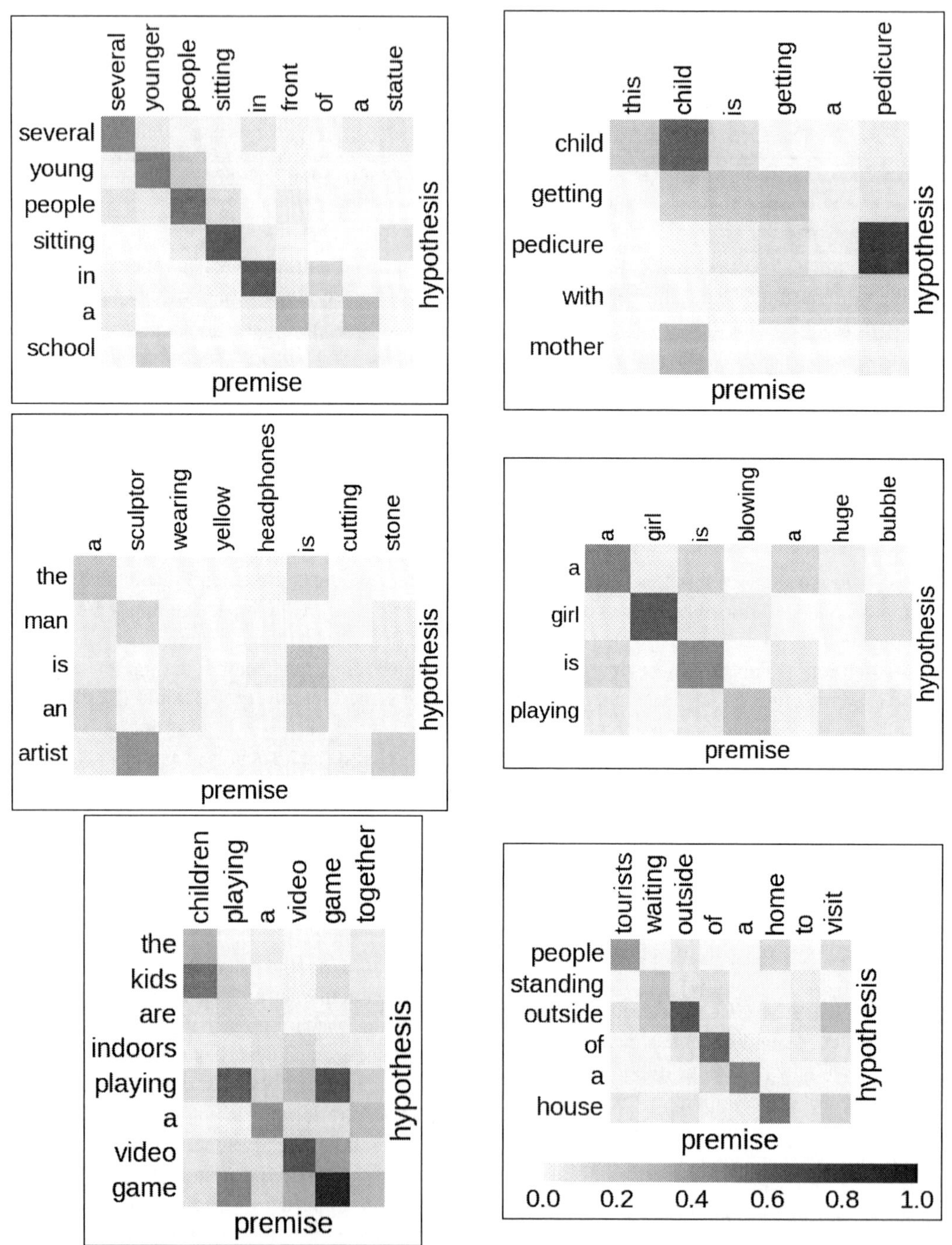

Figure 2: Heatmaps of cosine similarity between content that has been written to the associative memory at each time step of the premise (x-axis) and what has been retrieved from it by the Dual AM-GRU while processing the hypothesis (y-axis).

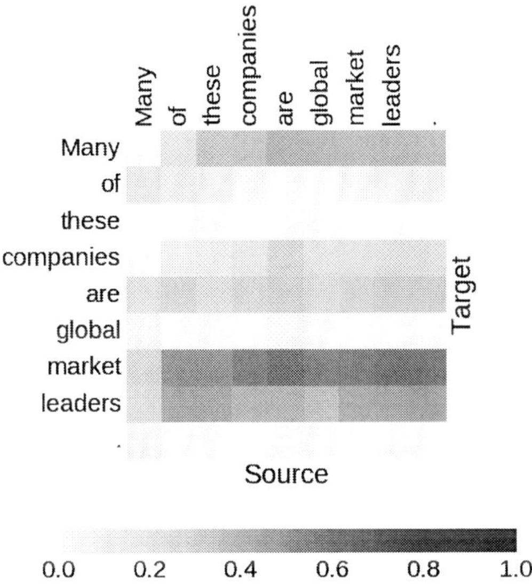

Figure 3: Heatmap of cosine similarity between content that has been written to the associative memory at each time step by the encoder (x-axis) and what has been retrieved from it by the Dual AM-GRU while decoding (y-axis).

not naively transferable to the task of sequence-to-sequence modeling. We believe that the main difficulty lies in the computation of an appropriate key at every time step in the target sequence to retrieve related content. Furthermore, the encoder should be enforced to not always use the same key. For example, keys could be based on syntactical and semantical cues, which might ultimately result in capturing some form of Frame Semantics (Fillmore and Baker, 2001). This could facilitate decoding significantly. We believe that this might be achieved via regularization or by curriculum learning (Bengio et al., 2009).

6   Conclusion

We introduced the Dual AM-RNN, a recurrent neural architecture that operates on associative memories. The AM-RNN augments traditional RNNs generically with associative memory. The Dual AM-RNN extends AM-RNNs with a second read-only memory. Its ability to capture long range dependencies enables effective learning of dual-sequence modeling tasks such as recognizing textual entailment. Our models achieve very competitive results and outperform a comparable attention-based model while preserving constant computational and memory resources.

Applying the Dual AM-RNN to a sequence-to-sequence modeling task revealed that the benefits of bridging long range dependencies cannot yet be achieved for this kind of problem. However, quantitative as well as qualitative results on textual entailment are very promising and therefore we believe that the Dual AM-RNN can be an important building block for NLP tasks involving two sequences.

Acknowledgments

We thank Sebastian Krause, Tim Rocktäschel and Leonhard Hennig for comments on an early draft of this work. This research was supported by the German Federal Ministry of Education and Research (BMBF) through the projects ALL SIDES (01IW14002), BBDC (01IS14013E), and Software Campus (01IS12050, sub-project GeNIE).

References

Martín Abadi, Ashish Agarwal, Paul Barham, Eugene Brevdo, Zhifeng Chen, Craig Citro, Greg S. Corrado, Andy Davis, Jeffrey Dean, Matthieu Devin, Sanjay Ghemawat, Ian Goodfellow, Andrew Harp, Geoffrey Irving, Michael Isard, Yangqing Jia, Rafal Jozefowicz, Lukasz Kaiser, Manjunath Kudlur, Josh Levenberg, Dan Mané, Rajat Monga, Sherry Moore, Derek Murray, Chris Olah, Mike Schuster, Jonathon Shlens, Benoit Steiner, Ilya Sutskever, Kunal Talwar, Paul Tucker, Vincent Vanhoucke, Vijay Vasudevan, Fernanda Viégas, Oriol Vinyals, Pete Warden, Martin Wattenberg, Martin Wicke, Yuan Yu, and Xiaoqiang Zheng. 2015. TensorFlow: Large-scale machine learning on heterogeneous systems. Software available from tensorflow.org.

Dzmitry Bahdanau, Kyunghyun Cho, and Yoshua Bengio. 2015. Neural machine translation by jointly learning to align and translate. In *The International Conference on Learning Representations (ICLR)*.

Yoshua Bengio, Jérôme Louradour, Ronan Collobert, and Jason Weston. 2009. Curriculum learning. In *Proceedings of the 26th annual international conference on machine learning*, pages 41–48. ACM.

Samuel R. Bowman, Gabor Angeli, Christopher Potts, and Christopher D Manning. 2015. A large annotated corpus for learning natural language inference. In *Proceedings of the 2015 Conference on Empirical Methods in Natural Language Processing (EMNLP)*. Association for Computational Linguistics.

Jianpeng Cheng, Li Dong, and Mirella Lapata. 2016. Long short-term memory-networks for machine reading. *arXiv preprint arXiv:1601.06733*.

Ivo Danihelka, Greg Wayne, Benigno Uria, Nal Kalchbrenner, and Alex Graves. 2016. Associative long short-term memory. *arXiv preprint arXiv:1602.03032*.

Charles J Fillmore and Collin F Baker. 2001. Frame semantics for text understanding. In *Proceedings of WordNet and Other Lexical Resources Workshop, NAACL*.

Alex Graves, Greg Wayne, and Ivo Danihelka. 2014. Neural turing machines. *arXiv preprint arXiv:1410.5401*.

Edward Grefenstette, Karl Moritz Hermann, Mustafa Suleyman, and Phil Blunsom. 2015. Learning to transduce with unbounded memory. In *Advances in Neural Information Processing Systems*, pages 1819–1827.

Karl Moritz Hermann, Tomáš Kočiský, Edward Grefenstette, Lasse Espeholt, Will Kay, Mustafa Suleyman, and Phil Blunsom. 2015. Teaching machines to read and comprehend. In *Advances in Neural Information Processing Systems (NIPS)*.

Sepp Hochreiter and Jürgen Schmidhuber. 1997. Long short-term memory. *Neural computation*, 9(8):1735–1780.

Diederik Kingma and Jimmy Ba. 2015. Adam: A method for stochastic optimization. In *The International Conference on Learning Representations (ICLR)*.

Jiwei Li and Eduard Hovy. 2015. The NLP engine: A universal turing machine for nlp. *arXiv preprint arXiv:1503.00168*.

Jiwei Li, Minh-Thang Luong, and Dan Jurafsky. 2015. A hierarchical neural autoencoder for paragraphs and documents. In *53nd Annual Meeting of the Association for Computational Linguistics (ACL)*.

Jeffrey Pennington, Richard Socher, and Christopher D Manning. 2014. Glove: Global vectors for word representation. In *EMNLP*, volume 14, pages 1532–1543.

Tony A Plate. 1995. Holographic reduced representations. *Neural networks, IEEE transactions on*, 6(3):623–641.

Tim Rocktäschel, Edward Grefenstette, Karl Moritz Hermann, Tomáš Kočiskỳ, and Phil Blunsom. 2016. Reasoning about entailment with neural attention. *The International Conference on Learning Representations (ICLR)*.

Sainbayar Sukhbaatar, Jason Weston, Rob Fergus, et al. 2015. End-to-end memory networks. In *Advances in Neural Information Processing Systems*, pages 2431–2439.

Ilya Sutskever, Oriol Vinyals, and Quoc V Le. 2014. Sequence to sequence learning with neural networks. In *Advances in neural information processing systems*, pages 3104–3112.

Oriol Vinyals, Łukasz Kaiser, Terry Koo, Slav Petrov, Ilya Sutskever, and Geoffrey Hinton. 2015. Grammar as a foreign language. In *Advances in Neural Information Processing Systems*, pages 2755–2763.

Shuohang Wang and Jing Jiang. 2016. Learning natural language inference with lstm. In *Proceedings of the 2016 Human Language Technology Conference of the North American Chapter of the Association of Computational Linguistics*.

Jason Weston, Sumit Chopra, and Antoine Bordes. 2015. Memory networks. In *The International Conference on Learning Representations (ICLR)*.

Author Index

Association for Computational Linguistics
209 N. Eighth Street
Stroudsburg, Pennsylvania 18360

ISBN 978-1-5108-2762-2